Secondary School
Teaching Methods

THIRD EDITION

Leonard H. Clark
Jersey City State College

Irving S. Starr
University of Hartford

Secondary School Teaching Methods

Macmillan Publishing Co., Inc.

New York

Collier Macmillan Publishers

London

Macmillan Publishing Co., Inc.
866 Third Avenue, New York, New York 10022

Collier Macmillan Canada, Ltd.

Library of Congress Cataloging in Publication Data

Clark, Leonard H
  Secondary school teaching methods.

  Includes bibliographies and index.
  1. Education, Secondary—1945–   I. Starr,
Irving S., joint author.   II. Title.
LB1607.C49   1976   373.73   75–9866
ISBN 0–02–322800–8

Printing: 1 2 3 4 5 6 7 8   Year: 6 7 8 9 0 1 2

Preface

This is the third edition of this book. Since the publication of the first edition many pedagogical innovations and experiments have been launched. The authors have attempted to incorporate the important changes into this revision. Otherwise the purpose and treatment, except for minor reorganization to make the book more useful and cohesive, remain the same in this edition as in the first, for despite innovations and experiments, the basic pedagogical principles have not changed.

This book was written to help prospective teachers learn how to teach. It is designed as a college textbook for a single semester course in general methods of teaching in the secondary school, although it might serve well as a reference work for student teachers and teachers in service. The authors have attempted to make the book as practical and useful as possible. To achieve this end, they have tried to write from a middle-of-the-road point of view, and to describe methods suitable for use in the type of school in which the student is likely to teach when he goes to his first position. For this same reason, they have attempted to write simply and clearly, to use numerous examples, to point up important understandings by means of questions at appropriate places within the text itself, and to keep quotations and references to scholarly works to a minimum. In general, discussion of educational theory has been omitted except when it seemed necessary to explain the why of the methods advocated. Nevertheless, the emphasis is, of necessity, on principles rather than recipes. There are no sure-fire recipes in teaching.

The authors wish to acknowledge their indebtedness to the many persons—students, teachers, and friends—who have helped them write this book. Grateful thanks are expressed to the students, teachers, superintendents, principals, and publishing houses who allowed the authors to reproduce their materials. A particular debt of gratitude is owed to Roy O. Billett, formerly professor of education at Boston University, in whose classes the authors formed many of their ideas concerning education; to Professor William T. Gruhn of The University of Connecticut, who went considerably beyond the call of duty in reading and criticizing the manuscript of the first edition; to Idella M. Clark, whose help in the collection of the necessary data for earlier editions has been immeasurable; and to Maria A. Clark, who not only typed the manuscript for each of the editions innumerable times, but also read the copy and made suggestions for improving the wording, and without whose help the book could never have been finished.

Chatham, New Jersey   L. H. C.
Hartford, Connecticut   I. S. S.

Contents

Contents

Contents

I

Foundations
of Method

What Is Teaching?

1

Teaching is exciting, rewarding work. It has always been so, but today new knowledge about the psychology of learning and teaching, innovations in teaching technology, the increased professionalization of school staffs, and new curricular patterns are making teaching more satisfying than ever before.

However, like all other professions, it is demanding. The teacher must base his practice on firm knowledge of the nature of the learner, the nature of the teaching process, and the nature of subject matter. To be really proficient the professional teacher must have a vast reservoir of skills and knowledge from which to draw the right approach for each particular situation. Take the case of Joe, a tenth-grader.

Joe is slightly under middle height. In class he is very quiet. He never causes disciplinary disturbances. Neither does he do any work. In fact, one would hardly know he was in the class at all. He just sits there. When the teacher cajoles him, he says that he is "dumb and can't do it, so there's no use trying." But this is not true. Test scores show him to be well within the normal range. His other activities do not indicate excessive dullness. He cannot read well (he is reading at a sixthgrade level), but he is one of the best soccer and basketball players in the school. On the field his playing is marked by its aggressiveness. As a matter of fact, his aggressiveness largely makes up for his lack of height in basketball. The coach says that he is one of the "smartest" forwards he has seen on the soccer field in the last few years.

Joe has never been known to pick up a book voluntarily. It has been a long time since he has turned in an acceptable paper. He knows that his failures will make him ineligible for varsity athletics, but he sees no reason for working because he believes that he will fail anyway. If he should pass, he will say that it is only because the teacher is "giving him a break." Seemingly, he has no interest other than athletics.

Difficult cases like Joe's challenge the ingenuity, the resources, and the skill of the teacher. The unskilled teacher might be overwhelmed by Joe's lack of enthusiasm and decide to give up. Not so the professional teacher. He knows that he must teach Joe—whether Joe wants to learn or not—and he has the knowledge and the resources with which to undertake this task.

Joe poses a difficult problem, but even cases like that of Billy need skillful teaching. Billy is an average eighth-grader with average intelligence. Usually a happy person, he gets along well with his teachers and his peers. Billy's mother is a homemaker and his father is a mechanic. There are two other children at home, one younger and one older than Billy. Home is the focal point of life in the family. Billy seems to have no great problems. Yet he does have trouble with some of his schoolwork. All normal pupils do, and Billy is normal, not brilliant. Although he is a willing worker and as cooperative as he can be, he finds many of his assignments too much for him. It will take plenty of skillful teaching if Billy is to get the most out of his mathematics, for instance.

Cases like these are commonplace for the professional teacher. When one is a master of teaching techniques, helping pupils like these is a challenge which never allows the work to become humdrum. And when one's efforts are finally crowned with success, nothing could be more gratifying.

TEACHING, A DEFINITION

In the final analysis teaching is an attempt to help someone acquire, or change, some skill, attitude, knowledge, ideal, or appreciation. In other words, the teacher's task is to create or influence desirable changes in behavior, or in tendencies toward behavior, in his pupils. Some authorities say that as far as school classes are concerned, if the pupils have not learned anything, the teacher has not taught anything. This statement is probably too harsh, but it does introduce an important point: The goal of teaching is to bring about the desired learning in the pupils. Therefore, it is said, the only valid criterion of success in teaching is the degree to which the teacher has been able to achieve the desired learning in his pupils. Thus the teacher must know (1) what learning is desirable for his pupils, and (2) how to bring about this learning. The basic problem to be solved, then, in any teaching situation concerns the selection of content and method.

*

Discuss the phrase: "There is no teaching unless there is learning." Is it true or partially true? What implications does it have for the teacher?

Do you agree that it is the teacher's job to teach Joe whether Joe wishes to learn or not?

*

ACCOUNTABILITY

Recently the notion that success in teaching can be gauged only by the pupils' success in learning has been incorporated into the modern concept of accountability. Many of the lay public and some school administrators are assuming that the performance of the pupils is the criterion by which they should judge the success of our schools and our teaching. They contend that teachers are supposed to teach and pupils are supposed to learn and that if pupils cannot perform at the level one can reasonably expect of pupils their age, then the schools and teachers have failed. If teachers wish to qualify for their pay, these parents and administrators say, they must make sure that pupils learn well enough to perform at the appropriate level.

Perhaps such an approach to accountability is too simplistic. Maybe, instead of judging success or failure of teaching by pupil progress, more attention should be paid to an assessment of teaching procedures and adherence to the curriculum. Such is the method used for judging the competence of other professional practitioners, physicians, for example. Be that as it may, accountability is here to stay, at least for a while, and teacher competence will be judged more carefully in the future. Whatever the criteria used in accountability formulas, it is certain that the accountability movement will require teachers to be more knowledgeable and skillful in the selection and execution of teaching strategies and tactics than ever before.

*

Do you agree with the lay people and administrators who say that if teachers wish to qualify for their pay, they must make sure that pupils learn well enough to perform at their appropriate age level? If you do, would you make exceptions to the rule?

*

THE ROLE OF METHOD

Content vs Method

Throughout the past decade educators have indulged themselves in debates between "content" and "methods"—one group holding out for the primacy of teaching method and the other insisting that course content is all important. These positions are exemplified by two commonly held misconceptions: (1) "Anyone who really knows how to teach can teach anything," and (2) "All that anyone needs to be able to teach a subject is to really know it."

A FALSE DICHOTOMY

Content and methods of teaching are not really dichotomous. Whenever one teaches one must teach someone something. That something is *content,* or subject matter. Without it no teacher can teach anything. But also, in order to teach anything to his pupils, the teacher must use some sort of technique or approach. This technique or approach is *method,* and it is to a large extent the method that determines what a pupil learns, how

he learns it, and how viable this learning is to him. In fact, because selecting content for lessons, units, and courses is part of teaching method, method determines the content actually taught as well as the content actually learned by the pupil.

To a large extent the teaching method determines the pupil's conception of the nature of the subject matter that he studies. In a sense it even changes the nature of the subject matter for, although the basic nature of the discipline remains constant, the teaching method determines the relationships, emphases, and methods of investigation and the overall impact of the subject matter of each of the academic disciplines as taught in the school. It is time that we drop this method versus content dispute and realize that they both are legs on which the teaching process stands. Without either one of them the teaching process will collapse.

THE IMPORTANCE OF CONTENT

Because this is a book on teaching methods, we wish to state early and emphatically that teachers must know their subject matter. Modern secondary school teaching techniques are dependent on the teacher's having considerable knowledge of the materials and resources available in the field and mastery of its content. To give a satisfactory lecture or to hear lessons based on a textbook does not require much scholarship, but to conduct unit assignments, laboratory classes, differentiated lessons, research activities, the solving of real problems, or true discussion groups requires that the teacher have the flexibility that only the command of a large fund of immediately usable knowledge can give. Moreover, the teacher must be familiar enough with the material available in the field to be able on short notice to put each pupil in touch with sources of information pertinent to the pupil's topic and suitable for his reading and interest levels. As a rule, the teacher who is not knowledgeable about and comfortable with the content he teaches is doomed to dullness. Two of the keys of good teaching—and good teaching has many keys—are flexibility and the encouragement of inquiry. They both require of the teacher knowledge of content—much knowledge constantly renewed.

At the secondary school level, of course, one is not expected to be a research scholar. Rather, teachers are the mediators who present and interpret the work of scholars to others. Therefore, teaching requires more of the teacher than knowledge of the subject alone; he must assimilate it well enough to mediate it to his pupils.

SKILLS AND CONTENT

To be sure that there is no misunderstanding, perhaps at this point it should be emphasized that the content of one's field includes more than just information. Attitudes and skills are basic subject matter for every course. Thus, for instance, appreciation is essential content for literature courses, and objectivity for science courses. Such intellectual skills as critical thinking, problem solving, and writing are essential content for any course. In fact, in many cases these skills and appreciations are much more important than the informational content. So much so, in some instances, that the only real value of the informational subject matter in the course is as a medium by which to teach essential skills and attitudes. Knowledge of one's content requires that one have mastered the intellectual skills and acquired the attitudes and appreciations essential to the subject field.

Selecting Strategies and Tactics

Method in teaching concerns the way the teacher organizes and uses techniques of teaching, subject matter, teaching tools, and teaching materials to reach teaching objectives.

Evidently there is no one best method of teaching or any one method that will suit all occasions. Different objectives, different subject matter, and different pupils require different strategies and tactics.

By teaching strategy we mean the general approach to a relatively large goal. A strategy, then, includes the selection of suitable subject matter and the general organization of the subject matter for instruction as well as the modes of instruction. Tactics, on the other hand, concern the handling of specific individual episodes. Combined, they determine the success of the strategy, i.e., whether or not we succeed in reaching our teaching goal.

Tactics are as likely to be spontaneous as preplanned, but must, of course, be harmonious with the strategy. They are often called operations and are the procedures used to achieve the goals of our strategy.

Thus, if one should decide to develop a certain concept by the use of Socratic questioning, the subject matter, the general method of procedure, and the key questions would be the strategy. The specific questions asked, the techniques used to elicit the answers, and the ways in which specific answers were handled and followed up, would be the tactics employed to implement the strategy. Some of these tactics would have been planned in advance, but many of them would have to be improvised at the spur of the moment as the situation developed. In addition to strategy and tactics, there are also grand strategies which concern the overall approach to entire courses or curricula.

In any teaching situation the first and most important consideration is to determine the aims or objectives. What exactly are our purposes in teaching these young people? What changes do we want to bring about in them? These considerations are all important, because in planning lessons and units, the teacher should select approaches and teaching activities, that is, strategies and tactics, that seem best suited to the type of objective he is after and then aim these approaches and activities directly at the objective. Only in this way can we obtain effective instruction that will bring about the goals desired.

It follows, then, that the basic problem of method is selection. The teacher must first of all select the goals and set his direction. Next he must select the strategy by which he can reach those goals. As part of the strategy he must select the content and the general approach. Then he must select the materials and teaching tools to use and, as he goes along, select the tactics to meet specific contingencies so as to carry out and implement the strategy. Finally he must select the proper instruments and techniques to evaluate and follow up what he has done.

*

To what extent and in what ways does method determine content? And content method?

The basic problem of method is said to be selection. Do you agree? Explain.

*

The necessity for selecting appropriate tactics and strategies can hardly be overemphasized. Using inappropriate strategies and tactics can defeat the purpose of our teaching. It is one of the major causes of teaching failure. The inordinate amount of verbalism (repeating the words without understanding their substance) in some of our secondary school classes is an example of what can result when one selects the wrong strategies and tactics.

Probably the reason teachers so often pick an inappropriate strategy or tactic is that they have never thought through what it is they are trying to do and do not comprehend what understanding and knowing entail.

To understand something one must have clear concepts. Many times we think we know something when actually we have only a vague notion. When we try to explain the meaning of a word and find that we cannot do it, we say "I know what it means, but I just can't explain it." More often than not, the truth is that we really have only a fuzzy idea and do not really understand what the word means. If we do not know clearly enough to use the knowledge, we do not really know at all.

There are several types of knowing: we can know *about;* we can know *that;* and we can know *how.* Learning about something is not the same as learning it, nor learning how to do it. Studying about political campaigning by reading a textbook and sitting through class lectures and discussions results in learning that is quite different from what one gets from active participation in a political practicum. The boy who only reads about how to swim may sink like a rock when he gets into the water. Neither does one learning product guarantee another. The girl who learns the rules of grammar and can do all the exercises in her grammar workbook perfectly may not be able to write a clear, idiomatic sentence. Or again, a graduate student may find that studying technical French has not helped him a bit when ordering a dinner in Paris. Neither does studying American history necessarily produce good citizens. To learn something we must study *it*—not about it or something like it. To learn to do something we must study and practice how to do it.

An example of this confusion is the common error of mistaking memorizing for understanding. We confuse the word with the deed, the name with the object. Children are often asked to learn words and phrases which mean nothing to them. It is quite possible to repeat that in a right triangle the square of the hypotenuse is equal to the sum of the squares of the opposite sides and yet not have the slightest idea of the meaning of square, hypotenuse, opposite sides, or right triangle. Thousands of persons can glibly recite that a noun is the name of a person, place, or thing, and yet not be able to pick a single noun out of a sentence. The cartoon of Miss Peach's class illustrates how well some elementary school children understand the pledge of allegiance to the flag. This parroting is called verbalism. It is one of the banes of both the elementary and secondary school. Really to know something we must know it well enough to use the knowledge.

NEED FOR BOTH VICARIOUS AND DIRECT LEARNING

In some instances verbalism, parroting without understanding, is the result of an overuse of vicarious learning. Much of our best learning comes through direct experience like that of the burned child who learned to fear the fire. Fortunately, it is not necessary to get burned. We can learn vicariously, through the experiences of others. Not everyone can go to see the pyramids, but anyone can learn about them from descriptions and pictures. The direct experience usually results in more vivid

Figure 1–1
Miss Peach's Pupils Recite the Pledge of Allegiance to the Flag.
Copyright, 1957, New York Herald Tribune, Inc. Reproduced with permission.

learning, but it is not always efficient. Sometimes it is quite inefficient, time-consuming, and costly, as in the case of the burned child. "Learning the hard way," we call it. For this reason we must rely on vicarious experience for much of our schoolwork. To do so is quite proper. It saves time, money, and effort. Used correctly it can be quite effective. In many instances it is the only type of experience possible. However, many high school teachers rely too much on vicarious learning. This may lead to verbalism. A balance between vicarious and direct learning is imperative. In general, learning situations should be as realistic as possible.

NEED FOR REALISTIC LEARNING

Realistic learning situations help make the learning meaningful to the pupil and thus help to avoid verbalism. Only meaningful material can be learned efficiently. To require boys and girls to learn things that they do not understand is absurd. In the first place, if the learning is meaningless to the learner it is useless. In the second place, meaningless material is much more difficult to learn than meaningful material. Yet many youngsters are required to learn things meaningless to them every day. How many youngsters have strived to learn:

> Once upon a midnight dreary, as I pondered, weak and weary,
> Over many a quaint and curious volume of forgotten lore,
> As I nodded, nearly napping, suddenly there came a tapping
> As of someone gently rapping, rapping at my chamber door.

even though they had not the slightest idea of what it was all about and could not translate "midnight dreary," "quaint and curious volume," "forgotten lore," or even "chamber door."

In order to avoid mere verbalism and inefficient learning among his pupils, the teacher should see to it that all learning situations in his classes are meaningful. To do so, he must eliminate meaningless material either by omitting it altogether or preparing the pupils for it so that it will be meaningful when they study it. In the foregoing example one might substitute a less difficult poem for Poe's *The Raven,* or one might prepare the pupils by

studying the poem, its message, and its vocabulary before the students attempt to learn it. In any case, in guiding the pupils' activities the teacher should make every effort to ensure that the experience is meaningful to the pupils.

LEARNING BY BUILDING CONCEPTS

One reason for the prevalence of verbalism in our schools is that it has become a general practice to teach (1) isolated facts or bits of information, (2) generalizations presented as isolated facts or bits of information, or (3) a combination of facts and generalizations stated as isolated facts or bits of information. Of course, a certain amount of teaching must be information giving, but the object of teaching is not the amassing of information but the building of concepts, skills, attitudes, ideals, and appreciations. To build concepts efficiently one must give pupils opportunities to learn specifics and then encourage the pupils to build the desired concepts or generalizations themselves by inference from the data. In this process the pupils need to examine the information, to establish the relationships among the facts, and to draw conclusions. When pupils learn concepts in this way, the concepts will become real to them because they are their own.

LEARNING BY DOING

Skills must be learned directly by actually performing the skill. Of course, one can, and probably must, learn a lot about the skill in other ways, but the only way to master a skill is to practice it. As Comenius pointed out in 1657,

> What is to be done must be learned by practice. Artisans do not detain their apprentices with theories, but set them to do practical work at an early stage; thus they learn to forge by forging, to carve by carving, to paint by painting, and to dance by dancing. In schools, therefore, let the students learn to write by writing, to talk by talking, to sing by singing, and to reason by reasoning.

All too often teachers forget this obvious, long-known fact. And so they make the mistake of trying to teach pupils how to write by teaching them grammar, and how to reason by memorizing rules and facts.

ATTITUDES, APPRECIATIONS, AND IDEALS

One must develop attitudes, appreciations, and ideals by suitable, purposeful approaches. If a teacher wishes to develop an attitude in his pupils, he must provide opportunities that will foster that attitude. Critical attitudes suitable for scholarly work are not engendered by swallowing lectures whole. Appreciation of literature is not learned by studying literature as though it were content to be learned rather than to be savored and judged. To avoid making the teaching of attitudes become sheer mockery, teachers must attempt to provide an atmosphere conducive to the attitudes sought and to give pupils plenty of opportunities to practice the desired attitude or behavior.

*

Can you give examples of different types of knowing? What implications do these different ways of knowing have for the teacher?

Can you cite examples of verbalism from your own school experience?

*

Pattern of Teaching Strategy

In general, the procedure in most good teaching follows the same five-step pattern:

1. Diagnosing the learning situation.
2. Preparing the setting for learning.
3. Guiding learning activities.
4. Evaluating the pupils' learning.
5. Following through.

To be competent a teacher should be a master of the techniques necessary to carry out each of these steps for they are, or should be, the basis of all teaching strategies.

DIAGNOSING THE LEARNING SITUATION

The first procedure in good teaching is to diagnose the teaching-learning situation. Somehow the teacher must find out what the needs of the pupils are so that he can plan experiences that will help them satisfy their needs. This entails knowing every youth as well as possible. Any physician will tell you it is impossible to know too much about a patient. In a sense the pupils are the teacher's pa-

tients. When the pupil is in good academic health the teacher tries to keep him so. When he is not, the teacher's job is to bring him back to health as soon as possible.

A case in point: Learning is usually developmental. That is to say, *new learning builds upon previous learning.* A child needs to understand simple multiplication before he can succeed with long division. A pupil who does not know the principles of solving simple equations will probably have a difficult time with quadratics. Since this is so often so, learning should follow an orderly sequence with the new learning building upon past learning.

Moreover, learning is not merely the accumulation of new concepts, skills, ideals, attitudes, and appreciations. Rather it is the integration of these new learnings and the concepts, skills, ideals, attitudes, and appreciations already present. The new learning becomes interwoven into one's personality. The result is really a personality change of some sort or another. This takes time. Although many pupils learn many things rapidly, thorough learning is apt to be a relatively slow process.

Since learning is developmental, it follows that one learns better when one is ready to learn. The principle of readiness has confused both teachers and lay people. Psychologically it can have many ramifications, but for our classroom purposes it can be defined quite simply. Readiness is a combination of maturity, ability, prior instruction, and motivation. A person is ready to learn something when he has matured enough to learn it efficiently, when he has acquired the skills, knowledge, and strengths prerequisite to learning it, and when he is sufficiently motivated. When a pupil has reached such a state of readiness, the teacher's job is relatively easy; when he has not, the teacher's job is more difficult and sometimes absolutely impossible. No one would attempt to teach a toddler the classic ballet: One must learn to walk before he can learn to run. Therefore, an essential part of diagnosis is to determine what kinds of learning the pupils are ready for.

PREPARING THE SETTING FOR LEARNING

The job of a theatrical producer is to provide a setting in which the action of the play can take place. So it is with the teacher. He must provide a setting for learning. This setting for learning includes many things. It includes creating a pleasant physical environment that will invite the pupils to learn. It includes providing the materials of learning so that they will be in the right place at the right time. But more than that, it includes providing an intellectual setting that will cause boys and girls to want to learn and an emotional setting that will provide the security and support that fosters learning.

GUIDING LEARNING ACTIVITIES

Once the stage has been set and the pupil is ready to work, the teacher must guide his learning. This can be done in many ways. The first job of the teacher is to help select the activities that are most appropriate for the pupil's goals and needs. As the pupil proceeds on the path selected, the teacher must help him toward the goal. The teacher can do this by showing the pupil how to do things, by presenting new facts and concepts, and by explaining and expanding old ones through such techniques as asking questions, giving vivid examples, and using audio-visual aids. The teacher can also guide the pupil by pointing out his errors. As the teacher watches the pupil's progress, he shows the pupil that here he has taken the wrong approach, here he has gone off on a tangent, here his thinking is illogical, here his premises are false, or here he is inconsistent. Praising good work and encouraging successful and profitable lines of endeavor are also among the effective techniques in guiding learning.

EVALUATING THE PUPILS' LEARNING

Guiding pupils' learning is also a continuous process of evaluation and reevaluation. In order to ensure that learning proceeds on its proper course, the teacher must examine the progress of the learning. On the basis of this evaluation the teacher can determine what the next steps should be. From it he can learn what has been missed and what must be retaught, and where the emphasis should be placed in succeeding classes. Evaluation also tells the pupil where he has hit or missed the mark. It is essential to diagnosis and necessary to good instruction.

FOLLOWING THROUGH

Much teaching is not truly effective because teachers often forget the final step of the pattern—the follow-through or follow-up. Without it teaching all too often becomes a case of "so near and yet so far," for it is the follow-through which drives home and clinches the learning. The follow-through can take any of many forms. At times a simple summary will do. Other times the teacher must repeat a point week after week. Often it consists of applying the learning in new practice situations. Then again it may be a simple matter of occasional review or a reminder. But in every case the teacher makes the learning a little more thorough than in the original teaching-learning situation.

In many instances this extra effort must consist of reteaching those things that the evaluation tells us the pupils have not learned, for the follow-through is not only an opportunity to clinch pupils' learning but also a chance for correcting mistakes and filling in gaps. Thus, any good mathematics teacher who, upon checking his pupils' work, found that they had not mastered one of the principles of the latest unit would stop to go over the principle again to be sure the pupils understood it before moving on to the new unit. The teacher's failure to clinch basic learnings is an all too frequent cause of pupils' failure at more advanced levels. Whatever is worth teaching is worth teaching well, and, if pupils miss it the first time around, the follow-up gives them a chance to make up the loss. A little additional effort can make the difference between half-baked learning and real understanding.

*

Is the fact that a pupil has successfully passed the prerequisites to a course any guarantee that he is ready for it? How might one tell if the pupil is ready?

Without continuous evaluation teaching is seldom efficient. Why?

Can you think of any teaching-learning situation in which any of the five steps of the general pattern of teaching strategies should be omitted?

Evaluation usually shows that not all pupils have reached the same point. What implications does this have for the guiding of learning activities?

*

Teaching Tactics

Teachers have a multitude of teaching tactics, or operations, available. Hence the problem of selecting the best tactic for the immediate situation and using it in the way most likely to bring about teaching success in that particular situation requires considerable skill. This problem is complicated by the fact that no situation is identical with any other and so the teacher must adapt or create a new tactic for each situation he encounters. It is for this reason that no textbook in methodology can prescribe exactly what a teacher should do in the classroom at a particular moment. Anyone who claims to give definitive prescriptions to specific problems that may arise should be viewed skeptically. Certainly any claim that any single method or approach to the teaching of any subject is the best way to teach that subject has the elements of quackery latent in it—no matter who makes the claim or who supports it. However, the teacher who has a sound grasp of educational principles and mastery over a large store of teaching techniques will find himself ready to provide the tactics necessary for almost any situation that could arise in any of his classes.

FLANDERS' CATEGORIES

Most teaching tactics are largely verbal. Amidon and Flanders[1] have divided the verbal teaching operations into ten categories. These categories are shown as Table 1–1. Seven of these categories describe operations in which the teacher does the talking or initiates the talking. Of these seven, four categories describe operations in which the teacher influences the pupil indirectly by accepting his feelings, praising or encouraging him, accepting his ideas, or asking questions. The remaining three teacher-talk categories include operations by which the teacher influences the pupils directly. In these categories we find such operations as lecturing, telling, giving facts or opinions, asking rhetorical questions, giving directions, criticizing, scolding, and justifying class procedures.

On the basis of a two-year study of junior high school teachers and pupils findings indicate that "all types of students learned more from working with the more indirect teachers than with the direct teachers"[2] and that in "both social studies and mathematics classes the students of the more indirect teachers scored higher on achievement tests than did the students of the more direct teachers"[3] However, the most successful teachers were the ones who could "shift their behavior as necessary. That is, they could be just as direct as any teacher in certain situations, but they could be far more indirect in other situations." In other words *the teachers who could best adapt their behavior to the situation were the most successful.* As a rule, however, the teachers who had this flexibility were the indirect teachers. The direct teachers were seldom able to adapt themselves to the situation requiring an indirect operation.[4]

IMPLICATIONS OF INTERACTION ANALYSIS

This research seems to have several implications for teaching. One is "that where the learner's goals are not clear to him an indirect approach which allows the pupil to set up his own goals is more effective than an approach in which the teacher tells the pupil what to do." Another is that recent tendencies to base courses upon classroom lectures are probably less efficient than courses in which the pupil is largely self-directing. A third is that the teacher who has developed the social skills of accepting, clarifying, and using pupils' ideas is probably potentially more effective than a teacher who does not possess those skills even though he may be a skillful director and lecturer. A fourth is that the most capable youth probably develop intellectually more and more rapidly with teachers who use indirect tactics than with teachers who use direct tactics. It is therefore somewhat alarming to find Flanders' statement that

> Two-thirds of the time spent in a classroom, someone is talking. Two-thirds of the time someone is talking, it is the teacher—for the teacher talks more than all the students combined. Two-thirds of the time that

---

[1] Edmund J. Amidon and Ned A. Flanders, *The Role of the Teacher in the Classroom* (Minneapolis, Minn.: Paul S. Amidon and Associates, 1963), p. 12.

[2] Ibid., p. 56.
[3] Ibid., p. 57.
[4] Ibid., p. 57.

Table 1–1

Summary of Categories for Interaction Analysis*

*Edmund J. Amidon and Ned A. Flanders, The Role of the Teacher in the Classroom. (Minneapolis, Minn.: Paul S. Amidon and Associates, 1963).

Teacher Talk	Indirect Influence	1. ACCEPTS FEELING: accepts and clarifies the feeling tone of the students in a nonthreatening manner. Feelings may be positive or negative. Predicting and recalling feelings are included.
		2. PRAISES OR ENCOURAGES: praises or encourages student action or behavior. Jokes that release tension, not at the expense of another individual, nodding head or saying "uhhuh?" or "go on" are included.
		3. ACCEPTS OR USES IDEAS OF STUDENT: clarifying, building, or developing ideas or suggestions by a student. As teacher brings more of his own ideas into play, shift to category five.
		4. ASKS QUESTIONS: asking a question about content or procedure with the intent that a student answer.
	Direct Influence	5. LECTURES: giving facts or opinions about content or procedure; expressing his own ideas; asking rhetorical questions.
		6. GIVES DIRECTIONS: directions, commands, or orders with which a student is expected to comply.
		7. CRITICIZES OR JUSTIFIES AUTHORITY: statements intended to change student behavior from nonacceptable to acceptable pattern; bawling someone out; stating why the teacher is doing what he is doing, extreme self-reference.
Student Talk		8. STUDENT TALK-RESPONSE: talk by students in response to teacher. Teacher initiates the contact or solicits student statement.
		9. STUDENT TALK-INITIATION: talk by students, which they initiate. If "calling on" student is only to indicate who may talk next, observers must decide whether student wanted to talk. If he did, use this category.
		10. SILENCE OR CONFUSION: pauses, short periods of silence, and periods of confusion in which communication cannot be understood by the observer.

the teacher is talking, he is lecturing, giving directions, or criticizing the behavior of students. One-third of the time he is asking questions, reacting to student ideas, or giving praise.[5]

[5] Ibid.

TYPES OF TEACHING TACTICS

Obviously each teacher must use a large number of teaching tactics of various kinds. Among them are such tactics as the following:

Tactics designed to make the pupils' ideas clear.

Tactics designed to present new or different materials.

Tactics designed to show pupils how to do things.

Tactics designed to affect or change attitudes, ideals, appreciations.

Tactics designed to give security.

Tactics designed to motivate.

Tactics designed to evaluate, or measure.

Tactics designed to guide or direct pupils' work.

Tactics designed to arouse, direct, or assuage emotions.

These are often called operations. The important thing is to select the proper tactics for the result one desires. Presumably in the Amidon and Flanders studies it was the indirect teachers' ability to select their tactics more skillfully than the direct teachers that made them more successful.

The Clarifying Tactics. The clarifying tactics are operations by which the teacher helps the pupil make his ideas clear. For one must remember that no one can clarify understandings for anyone else. Neither can he have insights for anyone else, nor do anyone else's thinking. Each person must do these things for himself. But it is possible for a teacher to help and guide a pupil to clearer understandings and insights. The clarifying tactics are the tactics the teacher can use to accomplish this purpose. Some of them are described below. Note that almost all the operations described are based on questions and are examples of what Flanders calls indirect teaching.[6]

A typical clarifying tactic is to ask the pupil to define what he means in his own terms. Another is to ask him to illustrate or demonstrate his meanings. Yet another is to ask him where he got his idea—what is its basis and is this basis a tenable one? Still another would be to throw back the pupil's idea to him, perhaps rephrased, to ask him whether that is what he means. If it is what he means, then another tactic would be to ask him to forecast the implications or logical consequences of this idea. In other words, if so, then what? Still another tactic is to ask the pupil to summarize what he means or to organize his meaning into the logical outline. Another is to question his basis for belief.

[6] The descriptions are largely derived from Louis Raths' *What Is Teaching?*, undated, mimeographed.

Is he dealing with fact or opinion, fact or feeling, fact or emotion? Questioning the pupil about what causes his difficulty in order to help him solve it is still another example of a clarifying tactic.

Show-how Tactics. The show-how tactics are mostly concerned with skills. They include such operations as demonstrations using visual and audiovisual aids, and helping pupils to perform the task, perhaps by showing them alternate or better methods to use, or by analyzing the pupils' present techniques to see where they are at fault. Telling a pupil how to do something and taking him through the task step by step can also be included as show-how tactics even though they are often not so much "show-how" as "tell-how." So can correcting of faults in techniques or form during practice, as when the golf instructor tells the pupil to hold the club like this and not like that. (In this case practice is a teaching strategy.)

The Security-giving Tactics. The security-giving tactics are the operations that make it possible for pupils to feel free to learn. For many pupils school is a challenging and frightening experience full of many strong pressures. Teachers need to help pupils gain the confidence they need to meet the pressures and to cope with the challenges. The tactics that provide these qualities are the ones by which the teacher lets the pupil know that he is welcome in the class and that the teacher respects his individuality and will support him in his efforts to learn, even when he makes mistakes.

One of the most important aids to security giving is consistency in the teacher's behavior and in the types of operations he uses in his teaching. Although variety is supposed to give spice to life, and one should, of course, use many different types of activities, variety should not be confused with inconsistency. The teacher who is authoritarian one day and permissive the next, or one who swings from using very conservative to very progressive procedures without adequately preparing the pupils for the change, adds not interest, but insecurity, confusion, and chaos.

OTHER KINDS OF TACTICS

Teachers may use many other kinds of tactics. Among them are tactics in which teachers direct, request, explain, suggest, praise, point out possibilities and alternatives, create problem situations, and show materials and methods; tactics by which teachers try to motivate pupils, tactics in which teachers compare and judge correctness, tactics in which the teacher praises or condemns pupil behavior; tactics in which he presents an attitude or behavior in a favorable light, or reinforces it with emotion or emotionally toned behavior; dramatic or musical presentations; and the pointing out of suitable models for pupils to follow. These tactics are especially significant because the operations that bring about the learning of knowledge and skills will not suffice if teachers wish to change their pupils' attitudes, ideals, and appreciations.

*

Perhaps you would like to arrange the various tactics in a set of categories of your own.

List all the tactics you can think of according to their categories.

How can a teacher determine which tactic to use in any specific situation?

What differences in strategy and tactics would be called for in teaching situations in which the main objective was (a) an appreciation; (b) a skill; (c) an attitude; (d) information?

*

The New Technology

In the middle years of the twentieth century educational technology developed with astonishing rapidity. The period since World War II has seen the development of new teaching tools, educational machines, instructional materials, new curricular and administrative organizations, and new kinds of school buildings and classrooms. These innovations have had and are having considerable impact on secondary education.

THE SYSTEMS APPROACH

One result of the advent of the new technical innovations seems to be the possibility of developing a systems approach in teaching in which the teaching aims can be laid out very specifically and the human and material resources needed to achieve these goals can be utilized most effectively and efficiently. By using teaching machines and computer-assisted instruction, teachers should be able to individualize instruction and to teach facts and information with a thoroughness quite rare in standard classrooms. Certainly a language laboratory properly constructed and used should be able to take on the onerous foreign-language pattern drills period after period without a bit of the fatigue that can overwhelm a teacher. Similarly, we can capitalize on the various talents of our teachers and support personnel. If certain jobs can best be done by clerks, we should turn them over to clerks. If some teachers are showmen and lecturers, then they should be the teachers who lecture. On the other hand, if some teachers are excellent at leading discussions or at helping individuals, they should be the discussion leaders or the directors of pupils' individual study. In addition, if some teachers have superior guidance skills, then they should be homeroom teachers. In other words each teacher's work should be arranged according to his ability and he should be given the tools and the help that will enable him to do the best teaching possible.

Whether we shall ever achieve this utopia that the dreamers visualize is still to be revealed. Not all the innovations have been accepted universally, nor have all the new devices been completely successful. Some people find instruction by teaching machine boring. Some schools have rejected the language laboratories after a few years of trials. The real danger, in the eyes of many critics, is the fear that the new technology may lead to impersonal indoctrination. There is little doubt, however, that eventually technology will be able to overcome most of its present faults. There is good reason to believe that, for good or evil, the age of educational specialization has begun.

HUMANE TEACHING

No matter what the future holds, the principle of the need for selecting the right tool or approach to do the job required applies more than ever. The new teaching technology makes, and will continue to make, it necessary to match tool and task better than ever before so that we can become more productive teachers. This result can be accomplished only if we teachers become more humane—turning the mundane, routine teaching tasks over to the machines and clerks and really concentrating on the higher cognitive and affective aspects of learning.

*

In what ways is the new technology affecting teaching method?

What types of teaching jobs are best done by teachers? What, if any, can be safely turned over to machines?

Investigate team teaching as one aspect of the movement towards a systems approach.

*

THE ROLE OF SUBJECT MATTER

Three Positions

The professional teacher also selects his strategies and tactics on the basis of the subject matter to be taught and his notion of the role of subject matter. There seem to be three ways to think of subject matter. One is to consider it something valuable in and of itself. According to this position, one should learn the subject matter, whatever it is, not for any contingent values that may come from knowing it, but because to know it is good. The second position is to think of subject matter as having some utilitarian value. According to this position one should learn the content, whatever it is, because one can use that particular knowledge for some practical purpose, for example, to earn a living or to get into college. The third position is to think of subject matter as a means of teaching process, methods, or structure. According to this way of thinking it is not so much the content that has value, as the skills, attitudes, and generalizations we gain by means of learning the content. Thus if the real object of learning history is to learn historical method or to think historically, then it does not matter particularly what history we learn as long as we learn it in such a way that we learn the method. In this view content is only a vehicle to use to teach process.

Even though many teachers have never considered their own views about subject matter, their views tend to influence the content they select for their courses and the ways in which they teach. The philosophical orientation of the teacher, then,

is, whether he is aware of it or not, a determiner of educational method.

From this discussion perhaps we can draw the inference that *content is not necessarily information or fact, but it is also processes, skills, and attitudes.* Knowing how is as much part of curriculum content as knowing what.

The Structure of the Disciplines

Another determiner of teaching method is the structure of subject matter. By structure we mean the interrelationships or organization of parts. Thus the structure of subject matter includes the scope and sequence and vertical and horizontal organization of its content which in turn must be based upon the organization of the disciplines or selections from which the subject matter is obtained.

DIFFERENT STRUCTURES FOR DIFFERENT DISCIPLINES

An important point that has been lost sight of for many years by many teachers and administrators as well as parents and pupils is that the structures of the different disciplines vary from each other. Not only that, but the disciplines themselves have subdivisions whose structures vary from each other. That this important fact has not figured more prominently in educational thinking is strange, because persons who have stopped to consider have been well aware of it since the time of Aristotle.

ARISTOTLE'S THREE CATEGORIES

Aristotle divided the disciplines into three categories: the theoretical, the practical, and the productive. By the theoretical he meant those studies which consist of knowledge that we know absolutely; by the practical he meant those studies that require choice and decision like political science or logic; by the productive he meant the disciplines like the fine arts, practical arts, or engineering that bring forth some tangible result or product. Schwab explains these three categories more explicitly.

The theoretical disciplines, devoted to knowing, concern themselves with those aspects of things which are fixed, stable, enduring. Hence, the theoretical disciplines are concerned with precisely these aspects of things which we cannot alter by making or make use of by doing. The productive disciplines are concerned with what is malleable, capable of being changed. The practical disciplines are concerned with another sort of malleability of human character, its ability to deliberate on its future and (within limits) to do as it sees fit.[7]

THE NEED TO DIFFERENTIATE

The Aristotelian analysis of the disciplines is only one of many. The interesting and alarming thing about this analysis of the disciplines, as Schwab points out[8], is that teachers have tended to teach all disciplines in the school curriculum as though they were theoretical. For example some teachers teach literature, composition, and even music and art as though they were history or science, and so, instead of reacting to poetry, treat it as fact to be learned. Such malpractice is tragic. The structures of the disciplines and their subdivisions require different teaching strategies for different studies. The disciplines differ according to purpose, substance, organization, and method of inquiry by which knowledge in the field is discovered and verified.

THE REVISIONIST NATURE OF KNOWLEDGE

The common tendency of teachers to treat all knowledge as though it were indubitable, permanent truth is particularly regrettable because of the revisionist nature of all disciplines in modern times. The middle-aged teacher of history today finds in modern historical research interpretations of the Colonial Era, the American Revolution, and the Civil War and the Reconstruction quite different from those he learned in the works of Beard and Muzzey he read in his student days. Similarly, a great number of the facts about the immutable elements so earnestly taught to high school pupils thirty years ago have turned out to be not so. In literature, too, styles of criticism have changed, and

even the mighty rules of grammar are losing face.

Every day knowledge changes faster and faster. Consequently to attempt to teach pupils facts alone is to lead pupils to dissatisfaction when they learn that new discoveries have proved that the facts they learned are facts no longer. Instead of facts and information the pupil of the future needs to know how to cope with new knowledge. For this purpose he needs familiarity with the structures of the disciplines and knowledge of the mechanisms by which knowledge in the disciplines is created. Above all, he needs to master the intellectual skills and attitudes that allow him to keep himself well informed and well educated no matter what new knowledge appears. To meet these needs the teacher must adopt teaching strategies that will teach pupils to seek out rather than to accept knowledge.

THE FUTILITY OF SUBJECT COVERING

He must also find strategies that give depth rather than superficiality. In the modern world to attempt to cover the subject is obsolete. No longer can anyone hope to cover the entirety of any subject. We can only attempt to select whatever material seems the most desirable in view of our goals. Again, as with the revisionist nature of knowledge, the situation calls for an emphasis on the teaching of process and structure. What our criterion will be for the selection of subject matter depends somewhat on our philosophy. But no matter what that may be, we have come to the point where it is more important to eliminate well than to include. The watchword that must guide every teacher of every subject is: *Teach more effectively and thoroughly by concentrating on the most useful and ornamental and eliminating the rest.*

*

Aristotle says that disciplines differ. What are the implications of these differences for teaching?

How can we teach so that what the pupils learn will not be soon out of date?

According to one educationist any high school teacher who believes that he must cover the subject is incompetent. What then should the teacher be doing?

In what way is the teaching strategy one uses likely to determine the nature of the subject matter pupils learn?

*

---

[7] Joseph J. Schwab, "Structure of the Disciplines: Meanings and Significances," in G. W. Ford and Lawrence Pugno, *The Structure of Knowledge and the Curriculum* (Chicago: Rand McNally & Company, 1964), p. 17.

[8] Ibid.

KNOWING THE PUPIL

The Nature of the Adolescent

In addition to a knowledge of boys and girls and how they learn, teaching also requires a particular knowledge of each boy and girl in the class. The teen-ager who is our secondary school pupil is an individual of complexities and enigmas. The business of growing up is a complicated one. The adolescent is torn by many conflicts and many moments of indecision. At one moment, he may struggle for complete independence; at the next moment he may need the reassurance and protection he required when he was younger. As he enters early adolescence, he brings with him personal, social, educational, and vocational problems which he is incapable of analyzing and for which he is incapable of setting up any logical solution. For example, let us examine the case of Judy.

Judy, a pleasant girl of fifteen in the tenth grade, is a typical example of a teen-ager beset by the many problems of the adolescent. She is more concerned with the telephone than with homework; more concerned with her personal appearance than with that of her room or her locker; more interested in going on dates than in studying at home. Judy's schoolwork is suffering, and feelings of antagonism have developed between her and her teacher. It seems as if Miss C. is usually punishing Judy for one thing or another. At home antagonism between mother and daughter also prevails, although Judy is doted on by her father. In fact, the parents often argue over Judy.

This picture of Judy is not at all unusual. The lives of many adolescents are quite stormy. Of course, most youngsters, especially those who come from healthy home and school environments, overcome these difficulties relatively unscathed. Still, the teacher who understands the reasons for an adolescent behavior can do much toward helping the pupil during this trying period. By getting to know and to understand the pupil the teacher is in a position to help the pupil solve these problems and to adapt his program to make the most of the situation.

It is here that the teacher must be aware of factors that contribute to many of the changes in behavior taking place. The early adolescent, beset with the mysteries of physiological changes, and concerned over the development of secondary sex characteristics, needs strong support, not only from home, but from school as well. The rebellion of the middle adolescent is understandable, too, if the teacher is cognizant of the conditions of life that help create the uncertainty, confusion, concern, and rebellion within the youngster.

Dr. William C. Kvaraceus has said that "in today's complex and mobile society, youth continues to be the most vulnerable segment of any group." [9] He goes on to say that he considers being a youth or teen-ager the most dangerous occupation in every society today. The rapid changes now going on are steadily increasing the hazards to youth.

Obviously then, if teachers are to be able to diagnose the teaching-learning situation accurately and formulate effective teaching strategies, they must be familiar with the characteristics of secondary school pupils in general and their own individual pupils in particular.

Some Generalizations About Secondary School Pupils

Diagnosis is complicated by the fact that the characteristics of secondary school pupils in general do not necessarily apply to every adolescent boy or girl. Each secondary school pupil is unique. The set of characteristics that make up his physical, mental, emotional, and social being can never be duplicated exactly. Yet there are a number of generalizations true enough of youth in general to be used as a tentative guide if we remember that when one applies these generalizations to any individual, one must be prepared for variations from the norm. With this caveat in mind, let us look at some generalizations about the characteristics of adolescents.

1. A pupil is an entire organism. Anything he learns or does affects him as an entity. All activity has emotional, mental, and physical aspects. This applies to school learning as well as to other activities.

[9] William C. Kvaraceus, Director of Youth Studies, Lincoln Filene Center for Citizenship and Public Affairs, in a speech at the University of Hartford, October 28, 1964.

2. Pupils are plastic. They can be shaped, but in the process they interact with the environment. They are not just wax tablets to be written on. They are not passive, nor do they just react to environmental stimuli—although the environment has a great deal to do with what a pupil is, what he becomes, and how he behaves.

3. Adolescence is a period of change accompanied by rapid and uneven growth. These changes may cause many conflicts within a youth and in his social relations.

4. Secondary school age pupils and middle school age pupils tend to be emotional, moody, and flighty. Schools are likely to be sources of frustration, failure, humiliation, and punishment to them. They are a combination of naïveté and sophistication.

5. Secondary school pupils need to establish themselves as young men and young women. They need to learn how to live their roles in a heterosexual world and to make adjustments to their new evidence of sexuality and its attendant problems. In this connection, secondary school pupils have certain developmental tasks to perform. They, consciously or unconsciously, try to carry out those tasks by, quite properly, giving them a higher priority than schoolwork and other tasks. According to Havighurst these developmental tasks are:
   a. To learn to understand oneself, to live with and compensate for one's inadequacies, and to make the most of one's assets.
   b. To learn what it is to be a young man or young woman and to act accordingly.
   c. To develop a suitable moral code.
   d. To learn how to act one's part in a heterosexual society.
   e. To determine, prepare for, and become placed in his vocation.
   f. To acquire a suitable philosophy of life.
   g. To build a system of values.
   h. To establish himself as an independent individual free from his mother's apron strings.
   i. To learn how to make reasonable decisions in serious matters of his own responsibility without undue reliance on an older person.
   j. To master the social and intellectual level and knowledge necessary for adult life.
   k. To learn the skills of courtship and to establish close friendships with persons of the opposite sex as preparation for finding a suitable mate.
   l. To break away from his childhood home.
   m. To learn what kind of person he is himself and to learn to live with himself.[10]

6. Secondary school pupils are trying to establish their independence. They tend to be very critical of adults and of the adult world and to reject adult authority and domination. They tend to associate school learning with adult domination and so reject it.

7. In spite of their desire for asserting their independence, secondary school age pupils have great need for security. They are greatly concerned about themselves—their bodies, social relations, future, image, status, and so on. This accounts for such phenomena as going steady, early marriage, conformity, and the like. It also accounts for many rapid extreme alternations in behavior. It follows then that secondary school programs should be supportive.

8. Secondary school pupils tend to be obsessed by conformity. Even the "nonconformists" are conformists. Adolescents tend to conform to the standards of the adolescent community rather than those of adults—although these standards may be the same.

9. In their efforts to establish themselves as grown-ups, youths are likely to experiment with undesirable behavior calculated to illustrate their independence, manliness or womanliness, and adulthood.

10. Secondary school pupils desire self-realization and so need to achieve, to feel important, and to be accepted by their peers and by adults. They don't want to be talked down to or to be treated like children. They need responsibility. They need the chance to be leaders sometimes. Therefore teachers should give all pupils a chance to shine, to show off a little, and to assume some real responsibility.

11. Because of his desire for recognition and achievement the pupil of secondary school age

[10] Robert J. Havighurst, *Human Development and Education* (New York: Longmans, Green & Co., 1953) , Ch. 1, pp. 9–15, 19, 20; also *Developmental Tasks and Education,* 2nd ed. (New York: Longmans, Green & Co., 1952) .

is likely to be sympathetic to the desires of others, particularly the disadvantaged and downtrodden in their search for civil rights, economic opportunity, freedom, and so forth. Secondary school pupils tend to be "suckers for causes" whether well deserved or not.

12. Secondary school pupils are concerned about the meaning of life and self. They are concerned with vocational choice (some of them at least). They do not see much relevance or pertinence to most of the content in the secondary school curriculum.

13. Youth of secondary school age are more ready to learn through verbal means than younger ones. They are not as dependent on demonstration, manipulation, nonverbal perception, and the like as younger pupils are. On the other hand, they cannot learn everything from entirely verbal presentations. (Neither can adults for that matter.)

14. Pupils have long attention spans, but low tolerance to boredom.

15. Youth are self-motivating. It is not a matter of getting pupils to do something so much as getting them to direct their activities into desirable directions. Schools and teachers need to provide relevant curricula, courses, and lessons that have meaning to pupils and that they can see real reasons for doing.

16. Pupils are interested by activity, novelty, adventure, and the like.[11]

Learning About the Pupil

Because pupils are so different, if the teacher is to provide the sort of teaching best suited for each pupil, he must be well acquainted with their abilities, potentialities, goals, backgrounds, problems, and needs. Without this knowledge the problems of motivation, provision for individual differences, adjusting curriculum and methods to meet pupils' needs, and selecting the proper goals and instructional strategies and tactics becomes very difficult. Fortunately teachers have many tools available to help them learn about pupils. These tools make it possible for a teacher to become fairly well acquainted with his pupils even though he may have five sections of thirty pupils each.

INVENTORIES AND SCALES

One effective means of finding out what worries, problems, or concerns a pupil may have is the problem inventory. These inventories are intended to provide the means of identifying the personal problems of individual pupils. Similarly, the teacher has available data compiled by the use of instruments designed to find out pupils' attitudes, vocational leanings, aptitudes, interests, and the like. Inventories of this sort are ordinarily given by guidance personnel who make the results available to teachers. Not only is the administering of such instruments usually a sensitive task, but often interpreting their results requires professional skills that few beginning teachers have mastered.

OBSERVATION AS A SOURCE OF INFORMATION

Observation is one of the best means of getting to know a pupil. Through its use an alert teacher, properly trained, can often find clues to the causes for a pupil's behavior. However, one should not limit his observation to the pupil. Many times the teacher can understand a pupil's problems better after observing and talking with the parents. Therefore the teacher should meet the parents early in the school year—especially if the pupil shows signs of having difficulty in the classroom or elsewhere in school. By utilizing the information gleaned through observing and talking with his pupils and their parents, the teacher can often help the young people in his charge solve their problems. Techniques to help one in observing include check lists, rating scales, behavior logs, and anecdotal records. They will be described more fully in later discussions of evaluation and diagnosis.[12]

INFORMATION FROM OTHER TEACHERS

The teacher who wishes to learn about his students should confer with other teachers also. Objective discussions with one's colleagues can re-

---

[11] Leonard H. Clark, *Teaching Social Studies in Secondary Schools: A Handbook* (New York: Macmillan Publishing Co., Inc., 1973), pp. 11–13.

[12] See Ch. 15.

Figure 1–2
A Sample Cumulative Record Folder (First Page).

1 [A]	LAST NAME	FIRST	MIDDLE	RELIGION	PLACE OF BIRTH	DATE OF BIRTH	M F W C
2	YEAR AND AGE						
3	ADDRESS — HOME						
4	ADDRESS — TELEPHONE						
5	ADDRESS — SCHOOL						
6	PHYSICAL DISABILITIES						
7	HEALTH PHYSICAL						
8	HEALTH MENTAL						
9	SOCIAL ADJUSTMENT HOME CONDITIONS						
10	STUDY CONDITIONS AND HOURS STUDY PER WEEK						
11	COMMUTING HOURS PER WEEK						
12	INTERESTS REPORTED						
13	VOCATIONAL PREFERENCE						
14	EDUCATIONAL PLANS						
15	EDUCATIONAL SUGGESTIONS						
16	LOANS OR SCHOLARSHIPS						
17	SUPPORT OF SELF OR DEPENDENTS						
18	PERSONALITY RATINGS — +2						
19	PERSONALITY RATINGS — +1						
20	PERSONALITY RATINGS — N						
21	PERSONALITY RATINGS — −1						
22	PERSONALITY RATINGS — −2						
23	PERSONALITY TESTS USED						

	NAME OF	HEALTH	RELIGION	DIED	BIRTHPLACE - NATIONALITY	ARRIVED U.S.A.	EDUCATION-WHERE-KIND-DEGREE	OCCUPATION	ADDRESS (IN PENCIL)	TELEPHONE
24	FATHER									
25	MOTHER									
26	STEP PARENT OR GUARDIAN									

	HOW MANY	NOW ATTENDING WHAT COLLEGE	GRADUATED FROM WHAT COLLEGE	AUTHORITY OF BIRTH CERTIFICATION		HOME	BEFORE 10 YRS OLD	AFTER 10 YRS OLD
27	OLDER BROTHERS			31 PASSPORT	35 CHURCH RECORD	38 LANGUAGE SPOKEN IN THE HOME		
28	YOUNGER BROTHERS			32 OATH	36 HOSPITAL RECORD	39 TYPE OF HOME COMMUNITY		
29	OLDER SISTERS			33 BIRTH CERTIFICATE	37			
30	YOUNGER SISTERS			34 OTHER EVIDENCE		40 IF PARENTS ARE SEPARATED GIVE DATE		

K. P. 14196

veal much. The discussions, however, ought to be planned; even if sometimes greatly illuminating, chance conversations are liable to be unproductive. On the other hand, planned conferences of all the teachers and guidance counselors concerned are often extremely helpful in bringing about an understanding of the personality and problems of a particular boy or girl.

The opinions and observations of faculty members can also be gathered from anecdotal reports, behavior logs, and cumulative records. The cumulative record may include much significant information because it is the repository of such records as

1. Pupils' personal goals.
2. Records of significant experiences.
3. Records of conferences.
4. Test data.
5. Health records.
6. Family history.
7. Course records.
8. Activity records.
9. Personality ratings and descriptions.

Figure 1–3
A Sample Cumulative Record Folder (Second Page) .

1	B	YEAR AND AGE					
2	COUNSELLORS						
3	DISCIPLINE						
4	NUMBER OF DAYS ABSENT						
5	NAME AND TYPE OF SCHOOL						
6	DATE AND REASON FOR LEAVING						
7	NOTABLE ACCOMPLISHMENTS OR UNUSUAL EXPERIENCES						
8	CLUBS AND OFFICES						
9	EXTRA CURRICULUM EXPERIENCES	ATHLETIC					
10		HRS A WEEK					
11		NON ATHLETIC					
12		HRS A WEEK					
13	VOCATIONAL EXPERIENCES	TYPE AND DURATION					
14		WEEKLY PAY					
15		HRS A WEEK					
16	SUMMER EXPERIENCES						
17							
18							
19							
20	OBJECTIVE TEST SCORES						
21							
22							
23							
24							
25							
26							

10. Questionnaires.
11. Administrative records.
12. Anecdotal reports.

Most cumulative records are made up of a folder or envelope on which one can record pertinent data and in which one can place other records and reports. An example of a cumulative record folder appears as Figures 1–2, 1–3, 1–4, and 1–5.

*

An example of a cumulative record form is shown in Figures 1–2, 1–3, 1–4 and 1–5. What information of value might you find in it? In what ways might the information in this cumulative record help the teacher in his teaching? What physical and health data would be helpful? Is there any information omitted from the printed form?

How might each of the records suggested in the list above be used by a teacher?

*

Three Basic Questions

In short, knowing the pupil boils down to three basic questions.

Figure 1–4
A Sample Cumulative Record Folder (Third Page).

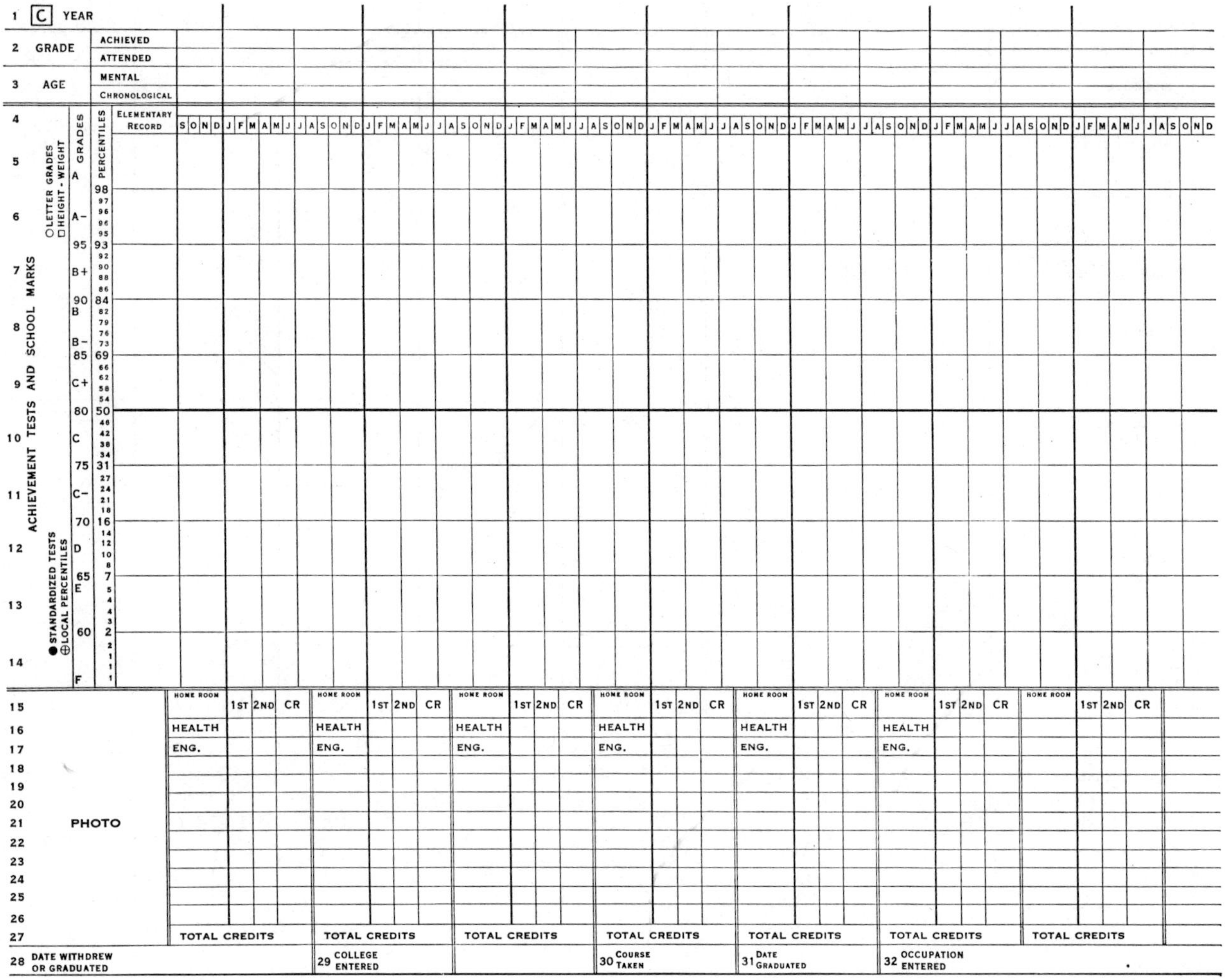

1. What should a secondary school teacher know about each pupil?
2. Where can he find this information?
3. How can he use this information once he has found it?

The following outline is a summary of the answers to these three questions as given by five graduate-class discussion groups.

WHAT SHOULD A SECONDARY SCHOOL TEACHER KNOW ABOUT EACH PUPIL?

a. Vital Statistics
  (1) Name, grade, course, and so on
  (2) Health record—mental and physical (defects?)
  (3) Any standard test results (reading grade level, aptitude and ability, and so on)

Figure 1–5
A Sample Cumulative Record Folder (Course Selection Insert).

SUBJECT SELECTIONS

NAME_____   YEAR OF GRADUATION_____

GRADE 9	Points	GRADE 10	Points	GRADE 11	Points	GRADE 12	Points
1. Phys. Ed. & Health	1	1. Phys. Ed. & Health	1	1. Phys. Ed. & Driver Ed. & Health	1	1. Phys. Ed. & Health	1
2. English I	5	2. English II	5	2. English III	5	2. English IV	5
3.		3.		3. U.S. History I	5	3. U.S. History II	5
4.		4.		4.		4.	
5.		5.		5.		5.	
6.		6.		6.		6.	
7.		7.		7.		7.	
Total Points		Total Points		Total Points		Total Points	

IOWA TESTS	GRADE 7	8	9
Vocabulary			
Reading Comprehension			
Language Skills			
Work Study Skills			
Arithmetic			
Total			
DIFFERENTIAL APTITUDE TESTS			
Verbal			
Numerical			
Abstract			
Spatial			
Mechanical			
Clerical			
Spelling			
Sentences			

COOPERATIVE TESTS	GRADE 9	10	11
(Vocabulary)			
Reading Comprehension			
Mechanics of Expression			
Social Studies			
Mathematics			
Science			
Foreign Language			
OTHER TESTS:			

	GRADE 8	9	10	11
Vocational Plans				
Educational Plans				
Rank in Class				
Scholastic Aptitude				
Interest Inventory	Grade 8 — California 1. 2. 3.		Grade 11 — Kuder 1. 2. 3.	
Counselor's Approval				
Parent's Signature				

(4) Attendance record
b. Home Situation
   (1) Family background
   (2) Intrafamily relationships
   (3) Social contacts with community (club membership, and so on)
   (4) Religious attitudes and affiliations
   (5) Economic status
c. Social Outlook
   (1) Friends
   (2) Social activities
      Spare time
      School extracurricular
   (3) Group acceptance
d. Personal Qualities
   (1) Ethical standards and attitudes

(2) Talents and capabilities

(3) Goals and ambitions (immediate and future)

(4) Interests and hobbies (in or out of school)

(5) Antisocial traits causing discipline problems

a. Records

(1) Cumulative record folder (Permanent Record Card)

(2) Test results (vocational, interest, aptitude, ability, intelligence, achievement, and so on)

(3) Anecdotal records

(4) Physical examinations (dental, visual, auditory, and so on)

b. Indirect Contacts

(1) Home visitations

(2) Reliable members of community (Boy Scout leaders, priests or ministers, police, and so on)

(3) PTA contacts with parents

(4) Guidance nurse or guidance counselor

(5) Other dependable teachers

c. Direct Contacts

(1) Personal observations during
    informal discussions
    conferences
    special help periods
    nonschool activities

(2) Conclusions drawn from
    autobiographies
    questionnaires
    sociograms

Employing the preceding data and experience the teacher can

a. Judge more accurately what to expect intellectually from the student and in so doing perform the following functions:

(1) Select and plan the subject matter of his course at such a level and in such a manner that it challenges the student if he learns rapidly or encourages him if he learns slowly.

(2) Transfer a student to classes or courses that are at the level of his ability before a critical situation arises where disciplinary action is needed as a result of the pupil's maladjustment.

b. Plan a seating arrangement and class grouping that will promote the greatest social, physical, and intellectual adjustment or progress for the student.

c. Encourage and use leadership qualities more effectively.

(1) to further individual development and

(2) to secure greater class interest and cooperation.

d. Refer to the proper authority any problems arising from health difficulties.

e. Prevent many discipline problems and deal more intelligently with those that do arise.

f. Encourage the student to use any special abilities through recognizing his efforts, achievements, and so on.

g. Aid more effectively in helping to guide the student's program.

h. Assist in home and group adjustments.

i. Integrate class as a group by preventing the formation of cliques.

j. Stimulate interest in hobbies and outside activities.

*

What do you think of the answers given by these students? Would your answers to these three questions agree with theirs?

Turn back to the description of Judy. What information about Judy would help you understand her problems better? In what ways would a better understanding of Judy's problems help Miss C. in her teaching?

*

SUMMARY

The criterion for success in teaching is the extent to which the teacher is able to bring about changes in pupils' behavior or tendency toward behavior. To meet his responsibilities the teacher needs much skill. As a rule, in spite of pupils who are recalcitrant, ill, or meagerly endowed, most failures in teaching result from poor teaching or poor curricula. One result of poor teaching is meaningless parroting which can be avoided if one teaches realistically and aims his instruction at the knowledge, skill, or attitude to be learned rather than at empty skills.

The role of method is to bring about learning. It includes both content and techniques, strategies and tactics. The key to method is to bring about the desired learning in pupils by selecting the proper strategies and tactics and consequently the proper content and techniques. To achieve this conclusion one must diagnose the situation, prepare for the learning, guide the activities, evaluate the learning, and follow up. Teaching tactics are the techniques and content by which one carries out a strategy. There are many different tactics, or operations. The objective is to select the one best suited to carry out the goal of the moment. Unfortunately the operations most frequently used do not seem to be the most promising for most teaching-learning situations. The discovery of new technology has made it more important than ever that teachers choose and use the instructional tool or technique most appropriate for the kind of learning at hand so that the teaching can be most effective and efficient.

Subject matter is not all the same and so all subjects should not be taught in the same way. Rather, the teaching approach should vary according to the structure and methods of the disciplines concerned. No longer can teachers be content to teach pupils information and to cover the subject. The modern world contains too much information to cover and the facts are changing too swiftly. Modern teaching must concentrate on organization, method, process, structure, skills, and attitudes so that young people can cope with the new and different knowledge that will be discovered before they get the old knowledge well digested. It is for these reasons that the teacher must teach more by teaching less.

To be effective, teaching methods must be adjusted to the nature of the pupil, including how he learns. In general the secondary school learner is a complex individual. In order to understand and deal with individual pupils as individuals, one can make use of a number of techniques and devices among which are various inventories and scales, observation, anecdotal reports, behavior logs, and cumulative records. As a rule the more one knows about each pupil, the better his teaching will be.

The American
Secondary
School Today

2

Every country on earth has evolved a school system peculiar to its own tradition, needs, and culture. The United States is no exception. The American school system and the American secondary school are both unique.

A DECENTRALIZED SYSTEM

Unlike school systems in many foreign lands, the American school system is decentralized. The constitution of the United States gives the responsibility for education to the various states. The states, in turn, have delegated a large measure of their authority to local school districts.[1] In effect, the state education agency, e.g., the State Board of Education, sets up general guidelines and then allows the local districts to run their schools pretty much as they please as long as they follow the guidelines reasonably well. The states also make some financial contribution to the local school districts and use this state aid to induce districts to follow state

[1] The state of Hawaii is an exception to this rule.

regulations. On the whole, these regulations are rather lenient and general so that the local districts do not find them overly restrictive. If anything, they are more likely to be influenced by the standards set forth by the regional associations of schools and colleges which act as accrediting agencies.

THE TWELVE-GRADE LADDER

Despite the lack of rigid central control, school districts throughout the country follow similar organizational and curriculum patterns. One distinctive feature common to American schools is the twelve-grade ladder system in which the pupils move from grade one to grade twelve in annual steps. This system differs from the traditional European plan which consists of at least two educational ladders, one for the elite and one (or more) for the rest. As a rule the elite track in these countries carries pupils through the equivalent of the American fourteenth grade (junior college), although not all students continue so long in the program, and is much more academically oriented than in the American schools. The fact that the American school system, by design, extends only through the twelfth grade and provides only one institution in which the elite and ordinary pupils are schooled together, has caused a number of misconceptions about the comparative effectiveness of traditional European and American schools.[2]

Although the typical American school system is a twelve-grade system, it is not limited to just twelve grades. Many school systems provide kindergartens and nursery schools for children who are not yet ready for the first grade.[3] Neither are the twelve grades organized in the same way in different school systems. Common plans of organization are

The 8–4 plan (i.e., 8 grades elementary, 4 high school).

The 6–6 plan (i.e., 6 grades elementary, 6 junior-senior high school).

The 6–3–3 plan (i.e., 6 grades elementary, 3 junior high school, 3 senior high school).

The 6–2–4 plan (i.e., 6 grades elementary, 2 middle school, 4 high school).

The 5–3–4 plan (i.e., 5 grades elementary, 3 middle school, 4 high school).

Proponents of the various plans have developed rationales to justify their adoptions, but, to tell the truth, the plans are frequently the result of sheer expediency or of a current fad.

PUBLIC SECONDARY SCHOOLS

By and large public secondary schools in the United States are extremely similar to each other. In almost every instance they try to offer *universal public* education in *comprehensive* schools. In this context *universal* means that the schools are open to all youths of the proper age group who have completed the elementary school program. Theoretically no one is denied admittance because of race, social status, wealth, intelligence, or class, although, in fact, the schools have not always lived up to this ideal. They are seldom selective in the sense of catering to an academic elite as many private and foreign schools are, however. *Public* means that the schools are financed by public funds. Theoretically pupils can attend without incurring any expense. Actually, in some instances, travel, materials, and incidentals make public secondary education fairly expensive. *Comprehensive* means that the school tries to provide for all the needs of all the youth in a single institution. Some school districts, however, provide specialized high schools for pupils with special talents or vocational goals. New York City, for instance, has high schools for the performing arts, needle trades, science, and other academic and vocational specialties. Actually few American high schools are truly comprehensive; rather they are academic high schools with other curricula added. To present a program that would meet the needs of all youth seems to be just too much for the average high school to handle.

The curricula in American secondary schools tend to be somewhat conservative. Despite the numerous allegations of educational critics and the press, the schools have been slow to accept innovations. Neither in the past nor in the present have progres-

---

[2] We must note that in some cases European countries are moving away from their traditional patterns toward comprehensive secondary schools like those in the United States, and that research studies indicate that academic results of the better American students compare favorably with those of their European counterparts.

[3] New York City provides education from preschool years through the graduate schools.

sive education and educational alternatives ever really taken hold. Today most secondary schools remain, as they have been in the past, subject centered—i.e., their curricula are centered around the scholarly disciplines. In almost every instance it is the content of the disciplines rather than the needs of the pupils or society that determine course offerings and course content.

PRIVATE SECONDARY SCHOOLS

On the whole, private secondary schools in the United States offer about the same programs as the public schools do. Being relatively free of state supervision and control, they are more independent. Consequently some of them are more innovative while others are more conservative. Still most independent secondary schools, including the parochial schools, differ from the public secondary schools only in their efforts to meet certain needs and desires of their clientele. Thus the preparatory school concentrates on preparing youth for college while most parochial schools try to provide a comprehensive program within a religious context. Other schools are frankly experimental. Because the independent schools are in a large measure dependent upon tuitions and contributions for their financing, they are sometimes more responsive to the wishes of parents than public schools are.

*

Do you feel that secondary education should be universal or selective? Why? What advantages are there to each?

Would you prefer your own secondary school to be comprehensive or specialized? What advantages do you see in each type?

*

THE HISTORY AND DEVELOPMENT OF SECONDARY SCHOOLS IN THE UNITED STATES

No one can understand the American secondary school of today unless he is familiar with its history. Although it may be too much to say that the present American secondary school curriculum is a historical accident, it is true that today's curriculum is largely the result of historical accidents and the forces of tradition. Relatively few educators and still fewer lay people have ever thought through what the role of the school should be or what would be the best program for boys and girls. Perhaps if we had a better understanding of educational history, we could free the schools of the unnecessary baggage they carry and also stop the current practice of reforming education by repeating the mistakes of the past.

Early American Secondary Schools

THE LATIN GRAMMAR SCHOOL

As one might expect, the first American secondary schools were transplants from Europe. As early as 1620 an attempt was made to found a Latin grammar school in Virginia, although on the southern plantation some form of the tutorial system, or family school, so common in the homes of the British nobility, was more usual. In more thickly settled New England, Latin schools were found more frequently. The Boston Latin School was established in 1635. In 1647 Massachusetts towns were required by law to maintain Latin schools so that boys might prepare to enter college and train for the ministry. However, these Latin schools were never really popular for reasons that may soon appear obvious.

The European Latin grammar school had been a very practical school in the days when Latin was the spoken and written language of all educated men. When Latin was replaced by the modern languages, the Latin school lost most of its validity. The school curriculum degenerated into the formal shell called Ciceronianism. Instead of learning and reading Latin as a source of knowledge and enjoyment, pupils studied Latin only for the sake of studying Latin. Probably very few boys ever progressed to the point where they could read Latin freely without constant reference to a Latin dictionary.

The Latin grammar school never became really popular in the colonies. The reason why the Massachusetts General Court passed its 1647 law was, evidently, that the towns were not providing their youth with secondary schooling. Even after the passage of this law many towns did not live up to its requirements. After all, for most practical men in a rapidly developing society the amenities of a Latin education seemed to have little real value.

PRIVATE VENTURE SCHOOLS

Because the Latin schools did not meet the needs of many families, independent entrepreneurs set up private venture schools in every city in the colonies. In these schools youths could learn the practical subjects that they needed in order to master the skills required in the trades and professions of the day. Thus we find teachers who offered to teach mathematics, astronomy, navigation, bookkeeping, English composition, and similar practical subjects to boys who hoped to become merchants, navigators, surveyors, or practitioners of other businesses and professions. These schools were literally private ventures in which the teacher earned his living by teaching people what they were willing to pay to learn. Their popularity shows that there was need for them. The Latin school was just not delivering the goods people wanted.

THE ACADEMY

The success of the private venture school showed the need for a new institution. In 1749 Benjamin Franklin proposed a plan for an academy which he hoped would provide a functional education for boys and girls of the middle classes. Many of the ideas for this school he took from European realists such as Comenius and John Locke. In its curriculum much attention was to be given to the English language and to practical studies such as accounting, public speaking, logic, and commerce. Each of these subjects was to be taught for its practical value to men of affairs. Pupils were not to take all subjects but to choose from those most useful. As Franklin expressed it, since the school could not teach everything, he hoped it would teach those things likely to be "most useful and most ornamental. Regard being had for the several Professions for which they are intended."

Much to Franklin's distress the academy established in Philadelphia did not develop into the functional school he had envisioned. Instead it degenerated into a Latin school and eventually became a university. Educators were conservative

then as now and did not accept this newfangled school.

The academy idea was not lost, however. In 1778 the Phillips (Andover) Academy in Andover, Massachusetts, opened both a Latin and an English department, with the avowed purpose "more especially to learn them the great and real business of living." From that time on the academy's popularity increased. By the middle of the century it had become the typical American school.

The American academy was a tuition school living off its tuitions. Because it needed students in order to exist, its programs were sensitive to public demand. It tried to provide a suitable education for any boy or girl who could pay the costs. In many academies the policy seemed to be that if enough students wanted to study a subject, the academy would offer it.

Although most academies started out as utilitarian institutions, many of them gradually became little more than college preparatory institutions. Some had been Latin schools in all but name from the very first. In the latter half of the nineteenth century the academy began to decline and was replaced by the high school.

THE HIGH SCHOOL

On the whole, the academy was a successful institution, but it was also a private institution. Parents found it expensive. In 1821 the Boston School Committee[4] established the first American public high school, the Boston English Classical High School. It was founded, they said, because the public schools (i.e., the Latin Schools) in Boston did not give "a child an education that shall fit him for active life and serve as a foundation for eminence in his profession" and so forced parents to send their children to private academies at "heavy expense." [5] As originally conceived, the high school was to be a terminal institution for pupils who, it was expected, would enter the mercantile or mechanical employments. The curriculum adopted was very much like that of the academy.

[4] I.e., Board of Education, or School Board.
[5] From report of the subcommittee report on the basis of which the School Committee voted to establish the English Classical School. I. L. Kandel, *History of Secondary Education* (Boston: Houghton Mifflin Co., 1930), pp. 426–427.

The high school idea soon caught on and spread. Some academies were taken over by towns and made into public high schools, or free academies. Some elementary schools added advanced courses and gradually developed high school programs. After a while the idea that the high school should be an extension of the common elementary school became accepted. Of course, many people objected to being taxed so that high school aged youths could go to school, but the right of school districts to establish high schools was soon supported by numerous court decisions (notably the Kalamazoo case of 1874 and a Pennsylvania case of 1851).

Until about 1890 the high schools were rather small. Only 6.7 per cent of the fourteen-to-seventeen year-olds were enrolled. Many high schools were little more than college preparatory schools. This tendency was reinforced in 1892 by the famous report of The Committee of Ten which, although it stated that the business of the school was not preparation for college but preparation for life, recommended that all pupils be taught the academic college preparatory subjects. At about this time, also, efforts were made to standardize and improve secondary education. Regional associations of colleges and secondary schools were formed to inspect and accredit high schools. In 1899 the College Entrance Examination Board began its program. To this day, many educators and laymen continue to support this highly academic curriculum, and only this curriculum, on the basis of the general theory that it "trains the mind." To many more the principal criterion by which to judge the worth of a school is how well its pupils do on the College Board examinations.

By the end of World War I, one third of fourteen-to-seventeen year-old youths were in the high school. By World War II this number had risen to almost three fourths. As the schools enrolled more and more pupils it became evident that academic college preparation was not enough. High schools added such subjects as manual training, art, music, homemaking, and business. In 1918 the Commission on the Reorganization of Secondary Education declared that secondary education should be extended into all areas of human life. Although the curriculum was somewhat broadened, it still remained, however, largely subject-centered and academic.

Junior High Schools and Junior Colleges

At the turn of the century, secondary education began to extend upward and downward. Junior high schools were formed to provide a school for young adolescents in which they would study a curriculum different from that of the elementary school but not as advanced as that of the high school. It was hoped that such a school would reduce the number of pupils dropping out of school by making the work more interesting and relevant to pupil needs than the elementary school work and also by enrolling pupils in a new school before the end of the compulsory attendance period. Junior colleges were introduced as a bridge to the university and a stepping stone for students who wished a practical post-high-school technical or vocational education as a preparation for their life's work.

Life Adjustment Education

The high school and junior high school never did learn how to cope with their tremendous growth. This growth became more and more of a problem as the states raised the school-leaving age in order to keep boys and girls off the job market. Some schools introduced general curricula that were simply watered-down versions of college preparatory courses. Some schools introduced homogeneous grouping. Some introduced general courses and curricula for pupils who planned neither to go to college or to go into business. In 1947 a Chicago conference heard the famous Prosser Resolution which advocated "life adjustment" education for the 60 per cent of youth who were not reached by the college preparatory and vocational curricula of the secondary schools. Life adjustment education, as its advocates visualized it, was to be devoted almost entirely to instruction in such studies as citizenship, health, family living, and moral and social conduct. This program never became really popular in American secondary schools.

Progressive Education

The first three or four decades of the twentieth century saw the advent of the often talked about (and sometimes practiced) movement called progressive education. This program was intended to make education relevant and real to boys and girls. It emphasized pupil-centered education in which pupils developed naturally, planned and governed their own activities, engaged in lifelike rather than bookish activities, followed their own bents in individualized classes, and learned by thinking and doing rather than by lecture and rote memory. It fostered complete living and education for complete living. It had its beginnings in the works of Jean Jacques Rousseau and other eighteenth and nineteenth century writers and educators and has become popular in the alternative schools of the 1970's, but it has seldom been incorporated in full into American secondary schools.

Because of progressive education's popularity with theorists, it has had considerable influence on the school curriculum and methodology. One important innovation was the core curriculum which became popular in the junior high schools. The core curriculum was an attempt to make subject matter more meaningful and relevant to pupils' lives by integrating subject-matter content and doing away with artificial subject-matter boundaries.

The Conservative Reaction

After World War II there came a period of bitter complaints about the public secondary school. The basic complaint was that the schools were not providing good intellectual education. The critics evidently based their conclusions on fears that progressive education, life adjustment education, and child psychology were softening the American people and diluting the American school program. They claimed (erroneously) that American youth fell far behind European pupils intellectually. They accused the schools of soft pedagogy which allowed pupils to get by without learning fundamentals. They were particularly virulent in their attacks on the core curriculum, progressive education, and new methods that allowed pupils more freedom.

In 1957 the launching of the first Sputnik satellite by the Russians spurred the critics into greater action. Groups of college professors, who often knew little about teaching or education, at least on the elementary and secondary school level, set out to reform the schools. As a result there came a new emphasis on teaching the disciplines. Coupled with this call for a return to an accent on discipline was an increased interest in the inquiry methods. These methods were essentially the old problem-solving and Socratic-questioning techniques in new guises. The major concern of the reformers was to raise standards. Among the measures they recommended were

Increased rigor in courses and assignments.
Elimination of all broad field courses and return to discrete subject courses.
Elimination of life adjustment education.
Elimination of the junior high school.
Abandonment of modern progressive methods of teaching.
Adoption of statewide or national systems of examinations.

As Alcorn, Kinder, and Schunert [6] point out, most of these proposals represented "three positions on curriculum development: a return to the past, an emphasis on intellectualism, and an adoption of European patterns of education." One result of this movement has been the adoption of assessment programs at the national and state levels. Another result has been a movement to make teachers accountable for what pupils learn, although the movement is more directly the result of public disenchantment over the failure of city schools to cope with the educational problems of the inner city.

The Reaction to the Reaction

As one might expect, the conservatism of the 1950s and early 1960s brought on a reaction in the late 1960s and the 1970s. This new movement emphasized student freedom, relevant (by which the proponents sometimes meant nonacademic) education, pupil participation in decision making, individualized instruction, and other progressive notions.

[6] Marvin D. Alcorn, James D. Kinder, and Jim R. Schunert, *Better Teaching in Secondary Schools*, 3rd ed. (New York: Holt, Rinehart and Winston, Publishers, 1970), p. 396.

These influences can be seen in the introduction of modular schedules in which the pupils program much of their own time, middle schools that returned to what was basically the core curriculum in all but name, integrated humanities programs, completely pupil-centered schools, and alternate schools and schools without walls that have rejected traditional subject matter. The early 1970s also brought forth a renewed interest in the vocational curriculum in the shape of the career education program that seeks to make the curriculum more down to earth.

Just what direction education will take in the future is problematical. However, in spite of all the educational movements the basic curriculum and methodology of the average secondary school has not changed so very much from those of the secondary school of a half century ago.

*

It is said that the history of education consists of constant swinging from action to reaction and back again. Do you see evidence of such a pattern in this short history of the secondary school in the United States? If so, what? If not, do you spot any definite trends in American secondary education in this short history?

*

THE AIMS OF THE SECONDARY SCHOOL IN THE UNITED STATES

As we have seen, in many respects American secondary education "just keeps rolling along." Very few persons have really thought carefully about what the secondary school should do or what a secondary education should accomplish. The first schools in New England were formed to prepare an educated clergy. Up until 1890 most secondary schools concentrated on middle class vocational and class goals, especially college preparation, statements about the "more serious business of living" notwithstanding. With the twentieth century, scholars began to give more serious attention to the purposes of secondary education. Most of them evidently decided that the objective was the "full life." They thought that the schools should prepare pupils for all areas of living: health, command of the fundamental processes, worthy home

membership, vocational efficiency, civic competence, worthy use of leisure time, and ethical character.[7] In short, secondary education was to serve the needs of all the children of all the people. These needs, as summarized by the Educational Policies Commission are

1. All youth need to develop saleable skills and those understandings and attitudes that make the worker an intelligent and productive participant in economic life. To this end, most youth need supervised work experience as well as education in the skills and knowledge of their occupations.
2. All youth need to develop and maintain physical fitness.
3. All youth need to understand the rights and duties of the citizen of a democratic society and to be diligent and competent in the performance of their obligations as members of the community and citizens of the state and nation.
4. All youth need to understand the significance of the family for the individual and society and the conditions conducive to successful family life.
5. All youth need to know how to purchase and use goods and services intelligently, understanding both the values received by the consumer and the economic consequences of their acts.
6. All youth need to understand the methods of science, the influence of science on human life, and the main scientific facts concerning the nature of the world and of man.
7. All youth need opportunities to develop their capacities to appreciate beauty in literature, art, music, and nature.
8. All youth need to be able to use their leisure time well and to budget it wisely, balancing activities that yield satisfactions to the individual with those that are socially useful.
9. All youth need to develop respect for other persons, to grow in their insight into ethical values and principles, and to live and work cooperatively with others.

[7] These areas represent the Seven Cardinal Principles, or Major Objectives, of the 1918 report, *The Cardinal Principles of Secondary Education,* of the Commission for Reorganization of Secondary Education.

10. All youth need to grow in ability to think rationally, to express their thoughts clearly, and to read and listen with understanding.[8]

Critics of education have often thought that this concept of educating for complete living was impractical. Folk wisdom tells us that people who try to do everything end up doing nothing well. Schools, they say, should give up all the folderol and concentrate on their prime mission, intellectual education. In 1961 the Educational Policies Commission reviewed its position and announced that, although it reaffirmed its belief that the schools should educate broadly, the central purpose of American education should be to teach pupils to think independently.[9]

Although the primacy of the intellectual goal of the secondary school seems self-evident to many observers, during the early 1970s there was a great deal of pressure to place more emphasis on the affective and social aspects of life in secondary education.

*

Is the notion that the secondary schools should try to serve the needs of all American youth impractical? Should the primary goal of the secondary schools be intellectual?
What stress should be placed on the affective and social aspects of pupils' lives?

*

THE CURRICULUM OF THE AMERICAN SECONDARY SCHOOL

The curriculum is the totality of the experiences that a school plans for its pupils. It is not restricted only to courses; the extracurriculum and auxiliary services such as the guidance and health services are also part of the curriculum. On the other hand, the curriculum does not include every-

[8] Educational Policies Commission, *Education for All American Youth* (Washington, D.C.: National Education Association, 1944), pp. 225–226.
[9] Educational Policies Commission, *The Central Purpose of American Education* (Washington, D.C.: National Education Association, 1961).

thing the pupils learn in school. Much of that is part of a hidden agenda that influences pupil learning in spite of the school's best intentions. Many boys and girls learn to smoke at school, for instance, but smoking is not really part of the school's curriculum. Neither are many of the attitudes and values pupils pick up from their teachers and colleagues. Still, the curriculum does include much more than the courses that the school offers.

The course offerings are contained in the program of studies. In most elementary schools these are arranged into a single curriculum which is required of all pupils. In the senior high school the program is more likely to be arranged in a flexible pattern that allows pupils to select the sequence of courses that seems best to fit their needs and desires. Thus a high school pupil may elect courses that will meet college entrance requirements or prepare him to become a bookkeeper or a mechanic. Classes and curriculum tracks may also be differentiated on the basis of academic ability. In some high schools academically talented pupils may move through the curriculum much more quickly and proceed to studies much more advanced than average pupils, while slow pupils may spend most of their career on basics.

General Education

The total curriculum is made up of both general and specialized education. General education consists of the learning that every person should have a chance to acquire. It is sometimes called common learnings. At the elementary and middle school level most of the curriculum fits into this category. Presumably everyone should have a chance to learn to read, write, and figure, for instance. At the secondary school level it is more difficult to demonstrate that any particular learning is essential for everybody. Yet there are many things that would be valuable for everyone to learn. Among them are personal relationships, home management, health, ethical values, good citizenship, and a reasonably good background in subject matter relevant to making one's life fuller and richer both as a citizen and as an individual. Perhaps most important of all are the various skills that enable a person to think critically.

Specialized Education

General education is for everyone. It does not prepare pupils for any particular vocation or avocation. Specialized education is ad hoc education—education designed to meet the particular needs of particular people. It provides for the differences in pupils by giving them opportunities to develop the ways that suit them best as individuals. It does prepare pupils for particular vocations or avocations. Both vocational education and college preparatory education are examples of specialized education.

Theoretically the early years of one's education should consist largely of general education. As one moves toward the terminus of his formal schooling one would expect his education to become more and more specialized so as to prepare him for his life work and his role as an adult. The problem is to create a curriculum with an appropriate balance between general and specialized education at each academic level.

PROVIDING FOR INDIVIDUAL DIFFERENCES

The secondary schools of the nation have never satisfactorily solved the problem of what to teach a student body that includes pupils from almost every intelligence level, from every social and economic level, from a variety of racial and ethnic backgrounds and with a tremendous range of ambitions and interests. The specialized education portion of the curriculum is part of the schools' attempt to provide for the differences in individuals. Curricular provisions for individual differences also include

Elective courses.
Mini-courses.
Homogeneous grouping.
Curriculum tracks.
Continuous promotion schemes.

Some of these provisions are discussed in Part IV "Providing for Pupil Differences" and in other sections of this book.

The Subjects

Theoretically curricula may be classified as subject-centered or experience-centered. The subject-centered curriculum is based on formal courses and emphasizes the learning of subject matter and the study of the disciplines. The experience-centered curriculum, on the other hand, focuses on the problems and concerns of youth living in contemporary society. It accentuates the processes of learning and thinking and plays down the study of the disciplines; subject matter is introduced only as it pertains to the problems being studied. In the experience-centered curriculum pupils take a major role in deciding just what will be studied and how it will be studied.

Most secondary schools hold to the subject-centered curriculum. The faculty and administrators determine what the curriculum will be without much consultation with the pupils. Presumably they select the curriculum content on the basis of the pupils' needs. More often the courses are just blocks of more or less logically organized subject matter having little relation to the needs of anyone. At times it has seemed as if the schools were moving toward an experience-centered curriculum relevant to the needs of the pupils and the community, with increased pupil participation in curricular decision making; so far, however, most of these movements have been abortive.

Ordinarily then the program of studies consists of separate, discrete courses in the academic disciplines. These can be classified into the following categories

English Language Arts.
Foreign Language.
The Social Studies.
The Sciences.
Mathematics.
The Fine Arts.
Business Education.
Vocational and Practical Arts.
Health and Safety.
Physical Education.

Table 2–1 is a typical list of course offerings.

Curriculum Problems and Issues

Aristotle once wrote

That education should be regulated by law and should be an affair of state is not to be denied, but

Table 2–1
Course Offerings Grades 9–12

Students *will usually take the subjects at the level designated.* However, individual needs are always the determining factor. It is suggested that students make the most use of the high school program and elect offerings which meet their individual needs and goals. Counselors are available to aid you in your selection and to review all standardized testing results with you and your parents. All courses are offered on a semester basis. Each semester course for all classes except the class of 1975 is worth $2\frac{1}{2}$ credits, unless noted below.

Subjects	Grades	Credits
English 9	9	
English 10	10	
English Electives	11, 12	
Seminar	12	
Reading Skills Improvement	9–12	0
Vocabulary Development	9–12	0
Reading Comprehension Analysis	9–12	0
Remedial Reading	9–12	0
Modern Euro. History I–II	9	
U.S. History I (1–2)	10–11–12	
U.S. History II (1–2)	10–11–12	
U.S. History I	10–11–12	
(semester followed by electives)		
U.S. History II	10–11–12	
(semester followed by electives)		
Economics	12	
International Relations	12	
General Math	9–10	
Intro. to Algebra	9–10	
Algebra I	9–10	
Geometry	9–10	
Algebra II	10–11–12	
Senior Math	12	
Modern Analysis	12	
Calculus	12	
Computer Science	9–12	
Business Math	9–11	
Probability & Statistics	12	
Engineering Math	12	
French I	9–10	
French 9	9	
French 10	10	
French II	10–11	
French III	11–12	

Table 2–1 *Course Offerings Grades 9–12 (cont'd)*

Subjects	Grades	Credits
French IV	11–12	
French V	12	
German I	9–10	
German II	10–11	
German III	11–12	
German IV	12	
Spanish I	9–10	
Spanish 9	9	
Spanish 10	10	
Spanish IIA–IIB	10–11	
Spanish III	11–12	
Spanish IV	12	
Earth Science I	9–10	
Earth Science II	11–12	
Biology (Gr. & Blue)	10–11	
Chemistry	11–12	
Physics	11–12	
Adv. Biology I, II	11–12	
Adv. Science I, II	11–12	
Personal Typing	9	
Typing I	9–10	
Typing II	10–11	
Typing III	11–12	
Office Practice	11–12	
Shorthand IA–B	10–11	
Shorthand IIA, B	11–12	
Accounting I	10–11	
Accounting II	11–12	
Accounting III	11–12	
Accounting IV	12	
Bookkeeping I, II	9–10–11	
Consumer Law I, II	9–10–11	
General Business I, II	9–10	
Intro to College		
Business Subjects	9–12	
Intro to Fine Arts	9–12	
Drawing & Design I, II	9–12	
Painting I, II	9–12	
Graphics I, II	9–12	
Ceramics I, II	9–12	
Sculpture I, II	9–12	
Crafts I, II	9–12	
Photography I, II	9–12	
Contemporary Bachelor		
Living I, II	12	

Table 2–1 *Course Offerings Grades 9–12 (cont'd)*

Subjects	Grades	Credits
Contemporary Living I, II	9–12	
Contemporary Living III, IV, V, VI	10–12	
Contemporary Living VII, VIII	12	
General Shop	9–12	
Manufacturing	9–12	
Power I, II	9–12	
Construction/Cabinet Making	9–12	
Architectural Drafting	9–12	
Architectural Design	9–12	
Mechanical Drawing	9–12	
Mini-courses in Industrial Arts and/or Resource Center for Industrial Arts	9–12	
Chorus	9–12	
Band	9–12	
Music I	9–12	
Music II	10–12	
Phys. Ed. & Health	9–12	
Driver Education	11	0
Occupational Ed.	9–12	
Morris County Vocational School Offerings—open to	11–12	15

* Program of Studies, 1974–1975. Chatham Township High School, Chatham Township, N.J., pp. 6–7. By permission of Ellwood Jacoby, Superintendent of Schools.

what should be the character of this public education, and how young persons should be educated, are questions which remain to be considered. For mankind are by no means agreed about the things to be taught, whether we look to virtue or the best life. Neither is it clear whether education is more concerned with intellectual or with moral virtue. The existing practice is perplexing; no one knows on what principle we should proceed—should being useful in life, or should virtue, or should the higher knowledge be the aim of our training; all three opinions have been entertained.[10]

The problems and issues Aristotle spoke of, and many more additional ones, have never been entirely solved. In many respects the modern curriculum is a compromise of irreconcilable positions.

[10] *Politics,* VIII.

Let us look at a few of the problems and issues that face the school.

ARTICULATING THE CURRICULUM

Vertical and horizontal articulation of the curriculum are two problems that continually perplex school administrators and teachers. Vertical articulation is the fitting together of courses and units so that pupils can make a smooth progression up the educational ladder. The problem is to prevent gaps and overlaps. This problem is particularly troublesome at the break between lower and upper schools, e.g., between the middle school and the high school or the elementary school and the junior high school. School officials and teachers try to achieve vertical articulation by paying close attention to the sequence of courses, units, and subject matter content. Through these efforts they hope to prevent gaps and unnecessary repetition in pupils' programs.

Horizontal articulation has to do with the correlation and coordination of what pupils study at the same level or grade. It seems obvious that if a pupil's efforts in English can be coordinated with his work in history, his learning will be more efficient and teaching will be more effective.

Attempts to articulate horizontally take many forms. First is the simple correlation of courses in which teachers point out the application or relation of the content of their courses to other courses. Another method is for teachers to plan their courses to support each other. Many junior high schools and middle schools set up interdisciplinary teaching teams in which teachers who instruct the same pupils plan together. Another approach is to fuse two or more courses into one. For instance, in some seventh and eighth grades English and social studies are integrated into a block. Another plan is to center all the school work around problems or themes and to introduce the subject matter of the various disciplines only as it pertains to the problem or theme. For example, in the study of the city pupils might study literary works, history, sociology, political science, geography, the physical and biological sciences, statistics, and even the fine arts.

Unfortunately in many high schools the courses offered in the different disciplines have no relation to one another. At the upper levels this practice is the rule rather than the exception as all college students know.

BALANCE IN THE CURRICULUM

Ideally the secondary school curriculum should be made up of courses from the various fields in proportion to their importance to pupils' present and future lives, and the needs of society. Such a nice balance has never been maintained. Historically the curriculum has favored the bookish and the literary. In the 1960s there was a great attempt to emphasize the sciences, but the humanities, social sciences, health, and physical education were neglected. In many schools college preparation has been emphasized to the detriment of all the other roles of public education. Health and the social sciences are often given short shrift. Vocational education has not fared very well either.

Not only should the secondary school provide a balance in the subject matter offerings it must also try to keep its various roles in balance, e.g., provision for the needs of the individual pupils vs. the needs of society, education for social change vs. education for social stability, needs of pupils education for the present vs. education for future needs, education for world citizenship vs. education for patriotism; education for diversity vs. education for unity. It should also take care that the provisions for the needs and desires of one group do not overshadow the provisions for the needs and desires of another group.

To keep the curriculum in balance faculties and school officials must avoid falling for fads and climbing on bandwagons. All positions in controversial matters should have a fair hearing. In building a curriculum, to be an advocate is seldom wise. One should never sacrifice Peter, just so Paul can be paid. Perhaps also, if the curriculum is to be truly balanced, the pupils should have a chance to make at least some contribution to the decision making. Certainly no one should be cut off from his goals and needs because of an imbalance in the curriculum.[11]

11 Association for Supervision and Curriculum Development, *Balance in the Curriculum* (Washington, D.C.: Association for Supervision and Curriculum Development, 1961).

WHAT SHOULD BE TAUGHT?

Determining what to teach and what to leave out is a major problem. It is, of course, axiomatic that the curriculum should be relevant to both the needs of the pupils and the needs of society. But when in fact is a curriculum relevant? Is, as some hold, the best curriculum made up of eternal truths that everyone should learn in a common curriculum, or should the curriculum be so individualized that everyone can have his own curriculum? Similarly, should there be different curricula for different ethnic or racial groups or for pupils with different vocational goals? Should, as essentialists claim, the curriculum be aimed at providing the skills, knowledge, and attitudes that youth will need when they become adults or should it, as the progressivists believe, meet the needs of pupils now and let the future take care of itself?

Is a relevant curriculum one that brings pupils face to face with the materialistic facts of society through active participation or is a curriculum that concentrates on intellectual development alone really more relevant? Is a curriculum the student selects for himself more relevant than one selected for him by knowledgeable adults who have been through the mill? Should the accent be on liberal education, or should it be on vocational education? Should the curriculum give boys and girls an opportunity to learn to be good citizens by practicing good citizenship, or should it concentrate on the intellectual?

What is the role of subject matter anyway? Should one select subject matter content because it has its own intrinsic value, or should one select it because presumably someday it will be useful to the pupils? Or is it possible that subject matter content does not matter at all, but that it is only important as a vehicle for teaching intellectual processes and attitudes, such as the ability to solve problems, to ferret out facts, or to view and analyze conflicting data objectively.

*

Think back over your secondary school career. Was the work you took integrated vertically, i.e., did your work move in an even line straight through from grade 7 to 12? Or were there repetitions and gaps? Was your secondary school work articulated horizontally, i.e., was the content in the different subjects each year taught in such a way that the interrelationships between the content of the various fields were clear? Did the teaching and learning of the various subjects consciously support the teaching and learning in other subjects? What attempts that you know of were made to solve the problems of vertical and horizontal articulation? Can you think of anything teachers might have done to improve articulation?

Was your own school program well balanced? Was your personal program well balanced? What areas, if any, were overemphasized? What areas, if any, were neglected?

What aspects of your own teaching field are really relevant to the lives of youth in the last quarter of the twentieth century?

*

WHOM TO TEACH?

At the present time all youths are required to attend school until they have finished high school or reached a specified age (sixteen in many states). Some critics of education doubt whether such practice is wise. Some of the pupils, they say, cannot benefit from a high school education and would be better off doing something else during their teens. Is it really right for secondary schools to be required to provide remedial work for pupils who have not met the prerequisites? Perhaps secondary education should be reserved for an academic elite who would enjoy and profit from academic secondary education. Education for only the college-bound would be cheaper and simpler to provide, they say. If, on the other hand, formal secondary education should be the right of all youth, presumably the curriculum must provide a wide choice of subjects and activities, or attending school will not be worthwhile for everyone. Furthermore, if the society at large is to benefit from its investment in secondary education, the schools must provide for the needs of all youth.

WHAT METHODS SHOULD BE USED?

How one teaches is just as much part of the curriculum as what one teaches. The use of inquiry and problem-solving techniques produces learning different from that produced by the lecture or recitation. Individualized instruction generates a curriculum different from that derived from large group instruction. When teachers or curriculum committees decide on one or another strategy they are making curriculum decisions. Unfortunately

many parents and teachers have not been able to see the relationships between their educational goals and teaching methods. All too often the methods they advocate for their classrooms are incompatible with the goals they desire.

Building the Curriculum

Curriculum building has always been a source of controversy. Teachers naturally feel that they, as the professionals closest to the problem, should make, as well as implement, the important curriculum decisions. Pupils, the people most intimately concerned, feel that they should have at least some say. Parents and other laymen feel that they should call the tune because they foot the bill. The local and state boards of education and the legislature are charged with the legal responsibility for maintaining appropriate and effective curricula.

Lately numerous pressure groups and self-annointed lay authorities have had much influence on curriculum decisions. It seems as if every group that has an axe to grind wishes to grind it in the public school. In a number of instances the professionals have been treated as menials. Books, programs, methods, and innovations have been adopted or dropped without consultation with the teachers, who presumably know most about them. Oftentimes the decisions made have been made in ignorance and have done little to advance quality education. For instance, some of the secondary school curricula written by university specialists in the academic disciplines and imposed on the secondary schools by pressure groups and laymen have turned out to be impractical for secondary school boys and girls, who after all are not college majors or graduate students in the subjects.

Ultimately, however, what is actually taught in the classroom and the way it is taught, are largely decided by the classroom teacher. The real curriculum is what the teachers teach.[12] Innovations forced on the teachers usually backfire no matter how meritorious they may be.

[12] Remember that the curriculum is the planned experiences. Sometimes what the pupils learn comes mostly from a shadow curriculum of unplanned experiences that boys and girls encounter in spite of the plans of the teacher.

INFLUENCES ON THE CURRICULUM AND TEACHING

Although in the long run the teacher is the most important factor in teaching, what actually is taught, the curriculum, is the result of many other influences. Perhaps the most influential of these is the textbook publisher. Often curriculum building, as practiced, amounts to little more than deciding what courses to offer and then selecting textbooks. Many teachers use the textbook as a course of study. Each year they begin at the beginning of the textbook and work their way through it. Test publishers are also influential. When teachers know what their pupils will be tested on, they teach accordingly. It is quite possible that the introduction of a national or state assessment (i.e., testing) program would dictate the exact content of future curricula. Assessment programs could very well stifle innovation and reform and harden the curriculum into an archaic mold. This, at least, seems to be the European experience.

Business and Industry. Business and industry are also influencing the school curriculum—partly through the introduction of new hardware and software. Computer-assisted instruction, for instance, is a product, at least in part, of industrial initiative. Business firms, such as Westinghouse, have taken over the designing of curricula in some instances. A number of firms, e.g., Educational Technology Publications, Inc., provide workshops and training programs for teachers. Business firms also exert pressure on the school curriculum both directly and through such organizations as the Chamber of Commerce to see to it that the schools present to youth points of view congruent with their own. A surprising number of firms and business associations, e.g., U.S. Steel and the American Petroleum Institute, have developed instructional materials about the industries they represent which they distribute to teachers gratis on request. Similarly other pressure groups of all sorts, representing such interests as labor, political groups, patriotic organizations, religious organizations, and the like, seek to influence the curriculum. Driver training, for instance, was introduced largely through the efforts of the insurance companies and the American Automobile Association. The private foundations have also exerted pressure by granting support to new programs and research that support their objectives and biases.

Professional Organizations. The educational profession itself influences the curriculum through its teachers' organizations. These organizations both at national and state levels publish journals and newsletters that speak with some authority on matters of curriculum and method.[13] These organizations from time to time sponsor research and commissions that influence teachers' opinions and beliefs on curricular matters. They also sponsor workshops and conferences at which teachers and administrators can learn and discuss new ideas and practices. Some local teachers' unions[14] include curricular matters in their negotiations with the local school authorities. Similarly the curriculum is influenced by the work of colleges and universities, teacher education specialists, educational researchers, and curriculum consultants.

Governmental Agencies. Local communities have peculiar characteristics that are reflected in the curriculum. A suburban community that sends more than 90 per cent of its high school graduates to college wants its secondary schools to do a good job of college preparation. In the large city bordering the suburban community vocal citizens are anxious that the school provide good programs in black studies, Italian, and vocational education. The type and content of the curriculum that the community wants are colored by its social, economic, racial, and ethnic backgrounds.

In most communities, as in this large city, there are diverse interests and groups seeking to influence the curriculum. Oftentimes the goals of these groups are antagonistic and incompatible. It is the job of the school authorities and teachers to reconcile differences and to come up with a curriculum beneficial to all the pupils. In their deliberations the local curriculum builders must consider the edicts of the state education agency and the state legislature. Regulations made by these bodies have the force of law. Although some states give the local secondary schools great freedom, while others

---

13 E.g., *The English Journal* of the National Council of Teachers of English.

14 E.g., the local chapters of the American Federation of Teachers and National Education Association of the United States.

are relatively more restrictive, legislatures all too frequently try to dictate what should be taught and how it should be taught. Usually state dictation of anything other than broad policy is self-defeating. However, if the state did not specify minimum standards and conduct inspections, some communities might not support their schools at all.

The state government uses both its authority and the power of the purse to enforce its mandate. The Federal government, on the other hand, has had little power over the curricula of local schools. During the Lyndon B. Johnson administration the government tried to foster curricular and methodological reforms by funding research and innovative practices. Since then money from the Federal government has had considerable impact on the schools and their curricula, although lately many federally funded programs have been curtailed because of cuts in the federal budget.

Higher Education. Higher education has also made an impact on the secondary school curriculum. College entrance requirements have always been an important consideration for curriculum makers. The biases of secondary school teachers toward content and method were learned in college and graduate school. (Most high school teachers have been liberal arts graduates. That may be one reason why the high school has been so academically oriented.) Furthermore, many college and university subject specialists write secondary school texts and participate in the numerous curriculum writing projects that have been sponsored by scholarly groups. University colleges of education have sponsored much educational research and many development projects. They have also provided schools with consultant services, workshops, and in-service education courses designed to update the curriculum. Many universities maintain curriculum laboratories and experimental centers which develop and test new curriculum materials and methods and educational theories.

THE TEACHER AND THE CURRICULUM

There was a day when teachers were given syllabi that they were expected to follow to the letter. But today secondary school teachers are taking a more and more active role and a freer hand in determining what and how they teach. Rather

than be directed to follow a prescribed syllabus the modern teacher is more likely to be given a curriculum guide or resource unit which provides him with suggestions and aids which he adapts and uses as he sees fit.

Teachers are also taking more active roles in formal curriculum development. In the hierarchy of the school system the person responsible for curriculum development is the school superintendent. In all but the smallest school systems the superintendent must delegate leadership. If the curriculum revision is to be system-wide, he may turn the leadership over to the curriculum director or perhaps to subject supervisors; if the curriculum revision is to be only building-wide, the key person is the building principal. Revision of single subject offerings within a school may occur under the direction of a department chairman. But no matter who is in charge or who gives the project direction, the real work is done by the teachers. It is they who are formed into committees or teams to dig out the necessary information, make the necessary decisions, and construct the necessary curriculum guides, resource units, and instructional materials. Young teachers would do well to volunteer to serve on curriculum committees. They provide an opportunity to be of service and to influence curriculum development. They also give one an opportunity to learn more about one's subject and about teaching it and to become recognized as a professional.

CURRICULUM GUIDES AND RESOURCE UNITS

Curriculum committees work out such things as the instructional objectives, scope and sequence of courses and unit, course and unit content, instructional resources, materials of instruction, methods of instruction, and evaluating devices. These they write up in curriculum guides or resource units. A curriculum guide contains a suggested plan for a course or sequence of courses. Ordinarily it is not a syllabus to be followed but rather a series of suggestions that will guide and aid the teacher who, being a professional, will accept or reject the suggestions and add to or subtract from the plan suggested as the situation and his own expertise dictate. The Table of Contents of a curriculum guide appears as Table 2-2.

The resource unit is a resource that a teacher

Curriculum Guide—Table of Contents

Table 2–2
*Table of Contents, Curriculum Guide**

* *A Guide for Social Studies, American Studies 9.* Independent School District 77, 51 Park Lane, Mankato, Minn.. 1969.

might use in building a teaching unit. It provides the teacher with suggested objectives, content, methods, materials, resources, and so on that he might draw on in building his own unit. It is not written for any particular class or grade. Its contents might be equally useful to teachers of different grades or courses. It is simply, as its name suggests, a resource that a teacher can go to when planning. Good resource units can save teachers much grueling hackwork and allow them to plan well and still have time for other activities.

THE EXTRACURRICULUM

The extracurriculum is that part of the curriculum that is not included in pupils' regular courses and does not carry credit for graduation. The dividing line between the curricular and the extracurricular has become very indistinct as the result of two concurrent trends. One is a trend for curricular activities to spread into the extracurriculum (e.g., French clubs, mini-courses, and volunteer Saturday morning laboratory classes and field trips). The other is the trend for the extracurriculum to become curricular (e.g., the school newspaper published by the journalism class or the credit-bearing school chorus).

The aims of the extracurriculum are the same as those of the curriculum. The extracurriculum contributes to the achievement of these aims by (1) reinforcing classroom learning, (2) supplementing formal studies, (3) aiding total life adjustment, (4) integrating learning, and (5) democratizing school and American life.[15] Although regular classes can also offer some of these contributions, the informality of the extracurriculum and its freedom from the pressures of marks and academic credits make it easier to carry out these shared aims.

CRITERIA FOR EXCELLENCE IN THE EXTRACURRICULUM

In many respects the extracurriculum's contribution may be fully as important and even more effective than the more formal portions of the cur-

---

15 Robert W. Frederick, *The Third Curriculum* (New York: Appleton-Century-Crofts, 1959), p. 55.

riculum. Like the more formal portions of the curriculum, the extracurriculum should be carefully planned and carried out. The best extracurricula meet the standards suggested by the following principles.

1. It is planned so as to contribute directly to the educational aims of the school.
2. It supplements and reenforces curricular activities. It does not repeat classroom activities. Rather it introduces learning, approaches, and materials not available in regular courses.
3. It is pupil-centered, and in so far as feasible, pupil-planned and -directed.
4. It provides every pupil ample opportunity to participate up to the limits of his abilities and interests. No one is eliminated because of race, religion, financial ability, social position, or academic standing.
5. It provides enough different activities to allow every pupil to participate in something he finds congenial.
6. It provides pupils with adequate opportunities to develop leadership and followership abilities.
7. It fosters the development of healthy attitudes, ideals, and value systems and avoids the development of false and inadequate attitudes, ideals, and value systems.
8. It is flexible. It is easy to add new activities and drop old ones that are no longer useful.
9. It is adequately supported by competent, sympathetic faculty sponsors or advisors.
10. It is adequately funded.
11. It is recognized by being properly scheduled.
12. It is constantly being evaluated and reevaluated.

WHO SHOULD PARTICIPATE IN THE EXTRACURRICULUM?

The answer to this question is *everyone*. Schools are provided to educate everyone enrolled. Therefore, all school activities should be open to all boys and girls. Each pupil should be given a chance to participate, enjoy, and explore his interests to the best of his ability. Of course, certain extracurricular activities require skills and abilities that some pupils do not have. After a fair trial these pupils may be guided into some other activity, or perhaps some other job within the same activity. For instance, the boy who cannot hit the basket will not add much to the basketball team as a player but may make a good manager or publicity agent; similarly, the girl whose dramatic ability is nil but who is good at makeup can find an important place in the dramatics club.

This principle of making extracurricular activities open to all has been most seriously violated in school social activities. There is no room in the school for activities that bar boys and girls on the basis of social position, class, or wealth. Junior proms, sororities, clubs, and parties that require a considerable expenditure of money by pupils cannot be justified in a public high school because the expense automatically rules out participation by the less wealthy pupils. Equally out of place are secret societies, fraternities, and sororities whose membership is determined by social favor and secret ballot. Such activities do not belong in the program of the modern public secondary school. The sponsor should guide the pupils into desirable social habits and see to it that no pupil is barred because of wealth, race, religion, or social status.

THE DANGER OF OVERPARTICIPATION

While it is true that every pupil should be allowed to pursue his interests, many pupils must be protected from overparticipation. Even for teenagers the day is limited to twenty-four hours. To do all the things some high school youngsters attempt to do is impossible. Many youths spend so much time and energy on the extracurriculum that they have little or no time left over to spend on their classwork. To prevent these pupils from attempting too much, it may be necessary to limit their participation in extracurricular activities.

Besides causing pupils to neglect their studies, individual overparticipation in extracurricular activities tends to limit participation to a relatively small group of pupils, thus preventing other equally talented pupils from participating. Particularly troublesome is the fact that the positions of leadership are frequently monopolized by a small group of pupils. Such situations are common because both teachers and pupils tend to select those who have already shown themselves willing and able.

Properly guided, extracurricular activities can involve many youngsters in positions of trust, responsibility, and leadership, thus developing these qualities in a larger part of the student group.

THE GUIDANCE PROGRAM

Every Teacher a Guidance Worker

In recent years the need for guidance and guidance services has grown enormously. The great increase in secondary school enrollment and the consequent diversity in the student population have made the problems of providing adequate secondary school curricula for individual pupils much more complex than in the college-oriented school of a half century ago. To date, American secondary school educators have not been able to solve these problems satisfactorily. About one third of American youth do not finish their secondary school courses, while others who keep on to the bitter end find that, after all, their secondary school years have given them little of value. In 1958, Congress recognized the seriousness of pupils' need for help and direction and provided federal support for programs to improve guidance, counseling, testing, and the training of counselors.

Every teacher's job includes guidance duties. If he does no actual formal counseling or homeroom guidance, he must cooperate with the persons charged with such responsibilities. If he teaches in a school which, as yet, has no, or insufficient, specialized guidance personnel, he will undoubtedly have to perform some of the duties ordinarily assigned to the specialist. In any case, no matter where he teaches, the good teacher finds it necessary to guide pupils in his classes in ways not included in the course of study. Indeed, every teacher should contribute eagerly to the guidance program, for it can be extremely helpful to him and his pupils. As a matter of fact, the functions by which a classroom teacher contributes to the guidance program are pretty much what a good teacher would expect to do anyway. Since there is a trend toward broadening guidance activities in the secondary school, new teachers will be more and more likely to find guidance duties formally recognized as part of their assignment. But whether there is a guidance program or not, the good teacher will engage in many guidance activities as part of his normal teaching responsibilities.

The Guidance Services

What, then, is the guidance program? It is not, as many people seem to think, designed to provide a place where troubled pupils can go to have a counselor solve all their problems and make their difficult decisions for them. Rather, it is a program designed to help pupils to understand themselves and to direct their own lives more efficiently. At the same time, the guidance program attempts to provide the information necessary for efficient teaching of each individual and for improvement of the total school program. Through the guidance program the school tries to help all pupils shape for themselves fuller, happier, and more useful lives and become better students and citizens.

To accomplish these purposes the complete guidance program provides the following services: individual inventory service, occupational and educational information service, counseling service, placement service, and follow-up service.[16] These services are not separate offices or departments of the guidance program. In actual practice no formal distinction is made between the services. Many guidance workers engage in all the services every day and would be hard put to tell when they are providing one service or another. These services are similar to those the teacher uses in his teaching but are greatly amplified in scope.

THE INDIVIDUAL INVENTORY SERVICE

The individual inventory service includes all the data-gathering devices and records by which the school gets to know the pupils. Included in this service are cumulative records, anecdotal reports, health records, reports of home visits, and intelligence and other psychological test scores—in short, all the information the school has been able to gather about the pupils. Among the information gathered here are personal statistics, home environ-

16 Harold Mahoney, "The Guidance Program, Bulletin 45," Connecticut State Department of Education, 1948, pp. 19–28.

ment, preschool history, health information, school history, aptitudes, abilities, personality traits, nonacademic and out-of-school activities, and plans and interests. To gather this information, the guidance workers use the same devices that teachers use to learn about the pupils in their classes, plus data from other sources not readily available to the classroom teacher. Among them are previous school records, school testing programs, case studies, interviews with pupils, their parents, and others, questionnaires, autobiographies, and routine and extraordinary reports from teachers and other sources. The data gathered through the individual inventory service are used as a basis for counseling by the guidance workers and are made available to teachers for use with their pupils.

A good school testing program is an essential part of an adequate individual inventory service. Properly used, modern tests provide much information indicative of pupils' potentialities. When misused, however, test results can be harmful. They should never be considered the final authority in making decisions or in studying an individual. To avoid misuse and misunderstandings teachers and counselors should use test scores for only well-defined purposes. When dealing with pupils and parents, teachers should be particularly careful to explain and interpret test results to them. Failure to do so may allow parents and pupils to come to erroneous conclusions.

THE INFORMATION SERVICE

The occupational and educational information service is a repository for information of all sorts. In addition to occupational and educational information, this service may also make available information about oneself (collected through the individual inventory service), boy-girl relations, and extracurricular opportunities. The following description of the Wichita, Kansas, program illustrates the type of information made available to pupils.

1. Information concerning educational requirements and opportunities beyond the secondary school.
   a. Current catalogues available for colleges, universities, and special training institutions.

b. Current information regarding financial assistance as scholarships, loans, and other forms of student aid.

2. Information about local and national occupational opportunities, requirements, trends, and employment conditions.

3. Special programs to inform parents and students, such as "Career Days" and "College Nights."

4. Visual aids in the form of posters, graphs, charts, photographs, pamphlets, and other materials to present information of guidance value.

5. Information concerning agencies and persons qualified to render assistance for physical, emotional, educational, vocational, or employment needs.[17]

The information may be disseminated to pupils in several ways, such as through homeroom classes, orientation classes, units in core and other courses, and so on. In libraries, homerooms, and the counselor office waiting room, information is frequently stored in open shelves, so that shy or embarrassed pupils may look things up without "bothering" anyone. Also, trained guidance personnel suggest references to guide the pupil to the information he desires.

THE COUNSELING SERVICE

The counseling service is the heart of the guidance program. By means of counseling, the guidance workers do most of the actual guiding. We shall discuss this aspect of the guidance program more thoroughly later in the chapter.

THE PLACEMENT SERVICE

The placement service attempts to place boys and girls in their proper niches in the curriculum, the extracurriculum, and in post-high-school activities. This service has long been a function of the school. Nowadays, however, it is no longer simply a matter of trying to match youths and jobs or curricula. Rather, it is an attempt to develop in the young people the attitudes and understandings necessary for making their own decisions. At the

present time, counselors are devoting much of their effort to selecting and preparing pupils for the right college and college curriculum. Another relatively new concern is the finding of jobs for dropouts and for former graduates who need assistance.

THE FOLLOW-UP SERVICE

The follow-up service tells us how well our school programs have succeeded and helps us prepare to do a better job for pupils to come. By following up one can check on the success of counseling or therapy for individual pupils. From follow-up studies of the school's graduates, counselors can examine the effectiveness of the curriculum in whole or in part. A study of graduates might show whether the college-preparatory, business, or other curricula are sufficiently effective and, if not, in what ways they might be improved.

A TOTAL PROGRAM

The foregoing paragraphs should make clear that the guidance program is not fractionalized into special types of guidance. One no longer thinks of educational guidance or vocational guidance; one thinks of guidance. Educational and vocational guidance are not special types of guidance; they are different aspects of guidance. Similarly, the five pupil-personnel services should not be thought of as separate functions but as different facets of the guidance function.

*

In what ways does guidance differ from teaching?

What contributions might you as a teacher make to each of the guidance services?

Of what value are the guidance services? If you were asked to prepare a defense for including a guidance program in your school, what would your arguments be?

*

Guidance Service to Teachers

The guidance program helps the teacher in many ways. In the first place, it can provide the teacher with information that enables him to know the individual pupils better. The teacher, of course, can gather considerable information himself. However, by means of its specialized techniques and

[17] Robert H. McIsaac, "Guidance Services," in Lester D. and Alice Crow (eds.) *Readings in Guidance* (New York: David McKay Co., Inc., 1962), pp. 562–563.

trained personnel, the guidance program can provide the teacher with information he otherwise could not obtain except at great cost. Furthermore, information can often be collected more effectively through the guidance program, and the teacher is left with more time to devote to other matters.

The guidance program can also help the teacher with difficult pupils and their problems. Through the use of his specialized resources, the guidance worker can often find the cause for a difficulty and help resolve the problem. Sometimes he can do this quickly. Usually, however, the problems given to guidance workers are not easy to solve; they often involve changing habits and attitudes that the pupil has taken years to develop. Therefore, teachers should not expect quick results. It is more realistic to look for long periods of slow improvement. Patience, cooperation, and understanding should be the watchwords in the teacher's relationship with the guidance worker, for they each need the other's help and support.

DEVELOPMENT AND TRENDS IN SECONDARY SCHOOLS

The 1960s were a period of great educational change, experimentation, and innovation. Some of these innovations are continuing in the '70s and probably will result in permanent change. Others are being dropped in favor of a return to the *status quo ante* or of new innovations or experiments. Of course, not all of these innovations and experiments are either very new or very experimental. Some of them, in fact, are reintroductions of very old practices, sometimes in new guises, sometimes not. The following list briefly describes some of the trends and developments in curriculum and school organization in secondary education in the United States.

1. Probably organizational changes will make the schools more responsive to the needs of the pupils. Priority might be given to developing a continuous series of learning experiences. Harold G. Shane, who advocates such a continuum, states that, if it should be adopted, schools in the future would have the following characteristics.[18] (a) Since any one learner is

[18] Harold G. Shane, "A Curriculum Continuum: Possible Trends in the 70's," *Phi Delta Kappan*, 51:389 (March, 1970).

merely progressing at a different rate than any other, there would be no failure or acceleration. (b) Much of the remedial or special education efforts or all of them would be eliminated. (c) Since each pupil progresses at his own rate, whether handicapped or not, all education would be "special" for the individual. Promotion and dropouts would be eliminated. (d) In this personalized program, a student could continue his education outside of school and return weeks or months later to the school experiences. (e) Other changes would involve the termination of compensatory education and report cards.

2. More people are becoming involved in curriculum determination. Students and teachers are in the process of securing a greater voice in determining the kinds of educational experiences that are to be the requirements and electives for the completion of secondary education. Parents and the general populace are also assuming a larger role than ever before in recent times.

3. Progressive education is returning. Since pre-World War II, education has come almost full circle. The progressive proposals and practices of the 1930's which were rejected to be replaced by subject matter for its own sake in the 1950's are coming back. At least there seems to be a continued movement to humanize the schools and make them more relevant to contemporary society. Evidently the trend toward a continuation of relevancy, and pupil and problem-centered classes, will continue.

4. Considerable influence is being exerted by minority groups upon the curriculum. Probably this influence will continue to be felt. However, there is a chance of a reaction of the majority against the minority influence, if it should receive undue emphasis.

5. There is a movement to make educators accountable for the school's product. Laymen are demanding that educators guarantee the learning of a specified quantity and quality as a condition for paying them and underwriting the school program.

6. The need for humaneness and "relevance" has caused a trend toward individualizing the curriculum.

7. There appears to be a slight trend toward a reexamination of the worth of particular disciplines. Citizens are once again asking what benefits pupils derive from studying the various academic subjects. This concern is tied to the growing concern for curricular relevance.

8. There seems to be a trend toward including an even greater number of subjects in the curriculum of the secondary school. New subjects are being added, but old ones are not being deleted.

9. Many lay people believe that the public school is an inefficient monopoly and have therefore begun a movement to search for new agencies to educate the nation's school children and youth.

10. The improvement in technology, both in teaching methods and in teaching tools, is continuing and will soon make a considerable difference in the curriculum, instruction, and organization of the schools.

11. Recently a number of organizational changes have taken place in the secondary schools. Among them are flexible scheduling, team teaching, advance credit courses offered in the high school, the ungraded school, continuous progress schemes, teacher aides, honor study halls, differentiated staffing, team teaching, the work-study programs, a school-within-a-school, small school agreements, cultural enrichment programs, mini-courses, student exchange programs, educational parks, optional class attendance, a shorter or longer school year, independent study, no-wall schools, and the accountability concept. Some of these changes are relatively recent; others were initiated years ago but have not been widely accepted until recently. Many of the changes instigated are quite transitory—often ceasing to exist after a year or two; others have been quite successful resulting in permanent change.[19]

The sum total of these trends seems to be a movement toward a more humane, responsive school in which the curriculum will be much more down to earth and the needs of the community and of youth will be better and more democratically served than in the past.

SUMMARY

The American school system is based on a twelve-grade ladder. The organization of schools within the twelve-grade system varies, but in spite of the variations the twelve-grade system is almost universal. Public secondary schools in the United States are much like each other. They, with a few exceptions, offer universal public education in a comprehensive school. Private secondary schools follow much the same pattern, although they are, of course, not public. As a rule, the curriculum of both private and public schools is conservative.

To a rather large extent the American secondary school is a creature of its past. Because of tradition and inertia "its curriculum and organization are weighted down with considerable unnecessary baggage." Over the years attempts to make the curriculum more relevant, meaningful, useful, and practical have bogged down because of academic, lay, and professional reaction. Because of this academic reaction the secondary school curriculum,

public and private, has remained basically conservative.

The American people have never really decided what they expect of the American secondary school. Educational experts have proclaimed that the secondary schools should serve the needs of all American youth. Other experts have maintained that although the schools should strive for such major goals as health, command of the fundamental processes, vocational efficiency, civic competence, worthy use of leisure time, and ethical character, their primary mission was intellectual—to teach pupils to think. Lately other writers have been calling for greater emphases on the affective and social goals of secondary education. Issues concerning the role and purpose of the secondary school in the United States are no more settled today than they were years ago. Although the American secondary school consists of discrete academic courses, some schools have experimented with alternative programs of one sort or another. Among the curriculum problems that face secondary school personnel are the relative roles of general and specialized education, how to best provide for individual differences, whether the curriculum should be subject- or experience-centered, how to articulate vertically and horizontally, and the question of when the curriculum is in proper balance. In addition there are such basic problems as what to teach, to whom, and by what methods. So far none of these problems has been solved.

The curriculum is the result of many influences —not the least of which is the secondary education's history. Textbook publishers, business and industry, pressure groups, professional organizations, governmental agencies, institutions of higher learning, all have considerable input into the curriculum-making process, but it is the local teachers, administrators, and lay public that are responsible for the local curriculum. The roles of the teacher, the layman, and the pupils in curriculum building are growing greater. Of course, in the final analysis, what is actually taught is really determined by the teachers in the classroom. Curriculum guides and resource units provided by the school system make the teachers' work easier and serve to standardize the teaching and curriculum throughout the system.

The curriculum is not confined only to the

[19] Leonard H. Clark, Raymond L. Klein, and John B. Burks, *The American Secondary School Curriculum*, 2d ed. (New York: Macmillan Publishing Co., Inc., 1972), pp. 487–488.

courses taught in the school; it includes the extra-curriculum and the guidance program as well. The extracurriculum may well provide educational essentials that are impossible in the regular academic program. It should therefore be both open to and attractive to all pupils. The guidance program, when well-organized, also provides essential services. Its purpose is to help pupils to understand themselves and to direct their own lives more efficiently. To accomplish these purposes it provides individual inventory services, occupational and educational information services, counseling services, placement services, and follow-up services. Usually these services are not separate, but part of one large service by which the school tries to help its pupils become happier and more useful students and citizens.

It is somewhat difficult to spot trends in secondary education because of the prevalence of transient fads and the constant pulling and pushing of action and reaction in educational circles. However, it appears that schools are becoming more responsive and humane and that they are attempting to provide curricula and methods that are really relevant and .practical in so far as the wishes and needs of youth and society are concerned.

Suggested Readings for Part I

ALCORN, MARVIN D., JAMES S. KINDER, AND JIM R. SCHUNERT, *Better Teaching in Secondary Schools,* 3rd ed. New York: Holt, Rinehart and Winston, Publishers, 1970. Chs. 1, 2, and 15.

ALEXANDER, WILLIAM M., *The High School Today and Tomorrow.* New York: Holt, Rinehart and Winston, Publishers, 1971.

ALLEN, DWIGHT W., AND ELI SEIFMAN, *The Teachers Handbook.* Glenview, Ill.: Scott, Foresman and Company, 1971. Sec. 4–7.

"Alternatives in Public Education," *NASSP Bulletin* (September 1973). Entire issue.

AMIDON, EDMUND J., AND ELIZABETH HUNTER, *Improving Teaching.* New York: Holt, Rinehart and Winston, Publishers, 1966.

———, AND NED A. FLANDERS, *The Role of the Teacher in the Classroom.* Minneapolis: Paul S. Amidon and Associates, 1963.

BAUGHMAN, DALE, *What Do Students Really Want?* Bloomington, Ind.: The Phi Delta Kappa Educational Foundation, 1972.

BELLACK, ARNO A., *Theory and Research in Teaching.* New York: Teachers College Press, 1963.

BIDDLE, BRUCE J., AND WILLIAM J. ELLENA, eds. *Contemporary Research in Teacher Effectiveness.* New York: Holt, Rinehart and Winston, Publishers, 1964.

BIEHLER, ROBERT F., *Psychology Applied to Teaching.* Boston: Houghton Mifflin Company, 1971.

BRAUNER, CHARLES J., *American Educational Theory.* Englewood Cliffs, N.J.: Prentice-Hall, Inc., 1964.

BROWN, B. FRANK, *The Non-Graded High School.* Englewood Cliffs, N.J.: Prentice-Hall, Inc., 1963.

BRUNER, JEROME S., *The Process of Education.* Cambridge, Mass.: Harvard University Press, 1960.

BUGELSKI, B. R., *The Psychology of Learning Applied to Teaching,* 2nd ed. Indianapolis: The Bobbs-Merrill Co., Inc., 1971.

CAWELTI, GORDON, *Vitalizing the High School.* Washington, D.C.: Association for Supervision and Curriculum Development, 1974.

COLEMAN, JAMES S., *Adolescents and the Schools.* New York: Basic Books, Inc., Publishers, 1965.

———, *Youth: Transition to Adulthood.* Chicago: University of Chicago Press, 1974.

Coop, Richard H., and Kinnard P. White, *Psychological Concepts in the Classroom.* New York: Harper & Row, Publishers, 1974.

Cusick, Philip A., *Inside High School.* New York: Holt, Rinehart and Winston, Publishers, 1973.

Disque, Jerry, *In Between: The Adolescent's Struggle for Independence.* Bloomington, Ind.: The Phi Delta Kappa Educational Foundation, 1973.

The 80's: Where Will the Schools Be? Reston, Va.: The National Association of Secondary School Principals, 1974.

Eisner, Elliot W., and Elizabeth Vallance, *Conflicting Conceptions of Curriculum.* Berkeley, Calif.: McCutchan Publishing Corporation, 1974.

Fantini, Mario D., *Public Schools of Choice.* New York: Simon & Schuster, Inc., 1973.

Filbeck, Robert, *Systems in Teaching and Learning.* Lincoln, Nebr.: Professional Educators Publications, Inc., 1974.

Friedenberg, Edgar Z., *The Vanishing Adolescent.* Boston: Beacon Press, 1973.

Frymier, Jack R., *The Nature of Educational Method.* Columbus, Ohio: Charles E. Merrill Books, Inc., 1965.

Gagné, Robert M., *The Conditions of Learning.* New York: Holt, Rinehart and Winston, Publishers, 1965.

Gottlieb, David, *Youth in Contemporary Society.* New York: Sage Publications, Inc., 1973.

Grambs, Jean D., John C. Carr, and Robert M. Fitch, *Modern Methods in Secondary Education*, 3rd ed. New York: Holt, Rinehart and Winston, Publishers, 1970. Chs. 1–4 and 18.

Grinder, Robert E., *Adolescence.* New York: John Wiley & Sons, Inc., 1973.

Gronlund, Norman E., *Determining Accountability for Classroom Instruction.* New York: Macmillan Publishing Co., Inc., 1974.

Highet, Gilbert, *The Art of Teaching.* New York: Vintage Books, 1955.

Hullfish, H. Gordon, and Philip D. Smith, *Reflective Thinking.* New York: Dodd, Mead & Company, 1961.

"Humanizing the Schools," *NASSP Bulletin*, February 1972. Entire issue.

Hyman, Ronald T., *Ways of Teaching*, 2nd ed. Philadelphia: J. B. Lippincott Company, 1974. Introduction and Ch. 1.

Jewett, Ann E., and Clyde Knapp, *The Growing Years*, 1962 Yearbook, American Association for Health, Physical Education and Recreation. Washington, D.C.: The National Education Association.

Lee, Gordon C., "The Changing Role of the Teacher" in *The Changing American School,* Sixty-fifth Yearbook, Part II, National Society for the Study of Education. Chicago: University of Chicago Press, 1966.

Lesser, Gerald S., *Psychology and Educational Practice.* Glenview, Ill.: Scott, Foresman and Company, 1971.

Mood of American Youth, Gilbert Youth Poll. Washington, D.C.: National Association of Secondary School Principals, 1974.

Mouly, George J., *Psychology for Effective Teaching*, 3rd ed. New York: Holt, Rinehart and Winston, Inc., 1973.

Mueller, Richard J., *Principles of Classroom Learning and Perception:*

An Introduction to Educational Psychology. New York: Praeger Publishers, Inc., 1974.

The National Commission on the Reform of Secondary Education, *The Reform of Secondary Education*. New York: McGraw-Hill Book Company, 1973.

National Society for the Study of Education, *The Curriculum: Retrospect and Prospect*, Seventieth Yearbook, Part I. Chicago: University of Chicago Press, 1971.

———, *Theories of Learning and Instruction*, Sixty-third Yearbook. Chicago: University of Chicago Press, 1964.

———, *Uses of the Sociology of Education*, Seventy-third Yearbook, Part II. Chicago: University of Chicago Press, 1974. Section I, Youth Culture.

POSTMAN, NEIL, AND CHARLES WEINGARTNER, *How to Recognize a Good School*. Bloomington, Ind.: The Phi Delta Kappa Educational Foundation, 1973.

RIORDAN, ROBERT C., *Alternative Schools in Action*. Bloomington, Ind.: The Phi Delta Kappa Educational Foundation, 1972.

RYLE, GILBERT, *The Concept of Mind*. New York: Barnes and Noble, Inc., 1949.

SMITH, B. OTHANEL, AND ROBERT H. ENNIS, *Language and Concepts in Education*. Chicago: Rand McNally & Company, 1969.

SMITH, VERNON, et al., *Optional Alternative Public Schools*. Bloomington, Ind.: The Phi Delta Kappa Educational Foundation, 1974.

STINNETT, T. M., AND ALBERT J. HUGGETT, *Professional Problems of Teachers*, 2nd ed. New York: Macmillan Publishing Co., Inc., 1963.

STUART, JESSE, *To Teach, To Love*. New York: Penguin Books Inc., 1973.

"Student Activities," *NASSP Bulletin* (September, 1971).

"The Subject Is Curriculum," *NASSP Bulletin* (November, 1969).

UNRUH, GLENYS G., AND WILLIAM M. ALEXANDER, *Innovations in Secondary Education*, 2nd ed. New York: Holt, Rinehart and Winston, Publishers, 1974.

VARS, GORDON F., ed. *Common Learning: Core and Interdisciplinary Team Approaches*. Scranton, Pa.: International Textbook Co., 1969.

WEIGAND, JAMES E., *Developing Teacher Competencies*. Englewood Cliffs, N.J.: Prentice-Hall, Inc., 1971.

WILHELMS, FRED, *What Should the Schools Teach?* Bloomington, Ind.: The Phi Delta Kappa Educational Foundation, 1972.

WILSON, CHARLES H., *A Teacher Is a Person*. New York: Holt, Rinehart and Winston, Publishers, 1956.

WILSON, ELIZABETH C., *Needed: A New Kind of Teacher*. Bloomington, Ind.: The Phi Delta Kappa Educational Foundation, 1973.

WILSON, L. CRAIG, *The Open Access Curriculum*. Boston: Allyn & Bacon, Inc., 1971.

WINDER, ALVIN E., *Adolescence*, 2nd ed. New York: D. Van Nostrand Co., 1974.

Youth into Adult. Washington, D.C.: National Commission on Resources for Youth, 1974.

II

Motivation, Discipline, and Control

Motivation

3

THE IMPORTANCE
OF MOTIVATION

People learn through activity. The human mind cannot absorb knowledge like a sponge. Neither is the mind a wax tablet upon which the teacher can write. Nor is it a lump of clay the teacher can mold into the shape he desires. Rather, learning results from one's interactions with the environment—both what he does to the environment, and his reactions to what the environment does to him. Thus the burnt child who learns to fear the fire learns from the effect of the environment on him, while the boy who solves a puzzle learns from his effect on the environment. In short, people learn from experiences and only from experiences. Without experiences there would be no learning. In order to learn a person must act (or react). He may solve problems. He may read. He may listen to his teacher or fellow pupils. He may practice. He may react to the beauty of a sonnet or a sentimental thought. But if he is to learn, he must *do something*.

Not all experiences result in learning, however. After constant repetition, for example, an experience seldom produces much learning; neither do experiences which lack meaning or in which the learner is not paying attention. How many steps are there between the first and second floor of your home or your dormitory? How many chairs are there in a row in your classroom? The chances are that unless you have paid particular attention to these details, you do not know. Any experience may result in learning, but many do not. In fact, many activities, such as misbehavior in the classroom, actually prevent desirable learning.

Since all this is so, the teacher must somehow get his pupils to engage in activities that will result in the desired learnings. This process is the essential ingredient in both instruction and discipline.[1] We call this process motivation.

Blocks to Learning

FALSE CAUSES FOR NOT LEARNING

Why is it that so often pupils do not learn in our classes and schools? There are many reasons, of course. But often the reasons we assume to be the causes are false ones. For instance we say

"Eileen is the silliest girl you've ever seen. She never pays attention to a thing. She can't keep her mind on anything." (But watch her at the theater. Engrossed in dreamland she sits. Seemingly no commotion in the theater could draw her attention from the plot.)

"John is the stupidest boy I've ever seen." (Yet he was able to learn to read music and become the highly successful leader of his own orchestra.)

"Joe is the laziest boy in school. He just won't do a thing. I don't think he has finished one algebra assignment this year." (But think of the hours of hard physical and mental work he has spent putting together his hot rod. His mother has a hard time getting him away from that car long enough to eat his dinner.)

---

[1] In a sense instruction and discipline, or control, are really synonymous. One cannot have good instruction without good discipline.

REAL CAUSES FOR NOT LEARNING

Obviously these accusations do not really explain why pupils do not learn. If anything, they describe symptoms, not real causes. Too often such statements are only alibis by which we teachers explain and attempt to justify to ourselves our lack of success. We can no longer fall back on such excuses. Our clients—the pupils, parents, and community—will no longer let us pass the buck down to the pupils. We must assume the responsibility ourselves when it is ours. What then are the real causes for pupils' not learning? Let us look at a few of them.

First and most important is poor teaching. Teaching is often ineffective, because it is inadequately planned or because it violates the laws of learning. Some courses are poorly organized and lack direction. Some classes are poorly motivated. In some courses the work is too hard or too easy. Some teachers attempt to cover the subject rapidly instead of giving it time to sink in. Some teachers ignore the fact that pupils are individuals with varying backgrounds, talents, and interests, and attempt to teach everyone the same material at the same rate in the same way.

The curriculum itself is often a major cause of nonlearning. Too much of what is taught in the secondary school has little bearing on the lives or needs of the pupils. At least one educational philosopher has come to the belief that probably half of the high school curriculum could be dropped from the school program tomorrow without anyone's noticing its passing. Be that as it may, in truth, all too frequently high school curricula do little to interest pupils or to prepare them for life today or in the future in any significant way. It is not surprising that for many pupils their studies seem too futile and dead-end to be worth their exerting any real effort to learn them. If we wish pupils to make an effort to learn, we ought to provide something for them to learn that at least seems worthwhile to them.

Poor teaching and poor courses probably cause most failures to learn, but they are not the only causes. Pupils are often handicapped by poor health, fatigue, physical or mental limitations, emotional difficulties, environmental factors, family attitudes, or peer pressures. If a pupil's parents and friends feel that studying a Shakespearean sonnet is a waste of time and money, it probably will not be easy to convince the youth that he should devote much time to it. Or again, a young person may believe, as did the poet, in burning the candle at both ends. Although this practice may give "a lovely light," it is not helpful because fatigue hinders learning and too many interests distract pupils from the desired learnings.

These, then, are some of the blocks to learning. If the teacher is to do his job—helping pupils learn—the blocks must be overcome. Of course, the teacher is not always in a position in which he can do much to overcome them. But a good teacher will take each youngster and try, by using the best methods and materials he knows, to help the pupil learn what he should learn in spite of any obstacles. This is a key challenge of teaching. It is the heart of motivation—and of discipline.

THE MAJOR BLOCK TO LEARNING

That brings us to a major block to school learning. Few teachers and few faculties do much to make school learning seem important or attractive when compared to life's other activities. In fact, many of the things we teachers do seem to be designed so as to convince the pupils that learning is undesirable and unpleasant. In what other endeavor would one try to sell a product by using it as a punishment? Yet every day some teacher assigns class work as a punishment.

*

Do you recall what your teachers did in your high school classes that made you wish to study and work in their courses? What did they do that caused you to dislike schoolwork in general and the assignments in their courses in particular? What types of teacher actions particularly turn pupils off?

*

Causes of Misbehavior

The real causes for not learning and the causes of pupil misbehavior are pretty much the same. That is to say that discipline problems, like learning problems, are usually motivation problems. Recognizing this fact does not make it easy to solve problems having to do with control, but it does give one a perspective from which to view the problems and to shape strategies.

MANY CAUSES FOR EACH INCIDENT

As in the case of not learning, each act of misbehavior ordinarily has many causes. Seldom is any one motive the sole cause of any particular action, good or bad. What is it that makes a normally pleasant youth rebel toward the end of the last period on a sunny June day? Let us look at a few of the possibilities.

A certain young man has been sitting in a hot classroom for almost an entire class period. For much of that time the sun has been shining into his eyes because of a broken window shade. This is the last period and he has had no food for several hours. He is tired, hot, and hungry. His head is beginning to ache. The class is deadly dull. All period long the class has been reviewing subject matter detail by answering questions. Around and around the class go the questions. What are the properties of chlorine? What is the formula for sulfuric acid? What is oxidation? The pupils do not seem to know the answers very well, and this exasperates the teacher. As each pupil fails to get an answer, the teacher berates him and threatens him with dire results on the final examination for which they are reviewing. The glumness of the class increases. Our young man's mind wanders. He watches the freight train going down the track toward New York and counts the cars. Then he falls to dreaming about the new stereo albums he plans to add to his collection. Suddenly he hears his name.

"I am sorry, Mr. ———, I did not understand the question."

"You would have understood it all right if you had been listening. How do you expect me to get you thick-headed nincompoops ready for this examination if you don't pay attention? I asked you, who was Lavoisier?"

At the moment our young man hasn't the slightest idea and mutters something to that effect in an undertone.

"What did you say? What are you muttering?"

Goaded beyond repair our young man blurts out, "I said I don't know and I don't care."

And then the sky falls. Who can say what caused the pupil to blow up? The heat, the sun, the headache, the hunger, the poor teaching, the boredom, the woolgathering, the teacher's exasperation, the nagging, the abuse? All these things contributed, with perhaps many others we do not know of. Almost every incident of misbehavior is the result of a multitude of causes.

THE COMMUNITY

One source of misbehavior is the environment in which the youth lives. In an area where crime, sex irregularities, drunkenness, drug addiction, barroom fights, and knifings are common, it would be naïve to expect pupils to rise overnight to the prim middle-class mores of the ordinary school and school teacher. For youths from such areas achieving acceptable standards of behavior can be a long, hard process. Fortunately, these youths after their fashion want to be respected and be respectable. The idealism of youth may be warped in some of them, but it is there.

A school administrator never tired of relating an incident which occurred many years ago. Two elementary school girls were fighting in the age-old manner of fishwives. The coming of the superintendent of schools brought the fight to a quick halt, but one of the girls thought that she should apologize and explain. She hurried up to him and blurted, "I know I shouldn't swear, Mr. C., but, honest to God, she made me so God damned mad . . ." This young lady had not as yet achieved the standard of speech and conduct one would hope for, but, after her fashion, she was trying.

Home situations cause much school misbehavior. Boys and girls carry sibling rivalries, jealousies, and attendant high feelings to school with them. Pupils are often under parental pressure of one sort or another. Resentment and rebellion against such pressures can carry over into the classroom. Both neglected and overprotected pupils have not established desirable behavior patterns in many instances, and continue their misbehavior in school. Homes in which values differ from those of the school make the work of the teacher more difficult—particularly homes in which the parents have little interest in secondary education.

EMOTIONAL DIFFICULTIES

Teen-agers seem to have more than their share of emotional troubles. These disturbances may not be serious, but they are frequently upsetting. The cause of the upset may have nothing whatsoever to do with the class or the school. Let us suppose, for instance, that a boy has been late for breakfast and has missed his bus. His father, who has had to drive him to school, has let him feel the sharp side of his tongue. Before school starts, the boy is already emotionally upset. A trifle may set him off.

Any threat to a pupil's security may lead to undesirable behavior. To prevent the loss of security, or to regain it once it is lost, the pupil may resort to subterfuge, escape, or something else equally undesirable. Many common classroom conditions are serious threats to the security of pupils. Threats of failure, rejection, ridicule, and inconsistency on the part of teachers are some of them. The misuse of tests is one of the most common. Overly difficult tests and unnecessarily high and rigid standards of achievement may cause fear, jealousy, and antagonism. The natural result is cheating. Similarly, ill-conceived practices such as sarcasm and criticism of individuals in front of the class cause embarrassment, resentment, and class tension. In such an atmosphere many pupils resort to misbehavior as a defense.

At times, misbehavior is symptomatic of social maladjustment. Boys and girls who are not accepted by the group often make nuisances of themselves in order to gain status. Indeed, some of them want attention and recognition so much that they welcome being punished to get it.

ADOLESCENCE

A certain amount of school misbehavior is simply the result of what our forefathers called an "excess of animal spirits." By nature adolescents are a restless lot whose basic needs and drives do not always run in complete harmony with even the best curriculum. In ordinary situations adolescents very quickly get tired of just sitting. Much pupil restlessness in class may be laid to a simple need to work off energy.

At this time of life, also, boys and girls are in the midst of carrying out some of their most critical and difficult developmental tasks, in particular learning to achieve a role in adult heterosexual society. The great growth and physical changes of adolescence often confuse pupils and lead to untoward behavior. Both boys and girls find it difficult to adjust to their new bodies and their resulting new social roles. Similarly as their horizons expand they find themselves confronted with perplexing conflicts of values in the home, school, and peer groups that make it difficult to know how to behave. Thus an adolescent's classroom misbehavior may be an attempt to establish himself and his personality in the society of his peers. It may also be just a carry-over from his life away from school. After all, to most boys and girls social activity and love affairs seem to be fully as important as algebra and geography. Life does not stop just because class is in session.

SCHOOL-CAUSED MISBEHAVIOR

Proper handling of problem cases is, of course, a difficult and time-consuming business. Fortunately, most classroom offenses stem from causes within the teacher's control. Some of these causes are poor teaching, poor curriculum, poor classroom management, poor techniques of discipline, and personality defects in the teacher. *Curricula which do not provide for the needs and interests of youth sow the seeds of misconduct.* The further the curriculum gets from the life of the youth, the less likely he is to see its worth, and the more liable he is to seek entertainment during school hours. Similarly, poor teaching produces dead, pointless classes which breed misconduct. Long lectures by unskilled lecturers make even hardened adults bored and restless. Grading practices that force nonacademically inclined pupils to compete on equal terms with the talented cause discouragement, frustration, and consequent hell raising.[2] Like poor teaching, poor methods of discipline engender misbehavior by causing dissatisfaction, discontent, and tension. A succeeding section will discuss these

[2] Only in schools are people required to compete with people out of their league.

causes more fully and attempt to show how to avoid them.

TEACHER-CAUSED MISBEHAVIOR

Frequently the cause of pupil misbehavior is the teacher himself. That teachers cause behavior problems by using poor methods of teaching and control has already been pointed out. Lesson planning is the key to good teaching. Yet many teachers never seem to plan well. Their classes never seem to go anywhere because they have no real objective. There are no provisions for motivating the pupils. There is no variety; every day the classes repeat the same monotonous grind. Boring classes are always invitations to misbehavior. Sometimes the classes contain dead spots in which pupils have really nothing to do. The assignments are vague; pupils are not sure what they are supposed to do and how they are supposed to do it. Such assignments are frustrating. Also frustrating are lessons that are too hard or too easy, too fast or too slow.

In addition to using poor methods, some teachers act as though they wanted to create behavior problems. They come to class late or start class late. They waste time. Their classes have dead spots in which nothing is really happening. Their work habits are sloppy, and so is their class organization. They abuse their pupils by being sarcastic, calling them names, making fun of them and their mistakes, giving them injudicious tongue lashings, and generally treating them like dirt. Other teachers are unconsciously discourteous, brusque, and unsympathetic. They are unfair and inconsistent in their demands. Some act as though they disliked pupils. It is difficult to get cooperation from people who feel you dislike them.

*

Think back over the classes you have attended in which there have been disciplinary incidents. What seemed to be the cause? What were the causes of disciplinary incidents involving you or your friends when you were in secondary school?

Why do pupils misbehave? List all the possible causes for misbehavior that you can name. How might knowledge of the causes of misbehavior influence the teacher's action?

Many (some say most) behavior problems are teacher-created. Can you think of some examples? How can the teacher avoid creating such situations?

*

SOME PRINCIPLES
OF MOTIVATION

WHAT MOTIVATION IS NOT

As we have already tried to point out, motivation, in schooling, is the process of getting pupils to engage in activities that will presumably result in their learning those things they ought to learn. At this point, so as to allay any misapprehensions, it may be wise to point out what motivation is not. Motivation does not imply that pupils should do only those things that interest them or that teachers should always make classes enjoyable. Nothing could be farther from the truth. At times pupils must learn lessons and participate in activities that they dislike. It is not the teacher's job to get each pupil to like every subject or activity, although it would help if he could; it is rather to get the pupil to learn as well as he possibly can whether he likes it or not. In many a classroom the problem of how to motivate the pupils is by far the most pressing one to the teacher.

A common manifestation of the problem of motivation is the nonacademically inclined youth who, the teachers say, has a short attention span. Such pupils are legion in our secondary schools. But the notion that they have short attention spans is a myth. Every normally healthy secondary school youth within the normal range of intelligence has a long enough attention span when he is confronted by a situation interesting and challenging to him. Watch him at the movies or trying to learn the techniques of his favorite sport. The trouble is not that normal adolescent boys and girls have short attention spans, but that they have low tolerance for boredom. Naturally they find it hard to keep their minds on lessons that they hate and see as pointless.

When pupils find their classes interesting, exciting, and personally worthwhile, teachers have few problems because of short attention spans even among the least academically inclined pupils. (That is why skillful speakers are able, by the use of striking illustrations and homely examples, to capture and hold the attention of listeners of all ages.)

*

What is motivation? What are its implications for teaching?

"Learning takes place only through activity." What does this mean? What are the implications for teaching?

What causes people to do things? List the reasons why you have done the more important things you have done today.

*

HOW TO MOTIVATE PUPILS

How, then, does one motivate pupils? Unfortunately it is not easy. No royal road to learning exists; neither is there a surefire method of motivating young people.

Techniques that work well in one situation may be useless in another. Incentives that enthuse some individuals in a class leave others completely indifferent. About all one can do is to point out that the teacher must try to create the desire to learn and to suggest principles and possible techniques for creating that desire. Therefore, in the next few pages we shall examine several principles of motivation.

1. Take advantage of the pupil's present motives.
2. Make the potential learnings seem worthwhile.
3. Help the pupil establish suitable tasks and objectives.
4. Keep up the pace.
5. Develop a receptive mood in the learner.
6. Cultivate in the learner ideals and attitudes conducive to learning.
7. Utilize reinforcement theory as much as feasible.
8. Provide good models for pupils to fashion themselves after.

It should be emphasized that the best motivational devices and techniques are positive in nature. We teachers have in the past placed too much emphasis on negative aversive measures in an attempt to motivate and discipline. It is time for us to turn from negative motivation to positive motivation. Success breeds success.

Utilizing Present Motives

THE IMPORTANCE OF INTEREST

Pupils undoubtedly learn more efficiently those things that interest them. Therefore, that teachers should try harnessing pupil interest as a means to effective teaching seems to be self-evident. This doctrine of interest does not imply that the whims of pupils should determine the curriculum. It does imply that when possible the teacher should use pupil interests already established or, if suitable pupil interests are not established, the teacher should somehow create interest or the lesson will fail.

As we grow older most of us find it increasingly difficult to know and understand the interests of young people. The goals of youth are not the same as the goals of adults. Adults are sometimes shocked to find that what they feel ought to be of the utmost intrinsic value to all youth, seems to be quite worthless to young eyes. Even young adults find that what is intensely interesting and exciting to them at twenty-two may not find a single response in a group of fifteen-year-olds. For this reason the beginning teacher should make a point to find out the interests, attitudes, ideals, and goals of his pupils. Once he knows what his pupils think is important, he can adapt his motivational techniques accordingly. This information can be gathered by using the devices and techniques discussed in Chapters 1 and 15. In addition, the teacher may use devices designed specifically for the gathering of information about pupils' interests.

An example of such a device is the interest inventory. Through the use of such inventories, the alert teacher may gain insights into the reading interests and hobbies of his pupils. Such instruments may be devised by teachers quite easily. For example, one can build an interest finder by simply preparing a questionnaire of items designed to find out what the pupils' interests are, such as:

What is your favorite way of killing time?
If you could do anything you wanted to do, what would you want to do most?
What kind of movies or television programs do you like most?

USING PUPILS' ATTITUDES AND IDEALS

Among the motives pupils bring to school are their ideals and attitudes. Insofar as he can, the teacher should attempt to harness such attitudes as cooperativeness, neatness, industry, fairness, courtesy, patriotism, and honesty, and utilize them in his teaching. A young person assigned to a group project role he does not particularly like might do his job well because the teacher has appealed to his cooperative attitude. Undoubtedly you can think of examples in your own school life in which you have performed downright distasteful tasks simply because an attitude or ideal told you that this was the thing to do under the circumstances. Frequently this type of experience leads us to our most useful and valuable learning. Sometimes, in spite of our prejudice, the experience itself turns out to be extremely rewarding. Many older students find great enjoyment in academic activities they thought to be distasteful when they first encountered them. Adults have had a lifetime of happy fulfillment in careers stemming from academic tasks they had to do against their will.

HARNESSING THE NATURAL MOTIVES

Every boy and girl comes to school with certain basic drives. These natural motives are often more powerful than any incentive the teacher can invent. The competent teacher is alert to these drives and uses them in his teaching, if he can. If he cannot utilize them, he at least strives to adapt his classwork so that it seldom conflicts directly with them.

One winter day an English teacher suddenly found the attention of his class leaving him. Something outside the window had stolen it away. A little irked, he looked out to see what the matter was. No wonder the class was diverted. A big gray cat was stalking a rabbit in the heavy snow. Stealthily, the cat sneaked up on the rabbit and just as he seemed to be within range and ready to pounce on his prey, the rabbit hopped out of reach. Undaunted, the stubborn cat tried again and again, but the deep snow prevented him from closing in. Few English literature classes can compete with such real life melodrama. In this instance, the teacher allowed the class to watch the struggle for a while and then dispatched someone to chase the animals away—ostensibly to save the life of the rabbit, although after a few minutes of watching it was obvious that the rabbit was in no danger. By doing this, the teacher avoided competing with the pupils' natural curiosity. Perhaps he could have harnessed this curiosity and interest by diverting the class to a discussion of the incident and tying it up with literature—plot, incident, suspense, conflict, characterization—or possibly he could have encouraged pupils to turn the incident into a bit of creative writing. Certainly he was wise not to attempt to continue with his original plan in the face of this strong natural motive.

Incidents like the above are not commonplace, but still it is typical of the kinds of incidents that bring into play strong natural motives. Let us look at a much more prosaic example. In a social studies class one morning the juniors were all upset because they had had a most interesting and exciting speaker on Russia at assembly. However, because some faculty members dominated the discussion, the students had not had a chance to ask the speaker their questions. So, rather than go on with his prepared lesson, the teacher took time to discuss their questions, in this way easing their frustration and taking advantage of their interest.

*

The English teacher's predicament, although an actual incident, was very unusual. The second example is quite commonplace. Perhaps you can think of more commonplace examples of natural motives interrupting the normal course of learning. Have there been any instances in your college classes when the teaching has been hampered by the natural motivation of the students? What, if anything, did the instructor do? What might he have done?

*

Capitalizing on Pupil Curiosity. People are naturally curious. Watch a little child examine things. Listen to him asking questions: Why? Why? Why? This curiosity abides in adults also, and it is probably just as strong. Witness the crowds that gather whenever there is an accident. When people are not naturally curious about a certain thing, it is usually fairly easy to arouse their curiosity. One way of doing so is to puzzle them a little so that they ask themselves what will happen next, or what will this result in. Another is to make use of suspense. If teachers can capitalize on the curiosity of youth, the youngsters will do their schoolwork more eagerly because they will want to find out. This is an important type of motivation.

Suspense catches and holds the pupils because they want to find out the ending. Everyone has sat through poor movies and bad television shows

because he wanted to see how they came out. In such circumstances, because the author has kept us in suspense, we stay on to the end in spite of our better judgment. In the same manner, teachers who can create a feeling of suspense in the classroom can arouse the pupils' curiosity and hold their interest.

A student teacher in a junior high school general science class performed an experiment in which he attempted to demonstrate the power of air pressure by creating a vacuum in a large can. He first talked to the pupils telling them what he intended to do, and asked them what they thought would happen when he created the vacuum. Several theories were proposed, of course; among them the theory that the pressure of the atmosphere would "smash the can." "All right," he said, "let's see if the atmosphere can crush the can." He then heated some water in the can filling it full of steam. Capping the steam-filled can he said, "O.K., now let us see what happens." An air of intense expectancy hung over the classroom as the eighth graders stared at the can. Suddenly one yelled, "There it goes," as the can slowly started to crumble. In a few minutes the class was off on a lively discussion of what had "smashed the can." By harnessing the natural appeal of curiosity, through the medium of suspense and a simple experiment, the teacher had aroused the class to productive activity.

Social Approval, Self-esteem, and the Desire for Success. Quite often praise and rewards spur us on to heights when we might otherwise rest on our laurels. Everyone wants to feel that he is important and respected by his friends and associates. This is particularly true of adolescents who oftentimes will do almost anything to win approval. All of us want to be proud of ourselves. We desire and need success in order to build up our self-esteem and the approval of the group. No one wants to be a failure. For this reason the competent teacher gives his pupils plenty of opportunity to preen their feathers. He does his best to find something to praise in even the least successful of them. Recognition of one's success by others is most enjoyable. When this recognition takes a tangible form, it is usually even more enjoyable. In addition, just the feeling of having succeeded, whether anyone praises you or not, can be motivating. Teachers should see to it that pupils have many successes in their schoolwork. They can do so by differentiating the work to be done and seeing to it that pupils are assigned tasks commensurate with their abilities. Repeated failure soon puts an end to the desire to try.

Need for Security. Any threat to a young person's security makes learning a more difficult problem. For this reason one should probably avoid the use of fear as a classroom motivational device even though fear is one of the most powerful of motives.

The frightened person cannot think well. When intensely afraid he may become completely disorganized. Constant worry, a milder form of fear, may lead to mental and emotional idiosyncrasies if not to actual illness. Youths have fears and worries enough without our creating more. Fear should be saved for such important things as life and death situations, for example, preventing young people from driving too fast or little children from crossing the highway alone.

It is for these reasons that the overemphasis on tests and marks should be discouraged. Also to be avoided are class recitations in which pupils are shamed if they answer incorrectly. Ignorance is not a crime to be punished. Overharsh attitudes keep pupils from trying their best and tend to make pupils who do try rigid so that they cannot think their best. Pupils learn better in a more relaxed atmosphere.

*

What does psychology tell us about the effect of praise, reproof, rewards, and punishment upon learning? What are the implications for teaching?

Should emulation, competition, and rivalry be used to motivate classroom learning? What are the advantages and disadvantages of each?

Evaluate the following as motivating techniques: sarcasm, ridicule, fear.

*

Desire for Adventure and Action. Paradoxically, the need for security is accompanied by a desire for action, adventure, and excitement. This often causes youngsters to take chances that seem to belie their desire for security. Often the adventurer finds his security by seeking his adventure in groups and by soliciting the approval and admiration of his peers for his adventuresomeness.

The teacher would do well to feature activities and materials that have plenty of excitement and action at least part of the time. In the junior high school grades teachers sometimes use competitive games to give excitement to practice and drill lessons. Alert history and English teachers can utilize stories of adventure to stimulate their classes. History is full of heroic adventures by heroic men. Teachers would do well to harness the exploits of such men as George Washington, Zebulon Pike, Lewis and Clark, Coronado, and Daniel Boone to furnish their history courses with excitement and high adventure.

Desire to Play and Have Fun. Enjoying oneself is a prominent goal in every person's life. We all need to play and amuse ourselves—even the hypochondriac who enjoys poor health. This motive is closely akin to the need for action, adventure, and excitement. The ordinary class abounds with opportunities to use games—an example is the use of pseudobaseball games in drill activities. Another example of making a dull activity fun was that used in a midterm test in a college course in German. The test was given just prior to the annual fall dance weekend. The test consisted largely of translating a hilarious account of the *Tanzwochende* to come and all the fun the *Mädchen* and *Knaben* were to have. The test was fun and many of the students found it enjoyable —if a midterm test can ever be described as enjoyable. Similarly at least one New Jersey high school teacher adds spice to his tests by including silly questions such as "In ten words or less explain why this is the best course you ever heard of."

The Need for Friendships. Youths are gregarious. One of the most powerful natural drives is the desire for friendship. Any attempt to keep boys and girls quietly working by themselves in a crowded classroom for long periods of time is against the laws of nature. Capable teachers will usually refrain from making such periods overly long and will not be too harsh on boys and girls who feel the need for conversing with their friends. Youth's gregariousness and friendships can be of considerable help to the able teacher—especially in grouping and in conducting group activities. Means of determining and profiting from natural groups and friendships in one's teaching are explored further in Chapters 2 and 11.

To have friends is exceedingly important for adolescents but most important of all perhaps are the heterosexual friendships which begin to form at this stage of life. Sex and the desire for one's own home are basic drives. Their power and importance should not be underestimated. It is too much, for instance, to expect a pretty girl to concentrate on Ohm's law when she has a complexion problem the day before the junior prom.

Heterosexual interests also have some bearing on the type of subject matter and activities selected for a class. This drive does not play the same role in the lives of seventh graders that it does in the lives of twelfth graders. Romantic literature may have little meaning to a seventh-grade boy, but it may be of major importance to his older sister. The teacher should bear in mind the sex and age of his pupils in selecting the activities and materials of instruction.

Making Learning Worthwhile

TEACHER ATTITUDES AND MOTIVATION

If a teacher wants his pupils to feel that the learnings of his course are valuable, he must feel so himself. The teacher who is sincerely enthusiastic about his subject is a much better salesman than the teacher bored by his own course. Some teachers' enthusiasm is hard to resist. Before the pupils realize it they begin to catch the teacher's spirit—sometimes in spite of themselves. Of course, enthusiasm alone will not fire up every member of the class, but it helps. No one should teach a subject he does not like.

One of the most successful teachers of English the authors ever knew was a literature enthusiast. One had only to sit in his class a minute to know that literature was important to him. His enthusiasm was infectious. It was hard to leave his classroom without feeling the fascination of literature. Moreover, he had the habit of selecting things to read and handing them to a pupil with such comments as, "You know, here's a story I bet you'll enjoy. It is about. . . . . Why don't you read it and tell me how you liked it?" Even his supervisor was not immune from his blandishments; frequently he left the classroom with an assignment.

This teacher's eagerness and enthusiasm trapped pupils into wanting to read literature.

This same teacher also used effectively a technique which combined his enthusiasm for literature with an appeal to curiosity. With all the proper histrionic effects he would start to read a story to the class. Then, at a crucial point, he would stop to ask questions which could be answered only by completing the story. Often the pupils could hardly wait to turn to their books to find the answers.

THE IMPORTANCE OF PUPIL VALUES

Once a pupil is convinced that learning is vital he is usually willing to work to acquire it. It is well known that some pupils see little value in much of their school work and find it difficult to arouse much enthusiasm for their tasks. The teacher should try to make his classes seem worthwhile to all of his pupils. Unless the pupils think their lessons are worthwhile, their participation will be only grudging, no matter how valuable the lessons really are.

Immediate Values and Deferred Values. If a pupil really wants to learn something now, he will usually attempt to learn it at once. If he thinks that he would like to know something about the matter when he grows up, he is apt to turn to other problems which seem more immediate to him. Whenever possible, the teacher should make the pupils aware of the immediate values of his lessons if he hopes to raise their motivation to a high pitch. This can often be done by centering the classwork around everyday concerns of pupils, by including current issues in the school and community, by pointing out how the classroom learning may be used in other classes and activities, and by consciously attempting to tie the lessons to the present attitudes and interests of pupils. For example, in a mathematics class one might use graphs to illustrate problems being studied in the social studies class, or the study of percentages might be related to the standings of the major-league baseball teams. Such techniques are much more likely to succeed in setting pupils to work than exhortations to "study because you will need to know it in college."

Something Suitable for Everyone. What we

know about individual differences tells us that boys and girls are not all interested in the same things. This variety may give spice to life, but it also complicates the motivating of a class of adolescents. We want our classes to seem worthwhile to the pupils in order that the pupils will work at high levels. But what one pupil finds worthwhile another may find a waste of time. What is the answer? Obviously the way out is to provide sufficient types of activities and materials so that everyone finds something interesting and worthwhile.

Pupils' notions of what is worthwhile are, of course, constantly subject to change. Consequently, teachers can frequently convince pupils that their assignments are truly worthwhile by simply presenting convincing arguments. But merely stating that so and so is important, or will be important, is not enough; the teacher should be prepared to show why. For example, one day a young beginning teacher asked his supervisor what he should do when his seventh-graders asked him why they should learn the names of the different climatic zones in their geography. "Why, tell them, of course," was the answer. "Yes," he said, "but I can't think of any reason for their learning them myself." If the teacher does not know why a certain learning is worthwhile, how can he expect a boy or girl to make the effort necessary to learn it?

*

How would you have answered the seventh-grade geographers?

Can you justify teaching your major fields?

Go through a textbook you might use in your teaching. How can you make this material seem worthwhile to a group of teen-agers? Why is it worthwhile?

*

Intrinsic and Extrinsic Values. Any particular learning seems worthwhile to a pupil if it has either intrinsic or extrinsic value for him. If the learning is valuable enough to cause the pupil to act, he is acting because of its intrinsic value. This is intrinsic motivation. An example of intrinsic motivation is learning to drive a car. Most young people learn to drive because knowing how to drive has intrinsic value to them.

Some learnings seem to have no intrinsic value to the pupil although they have an extrinsic one, i.e., the learner sees relatively little value in the learning itself but does see value in what the learning may get him. An example of this may be the case of the youth who learns geometric theorems because he wishes to earn an A in the course or because his father has promised him a prize if he learns them. Here the goal is not the learning itself but something that can be obtained through the learning. Such goals are called incentives. They are really ulterior motives for undertaking activities otherwise considered not worth doing. Ordinarily, we should prefer that boys and girls do their schoolwork because of its intrinsic value to them. When this proves impossible or impractical, the teacher should use incentives that will create the desired response.

The incentive most frequently used in our schools is the school mark. That it should have become so important is most unfortunate because in many classes the only thing that matters is the mark. Real learning and understanding tend to be lost in the race for marks. When this happens, too much stress on the incentive has defeated the purpose of education. One result is cheating. Another is the transient learning that results so often from cramming for tests. Here today but gone tomorrow.

The mark has equally failed as a motivating force for the nonacademic, non-college-bound pupils. Our grading practices are very discouraging to them. Only in schools is it necessary to compete with everyone in the total population. Because they know they will not do well and because they suspect that their marks will never really have much influence on their lives, many of these young people could not possibly care less about school marks. To them good marks are unattainable and not very desirable. Even to the average pupil they are not a very sharp goad. Their only effect seems to be to arouse spasmodic bursts of effort to cram in as much knowledge as possible during certain periods of stress.

TEACHER-PUPIL PLANNING AND MOTIVATION

What a person elects to do himself usually interests him more than something imposed by someone else. At least, he is likely to think it is more interesting and is, therefore, more willing to start it. Consequently, boys and girls who plan their own activities may begin them more willingly than the pupils who do not. If the teacher allows the students to pick what they will read, or which of the activities they will do, or which order they will do them in, or to discuss what is important to learn in the new unit or topic, this may engender a favorable attitude in the pupils toward the work to be done. It also gives the teacher a considerable advantage. If he can capitalize on this start, quite often the pupils' enthusiasm will carry throughout the study of the topic or activity. The capable teacher will encourage pupil participation in the selection of topics and activities in order to capitalize on their motivational value.

*

It has been suggested that pupils could well participate in determining which short story or novel the class should read, or deciding in what order units should be taken up, or discussing what should be emphasized in a particular unit. Give specific examples of matters pupils could decide in teacher-pupil planning in your own field.

*

Establishing Suitable Objectives

THE NEED FOR AN OBJECTIVE

Both long-term and short-term goals are necessary to keep pupils moving in the way they should go. Long-term goals are necessary for giving overall direction, but it is the short-term goals that move us through the daily tasks and keep us going forward. For this reason, if classes are to be worthwhile, the teacher should have a definite goal for each lesson. Furthermore, the pupils should know approximately what this goal is and why it is important and adapt the goal for themselves.

As a matter of fact, the pupil always participates in the selection of his own objectives. Everything he does is instigated by the occasion, by self-instruction, or by instruction from another. As a result of one of these influences, or a combination of them, the pupil elects to do something. That is to say, he establishes a task. This task is his objective. It may be considerably different from what the teacher had in mind. However, the teacher's role is to provide situations in which the pupil will select, or accept, tasks that will help him toward

the learning desired. The teacher can do so through the use of directions and assignments.

THE ASSIGNMENT AS A MOTIVATING DEVICE

A famous professor of education used to remark that boys and girls usually would be glad to do their schoolwork if they could only figure out what the teacher wanted them to do. There is more than a germ of truth in this statement. Most of us have been in classes in which we did not know what to do. This fault is all too common. When the teacher finds his pupils are not doing their assignments but instead are crying, "I did not know, I had no book," and the like, he should check his directions. As often as not the fault lies in the assignment. If teachers hope to keep pupils working, they must be sure their assignments are definite, the directions clear, and the materials available.

In the past the assignment has been almost synonymous with homework. In many classrooms, even today, the assignment consists of a hurried shout at the end of the period—often drowned out by the clamor of the bell and the scuffling of feet eager to be on their way. Today one should think of a good assignment in a different way. An assignment is a job to be done, whether at home or in class. It may be assigned by the teacher or arrived at through the cooperative effort of both teacher and pupils. No matter who prepares the assignment it should serve the following purposes.

1. Set the direction of study and outline the scope of the task.
2. Motivate the pupil and prepare him for the task.
3. Help the learner to the means for accomplishing his task, i.e., establish possible methods and materials.
4. Adapt the tasks to the needs of the various pupils.

Thus the assignment is an essential factor in motivation and a basic part of any lesson. Let us look at these functions briefly.

The Functions of the Assignment. The first purpose of the assignment is *to set the direction and the scope of the task.* It is almost impossible to do anything unless one knows what to do. The purpose of the assignment is to make each pupil's task clear and definite to him. Some teachers tell the pupils just what is to be done. Others develop the task cooperatively with the group. In either case, however, the teacher should try to make sure that each and every pupil knows exactly what his task is. In case of a problem, for instance, the teacher must be sure that the pupils understand the problem, that the problem is well enough defined to be manageable, and that the pupils know how to go about solving it.

An example: Let us suppose that the class had just completed studying the Civil War period and was ready to go on to study the Reconstruction period. Let us further assume that as a result of class discussion the class had decided that they wanted to know the answer to some of the following questions:

> After the war was over, how did the Confederate states get back into the Union?
> How did the Southerners feel about the North? And vice versa?
> If much of the South was destroyed, as by Sherman in his march to the sea, how did the people live in the South after the war?
> What happened to the slaves?
> What happened to the Confederate soldiers?

These questions could lead a group of students into all sorts of problems. These are not easy problems. Books have been devoted to them. On the other hand, impatient, subject-centered, ground-covering teachers often have tried to answer each of them summarily in a few sentences. If these questions are to serve as a basis for future study they must be delimited.

In any case, the assignment must be clear and definite before it is finally made. Probably it is best to give it to the pupils in writing. Short assignments may be placed on the chalkboard. A wise practice is to reserve a specific spot on the chalkboard for assignments and to always write the daily assignment on that spot. Longer assignments should be duplicated. Written assignments minimize pupils' forgetting what it is they were going to do. Also, setting the assignment down helps to lessen chances for misunderstandings—both on the part of the pupil and the teacher—of what the task is.

The second function of the assignment is *to prepare the pupils for the job to be done.* This preparation includes supplying the background material the pupils need before starting the new task and providing for adequate motivation. Since the assignment determines what is to be done, it is particularly important in motivation. It is during the assigning that the teacher makes sure that the pupil knows why he should do this job and that the reasons for doing it are worthwhile.

Not only should the assignment make clear what is to be done, and motivate the pupil to attempt the task, but *it also must point out to him how to do it.* This is the third function of the assignment. Although teachers should avoid spoon-feeding the pupils, they should also be sure that each pupil knows how to go about his task. If it is a job of studying through reading, the key words should be pointed out, and suggestions concerning what to look for should be made. In other words, the teacher should try to be sure that the pupils know how to use the methods and materials available to them.

Thus, if in a history class the teacher wants the pupils to prepare a map exercise in which they map the boundaries of the grants made to the London and Plymouth Companies by King James in the charter of 1606, he needs to make sure that the pupils understand what they have to do, that they know how to plot latitude and longitude on a map, and that they can read the charter provisions. To prepare for their assignment he might well have to devote a half period to a review of map reading and another to the close reading of the charter as preparation for the assignment.

The fourth function of the good assignment is *to provide every pupil with a task appropriate for him.* It is hard to prove any subject matter is truly essential except as it meets the needs of youngsters. If this is true, any assignment which places subject matter above the individual differences of the youngsters is of doubtful validity.

The Marks of a Good Assignment. What, then, are the marks of a good assignment? The following list will suggest some criteria for evaluating an assignment.

1. Is it worthwhile?
2. Does it seem worthwhile to the pupil? In

other words, does it capitalize on pupil interest or create pupil interest?

3. Is it clear?
4. Is it definite?
5. Does it provide for the differences in pupils —i.e., their different aptitudes, abilities, and interests?
6. Is it reasonable as far as length and difficulty are concerned?
7. Does it show the pupil how to go about it? Does it suggest methods and materials which may be used profitably?
8. Does it provide the pupil with the background necessary for completing the assignment satisfactorily, e.g., vocabulary?

*

Use these criteria to judge assignments given in your college courses.

Do your college assignments perform the functions assignments should perform? If they fail, in what ways do they fail?

A student teacher's assignment to his United States history class was, "Read pages 184–297 for tomorrow." In what way is this assignment deficient?

*

Making the Assignment. In order to make an effective assignment, the teacher must take time to develop it sufficiently. Even for a short assignment the teacher will ordinarily need to allow at least ten minutes for his presentation. The use of one or more entire periods is not unusual. In fact, to develop properly a long-term assignment or a unit assignment in less than a period is virtually impossible, particularly if the assignment is developed by the teacher and class cooperatively. Beware of giving an assignment at the last minute just as the bell is going to ring (or has started to ring). Pupils seldom take such assignments seriously. They cannot listen to orders carefully in the last minute rush. There is not time for them to digest the assignment, to ask questions, or to make notes, or for the teacher to give the pupils direction, to clarify what is to be done, and to motivate the pupils. Last-minute assignments are almost always disasters.

It matters little whether the assignment is developed at the beginning, middle, or end of a period as long as the teacher allows time enough to do the job properly and makes sure that the assignment fits into that spot naturally. To be most effective, the presenting of the assignment should probably immediately precede the task to be done. Homework assignments should be presented at the propitious moment in the lesson when the content of the lesson is most suitable as a background for making the assignment.

MOTIVATING BY MEANS OF PROBLEMS

Pupils are seldom interested in work that is too easy and that they already know. The teacher should try to challenge every pupil to do his best. Problem solving is particularly useful in challenging the interests of boys and girls. From time immemorial people have loved to try to solve problems. Challenging problems appeal to the natural drives of activity, success, and curiosity. They are effective motivating devices.

*

It has been stated that marks, prizes, and punishment are poor motivating devices for school use. Why do some authorities take this position? Do you agree? Defend your position.

What techniques might a teacher use to induce pupils to adopt goals that will lead to the learnings desired by the teacher? Consider such things as

teacher talks and lectures   demonstrations
field trips   suspense
moving pictures   problem raising
stories   quizzes and tests
dramatizations

Criticize some of the assignments given to you in your college work. How could they have been improved?

*

Keeping Up the Pace

NECESSITY FOR LIVELY LEARNING

Once a class is interested, the teacher must be constantly alert to keep the class free from dead spots. A dragging class can kill all the enthusiasm of the most eager group of pupils. Dull classes lead to wool-gathering and switching of attention and interests to other less desirable activities and goals. In every meeting of every class the pupils should feel that the class is going somewhere important. They should also feel a certain amount of pressure, however light, to exert themselves to go along too.

Participating in One's Own Learning. Learning may be its own reward. Learning is always emotionally tinged and usually quite gratifying to the learner. The opening up of new vistas and the excitement of new ideas and skills and the sheer involvement in the learning process can catch the young person up in the excitement of intellectual attainment. For many of us the intellectual experience alone is enough to keep us working diligently all the rest of our lives. It is important that we teachers give the pupils opportunities to really participate in true learning experiences. When we do, we give the pupils a chance to share the emotional experience that Keats had "On First Looking Into Chapman's Homer."

> Then felt I like some watcher of the skies
>   When a new planet swims into his ken;
> Or like stout Cortez[3] when with eagle eyes
>   He stared at the Pacific—and all his men
> Look'd at each other with a wild surmise—
>   Silent, upon a peak in Darien.

Such experiences make learning worthwhile; for the person who has a real chance "to participate in his own learning" these experiences are rather frequent occurrences. Many scholars derive their greatest motivation from their involvement in the learning. Fresh ideas and fresh insights really make life exciting.

A Variety of Learning Activities. Although it is probably true that too much variety in method and activities may sometimes confuse the learner, it is just as true that the same activity or same kind of activity repeated endlessly usually bores him. In order to keep interest at a high level, the teacher should change his methods from time to time. Especially helpful are such interest-catching devices as vivid illustrations, audio-visual aids, field trips, demonstrations, dramas, and television programs.

Humdrum recitations with their continual repetition of boring answers to boring questions day after day should be avoided.

Lively Activities Rather than Passive Activities. Pupils are naturally active. They do not relish sit-

[3] Keats was mixed up. It was really Balboa who stared at the Pacific from a peak in Darien.

ting still all day. Because they enjoy doing things, activities in which they can actively participate interest them. Moreover, once they are actively participating, their interest is much more easily kept at a high level. Witness the difference between the lecture and a workshop or laboratory. Quite often, the very persons who anxiously wait for the bell in lecture classes do not know when to stop in a workshop or laboratory situation. To keep motivation high, teachers should use such activities to the optimum.

CHALLENGING BUT NOT DISCOURAGING WORK

One way to keep up the pace is to see that the work is challenging but not discouraging. Some boys and girls do not do their schoolwork well because it does not challenge them. This is particularly true of the bright pupils. Youth wants to test itself. It wants to fly high. Boys and girls do not want baby work. An industrial arts teacher, for instance, was having trouble with discipline. This was not surprising because the class consisted largely of troublemakers, who were impatiently awaiting their sixteenth birthdays. Yet the problem was largely teacher-caused. In an attempt to make the instruction fit the needs of these boys, the teacher had devised a course in home mechanics. The activities of this course consisted of such things as puttying windows, changing fuses, and the like. These activities were not interesting and provided no challenge. When the teacher switched to assigning more challenging activities, his discipline problems abated considerably. On the other hand, work that is too difficult can be frustrating. No one can keep up a major effort long when he feels that he has little hope of succeeding.

KNOWLEDGE OF ONE'S OWN PROGRESS

Knowing how one is getting along also tends to keep one on his toes. Pupils like to know how they are progressing. Knowledge of one's progress makes it possible to reform one's goals and take further strides ahead. Nothing succeeds like success. The knowledge that one has accomplished a certain amount is often sufficient cause to go further—with renewed vigor. To make the most of this phenomenon teachers should try to see that pupils understand and appreciate their own achievement. For this knowledge to be really effective the pupil needs to know "how he did" almost immediately. If, for instance, a teacher takes a couple of weeks to read and evaluate papers, their motivational value will have pretty well evaporated by the time he hands back the papers to the pupils. A simple mark on the paper does not really help the pupil's motivation much either. If the pupil is going to understand "how he did," the teacher must provide the pupil with some analysis of his paper's strengths and weaknesses. Pupils can improve only if they understand where they hit and where they missed the mark. To make the most of this phenomenon teachers should try to inform pupils of their achievement just as soon as possible after they have attempted the learning task.

*

Why is it that youngsters in laboratory-type classes seem to be more interested in their studies than pupils in other classes?

What activities might you use to keep a class in a subject in your field moving rapidly?

Some authors say that the lecture should not be used in secondary schools. What is your opinion? Why?

*

Creating a Receptive Mood

A PRINCIPLE OF SALESMANSHIP

Quintilian, the Roman teacher of rhetoric, once remarked that harsh discipline raises resentment which is transferred to the subject matter. He was right. Therefore, for the sake of good motivation, harsh, restrictive, disciplinary measures, unpleasant teaching methods, and anything else that may cause dislike and antagonism should be avoided. Remember that you are trying to sell a valuable commodity. People who dislike you, your product, and your store will not buy from you. Of course, punishment can also motivate, but it should seldom be used for classroom motivation because it tends to create an atmosphere of surly, sullen repression. In such an atmosphere pupils' work is usually halfhearted. Since the object of teaching is learning, we need to find a more efficient motivating device than punishment. Still, boys and girls

must learn that if they misbehave or neglect their work they must suffer the consequences. Occasionally, the teacher will have to use negative measures to make these points clear. Poor papers should be redone. Neglected responsibilities should lead to loss of privileges. Undone work should be made up—perhaps in after school hours or detention periods, or even, on occasion, next term as a repeater. Such treatment should always be fair, just, reasonable, and preceded by fair warning.

That a customer must be put in a receptive mood is almost axiomatic among salesmen. As Risk has suggested, it is not often that we find salesmen who try to sell their products by insulting the customers.[4] So it is with teaching. What we are after is to get learning across to the pupils. To make the learning or the learner disagreeable is unrealistic. Perhaps making your subject pleasant may seem to be sugarcoating it. If so, remember that it is the learning that counts. *Any method or device, within reason, that you can use to expedite learning is legitimate.* If to expedite learning one must sugarcoat the subject, then do not spare the sugar.

A "PLEASANT HOUSE"

One method of placing your customers in a receptive mood is to provide a pleasant environment. It is axiomatic that boys and girls (and for that matter men and women) work better in pleasant surroundings. A dark, dirty, repressive atmosphere seems to hold back the average person. In a bright, cheerful atmosphere pupils are more likely to become interested in their school work and perform it conscientiously. A bright atmosphere tends to remove the tensions which so often hold back the learning process. Therefore, the teacher should strive for a pleasant classroom. It may be that he can do little about the classroom's decor, although he can usually help that considerably, but he can do much for the spirit of the pupils by eliminating overseriousness in the classroom. Learning is not necessarily solemn. People learn better in a happy frame of mind. Laughter, fun, humor, cooperation, pleasantness, and politeness all go to make the

---

[4] Thomas M. Risk, *Principles and Practices of Teaching in Secondary Schools*, 3rd ed. (New York: American Book Company, 1958), pp. 324–327.

classroom a happy place. Vittorino da Feltre, the great Renaissance schoolmaster, called his school "The Pleasant House." As part of our motivational technique we should strive to make our schools "Pleasant Houses."

Cultivating Desirable Attitudes and Ideals

Earlier in the chapter an attempt was made to show how one might harness the pupils' attitudes and ideals. Fortunately for the teacher, attitudes and ideals are acquired, or learned, characteristics. Since this is so, it is possible to teach pupils new attitudes and ideals and change old ones. Teachers have frequently been able to convince pupils that what seemed to be a complete bore is really fascinating. Therefore, the teacher should do his best to create and cultivate attitudes and ideals that foster learning. Reinforcement theory and modeling are most useful for this purpose.

REINFORCEMENT THEORY

Use of Reinforcement Theory

From reinforcement theory one can learn a number of techniques and strategies that can be very helpful in both the motivation of learning activities and in the establishing and maintaining of well-disciplined classes. Basic to the theory is the belief that people tend to behave only in ways that pay off with some sort of reward valuable to them. That is to say, when a behavior results in some sort of reward it is reinforced and so more likely to be repeated. Therefore, in order to encourage pupils to engage in a certain action one should reward them when they engage in that action, and when we wish to discourage pupils from certain misbehavior, we should reward them when they engage in behavior incompatible with the misbehavior. In teaching, the theory tells us that the basic principle to follow is to give praise and attention to pupil behavior that facilitates learning and to avoid rewarding behavior that hinders learning.

Neglect of this principle is a primary cause of discipline problems in the school. Very frequently we teachers reinforce the behavior we wish to eliminate, e.g., we encourage "the negativistic student by arguing with him, the aggressive student by paying attention to him, the dependent student by doing things for him, or the whiny student by eventually giving in to him." [5] On the other hand, most teachers neglect to reward or to recognize "the talkative child when he is quiet, the hyperactive child when he is in his seat, or the impossible student when he turns in an assignment." [6] All too often good behavior does not pay off, whereas misbehavior is rewarded because it commands attention from the teacher and establishes the pupil's prestige and status among his peers.

Reinforcement Principles

The following list of reinforcement principles should be a useful guide to teachers in their attempts to change pupil behavior.

1. Try to reinforce new behavior by rewarding it every time it occurs.

2. Then, when the behavior has been established fairly consistently, gradually reduce the frequency of reinforcement until finally the reinforcement occurs only occasionally at haphazard intervals. Such intermittent reinforcement is much more effective for maintaining an established behavior than frequent or regular reinforcement.

3. At first, reward the behavior as soon as it occurs. Then, as the pupil becomes more confident, you may delay the reward somewhat.

4. Try to use rewards suitable for the pupils. Remember that what is rewarding for one pupil may be punishing to another. (Conversely, what may be a punishment for one pupil, or what you may think to be a punishment, may be rewarding to another.) Remember also that performing the act, or improving one's competency, may be its own reward. Probably a mix of tangible rewards, social rewards, rewarding activities and feedback, and success activities will be the most satisfactory.

---

[5] Harvey F. Clarizio, *Toward Positive Classroom Discipline* (New York: John Wiley & Sons, Inc., 1971) p. 15.
[6] Ibid.

If possible, try to see to it that the performance itself is rewarding.

It is, of course, advantageous if the pupils can select their own rewards. For this purpose the reinforcement menus described in a later section of this chapter can be very helpful.

5. In using rewards with recalcitrant pupils it is wise to start small. Sometimes it is very hard to find anything really commendable in a pupil's work at first. Therefore you should reward such pupils when they do better and keep rewarding small improvements until the pupil achieves the behavior desired. This process may take a long time, as the following steps from a sequence worked out by Clarizio for a pupil who refuses to do his arithmetic illustrate.[7] In this sequence Clarizio recommends that the teacher reward such improvements as

Being in his seat even though he is not working.
Taking out his book.
Opening the book to the assignment.
Looking at it.
Doing one problem.
Doing two or three problems.
Completing the assignment.

[7] Ibid., p. 34.

Figure 3–1

Educational Contract *

*Harvey F. Clarizio, *Toward Positive Classroom Discipline*, New York: John Wiley & Sons, Inc., 1971, p. 15.

Between (Student's name) and (Teacher's name)

Student agrees to

1. Complete assigned homework—	5 points	
if well done and accurate	2 extra points	
2. Hand in assignments on date due—	5 points	
if handed in before due date	2 extra points	

Teacher agrees to

1. Check homework and give appropriate number of points to the student (as indicated above).
2. Not reprimand or comment when homework is not completed or handed in.
   (a) If two consecutive assignments are not handed in—3 points are subtracted from accumulated total.
   (b) If three consecutive assignments are not completed and handed in the contract is considered void.

Student can exchange his points for

(1) Free period time during class (5 points per 5 minutes).
(2) Access to the driving range (10 points per 15 minutes).
(3) Excuse from the weekly social studies quiz (30 points each week).
(4) Being helper to shop teacher (10 points per 15 minutes).
(5) Credits for purchase of pocket book (5 points per credit—10 credits for free book).
(6) Being a student referee for a varsity game (30 points per game).
(7) Access to student lounge during free period (study hall) (30 points per period).

Signed ————————————————————
                                            STUDENT

Signed ————————————————————
                                            TEACHER

1. Challenging teacher or another student to a game of chess.
2. Using the portable computer.
3. Doing extra credit problems and seeing how they can raise his grade.
4. Making up a geometry quiz and then giving it to the class.
5. Sitting at the teacher's desk while doing homework problems.
6. Preparing the bulletin board using a display of the student's choice.
7. Writing letters.
8. Playing chess.
9. Reading.
10. Playing charades.
11. Talking over past or forthcoming athletic or social events.
12. Having a creative exhibit period (a grown-up version of show-and-tell).
13. Comparing a 1902 Sears-Roebuck catalogue with the current one, discussing changes in style, price, and the like, and trying to discover why the changes occurred.

Daily Specials

Monday.   Appear as guest lecturer in the other math classes.
Tuesday.   Do the special crossword puzzles involving geometry concepts learned.
Wednesday.   Time in which you can play a math game with another student.
Thursday.   Construction of special paper models using geometrical figures to complete.
Friday.   Do mystery problems involving mathematical solutions. *

Table 3–2
Reinforcement Menu:
High School Geometry Class

* Ibid., p. 30.

These steps are only a portion of the entire sequence.

6. Utilize contingency contracts and reinforcement menus.

CONTINGENCY CONTRACTS

L. E. Homme has developed a reinforcement device he calls the contingency contract. Contingency contracts are particularly effective at the secondary school level, according to Clarizio.[8] They are based upon the common practice Homme calls Grandma's law: that is "if first you do this, then you can do that (or have that)." Most of us probably remember this law in the form of "If you first eat your vegetables, then you can have some dessert." To be effective the contingency contract must lead to an extremely desirable reward that

8 Ibid., p. 41.

the pupil cannot attain outside of the contract. These contracts are best worked out by the teacher and the pupils together before the term of the contract begins. Occasionally teachers may set up the details of the contract unilaterally and get the pupils to agree to its terms but this procedure is usually not really satisfactory. Sometimes pupils may work out the terms of the contract and present them to the teacher. Figure 3-1 is an example of a contingency contract.

REINFORCEMENT MENU

A reinforcement menu is similar to the contingency contract. It consists of a list of highly desirable activities that pupils can do once they have completed a set assignment. Ordinarily these activities should be congruent with one's educational goals, but not always so. Sometimes activities that are pure fun or relief from class activities may be more effective. An example of a reinforcement menu appears as Table 3–2.

Modeling

Much of the behavior one learns he learns by imitating a model. It is imperative then to try to provide pupils with good models to copy. To be effective, these models should be highly esteemed by the pupil. Models whom pupils do not respect or identify with are usually of little value. Nevertheless, pupils will model themselves after the behavior of a person whom they do not regard especially highly if they know that they will be expected to demonstrate that they can reproduce that person's behavior and that they will be rewarded if they can do so.

A model may be almost anyone pupils admire and can identify with. Obviously the teacher himself may be a model. In addition, teachers should seek out models among the pupils' peer group and in the community. Admired personalities such as the stars of stage, screen, sports, and television, and other public figures in the news are natural models that some youth imitate.

Pupils can also look to certain of their peers as role models. In this respect there seems to be a "ripple effect" [9] which causes pupils to learn from the experiences of others in their classes. Thus if pupils see a certain behavior in Pupil A, they are likely to adopt that same behavior themselves. Consequently, it seems desirable for the teacher to utilize methods by which pupils can learn from one another, i.e., from each other's example and from the effects of their behavior on others.

Unfortunately live models are not always predictable. They sometimes act in ways one would rather pupils did not imitate. Consequently, it is often necessary to resort to symbolic models—films, tapes, stories, drama, simulations, role playing, and the like—in which pupils can see the behavior to be imitated at the appropriate time and place and in the proper sequence.

*

What pupil attitudes and ideals would be desirable aids to classroom motivation? How might you use them? How might you develop them?

[9] J. Kounin, *Discipline and Group Management in Classrooms* (New York: Holt, Rinehart and Winston, Publishers, 1969) .

A certain teacher says that it is impossible to teach her pupils anything because of the no-failure policy of the school. The supervisor says that the teacher is merely excusing her ability to make her teaching interesting. React to these statements.

Prepare a list of motivational devices for possible use in a class you expect to teach.

Show how you could use a contingency contract in a class you expect to teach. What would you use as point-getting devices? What for rewards?

What rewards could you include in a reinforcement menu?

*

SUMMARY

Motivation is too important in the teaching-learning process to be left to chance. It is the key both to good learning and to good discipline. Only pupils who are well motivated learn well. When pupils fail to learn, the chances are great that the basic cause of the trouble has to do with motivation. Modern discipline emphasizes cooperation and self-discipline rather than authority. Incidents of misbehavior can have many causes. Among these causes are faulty personalities, poor home and neighborhood conditions, emotional difficulties, social maladjustment, fatigue, bad physical conditions, poor teaching, poor curricula, and poor classroom management. The fault lies with the teacher and the school as often as it does with the pupils, for they have not taken the steps necessary to motivate pupils to work and study. Fortunately all kids are motivatable.

Since each teacher has a valuable commodity to sell to sometimes unwilling clients, it is important that he find a way to motivate them. If he can do so by positive means, the chances of successfully teaching his students will be greatly enhanced. Unfortunately, such positive motivation does not always come naturally. More frequently than not, the teacher must convince reluctant pupils of the value of his wares and create in them an inclination to buy. For this purpose the teacher has many tools and techniques at his command. One of them is to harness as far as possible the pupil's natural motives, such as his curiosity, his attitudes and ideals, his desire for success, self-esteem, and security, his love of fun, adventure and action, and his need for friendship. Another method is to try to make the subject matter seem valuable to the pupil. Perhaps the best way to do this is to really believe in the material's importance yourself. In this connection one should remember that pupils are more likely to be moved by immediate rather than deferred and intrinsic rather than extrinsic values. Because people respond differently to things, individual motivation may be fostered by making adequate provisions for individual differences. Marks have not proved to be adequate motivating devices for most boys and girls; teacher-pupil planning has been somewhat more successful.

New ammunition for the development of techniques and strategies that can be helpful in the motivating of pupils can be found in reinforcement theory. Basically this theory holds that one should reward a person when he behaves in the way one desires, but not reward him when he behaves in undesirable ways. Unfortunately many of our present disciplinary procedures tend to reward untoward behavior. As we develop and use teaching methods that utilize reinforcement techniques properly, we should find our pupils becoming better motivated and better behaved. Among the techniques recommended are judicious use of rewards and the use of contingency contracts, reinforcement menus, and modeling.

Perhaps the best motivating device is a clear, definite, reasonable assignment. A good assignment serves the following functions.

1. It sets the direction of study and outlines the scope of the task.
2. It motivates the pupil and prepares him for the task.
3. It helps the learner to the means for accomplishing his task; that is, it establishes possible methods and materials.
4. It adapts the tasks to the needs of the various pupils.

If the assignments are good and the class proceeds at a lively pace in a friendly atmosphere, a teacher can expect relatively little "customer resistance," especially if the assignments let the pupils feel the thrill of participating in their own learning and creating their own knowledge. If, in addition, a teacher engenders and cultivates in his pupils attitudes and ideals favorable to learning, his efforts should be well rewarded.

Discipline
and Control

4

Discipline has always been a problem for teachers. In the last century many schoolmasters controlled their classes by might. So long as a teacher could lick any boy in the class, he could maintain discipline. If he was not up to a fight, as often as not the "scholars" would run him out of town. Certainly such was the case with the Hoosier Schoolmaster in nineteenth-century Indiana.[1] Discipline was also a problem in eighteenth-century England. In those days when caning was king and when Headmaster Keate of Eton obtained control by assembling the entire school to see the sixth form flogged, many of the famed public schools were rocked by student rebellions. In fact, on at least one occasion, the master had to call in the troops to rescue the school from the boys.

Motivation: The Key to Good Discipline

Today, even though they may not rely on fisticuffs or call in the militia to gain control of their

[1] Edward Eggleston, *The Hoosier Schoolmaster,* a famous novel first printed in 1871 and well worth reading today to get the flavor of our profession a century ago.

classes, many teachers still find it difficult to maintain well-disciplined classes. Most new teachers find discipline their major problem. Many experienced teachers are no less concerned with it. It is one of the most frequent causes for teachers' failing and leaving the profession.

This is especially true in secondary schools because maintaining discipline in secondary schools is sometimes especially difficult. Many pupils, particularly youths from ethnic or racial minorities, are disenchanted with school. Many, because of unfortunate experiences in school and community and because of a belief that the system is rigged against them, have rejected school. Also, as Lueck et al. point out, in the departmentalized secondary school there are so many pupils, it is difficult for a teacher to know his pupils well[2] and there is little chance to study them in advance. As a result, secondary school teachers cannot really know all of their pupils well enough to understand why they act as they do, or to predict how they will act in a given situation. Nevertheless, order must be maintained, and the pupils must do the necessary work. No matter how difficult the classes or unruly the pupils, the job must be done. No alibis can be accepted. That the job can be done is evident when we consider the number of teachers in the most difficult situations whose classes are productive and virtually free from discipline problems. *The key to good discipline is good motivation.*

Good Discipline

Nowadays our concept of the well-disciplined class has changed. Not many years ago the basic criterion was quietness. One could literally hear a pin drop. Some teachers and principals still believe silence to be a sine qua non, but, on the whole, modern thinking has adopted a more reasonable point of view. In the modern classroom the atmosphere is likely to be less repressed than in the classes of our ancestors. The amount of freedom varies with the type of instruction, of course. Lectures and demonstrations require a high degree of quiet attentiveness; work sessions and laboratory classes are likely to be buzzing with free activity.

[2] William R. Lueck et al., *Effective Secondary Education* (Minneapolis: Burgess Publishing Company, 1966) p. 340.

Accordingly, in the modern classes one may find some boys and girls talking quietly to each other about their work while others are moving about the classroom on one errand or another and still others are working alone at their desks. The scene is like that in a large office or business enterprise in which it seems as though everything was happening at once. At first glance it may seem confusing; yet all the activities are purposive—all aimed at getting a job done. So it is with the modern class. In comparison with classes of an earlier age the modern classroom may seem noisy and confused. But the seeming confusion is purposive—the many activities are all directed at the same goal. The noise is the whirring of the classroom machinery at work.

This changing concept of classroom discipline has led some neophytes to believe that order is not necessary. Nothing could be further from the truth. The classroom is a place for learning. Any disturbance which prevents or hinders learning is unpardonable. Orderliness is a must. The difference between the classroom of today and that of yesterday is in the type of order. The teacher in today's ideal classroom tries to emphasize courtesy, cooperation, and self-control. Instead of the complete totalitarianism of some traditional teachers, who were in every sense dictators, the ideal modern class stresses the freedoms of democracy. The class is free from fear. The pupils are citizens of the class, not subjects of the teacher. Their job is to cooperate for the common good, to obey the laws of their classroom democracy, and to respect and obey proper authority. Their role in class is similar to our own as citizens of our country. Perhaps, on the whole, today's adolescents take their roles more seriously and are more law-abiding than adults.

Some teachers are under a misapprehension about discipline, permissiveness, and mental health. They are afraid that any thwarting of pupils' desires and impulses may ruin the pupils' mental health. Not so. In fact, strict control in itself can be a virtue leading to the development of worthwhile learning for the future and desirable behavior in the present. An orderly no-nonsense atmosphere is probably more healthful than a laissez-faire, overpermissive atmosphere. Teachers may not hide behind the shibboleths of permissiveness and mental health. Classes should be permissive only to the extent that they are supportive. The mental health of the pupils will be fostered best in an orderly, democratic class.

*

What is good discipline? How can you tell a well-ordered classroom?

How much freedom should there be in a classroom?

*

CREATING SELF-DISCIPLINE

Since modern schools advocate self-discipline rather than imposed authoritarian rule, teachers must consciously try to develop self-discipline. Self-discipline does not come naturally; it must be learned. Becoming self-disciplined is a time-consuming process; the result of much practice. Teachers who are attempting to teach self-discipline should expect to proceed slowly.

Developing a Code of Conduct

The first step in achieving self-discipline is for boys and girls to find out what good behavior is. Seriously and carefully working out a class code of conduct can make a vital contribution to developing excellent personal behavior standards in the pupils.

One teacher had great success with the following technique. For many years at the beginning of the term he addressed his class in the following manner: "We are going to have to spend the rest of the year here together. In order to keep out of each other's hair we need some rules. Let's talk the situation over and see if we can figure out what rules we want to have in this class." Then the class set to work to discuss why they needed rules and what kind of rules they needed. Finally, they drew up a set of rules which a committee put in final form for class adoption. During the discussion the teacher presided and made suggestions. Most of his comments were questions such as, "What about chewing gum? Is that what you really want to do? Do you need that? Aren't you being a little strict?" The resulting rules were usually a workable code that the pupils could follow quite well. The teach-

er's greatest difficulty was to keep the rules from becoming too strict and too detailed. Sometimes, after a few weeks, the teacher had to suggest that the rules be reviewed and revised.

The technique just described worked for this social studies teacher for more than twenty years, but it may be unsuitable for other teachers in different situations. Each teacher must suit his methods to his class and his own personality. Some classes of teen-agers are not ready for democratic procedures and could not satisfactorily work out their own code of conduct. The important thing is to develop for each class standards of conduct the pupils will accept as reasonable and worthwhile. Extra time spent on this important task at the beginning of the year may result in much greater class progress throughout the rest of the year.

Helping Pupils Improve Their Own Standards

Frequently youths' standards are not quite what we would like them to be. Sometimes they live in homes and neighborhoods that see no value in the standards set by the school. When this is so, their teachers should help them arrive at suitable standards. This they cannot do by legislating standards; neither can they do it by criticizing the standards of the youths' families and friends. Doing so may serve only to arouse hostilities. The teachers must depend on the reasonableness and workability of the standards rather than on authority alone. They can show youths how many people make their lives more enjoyable by living by good codes. They can also let their pupils know how teachers and other people feel about proper conduct. In this way teachers can often convince pupils that these standards will make life better for them and induce them to adopt more suitable patterns of behavior voluntarily.

Enforcing Rules as a Way to Self-discipline

Enforcing rules may itself be an opportunity to teach the fundamentals of self-discipline. Whenever a youth commits an offense of any magnitude, the usual procedure is for the teacher and pupil to have a private conference. In this conference the teacher can analyze the incident with the pupil. Together they can determine exactly what the misconduct has been, why it is unacceptable, and what the pupil should do for reparation. Used skillfully this type of conference can produce real learning in self-discipline.

In some schools, teachers encourage the pupils to carry out the enforcement of class rules. Properly guided, this technique can help pupils to achieve self-discipline, but it should be reserved only for classes that are ready for it. Throwing too much responsibility on a class newly introduced to democratic procedures may cause the program to break down. Like other democratic organizations, the group is much more adept at determining policy than at carrying it out. Enforcing the rules must be left up to the executive. Therefore, the enforcement of classroom rules should be the job of the teacher himself.

ACHIEVING CLASSROOM CONTROL

Teacher Personality and Classroom Atmosphere

The personality of the teacher does much to create the atmosphere of the class. The teacher should work hard in order to win a pupil's respect. This can be done only "by treating him fairly and compassionately over a sustained period of time." [3] Teachers who rub pupils the wrong way, who do not like adolescents, who are more interested in the subject than in their pupils, who are inconsiderate, unhappy, and lack a sense of humor are likely to have disturbances in their classes. The characteristics the teacher most needs are empathy, warmth, and genuineness[4] according to C. B. Truax. That is to say the teacher should be friendly, cheerful, fair, consistent, interested, honest, interesting, and helpful. The teacher who can create a feeling of rapport with his pupils, like the skipper running a happy ship, usually has little difficulty.

[3] William G. Spady, "Authority, Conflict, and Teacher Effectiveness," *Educational Researcher*, 2:4–10 (January 1973).

[4] Duane Brown, *Changing Student Behavior: A New Approach to Discipline* (Dubuque, Iowa: William C. Brown Company, Publishers, 1971), p. 12.

For this reason as soon as possible the teacher needs to get to know his pupils as individuals and treat them so. Most particularly, from the very first he should learn each pupil's name and use it in class. This practice is not only good for the pupil's ego but also serves to notify the pupil that any misbehavior on his part will not be anonymous. In addition, if the teacher knows something of the pupil's background and interests, he can use this knowledge to cement friendly relations and to direct pupil interests in desirable directions.

Teachers' attitudes tend to spread to the class. If the teacher dislikes schoolwork, the class will probably dislike it too. Tense teachers usually convey their tensions to their pupils, and teachers who expect misbehavior usually get it. Perhaps the first rule to follow is not to look for trouble, for "he who looks for trouble shall surely find it." In the classroom his approach should always be positive; the emphasis should be on the *do's,* never on the *don'ts.* By acting on the assumption that everything is going to be all right, and by concentrating all his efforts on the main job, i.e., teaching, the teacher will eliminate a good share of the potential disturbances. In securing and maintaining good classroom relationships a businesslike, matter-of-fact bearing can be very persuasive.

Nevertheless, even in the best-regulated classes and schools, youngsters do misbehave. In some neighborhoods they seem to do little else. The teacher must try to take misbehavior in his stride. This calls for keeping a tight rein on his own emotions—not always an easy thing to do.

ACHIEVING THE PROPER PERSPECTIVE

Perhaps the best technique for keeping on an even keel is not to take one's self too seriously. Teachers are human, too. They do not know everything, and they do make mistakes. What is more, the pupils know it. No amount of dissembling can keep the truth from them. The sooner the teacher realizes this and relaxes, the better off he will be.

Many young teachers seem to think that every incident of pupil misbehavior is a personal insult. This is not so. Actually most teachers are not important enough in the pupils' scheme of things to be acted against personally. Teachers should not be upset by pupils' misconduct any more than they should be upset by pupils' lack of knowledge. This is the way youngsters are; the teacher's job is to help them achieve the highest goals they can. If a teacher views pupil misdemeanors as personal insults, he may soon find that they have become just that.

In other words, a teacher needs a sense of humor and a sense of proportion. When the teacher gets to the point where he can laugh at his own failings, he is well on the way to developing a pleasant classroom atmosphere and good classroom control. Clowning in the classroom should not be encouraged, but when something is funny, laugh at it and then turn the good feeling toward the work of the day. Laughing with pupils clears the atmosphere. It is always easier to learn in a pleasant class than in a repressive one, and after all, pupil learning is what you are after. The teacher needs a sense of perspective, too. He needs to put first things first. He is not a policeman. He is a teacher. His primary job is not to enforce rules, but to draw out learning. He should not let little things upset him.

CREATING A FRIENDLY ATMOSPHERE

The teacher should also try to make the classroom a friendly place. By his actions, rather than by his words, the teacher should let the pupils know that he would like to be a friend. This does not mean that he should attempt to be a buddy. In such cases familiarity may breed contempt. No one can be a boon companion to everyone, and teachers must avoid creating favorites. Besides, adolescents prefer that adults act their age.

Perhaps the best summary of what we have tried to say is that the teacher should set a good example. Remember, you, the teacher, are "one source of reinforcement for both positive and negative behavior patterns."[5] In fact, as Marx and Tombaugh point out, "the most critical determinants of motivation to learn are the personality and training of the teacher."[6] Aloofness, sarcasm, and coldness can hurt motivation. If the teacher's behavior is truly considerate, patient, pleasant, and sympathetic, and shows that he cares for the pupils as in-

dividuals and is truly trying to teach them well, then the class will probably respond favorably to his teaching.

*

What can you do about the pupil whose behavior problems arise from the home? From emotional difficulties? From social problems?

Think back to your high school days. Try to picture the teacher who had the most trouble and the teacher who had the least difficulty. What was it about those teachers that made the difference in their relations with pupils?

*

An Ounce of Prevention

Proper planning is indispensable for establishing and maintaining good classroom discipline. As a general rule, boys and girls wish to behave properly, and, what is more, they usually want to learn if the subject matter seems to be worth learning. Many, if not most, disturbances result from poorly organized classes—classes that lack purpose, classes that start late, classes in which pupils have nothing to do. Careful planning can usually eliminate faults of this sort. It is always wise, for instance, to provide activities for the more active and impatient boys and girls that will let them work off their energies.

Many teachers bring troubles on themselves by neglecting individual differences. Picture the discipline problem of the tenth-grade teacher who planned to spend four weeks on *The Tale of Two Cities.* Four or five of her brightest boys read the story over the weekend and so had time on their hands. To find something to do, they organized a ball game, using a soap eraser and a ruler. Providing for individual differences might have eliminated this problem.

"Our teacher is funny," a small boy reported to his mother during his first school experience. "She wants you to keep at work all the time whether you have anything to do or not."[7] This anecdote is no less true today than it was in 1893. The devil makes work for idle hands. Pupils who have nothing to do will find things to do. Planning that

5 Ibid., p. 74.
6 Melvin H. Marx and Tom N. Tombaugh, *Motivation: Psychological Principles and Implications* (San Francisco: Chandler Publishing Company, 1967), p. 202.

7 Sarah L. Arnold, "Waymarks," *Journal of Education* (February 4, 1893).

leaves dead spots in the class encourages trouble. To avoid these empty spots, the teacher must be sure that everyone has plenty of worthwhile activities to do. Classes in which the teacher does all the work and the pupils just sit and vegetate should be avoided. This is why the teacher should be wary of the beginner's tendency to overuse the lecture. Few lecturers can hold the interest of a group for long—particularly when the group is large, young, or not intellectually inclined. To lecture more than 20 per cent of the time may be disastrous.

Not only should the pupils have plenty of worthwhile activities to do, but the teacher should be sure that the pupils know how to carry out the activities. Many discipline problems are caused by pupils who do not know what they are supposed to do or how to go about doing it. A little instruction in how to study, or how to use the tools of learning, or how to carry out the assignments may pay off in serener classes.

The teacher should also make a point to get the lesson going the moment the period begins. Neophytes, a little unsure of themselves perhaps, are sometimes tempted to give themselves a little respite by stalling a minute or two at the opening of the class. Doing so is dangerous; the class that has time to fool around before the lesson starts may never find time to get down to business before the period ends. It is wise, however, for the teacher to wait until the group is quiet before he begins to talk to them. The teacher who allows pupils to be noisy while he is talking, is wasting his time and at the same time encouraging discourtesy.

An essential of good planning is to provide plenty of good materials for pupils to work with. Failure to provide enough of the right materials can cause the worst dead spots of all. In order to eliminate mischief-breeding periods of waiting, the teacher's lesson planning should ensure that the materials needed for the lesson are on hand and include procedures for rapid delivery and collection of materials.

Much misbehavior is caused by teachers' ignoring pupils' predispositions. Any class procedure that violates the natural inclinations of boys and girls creates a situation that can lead to misconduct. Adolescents are naturally gregarious social creatures. It is unreasonable to insist on an absolutely quiet classroom in which "you can hear a pin drop." A class that is all keyed up—having just come from an exciting assembly, perhaps—cannot easily settle down to a placid routine. By adjusting the material and tempo of the instruction to the predispositions and mood of the class and of individual members of it, the predispositions of pupils may be made an aid to learning rather than a threat to peace. In his planning, the teacher must allow for these predispositions; he must also be flexible enough to be able to change his plans, when necessary, to fit the mood of the class. Switching from lecture or recitation to a snap quiz or written assignment is a most effective example of this principle.

To keep the class moving smoothly and to avoid dead spots, the teacher should carefully routinize all organizational and administrative details such as passing out and collecting papers. The work necessary to provide plenty of good materials and a proper plan is usually rewarded by easier discipline. It lessens both the opportunity and the need for mischief. One might call this approach preventive discipline.

Above all the teacher must keep the class highly motivated. He will have little need for worry about discipline if his planning keeps the pupils busy doing things that appeal to them or that they know will pay off in a gratifying way. To this end he should avoid letting his classes fall into the same routine day after day. Use variety to keep the pupils on their toes.

THE FIRST DAY

The first days of the school year are crucial as far as establishing relationships with the pupils is concerned. These first classes will bring you together with new pupils in a new situation. In this situation your position is much the same as that of a stage star at an opening performance. Under the circumstances, it is not at all unusual for a beginning teacher to feel nervous. You will certainly be tense; you may even suffer from stage fright. But no matter how nervous you are, you should display as much confidence as you can muster and go ahead with your work. If you act as though this were a commonplace occurrence which you are enjoying, the pupils will probably be convinced by your performance.

However, you are new and you can expect some boys and girls to try you out. In the interest of good discipline, it may be wise to be fairly strict for a few days. During this period, minimize the amount of pupil movement around the classroom. A wise precaution is to have a written assignment ready so that you can give the class written work if the pupils become restless. In any event you should have an alternate plan of some sort to fall back on if your first plan does not work.

In order to establish good teacher-pupil relationships and teacher control, learn the names of the pupils immediately. During the first period you should probably prepare a seating plan. One way to do so is to assign some written work to the pupils and then circulate about the room to copy their names from their papers. Another method is to have the names of the pupils written on a slip of paper before the period starts, and, as you call the roll, to put these slips in the proper places in a pocket-type seating plan. No matter how you prepare the seating plan, associate the names of the pupils with their faces as quickly as possible. If a pupil realizes that you know his name, you will more readily establish good rapport with him.

A Few Definite Rules

Unfortunately, a teacher can seldom plan a class so well that all his problems are completely solved. The best laid plans "gang aft agley"; consequently, each class must have rules. One of the maxims of our country's forefathers was that the government which governs least governs best. This maxim seems to apply, to some extent, to the modern classroom. Well-disciplined classes are classes with few rules. Every class needs some rules; no class needs many. Too many rules are confusing to pupils, and may become unenforceable. A few definite rules which make sense to pupils and teachers alike will prove to be the most successful. Or perhaps just a few general principles such as "You must not interfere with the learning of others by being rowdy" may work just as well.

In any case, it may be best not to have a rigid set of rules at first. Rigid sets of rules tend to encourage rule breaking. Furthermore they are likely to inflict on the teacher the necessity of enforcing rules he does not wish to enforce. A few definite rules or general principles of conduct give the teacher room to maneuver.

There must be some rules, however. These rules should give the pupils considerable freedom, but let them know exactly what the limits are. A rule can be considered a good rule when it clearly spells out what it is the pupils must do, seems reasonable, and can be enforced. It may be best to make rules as they are needed rather than to concoct a rigid set of rules beforehand.

It goes without saying that every class rule should seem reasonable to the pupils. Any attempt to enforce what pupils find unreasonable is bound to lead to a struggle. Rules that are too strict create tensions. Rebellion, misdemeanors, and an occasional blowup may be the result. On the other hand, teachers who let pupils do whatever they please create equally severe difficulties for themselves. Such classes are bound to become noisy and disorderly. Teachers—and there are some—who believe that by removing all controls they are creating a permissive atmosphere are mistaken. A permissive atmosphere is a friendly atmosphere in which the pupil is not afraid. Freedom from controls is not permissiveness; it is laissez-faire. Generally speaking, little worthwhile learning comes from laissez-faire teaching. Clear, definite rules which specify the expected norms and limits of behavior help clear the air and avoid clashes caused by pupils' attempting to go too far. It is unusual to have good teaching without good rules.

To establish classroom rules one should use a method that will develop positive behavior in the pupils. Probably the best way to develop acceptable rules is to have the pupils develop their own standards of behavior. Pupils usually abide by their own rules willingly. One method of developing rules has been described in the beginning section of this chapter entitled "Developing a Code of Conduct." Using this type of procedure tends to take the onus of rule making and enforcement off the teacher. Arbitrary imposition of rules on pupils is an invitation to rebellion.

*

What rules or standards for behavior are appropriate for a high school class?

Should a set of rules for classroom behavior be provided? (Some texts say, yes; some say, no.) If so, who should make it and how should it be enforced? Be prepared to defend your position.

Do you agree with the practice of having the pupils develop their own rules for behavior? How would you go about developing such rules?

*

ENFORCING THE RULES

Once rules are made, they must be enforced. The pupils should have no doubt that these rules are operative and that breaking them will not be countenanced and that living up to them pays off in some worthwhile reward. Laxity in the enforcement of rules makes them worthless. The pupils lose respect for them and resent subsequent attempts to enforce them. The American Revolution was caused, at least in part, by a British attempt to enforce laws, some of which were quite reasonable, after a long period of laxity.

Although it is possible to be too rigid, one characteristic of the teacher with good control is consistent enforcement of the class rules. Boys and girls like to know where they stand. The teacher whose rules are sacrosanct today and of no importance tomorrow is anathema to them. Also, since getting away with mischief may be possible, the pupils will be tempted to try their luck.

In this connection firmness[8] pays off because of its "ripple effect." The way you handle one case of misbehavior has considerable effect on other pupils who see or hear of the incident. Thus if pupils find that a teacher is consistently firm in the handling of a few cases initially, they will assume that he is strict and they will act accordingly. The ripple effect is particularly strong when high-status pupils are involved. Consequently teachers should work hard to control these pupils. If the high-status pupils are brought into line, the other pupils will follow along. Obviously the ripple effect can make a great difference in your relationship with pupils. If pupils find you to be fair, just, pleasant, and empathetic in your dealings with others they will tend to respond to you in the same way.

Along with consistency goes fairness. The teacher must treat all pupils alike. The teacher who has favorites or who treats some pupils preferentially may be creating behavior problems. Playing favorites loses the teacher the respect of his pupils and engenders active dislike in the pupils not so favored.

[8] Harvey F. Clarizio, *Toward Positive Classroom Discipline* (New York: John Wiley & Sons, Inc., 1971), p. 65.

The teacher, then, should try to be consistent and fair. This, of course, does not mean that one should never make an exception to a rule. As long as pupils have different personalities, they must be treated differently from one another. The punishment that one pupil might take as a lark could be devastating to another. To this extent the punishment must suit the offender. Nevertheless, the enforcement of the rules must remain consistent even if the means of enforcement may vary. Exceptions to this rule should be truly exceptional and made only for extraordinarily good reasons. It helps considerably if the reasons and their merits are evident to the class as a whole. Otherwise, the pupils may accuse the teacher of favoritism and unfairness.

AVOIDING POOR ENFORCEMENT TECHNIQUES

The teacher should guard against nagging for it disturbs the lesson and may cause additional pupil misbehavior. At times, he will do better to disregard minor infractions than to attempt ceaselessly to correct the pupils. Criticizing or scolding a pupil too much will result only in arousing the support and sympathy of his peers.

Nagging often results from insistence on unnecessarily high standards of pupil behavior and from poor organization of classes. If a teacher finds it necessary to keep admonishing a pupil, he should check to see whether the pupil has something worthwhile and appropriate to do. Sometimes a good remedy is to direct a question to the youth whose mind seems to be wandering or to start the restless pupil off on a new activity. Often just a reproving glance, a gesture, or moving in the direction of an incipient behavior problem will bring the potential culprit back in line before anything really untoward has had a chance to happen. Such techniques distract youths from mischief. The teacher who keeps alert can often head off cases of misbehavior before they start.

Besides nagging, other poor methods of enforcing rules also cause misconduct. Harsh punishment, for example, often brings about resentment and revolt. In the old English public schools it sometimes resulted in open rebellion and the thrashing of the teachers by the pupils. In spite of the number of people who believe in force as the supreme disciplinary agent, harshness has never been really successful. Quintilian, the great Roman teacher, shows why. Corporal punishment, he says, will make the pupils hate their studies and often causes them to rebel or to stop trying. Besides, it may lead to more trouble since harshness often merely hardens pupils in their misbehavior. A good teacher, he said, can do better without it. These warnings are still valid after 1,900 years. Harsh punishment is likely to create more discipline problems than it cures.

In enforcing his rules, the teacher should avoid making big scenes out of insignificant acts. To do so is utter folly. Most little things can be brushed off lightly. Often a look or a pleasant word will suffice. The teacher who makes major issues of minor transgressions soon finds that they do not remain minor. He would do better to save his fire for something important. Such a policy will not only help the teacher avoid unpleasant scenes, but will also prevent nagging and a repressive, punitive atmosphere in the classroom. The latter should be avoided at all costs because it is a deterrent to learning.

In this connection, the teacher should also shun threats and ultimatums. These create scenes and, if a pupil misbehaves, fetter the teacher's course of action, since he must carry out his threats if he is to keep the pupils' respect.

Stopping Misbehavior

The key to maintaining good classroom discipline is motivation. Pupils who are actively at work are not discipline problems. An earlier chapter has attempted to show how to get pupils to work. It indicated that a combination of modeling and positive reinforcement is probably the most efficient method for motivating new behavior and that intermittent, positive reinforcement is probably the most effective method for maintaining behavior once acquired. Now let us turn to the correcting of bad behavior.

FOUR BASIC METHODS

According to Krumboltz and Krumboltz,[9] there are four ways to stop bad behavior:

[9] John D. Krumboltz and Helen B. Krumboltz, *Changing Children's Behavior* (Englewood Cliffs, N.J.: Prentice-Hall, Inc., 1972), p. 136.

1. To force the miscreant to continue doing the misbehavior until he gets sick of it (the satiation principle).
2. To arrange it so that he gets no reward from the misbehavior (the extinction principle).
3. To reward behavior incompatible with the bad behavior (the incompatible alternative principle).
4. To set up an aversive situation which he can end only by improving his behavior (negative reinforcement principle).

Punishment, that is arranging that the misbehavior yields a result so distasteful or unpleasant that the miscreant will not behave in that fashion again, is really a fifth method although it may be considered negative reinforcement.

Only occasionally can one use the satiation principle in secondary schools. Although there may be occasions when one can force a pupil to continue a misbehavior to the point at which he never wants to do it again, such opportunities are rare. Extinction is also difficult to use in secondary schools, partly because the teacher does not always have full control of all the reinforcing agents. Nevertheless, Clarizio wisely states "The teacher, even though he might initially feel uncomfortable, will do a more adequate job of managing classroom behavior if he can learn to avoid responding to certain misbehavior. Remember that teacher disapproval can strengthen deviant behavior, whereas ignoring it can weaken such behavior by removing the payoff. The student has to learn that unacceptable behavior is worth nothing."[10]

The incompatible alternative principle can be useful. The idea is to set up a desirable alternative behavior which would result in a reward so great that the pupil would choose it above the misbehavior. To be effective, the reward for the alternative behavior must be really powerful—powerful enough to offset the reward gained from the deviant behavior.

The negative reinforcement principle consists of setting up a mildly aversive situation which you terminate as soon as the pupil's behavior improves. Thus every time the pupil misbehaves he gets into trouble which ceases as soon as he starts behaving. The difference between negative reinforcement and punishment is that in negative reinforcement the aversive behavior stops just as soon as the pupil's

[10] Harvey F. Clarizio, op. cit.

behavior improves. Thus it is more effective than punishment. Sometimes punishment is necessary, however, to shock pupils into trying the alternative behavior.[11]

THE ROLE OF PUNISHMENT

Sooner or later, no matter how sensible the rules and how careful the planning, some pupil will commit an offense for which he must be punished. The Mikado probably meant well when he sang

My object all sublime
I shall achieve in time—
To let the punishment fit the crime—
The punishment fit the crime;
And make each prisoner pent
Unwillingly represent
A source of innocent merriment,
Of innocent merriment![12]

But his scheme would not have worked well. Punishment should never be used as a source of "innocent merriment." But it should be appropriate and, whenever possible, constructive. If a pupil smashes a window willfully or carelessly, let him clean up the mess and make proper restitution for it. In general, if his punishment is the logical result of his misconduct, the pupil is likely to accept it without resentment and may learn not to offend in the same way again. For that matter, any punishment is more likely to be effective if the pupil sees its reasonableness. The teacher should always try to help the pupil see the appropriateness of his punishment before initiating it.

Punishment should be used sparingly because overuse of it creates the repressive atmosphere teachers wish to avoid. Furthermore, overusing punishment takes the force out of it. Sometimes it causes lying, cheating, truancy, and rebellious behavior. Punishment should be held as a reserve for specific important offenses. It should never be used as a general disciplinary measure. The teacher who commits this reserve too soon, or too often, or on too wide a front, finds he has little to fall back on in real crises. Rewarding alternative behavior and negative reinforcement are much more useful techniques.

[11] Ibid., pp. 182–186.
[12] W. S. Gilbert and Arthur Sullivan, *The Mikado*, Act. II.

When punishment is used, it should be swift, sure, and impressive. The teacher should never punish on impulse; he should think twice before he acts; but he should act at once. Should he himself become emotional, however, he would do well to calm down before prescribing the punishment, for punishing pupils in anger can be disastrous. It requires a cool head to ascertain without the shadow of a doubt that one has correctly identified the guilty one and to select a punishment appropriate for both the offense and the offender. To make punishment effective, combine it with positive measures. It is important to be sure that the pupils know just what behavior is expected from them. Positive reinforcement techniques, modeling, and direct instruction in how to behave will give point to the punishment and lead to the behavior desired when punishment alone will not.

Harsh punishment should be avoided. Sarcasm, ridicule, humiliation, corporal punishment, and unnatural punishment often do more harm than good. Verbal punishment should be delivered in private. Although punishment should not be harsh, it should be severe enough to impress the pupil. Demerits and detention quite often do not have much meaning to the pupil. For instance, a certain teacher kept a boy after school every afternoon for a month, apparently without effect. One afternoon he found out why: the boy had to wait for his father every afternoon anyway and was sometimes hard put to find ways to kill time. Detention to him was no hardship at all and so was quite ineffective. As a matter of fact to some pupils detention is fun.

A Word About Corporal Punishment. Some teachers, clergymen, and newspaper editors blame all the ills of modern civilization on the schools which no longer beat out the tune with a hickory stick. That anyone should have so much faith in corporal punishment is astonishing in view of its centuries-long history of little success. Although it may be true, as some writers claim, that certain types of youngsters, particularly those from disadvantaged areas, may understand and accept physical punishment better than any other kind, it is almost always wiser to use some other method in punishing secondary school pupils. Pupils of this age are too nearly grown up for this type of punishment. High school girls are young ladies and fall under the taboo against striking women. High school boys are young men who may not accept such punishment graciously.

The wise teacher never touches a secondary school pupil except in a formal situation with suitable witnesses according to the laws of his state and school district. Otherwise, he may lay himself open to accusations and legal difficulties. All in all, if such drastic measures as corporal punishment must ever be used, discretion tells us to send the pupil to the principal and let him take over. A wiser policy would be never to use it.

Detention.   Detention, or staying after school, is one of the most frequently used punishments. In general, there are two types of detention periods. One is the sort common in large schools in which the pupils must report to a detention hall. The other is a do-it-yourself arrangement whereby each teacher looks after his own detainees. In spite of its widespread use, detention is not very effective except when the pupil has something else vitally important to do after school—a condition that, surprisingly, does not obtain so very often. Also, detention is all too often a source of difficulty in other areas of a student's life. It can, and often does, cut into other activities that the pupil needs more than disciplining. In at least one school, detention sessions assigned by one teacher kept a potential dropout from attending remedial tutorial sessions scheduled by another teacher. Likewise, pupils' part-time jobs may conflict with detention. For a pupil to lose his job for a simple infraction of school rules can be a severe and unjust punishment. Still another difficulty in some schools comes from the bus schedule. Further, detention periods are a waste of time unless they are used constructively. Their force as a deterrent is not strong enough to warrant keeping the pupil sitting doing nothing. If a school must use detention periods, they should be combined with a conference or some educationally valuable activity.

Verbal Punishment.   The reprimand is probably the commonest and most poorly used kind of punishment. An occasional scolding never really hurt anyone who actually needed it and knew he needed it. Yet like many other measures its effect soon dissipates when it is overused. Then it becomes mere nagging, the futility of which we have already discussed. Loud, frequent reprimands are ineffective. They only add to the turmoil. Calm, firm repri-

mands are much more effective. As a rule, reprimands should be given in private. Frequent public reprimands tend to reinforce misbehavior. The class may either sympathize with the pupil being reprimanded or make him a folk hero. However, a quiet, calm, firm reprimand given in the course of things when needed by a teacher who is fair and gives plenty of honest praise for what the pupil does well, will be effective and have no deleterious side effects. From time to time, however, a whole class may need to be told the hard facts of life. Whenever such explanations are in order they should be businesslike and matter-of-fact. It is not a time for emotionalism.

Sarcasm and ridicule are two other common types of verbal punishments. Educational methods textbooks customarily point out that neither of these punishments should be used, although in faculty lounges one is likely to be regaled with stories of the Mr. Chips type who ruled his classes with a tongue of acid and so endeared himself to the hearts of generations of his pupils. Of course, the effectiveness of such weapons depends upon the pupil, the teacher, and the teacher-pupil relationship. Where some youngsters might relish a teacher's sarcasm as a big joke, others might wither in spirit; where some could brush off ridicule without a qualm, others may be blighted. Because the teacher can never be sure just what the effect will be, he would be wise to avoid such punishments.

Isolation.   Changing seats to break up seating arrangements that permit cliques and friends too much opportunity for social visiting is a common practice. This procedure has much to recommend it as long as the teacher does not create a situation in which the pupils who formerly whispered to each other now shout and pass notes. Another similar plan is to change the seat of a chronic offender so that he is isolated from the rest of the class all alone somewhere in the back of the room. Other teachers like to put their behavior problems up front in the first row next to the teacher's desk or podium. Placing the pupil up front may be objectionable for two reasons: (1) It places the pupil where he is assured of an audience if he wants to show off, and (2) it seems to assume that the teacher will work entirely from his desk at the front of the room, a practice not generally recommended. In the case of an extraordinarily bad incident one can, of course, send the pupil out of the classroom. One should do this sparingly—only when faced with a major problem with which, for one reason or another, one cannot cope at the time.

Assigning Extra Work. At one time the most common method of punishing secondary school pupils was to assign them a number of lines of Latin verse to translate. Today the assignment of extra work continues to be a common punishment in spite of the fact that experts advise against it. Their objection is that associating school work with punishment creates a prejudice against the subjects in the minds of the pupils. This objection is probably well founded. However, there should be no objection to making pupils redo sloppy work again and again—in fact, the teacher who accepts papers that have been carelessly prepared encourages poor work habits. Likewise, there should be no objection to keeping pupils busy at class assignments during detention periods.

Deprivation of Privileges. One of the few punishments that seems to be both effective and acceptable to experts in pedagogy is to take away privileges from pupils who misbehave. In general, this practice is a good one. Unfortunately all too many pupils do not have any privileges the loss of which would greatly concern them. In poor schools and for chronic offenders it may carry no weight at all. One can capitalize on this type of punishment by combining it with a system in which the teacher rewards good behavior by granting the pupils desirable privileges.

Deducting from Academic Mark. Punishing pupils by lowering their marks in the course is a tempting technique which should be avoided. Academic marks, if they are to have any validity at all, must be based upon pupils' achievement. To lower a pupil's course mark because he misbehaves is unfair to him, his parents, and prospective employers or college admissions officers. Under no circumstances can such punishments be tolerated.

After reading such a devastating description of the punishments at his disposal, the prospective teacher may be somewhat discouraged. Is there nothing that can be done? Yes, of course, there is. The answer to the problem lies almost entirely in positive measures many of which have been described early in the chapter.

*

Why should the teacher avoid use of the following?
  sarcasm
  threats
  nagging
  yelling
  constant vocal correction
  arguments with pupils
  corporal punishment.
Are any of the above ever permissible? If so, when? Justify your reply.

*

Sending Pupils to the Office. Sometimes behavior is of the sort which makes it necessary for the teacher to send the miscreant to the office. As a general rule, principals and vice-principals are not overjoyed by the visits of these young people. A certain vice-principal was discussing an important matter with a visitor when a surly-faced girl of fifteen arrived in his office with a note from her teacher. He looked at it and then sent her into another office to wait. As soon as she had left he exclaimed to his guest, "Now what am I supposed to do with her? I don't mind having them come up here once in a while, but you'd think that woman could handle some of her own discipline!"

Each teacher is responsible for his own discipline. Sending the pupil to the office should be reserved for really serious offenses. The principal or his assistant is not in a good position to deal with routine cases. He is handicapped by not knowing exactly what has happened, and his special disciplinary powers are best suited to dealing with major offenses. Sometimes his sympathies lie with the pupil. Furthermore, sending the pupil to the office may be taken as a sign of weakness in the teacher and lower his prestige among the pupils. Doubtless there are crises in which the teacher must cast pupils into outer darkness, but these occasions should be kept to a minimum. If he handles his own discipline problems, the teacher will usually rise in the esteem of his pupils and of his principal as well.

In spite of the warning contained in previous paragraphs, the teacher should not hesitate to send bad actors to the office for correction when it is necessary—for example, when dealing with the pupil would disrupt or interfere with the progress of the class lesson, or when the offense is beyond the scope of the teacher's power and authority. In no case should the misbehavior of one pupil be allowed to break up a class. When sending a pupil out of class the teacher should be sure to inform the pupil just where he is to go and what he is supposed to do, and also to inform the official to whom the pupil is to report just exactly why the pupil is coming to him, either by a note or by the intercommunications system.

Although most principals and other superiors expect teachers to handle their own discipline problems, they welcome the opportunity to be of help. The beginning teacher should certainly go to his superior for assistance. The latter will gladly give the teacher sound advice and practical help, if he can.

HELPING THE DIFFICULT CHILD

Every school has difficult pupils who for some reason or other do not seem able to adapt to the school program. This inability to adjust to a school situation may be caused by problems at home, the social environment in the community, or personality defects. Frequently such pupils seek release from their problems in undesirable ways. These pupils need to be helped. They should be treated with sympathy and understanding. In most cases, they should be referred to guidance counselors for help. In the meantime the teacher should try to find out as much as possible about these pupils and treat them accordingly.

Some youths deviate far from the normal. Although the teacher should attempt to help each boy and girl if he can, the time necessary for attending to difficult cases may cause him to neglect the rest of the class. Besides, the teacher probably does not know what to do anyway. The teacher's job is to get problem pupils specialized help as soon as possible. For him to try to provide the help himself might well be unethical.

Teachers are usually well aware of the obstreperous pupil. However, a behavior problem which is fully as dangerous is presented by the quiet, withdrawn pupil. Such pupils often develop severe emotional problems. Any person who seems to be too quiet and withdrawn should also be referred to the guidance counselor.

In spite of the desirability of referring pupils with difficult emotional problems to specialists, much of the time teachers must be prepared to cope with these pupils and their problems in regular classes. Specialist help is not always available. Furthermore the track record of the specialists is nothing remarkable. When he must do the job himself the teacher should focus on attempting to improve the overt behavior of the pupil rather than finding and correcting the underlying causes. After all the teacher's job is to teach and he cannot allow one pupil, even a pupil with problems, to upset the entire class. Besides, as Clarizio points out, teachers are not trained to treat mental or emotional problems, nor should they be. Even if they could identify the underlying problems, teachers are not in a position to do anything about them, and if they were, the behavior might continue to exist after the causes had been treated. (At least, they often continue after the pupil returns from the specialist.) So there is nothing one can do except to deal directly with the behavior. Fortunately direct instruction in how to behave using the motivational and disciplinary techniques at the teacher's command can and frequently does change misbehavior to acceptable behavior.[13] There is no excuse for allowing pupils to continue to misbehave just because they have problems. After all, discipline is primarily a matter of motivation and training.[14]

*

Criticize the following rules for discipline:
1. Watch carefully for the first small signs of trouble and squelch them at once *with no exceptions.*
2. Hold your group to very high standards at first. You can relax later if the situation warrants it.
3. Be a real friend to the children.
4. Employ self-government only if you are sure the class is ready for it.
5. Be fair.
6. Be consistent.

Criticize the following practice reported by a national wire service: "The Boston School Committee recently directed that the following commandments be read biweekly to pupils in grades seven through twelve.
1. Don't let your parents down; they've brought you up.
2. Be smart, obey. You'll give orders yourself some day.

[13] Clarizio, op. cit., pp. 6–7.
[14] Daniel N. Wiener, *Classroom Management and Discipline* (Itasca, Ill.: F. E. Peacock Publishers, Inc., 1972), Ch. 8.

3. Stop and think before you drink.
4. Ditch dirty thoughts fast or they'll ditch you.
5. Show-off driving is juvenile. Don't act your age.
6. Pick the right friends to be picked for a friend.
7. Choose a date fit for a mate.
8. Don't go steady unless you're ready.
9. Love God and neighbor.
10. Live carefully. The soul you save may be your own."

*

SUMMARY

The key to good discipline is good motivation. In this respect positive measures always seem to be more successful than negative ones. If one could successfully carry out all of the principles outlined in Chapter 3, there should never be any problem of discipline or control in his classes. Such a utopia will be hard to find, however, and in the meantime the following rules should help the teacher achieve classroom control.

1 Set a good example:
   Don't take yourself too seriously.
   Develop a sense of humor.
   Do as you would be done by.
   Be friendly, but not too friendly.
   Control your own temper.
   Let sleeping dogs lie: Do not go looking for trouble. Expect good conduct.

2 Plan classes well:
   Eliminate lags and dead spots.
   Provide for individual differences.
   Vary classroom activities.
   Make classes interesting.
   Make classes seem worthwhile.
   Help pupils feel important.

3 Have a few definite rules and enforce them:
   Let pupils help make the rules.
   Be fair and consistent.
   Don't make mountains out of molehills.
   Avoid scenes.
   Avoid ultimatums.
   Avoid threats.
   Do not nag.
   Take it easy.

4 Punishment should be rare but, when necessary, swift and certain:
   Never use sarcasm, ridicule, harsh or humiliating punishments.
   Never embarrass pupils.
   Avoid corporal punishment. If it must be used, let one of your superiors do it.
   Don't punish the entire class for the faults of a few.

5 Try to develop self-discipline.

6 Refer serious cases of pupil problems to the guidance staff.

7 Stand on your own feet; assume the responsibility for your own classroom control.

ALCORN, MARVIN D., JAMES S. KINDER, AND JIM R. SCHUNERT, *Better Teaching in Secondary Schools,* 3rd ed. New York: Holt, Rinehart and Winston, Publishers, 1970. Chs. 12–14.

ALSCHULER, ALFRED S., *Developing Achievement Motivation in Adolescents.* Englewood Cliffs, N.J.: Educational Technology Publications, 1973.

ASCHNER, MARY JANE, AND CHARLES BISH, *Productive Thinking in Education.* Washington, D.C.: The National Education Association, 1965. Part II.

BROWN, DUANE, *Changing Student Behavior: A New Approach to Discipline.* Dubuque, Iowa: William C. Brown Company, Publishers, 1971.

CLARIZIO, HARVEY F., *Toward Positive Classroom Discipline.* New York: John Wiley & Sons, Inc., 1971.

DAVIS, JEAN E., *Coping with Disruptive Behavior,* What Research Says to the Teacher Series. Washington, D.C.: National Education Association, 1974.

Suggested Readings for Part II

DOLLAR, BARRY, *Humanizing Classroom Discipline.* New York: Harper & Row, Publishers, 1972.

FRYMIER, JACK R., "A Study of Students' Motivation to Do Good Work in School," *The Journal of Educational Research* 57:239–244, (January, 1964).

———, *Motivation and Learning in School.* Bloomington, Ind.: Phi Delta Kappa Educational Foundation, 1974.

GNAGEY, WILLIAM J., *Controlling Classroom Misbehavior,* What Research Says to the Teacher Series, No. 32. Washington, D.C.: Association of Classroom Teachers, 1965.

HAMACHEK, DON E., *Motivation in Teaching and Learning,* What Research Says to the Teacher Series, No. 34. Washington, D.C.: Association of Classroom Teachers, 1968.

HOOVER, KENNETH H., *The Professional Teacher's Handbook.* Boston: Allyn & Bacon, Inc., 1973. Ch. 4.

JAMES, DEBORAH, *The Taming.* New York: McGraw-Hill Book Company, 1969.

JESSUP, M., AND M. KELLEY, *Discipline: Positive Attitudes for Learning.* Englewood Cliffs, N.J.: Prentice-Hall, Inc., 1971.

KOUNIN, JACOB S., *Discipline and Group Management in the Classroom.* New York: Holt, Rinehart and Winston, Publishers, 1970.

KRUMBOLTZ, JOHN D., AND HELEN B. KRUMBOLTZ, *Changing Children's Behavior.* Englewood Cliffs, N.J.: Prentice-Hall, Inc., 1972.

MACMILLAN, DONALD L., *Behavior Modification in Education.* New York: Macmillan Publishing Co., Inc., 1973.

MADSEN, CHARLES H., JR., AND CLIFFORD K. MADSEN, *Teaching Discipline.* Boston: Allyn & Bacon, Inc., 1974.

MARX, MELVIN H., AND TOM N. TOMBAUGH, *Motivation: Psychological Principles and Educational Implications.* San Francisco, Calif.: Chandler Publishing Company, 1967.

MEACHAM, MERLE L., AND ALLEN E. WIESEN, *Changing Classroom Behavior,* 2nd ed. New York: Intent Educational Publishers, 1974.

National Society for the Study of Education, *Behavior Modification in Education,* Seventieth Yearbook, Part I. Chicago: University of Chicago Press, 1973.

———, *Learning and Instruction,* Forty-ninth Yearbook, Part I. Chicago: University of Chicago Press, 1950.

———, *Theories of Learning and Instruction,* Sixty-third Yearbook, Part I. Chicago: University of Chicago Press, 1964. Chs. 8 and 9.

RUSSELL, IVAN L., *Motivation.* Dubuque, Iowa: William C. Brown Company, Publishers, 1971.

SLOANE, HOWARD N., JR., AND DONALD A. JACKSON, *Guide to Motivating Learners.* Englewood Cliffs, N.J.: Educational Technology Publications, 1974.

STOOPS, EMERY, AND JOYCE KING-STOOPS, *Discipline or Disaster.* Bloomington, Ind.: The Phi Delta Kappa Educational Foundation, 1972.

"Student Interests," *NASSP Bulletin* (February 1974).

WIENER, DANIEL N., *Classroom Management and Discipline.* Itasca, Ill.: F. E. Peacock Publishers, Inc., 1972.

III

Planning

Planning
for Teaching

5

The key to successful teaching is good planning. There is no substitute for it. Good planning helps create correct discipline, pleasant atmosphere in the class, and purposeful activity free from dead spots and waste motion—in short, good planning promotes worthwhile learning. No one can teach well for long without planning well.

The Basic Ingredients

What are the basic ingredients of a good teaching plan? Probably in teaching they can be reduced to the following:

1. What we expect the pupils to learn.
2. How we hope to bring about this learning.

In addition, good evaluation is necessary for planning to be successful. What pupils should be taught depends, in part, on what they have already learned. Evaluation gives the teacher the feedback and other information by which he can determine what the pupils need to learn and what steps he probably should take to make that learning come about. Without adequate evaluation the two basic ingredients will not work.

These ingredients are fundamental to all educational planning. They apply to the building of an entire curriculum fully as much as they do to the teaching of individual lessons. That this should be so seems obvious, but in teaching much that should be obvious is never recognized by many practitioners.

Resources for Planning

Basically it is the classroom teacher who is responsible for the planning of lessons and courses. It is he who in the final analysis determines the goals and procedures of the lessons, units, and courses he teaches. In this planning process he has available to him certain resources from which he can seek aid and which suggest guidelines that he presumably ought to follow. Among the aids are textbooks, commercially developed courses and curriculum materials, curriculum guides and syllabi issued by local school authorities, curriculum bulletins from state and federal school agencies, and resource units. In some districts curriculum guides specify what should be taught and how it should be taught in great detail, but usually these materials are suggestive only. When this is true, how closely the teacher should follow the text or the school curriculum guide is up to him. Perhaps at first, at least until one feels at ease with teaching and the course, it is wise to follow the suggestions rather closely. In any case, the teacher would do well to consult as many of these resources as he can before he commits himself to any particular plan of action. You will find comments concerning the use of these resources in the preparation of course and lesson plans in the sections on planning courses and lessons.

Teacher-Pupil Planning

Although the responsibility for determining the goals and procedures of courses, units, and lessons falls squarely on the teacher, even when the course plan is largely prescribed by school officials, it is the pupils who most feel the impact of the plans. Because the pupils and their welfare are so involved, many people have thought that they should have at least some input into the planning of their own instruction. Consequently during the twentieth century there has been an accent on pupil participation in the planning of their own classes that has never been found in the formal schooling of any earlier period, although it has always been present to some extent in informal learning situations. This sort of planning is commonly called teacher-pupil, or cooperative, planning.

To what extent pupils participate in the planning of their own learning activities varies greatly from school to school and class to class, the range being from almost no participation at all to pupils' making almost all the decisions for entire units and courses. In almost every course, however, the pupils do some of the planning, if only to select and carry out their own projects, reports, outside readings, and similar activities.

How much pupils should be encouraged, or even permitted, to cooperate in the planning of class activities is open to debate. It seems obvious that pupils do not have enough knowledge about any of the secondary school subjects to know either what can be learned from them or what potential values they may hold for secondary school youth who learn them. It is also axiomatic that the teacher, having been appointed by the school authorities to guide the learning of pupils, cannot turn his responsibilities for the progress of his courses over to pupils. On the other hand, certain benefits do accrue from teacher-pupil cooperation in planning. Principally these benefits come as an increase in pupil motivation and the development of skills in planning and decision making.

MOTIVATING BY MEANS OF TEACHER-PUPIL
PLANNING

Pupil participation in planning can be an aid to motivation. No one knows what the pupil finds interesting and important better than the pupil himself. Since teachers should select material that is important and interesting for boys and girls to study, what could be more natural than to ask them to help select the topics and activities?

Once an activity is planned by the group, it becomes a group activity. In other words, if the planning has been really successful, the responsibility for completing an assignment becomes a group concern. The young man who fails to do his part no longer faces the displeasure of his teacher alone; he must also face the displeasure of the group he has let down. And, for an adolescent, the displeasure of one's peers is much more powerful than the displeasure of an adult.

A LABORATORY OF DEMOCRATIC CITIZENSHIP

One of the aims for which many teachers and educational theorists claim schools should strive is the ability to think. Another aim frequently mentioned in the literature on education is the ability to choose wisely. One of the reasons for advocating public education is to develop good citizens. All of these educational aims imply the ability to plan one's own work, and the ability to work with others in planning group activities. What better experience can one gain in this sort of thing than by participating in the planning of class activities and lessons? *Teacher-pupil planning offers one a laboratory in thinking, in making choices, in planning —in short, in democratic citizenship.*

Team Planning

The developments in instructional technology bring with them increasing need for team planning, in which various members of the staff cooperate to bring forth coordinated plans so that various aspects of the instructional program will fit together harmoniously. This type of planning may be part of formal teaching team arrangement or simply informal ad hoc arrangement between colleagues. An example of such a flexible arrangement is that in which a social studies teacher and an English teacher finding that they by chance shared the same group of ninth graders decided to collaborate on their assignments. Another more formal arrangement is that in which the social studies, science, and English teachers agreed to cooperate on the assigning and reading of major research papers. In this instance, the teachers of social studies and science suggested topics for the major research papers and read the papers for their content, while the English teachers taught the pupils how to pre-

pare a research paper and evaluated the papers for excellence in style, usage, format, and other elements of English. Another type of more formal team planning arrangement in a junior high school involves multidisciplinary teams which share the same pupils in their classes. The members of a team meet regularly to coordinate the planning in the various courses. Still another type of team planning is that of the formal teaching team of the so-called Trump Plan in which different teachers play different roles, some conducting large groups, some small groups, and so on. Teams of this sort require careful planning. To allow sufficient time for such planning, team-planning sessions may be incorporated into the daily schedule.

Except for the fact that it is done cooperatively by the team, team planning is not so very different from other planning. The problems of what, how, when, and where bear the same importance in cooperative efforts as in individual planning. The real difference is that the planning is complicated by the need to unite the varying notions and inclinations of several teachers into one unified, workable whole. Bringing about such harmony requires team members who are well versed in group process and careful attention to details so that everyone knows what he is supposed to do and how and when he is supposed to do it. It also requires an infinite amount of following through and checking to ensure that the plans are properly executed.

Team planning does not necessarily imply teaching teams of any sort. In most schools teachers who teach the same or similar courses collaborate on the planning of course sequences and course content. Such planning can be instrumental in making a harmonious, well-articulated curriculum.

OBJECTIVES AND PLANNING

That teaching should be purposeful is axiomatic. The citizens who tax themselves to provide schools do so in the hope that the schools will accomplish certain purposes. Just what these purposes are may not be very clear to them, but implicit in their action is the expectation that the schools will make their children into good citizens who will lead productive lives. Similarly teachers may not be really clear about what they wish to accomplish in their courses and lessons. Yet every teacher who teaches a lesson hopes that the lesson will result in some learning—if only the learning of a few facts or of certain items of prescribed subject matter. Everyone who teaches has objectives for his lessons, units, and courses, although some teachers do not seem to know what they are. When one considers how necessary it is to have good objectives, it is astonishing to find that many teachers have never carefully thought out what the objectives of their lessons are or should be. And it is even more astonishing to discover how many teachers do not realize the implication of their own objectives and so teach in a manner totally inconsistent with what they think they should be accomplishing.

Kinds of Objectives

Objectives are what one hopes the pupils will learn from one's courses and lessons. In other words, the objectives are the *learning products* or pupil *terminal behavior* for which one is striving.

GENERAL VERSUS SPECIFIC OBJECTIVES

Some of these learning products are extremely broad and general; others are very narrow and specific. The central purpose of education in the United States according to the Educational Policies Commission, for instance, is to teach pupils to

think independently.[1] Nothing could be much broader than that. On the other hand, an objective for a Latin drill lesson might be for the pupils to learn to conjugate without mistakes the verb *amare* ("to love") in the present tense or to learn by heart the chemical formula $NaSO_4$. Nothing could be much narrower and more specific than these.

Objectives, then, vary from the broadest statements which may be used to describe the general aims of the entire American educational system to the extremely narrow objective of a specific drill exercise. As Figure 5-1 shows they may also fall at any level between these two extremes. In other words, while there are general objectives and specific objectives, some objectives are more general or more specific than others. In theory, and in the best practice, specific objectives are subordinate to and contain the basic ingredients of the more general objectives (as in Figure 5-2). In general, the broadest objectives are those for all education, fol-

Figure 5–1
General to Specific Objective Continuum.

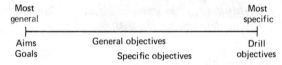

[1] Educational Policies Commission, *The Central Purpose of American Education* (Washington, D.C.: National Education Association, 1961).

Figure 5–2
Pyramid of General and Specific Objectives

Note that the pyramid extends from the very specific to the very general and that the specific objectives at each level make up the components of the general objective in the next level above it.

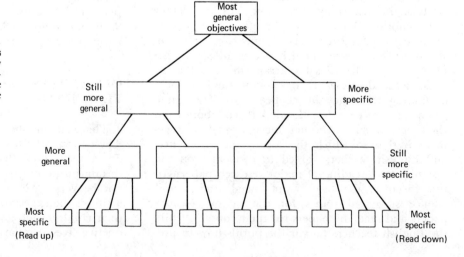

lowed by (in descending order) those for specific schools, those for specific curricula in schools, those for specific units, and finally, the least broad, those for specific lessons and exercises. If lessons, courses, and curricula are well built, the specific objectives of the lessons contribute directly to the more general objectives of the course, which in turn are the ingredients that make up the more general objectives of the curriculum. Similarly each unit, course, and lesson may contain a number of specific objectives which combine to form a more general objective. For instance, the teacher may set the learning of the conjugation of the verb *amare* as a beginning step toward his more general, although still rather specific, objective of learning to conjugate first conjugation verbs.[2]

OVERT VERSUS COVERT OBJECTIVES

Sometimes learning results in overt (i.e., observable) behavior. If the pupil learns to conjugate

[2] Writers on educational topics have developed a nomenclature that differentiates between the kinds of general and specific objectives. Unfortunately there is little agreement about the terminology. The terms *educational goals, educational aims,* and *educational objectives* are often used to denote the broad general goals of education in the United States or in a school system. The term *general objective* is most often used to describe the major goals of a unit or course. The terms *specific objective* or *instructional objective* are used to describe subsidiary objectives that go to make up general objectives. They are usually used to denote specific learnings to be taught in units or lessons.

the Latin verb *amare* in the present tense, he learns to say or write

Amo	I love
Amas	You love
Amat	He, she, it loves
Amamus	We love
Amatis	You love
Amant	They love

Similarly if the goal were for the pupil to be able to translate the simple Latin sentence *Nauta puellam amat* (The sailor loves the girl), the pupil would be able to tell what the sentence means and distinguish it from the equally simple Latin sentence *Puella nautam amat* (The girl loves the sailor). We can tell when the pupil has reached these goals because we can easily observe the behavior.

On the other hand, many objectives are covert, that is to say, the learning products are not easily or directly observable. *Understandings, appreciations, attitudes,* and *ideals* all fall into the category of covert objectives. If the object of our instruction is that pupils will appreciate the beauty of a Van Gogh painting, it is pretty hard to tell whether or not that objective has really been achieved. The observable behavior of the pupils may or may not give a true indication of appreciation. Pupils may be able to recite the right words and simulate the proper actions without having any real feeling or appreciation or understanding.

Figure 5–3

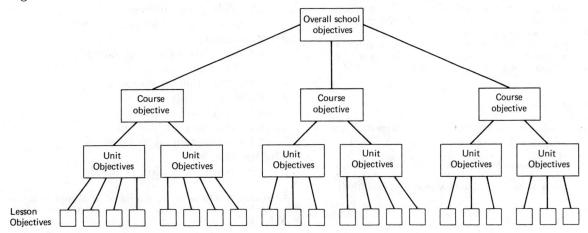

The present educational fad is to describe all teaching objectives in terms of observable behavior, i.e., as behavioral objectives. Unfortunately, many of the larger, more important teaching goals involve covert behavior and so do not lend themselves to such description. While it may be possible to describe overt behavior that may indicate the covert behavior required by these high-level goals, many of the goals simply cannot be described accurately in terms of overt behavior. It is important to remember this fact when one uses behavioral objectives. Otherwise the behavioral objectives are all likely to be trivial. The writing of behavioral objectives will be described in a later section.

THE COGNITIVE, AFFECTIVE, AND PSYCHOMOTOR DOMAINS

Teaching objectives may be understandings, skills, appreciations, ideals, attitudes, or any combination thereof. Bloom and his associates have divided all these various kinds of objectives into three domains:

> The cognitive domain: "Objectives which emphasize remembering or reproducing something which has presumably been learned, as well as objectives which involve the solving of some intellective task for which the individual has to determine the essential problem and then reorder given material or combine it with ideas, methods, or procedures previously learned. Cognitive objectives vary from simple recall of material learned to highly original and creative ways of combining and synthesizing new ideas and materials."[3]
> The affective domain: "Objectives which emphasize a feeling tone, an emotion, or a degree of acceptance or rejection."[4] Interests, attitudes, ideals, appreciations, and values are included in the affective domain.
> The psychomotor domain: "Objectives which emphasize some muscular or motor skill, some manipulation of materials and objectives or some act which requires a neuromuscular co-ordination."[5]

BLOOM'S TAXONOMIES

Bloom and his colleagues have attempted to place the objectives of the cognitive and affective domains into taxonomies, or hierarchies. In the cognitive domain the researchers classified educational goals into categories according to their complexity. The categories that they have proposed, arranged from least to most complex are 1.00 Knowledge, i.e., Remembering, 2.00 Comprehension, 3.00 Application, 4.00 Analysis, 5.00 Synthesis, and 6.00 Evaluation.[6] Whether or not these categories really progress from the least complex to the most complex in all instances is doubtful. However, there is no doubt that synthesis and evaluation are considerably more complex than just remembering. It is the objectives in these categories that develop higher cognitive powers in pupils. While it is, of course, necessary to be sure that pupils do acquire knowledge and remember it, unless we aim at least some of our teaching at application, analysis, synthesis, and evaluation, our teaching will not help pupils develop their cognitive powers fully. Unfortunately much teaching never aspires to anything beyond the lowest cognitive objectives. To make teaching most effective, it should include objectives from all levels. It is unnecessary, however, to attempt to arrange one's lesson objectives so that the pupils move in order from the lowest to the highest levels.

Krathwohl, Bloom, and Masia arranged the effective domain into categories according to the degree of internalization they represent. These categories, ranking from the least internalized to the most internalized, are

1.0 Receiving (attending)
    1.1 Awareness
    1.2 Willingness to receive
    1.3 Controlled or selected attention
2.0 Responding
    2.1 Acquiescence in responding
    2.2 Willingness to respond
    2.3 Satisfaction in response
3.0 Valuing
    3.1 Acceptance of a value
    3.2 Preference for a value
    3.3 Commitment (conviction)
4.0 Organization
    4.1 Conceptualization of a value

[3] David R. Krathwohl, Benjamin S. Bloom, and Bertram B. Masia, *Taxonomy of Educational Objectives, Handbook II: Affective Domain* (New York: David McKay Co., Inc., 1964), pp. 6–7.
[4] Ibid.
[5] Ibid.

[6] Benjamin S. Bloom et al., *Taxonomy of Educational Objectives. Handbook I: Cognitive Domain* (New York: David McKay Co., Inc., 1956.

4.2 Organization of a value system
5.0 Characterization by a value or value complex
5.1 Generalized set
5.2 Characterization[7]

As Figure 5-4 shows, there is a great amount of overlap among these categories.

It is not usual for teachers consciously to aim their teaching at categories in the affective domain, notwithstanding pious statements about the teaching of appreciation, interest, values, and attitudes. Nevertheless, it seems self-evident that teachers should attempt to achieve goals on the higher side of the affective domain taxonomy. These objectives are difficult to achieve, no doubt, but, because they represent a high degree of internalization, achieving them is essential if there are to be real changes in pupils' affective behavior. Probably achieving the objectives at the lower levels is necessary before pupils can achieve them at the higher levels in this domain.

Accountability and Objectives

As we have already noted, both the public and the school authorities have always had certain expectations concerning the products of schooling. These expectations have led to the development of the principle of accountability. In short, the essence of this principle is that (1) the pupils should learn certain skills, knowledge, and attitudes by certain points in their careers, and (2) the effectiveness of teachers and schools should be judged on the basis of whether or not the pupils do learn what they are supposed to learn when they are supposed to learn it. Thus, if the expectation is that all pupils will learn how to read with reasonable proficiency by the end of grade nine and the pupils do learn to do so, the teacher and school have succeeded; but if the pupils do not learn to read at that level by grade nine, the school and teachers concerned have failed. Carrying out the principle of accountability requires that the objectives for each course and unit be spelled out explicitly. If the effectiveness of the school program and the competence of teachers are to be judged by how

7 Krathwohl, Benjamin S. Bloom, op. cit., p. 35.

Figure 5–4

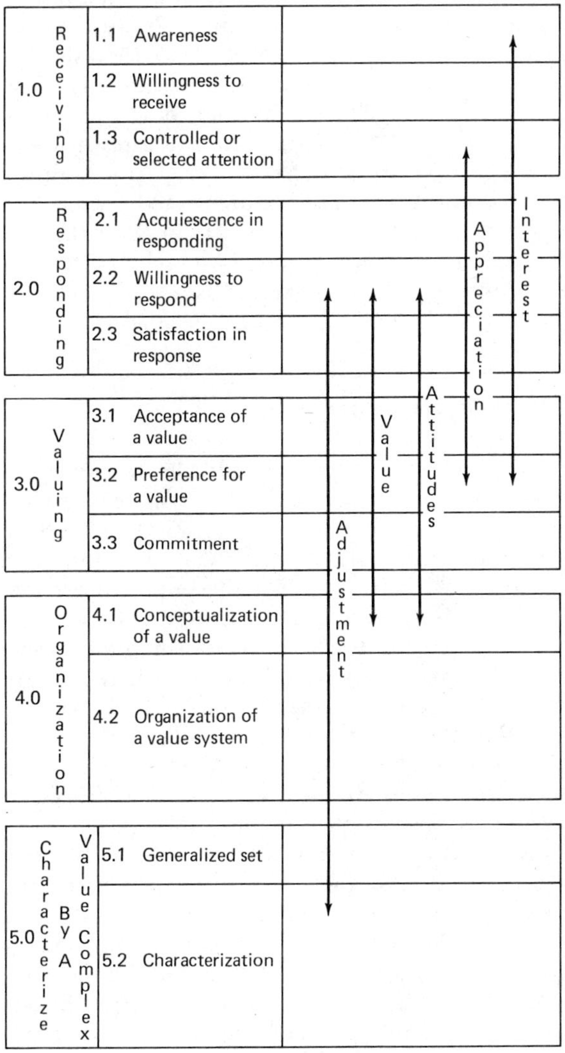

David R. Krathwohl, Benjamin S. Bloom and Bertram B. Masia, *Taxonomy of Educational Objectives. Handbook I: Cognitive Domain* (New York: David McKay Co., Inc., 1964), p. 37.

well the pupils achieve the objectives set for them, the objectives set forth must be clear, definite, reasonable, and measurable. For this reason many school authorities believe that the objectives of the school should be set forth as behavioral objectives.

Objectives expressed in terms of what the pupils can do are easy to measure. They also make it easy for the teacher to aim his teaching. Because school objectives expressed as behavioral objectives tell a teacher the criteria by which his teaching is to be evaluated, good definite behavioral objectives make the teacher feel more secure. In any case, if teachers are to be held accountable for pupil learning, definite objectives that picture exactly what the pupils are to learn are a must. Otherwise there is no standard by which to judge whether the teacher or the school has performed satisfactorily, and accountability becomes a mockery.

Pupil Objectives

So far we have discussed only the teacher's objectives: the objectives set forth by the teachers for the pupils to accomplish. These objectives will be futile unless the pupils adopt them, or compatible objectives, as their own. It is the pupil's objectives that cause him to act. For this reason it may be excellent policy for teachers to inform pupils early in the lesson, unit, or course just what it is they are supposed to gain from the instruction and convince them that the learning is worthwhile. If the pupils think the teacher's objectives are desirable and adopt them as their own, the learning process is well on its way. If they do not, the teacher must resort to some other motivational scheme, or fail. Knowledge of the goals and feedback concerning one's progress are among the best motivators of pupil learning. More often than not, if pupils know what it is they are supposed to learn, they will try to learn it. When teachers state their specific objectives as learning products, pupils are quite likely to accept them as legitimate objectives and work to achieve them.

Writing Objectives

In teaching, objectives are the learning products that it is hoped the pupils will acquire as a result of the teaching-learning process. The potential learning products are the teacher's goals. They are the skills and understandings and their attendant attitudes, appreciations, and ideals that the teacher is trying to instill in the pupils. Real learning products are changes in the pupil. Unless these changes occur, no lesson is successful. Of course, the same changes will not occur in every pupil. Some will learn more than others; some will learn more thoroughly; some may become enthusiastic about the learning; others may be left apathetic. The teacher's objectives then, do not represent the real learning products of the pupils; they represent what the teacher hopes the learning products will be. If a course or lesson unit is successful, the real learning products of the individual pupils will approximate the teacher's goals. We can judge the success of the instruction only by noting whether or not the behavior of the pupils is indicative of the behavior changes called for by the objectives.

Objectives as Learning Products

Since these objectives are descriptions of the potential learning products desired, they should be stated as learning products; that is, each objective should be expressed as a clear, declarative statement describing a specific understanding, skill, attitude, ideal, appreciation, or ability that the teacher hopes his pupils will have acquired upon the completion of the instruction. Some authorities recommend that objectives be presented in infinitive phrases. However, questions and infinitive phrases are usually not satisfactory statements of objectives because they do not describe understandings or skills that should be learned. Descriptions of the skill, understanding, or attitude that one is seeking to develop or of the behavior by which one would judge its presence or absence are much more likely to be satisfactory. Even the most general educational aims or goals should be stated clearly and precisely. For example, "to build good citizenship" is not explicit enough. To be useful, good citizenship must be defined and explained in terms of the type of behavior encompassed and excluded by this major educational goal.

For example, when the author of the unit entitled "From Empire to Commonwealth" presented her general objective as a short paragraph giving a rather precise description of the major concept to be learned, she gave a clear focus and definite limit to the understandings to be developed in that unit.

During the twentieth century there developed between the United States and the British Empire, now called the commonwealth, a real friendship based upon our common language, customs, and traditions. The great English-speaking nations, including all the British Dominions, linked by friendship, came to be recognized by the nations of the world as a tremendous force for keeping the peace and for success in war. Britain and the United States had many problems in common in dealing with colonial possessions, particularly those that wish to have complete self-government. In the period from 1919–1956 Great Britain changed from a solidly united Empire, one of the great powers of the world, to a great Commonwealth of Nations where the various parts that make up the whole are held together by reasons of trade and commerce.[8]

More specific objectives may also be described as potential learning products: understanding, skills, attitudes, appreciations, or ideals. The following are a few of the specific goals from the unit "From Empire to Commonwealth."

UNDERSTANDINGS
(CONCEPTS TO BE LEARNED)

1. Strong ties of friendship have developed between the United States and Great Britain during the twentieth century.
2. These ties which draw the United States close to the Commonwealth are based upon our common language, customs, and traditions.
3. The American State Department, beginning with the days of John Hay and continuing to the present, has cooperated with the British Foreign Office in matters of international importance to both nations.
4. The English-speaking nations have been a force by keeping the peace of the world as evidenced from the Hague Court, the World Court, International Conferences, and the United Nations.
5. The English-speaking peoples have banded together in wars of recent times, World Wars I and II and the Korean War, to carry on successful campaigns against aggressor nations who threatened the peace of the world.

ATTITUDES, IDEALS, APPRECIATIONS

1. No nation can depend entirely on itself.
2. The British people have done many noteworthy deeds and are worthy of respect.
3. Cooperation is more desirable than warfare in international relations.

[8] This unit was prepared by Dorothy Quigley while a graduate student at the University of Hartford.

4. In international affairs as well as private affairs one should deal justly with all—powerful or weak.
5. One should respect the rights and feelings of others.

Writing down the learning products as statements has several uses.

1. It ensures that the teacher has acquired the learning himself. A teacher who cannot describe the learning probably has never learned it thoroughly himself.
2. It gives the teacher a definite goal for which to aim.
3. It gives the teacher a standard by which to evaluate pupil achievement.
4. It helps to eliminate fuzzy thinking about the learning and thus helps to avoid soft pedagogy—i.e., pedagogy that results in no learning or little learning.

Writing Behavioral Objectives

Perhaps the most useful way to write instructional objectives, at least from the point of view of the evaluator, is to write them as behavioral objectives which describe the "terminal behavior."[9]

As we have already noted, behavioral objectives are statements that describe what the pupil can do or does do as a result of instruction. Behavioral objectives can be covert or overt, general or specific. However, they always describe the behavior that it is hoped the teaching-learning process will bring about. Thus, "Upon completion of the unit the pupils will understand the forces that caused the United States and the British Empire, now called the Commonwealth, to develop a real friendship," is a behavioral objective because it describes behavior that, it is hoped, will result from the study of the unit. It is covert, general, and perhaps a little vague. If the objective were revised to read "Upon completion of the unit the pupils will understand that one cause of the friendship between the United States and the British Empire was the commonality of language, customs, and tradition shared by the nations," the

[9] Some people object to the phrase terminal behavior because it suggests to them that progress completely stops at that point. If we think of terminal behavior as the behavior that takes place at the end of a trip or of a period of instruction, there seems to be no conflict. Thousands of commuters arrive at the Erie-Lackawanna terminal in Hoboken, N.J. every morning. Their terminal behavior is not to stop. Rather they run to catch the PATH train that races through the tunnel under the Hudson River to New York City. The term *terminal behavior* does not imply the end of progress.

objective would be perhaps somewhat more specific but still covert. However, if we should change the objective to read "Upon completion of the unit the pupil will be able to explain in his own words the significance of at least three of the principal reasons why the United States and the British Empire, now called the Commonwealth, developed a real friendship," the objective calls for overt behavior.

*

Formulate an objective requiring overt behavior for a lesson you might teach. When you do this remember that overt behavior is behavior one can observe; therefore, your objective must require the pupil to do something you can observe, e.g., explain, demonstrate, draw, describe, or compare.

*

General behavioral objectives are frequently written in terms of covert behavior—understanding, appreciating, valuing, and the like—but specific instructional objectives are more appropriately written in terms of observable terminal behavior. Specific behavioral objectives of this type are valuable because they give one really specific behavior to use as criteria for evaluating teaching and learning. Their worst drawback is that writers tend to make them picayunish so that instruction centers on trivia.

When using behavioral objectives, as when using other types of objectives, one needs general objectives and more specific subordinate objectives that contribute to the general objective. Thus we might have general and specific objectives such as the following:

GENERAL OBJECTIVE

The pupil understands that the great English-speaking nations came to be recognized by the nations of the world as a tremendous force for keeping the peace and for success in war.

SPECIFIC OBJECTIVES

1. The pupil can cite at least three evidences of the friendship of the United States and Great Britain in the first half of the twentieth century.

2. The pupil can demonstrate how the Hague Court, the World Court, and the United Nations were evidences of the role of the English-speaking nations as a force for keeping the peace.
3. And so on.

As with the other types of objectives the specific behavioral objectives are a sampling of the type of behavior that one would expect to elicit from the more general behavioral objective.

BEHAVIORAL OBJECTIVES AS STATEMENTS

Behavioral objectives should always be expressed as statements that begin "At the completion of the lesson (or unit, or course) the pupil. . . ." For purposes of brevity some or all of this beginning portion of the behavioral objective may be omitted so that the behavioral objective as written begins with a verb, e.g., "Types at the rate of forty words per minute without making more than one error per minute." When it is written this way, it is understood that the beginning words "At the completion of the instruction the pupil" have been omitted and that the objective in full would read "At the completion of the instruction the pupil will type at the rate of forty words per minute without making more than one error per minute." Although shortened objectives are satisfactory for most purposes, it may be better to write out the whole formula at first so that one is conscious that what he is describing is terminal behavior.

PUPIL BEHAVIOR, NOT TEACHER BEHAVIOR

Behavioral objectives describe pupil behavior, not teacher behavior. The objective "to discuss the picaresque novel" is not a behavioral objective because it does not describe the pupils' terminal behavior. Rather it describes the learning procedure. Similarly the phrase "the picaresque novel" is not a behavioral objective because it merely names a topic. "In this class I will demonstrate the cause and effect principle" is also not a behavioral objective because it describes teacher behavior rather than pupil behavior.

ONE AND ONLY ONE LEARNING PRODUCT

Each behavioral objective should include one and only one learning product. The objective "At the end of the unit the pupils will understand the principles underlying the problem-solving methods and apply them rigorously in their daily work" is not really satisfactory because it calls for two different learning products requiring different types of evidence. A pupil may understand the principles but because of an attitude or lack of skillfullness not use them. The objective should be made into two behavioral objectives:

1. At the end of the unit the pupil will understand the principles underlying the problem-solving method.
2. At the end of the unit the pupil will rigorously apply the principles of problem solving in his daily work.

OVERT SPECIFIC BEHAVIORAL OBJECTIVES

Specific behavioral objectives describe observable learning products. While general behavioral objectives may be described by such verbs as appreciate, understand, know, comprehend, and the like, specific behavioral objectives can be adequately described only in terms of overt terminal behavior by using such verbs as identify, describe, list, tell, explain, display, define, demonstrate, execute, state, tell, construct, organize, select, write, present, interpret, locate, compare, pronounce, perform, draw, and the like. In other words, at the level of specific behavioral objectives the objective should be what Tyler calls performance objectives, i.e., objectives that describe the performance of the pupils. For example, at the end of the lesson each pupil will be able to describe the procedure for constructing a map profile step by step without error. In this example the overt behavior is "describing." It can be easily observed and evaluated by the teacher.

AVOIDING THE TRIVIAL

Almost always the most striking thing about any list of behavioral objectives is their triviality. Behavioral objectives that measure the higher cognitive and affective mental processes are hard to write. Consequently most lists of behavioral objectives largely feature memory work, skills, and other comparatively simple objectives. This is unfortunate because the objective should be a sampling of all the relevant behavior in all domains. Teachers can write good behavioral objectives that sample the higher levels of the cognitive and affective domains, but doing so requires considerable skill and great effort. Although trying to write such behavioral objectives can be quite frustrating, it is worth the try because these are the important objectives that make education worthwhile.

Some examples.

Given a work of propaganda the pupil will be able to spot the propaganda devices and fallacious logic in the piece.

Given an unknown, the pupil will be able to outline a reasonable procedure for determining the chemical consisting of the unknown.

Given a nonfunctioning, small gasoline motor the student will be able to outline a valid step-by-step procedure for determining the cause of the motor's not functioning.

From a group of three paintings the pupil will be able to identify the one painting that most closely adheres to the principles of quality set forth in the course.

Criterion-Referenced Behavioral Objectives

Specific behavioral objectives may or may not be "criterion referenced." Criterion-referenced behavioral objectives are objectives that not only identify the pupil behavior sought, but also specify at what level the behavior must be performed. They may also specify the important conditions under which the behavior is to occur. Obviously criterion-referenced objectives must be specific overt behavioral objectives. Criterion-referenced behavioral objectives, when written out completely, contain four elements

Who (i.e., the learner).
Does what (i.e., the behavior required).
How well (i.e., the level of performance required or, in other words, the "criterion of acceptable performance").

Under what conditions (i.e., the givens and/or restrictions or limitations that govern an acceptable performance).[10]

For example, in the following sample criterion-referenced behavioral objective

Given examples of the type X^5/X^3 pupils will be able to solve the examples by subtracting the exponents in at least nine out of ten cases;

the four elements are

Who? The pupils
Will do what? Will be able to solve the examples by subtracting exponents.
How well? In at least nine to ten cases.
Under what conditions? Given examples of the type X^5/X^3.

Another example of a criterion-referenced objective is this:

The pupil will be able to pick out proper and common nouns from a page of his textbook with 90 per cent accuracy.

In this example the four elements are

Who? The pupil.
Will do what? Will be able to pick out proper and common nouns.
How well? With 90 per cent accuracy.
Under what conditions? From a page of his textbook.

Because criterion-referenced specific behavioral objectives are more precise than simple specific behavioral objectives, they usually provide (1) better targets for the instructor, and (2) more definite standards by which to judge the success of the teaching and learning than other types of objectives do.

*

Identify the four elements in the following objective: Given a quadratic equation in one unknown, the pupil will solve the equatic in eight out of ten instances.
Who?
Will do what?

[10] Robert F. Mager, *Preparing Instructional Objectives* (Palo Alto, Calif.: Fearon Publishers, 1962), p. 43.

How well?
Under what conditions?

*

A RECAPITULATION

In summary then, when writing behavioral objectives one should

1. State each general behavioral objective as a statement that describes the behavior sought in general terms, such as understands, comprehends, knows, or appreciates.
2. Be sure that each behavioral objective, general or specific, describes pupil performance rather than teacher performance.
3. Be sure each behavioral objective, general or specific, describes the terminal behavior of the pupil rather than subject matter, learning process, or teaching procedure.
4. Be sure that each behavioral objective is stated at the proper level of generality.
5. Be sure that each general behavioral objective is defined by a sampling of specific behavioral objectives that describe terminal behavior that will show when the objective has been reached.
6. Be sure that there is a sufficient sampling of relevant specific behavioral objectives to demonstrate that each of the more general objectives has been achieved.
7. Be sure that the behavioral objectives include the complex high-level cognitive and affective goals that are so frequently omitted because they are so difficult to write.
8. Be sure that each specific behavioral objective includes only one learning product rather than a combination of learning products.

*

Criticize the following objectives showing why they do not qualify as behavioral objectives. Rewrite each of them as a viable specific objective suitable for a single lesson.

My goal in this lesson plan is to teach a geography course. I will attempt to show regions of Anglo-America as to its original occupants—the American Indians. I will attempt to show how these people in their specific regions developed specific cultures in relation to their surroundings.

Aim: To review the four major parts of speech.

Purpose: To reaffirm the definition, recognition, and the use of the parts of speech.

What are the effects of a volunteer army on military security?

*

TO CONDUCT TEACHER-PUPIL PLANNING

In a social studies classroom a group of junior high school pupils were conducting a lesson. This lesson consisted of a series of committee reports on research projects just completed and a class discussion of the implications and significance of each of the reports under the quite capable direction of the young lady in charge.

This young lady was a ninth grader. The lesson, the culmination of several weeks work, had been organized and conducted by the pupils under her chairmanship. Three or four weeks before, the pupils had selected their topic from a short list of alternatives suggested by the teacher as one naturally following from their previous unit. In a group discussion they had decided the various facets of the topic they thought ought to be the most important to investigate. Committees were formed to look into the various aspects of the topic to be investigated and to report to the group what they had learned. But before letting the committees start their work, the class as a whole had set up a set of standards to guide them in their research and to use in evaluating their success. Now they had come to the last step.

Almost every activity in this unit had been planned by the pupils themselves under the surveillance of the teacher. At no time had the teacher dictated to them just what they must or must not do. Neither had she ever left them without support or guidance. She was always there to remind them of the essentials, to suggest alternatives, to point out untapped resources, to correct errors, to question unwise decisions. This sort of teaching is teacher-pupil planning at its best. To do it well requires great skill, much forbearance, and the careful training of one's pupils.

It also requires careful preparation by the teacher. Since cooperative planning may take the group off in any one of several directions, the teacher-pupil planning situation often necessitates the teacher's having several possible plans ready to suggest so that he can provide the pupils with guidance no matter which direction they take.

Teacher-Pupil Planning for Beginners

One good way to start on the road to teacher-pupil planning is for pupils to begin by helping plan their own individual activities. From this point they can move up to the planning of small group activities. In these activities the teacher must expect them to make some errors. He should be ready with help; in this respect the use of guide sheets can be quite helpful.

As they develop more maturity and skill in working as groups, they can proceed to the more difficult task of planning class activities. Later, when they have become more sophisticated, they can move on to such difficult tasks as planning what to include in a topic, and, finally, what topics to include in a course. With inexperienced pupils one should not expect great success initially. The secret of success is to give them small responsibilities at first and gradually to increase these responsibilities as the pupils show they are ready. This principle of moving from a small beginning shows up in other techniques recommended for introducing teacher-pupil planning. One of these is to present alternate plans and to allow the pupils to select the plans they prefer. Thus, in a general mathematics class which is studying how to prepare a budget, the teacher might ask the class whether they would prefer to make up a personal budget or to set up an organizational budget. In a music class the teacher might ask the group to choose between preparing "The Soldiers Chorus" or "When the Foeman Bares His Steel." In an English class the pupils might decide whether to study the short story or the drama next.

Another way to involve pupils in the teacher-pupil planning is for the teacher to propose a plan of action and then ask for their suggestions and approval. In business education, for example, the teacher might ask the pupils if they would like to go to a bank and see how a bank operates.

If they agree that this idea has possibilities, then they might discuss ways and means of making the visit and things they might wish to see when they get there.

DISCUSSION TECHNIQUES IN
TEACHER-PUPIL PLANNING

As groups become skillful in using teacher-pupil planning techniques, they can do much of their planning in group discussion. *Discussion techniques are especially useful in deciding what to include in a topic.* As a class is about to begin the study of insects, the teacher might ask, "What do you think we should learn about insects?" During the discussion the pupils might propose such things as

What do insects eat?
How do they reproduce?
What are insects anyway?
How do you make an insect board? And so on.

The teacher will undoubtedly have some things to suggest. Somewhere in the discussion he might ask: "Don't you think we ought to know something about the insect's life cycle?" Perhaps the pupils will not know what a life cycle is. Probably when they do know, they will want to include it. If they do not, the teacher should indicate the importance of the life cycle and point out the necessity for including it in the study.

Discussion techniques can also be used to plan learning activities. For example, as the class decides what it wants to study, the teacher or leader can bring up the question, "How do we go about it?" Thus, through class discussion, committees can be formed, readings can be suggested, dramatic roles can be cast, and field trips can be projected. Sometimes the class may ask a pupil or group to investigate and report on the feasibility of a project. Included in these plans should also be plans for evaluating what has been learned.

The same group discussion techniques can be used by a relatively mature group to select a topic for study. A good way to launch such discussion is to ask the pupils to suggest possible plans for consideration. Perhaps one might ask the pupils to skim a chapter or a book to find topics in it they would like to learn about. Perhaps their curiosity may be piqued by a movie, a story, a teacher talk, or a discussion of some current event. Consider what happened in a certain general science class the day after the first artificial earth satellite was launched. After a short discussion of the new satellite, it was obvious to all that the boys and girls of that eighth grade were anxious to know more about astronomy and were ready to work on it.

If discussion techniques are used in teacher-pupil planning, someone should keep a record of the decisions as they are made. If this record is kept on the chalkboard where everyone can see it, it makes the planning easier. As soon as the group has finished its planning, the final plan should be reduced to writing and given to the pupils, or posted on the bulletin board or the blackboard, so that the pupils will have it for ready reference.[11]

SOME WORDS OF CAUTION

As you can see, cooperative planning is a difficult technique. It is an excellent method of involving pupils in the learning process. It is particularly effective in long-term planning such as weekly or unit planning, but it is hard work, for cooperative planning is not pupil planning but teacher-pupil planning. Under no circumstances can the teacher abdicate his responsibilities and role as mentor. The teacher must guide and limit; seldom, if ever, should he turn the pupils completely free. The

11 In making group decisions, straw votes are usually helpful. The technique seems to be to avoid putting the question to a formal vote, but frequently to seek an expression of opinion. This allows easy elimination of unpopular alternatives and avoids foundering on difficult decisions. When the straw vote shows a split decision, further discussion can often bring the pupils to agreement. If no agreement is reached, the pupils will usually be willing to compromise, e.g., "first your topic, then ours." If necessary, one can resort to a formal vote, but doing so may defeat the purpose of teacher-pupil planning and is liable to split the group.
Teacher-pupil planning is usually more satisfactory when the group has some criteria on which to base its decisions. These criteria can be made jointly or by the teacher with class approval. During the planning session the teacher may often have to remind the class of the criteria. "Is this the sort of thing you really wanted to do? Is this really pertinent to our problem?" By so doing he can usually improve the quality of group decisions without seeming to impose his own will on the pupils.

amount of freedom the pupils should have depends upon many things, such as the pupils' maturity, their ability level, the subject, and their previous experience in cooperative planning. Pupils who have not learned how to plan will be overwhelmed if suddenly allowed to direct themselves.

Moreover, in order to plan, a teacher needs some information to use in his planning. The following anecdote, concerning a professor who found himself substituting for a sick colleague at a moment's notice, may be illustrative. The class he was to teach was the first one in a course in educational psychology. His only instructions from his stricken colleague were for the students to discuss what they would like to get out of the course. The discussion failed because the students did not know what they could get from such a course, and the instructor was not well enough prepared to help them out. Secondary school pupils who do not know the possibilities open to them cannot be expected to do what college students cannot do. Either the teacher should explain to them potential directions they can take, or he should direct them to activities that will give them the knowledge they need, even if to do so he must assume the major role in the planning and make most or even all of the decisions.

Teacher-pupil planning is probably not suited for every course and every teacher. To ask pupils to plan the topics in a course whose sequence is largely determined by the nature of the subject matter—as in mathematics—seems pointless. Pupil-teacher planning should not be used in the same way with all pupils, nor in all subjects.

Moreover, such planning may not be appropriate for all teachers. Conducting courses in this fashion requires considerable skill. It requires a teacher who is not afraid to subordinate himself to the group, who does not need to be the center of the picture, who is not afraid of making errors, who can command respect without demanding it, and who is relatively sure of his control of the pupils. The new teacher should go slowly in introducing teacher-pupil planning. Not to do so may result in chaos. Sometimes teachers are tempted to utilize teacher-pupil planning as a device for coercing pupils to do what they had already planned for their pupils to do. Such planning is not

teacher-pupil planning. It is fakery. In all things the teacher should be honest with his pupils. If he plans for them to choose within limits, let him prescribe the limits in advance. If he does not, he should go along with the pupils' decision even though it be a poor one. To allow the pupils to plan and then to veto or revoke the plan is dishonest and it destroys the pupils' faith in their teacher. So do attempts to manipulate pupils' decisions.

*

What are the advantages of teacher-pupil planning? What are its dangers? When and where would you use it? How would you set about to use it?

Is teacher-pupil planning really better suited to certain subjects and courses than to others? Explain your answer.

How would you introduce pupil-teacher planning to a high school class that had never had experience in planning?

*

Teacher-Pupil Planning for Individual Pupils

So far this discussion of teacher-pupil planning has been limited to group activities and group planning in which the entire class cooperates in the planning of a unit or topic. Teacher-pupil planning should also be used with individual pupils and small groups.

If their goals are firmly fixed and the pupils know what activities they may choose from, or what activities may help them learn what they want to learn, then individuals can do much of their own planning without the teacher's doing much more than approve their plans. Of course, the teacher will usually need to suggest a few changes of plan, recommend sources of materials and references, and guide the pupils as they work along. This procedure relieves the teacher of much of the detail, so that he has more time to work with individuals. In addition, the pupils learn through their own planning. It is unfortunate that many pupils have been deprived of this type of learning by overzealous teachers. *If people are ever to develop into scholars they need to learn the skills of planning and carrying out their own learn-*

ing activities. The sooner they learn these skills the better.

SUMMARY

Planning is a key to successful teaching. It is absolutely essential if the teacher is to make full use of his knowledge and skill. Poor planning has ruined many classes. In fact, it has been described as the most common cause of not learning.

The basic ingredients of a good teaching plan map out (1) what one plans for the pupils to learn, and (2) how one plans to bring about this learning. In addition, the planning must provide for evaluation, for without evaluation the two basic ingredients will not work. Good planning must be based on adequate diagnosis. Also helpful as a basis of planning are such instructional and curricular aids as textbooks, curriculum programs, curriculum guides and bulletins, and resource units. Teachers would do well to consult these resources carefully before they commit themselves to any particular plan.

Although the responsibility always rests on the teacher's shoulders, the pupils can often cooperate with the teacher in planning. If such planning is to be successful, pupils must be taught to plan. Usually the teacher and the pupils should start by designing class activities together. For a class to decide what it hopes to learn from a topic and what the topics of a course should be requires considerably more sophistication. With inexperienced pupils one should not expect great success initially. The secret is to give them small responsibilities at first and then increase the responsibilities as the pupils show they are ready.

Perhaps determining one's objectives is the most crucial part of planning for teaching. Many teachers neglect this aspect of planning, and as a result, their teaching is pointless and ineffective.

Teaching objectives should be thought of as learning products or pupil terminal behavior. They vary from extremely broad general objectives to very narrow specific objectives. Each specific

objective should contribute to the achievement of a major objective. The behavior called for by an objective may be either overt or covert and also either cognitive, affective, or psychomotor. Bloom and his associates have invented taxonomies of educational objectives for the cognitive and affective domains. In these taxonomies cognitive objectives are ranked from least to most complex, and the affective objectives from least to most internalized. In actual practice in our schools it seems that the high categories in these taxonomies have been neglected by many teachers and so pupils are not developing the higher mental processes as well as they probably should develop them. The present movement toward making schools more accountable for pupils learning what the people want them to learn is making it more important than ever that the instructional objectives at all levels be defined clearly. Even so, instructional goals are effective only when pupils adopt them or when they are compatible objectives as goals for their own behavior.

Since teaching objectives are potential learning products, they should be stated as learning products. They should be stated clearly and precisely as descriptions of the skill, understanding, or attitude one is seeking to develop or of the behavior by which one can judge the presence or absence of the desired skill, understanding, or appreciation. Perhaps the more useful type of instructional objective is the behavioral objective. Behavioral objectives may be either overt or covert, simple or criterion-referenced. Criterion-referenced behavioral objectives consist of four elements: Who (i.e., the learner); does what (i.e., the level of performance); how well (i.e., the behavior required); and under what conditions (i.e., the givens and/or restrictions or limitations that govern an acceptable performance). In any case, to be acceptable a behavioral objective must describe pupil behavior not teacher behavior. Further when preparing behavioral objectives teachers should guard against becoming involved with trivia and neglecting the larger more important educational goals.

Planning
Courses
and Units

6

COURSE PLANNING

Every course should be planned carefully and imaginatively. The proceedings and facilities for the planning of courses differ greatly from school to school and school system to school system. Some school administrations furnish courses of study, syllabi, or curriculum guides. These provide suggestions concerning the goals that should be achieved, the content of the course, the methods that might be employed, and the materials that might be used. Some schools provide source or resource units. These units give suggestions for topics, objectives, and activities for the units to be used in the courses. Some systems provide no course outline or guide of any sort other than texts, workbooks, and teaching materials.

Still, no matter what the system has provided to aid the teacher in designing his courses, the responsibility for the content of the course rests squarely upon the teacher. If the school provides a course of study, syllabus, or curriculum guide for a course, the teacher should make use of it.

Not to do so may introduce confusion into a carefully planned school program. Even so, courses of study are usually suggestive and allow for considerable variation. Even when courses are rigidly laid out, the good teacher must vary the course to suit the interests, needs, and abilities of his pupils. This he can do by such procedures as changing the course sequence, modifying the time spent on various topics, determining which topics should receive most emphasis, and varying the methods of teaching. In the final analysis it is the teacher who decides precisely what is to be taught and how it is to be taught.

*

A well-known teacher once said that there are three things important in good teaching. They are determining what the children are to learn, why they are to learn it, and how they best can learn it. Criticize this statement.

*

The Steps in Course Planning

Whatever one uses as a basis for his planning, the procedure for planning a course is relatively simple. The teacher may enlist the aid of his pupils in carrying out the procedure, or he may do it all himself. In either case, the responsibility for all the decisions made is his. The procedure consists of the following steps.

1. Decide what it is that the pupils are to learn from the course. These are the course objectives which should determine the nature of all later procedures. This step may require considerable evaluation and diagnosis before it can be completed.
2. Decide what course content will bring about the desired objectives. This course content consists of two parts: (a) the subject matter of the course, i.e., the sequence of topics, and (b) the approach or strategy to be used in teaching the topics.
3. Decide the amount of time to be spent on the various topics in the sequence. This step is essential to ensure that the various portions of the course receive the attention they deserve. Neglect of this step is one cause of the all too common practice of proceeding slowly in the beginning of the course and then rushing through the last weeks of the course because of lack of time.

Some Principles of Course Planning

These steps are quite simple, but they should be done carefully to provide a course of maximum benefit to the pupils. When executing them the teacher should keep the following principles in mind.

1. The teacher should determine the course objectives on the basis of their presumed ultimate value to the pupils and their contribution to the school's major educational goals. Once he has clearly established the course objectives, he should constantly keep them in mind. The objectives should be the touchstones he uses in making decisions in later steps.
2. The subject matter and procedures which make up the content of the course should be such that they will contribute toward achieving the objectives of the course. Subject matter and procedures which are not consistent with the objectives should be discarded.
3. The course should be psychologically organized.
4. The course content should be so selected and so organized that it gives the maximum amount of transfer and retention.

These principles apply to all course planning. At first glance they seem so axiomatic that they do not need repeating. Yet more teachers ignore them than follow them. One reason so much teaching is ineffective and irrelevant is that teachers do not follow these four simple, but basic, principles.

In modern individualized programs curricula may be broken down into a series of modules instead of the traditional course. Planning sequences of modules will be explained in a later section. However the four principles apply equally well to modular sequences as to traditional course plans.

The Objectives

SELECTING THE OBJECTIVES

The objectives of the course are extremely important. Ideally they should be the most important *examples*

Planning Courses and Units   **109**

factor in determining both the subject matter and method of teaching in the course. Let us assume that the objectives for Level I French as set forth by school authorities are

1. To develop facility and fluency with spoken French.
2. To develop the reading and writing skills to the point where the students can read and write anything they say.
3. To develop, through the language, an insight into and an appreciation of the French civilization and its influence on the United States.[1]

We know that in laying out the rest of our plan for Level I French we must (1) place our primary emphasis on the spoken word, (2) limit instruction in reading and writing French to material the pupils have already learned to speak, and (3) select French literature for reading that not only does not exceed their spoken vocabulary but that will also highlight French civilization and show French influences on our own culture. We also know that we should minimize the teaching of such things as grammatical laws because they are not directly pertinent to the objectives of the course. In this way the course objectives determine the content of the course.

The major consideration in selecting the objectives is the potential value of the learning to the pupil and to society. To an extent this value is dependent upon the nature and structure of the subject matter or discipline concerned. Therefore in assessing what will be of the most worth, the teacher must make his decisions in relation to the discipline and subject matter. Thus the objectives of the course of study for Level I Latin in Nevada are different from those for Level I French, even though they are both beginning foreign language courses.

1. To develop the ability to pronounce and use Latin words.
2. To develop sufficient knowledge of syntax and inflection forms for comprehensive reading.
3. To develop the ability to recognize, define, and use English derivations encountered during Level I.
4. To develop an appreciation for Roman life

and culture and its contributions to Western civilization.[2]

In general, knowledge of subject matter has very little value in and of itself. Rather, its value lies in its availability for use. Ordinarily, therefore, one should select as his course objectives concepts, skills, attitudes, ideals and appreciations that the pupil can use now or later—not just a mere accumulation of knowledge. In other words, the course objectives should consist of things that are useful now and that appear most likely to be useful in the future in view of the goals, potentialities, and opportunities of the pupils and the needs and expectancies of the nation. This doctrine is sometimes called the *doctrine of contingent value.*

PLANNING THE OBJECTIVES

With these principles in mind, you are now ready to decide what you wish to achieve in the course. In theory, you should be able to determine the course objectives from your study of the subject and your knowledge of the pupils. In practice, many teachers find this task too demanding and too time-consuming. For this reason, many school departments have provided curriculum guides or courses of study that contain suggestions. These documents usually contain statements of objectives with which you may, or may not, agree. For instance, a language arts curriculum guide gives the following general objectives for the English program.[3]

1. To foster an appreciation of the English language.
2. To further a correct usage of language.
3. To acquire such knowledge of grammar as will furnish the student with standards for measuring his own construction.
4. To build an adequate and an enriched vocabulary.
5. To develop effective organization and expression of thought in writing, in conversation, and in public discussion.
6. To listen courteously and objectively.
7. To create a permanent interest in reading

---

[1] Philip D. Smith, Jr., *Course of Study for Foreign Languages,* Department of Education, State of Nevada, Carson City, Nevada, 1962.

[2] Ibid., p. 45.

[3] *Program for the Low, the Average and the High Student for the 7th through the 14th Grades,* ed. Robert S. Shannon, Chairman, Language Arts, Santa Barbara Schools, Santa Barbara, California, 1956–57.

that the student may find in it both enjoyment and information.

8. To fit the individual student in his need as well as in his ability.
9. To promote good citizenship.
10. To instill a desire for truth and beauty.

These objectives are very general. At first glance they may seem to be so general as to give us no help at all. Yet, on closer examination, they do establish directions. We know that grammar should be a means rather than an end in itself, that the program should vary for different pupils, that considerable importance is attached to the spoken word, that attention should be given to correctness and clearness of usage and expression, and that the pupils should get some understanding of the language and its beauty. If we should go on now to examine the scope and sequence charts or content outlines of the various courses and various levels, we would have collected ideas enough to use as a basis for preparing our own objectives.

If no curriculum guides are available, the teacher can determine what goals to pick for his course by studying the textbook or books commonly used in courses of this sort. The content of the texts will show him what others have thought the course should contain. After studying these books he can decide how much of their thinking to accept, how much to reject, what he wishes to add, and what he wishes to emphasize. Then, once his decisions have been made, he can write down his objectives as the concepts—probably generalizations—skills, and attitudes he hopes to achieve, or as terminal behavior.

*

Criticize the objectives we have quoted from the language arts curriculum guide and foreign language course of study. In what ways are they helpful? In what ways could they be made to be more helpful? Can you rewrite any of the objectives so that they would be more valuable?

*

The Content

FITTING TOPICS TO THE OBJECTIVES

Once the objectives have been selected, the teacher must select a sequence of topics and approaches for teaching those things that will bring out the objectives. Too often planners forget this necessity. To reduce the argument to absurdity, if in French I your primary object is to teach pupils how to speak French, then the bulk of your coursework in Level I should consist of exercises in speaking French, not in translating written French or written English or in learning rules of grammar. In some courses the subject matter and the manner of teaching it seem to have absolutely no relationship to the goals the teachers claim to have.

*

Who should decide what the goals of a course should be? How would you decide what a course should include?

*

ORGANIZING THE COURSE PSYCHOLOGICALLY

A teacher can organize his courses in two ways: (1) according to the logical development of the subject matter, or (2) according to the psychological development of the pupils. At the secondary school level, courses should be organized psychologically. That is to say, they should be organized around the pupils rather than around the subject matter and therefore should

1. Be adapted to the level of the pupils.
2. Allow for variation from pupil to pupil and for the same pupil from time to time.
3. Be selective, making important omissions in subject matter.
4. Encourage logical memory and problem solving and emphasize teaching through guidance of experience.
5. Use both vicarious and direct experience in a proportion suitable to the level and experience of the pupils.[4]

From the foregoing list one can see that the topics for any course must be selected with greatest care. The competent teacher selects topics suitable to the pupils' activities and interests. If possible, he picks topics of immediate intrinsic value to them, frequently with the help of the pupils. He sees to it that the course does not limit the pupils to book learning alone, but that it is a judicious mixture of vicarious and direct experience.

4 Adapted from Roy O. Billett, *Fundamentals of Secondary School Teaching* (Boston: Houghton Mifflin Company, 1940), pp. 162–163.

Furthermore, the competent teacher adapts the topics he has selected to the needs of his class. Since all pupils are individuals, a predetermined selection of topics will not be appropriate for all pupils. The teacher should provide opportunities for differentiation within the topics and, if necessary, addition to, deletion from, or substitution for the normal sequence for some individuals.

Some highly gifted pupils, for instance, go all the way through junior high school without ever having a new topic introduced in many of their subjects because they have learned the ordinary course content years before. Such pupils should not have to walk lockstep with the other pupils. The teacher should find out what they can do, and then proceed to a point that is new and challenging to them.

PLANNING FOR RETENTION AND TRANSFER
OF TRAINING

Using the outcome of one learning situation in another situation is called transfer of training. Thus, when a pupil uses in a history class skills he originally learned in English, transfer has taken place. If such transfer does not take place, the learning is of little value.

Transfer is not usually automatic. It is more likely to result when the application of the learning to other situations is pointed out. When that is not done, transfer may not take place because the learner does not make the necessary connections. Transfer also takes place when components common to the original learning situation are present in the situation in which the learning is to be used. In other words, the more the learning situation is like the using situation, the greater chance there is that the learning will transfer.

Another aid to transfer is thorough learning. One can transfer what one knows and understands thoroughly much more readily than something less well known. Thorough knowledge also helps us retain our learning, but the best way to retain what we learn is to use it. What we do not use we tend to forget. Of course, we remember extremely vivid happenings well and we have learned some things so well that it seems we can never forget them. Still, in spite of exceptions, the rule holds. Even one's native tongue becomes

rusty if one does not use it. The key to retention is renewal through frequent use.

Both transfer and retention are encouraged by the mastering and use of generalizations for, as a rule, generalizations can be remembered and used better than detail. The best remembered generalizations (and therefore the generalizations most available for use) seem to be the ones the pupil derives for himself from specifics. Predigested generalizations worked out by the teacher and handed to the pupil are liable not to take at all, or to remain at the level of mere verbalism. (When a teacher does present generalizations to pupils, he should probably support them by much "forgettable detail," in order to make the generalization stick. Ordinarily, however, it is more effective to give the pupils the details and encourage them to draw their own generalizations.)

In preparing course plans, then, teachers should strive for a maximum amount of transfer and retention. To do so, they should provide for an optimum of usable learning and opportunities to use the learning in their classes and many occasions in which the pupils can both draw their own generalizations and also utilize these generalizations in new situations. Teachers will find the problem approach particularly useful for these purposes.

PLANNING THE SEQUENCE

With all these principles in mind, the teacher can set up the sequence of topics for the course. This sequence should consist of broad topics that can be expected to take two to four weeks of class time to accomplish. At this time it is not advisable to map out the course in great detail day by day, because, at this stage, no one can forecast just how the course will develop. One should delay filling in the details until one sees how the pupils are progressing.

As he picks his topics and arranges them in order, the teacher should also estimate the amount of time to be spent on each topic. Again the decisions should be approximate—in weeks and fractions of weeks rather than days. The teacher should, however, base his course calendar on the days available in the school year. In making this estimate he should remember to allow for assemblies, examinations, storms, and other contingencies that cause class periods to be cancelled. Ten days is a reasonable allowance for missed periods. If at the end of the year the teacher finds that this allowance is too great, he can use the extra time for review or for a special topic at the end of the term.

At this time one should also consider the general approach for the various topics and any major assignments such as research papers and projects. These items need to be considered because they will to some extent affect the time allotments of the various topics, and also, of course, they need to be scheduled as to be integral parts of the course.

Courses of Study and Curriculum Guides. In deciding the sequence of topics, a course of study or curriculum guide can be a great help to the teacher. Many courses of study or curriculum guides outline in great detail suggested topics and sequences. A course outline for Physical Science, for instance, lists a sequence of sixteen units for the course with a suggested course calendar.[5]

1. Air. Introduction to Physical Science. The Scientific Method. (4 weeks)
2. Water (2 weeks)
3. Fuels (3 weeks)
4. Forces (3 weeks)
5. Chemicals (5 weeks)
6. Metals (2 weeks)
7. Plastics (2 weeks)
8. Textiles (2 weeks)
9. Food and Drugs (2 weeks)
10. Sound (1 week)
11. Light (2 weeks)
12. Electricity (2 weeks)
13. Vacuum Tubes (1 week)
14. Atomic Energy (1 week)
15. Earth Science (8 days)
16. Astronomy (8 weeks)
    Review (2 weeks)

Other courses of study and curriculum guides, although they do not suggest the topics to be studied, do suggest what content should be covered. The language arts curriculum guide previously cited is an example of such a guide. In the area of sentence structure and punctuation for low ninth graders the guide suggests among other things that teachers

[5] Physical Science, Teaneck High School, Teaneck, N.J., August 6, 1959, pp. 3–9.

1. Insist upon legible handwriting.
   . . .
3. Improve the quality of the simple sentence.
4. Use simple dictation frequently.
   . . .
7. Reteach the distinction between the fragment and the sentence.

Frequently this sort of information can be found in the scope and sequence charts contained in courses of study and curriculum. However presented, it can be a boon to the teacher.

The Textbook and Course Planning. Obviously courses of study and curriculum guides can be of great help to the teacher planning a course. If they are not provided, the most common method of selecting the content of a course is to follow a basic textbook. The chief merit of this plan is that it gives the beginning teacher an organized outline of the subject content to follow. However, the teacher should recognize that all chapters are not of equal importance.

Furthermore, the text sequence is not always the best for every class. Slavishly following a textbook is poor practice. It may cut one off from many opportunities for creativeness, from new ideas, from flexibility of approach, and from variety of method. It often leads to merely covering the subject rather than to significant learning.

Covering the Subject. In laying out the sequence of topics one should remember the principles of psychological organization of courses that were mentioned earlier in the chapter. Not only should we be sure that the sequence of topics follows a proper order psychologically, e.g., earlier units should lay a firm foundation for later units, but also we should guard against violating the principle of psychological organization in other ways. Perhaps the greatest danger to guard against in planning a course is the temptation to include too much. One of the worst diseases in American education is the belief of so many secondary school teachers that they must "cover the subject" by which they mean that they feel that they must squeeze into the course everything alluded to in the textbook or, perhaps, even all the topics in the field. When they attempt to "cover the subject," teachers usually try to cover too much content for the time allotted. Consequently they whiz through a multitude of topics superficially. As a result, pupils usually end up learning nothing about everything or at best a little about a lot. It would be much more satisfactory for them to gain clear concepts and skills in a smaller area. One cannot teach pupils everything on any subject. The modern teacher must limit his course to the most important topics. He does not have time for unnecessary and marginal topics. Better to teach more by attempting less than to attempt more and teach nothing.

*

One author says that one should not follow a text in planning a course. Do you agree? Why, or why not?

Of what value are textbooks, curriculum guides, and courses of study in the planning of a course? How should each of them be used? How rigidly should they be followed?

*

The Continuous-Progress Modulated Course

Planning individualized modulated curricula or courses is little different from planning ordinary courses. About the only difference is that one must divide the course into modules and provide the pupils with instructional or learning-activity packets.

Briefly, the procedure for preparing a continuous-progress individualized modulated course or curriculum consists of the following steps:

1. Lay out the over-all goals. These may be written as general concepts, skills, attitudes, appreciations, and ideals to be learned; or as general behavioral objectives. These over-all goals will set up the limits of the content to be taught, specify the points of emphasis, indicate potential teaching strategies, and in general set the direction for the sequence of the modules.

2. Divide the course into modules.
   a. Determine the sequence of topics which will be the modules. (Textbooks, curriculum bulletins, and courses of studies are excellent references to use when selecting topics.)
   b. Prepare general and specific *behavioral* objectives for each module.
   c. Select the content that will result in the terminal behavior called for by the behavioral objectives in each module.

3. Prepare an instructional packet for each module. In it include the objectives, instructional activities and directions for doing them, and the materials of instruction needed (or instructions for procuring them).

As a rule, pupils work through the modules according to the sequence set up by the instructor. However, in many courses it is much better if the modules are built so that the pupils can choose their own sequence of units on the basis of their interests and abilities rather than to follow a set sequence of modules in courses in which a set sequence is not essential. More about conducting courses and the continuous progress plan can be found in Chapter 8, "Providing for Individual Differences."

*

To what extent and in what ways should the pupils participate in planning of a course?

How can you prepare for individual differences in the initial planning of a course?

What would you look for in selecting materials for your course?

*

UNIT PLANNING

The Unit Approach

Unit is one of pedagogy's weasel words. Because of slipshod usage, imprecise definitions, and pseudo-scholarship, many educational terms no longer have any real or definite meaning. Unit is one of these words. It has been used as synonymous with chapter, topic, learning module, or long-term assignments. From our point of view, a unit is a planned sequence of learning activities or lessons covering a period of several weeks and centered around some major concept, theme, or topic. Learning modules and learning contracts may be considered to be special kinds of units.

THE ESSENTIAL ELEMENTS OF THE UNIT

Although in many schools the unit is just a series of lessons grouped around a topic, e.g., the Reconstruction Period, in other more sophisticated classes the unit is a method of organizing subject matter, teaching techniques, and teaching devices so as to facilitate individualization of instruction, motivation, pupil planning and pupil responsibility for their own learning, and teaching emphasis on the higher levels of cognitive and affective learning. It is our belief that only such units should be considered *true* units.

In this type of unit, although all the activities and experiences should be designed to bring about the realization of the unit's objectives, not all of the activities and experiences need be required of every pupil. Rather, the pupils should find a wide selection of activities and experiences from which they may choose. Still there are, however, some activities that are required of all pupils. We shall call these activities the basic or core activities. Other activities may be purely optional. Pupils usually select the optional or related activities from a list given by the teacher or developed by the class. In carrying out a unit assignment, much of the direction and planning comes from the pupils themselves. Each pupil may be provided with a mimeographed study guide. With this guide and the teacher's help the pupils can plan their individual activities to a large extent. Thus they can begin new activities without waiting for the other members of the class, and the teacher is freed to work with pupils who need help, guidance, and counseling. As one can readily see, the unit assignment, usually lasting from two to six weeks, is a refined form of the differentiated assignment.

A UNIT IN ACTION

Mr. Jones teaches Problems of Democracy at Quinbost High School. In his course outline he has listed a unit on minority groups. Mr. Jones always tries to make his course interesting and challenging so that it will stimulate and motivate his students. On the day he was to begin the unit, he came to the classroom seemingly in an angry mood, tossed his books on the desk, and glared at the class. He then began a tirade on a particular minority group, telling the class about something a member of this group had done to him the day before, and concluded by saying that all members of that particular group were alike.

Immediately his class began to challenge him, disagreeing and telling him that he was unfair to generalize from one incident and that he shouldn't talk like that. Seizing upon this reaction, Mr. Jones then asked the class whether or not they had ever expressed such feelings toward any group. As the animated discussion continued, the class members began to see what the teacher was doing. Almost as one body they said that they wanted to discuss minority groups as a class topic.

The stage had been set! The teacher had fired their interest; the desire to study the topic was evident. He, then, set the class to talking about what subject matter they felt should be discussed and what outcomes there should be. This led to general teacher-pupil planning. Soon pupils were choosing committees and projects on which to work. Then, with the aid of study guides and their committee and project assignments, individual pupils completed tentative plans for their role in the unit.

The study guide they used consisted of three parts. The first part noted questions and problems everyone was to find answers for and suggested where the pupils might look to find these answers. The second part listed a number of readings and activities that the pupils might find interesting. All pupils were expected to do some of these, but no one had to do any particular one. In none of these optional activities or the required problems and questions was the pupil held to any prescribed reading or procedure. All he was asked to do was to carry out the activity, solve the problem, or find the information; he had free choice of ways and means. The third part of the study guide was a bibliography.

Once the teacher and pupils had finished the planning, they began to work. Except for two periods that Mr. Jones used for motion pictures, the next two weeks were devoted to laboratory work. The committees met; the researchers researched; the pupils carried out their plans.

Then the committees began to report. Some of the groups presented a panel. One did a play. Another conducted a question-and-answer game. In all of these activities pupils tried to bring out what they had learned. In between these reports, Mr. Jones and the pupils discussed the implication of the findings and other points they thought pertinent and important.

Finally the unit ended with everyone's setting down his ideas concerning the treatment of minority groups and with a short objective test based on the teacher's objectives as shown in the questions of the study guide.

Thus, after a little over three weeks, the unit was finished. Note that in the unit the pupils did a share of the planning and that much of the time was taken up in individual and group work laboratory-fashion. Note also that the unit consisted of four phases: an introductory phase that included motivating and planning activities, a laboratory phase that included individual and group work, a sharing phase in which pupils pooled their experiences, and an evaluating phase in which the teacher and pupils estimated the learning accomplished during the unit.

THE UNIT PLAN

All units must be planned even though in some units many of the activities pursued by the pupils are developed by teacher-pupil planning while the unit of work is in progress. In general, the unit plan contains the following components.

1. An overview that describes the nature and scope of the unit.
2. The teacher's specific objectives, which are the understandings, skills, attitudes, ideals, and appreciations he hopes his pupils will get from the unit. These may be, perhaps should be, behavioral objectives.
3. The unit assignment, which includes activities the class will participate in during the teaching of the unit. The activities will be of two types: (1) the basic activities to be done by all pupils to some extent in some time and (2) the optional related activities. A calendar noting when activities must be done would also be handy.
4. The study and activity guide, which will contain the instructions for carrying out the core activities to be done individually and in small groups.
5. Special study and activity guides that contain the instructions for carrying out the optional related activities and special activities, e.g., field trips.[6]

6 See Ch. 14 for a fuller discussion and for examples of study guides as well as the section in the latter part of this chapter.

6. A list of materials and readings for the boys and girls to use in their study.
7. A short bibliography and list of materials for the use of the teacher alone.
8. Test and/or other devices to be used in evaluating the success of the unit. These should test adequately each of the learning products described in 1 and 2.

The Teaching-Learning Cycle

As we have seen, the teaching-learning cycle in unit teaching consists of four phases: the introductory phase, the laboratory phase, the sharing of experience phase, and the evaluating phase.

These phases may or may not appear in order. It is quite possible that during the unit some evaluation activities may precede laboratory activities. In units which emphasize individualization different pupils may be working on each of the phases at the same time.

THE INTRODUCTORY PHASE

"A good beginning is half the battle." Perhaps this adage is an exaggeration, but it certainly has a point as far as teaching is concerned. A great deal of the success of any unit depends upon the introductory phase or, as it is often called, the approach. This phase consists of activities designed to launch the unit. In it the teacher attempts to

1. Arouse the pupils' interest.
2. Inform the pupils of what the unit is about.
3. Learn more about his pupils—their interests, their abilities, their present knowledge of the topic.
4. Show the relationship with preceding units and other courses.
5. Plan the rest of the unit with the pupils.

Sometimes an introductory activity sets the mood for an entire course or unit. If it is pleasant, friendly, and lively, perhaps the impetus of the first day will keep the class atmosphere pleasant, friendly, and lively. The first activities should also be purposeful and businesslike. If a class gets off to a fast start, the pupils are likely to get the impression that there will be no nonsense in the class because it is going somewhere. On the other hand, one can readily see what the pupils will expect of a class that starts late with much confusion and waste motion. Similarly, if the introductory activities are dull, it will be difficult to convince the pupils that later activities may be more interesting. An introductory activity is a device to get things going, and a good one does just that. Every course, unit, or lesson should start off promptly with an activity which tells the pupil, "Hold on to your hat, we are on our way."

*

The following were suggested as possible interest-catching introductory activities. What do you think of them?

1. Example One is a demonstration.

To get things moving quickly, one chemistry teacher makes a practice of starting his unit on oxidation with a *bang*. As he starts his introductory talk, he casually mixes together the ingredients for a demonstration that, he says, is yet to come. Suddenly an explosion nearly rocks the pupils off their seats. The teacher and pupils quickly follow the explosion with questions and discussion. What happened? Why? And so on.

2. Example Two is a laboratory procedure. The directions for it are

   a. Select five substances with characteristic odors, such as an onion, orange, fish, and peanut. Place them in small corked bottles.

   b. Blindfold your companion and be sure he holds his nose so he cannot smell. Let him taste each substance separately and describe it to you. Record each description carefully. Make two trials.

   c. Keep your companion blindfolded, but do not hold his nose. This time let him smell each substance and describe it. Make two trials.

   d. Compare the descriptions of the taste and smell of each substance as he gives them to you. How do they differ? Can you draw any conclusions about a person's relative ability to taste and smell? Do you think a cold in the nose makes any difference in the enjoyment of food? Why?

Are these examples really good interest-catching introductory activities? Why, or why not? If not suitable as is, how might you adapt them? Perhaps you will want to compare your answer now to your answer after you have completed reading this section.

*

Motivational Values of Introductory Activities. A good introductory activity may not only catch the interest of the pupils, it may set the pupils' mental gears in motion; it may start young minds to thinking about the topic; it may arouse their

curiosity; it may challenge them; or it may give them a taste which will make them crave more. In other words, a good introductory activity can and should motivate learning. Thus to motivate his pupils, a mathematics teacher may give the pupils a puzzle or problem of the "Mathematics for the Millions" variety to challenge the pupils' ingenuity. In a social studies class, the teacher might propose a troublesome problem facing the nation and challenge the pupils to seek possible solutions.

Pupil Planning in the Introductory Phase. A main purpose in the introductory phase is to give the pupil direction. Although the pupil need not know the teacher's goals for the unit, he should have some ideas of where he is going and what he can get out of it so that he can set goals of his own. Thus part of the introductory phase must be spent in planning. Planning is particularly necessary at this point because the class will spend much of the time in succeeding class sessions in individual and small groups. A good method is to distribute the study and activity guides here and let the pupils, under guidance, prepare their own plans. A sample form for a plan follows. The pupils should not be held closely to their plans; they should be permitted to change and amplify them throughout later phases of the unit.

Work Plan

NAME ——————————— CLASS ————
UNIT ——————————— DATE ————

Activities I plan to do.

Committees I plan to work with.

Materials I plan to read.

Things I plan to make.

Providing a Basis for Pupil Planning. Not only can the introductory activity give the class an opportunity for planning, it can give the pupils the basis on which to plan. By means of a teacher talk, a motion picture, a dramatization, a reading, or some such activity, one can orient the pupils so that they have the information necessary for each of them to know where he is and where he is going.

A good introductory activity can help the teacher get to know his pupils better both as a group and as individuals. Such information is essential to good planning.

*

What specifically might you do to challenge and motivate youngsters to learn in a subject which you plan to teach?

What are the merits of using a pretest as an initiatory activity? Under what circumstances would you recommend using a pretest?

*

Types of Activities in Introductory Phase. Teachers can use introductory activities for many purposes. However, they should not expect any one introductory activity to do everything they might wish in initiating a course or unit. Almost always one needs to use two or more different introductory activities to perform the functions desired in the introductory phase of any unit. For instance, it may be desirable to use one activity to help teacher and pupils get acquainted, another to arouse pupil interest, and still another to help pupils plan—all in the same unit.

The Teacher's Role in the Introductory Phase. The teacher's leadership is particularly important in introductory activities. Since the pupils are starting afresh, they have little or no framework in which to fit themselves, nor do they yet know in what direction they are going. Consequently the teacher must use better-than-average leadership or the class may flounder. This is particularly true in the introductory phase of the first unit of a course. For this reason introductory activities may well be teacher-centered.

One of the most popular introductory devices is for the teacher to talk to the pupils. If a teacher is good at it, this is an excellent method, but the talk must be interesting, sprightly, and pointed. It should hold promise, but not false promise. Perhaps it may outline what is to come, but the outline should not be overly detailed.

Other types of introductory activities high on

the list are demonstrations, motion pictures, discussions, pretests, questions, and planning.

Necessity for an Excellent Introduction As the course goes along the introductory phase often becomes vestigial as the natural carry-over from unit to unit eliminates the necessity of many of its functions and as the teachers begin to know their pupils better. But in every unit the teacher should use the most appropriate introductory activities he can employ. Because a good start is so important, introductory activities are worthy of one's best teaching. They can make or break a unit.

THE LABORATORY PHASE

In the laboratory phase the pupils go to work on their activities. During this phase they are free to attempt, under guidance, whatever activities seem best to them. In this way they can capitalize on their own interests and abilities. Activities during this phase will consist largely of individual and small group work: committee projects, construction activities, individual research activities, extensive reading, and the like. From time to time the class may be called together by the teacher or the pupils to engage in common activities such as talks, discussions, viewing films, and taking field trips. To a large extent the programming can be done by the pupils themselves. Many times the class selects a steering committee to coordinate the activities.

THE SHARING OF EXPERIENCE PHASE

Logically, the laboratory phase should be followed by the sharing of the interesting things learned during the laboratory phase. This part of the unit must be carefully planned. Nothing can be more boring, and less conducive to learning, than pupil reports repeated endlessly. Ordinarily, the pupils should do the programming themselves, but the teacher must guide them carefully to ensure variety and sparkle. Some devices which may be used are

1. Panels.
2. Oral talks.
3. Dramatizations.
4. Writing up the activities for publication.

5. Debates.
6. Group discussions.
7. Meetings of the class.
8. Exhibits.
9. Demonstrations.
10. Preparing an anthology of pupil work.
11. Presenting and defending a position.
12. Recordings and tapes.
13. Audio-visual materials.
14. Moving pictures.

The use of these techniques is described in Part V.

THE EVALUATING PHASE

Finally we come to the evaluating phase. Naturally, a good unit assignment will consist of many evaluations. The teacher evaluates the pupils' progress as they perform the activities, and so do the pupils. However, the end of the unit is a particularly good time for evaluation. Here the teacher stops to see how well pupils have progressed toward the goals, for he needs to know the pupils' present status in order to determine what to do next. Consequently the evaluative devices the teacher uses should be largely diagnostic. Information concerning the preparation and use of such devices may be found in Part VII.

THE FLEXIBILITY OF THE TEACHING-LEARNING CYCLE

Perhaps this description of the teaching-learning cycle makes it seem pretty rigid, but it is not so. It does not always roll forward relentlessly. Instead, it may vary from pupil to pupil. For some it speeds; for others it dawdles. For many pupils it starts, stops, turns back, and then starts again. If one group has finished the preparation of a dramatization and is ready to present it to the class early in the unit long before any other group is ready to share the experience, a good unit plan must be flexible enough to allow this group to present its dramatization then and there. Later the pupils may go to some other activities. Thus the unit has passed from the laboratory phase to the sharing of experience phase and back again.

*

Explain the teaching-learning cycle. What happens in each part of it? What are the introductory phase, laboratory phase, pooling and sharing phase, and evaluation phase? Give an example of each of the phases.

*

Planning the Unit

Planning a unit is a relatively simple matter. In general, the job can be reduced to the following steps.

First. Select the topic.
Second. Select your goals or objectives, i.e., the skills, understandings, attitudes, ideals, and appreciations which you hope the pupils will learn from their study of the topic.[7]
Third. Prepare the unit assignment.
  a. Select the teacher-pupil activities and subject matter by which the pupils will learn the learning products.
  b. Select the activities and subject matter all pupils should do to some extent at least.
  c. Select the activities that are to be optional.
  d. Organize the activities into a plan. Prepare for pupil programming of their own work.
Fourth. Plan, prepare, and secure the materials necessary for the activities.
  a. Study and activity guides.
  b. Special study and activity guides.
  c. Teacher bibliography.
  d. Pupil bibliography.
  e. Audio-visual materials.
  f. Equipment and supplies.
  g. Reading materials.
Fifth. Plan and prepare the evaluation materials and exercises. Prepare tests. *Note:* Tests should be planned before the class starts the assignment.

The ensuing paragraphs will explain in more detail what each of these steps entails and how to carry them out.

STEP ONE: SELECTING THE TOPIC

As in any other planning, the first step in unit planning is to select a topic. For practical purposes

---

[7] Some authorities advocate first selecting the objectives and then selecting the topic and activities to bring the objectives about. However, the beginning teacher will find the present order much easier even though theoretically perhaps not as desirable.

the topic is the name of whatever you are going to study. It may be an adolescent need or problem, or a bit of subject matter. In any case it should meet the criteria for topics suggested earlier in the chapter. It should

1. Center around some major understanding, problem, issue, or theme.
2. Fit the course objectives and further the course plan.
3. Be relevant to pupils' lives and to the society in which they live.
4. Be manageable—not too difficult, too big, or too demanding on time and resources.
5. Be suitable to pupils' abilities and interests.

*

How can a teacher determine whether a particular topic is worth the time and effort?

It has been stated that the basic criteria for judging a topic are (1) the nature of the pupil and (2) the society in which he lives. Is this a valid statement? Why, or why not?

Where might one turn to find suggestions for suitable topics?

*

STEP TWO: PREPARING THE OBJECTIVES

After the topic has been selected the teacher must decide what learning the pupils should acquire from the study of the unit. This selection is the responsibility of the teacher alone. However, in carrying out his responsibilities and selecting the objectives, he can get tremendous help from supervisors, administrators, and faculty committees. Written materials which may be of help are courses of study, curriculum guides, source or resource units, and curriculum bulletins. If such are available the teacher should study them carefully. They are usually a fruitful source of ideas. Sometimes the objectives suggested in such materials can be used without any change. More often they must be adapted and revised. Sometimes they will not be suitable at all. The teacher should not let the objectives suggested in such material fetter him and stunt his creativity. He is the person who must decide what learning products he should strive for.

The pupils can help greatly by telling the teacher what they want to know. Knowing what the pupils wish to know allows the teacher to select learning products of value to them. The pupils, of course, cannot themselves be responsible for selecting the learning products because they do not yet know enough about the subject.

The Overview. Once the teacher has decided what the objectives of the unit are, he should describe them in writing. It is usually helpful if the teacher writes a *general statement, or overview,* of what he is hoping to accomplish. This can be in the form of a paragraph or two describing what is to be learned in the unit, a table of contents listing the general objectives of the unit, or a series of problems or questions presenting the focus of the unit. The purpose of the overview is to establish the central thrust as well as the limits of the unit, this is to ensure that the specific objectives selected for the unit focus on the heart of the matter and are free from irrelevancies. The overview is, in other words, the general objective for the unit. Sometimes it is called the rationale.

The Specific Objectives: After the teacher has described the nature and scope of the unit in the overview, he is ready to state the specific objectives of the unit. These objectives, as we have noted earlier, are the understandings, skills, attitudes, ideals, and appreciations the teacher hopes the pupils will learn from the unit. Sometimes they are called terminal behavior. Their selection is important. What to leave out is as important as what to include.

All of the criteria for the writing of objectives that appear earlier in this book apply for the writing of unit objectives.

1. The objective should be expressed as a specific learning product or terminal behavior. Each objective should be expressed as a clear declarative statement describing either (1) the terminal behavior that should result from the unit (i.e., a behavioral objective) or (2) a specific understanding, skill, attitude, ideal, or appreciation that the teacher expects his pupils will have acquired upon completion of the unit.
2. The objective must be pertinent to this course. If it is not, it is obviously not valid, no matter how earthshaking it may be.
3. The objective must be achievable in the time

allotted. If it is not, it should be reexamined. Perhaps only a portion of the goal should be attempted.

4. The objective must be worthwhile and should be the most worthwhile of the possible objectives. If it is not, perhaps the teacher should change his objectives.

5. The objective must be suitable for the level of the pupils. If it is too hard or too easy, it can cause the unit to fail.

6. The objective should allow for individual differences. Unless the objectives allow some pupils to achieve more than others, and in different ways from others, the unit cannot succeed.

In listing the specific objectives, any order that seems desirable to the teacher may be used. Probably arranging the list in a logical order will help the teacher to understand his goals better and to organize his thinking. Under no circumstances should the list of specific objectives attempt to indicate the order in which the pupils will learn them. That sequence is a matter for each individual pupil.

However, some teachers find it helpful to list the skills, understandings, appreciations, ideals, and attitudes separately under definite headings. Although it is not essential, doing so seems to make it easier for the teacher to visualize his goals.

*

Do you agree with the authors that the teacher's objectives should be presented as learning products written in declarative sentences? Why, or why not? Give arguments both for and against. Would you rather use behavioral objectives?

Apply the criteria cited above to the following objectives in a biology unit on infectious disease, prepared by a student teacher.

Try to change at least some of these understandings, abilities, and attitudes to behavioral objectives.

INFECTIOUS DISEASE
Overview (General Understanding to Be Learned)
Infectious diseases are caused by parasitic bacteria which succeed in overcoming body defenses and enter the body of the host.

Certain hygienic and sanitary procedures are necessary for the prevention and control of disease.

Specific Objectives
UNDERSTANDINGS
1. Infectious disease is disease caused by parasitic

microorganisms.

2. A parasite is a dependent organism which gets its food directly from another organism, the host.

3. Bacteria are very simple one-celled plants classified into three main categories, the cocci, bacilli, and spirilla, by virtue of their form.

4. Bacteria reproduce by simple cell division or by spore formation.

5. All disease-producing bacteria are called pathogenic.

6. Infection takes place when disease germs overcome body defenses.

7. There are many ways bacteria enter the body of the host. Among these are through the nose, mouth, breaks in skin, eyes, ears, and the digestive tract.

8. The incubation period is the period between time of exposure to infectious disease and its development.

9. A contagious disease is one that is readily transmitted by direct or indirect contact between a diseased individual and one who is healthy.

10. Transmission of bacteria from one individual to another takes place through the following means: spit, spray, dust, air, contact, handkerchiefs, towels, utensils, food, water, insects, and animals.

11. Favorable conditions for bacteria are presence of organic matter (food), moisture, and moderate temperature.

12. Unfavorable conditions are dryness, extreme cold (not fatal), high temperature, sunlight, and chemical poisons.

13. To protect himself, the individual should
   a. Avoid taking into the mouth water, food, or the like, that may have been exposed to infection.
   b. Maintain personal cleanliness.
   c. Avoid use of common towel, cup, or the like.
   d. Disinfect cuts, wounds, or the like.
   e. Avoid contact with known or suspected cases of infectious illness.

14. To protect others we should
   a. Avoid spitting where germs may be carried away.
   b. Cover face when coughing or sneezing.
   c. Avoid touching food, dishes, or the like, to be used by others.
   d. Protect food, water, or the like, from dust.
   e. Cooperate with home and community in maintaining sanitary conditions.

ABILITIES
1. Ability to use compound microscope.
2. Ability to prepare slides for microscopic examinations of bacteria.
3. Ability to prepare materials for simple experiments with bacterial cultures.

ATTITUDES
1. A favorable attitude toward observing habits of

personal cleanliness in order to prevent the spread of disease.

2. A favorable attitude toward desirable and healthful practices in the home in order to prevent spread of disease.

3. A favorable attitude toward maintaining and observing health rules and regulations in the community for the preservation of health and the prevention of the spread of disease.

*

STEP THREE: PLANNING THE ACTIVITIES

After the objectives have been chosen and described, the teacher must plan the activities by which the class may achieve the objectives. These activities are the heart of the unit. If they are not carefully planned and organized, the chances of the unit's being successful are reduced to zero, since it is through the activities that the learning products are gained. The organization of the activities is the unit assignment.

Selecting the Activities. To develop a unit assignment one must first identify the activities one might use to achieve the desired learning. These activities will fall into two groups.

First, the activities that will help all pupils to reach the objectives and should be done to some extent sometime before the completion of the unit. These we shall call the basic, or core, activities.

Second, there are those activities that will help some youngsters reach the objectives but need not be attempted by all pupils. These we shall call the optional related activities.

What kind of activities should the teacher select? In the first place, *each activity should contribute directly to at least one of the teacher's objectives.* Time is too precious to waste on any activity not pertinent. Busy work wastes time; aimlessness discourages learning. The school can afford neither.

This brings us to the second criterion: *The activity should seem worthwhile to the pupil.* That the activity should be worthwhile is obvious, but that it must seem so to the pupil is perhaps not so obvious. Yet if the activity does not seem worthwhile, the pupil will not participate with maximum effort and no one can make him. The result is an inefficient teaching situation.

Maximum effort is often stimulated by challenging, thought-provoking situations. A third criterion, then, is that *the activity should be stimulating and thought-provoking.* To be maximally effective pupil activities should relate to the life of the pupil—for example, work in other courses, extracurricular activities, social functions, and home life. Thus a fourth criterion is that *the activities should relate to the pupils' aims and interests and pertain to their lives both in school and out.*

*

One authority on the unit says that the unit assignment should consist largely of a series of problems. Do you agree? What would the advantages be?

*

Organizing the Unit Activities. After the possible activities have been assembled the teacher must organize them into the best possible sequence for the teaching-learning situation. In organizing these activities, the teacher must allow for such things as the time available; the ability level of the pupils and their interests; the nature of the subject matter; the local school situation including rules, equipment, opportunities, and materials available. At this point the teacher may find that he should eliminate certain activities and add others. When doing this, he should always be careful to consider his objectives.

The organization arranged by the teacher before the class begins the unit must be flexible. It must allow the boys and girls opportunity to follow their various bents and to give each of them a chance to participate in the planning of the sequence of activities most desirable for him. No teacher can tell just what is going to happen in any class, so the plan must allow for any contingency. As the pupils progress, both teacher and pupils may want to change the sequence of activities to fit the situation as it develops. Frequently, current happenings, school, local, state, or national, will make a change in plan desirable and profitable.

The Basic Activities. The activities in which every boy and girl should participate may be called basic, or core, activities. These should be prepared so that all the pupils may have experiences suitable to their own levels. At least some of the activities should be appealing to the nonacademically minded youngsters. Many teachers reserve all the interesting projectlike activities for optional related activities or extra-credit work after the required work has been finished. This is poor practice. The youngster who needs stimulation most never has a chance to do anything stimulating.

The pupil should be able to reach all of the teacher's specific objectives by way of the basic activities. To be sure that the activities really do contribute to all of these learnings, the teacher should note just what learning product or products each activity is supposed to produce. This practice will help ensure that each activity does contribute to some objective and that all the objectives are provided for.

The Optional Related Activities. Optional related activities are activities that pupils may do if they wish. They should be truly optional. No pupil should be required to do any of them, although an effort may be made to interest particular pupils in whichever of these activities might be especially beneficial to them. The pupil's mark should not depend upon his completing any of them. If a pupil starts an activity that proves to be distasteful, the teacher may allow him to drop it if it seems desirable.

In a sense the optional related activities are projects. The pupils should be encouraged to suggest other activities not yet included in the unit assignment. Often pupil-suggested activities are the best of all.

Optional related activities are not necessarily activities to be done after the basic activities have been completed. A pupil might well start with an optional related activity. This is particularly true when the pupil has been difficult to interest in that subject or has a special flair.

*

How can a teacher provide for individual differences if he prepares a unit assignment in advance?

Should optional related activities be done only by the brilliant students who finish early?

*

STEP FOUR: PREPARING THE MATERIALS

The Study and Activity Guide. In order that the pupils may know how to proceed throughout the unit, each should be given a mimeographed study and activity guide. This guide should include the instructions for each core activity, except perhaps such activities as listening to a teacher talk. Since the activities in the unit should be geared largely to problem solving, the guide should consist mostly of questions, problems, and projects designed to stimulate thinking and investigating by the pupil. These should be presented in enough detail to allow the pupil to proceed on the activities without constantly resorting to the teacher for help. On the other hand, they should not be so detailed as to be recipes. Too detailed instructions of the recipe type can destroy initiative and prevent thinking. For instance, instead of saying:

Mix X and Y in a test tube. A precipitate should form. This is Z.

One could say:

Mix X and Y in a tube. What result do you observe? What should result? See references 10 and 13.

Or again, instead of saying:

Who said, "Give me liberty or give me death?"

A study guide might ask:

What was the importance of Patrick Henry's speech and what effect did it have on American history? Why did Patrick Henry say what he had to say? If you had been a member of the House of Burgesses how would you have reacted?

Some modern theorists decry the use of study guides on the basis that study guides may limit the creativity and originality of the pupil. To some extent this may be true, but good study guides seem to have advantages that outweigh the disadvantages.

1. They give the pupil a *source* to which he can refer if he forgets his assignment.
2. They give the pupil a *picture* of what activities he might want to do so that he can pick his choice of activities and the order in which he wishes to do them.
3. They give the pupil a *definite assignment* so that he can go ahead to new activities on his own without waiting for a new assignment from the teacher.

4. They give *definite instructions* which should eliminate misunderstandings about assignments and many excuses for incomplete or unattempted assignments.

A Sample Study and Activity Guide. This guide was developed for a unit on race relations in a twelfth-grade class in Problems of Democracy.

General Study and Activity Guide

1. What are the various groups that make up the population of the United States? 2:42–45.*
2. Make a classification of the different groups and give numbers. 14:521–527.
3. What is the composition of our population in Middletown?
4. What are the various sects (religious) in the United States? 1:101.
5. Give the names and numbers of the ten highest. 1:101.
6. How many of these religions are represented in Middletown? In Middletown High School?
7. How have these various groups affected the growth and development of the United States? Name the contributions of these groups. 14:512–517, 521–524.
8. What are some of the problems of harmonious relationships between different races and groups? 14:498–502.
9. When is a group regarded as a minority? 6:582.
10. How does prejudice destroy harmony between groups? 6:586–587.
11. What is prejudice? 26:Ch. 1.
12. How do we get our prejudices? 26:16; 22:29–33.
13. What are the principal races in the world? 6:84–89.
14. What is the meaning of discrimination? 6:89.
15. Give one example of political, social, and economic discrimination from your own experience.
16. How can we improve on the existing efforts to destroy prejudice and discrimination?

* These numbers refer to readings that the pupil may consult to find the answers to a particular problem.

17. What is the work of the Commonwealth Fair Employment Practices Commission?
18. What can you do to prevent discrimination?
19. Name four types of groups often regarded as minorities. 6:582–606.
20. What is the dominant group in America? 6:582–606.
21. What constitutes the differences between groups? 6:606.
22. Name the effects of prejudice on the person who practices it. 27.
23. Discuss the relationship of prejudice to Democracy. 27.
24. Is there such a thing as "racial superiority"? Explain your answer. 6:84–95.
25. Make a full report in writing on social adjustment involving the immigrant.
26. Read the Roll of Honor in your neighborhood for World War II. Copy ten names at random and try to determine their ancestry. Conclusion.

As part of each study guide the teacher includes a list of any materials needed by the students and a bibliography. The bibliography should consist largely of materials at the reading level of the pupils. However, there should be books difficult enough to challenge the brightest pupils, as well as others for the slow learners. References in the text may be keyed into this bibliography by a system similar to that illustrated in the sample study and activity guide.

Lists of materials required for specific activities should be part of the description of the activity. If including the list makes the description of the activity too long, the detailed description may be filed on 4 × 6 or 5 × 8 cards or placed on the bulletin board, thus keeping the size of the study guide reasonable.

*

Should all pupils begin at the beginning of a unit assignment and proceed with the suggested activities in order? Why, or why not? If not, how should they proceed?

At what point and how much should the pupils plan the unit assignment or their part in it?

*

Special Study and Activity Guides. Usually the optional related activities should be described by title and perhaps a brief notice in the study and activity guide or on a bulletin board. This serves to make the pupils aware of optional related activities which might interest them. Detailed instructions for such activities can be kept on 5 × 8 or 4 × 6 file cards. Should a pupil spot an optional activity that seems challenging to him, he can go to the file and examine the card. If the activity seems to be worthwhile, he can then elect to carry it out with the teacher's permission. This means, of course, that several cards must be available for each activity. If this seems impossible, the pupil can himself copy the instructions.

Another type of special study guide is that which is prepared to help the pupils get more out of such activities as field trips and moving pictures. Such special activity and study guides are used to point out the things that one should observe and the things one should investigate in such activities.

The following is an example of a special guide for an optional activity in the Problems of Democracy unit on Race Relations described earlier in the chapter.

Special Activity Guide
Report on Americanization Work in Middletown
1. Interview Mr. Rand in Room 310. Mr. Rand is head of the evening school in Middletown. Ask him questions along this line and take notes on his answers.
   a. What is the work of the Americanization classes?
   b. Who teaches these classes? What are their qualifications?
   c. What people are eligible for these classes?
   d. Why are the classes necessary?
   e. What subjects are taught and why?
   f. When a person completes the course what happens?
   g. How long does this course last?
   h. Who pays for it?
   i. What is the attitude of the people in the class toward America?
   j. How many people in Middletown have completed the course in the last ten years?
   k. Where do these people come from?
2. Write up the answers in the form of a report and submit it to the teacher for approval. Indicate whether you would be willing to give

the report to some other class if called upon to do so.

The Teacher's Lists of Materials, Equipment, and Readings. The teacher should also prepare for his own guidance, lists of materials, equipment, audio-visual aids and readings pertaining to the unit. Here he indicates the materials and equipment that will be needed and references the teacher should read to ensure that he is properly prepared.

STEP FIVE: PREPARING FOR THE EVALUATION

The evaluation in the unit goes on as the teaching goes on. Before one starts teaching the unit he should have worked out a complete procedure for evaluating the students' progress. This part of the unit plan should include decisions concerning what evidence to collect and what instruments to use in the evaluation. At the time he should also gather or construct the tests, scales, or other devices that he will need to use. You will find the procedures for devising an evaluation plan and constructing evaluative instruments in Part VII.

THE DAILY LESSON PLAN IN THE UNIT

The unit plan does not eliminate daily planning. Before each class the teacher must think through what is to be done that day and jot down the agenda for the day. This plan will include such things as announcements, programs of activities, reminders to work with certain pupils or groups, notes for teacher talks, and the like. Since the major part of the planning has been taken care of by the unit assignment the daily plan may be quite sketchy and informal. At times it may be as simple and brief as "continue laboratory session"; at other times it may be simply a list of the committee and individual reports or activities to be presented that period. Sometimes, however, experienced teachers find it preferable to use detailed lesson plans.

*

What part of the unit assignment should be placed on cards or on the bulletin board? Why?

What is the use of a study guide? Some authorities do

not approve of using study guides. Do you? What is the use of a special study guide?

*

PREPARING A LEARNING MODULE

Learning modules (sometimes called instructional learning packets, learning activity packets, instructional modules, instructional packets, or learning packets) are really a variation of the unit plan. They are especially useful for individualizing instruction. Basically the procedure for planning and building a learning module is the same as that for any other unit. It includes five basic steps.

STEP ONE

Once the subject content has been divided into topics or modules and the topic has been selected, the teacher should determine the learning objectives for the topic. These should be described as general and specific learning products or terminal behavior. It helps if one writes the objectives in the second person. They should explain to the pupil what he will have learned when he completes the module. The general objective can be written as an overview which includes not only a general description of the terminal behavior expected, but the reasons for studying the module and acquiring this learning. Frequently this is called the rationale. The specific learning products should be described as either simple or criterion-referenced behavioral objectives. In either case the teacher should take care to ensure that they contribute to terminal behavior called for by the general objective.

STEP TWO

When the objectives have been determined, the teacher should select the activities and content by which the pupils will be expected to achieve them. These activities will include the readings, exercises, problems, and so on, that will make up the pupil assignment during the module. These should be designed so that pupils can do the work on their own without having to depend on the teacher

as the source of knowledge. In the learning module the learner is largely self-directing and the teacher acts as a guide rather than as a master. In selecting the activities and content, the teacher should be very careful to be sure that the activities and content are pertinent to the goals. Any activities or content that do not contribute to the objectives should be dropped. This dictum, of course, assumes that the module objectives are broad enough to be worthwhile.

STEP THREE

After the content, activities, and objectives have been planned, the teacher should develop a plan for evaluating the pupils' achievement. This plan should probably include some sort of self-correcting pretest which will show pupils where their strengths and deficiencies lie. In individualized programs probably there should be some means for capable pupils to "test out" of a module by demonstrating that they have achieved its objectives. Teacher-administered pretest schemes can be used for this purpose. Self-correcting progress tests will also be useful for helping the pupil evaluate his own work as he progresses through the module. Some sort of post-testing device should be used to measure the pupils' final progress. Probably this should be some sort of teacher-corrected criterion-referenced post test or performance instrument. All the evaluating instruments should be prepared at this time.

STEP FOUR

By now all the necessary instructional materials to be used in the module should have been gathered or prepared.

STEP FIVE

Now one is ready to write the study guide. This is the document the pupil will use to guide himself through the module. Since it is the basis of individual study and self guidance, it should be prepared very carefully. In it the pupil will find
  a. Topic.

b. Rationale, including the general objectives and reasons why the learning is worthwhile.

c. The specific objectives stated as specific behavioral objectives—and addressed to the pupil, e.g., "At the end of this mod you should be able to locate the principal oceanic streams on the globe." Sometimes provisions are made by which the pupil can check off each of these behavioral objectives when he feels he has mastered the behavior called for.

d. Directions for the pupil to follow while completing the module. These directions should include

   (1) General directions: agenda, time limits (if any), and options.

   (2) Specific directions: that is, the directions and explanations for specific activities. For example,

      (a) Problem to be solved: What the problem is, what the background of the problem is, what requirements must be met to solve the problem successfully.

      (b) Reading: Purpose of the reading, what information is to be learned, what is to be done with the information, questions on the reading, exact citations.

      (c) Information to be learned: possible sources of the information.

   (3) Where to go for materials and information.

e. Bibliography.

f. Instructional materials that you have prepared for the module. (These may be included with the study guide or distributed separately.)

g. Self-correcting and other testing and evaluating materials. These should include both pretest and post-test material and perhaps intermediate progress tests. These may be included with the study guide or distributed separately. Note, however, that teacher-corrected mastery tests should be distributed separately as needed—not included in the original packet. Mastery tests should be administered separately under supervision and corrected by the teacher. Progress tests, on the other hand, are more useful when they are self-correcting.

PREPARING A LEARNING CONTRACT

The contract is another variation of the unit. In the contract the pupil agrees to do a certain amount of work during a certain period of time. If the contract is fulfilled satisfactorily, the contractor is rewarded with a certain mark. In general the procedure for planning under the contract plan is about the same as with the unit plan except that in the contract plan the pupil agrees to fulfill certain requirements in return for a certain mark. Basically the procedure for planning under the contract plan is

1. Set up objectives and activities whereby pupils may achieve the objectives.
2. Decide which activities will be required.
3. Decide which activities will be optional.
4. Decide what the requirements will be for the different grade levels (A, B, C, D).
5. Provide a written study and activity guide describing the activities.
6. Let each pupil decide how he will meet the requirements.
7. On the basis of these decisions have the pupil make out a contract in writing.

An example of a contract might be this.

Contract

Susan Q   To be completed by Nov. 1

During this unit I will
1. Read Chapter III of the text.
2. Do the problems on Worksheet A.
3. Participate in the panel on the Panama Canal.
4. Pass the unit test with a mark of at least C.
5. Demonstrate that I can perform all the requirements in group C.

Satisfactory completion of this contract will be awarded a unit mark of C.

signed   Susie Q.
                PUPIL
approved   Maria Alexandra
                TEACHER

The only real difference between the contract and an ordinary unit work plan is the element of quid pro quo.

SUMMARY

The responsibility for planning is the teacher's. He must plan his courses, his units, and his daily lessons, although he may have curriculum guides, courses of study, source units, textbooks, and other materials to draw from. In planning his courses, the teacher can find these devices greatly helpful, but he should guard against their restricting him too much. In selecting the topics and subject matter for the course, the teacher should try for psychological organization and for maximum retention and transfer.

The following is an outline of the type of unit plan suggested in this chapter.

1. An overview that describes the nature and scope of the unit.
2. The teacher's specific objectives which are the understandings, skills, attitudes, ideals, and appreciations he hopes his pupils will get from the unit.
3. The unit assignment which includes activities in which the class will participate during the teaching of the unit. The activities will be of two types: (1) the basic activities to be done by all pupils to some extent in some time and (2) the optional related activities.
4. The study and activity guide which will contain the instructions for carrying out the core activities to be done individually and in small groups.
5. The special study and activity guides which contain the instructions for carrying out the optional related activities.
6. A list of materials and readings the boys and girls may use in their study.
7. A short bibliography and list of materials for the use of the teacher alone.
8. Testing or other devices to be used in evaluating the success of the unit. These devices should test adequately each of the learning products described in 1 and 2 of this outline.

In carrying out such a unit plan the unit assignment should be introduced by introductory activities that will catch the pupils' interest and help the teacher know the pupils. Following the introductory phase comes individual and small group work interspersed by class activities. After this laboratory phase the pupils share their experiences and learning. Finally the unit of work ends in some sort of evaluative exercise.

These four steps, or phases, make up the teaching-learning cycle. In practice the four phases do not always follow in regular order, but vary to suit the occasion. Arranging the classroom as a laboratory increases the effectiveness of the unit assignment and the teaching-learning cycle.

Learning modules and learning contracts are really special types of units. The procedure for planning them is essentially the same as for other units. In carrying out the modules and packets, teachers will find that they are most successful when they use the laboratory approach.

Lesson
Planning

7

Once a course has been planned, the teacher must plan for the actual instruction. Some teachers use the unit plan as a basis for their planning. Others develop their topics solely on the basis of daily lesson plans. Of course, daily lessons are necessary in units too, but their role is not nearly as crucial, particularly when the units follow laboratory and long-term assignment procedures.

Sources of the Lesson Plan

Most teachers draw their lesson plans from their teaching experiences over the years. Teachers who have had little experience or narrow experience have relatively little to draw from other than their textbooks. The new teacher needs help in determining what goals to strive for, what activities to include, and what materials to use. Many school administrations provide such help through a variety of means. One way is through supervision. Almost always the supervisor will be willing to suggest techniques, approaches, and sources of materials if the teacher wants him to. Many supervisors make it a practice to go over teachers' lesson plans in order to point out ways of improving them. The new teacher should welcome such inspection. By following up his supervisor's suggestions he can usually learn much.

Other sources of help in building lesson plans are curriculum guides, curriculum bulletins, and resource units. Many of these list specific suggestions that can be particularly helpful for specific lessons in specific topics. Among the materials available for help in planning lessons, the resource unit is often the most valuable. The scope of the potential aid a good resource unit can give to teachers planning lessons is indicated by the content of the St. Paul resource unit *"Democracy vs. Communism"*[1] which includes

An overview.
A list of desired outcomes divided according to
  Understandings.
  Attitudes.
  Skills.
An outline of content.
A list of activities divided according to
  Initiatory activities.
  Developmental activities.
  Culminating activities.
An annotated bibliography.
An annotated list of films.
An annotated list of film strips.

Teachers who utilize sources such as this usually find it easier to prepare good lessons than when they go on unassisted.

PREPARING THE LESSON PLAN

A lesson is a short period of instruction devoted to a specific topic, skill, or idea. In preparing a lesson, the first thing to do is to decide what the pupil should learn from it. This is called the objective of the lesson. Deciding what these learning products should be is the responsibility of the teacher. That is true even though the lesson as a whole is developed cooperatively with the class.

Selecting the Objectives

In selecting the objectives, the teacher should keep certain criteria in mind.

[1] *Democracy vs. Communism, A Resource Unit for High School Social Studies Classes,* Curriculum Bulletin No. 86, St. Paul Public Schools, St. Paul, Minnesota, 1961.

1. The objective may be a concept, skill, attitude, ideal, or appreciation, or any combination of them. But no matter what it is, it should be a specific learning product or terminal behavior so definite and specific that the teacher can aim directly at it, and tell by means of educational measuring devices whether or not he has been successful. Many modern educators recommend that the objectives be written as behavioral objectives.

2. Each objective should be a worthwhile learning product pertinent to the course. One should always have a valid answer for the pupil who asks, "Why do we have to study this?"

3. The teacher should have each learning product clearly and definitely defined in his own mind. In order to be sure that his objectives are clear, the teacher would do well to describe just what the desired learning products are, in a few simple declarative sentences. He may be surprised to find out that he is not always so clear about them as he thought he was.

4. The objectives must be feasible. To try to teach something that is too difficult or something that cannot be completed in the time allotted is pointless. Do not try for too much. We reiterate: *It is better to do a little well than try to do a lot, and do it badly.* One or two major concepts are quite enough for one period.

5. The objectives should allow for differences in individuals. All pupils cannot learn the same things in any class. What is too easy for one may be too difficult for another. Therefore, one's objectives should allow pupils to achieve them in different amounts and in different ways.

*

What would be a suitable objective for a lesson on Edgar Allan Poe's *The Raven* to be given in grade ten?
How can one write objectives so as to allow pupils to achieve them in different amounts and different ways?

*

Selecting the Subject Matter

At this point it might be wise to mention the subject matter of the lesson. No lesson can get very far if the teacher neglects subject matter. The subject matter selected should, of course, lead to the objective of the lesson, and can hardly be separated from the activities. It is often wise to outline the subject matter to be studied or discussed. This outline might be included in the lesson plan itself, or placed on a separate sheet of paper. In choosing subject matter, it is particularly important to be selective. One cannot learn everything. Therefore the teacher should avoid attempting to include too much, and rather should include only that subject matter which seems to him to hold the most promise.

Planning the Activities

Once the teacher has chosen his objectives for the lesson he must decide how to reach them. The means he uses are the activities both he and the pupils pursue during the lesson. This phase of the lesson plan is often called the procedure. Experience is not just the best teacher; experience is the only teacher. Consequently, the planning of suitable activities is crucial. They are the experiences through which pupils learn. Unless the activities are properly planned, one can hardly expect the pupils to reach the desired goal.

Activities may be called the teacher's tools, and should be used accordingly. Just as a carpenter uses a ripsaw for cutting with the grain and a crosscut saw for cutting across it, so the teacher needs to select the proper activities for the job to be done. To this end, the teacher should learn to conduct many different kinds of activities. The more activities the teacher knows how to conduct, the more likely he will be able to find the activity most suitable for any given situation.

As in the planning of objectives, the teacher must be careful to choose suitable activities. If he wishes, he may enlist the help of pupils in deciding upon the activities. Still, the teacher is responsible for the quality and suitability of the activities chosen. Some criteria he may consider in selecting activities are

1. Will the activity lead to the goal desired? Is it suitable?
2. Is it efficient? Will it lead us to our goal directly and economically?
3. Is it suited to the pupils' abilities and interests?
4. Do we have time for it?
5. Do we have the material for it?
6. Does it allow for individual differences?

7. Is it suitable for the room in which it is scheduled to take place? If not, can we find a suitable place?

In addition to selecting the activities the teacher must also decide how to conduct the activities. He therefore tries to determine the sequence of the activities and the approximate time to be spent on each activity. He plans how to introduce the lesson and how to launch the various activities. He also provides for finishing each lesson with a culminating activity—a summary, for instance.

AIMING THE ACTIVITIES

Four points need to be emphasized in detail here because many new teachers never learn the truth about them until it is too late. The first is that every activity contained in every lesson should be aimed directly at an objective of that lesson. Anything less than that leads to soft pedagogy and drifting classes. If any activity does not contribute to your goal, leave it out. The only exception to this rule might be an activity that is designed to catch or hold pupil interest and to guide them into activities that do directly contribute to the objective. On occasion, circumstances may make it advisable to depart from the planned activities and substitute activities that serve other purposes. Such occasions should be relatively rare.

STEP-BY-STEP PROCEDURE

The second point that needs reiterating is that the portion of the lesson plan that outlines the activities, i.e., the procedure, should be detailed step by step. These activities should be explicit, definite, and detailed. It is not enough to say "Lecture on the amoeba—fifteen minutes"; you should plan what will be in the lecture. It is not enough to state that there will be a discussion on the civil rights law; plan the direction the discussion will take, the main points it will bring out, and the questions you will use. It is not enough to state that we shall have some problems done at the chalkboard; plan which problems and work out the answers.

MOTIVATION

The third point is that in setting up the plan for his activities, the teacher should consider the motivation of his pupils. Teachers should consider the activities to be sure that they have appeal and that the pupils are ready for them. If it appears that the activities do not have appeal, or that the pupils are not ready for them, the teacher should consider what steps he should take to be sure that the pupils put out their best effort. Sometimes he may need to withdraw the activities and substitute others; at other times he may wish to attach some extrinsic reward to them, or he may decide to postpone these activities until he has prepared the pupils for them. What the teacher does must depend upon his analysis of the situation. Many teachers provide a separate section in their lesson plan for motivation. Perhaps this is a good practice because so often, unless we make special provision for motivation, we are likely to neglect it altogether. Still, a special section in the plan for motivation should not be necessary. Rather, the teacher should attempt to ensure that, in so far as possible, at least some of the subject matter has natural appeal to the pupils. The more interesting and relevant to the lives of the pupils the subject matter is, the more motivating it will be. In addition, the teacher should incorporate activities that appeal to the pupils into his teaching methodology. Exhortations on the part of the teacher do not usually aid much in creating pupil interest and energy, but attempts to point out the usefulness or relevancy of the work may bear fruit. More effective are sprightly activities, interesting content, pupil planning and decision, and other techniques that catch the pupils' interest and convince them that the learning is worthwhile. If attention-catching activities come early in the lesson, they may catch and hold otherwise apathetic pupils through to the end.

CLINCHING THE LEARNING

The fourth point is that every objective needs to be driven home. Many teachers fail—when they fail—because they neglect to make the little extra effort that would clinch the learning that is their objective. Again, how to do this clinching depends upon the situation. In many lessons the clincher may be a summary at the end of the session. In others it may be a review or drill. In still others it may be a pupil summation to the question: "What was the main point that we were trying to get at in this discussion, John?" At times it might even be a short quiz. Even though sometimes lessons must carry over to the next classs, one can take it as axiomatic that any lesson plan that does not make provision for the clincher is not a complete plan.

THE PROBLEM OF TIME

In listing the activities in the procedure of his lesson plan the teacher should estimate how much time the class will spend on each activity. Beginning teachers find this estimate so difficult to make that they often ask for ways of determining just how long to allow for each activity. Unfortunately no one can give them this help, because there is really no way to tell how people will react. An activity that can be done in five minutes in one class may take fifteen minutes in another. All this notwithstanding, we shall attempt to provide a few rules of thumb to use as guides.

1. The first of these is to make your procedure too long at first. By doing so you may prevent the embarrassment of running dry with the period half over. Beginning teachers tend to talk fast and move swiftly, because of the tenseness caused by the newness of the classroom situation. As a rule this tendency wears off with experience. The new teacher often is troubled because he does not have enough material; the experienced teacher's trouble is more likely to be that he never has enough time.

2. The second rule of thumb is to provide a few minutes at the beginning of the period for taking attendance and the making of announcements, and five or more minutes at the end of the period for clinching the lesson. One also needs to provide, at some point, time enough to make an adequate homework assignment. It is this need to provide for classroom and teaching chores that accounts for the astonishing fact that a forty-minute moving picture may be too long for a fifty-minute period.

3. A third rule of thumb is to mark in your procedure by an asterisk or by underlining (some teachers use red ink) the activities that really must be covered during the period in case time starts to run out. This procedure can save one from such situations as never getting around

to showing pupils how to do their homework assignments, and so on.

4. A fourth rule of thumb is to give pupils time to learn. Don't rush. Points have to be made and remade. The fact that one of your bright pupils grasps the answer in a flash is no sign that everyone else does. Take time to be sure by asking others about the same point in different ways. One makes concepts clear by turning them over and over in one's mind. Give the pupils a chance to do that. Introduce your points and follow them up. If one takes time to be sure about ideas, he makes haste slowly but surely.

5. Finally, if you do run out of material, don't panic. Use the time for a review of what has gone on before, or for a chance to let the pupils start their homework under supervision. For a while at least, the new teacher would be wise to have some extra activities planned just for such a contingency.

Preparing for the Activities

The teacher must also prepare for the activities. If he plans to use questions, he decides what questions to ask, and notes down the wording of the more important ones. If he plans to use demonstrations or films, he gathers the necessary materials and equipment beforehand and checks them carefully to be sure that everything is in working order.

Before attempting any experiment or demonstration one should try it first to make sure of one's apparatus and technique. Nothing is flatter than a demonstration that will not work. Similarly, before one assigns a problem or exercise, one should check to see that it is solvable and that he himself knows how to solve it. Picture the plight of the beginning teacher who, in a physics class, was stumped by one of the exercises he had assigned to be worked on the board. A brilliant pupil finally showed him how to do it. Mistakes of this kind can cause pupils to lose respect for the teacher.

*

What activities might a teacher use to teach the objectives he decided were suitable for a discussion of Edgar

Allan Poe's *The Raven?* Plan the activities for a lesson designed to achieve these objectives.

*

Other Elements of the Lesson Plan

In his plan the teacher should list the materials and equipment needed for the lesson. He should also note special things he plans to do, such as announcements to be made. Also, he should write down things he wishes to remember to do or say, such as speaking to John about trying to be a little tidier or giving Joe a hand with setting up equations. Part of his planning will, of course, provide for any new assignments.

The Lesson Plan Format

The authors of this book do not insist on any particular format for the lesson plan. The format is up to the teacher. He should use whatever format is best for him. But he should use a format that is easy to follow, one that lists the activities in order of use, provides for the maximum amount of detail in the minimum space, and makes provisions for each of the following elements, although they all need not be present in every lesson plan.

1. The objective. A precise statement of what is to be learned in the lesson.
2. Subject matter. An outline of the subject matter to be covered is often very helpful. If it is to be used, it can be included here.
3. The activities (or class procedure). The activities through which objectives will be reached should be listed in order of occurrence with provisions for introducing them and for culminating activities. Evaluative activities should also be included.
4. The materials needed. Planning includes acquiring the materials needed for each activity and getting them ready for use. Preparing the classroom for the lesson should also be included.
5. Special notes. Reminders of anything that may be forgotten. This section usually includes matters that are out of the ordinary. Announce-

ments and special work for individuals are examples of the type of thing often included.
6. The new assignment. This section will be devoted to the assignment.

An outline based on the six headings above seems to be as satisfactory as any other format. However, in selecting a format a teacher should remember that his lesson plans are for his use alone (except in emergencies), and so he should use the format he finds easiest and most comfortable to use when he is teaching.

Using Plan Books

School officials often provide teachers with plan books with which to plan their lessons. These are valuable for planning the long-term sequence for the school year. Unfortunately, some of the commercial plan books do not allow enough space for one to enter an entire plan. Since this is the case, the teacher may want to prepare his daily plans on sheets of composition paper or in a notebook designed for that purpose.

Even though the teacher keeps more detailed plans elsewhere, he needs to keep in his plan book at least skeleton plans as he forecasts them for at least a week ahead. Here he should record the lessons to be studied, the assignments, and a word about the approach. Keeping these plans up-to-date is important because they may be used as the index for an estimate of the adequacy of the course by supervisors and as a basis for teaching the class if a substitute has to take over.

FOLLOWING THE PLAN

On the whole, the new teacher would do well to follow his plan fairly closely. Doing so is about the only way he can be sure to do what he has intended to do. Otherwise, in the hurly-burly of an active classroom situation a teacher can easily get sidetracked and lose sight of his objective. Nevertheless, a teacher should not let his plan handcuff him. There are at least two types of situations that require him to leave his plan: (1) when the lesson planned is going so badly that something must be done to save it, and (2) when something happens before or during the class to indicate that the pupils would benefit more from a different attack.

As a rule a teacher is foolish to stick by a lesson plan that is obviously not succeeding. Of course it should be only seldom that such a contretemps occurs, yet the new teacher would be wise always to have an alternate approach ready to use in case of emergency.

Often a change of pace is needed to cut off an incipient behavior problem. Pupils who are growing restless in a lecture or recitation may be ripe for a discussion or a problem-solving activity. Sometimes a written assignment can be quite effective for channeling energies that seem about to break the bonds of propriety. At other times a teacher can see by the looks on pupils' faces that what one is trying to teach is not getting through to them. In such cases a few well-directed questions may tell what the difficulty is so that the teacher can reorient himself and start off with a different approach or perhaps switch to a different, more elementary lesson.

At times pupils raise questions during the lesson that are sufficiently important to warrant immediate follow-up. Sometimes the point or problem is worth pursuing in detail. In such circumstances perhaps the teacher should discard his lesson plan completely and devote the class's attention to this new point. More often, the pupils' questions warrant only a short diversion from the planned procedure.

Sometimes events of importance may occur within or outside the class to make your plan obsolete. In the case of an event of national importance or of great importance to the school or community, it may be desirable to interrupt the class to talk about the event even though it has no visible relationship to the course or subject concerned. On December 8, 1941, teachers of mathematics, science, and English classes quite rightly turned on radios in their classrooms in order to hear President Roosevelt's speech asking Congress to recognize the existence of a state of war with Japan, *and a third of a century later many who were in those classes remember the lesson learned that day more vividly than anything else they learned in their high school programs.* In the case of an exciting school event, it may be wise to let pupils talk about it for a few minutes at the beginning of class so as to let them blow off steam a little before they settle down to work.

No one can tell any teacher when he should stick to his plan and when to depart from it. What a teacher does must be decided on the basis of what seems best at the time. The criteria on which to base one's decision are simple: (1) What will benefit the pupils most? (2) What will advance the cause of learning most? (3) How relevant and significant to the course is the change? The teacher should remember that, after all, his plan is only a means to an end. If something better comes along he should feel free to use it.

On the other hand, no teacher should change plans capriciously. Usually, if you are inspired by a "better" idea during a lesson it is wise to resist it and stick to your original plan. Good inspirations are hard to find. The chances are that your original plan will serve you better than any spur of the moment idea. Only rarely does it pay to be daring and discard your plans.

*

One day a supervisor visited a beginning teacher who was having difficulty. This young person had taken on a job which was almost too much for him. He was teaching material difficult for him and was having considerable trouble keeping up with the class. When the supervisor asked him for his plans, he replied, "I am so busy I have not been able to make any lesson plans yet." What would your answer be to this beginning teacher?

*

SOME SAMPLE LESSON PLANS

On the following pages you will find examples of lesson plans prepared according to various formats.

Most of these plans were prepared by college students. *None of them is perfect.* As you read them criticize them. Consider such questions as these:

1. Are the objectives clear and precise?
2. Are they attainable?
3. Could you write test items that would tell whether the objectives were actually achieved?
4. Will the procedure outlined lead to the attainment of the objectives?
5. Are the procedures detailed enough so that you feel the teacher really knows what he intends to do? Could you follow the plan if you were a substitute?
6. Are the procedures likely to encourage learning? Or will they be boring?
7. Do the activities allow for differences in the pupils in any way?
8. Does the plan note exactly what material and equipment the teacher needs to have ready so that he will not forget?
9. If you were a pupil would you enjoy the class?
10. If you were a pupil would you learn from the class?

Note that lesson plans are not always written in perfectly logical form—nor in finished prose. They are notes from the teacher to himself, and so quite personal. Consequently they frequently contain abbreviations and shorthand expressions. The important thing is that they be clear to the user. To make it easy to follow the plans, many teachers make ample use of underlining, capitals, asterisks, and other signposts. You will find examples of personal shorthand devices and signposts in these lessons. Do they help or hinder?

Lesson Plan 1

Senior English

OBJECTIVE: At the end of the lesson the pupils will
1. Perceive the mood of melancholy and retreat in Byron's *The Ocean*.
2. React to the emotional tone of the poem.
3. Realize that Romanticism was sentimental.

PROCEDURE:
2 min.   1. Take attendance.
4 min.   2. Read the poem to the students without their books.

4 min. 3. Now read it to them with their books. They should attempt to find the main meaning of the poem.

5 min. 4. Have the class list in their notebooks some of the attributes the poet gives to the human race, e.g.,

> Man marks the earth with ruin
> Man's ravage
> The vile strength he wields for Earth's destruction
> Men's empires have all disappeared yet ocean lives on unchanged.

5 min. Discuss the different attributes

5 min. 5. Is the picture of man created by the poet a happy or unhappy one?

Do you think that this is a true picture of man? Or is it too one-sided?

5 min. 6. List the attributes of the ocean, e.g., rapture on the lonely shore.

> Time writes no wrinkle on thine azure brow—
> Such as Creation's dawn beheld, thou rollest on.

The ocean is seen as great and powerful.
Does it have any qualities of kindness and sympathy with the human race or is it simply a blank force?

5 min. 7. Ask this question:
The poet says in the first stanza that he loves "not Man the less."

Later he urges the ocean to leave man lying dashed upon the earth.

Do you find that this poem seems to be a personal lashing out at man by the poet rather than an expression of a universal truth or an insight into man's condition?

5 min. 8. Give a quick lecture on the Romantic melancholy prevalent in Byron's time. The turning to nature for a source of strength.

  a. Sentimental contemplations of nature.
  b. For the Romantic, nature becomes a great restorative and spiritual guide.
  c. Nature is to be untouched by human hand. Celebration of nature in the ruin.

5 min. 9. Ask these questions:
Do you feel that this poem is applicable to modern-day life?
Are we marking the earth with ruin?
Do we have no control over the sea today?

MATERIALS: Textbooks

5 min. Assignment—Read "The Grave Digger" by Bliss Carmen.
Does his view of life vary from or resemble Byron's?
How does Carmen view man and ocean?

Lesson Plan 2

Biology

INTRODUCTION TO PLANT REPRODUCTION

OBJECTIVES: At the completion of the lesson the pupils will be able to
1. Identify corolla, sepals, calyx, perianth, stamens, pistil (stigma, style, and ovary), filament, and pollen grains.
2. Explain the purpose of each of the above.

SUBJECT CONTENT:
Text Reference: pages 370–373, covering topics, petals, corolla, sepals, calyx, perianth, stamens, pistil (stigma, style, and ovary), filament, and pollen grains.

CLASS PROCEDURE:

2 min. or 3 min.   1. Initiate class by forming four groups of five pupils each (out of a class of 20). Then distribute four orchids, one to each group.

15 min.   2. In each group have the third student from the end or the middle student hold the flower so that all may see the interior.

20 min.   3. With each group referring to the distributed flower, I will construct an artificial flower with the use of homemade (paper or cardboard) parts and a flannel board.

20 min.   4. Go over each part again, this time telling the use of the part.
     a. Petals (1) arranged in a circle to collect pollen grains in the bottom (2) are brightly colored to attract insects, (3) protect the reproduction organs of the flower against wind and the like.
     b. Sepals—are green (make food).
     c. Stamens—have a stem called a filament and an anther (sack which contains pollen).
     d. Pistil—usually one, but some flowers have more, composed of a stigma (sticky), which pollen attaches itself to; a style, which supports the stigma and transfers the pollen to the ovary; and an ovary, where pollenization takes place and where seed is produced.

5 min.   5. Terms:
     1. Corolla—all petals together
     2. Calyx—all sepals together
     3. Perianth—corolla and calyx together
   6. Without the pistils and stamens of flowers there would be no seeds and without seed the human race would not survive.

INSTRUCTIONAL MATERIALS:
1. Text—Biology—Kroeber, Wolff, and Weaver
2. Four orchids (real)
3. Flannel board—Homemade flower

ASSIGNMENTS:

3 min. Think about growing either lima beans or peas, collecting growth data, and reporting in a small paper a summary of root, leaf, and stem growth.

OBJECTIVE: At the completion of the lesson the pupils will understand that the corporation became the dominant form of business organization.

SPECIFIC OBJECTIVES: At the completion of this lesson the pupils will be able to

1. Give a valid operational definition of corporations in their own words.
2. Describe how a corporation is formed.
3. Describe the factors that caused the growth of corporations in the United States after 1865.

PROCEDURE:

1. What is a corporation?
   Ans.: *working definition*—a form of business organization in which the small savings of many investors are combined to provide the necessary funds for operating a business.
2. Prior to 1860 what forms of business organization were prevalent in the United States?
   a. *partnership*—owned by two or more individuals.
   b. *proprietorship*—owned by a single individual.
3. The corporation offers several advantages over the partnership and proprietorship. What are they?
   a. It can raise sizable amounts of money by selling stock.
   b. Stockholders risk only the money they invest. (Compare with partnership and proprietorship where owners may be sued for debts.)
   c. Ownership can change hands more readily.
   d. A corporation continues indefinitely.
4. How could we, as a class, form a corporation? (class discussion) *Put terms on blackboard.*
   a. *charter*—from state—legal right to conduct a certain type of business.
   b. *capital*—raising of funds for business purposes.
   c. *stock*—certificates of ownership.
   d. *directors* and *officers*—run corporation for stockholders—are elected by stockholders.
   e. *bonds*—means of borrowing money—fixed rate of interest.
   f. *dividends*—a share of the profits (if there are any) given to the stockholders.

Lesson Plan 3 *(Cont.)*

5. Corporations grew rapidly after 1865.
   a. Outburst of manufacturing after 1865. Production on a large scale for a larger national market seemed to offer the best hopes of a good profit.
   b. The new labor-saving machines and technological processes lowered production costs, but these machines were too expensive for the small local businessman to buy.
   c. By the 1890s corporations produced nearly three fourths of the total value of manufactured products in the United States.

MATERIALS:
Text—*The Making of Modern America.*

ASSIGNMENT: for tomorrow answer:
1. What are the chief features of the corporation? What are its advantages over other forms of business organizations?
2. How does the ownership of a corporation differ from its control and management?
3. Why did corporations grow rapidly after 1865? What happened to many small businesses? Why did the number of companies manufacturing a particular product decrease?

Answers can be found in todays notes and in text (pp. 368–372)
Ask students to begin thinking on a choice of an industrial tycoon (e.g., Carnegie, Rockefeller, and so on) or an industry (its development) for group reports.

Lesson Plan 4

Business English

OBJECTIVE:
The students will be able to use the telephone properly through the application of speech principles learned in the last two lessons.

CONTENT:
Working with the teletraining unit while the class uses evaluation sheets for criticisms of the participants.

PROCEDURE:
1. Outline for oral speeches (book reports) for next lesson written on chalkboard for all to copy.
2. Give a brief explanation of how the teletraining unit works.
3. Choose three students work the unit.
4. Distribute evaluation sheets to class.
5. Present a situation and let them make their own conversation.
6. Have the class evaluate and criticize (using evaluation sheets as a base) .

7. Present a situation from the workbook and let the students proceed according to the directions in the book.
8. Repeat step #6, using different situations each time, and new students.

MATERIALS:
1. Teletraining unit from Bell Telephone Co. (two phones, amplification unit, controls).
2. Ditto sheets for evaluation.
3. Teletraining workbook.

ASSIGNMENT:
Prepare oral book reports according to outline.

OUTLINE FOR BOOK REPORT

Enclosure 1

to Lesson Plan 4

FICTION:
1. Title of book
2. Author of book
3. State the author's purpose in writing the book (theme)
4. What is the prevailing mood of the book?—humor, sadness, despair, whimsy, etc. How does the author create and maintain this mood? (events, characters, etc.)
5. Give your frank criticism of the book, including reasons for your statements.

NONFICTION:
1. Title of book
2. Author of book
3. What topic does the author discuss? (science, adventure, biography, politics, etc.) Give examples from your book of what portion of the topic is discussed.
4. What is the author's purpose in writing the book? (what does he wish to tell us?)
5. Give your frank criticism of the book, including reasons for your statements.

N.B.
Be sure to include an original, arresting beginning and a strong, definite concluding statement.

Enclosure 2

to Lesson Plan 4

SPEECH EVALUATION CHART

Your Name and Section: _____ Date: _____

Names of Students: _____ And _____

	EXCELLENT	GOOD	FAIR	POOR	FAILING	COMMENTS
General attitude						
Voice (includes breath control, pitch, & steadiness)						
Articulation (pronunciation)						

Names of Students: _____ And _____

	EXCELLENT	GOOD	FAIR	POOR	FAILING	COMMENTS
General attitude						
Voice						
Articulation						

Lesson Plan 5

*Algebra I, Grade 9,
Modern Program of
Mathematics,
Accelerated Group*

OBJECTIVES:
1. The students should acquire the skill of finding the product of the sum of two variables, such as, x, y, and the difference of the variables, x, y. [$(x + y)\ (x - y) = (x - y)\ (x + y) = x^2 - y^2$].
2. They should also be able to recognize that $(x + y)$ and $(x - y)$ are the factors of $(x^2 - y^2)$. [$x^2 - y^2 = (x + y)\ (x - y) = (x - y)\ (x + y)$]

PROCEDURE:

Part I (Objective: By paper folding, acquire a rectangle whose dimensions are $(x + y)$ and $(x - y)$ and which is divided into two rectangles whose areas are easily calculated and add up to the desired solution (product).

1. Initiate the lesson by presenting the problem, $(x + y)(x - y) = ?$, and explain that they are going to discover the solution with your guidance and by using a rectangular piece of paper. (It would be possible to have students participate in the demonstration by working at their seats with a piece of looseleaf paper.)

2. Label rectangle A, B, C, D and let the dimensions be (x) and $(x + y)$ [Figure 1]

3. Next determine (y), by folding the upper left-hand vertex (A) down to the bottom edge (DC). Label points (E) and (F). Fold along (EF). [Figure 2]

4. Explain since $AD = DA = x$, that $DC = x + y$ and since $DC - DA = AC$, that $AC = y$. $[(x + y) - \alpha = y]$

5. Unfold paper so that original shape is assumed.

6. Ask what the dimensions of $ADEF$ are, what type of figure it is, and what the dimensions of $EBCF$ are. [Figure 3]

7. Next fold upper right-hand vertex B to fold line EF. Label S. Fold LS. [Figure 4]

8. Unfold paper and label all dimensions of the resulting figure. [Figure 5] Label rectangles with single letters G, H, I, J.

9. Point out that the rectangle composed of G and H has the dimensions $(x + y)$ and $(x - y)$ and that the area would be the solution we are looking for.

10. Show that if we find the areas of rectangles G and H and add them this will lead to the area of the rectangle composed of G and H.
    $\left. \begin{array}{l} \text{Area of } G = x(x - y) = x^2 - xy \\ \text{Area of } H = (x - y)y = xy - y^2 \end{array} \right\}$ by distributive property
    $x^2 - xy + xy - y^2 = x^2 - y^2$ (the solution product)
    $\therefore (x + y)(x - y) = x^2 - y^2$

11. Using rectangles G, H, and J, show that $(x^2 - y^2) = (x + y)(x - y)$ or that the whole rectangle (composed of G, H, and J and having dimensions $= x \cdot x$) minus rectangle J (dimensions $= y \cdot y$) leaves you with rectangles G and H which can be rearranged to form a rectangle with dimensions $(x + y) + (x - y)$. [Figure 6]
    $\therefore (x^2 - y^2) = (x + y)(x - y)$ or the factors of $(x^2 - y^2) = (x + y)(x - y)$.

Part II. Objective: To learn the algebraic technique of solving $(x + y)(x - y)$. Let students give reasons for each step.

1. Show by the distributive property that
    $(x + y)(x - y) = (x + y)x - (x + y)y$
    $\qquad\qquad\qquad = x \cdot x + y \cdot x - (x \cdot y + y \cdot y)$

2. Show by closure that now $(x + y)(x - y) = x^2 + yx - (xy + y^2)$

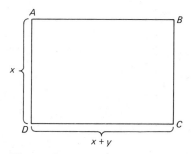

Figure 1

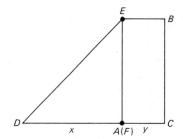

Figure 2

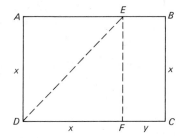

Figure 3

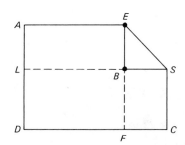

Figure 4

Lesson Plan 5 (*Cont.*)

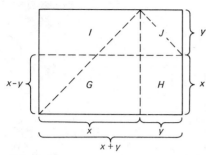

Figure 5

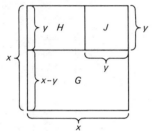

Figure 6

3. By the distributive property

$(x + y)(x - y) = x^2 + yx - xy - y^2$

4. $\qquad\qquad = x^2 + xy - xy - y^2$—by the commutative property of multiplication

5. $\qquad\qquad = x^2 + 0 - y^2$ — property of additive inverses

6. $\qquad\qquad = x^2 - y^2$ — property of additive identity
$\qquad\qquad\qquad\qquad (0)$

7. ∴ $(x + y)(x - y) = x^2 - y^2$

8. $\qquad (x - y)(x + y) = x - y^2$ —by commutative property of multiplication

9. Ask what property allows us to say that $x^2 - y^2 = (x + y)(x - y)$
Answer: Symmetric property of equality.

10. Ask for definitions of product and factor and stress.

11. Solve the following problems with class participation.
a) $(4 + y)(4 - y) = 16 - y^2$; b) $(x - 5)(x + 5) = x^2 - 25$;
c) $x^2 - 64 = (x + 8)(x - 8)$

MATERIALS:

1. Rectangular sheet of paper (backed with sandpaper).
2. Scissors.
3. Felt Pen.
4. Flannel Board.
$\qquad\qquad\qquad\qquad\qquad\qquad\qquad\qquad (3)\ (3)\quad (2)$
5. Cards with letters, $A,\ B,\ C,\ D,\ E,\ F,\ G,\ H,\ I,\ J,\ L,\ S,\ x,\ y,\ (x - y)$, $(x + y)$ all backed with sandpaper.

NOTES:

1. If students work with paper folding at their seats, suggest that they only label dimensions.
2. If there is additional time, work out
$(x + 2)(x - 2) = x^2 - 4$
$\qquad x^2 - 9 = (x + 3)(x - 3)$

ASSIGNMENT:

Five problems covering lesson product.

TIME ALLOTMENT:

10 min. — Homework review
30 min. — Present new material
 5 min. — Supervised study

Lesson Plan 6

Plane Geometry *

OBJECTIVE: To develop a method for proving
1. A ray to be the bisector of an angle.
2. A point to be the midpoint of a line segment.

3. A line to be the bisector of a line segment.
4. Similar conclusions that are an outgrowth of the congruence of triangles.

TEXT: Geometry—A Contemporary Course, pages 222–224.
(Background of students: The students are familiar with the method for proving triangles congruent through the use of the ASA and SAS postulates. They have also been taught how to prove line segments congruent and angles congruent by using the reverse of the definition of congruent polygons.)

PROCEDURE:
1. The following questions are designed to point up the information that the students already have that is a prerequisite for understanding the topic that is to be developed in this lesson.
    a. *Teacher:* "I wonder if one of you would summarize the nature of the material we have been exploring over the past few days?" *Ans.:* "We have been proving line segments congruent, and we have been proving angles congruent."
    b. *Teacher:* "Just what have we been using as a basis to conclude that a pair of angles are congruent?" *Ans.:* "We have been showing that these angles are corresponding parts of congruent triangles."
    c. *Teacher:* "Why are we in a position to say that two angles will be congruent if they are corresponding parts of congruent triangles?" *Ans.:* "The reverse of the definition of congruent polygons permits us to draw this conclusion."
    b. *Teacher:* "Hence, in general then, if we are asked to prove that a pair of line segments are congruent or a pair of angles are congruent, what will probably be our method of attack?" *Ans.:* "We will find a pair of triangles that contain these parts as corresponding parts and then try to prove those triangles to be congruent."
2. All of the preceding material is by way of review and the language used by the students in their responses should be by this stage of the work as mature as that noted in the answers given.
3. *Teacher:* "I would like to explore something with you today that is just a bit different from what we have been doing over the past few days. For instance, consider this situation in which we are asked to prove that AD is the bisector of $\angle BAC$." While talking, the teacher with the aid of a straightedge draws the accompanying figure and writes the following Given Data and Conclusion.

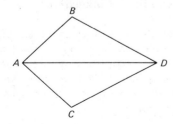

Given: $\overrightarrow{DA}$ bisects $\angle BCD$
$DB = DC$

Conclusion: $\overrightarrow{AD}$ bisects $\angle BAC$

* Courtesy of Prof. Harry Lewis, Secondary Education Department, Jersey City State College. The lesson illustrates the Guided Discovery Approach to the Teaching of Mathematics. Ordinarily the answers would not be spelled out in the lesson plan. They are included here only to illustrate the type of answer expected .

a. *Teacher:* "In searching for the proof to a problem such as this, what should be the *very first thing* we must examine?" *Ans.:* "The conclusion."

b. *Teacher:* "From what standpoint do we examine the conclusion?" *Ans.:* "We mentally try to come up with all the ways we have for proving a ray to be the bisector of an angle."

c. *Teacher:* "Well, how many ways do we have at our disposal for proving a ray to be the bisector of an angle?" *Ans.:* "Just one, the reverse of the definition of the bisector of an angle."

d. *Teacher:* "What does this imply we will have to prove before we can show that a ray is the bisector of an angle?" *Ans.:* "That the ray forms two congruent angles with the sides of the angle."

e. *Teacher:* "Then, in terms of the letters in our diagram, exactly what will have to be shown to be true before we can conclude that $\overrightarrow{AD}$ is the bisector of $\angle BAC$?" *Ans.:* "That $\angle BAD$ is congruent to $\angle CAD$."

f. *Teacher:* "Just what would you suggest we do in order to prove that these two angles are congruent?" *Ans.:* "Try to prove that $\triangle BAD$ is congruent to $\triangle CAD$."

g. (Now the teacher attempts to reverse the direction of the thinking of the students.) "Assuming that the two triangles can be shown to be congruent, what will follow?" *Ans.:* "$\angle BAD$ will be congruent to $\angle CAD$."

h. *Teacher:* "And on this information, what conclusion will we be able to draw?" *Ans.:* "That $\overrightarrow{AD}$ is the bisector of $\angle BAC$."

i. *Teacher:* "In view of our analysis, basically, what does the proof of this problem depend upon?" *Ans.:* "Proving two triangles to be congruent." *Teacher:* "And this we have done many times over during the past few weeks!"

j. *Teacher:* "Incidentally, why is it that we do not merely prove the triangles to be congruent and then simply say that $\overrightarrow{AD}$ is the bisector of $\angle BAC$ as a consequence of this?" (The teacher through this question is trying to anticipate and ward off an error frequently made by students during this unit of the course.) *Ans.:* "The information that triangles are congruent merely leads to pairs of congruent angles or pairs of congruent line segments and nothing else. The fact that triangles are congruent does not immediately imply that a ray is the bisector of an angle."

4. At this point the teacher asks for a volunteer (or possibly he simply calls on one of the brighter students in the class) to go to the board to give a formal proof of the problem. At the completion of the proof (which is given orally) the teacher returns to the front of the room and asks the following questions, calling on only the average or below average students in the class for the answers:

a. "In developing her proof, Dorothy stated that $\overline{DB}$ is congruent to $\overline{DC}$. How did she know this?"

b. "I notice that she has marked the diagram in such a way as to imply that $\angle BDA$ is congruent to $\angle CDA$. What enables her to do this?"

c. "What remaining parts of the two triangles did she have to prove congruent before she could conclude that the two triangles were congruent? What theorem, postulate, or definition permitted her to conclude that $\overline{AD}$ is congruent to $\overline{AD}$? Is the statement you have just given a definition, a postulate, or a theorem? (The purpose of this question is to keep alive the knowledge of the distinction between these basic elements. It is pursued no further than this in order not to distract the students' attention away from the major objective of the lesson.)

d. "Why did Dorothy want to prove these two triangles to be congruent?"

e. "Now that the triangles are congruent, what will follow?"

f. "And where does the fact that $\angle BAD$ is congruent to $\angle CAD$ lead us?"

5. *Teacher:* "There are other situations that are very much the same as the one we have just examined. As an illustration, consider the situation here (at this point the teacher makes a freehand drawing of the following figure). Suppose we are called upon to prove that B is the midpoint of $\overline{AC,}$ how would you suggest proceeding?" *Ans.:* "Prove that $\overline{AB}$ is congruent to $\overline{CB}$."

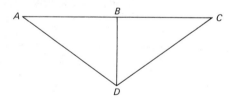

a. *Teacher:* "What would you probably have to do in order to arrive at this conclusion?" *Ans.:* "We would probably have to prove $\triangle DBC$ congruent to $\triangle DBA$."

b. *Teacher:* "Hence, here again, what seems to be our method of attack?" *Ans.:* "Prove a pair of triangles to be congruent. This leads to a pair of line segments being congruent and, in turn, this leads to a point as the midpoint of a line segment."

c. *Teacher:* "Let's consider that the conclusion we are asked to reach is that $\overleftrightarrow{DB}$ is the bisector of $\overline{AC}$ rather than that B is the midpoint of $\overline{AC}$. In what way will the attack just outlined have to be altered?" *Ans.:* "It would not have to be altered at all." *Teacher:* "Justify that." *Ans.:* "Well, to prove a point to be the midpoint of a line segment we have to prove two line segments to be congruent and to

Lesson Plan 6 (*Cont.*)

prove a line to be the bisector of a line segment we have to do the same." *Teacher:* "Is there any part of the write-up of the proof that will have to be altered?" *Ans.:* "Yes, the last 'Reason.' Rather than being the reverse of the definition of the midpoint of a line segment, it will be the reverse of the definition of the bisector of a line segment."

6. *Teacher:* "Let's all of us open our texts to page 223 and examine Exercise 1." (This exercise is very much the same as the first illustration developed with the students.)

a. The teacher now calls upon only the average or below average members of the class to answer the following questions:

1) What is the first thing you will examine in Exercise 1, John? In order to prove that $\overrightarrow{DB}$ bisects $\angle ADC$, what will you have to show to be true, Mary? How would you suggest that $\angle ABD$ is congruent to $\angle CDB$, James? What ways do we have for proving triangles congruent, Bill? Let's look at the Given Data for a moment. Which of the two ways of proving triangles will probably be applied in this situation, Eleanor? What makes you think that this is so? Once the triangles are proved to be conguent, what will follow, Henry? What reason would you write for that conclusion, Paul? What follows from the fact that those are congruent, Judith? And, finally, why can this conclusion be drawn, Ann?

2) (Notice that the students were not given the opportunity to volunteer but rather they were called upon at the teacher's discretion. The purpose of this was to try to make certain than even the slowest members of the class were familiar with the concepts that had been developed earlier in the period.)

b. Exercise 3 is examined in exactly the same manner as Exercise 1 had been.

HOMEWORK: If at all possible, this should be begun in class. Pages 223 and 224: Exercises 1, 2, 3, 7, and 9.

Lesson Plan 7

Geography

OBJECTIVE: (Concept to Be Learned)
The earth's grid is used for locating places on maps.

PROCEDURE:
1. Distribute globes.
2. a. What is a *grid?* Some examples?
    Ans.: Anything marked with *parallel* lines (draw grid on board).

b. What does parallel mean?

Ans.: Anything equally distant, as one line to another.

c. Examples:

Football field.

Patterns.

Lined paper, graph paper.

Crossing zone.

d. Point out something in the classroom that is a grid.

3. Can a grid be used in relation to the earth? How?

Ans.: Yes, it can be used to locate positions on the earth's surface.

4. What constitutes the earth's grid? Four things. How are they represented on a globe or map?

Write on board

a. *North and South Poles*—starting points, ends of axis on which the earth rotates (have students locate these and the following on their globes).

b. *Equator*—great circle considered to pass around the earth halfway between the poles.

c. *Parallels of Latitude*—smaller circles which are parallel to equator and mark off the *angular* distance in degrees north and between the poles and the equator.

d. *Meridians of Longitude*—great circles *perpendicular* to the equator and parallels which intersect each other at the poles. Measure distances east or west of an arbitrarily chosen starting line. (Demonstrate on board a perpendicular line and intersecting lines.)

5. Review all terms by having students relate them from globes to wall map.

6. We said that the earth's grid is used to locate positions on the earth's surface. How is this done?

Ans.: through units of measurement called *degrees*:

a. 1 = 1/360 of a circle.

b. Equator = 0.

c. North Pole = 90 N.

d. South Pole = 90 S.

e. Prime Meridian = Greenwich.

f. 180th Meridian = Pacific Ocean.

(Demonstrate all on board.)

7. Locate longitude and latitude of places in text, p. 86.

MATERIALS:

Globes.

World map—wall.

Pointer.

Text, manual.

NOTES: None.

Lesson Plan 7 (*Cont.*)

ASSIGNMENT:
Complete unfinished longitude and latitude problems on page 86 in text. Also prepare a grid for tomorrow's lesson on maps. Do this on white construction paper and make parallel lines 1″ apart from each other (give example on board). If any questions tonight, see sample grid on page 89 in text. Be sure to bring rulers and pencils to class tomorrow.

SUMMARY

Every lesson needs a plan. The essentials of a daily lesson plan are the objectives, the subject matter, the activities, the list of materials needed, the assignment, and any special notes. These essentials tell us what to do and how to do it. The format a teacher uses for his lesson plan is not so very important as long as the plan is clear and easy to follow. Sometimes daily lesson plans used in conjunction with units need not be very detailed. The important thing is to know what it is we wish to teach in the lesson and to provide activities that lead to these goals. One test of a lesson plan is to ask how each activity in the procedure will help to bring about the desired goal. Once the teacher has decided on his plan of action, he would be wise to keep to that plan unless there seem to be important reasons for changing course.

Suggested Readings for Part III

ALCORN, MARVIN D., JAMES S. KINDER, AND JIM R. SCHUNERT, *Better Teaching in Secondary Schools*, 3rd ed. New York: Holt, Rinehart and Winston, Publishers, 1970. Chs. 4–6.

ALDRICH, JULIAN C., *How to Construct and Use a Resource Unit*. New York: Joint Council on Economic Education, n.d.

ARMSTRONG, ROBERT J., et al., *The Development and Evaluation of Behavioral Objectives*. Belmont, Calif.: Wadsworth Publishing Co. Inc., 1970.

BLOOM, BENJAMIN S., et al., *Taxonomy of Educational Objectives, The Classification of Educational Goals, Handbook I: Cognitive Domain*. New York: David McKay Co., Inc., 1956.

CALLAHAN, STERLING G., *Successful Teaching in Secondary Schools*, rev. ed. Glenview, Ill.: Scott Foresman and Company, 1971. Chs. 3–8.

CLARK, D. CECIL, *Using Instructional Objectives in Teaching*. Glenview, Ill.: Scott Foresman and Company, 1972.

GAYLES, ANNE R., *Instructional Planning in the Secondary School*. New York: David McKay Co., Inc., 1973.

GRAMBS, JEAN D., JOHN C. CARR, AND ROBERT M. FITCH, *Modern Methods in Secondary Education*, 3rd ed. New York: Holt, Rinehart and Winston, Publishers, 1970. Ch. 8.

GRONLUND, NORMAN E., *Stating Behavioral Objectives for Classroom Instruction*. New York: Macmillan Publishing Co., Inc., 1970.

HARROW, ANITA J., *A Taxonomy of the Psychomotor Domain: A Guide for Developing Behavioral Objectives*. New York: David McKay Co., Inc., 1972.

HOOVER, KENNETH H., *The Professional Teacher's Handbook*. Boston: Allyn & Bacon, Inc., 1973. Chs. 2 and 3.

KIBLER, ROBERT J., LARRY L. BARKER, AND DAVID T. MILES, *Behavioral Objectives and Instruction*. Boston: Allyn & Bacon, Inc., 1970.

KIBLER, ROBERT J., DONALD J. CEGALA, LARRY L. BARKER, AND DAVID T. MILES, *Objectives for Instruction and Evaluation*. Boston: Allyn & Bacon, Inc., 1974.

KRATHWOHL, DAVID R., BENJAMIN S. BLOOM, AND BERTRAM B. MASIA, *Taxonomy of Educational Objectives, Handbook II: The Affective Domain*. New York: David McKay Co., Inc., 1964.

MAGER, ROBERT F., *Preparing Instructional Objectives*. Palo Alto, Calif.: Fearon Publishers, 1962.

McASHAN, H. H., *Writing Behavioral Objectives*. New York: Harper & Row, Publishers, 1970.

NOAR, GERTRUDE, *Teaching and Learning the Democratic Way*. Englewood Cliffs, N.J.: Prentice-Hall, Inc., 1963.

PARRISH, LOUISE, AND YVONNE WASKIN, *Teacher-Pupil Planning*. New York: Harper & Row, Publishers, 1958.

PLOWMAN, PAUL D., *Behavioral Objectives*. Chicago: Science Research Associates Inc., 1971.

POPHAM, W. JAMES, AND EVA L. BAKER, *Establishing Instructional Objectives*. Englewood Cliffs, N.J.: Prentice-Hall Inc., 1970.

———, *Planning an Instructional Sequence*. Englewood Cliffs, N.J.: Prentice-Hall, Inc., 1970.

———, *Systematic Instruction*. Englewood Cliffs, N.J.: Prentice-Hall, Inc., 1970.

SAMALONIS, BERNICE L., *Methods and Materials for Today's High Schools*. New York: Van Nostrand Reinhold Company, 1970. Chs. 1–5.

TANNER, DANIEL, *Using Behavioral Objectives in the Classroom*. New York: Macmillan Publishing Co., Inc., 1972.

VARGAS, JULIE S., *Writing Worthwhile Behavioral Objectives*. New York: Harper & Row, Publishers, 1972.

ZAPF, ROSALIND M., *Democratic Processes in the Secondary Classroom*. Englewood Cliffs, N.J.: Prentice-Hall, Inc., 1959. Chs. 4–6.

IV

Providing
for Pupil
Differences

Provisions for Individual Differences

8

A Description of Two Boys

Pete and Steve are tenth-graders in the same English class. Each of them lives in the same neighborhood, has approximately the same socio-economic status, is of Italian ancestry, and belongs to the same church. Yet they are completely different individuals.

Pete is a tall, thin boy. He looks as though he has not had a decent meal in a long time. His constant lack of energy seems to confirm this look. This may also explain his complete lack of interest in sports of any kind. He is exceptionally interested in music and plays the piano well. In fact, for the past few months he has been playing dinner music at a downtown restaurant as one of a trio. He is talented in other ways also. His I.Q. shows him to be well into the genius class. Yet his classwork is very poor; he does little or nothing in school. For several weeks he has not turned in a respectable paper. He has read few, if any, of the stories assigned in the study of the present topic—short stories. Still, he seems to have read recently many of the current best sellers and a quite a number of biographical works and popularized histories. Works having to do with politics and politicians seem to have a special appeal to him. He takes part in no school activities of any sort other than those assigned in class. He has few friends and keeps pretty well to himself, perhaps because he is inclined to give himself airs and to poke fun at the efforts of the other kids. In spite of an air of sophistication one gets the impression that this is an unhappy youngster whose many talents are going to waste.

Steve is about medium height and inclined to be a trifle stocky. His skin is dark and from time to time breaks out in a rash of pimples which annoys him somewhat. In the past he has been the victim of a serious speech defect. He still stammers badly at times, but his parents have been sending him to a local speech therapist who has helped him greatly. In spite of his disability Steve is one of the most popular boys in school and something of a ladies' man. He is president of his class and active in a myriad of other activities. His real hobby is sports, although he is not especially good at them. Still, he is captain of his intramural basketball team. His lack of skill is made up for, at least in part, by his aggressiveness. He is about the scrappiest player in the league. He is one of the varsity team's most ardent supporters. Probably he will be the varsity manager in his senior year, since he is leading all present contenders for that position.

Steve's great virtue, from the teacher's point of view, is his dependability. Rarely does he miss an assignment. Although he is only slightly better than average intellectually, he consistently does better than average, if not outstanding, work. His regular reading consists of popular magazines and the newspaper. Sometimes you may find him engrossed in a book of science, *Popular Science,* or a work of science fiction. Science is his best subject and we hear that at home he spends considerable time fooling around with a science hobby kit.

These two boys are individuals. Their personalities differ in many ways. The competent teacher tries to adapt his teaching so as to turn these differences to his advantage whenever possible.

*

Would you think it wise to try to teach both these boys the same material in the same way? In what ways,

if any, would you differentiate your teaching for them?

*

Individual Differences

Individuals differ in a multitude of ways—in physical makeup, in interests, in ability, in aptitude, in home background, in experience, in prior training, in social skill, in ideals, in attitudes, in needs, in vocational goals, and so on ad infinitum. This is an inescapable fact of human nature—a fact fraught with profound implications for the teacher. Because of these difficulties, to treat individuals as though everyone were alike simply will not work. Somehow, some way, teachers must adapt their teaching to individual differences.

Not only are pupils different, but each learns in his own way and at his own rate. No two persons ever learn exactly the same concepts from any learning situation. Nor do any two persons ever develop exactly the same method and degree of efficiency. Each individual's learning is shaped by his interests, his physical and psychic makeup, his past experiences, and his goals for the future and so differs from that of anyone else. Teachers should capitalize on these differences and make them a means of furthering learning.

*

Observe the members of your own class. In what ways do they seem similar? In what different?

If possible, visit a junior high school class or senior high school class. What evidence of individual differences do you find.

*

In other words, in so far as possible, schooling should be individualized. Curricula, courses, and lessons should be built in ways that allow pupils to adopt different goals, to study different content, to learn by different media and methods, to progress at different rates, and to be judged by different criteria—each in accordance with his own specific needs, ambitions, and talents.

All this seems to imply that much of the teaching in secondary schools should be laboratory teaching, that the pupils should share, at least in some measure, in determining what and how they will study, and that their success should be judged not by a single academic standard for all, but by the progress each pupil has made in view of the goals, content, media, and methods he has chosen.

Individualization of instruction of this type has much to recommend it. In addition to fitting the content and methods of teaching to the individual pupils, instruction *must* be individualized according to Keuscher, because of five "compelling reasons."

I. Philosophically it is consistent with the principles upon which our form of government, which spawned our educational system, is based.
II. The very nature of our democratic system and the way it functions demands knowledgeable, thinking participants.
III. Assembly line methods are tending to produce mass-produced, standardized citizens at the expense of individuality.
IV. As society grows increasingly complex there is a greater demand for a diversity of talents and skills.
V. It is probably the most efficient way to educate if one focuses on the product rather than just on the process.[1]

Most of the measures taken to provide for individual differences do not come up to the ideals that Keuscher implies. Individualization is not simply a matter of manipulating a certain body of content so that it is easier and simpler for some pupils and more difficult and complex for others. Neither is it a matter of giving certain pupils more or less of the same thing. Nor is it just a matter of making it possible for some pupils to progress more rapidly than others. Rather, in true individualization the emphasis is on the development of the individual to his fullest potential. The accent is not so much on the differences as it is on the development. Therefore individualized teaching goals and subject matter vary from individual to individual according to each one's needs, activities, and aspirations. Difficulty and speed are also considerations, to be sure, but the principal thrust should be on providing each individual with the curriculum best suited for him.

In this chapter we shall describe some of the procedures and devices that administrators and teachers use in their attempts to cope with the problems caused by individual differences and the need to individualize instruction.

*

A famous professor of education says, "We should not have a standard; we should have standards." What do you think he means? Is it advisable to require one pupil to do more or better work than another? How would you go about implementing the professor's statement?

*

ADMINISTRATIVE PROVISIONS FOR DIFFERENCES IN PUPILS

For a long time secondary school administrators have been trying, with rather indifferent success, to find answers for the instructional problems caused by individual differences. Most of the procedures that they have inaugurated to meet this problem have been based upon selecting or categorizing pupils. Recently, however, some schools have been moving toward attempting to provide for individual differences by making their curriculum organization flexible. Although none of these procedures or devices really solves the problem of individual pupil differences, they may reduce the scope of the problem somewhat by reducing the heterogeneity of the groups with which the teacher must deal.

Tracks, Streams, and Homogeneous Groups

To group pupils according to interest or ability is common practice in secondary and elementary schools both in the United States and abroad. American high schools usually offer several curricula based, supposedly, on the goals of the pupils. Thus we find a typical high school offering such varied curricula as college preparatory curricula for those pupils planning to go to college, secretarial curricula for girls planning to become office workers, vocational agriculture curricula for boys who plan to become farmers, home economics for girls planning to become housewives, and general curricula for pupils having no particular plans for the future.

The track or stream is another administrative device for reducing the range of heterogeneity in

[1] Robert E. Keuscher, "Why Individualize Instruction," in Virgil Howes, *Individualizing of Instruction* (New York: Macmillan Publishing Co., Inc., 1970), p. 7

classrooms. Usually tracks or streams are curricular sequences based upon pupils' ability in the area. Thus the mathematics program for a school might be divided into four tracks, the first for talented mathematic students, the second for ordinary college preparatory pupils, the third for noncollege preparatory pupils, and the fourth for slow learners.

HOMOGENEOUS GROUPING

Homogeneous groups are similar to tracks or streams except that they are not planned curricular sequences, but merely groupings of pupils made up for the year or term only. Although some homogeneous groups are based on homogeneity of interest or educational objectives and classes in such subjects as home economics, industrial arts, physical education, and biology may be grouped according to sex, most homogeneous groups are ability groups. By such grouping administrators hope to make it possible for teachers to teach more effectively and to adapt the curriculum to the varying needs of all the pupils.

Administrative grouping of pupils is not a direct responsibility of classroom teachers, but it does affect them and their teaching. The basic implication for the teacher is that he should differentiate his material and methods for the various groups so that he will be teaching the content best suited for each class in the way best suited for that class. Sometimes teachers find it frustrating to teach academic subject matter to slow groups. As a result they tend to blame their lack of success on the poorness of the group. Such a narrow view defeats the purpose of the ability grouping. Each teacher should try to adapt his teaching so that each pupil can learn to the best of his ability. Simply to water down the academic course for slower pupils or to cover it more slowly will not suffice. To make homogeneous grouping pay off the teacher must adjust both his content and his teaching methods to the abilities and interests of the various class members. Some comments on how to do this will follow in a later section.

One danger that comes from homogeneous grouping, tracking, and streaming is that the teacher may get the idea that the group is really homogeneous. It is not; no group of people is. All that can be done in grouping pupils is to reduce the range of one or another characteristic or group of associated characteristics. In a high-ability group the pupils may all be of relatively high ability, but they will differ in many other ways—in interests, in ambitions, in motivation, in goals, in personality, in aggressiveness, and so on. They even differ in intelligence and ability. Look at the IQ range of the pupils of a "good" college preparatory class in a New Jersey high school listed in Table 8–1. Although there is some doubt about the validity and meaning of IQ scores, these scores indicate that the range of intelligence in this "good" class extends from slightly above normal to very bright. Ergo, teachers who teach ability-grouped classes have problems of providing for individual differences just as other teachers do.

OBJECTIONS TO TRACKING AND GROUPING

Some teachers seriously object to tracking and homogeneous grouping because they believe them to be undemocratic. This objection probably stems from a misunderstanding of the principle that "everyone is created free and equal." These critics seem to believe that by placing pupils into homogeneous groups we are depriving them of their rights of equal treatment. However, the democratic concept is that everyone has an equal opportunity to make the most of his talents. The truly demo-

Table 8–1

IQ's of Homogeneous College Preparatory Tenth-Grade Class

James	136	David	125
Craig	135	Gerald	124
Charlene	135	Peggy	124
Sally	134	Bruce	123
Michelle	133	Jim	123
Judy	133	Margaret	123
Susan	131	Richard	122
Steve	130	Betty	121
Prudence	130	Christine	120
Tim	128	Guy	119
Gail	128	George	118
Joan	126	Wayne	116
Joanna	126	Neil	109

cratic teacher recognizes the differences in individuals and tries to make the most of them.

Theoretically, homogeneous grouping should make it easier for the teacher to accomplish this task. In practice, however, all too often homogeneous grouping, which is usually ability grouping, results in the short changing of the less academically inclined pupils who are only suffered rather than taught. Such classes for "slow pupils" may have a deleterious effect on the pupils' personalities. The pupils learn that they are not as good as other people. Consequently their levels of aspiration become low. They do not try because they know that teachers do not expect much from them. So we find that the pupils who need most to be challenged to try their best are not challenged at all. Furthermore, they are deprived of the help and example of their more successful peers. Pupils learn from each other. The nonacademically inclined pupils profit intellectually from being with the academically inclined; the academically inclined can profit socially and sometimes intellectually from being with the nonacademically inclined. Ability groups tend to be stifling.

Mini-courses

Many schools are introducing mini-courses in order to give pupils more opportunities to find course offerings suitable to their needs and interests than they can find in the standard curriculum. Mini-courses are short courses; they may be anywhere from a few weeks to a full quarter term in length and sometimes are not given for credit. Many require much pupil participation in the planning. Otherwise the preparation of a mini-course is similar to that of any other course. Of course, for mini-courses to be really valuable as tools for individualizing instruction, there should be a large enough choice of courses to allow pupils to find congenial courses.

*

How could one prevent a caste system from developing as a result of homogeneous grouping of class sections throughout the school?

Examine a high school honors class. What range interests, abilities, life goals, and academic backgrounds do you find?

Examine a mini-course program. In what ways does it provide for individual differences that a traditional program cannot? Or does it?

*

Other Administrative Techniques

In addition to plans involving grouping, administrators utilize varying promotion schemes to provide for individual differences. In some school systems pupils can move through grades seven to twelve in five years and spend the year saved at college or doing college work in the high school. Such acceleration is quite common although not all school administrators accept it as desirable. Also quite common is the old practice of making pupils who fail repeat a grade or course. In the past some administrators have tried to lessen the sting of failure by promoting every half year. Recently there has been a movement toward continuous promotion in ungraded schools. Basically, continuous promotion plans consist of dividing the course work of the curriculum into short steps, levels, or modules, and allowing the pupil to advance from step to step as he is ready. Similarly a number of plans to make the secondary school day more flexible have been introduced during the last decade or so. Some of these give a large portion of the school day over to independent study. Learning centers to which pupils may go to study independently under guidance have become quite common in some areas. In many schools the introduction of teacher aides has made it easier to provide guidance for independent and individualized study. The use of aides in these schools relieves the teachers from some of the busy work so that they can give more time to working with small groups and individuals. Among the ways aides can be used to good advantage in the individualizing of instruction are (1) to help pupils as they practice, (2) to help pupils with seat work, (3) to help with follow-up, (4) to tutor individuals, and (5) to supervise and guide small groups.[2] Undoubtedly all of these plans have merit. They should make providing for the differences in individual pupils easier and more effective. But they will not relieve the teacher of his responsibility of

2 Gertrude Noar, *Individualized Instruction* (New York: John Wiley and Sons, Inc., 1972), pp. 66–67.

providing for individual differences within his classes.

Providing for Differences Within the Classroom

In the ensuing pages we shall attempt to indicate some ways in which teachers can take advantage of individual differences within the classroom and make the instruction more profitable. This discussion is predicated on the assumption that adequate provisions for individual differences must be based upon thorough knowledge of the abilities, interests, ambitions, problems, and other characteristics of the pupil outlined in foregoing chapters.

DIFFERENTIATING THE ASSIGNMENT

The Differentiated Assignment

The first instructional procedure for coping with the problem of individual differences is the differentiated assignment. An assignment consists of activities laid out for the pupils to do. A differentiated assignment is a class assignment that allows different pupils to do different things during the time covered by the assignment. Many types of these assignments can be made. Ordinarily, the differentiated assignment is long, covering a period of several weeks. However, it can also be very short.

DIFFERENTIATING THE LENGTH OR DIFFICULTY OF THE ASSIGNMENT

Teachers often arrange their assignments so that slow learners will not have to do quite as much as their more able colleagues. In the sample assignment in the following section the teacher attempted to do this by assigning group 3, the fast group, considerably more work than group 1, the slow group. In a mathematics class he might have assigned five problems to the slow pupils, eight problems to the average pupils, and ten problems to the fast pupils. In the sample assignment the work assigned to the groups also varies in difficulty. Group 3 is reading in what the teacher considers a "hard" eighth-grade book; group 2, an "easy" eighth-grade book; and group 1, a sixth-grade book. All are studying about the same thing but at different levels of difficulty. In a mathematics class the teacher could have assigned more difficult problems to the better pupils. In actual practice many teachers vary both the amount and difficulty, as in the sample assignment.

DIFFERENTIATING THE TYPE OF WORK

Not only the amount but the type of work should vary from pupil to pupil. The pupil who thinks best with his hands should be allowed to create with them. The bright pupil should be encouraged to undertake minor research problems. Pupils who are interested might become specialists and keep the class up-to-date on the stock market or on the situation in the Middle East. Artistically inclined pupils might form a committee to keep the bulletin board attractive and persuasive. Scientifically minded students might be given different reading assignments from literary types. Thus, by varying the type as well as the amount of work, the teacher can provide tasks suited to the pupils' abilities and interests. The skillful teacher, by capitalizing on the pupil's interest and ability, may be able to enlist his enthusiastic cooperation and encourage him to learning unheard of in dull, humdrum, lockstep classes.

In every class there are pupils who have unique abilities which can make the class profitable and enjoyable. Each should be encouraged to make his special contribution. It may be that the socially promoted boy who reads at an abysmally low level can and will, if encouraged, draw illustrations for the novel that is being read, or build a setting for a dramatization for part of the plot. Another youngster or group of youngsters more literarily inclined might write the script for the dramatization. Pupils who are neither artistic nor literary might be the actors. Everyone should contribute. If pupils are encouraged to participate after their own fashion, then the class will be fuller and more meaningful and learning will be more likely to go on apace.

In order to capitalize on such different abilities and interests, the teacher should not only allow pupils to engage in different sorts of learning activity, but he should also accept different signs of growth, including different means of expression, when estimating and evaluating the academic progress of pupils.

For example, not everyone needs to express his understanding of the antebellum South by writing essays and answering questions about it. Many other media are available. Talented youngsters might produce illustrations of life in the South; a boy interested in mechanical drawing might draw a layout of a plantation; a girl interested in homemaking might investigate the menus of the era, or run up a costume appropriate to the period; a young engineer might construct a cotton gin; a young choreographer might score and dance a ballet in the *Gone with the Wind* motif; a poet might contribute some lyric poetry, perhaps an ode or two.

Also pupils with special interests might read and investigate in their fields of interest. In a science class the musically inclined might want to investigate why different tones result when varying lengths of catgut are scraped by horsehair, or why lightly scraping the strings of a violin can make a sound that can be heard all over the concert hall. In a mathematics class a pupil interested in design might solve problems having to do with the mathematics of design.

The teacher who would make the most of the potential of any class must permit boys and girls to learn through various media and evaluate their academic success on the basis of the growth and progress they exhibit through these media. Certainly a pupil who contributes by performing a well-conceived and executed original dance number deserves to be recognized more than a pupil who does a miserably sloppy research paper. The possibilities are limited only by the media available and the various talents of the pupils. However, the teacher must guard against the danger of encouraging boys and girls to participate in activities which in no way contribute to significant learning. If a boy or girl is to spend considerable time creating a dance in connection with the study of the antebellum South, that activity should result in real learning about the South. If it does not, that activity has no place in that classroom. One should not expect the learning to be identical with that of a pupil who constructed a cotton gin, however.

A SAMPLE SHORT DIFFERENTIATED ASSIGNMENT

The following short differentiated assignment was prepared and used by a beginning teacher while teaching "The Westward Movement" in an eighth-grade American history class. In this class the teacher divided the pupils into three groups on the basis of their presumed ability. Note that in this assignment group 1 is reading *Your Country and Mine,* which the teacher considers to be at the sixth-grade reading level; group 2 is reading *Your Country's Story,* which he considers easy reading for eighth-graders; and group 3 is reading *This Is America's Story,* supposedly a difficult book for grade eight.

A SHORT DIFFERENTIATED ASSIGNMENT

GROUP 1

Reading Assignment *Your Country and Mine,* pages 36–41:

1. Form into assigned groups.
2. Select one member to serve on each committee:
   a. Bulletin Board
   b. *Who's Who in American History*
3. Choose one of the following assignments:
   a. Write a story about Daniel Boone.
   b. Draw a picture of Boonesborough in its early days.
   c. Draw a map showing how Daniel Boone got to Boonesborough (page 43).

GROUP 2

Reading Assignment *Your Country's Story,* pages 160–163:

1. Form into assigned groups.
2. Select one member for each of the following committees:
   a. Bulletin Board
   b. *Who's Who in American History*
3. Choose one of the following assignments:
   a. Make a report on the nature and characteristics of the Indians as seen by the early settlers in Kentucky and Tennessee.
   b. Make a map showing the different routes to the West.
   c. Write a report telling why the Ohio Valley was so attractive to early settlers.

GROUP 3

Reading Assignment *This Is America's Story,* pages 223–231:

1. Form into assigned groups.
2. Select one member for each committee:
   a. Bulletin Board
   b. *Who's Who in American History*
3. Choose one of the following assignments:
   a. Prepare a short report on the history of political parties in the United States.
   b. Make a report on Hamilton's policies in solving this country's financial problems.
   c. Write a short report explaining why Jefferson and Hamilton had different views on many things.
4. Answer completely Check-Up Questions 1–3 (page 227) and 1–4 (page 231).
5. Give a brief account of the Northwest Territory and of its importance in the development of the West.

---

*

In what ways has this beginning teacher attempted to differentiate the assignment? How successful do you think this assignment would be?

How would you go about preparing a differentiated assignment for a course in your major field?

*

Groups Within the Classroom

Teaching is usually easier when the range of differences among pupils in a group is kept relatively small. As we have seen, the range can be reduced by homogeneous groupings, that is, by putting pupils of similar abilities, interests, ambitions, or other attributes together. Just as school administrators use homogeneous groupings throughout entire schools, teachers can group their pupils homogeneously within their classes. This grouping can be accomplished in several ways, such as

1. Placing the slow achievers in one group, the average achievers in another, and the rapid achievers in a third.
2. Placing pupils into groups according to their interests.
3. Placing pupils with similar interests and similar goals together in a committee to solve a particular problem or to do some sort of research.
4. Placing pupils into groups according to special needs.

Certain critics have objected to the use of ability groups within the class for several reasons. Many experienced high school teachers claim that to teach more than one group in the same room is impossible or too difficult. Yet anyone who has watched a skillful teacher conduct a one-room school or a primary room knows that this is not so. Teaching several groups at once is hard work, but then, all good teaching is hard work. Actually, using groups is often easier than attempting to teach the unready something they cannot learn or the uninterested something they will not learn. In the small rural high schools of the Catskills and other areas, teachers experimenting with multigrade classes in which they teach pupils of two or more grade levels (e.g., Spanish I, II, & III) in the same classroom have found that they can teach multigrade classes fully as successfully as they can single classes.

As we have already seen, another serious objection is that ability grouping labels some pupils as inferior. Although the danger does exist, ability grouping within classes may not be as dangerous as one might expect. The pupils usually know where the strengths and weaknesses of their classmates lie and recognize which ones are good students, which ones hate to study, which ones are social butterflies, which ones are wallflowers, which ones are sports-oriented, and so on, and take these differences in their stride. When teachers place their emphasis on helping the pupils in the groups to learn more effectively, there is seldom any stigma attached to belonging to any one group.

Nevertheless, these dangers are real ones. We must not allow a caste system to develop in any classroom. The danger may be avoided by seeing to it that the membership of the groups changes from time to time, that many types of groups and committees are used so that the pupil is not always in the same group, and that the pupil has ample opportunities to work as an individual and as a member of the entire class. To divide the class into three or four ability groups and to keep these groups together constantly for an entire term is malpractice. Small groups or committees centered around interests or problem topics or needs are probably more satisfactory.[3]

---

[3] See Ch. 10 for information on teaching by means of committees and small groups.

*

If you were to divide your class into groups, what basis for grouping would you use? How would you go about grouping the class? How long would you keep the same groups?

*

INDIVIDUALIZING INSTRUCTION

The differentiated assignment does not really individualize instruction. It merely reduces the problem of individual differences somewhat. If instruction is to meet the needs of individual pupils, ways must be found for individualizing assignments and instruction. At first glance this task seems to be insuperably difficult, but on closer analysis it is not as overwhelming a task as one might fear.

Accelerating the Brilliant Pupil

One way to help the brilliant pupil make the most of his talent is to let him proceed through the course more rapidly than his classmates. In a certain Latin class the teacher arranged the classwork so that the brilliant pupils could do most of the work independently at their own speed without waiting for slower classmates to catch up. One brilliant girl completed one year's work early in April and was well into the next year's work by the end of June. The teacher had made this acceleration possible by preparing units for the entire year in advance. When the pupil had completed one unit, she went right on to the next one.

In such teaching, since the accelerated pupil will finish the regular course work before the end of the school year, the teacher needs to provide additional work for the pupil. In the example cited, the pupil went on to units in the next year's work. In other instances one might prefer that the pupil study more deeply certain aspects of the present course or aspects of the course ordinarily omitted because of lack of time.

Differentiating the Work Completely

At times it is desirable to assign to certain pupils work that is entirely different from that of the rest of the class. An example of this is the case of Pete, the brilliant youth described earlier in the chapter who had been doing such poor work in his English class. Upon examining the situation, the teacher realized that the boy was finding the assignments too easy. He was bored. To remedy this, the teacher excused the boy from the regular assignment and substituted one he himself had had in college. Rising to this bait, the boy accomplished this assignment in a fashion acceptable for any college introductory literature course. By substituting an entirely different assignment, the teacher was able to inspire this boy to do work well beyond the level of his grade. This is an excellent way to help a gifted youth. If a pupil is competent in grammar and knows to perfection the parts of speech the class is presently studying, he should be studying something else. Why not put him to work on a problem in literature, or something else worthwhile? It does not matter particularly what the pupil does as long as it results in valuable learning.

*

What practical problems arise from allowing a pupil to go on to the next year's work? How might these problems be minimized?

In the example cited above, the accelerated pupils worked individually almost entirely. Is this a good practice? How might one accelerate pupils in a class without making the work entirely individual?

*

Conducting the Class as a Laboratory

A profitable way to provide for individual differences is to conduct the class as a laboratory. It is this feature that makes the unit method such a good approach to solution of the problem of individual differences. Here the pupils can work on their various tasks individually or in small groups under the teacher's guidance. In such a laboratory a committee might be working in one corner of the room preparing a dramatization, in another corner another group might be preparing a report. At their desks individual pupils might be working on research projects. Others might be reading required or optional readings. In the rear of the class a pupil might be putting the finishing touches on a model to be presented and explained to the class. Around the teacher's desk another group might be working with the teacher in planning a group project.

As the pupils work at their tasks, the teacher helps and guides them. Among the many things he can do to help them are

1. Observe pupils to diagnose poor study habits.
2. Show pupils where to find information.
3. Show pupils how to use the tools of learning.
4. Clarify assignments.
5. Show the pupils how to get the meat out of their studying.
6. Help pupils form goals for study.
7. Help pupils summarize.
8. Point out errors and incorrect procedures.
9. Suggest methods for attacking problems.

Laboratory classes of this sort allow the freedom necessary for different pupils to work at a variety of tasks at speeds suitable for them. To a lesser degree supervised study periods in which the pupils work on their assignments under the teacher's supervision and guidance can provide the same freedom.

Individualized Instruction Schemes

Whether he uses the laboratory approach or not, each teacher must somehow find time to work separately with each pupil. This does not usually take as much time as one might think. Many pupils need a minimum of guidance. If they are provided with clear instructions they can often work alone for considerable periods.

SPECIAL HELP

The most common type of individualized instruction is the special help given to certain pupils. Teachers have always helped boys and girls who were having trouble with their studies through extra help after school, during conference periods, in study halls, and in class. No matter what method of teaching is used, the teacher will need to provide special help for some pupils.

Not only do pupils having trouble with their studies need special help; pupils who are doing well need it also. Everyone at times needs encouragement, criticism, discipline, correction, and inspiration. Taking time to look over a pupil's paper, to

compliment him on his progress, and to point out possible modes for improving it can be beneficial for both the most successful and the least successful of one's pupils.

Nevertheless, in spite of the value of special help, it alone cannot meet the demands of individual differences. Stronger measures are needed. Insofar as possible the teacher must provide individual instruction designed for the individuals to be instructed. Such provision can usually be made most easily within the framework of the classroom laboratory, the differentiated assignment, the unit approach, or the learning packet. In the following paragraphs we shall discuss some techniques that can be used for individual instruction within such plans.

SELF-INSTRUCTIONAL DEVICES

The availability of self-instructional devices and materials has made individualizing instruction in ordinary-size classes much easier than in the past. The most spectacular of these devices are the many different sorts of machines now on the market. Pupils of foreign languages practice pronunciation, pattern drills, and other aspects of the spoken language by means of the language laboratory which is really little more than an elaborate tape recorder or combination of tape recorders. In some schools it is possible for pupils studying different languages, or different levels of the same language, to use the language laboratory at the same time. There is no reason why similar procedures cannot be used in language laboratories for oral English exercises.

Even without language laboratories such teaching is feasible. If each pupil has a tape of his own, he can use the tape recorder to record his voice and compare it to models. Using this recording as a basis of diagnosis, the teacher can then assign the pupils individual tape recorder exercises designed to help the pupils hear and correct their faults. Such exercises can be done during class laboratory sessions, free periods, or after school—in fact at any time that the pupil and a tape recorder are free. In some schools individual exercises of this type are the medium of much instruction in oral English.

Tape recorders can also present other types of lessons to individuals or small groups. Before a class the teacher might dictate·to a machine a lesson with instructions for an indivdual. During the class the teacher can turn the pupil over to the tape recorder and its pretaped lesson for a time. In one instance the teacher has prepared a tape recording of an account of the religious life of primitive man. This tape also includes a short introduction to tell what the tape is about and to direct the pupil's attention to important pertinent points and a short follow-up to reemphasize these points. An individual pupil can put on the tape recorder earphones and go to work on this lesson without bothering anyone else in the class. Whenever he finds a point difficult, if he wishes, he can turn the tape back and replay the bothersome section without disrupting anyone else's progress.

Similar lessons have been worked out for use on eight-millimeter self-loading individual-viewing motion picture projectors. Ordinary filmstrip projectors can be used in the same way. Sometimes two-by-two slides can be arranged in lessons for individual use by teachers who do not have desired filmstrips available. Pupils can follow the slide sequence on dittoed commentary sheets. Preferably such slide sequences should be presented in trays for automatic or semi-automatic projection. If such are not available and one must use a single-shot machine, one should be sure the slides are numbered in proper order and that the top right-hand corner is marked so that the pupil can tell which way to insert the slides into the machne.

Using Teaching Machines and Computers in Instruction. Teaching machines that use automated teaching programs and computer-assisted instruction are the most exotic of all the autoinstructional devices, although the secondary school teacher will probably find that in his school automated programs must be presented by means of programmed texts or similar devices rather than by machine. Because the programs are devised for individualized teaching, they should make it possible for teachers using them to cope with great ranges of ability within the class. The self-instructional features of the programs and machine make it possible for pupils to work through programs as rapidly or as slowly as seems most desirable and to pursue different topics or themes at the same time.

Computer programs can be most useful for individualizing instruction because through the use of the computer it is possible to program a separate course of instruction for each pupil. In effect, instruction via computer gives an intrinsic teaching program, i.e., a teaching program in which the instruction in successive frames is based on pupil behavior in earlier frames. Thus each pupil's performance at any instant determines what the computer will have him do next. So because Pupil A's responses to the computer's tutoring differ from that of Pupil B, the computer can and will give him an entirely different sequence of instructional episodes even if both pupils are studying the same topic in the same period. Teaching machines do the same thing, but without the aid of the computer they are not so proficient.

If the ordinary teaching programs have an advantage over other materials, it is because they are usually carefully built and tested. However, they are not the only type of self-instructional or auto-instructional material available. Examples of other self-instructional materials one can purchase or make include the self-administering and self-correcting drill and practice materials described in Chapter 12. Usually self-correcting materials can be used only for teaching information and skills; the self-correcting format cannot be adapted easily for instruction in the higher mental processes. Even so, such materials can help free the teacher from much busy work so that he can give more time to helping individual pupils learn at higher levels.

The use of programs, teaching machines, computers, and other self-instructional materials does not free the teacher from the necessity of selecting the material, preparing the pupil and setting for instruction, and guiding or supervising the instruction—including helping pupils with their difficulties and following up the teaching as well as evaluating the pupils' progress. Even the use of computer programs, teaching machines, computers, and other self-instruction cannot do all the job itself. The teaching task remains the same, but the use of these techniques and devices does make it possible for the teacher to spend more time with individuals and to develop the higher goals of instruction that so often are neglected.

Study and Activity Guides. Dittoed or mimeographed study guides can be a great help to teachers in individualizing instruction. Study guides can be of several kinds. One type is a general study and activity guide to be used as a guide by all pupils throughout a unit. Another is a special study and activity guide which is used with a certain book, movie, field trip, or other activity and which should help direct the study of any pupil engaged in this particular activity. Another type of special study and activity guide consists of directions for studying prepared for a particular pupil (or group of pupils) so that he can proceed at work different from those of other pupils without having to wait for special oral directions from the teacher who may be busy working with someone else. Similar study and activity guides can be recorded on tape for pupils whose reading level is not up to their understanding level.

Learning Packets.   Learning packets can be even more useful than study guides in the individualizing of instruction. Their use makes it possible for pupils to do a considerable amount of their schoolwork independently so that teachers can conduct classes in which the pupils work on different topics and different learning activities simultaneously.

In general, learning packets differ from study guides only in that learning packets are more complete. Whereas a study guide usually contains only directions, questions, problems, and other suggestions for study, a learning packet may contain

Diagnostic pretest.
Behavioral objectives.
Directions and suggestions for study, including required and optional activities—exercises, problems, questions, projects.
Progress tests.
Final mastery test (or post-test).
Materials for study.

These are discussed more fully in Chapter 6.

CONTRACT PLAN

As Chapter 6 points out, the contract plan is really a variation of the unit plan or the learning packet. In it the pupil agrees to do a certain amount of work. In preparing for the contract the teacher sets up learning objectives as in any other unit. These objectives may or may not be behavioral objectives. He also sets up activities—exercises, problems, readings, and so on. Some of these activities may be required, but most of them should be optional. These are listed in a study guide or learning packet. From this list the pupil decides which activities he will

attempt. In making his decision, he must include any activities that are required plus other optional activities that appeal to him. In addition, or perhaps in lieu, he may come up with ideas of his own. Once he has made up his mind what he wants to do, he presents his proposal to the teacher. Together they work out a contract. Usually the contract stipulates that if the pupil completes the activities contracted for and meets a certain standard of excellence doing so, he will receive a certain mark. Thus a pupil may contract to do such and such readings, exercises, problems, and so on, in order to win a "B." Many authorities frown at this element of the contract plan because they feel that it overemphasizes the mark. A sample contract appears in Chapter 6. Contracts are especially valuable because they provide an excellent procedure for differentiating pupils' assignments.

INDIVIDUAL AND GROUP PROJECTS

Both individual and group projects as described in Chapter 10 are useful for individualizing instruction. Since the basis of the project is that it be selected, planned, and carried out by the pupil because of some intrinsic value to him, the individual project is one of the techniques best suited for developing and capitalizing on individual interests and abilities.

INDEPENDENT STUDY

Noar says that bright pupils should do a lot of independent study on their own "without constant supervision, without the threat or reward of marks."[4] Probably this is the sort of opportunity that should be extended to all pupils on occasion. After all, one of the major goals of schooling is to help pupils to learn to work independently. Independent study is good for motivation. It may lead to better control. It should not, however, be the only method used to teach anyone.

To conduct independent study well requires considerable skill. It is important to give the pupil the right amount of support, help, and leadership without stifling his own ideas and initiative. The pupil must be guided into selecting independent study

[4] Noar, op. cit., p. 84.

appropriate to his abilities, experience, interests, and goals. Pupils tend to bite off more than they can chew. In the beginning of the independent study it is good to arrive at a pretty definite understanding of just what is to be accomplished and how it is to be done. These can be written down. Learning packets and study guides are excellent for this purpose. Once the pupil has started his work, the teacher must run frequent checks on his progress to see that he is working well; he also must provide help, direction, and redirection. To be sure that the pupils do have sufficient guidance, it is good to have a schedule for conferences with them. In addition, the teacher must make himself available to the pupils. When a pupil doing independent study needs help, he should have someone to go to immediately.

CONTINUOUS-PROGRESS PLAN

Some schools are organized on continuous-progress plans in which each pupil progresses through the curriculum independently at his own pace without regard to grade levels. Even in schools which are organized in the traditional grade levels, teachers can organize their own courses on the continuous-progress plan. One example of this type of course organization has already been cited in the section on accelerating the brilliant pupil. Of course, in a true continuous-progress course, some pupils will take longer than the normal time to finish the units. In conducting such courses it is wise to remember that speed is not always a virtue. The pupil who proceeds through the units slowly but thoroughly may, in the long run, prove to be more able than the star who flips through them at great speed.

Procedures for building modules, learning activity packets, and courses or curricula on the continuous-progress plan have been presented in Chapter 6.

To conduct a course of the continuous-progress type requires constant supervision and guidance. The teacher must be constantly available and watchful to prevent pupils from having to stand around waiting for help or from struggling through work they do not understand. Whenever possible, the teacher should utilize small-group instruction techniques to help pupils who are at the same point

in the module or who are encountering the same problems. However, the purpose for using learning packets in these courses is to give the teacher a better opportunity for giving pupils individual attention as much as it is to break the regimentation of the standard recitation.

PROVIDING FOR DIFFERENCES BY MEANS OF FREE PERIODS

Occasionally, pupils may be given free periods in which they are permitted to follow their own interests as much as possible. The activities of such a free period should be limited to those which are suitable to the classroom and to the subject. Such periods are usually more appropriate for reading and literature than for other subjects, although this does not need to be so. They are often instrumental in forming new tastes in reading, art, music, and other areas, and often open new vistas of appreciation to the pupil. They also have the additional advantage of giving the teacher opportunities to help pupils who need individual attention.

*

How can a teacher find material to suit the varying reading levels of his students on a limited school budget?

How can different types of work areas within a classroom help to provide for individual differences? How can they be used?

How can self-correcting material be used in providing for individual differences?

How can self-evaluation of a pupil's progress be used to motivate him?

*

Finding Time for Individual Instruction

PUPIL PARTICIPATION IN PLANNING AND EVALUATION

To provide properly for individual instruction takes time. One of the keys to finding the necessary time is to allow the pupils to take a greater share in the responsibility for their own studies. *Adolescent boys and girls, particularly the brilliant ones, are quite capable of planning, directing, and evaluating their own work, particularly if they have study guides to help them.* When the teacher allows them to do so, he not only helps them to acquire skills in self-direction, but he also frees himself for individual and small-group work. Moreover, the use of pupil planning and evaluation makes it possible for each pupil to map out an individual plan suitable to his own needs.

THE USE OF PUPIL HELP

Talented boys and girls often help other pupils who are having difficulty. This technique can be quite beneficial if done carefully. It gives the teacher some assistance so that he can find time to do more individual teaching. It teaches the gifted youngster how to share his talents and to communicate his ideas to others. It helps foster the idea of service. Most important of all, it helps the talented youth to learn the subject more thoroughly. Moreover, youths frequently learn more readily from their peers.

This is an excellent method, but, if not used judiciously, it can be dangerous. First, the teacher may call on a brilliant pupil to do teaching that the teacher should do himself. This could result in the exploitation of the brilliant youth, while the dull pupil is deprived of the professional help he deserves. Then, too, one must avoid holding back the gifted youth. *It is not right for the bright pupil to mark time repeating the same material when he might be going on to more advanced or deeper study. The minute it becomes evident that the pupil tutor is not learning from the tutoring project, the project should stop.* To help the brilliant youths make the most of their talents is one of the teacher's most important tasks. He must not sacrifice them to help the mediocre. Used with care, however, the practice of having bright pupils help the slow ones is an effective method of meeting individual differences.

Sometimes it is even more effective if pupils who are ordinarily not brilliant but who have mastered the skill or concept in question do the tutoring.

*

How can pupils help each other? How can such help be used to provide for individual differences?

How can a teacher of a large class find time to work and confer with individual pupils? List occasions when the teacher might consult with pupils informally.

How would you go about setting up a classroom laboratory in a course you might teach? How could you use a classroom laboratory?

*

Accepting Different Evidences of Accomplishment

Earlier in this chapter it was pointed out that if pupils are encouraged to learn through many different media, the teacher must accept different types of growth as evidence of achievement in the course. This point cannot be emphasized too much. Certainly the essential learning in any lesson should be common to all the pupils, but the teacher cannot let the matter rest there. He must also accept various kinds of evidence of growth. The youngster who has increased his stature through creative writing, the girl who has grown through art, and the boy who has increased his technical skill through building models have all grown in desirable ways. All pupils do not acquire identical learning in any unit. The teacher should recognize that various types of growth are desirable and therefore should accept them as evidence of progress in the course.

Need for Variety of Materials

Providing for individual differences requires a wealth of instructional materials. It goes without saying that one cannot expect every member of the class to be interested in the same thing. Therefore, we must provide instructional materials which will suit many interests. Materials too easy for bright pupils may also be so difficult that it may frustrate the slow pupils. Consequently, the teacher should no longer limit himself to just one textbook. He must provide readings suitable to the various levels and interests found in his class. In addition to the readings the teacher should provide ample materials for other types of activities. A later chapter will show in more detail how to obtain and use such materials.

Not only should we provide a wealth of materials, we should also make them available when the pupil needs them. One of the characteristics of the classroom laboratory is an abundance of attractive, appropriate materials immediately on hand, ready for use. Thus the pupil can get whatever he needs at the appropriate moment without disturbing anyone.

SUMMARY

Every pupil is different from every other one, and so each one's education should be different if he is going to benefit from it optimally. These differences cause many pedagogical problems. On the other hand, they also offer the teachers levers by which to make their teaching more effective.

In so far as possible, schooling should be individualized. Secondary school administrators have attempted to provide for the individual differences by organizational devices. Among these devices have been such things as tracks and streams, homogeneous grouping, mini-courses, acceleration of the brilliant, and ungraded schools. None of these plans have been able to provide the complete answer to the problem. Even when the administrative devices are successful, they can cope with only part of the problem. As in all other instructional matters, the final solution must be worked out by individual teachers.

Luckily the teacher has at his disposal many techniques for coping with individual differences in pupils. He may differentiate his assignments by varying the difficulty, length, or type of work from pupil to pupil. He may find it desirable to group his pupils within the classes according to need, interest, or abilities, or to partially differentiate the work through individual or group projects. Sometimes he may find it advantageous to allow pupils to move through the course more quickly, or more slowly, than the average pupil, or to encourage pupils to enrich their learning by going into topics more deeply than other pupils do.

Individualizing instruction is not as difficult as teachers fear, and it is necessary. One way to meet this need is by conducting the class as a laboratory. In laboratory periods many pupils can proceed with a minimum of guidance while the teacher helps pupils who need assistance. Particularly valuable as means of freeing teacher's time for those who need help are the many self-instructional devices which help pupils teach themselves. Among these devices are teaching machines and programs as well as older devices like self-administering and self-correcting practice material. Dittoed or tape-recorded study and activity guides and learning packets can be extremely helpful and should be used. Combined with the laboratory approach they are especially effective. The same comment is true of the contract plan, independent study, and continuous progress, all of which require a laboratory atmosphere plus some system of helping and guiding pupils as they work independently or in groups. Free periods in which pupils are allowed to follow their own bents are also useful.

Finding time for individual instruction is difficult, but when teachers give pupils more time to participate in the planning and evaluating of their own studying, they can free a lot of time without slighting any pupils. Also teachers can make time by encouraging pupils to help each other.

If one provides well for individual differences one must expect to have to evaluate pupils' learning on new bases because pupils will not learn the same things in the same way. As a corrolary, one must also expect to use a much greater variety of materials in traditional classes. Not only will many readings be required but also materials for many other kinds of activities.

Teaching "Special" Pupils

9

Providing for individual differences in pupils who deviate considerably from the norm requires special measures. All too often schooling is frustrating and deadening to them because teachers forgot this elemental fact.

In this chapter we shall discuss three types of pupils who deviate from the norm: pupils who find it difficult to learn because of lack of native ability or inadequacies in their prior schooling; children of the poor, particularly those from the urban and rural ghettos; and pupils talented in the academic and allied fields. In these discussions we have made a number of general statements and suggestions about teaching pupils who fit into these categories. But the reader should read these statements and suggestions with caution. Pupils do not fit neatly into categories. What is true of one talented youth may not be true of another. No two youngsters in the black ghetto are alike. In general, the statements and suggestions about any category are true, but teachers deal not with the long run but with individuals. Individuals are the exceptions that prove the rule.

THE ACADEMICALLY INEPT

Pupils who have difficulty learning academic material are an especially difficult problem for secondary school teachers because, as subject specialists, the teachers wish to teach their subjects well and these pupils are not able to learn them well. This in itself is frustrating. Furthermore, because they seldom have learned to learn by themselves, the academically inept are more dependent on instruction than other pupils are. This fact tends to place considerable strain on the teacher. Nevertheless poor academic learners must be taught and should be taught well. Although some teachers find teaching them burdensome, most good teachers look on teaching them as a challenge rather than a chore. Teaching them can be most rewarding.

Characteristics of Poor Learners

More often than not, the academically inept are dull intellectually. They cannot think fast or learn academic things quickly. They need time to learn. To rush them through an assignment may result in no learning at all. But when we give them enough time, they may be able to learn more than we expect of them. Problem-solving activities are sometimes too much for them because of their lack of intellectual ability. On the other hand, they may be able to memorize, albeit sometimes excruciatingly slowly, and to solve problems that are not too difficult. Sometimes they are really skillful at remembering and solving problems that they are interested in.

Because of their lack of ability and lack of interest, intellectually dull pupils are easily discouraged by difficult academic material. Further, their lack of ability, poor vocabulary, and inclination to inattentiveness often make it difficult for them to understand directions. When an intellectually dull pupil claims that he does not know what to do, he is probably telling the truth. Not understanding what to do and trying to cope with material that is too difficult can be particularly frustrating. One can readily understand why so many intellectually dull youths are bored and discouraged. As often as not,

such pupils become behavior problems of one sort or another.

Although the academically inept pupil usually has little interest in the abstract, he is not devoid of interests. Rather, his interests are likely to concern things and concrete situations. Similarly his thinking is more likely to deal with specific situations than with generalizations.

Many dull boys and girls are much slower than they need to be. Sometimes they are only very poorly prepared. Because former teachers did not realize the problems and potentialities of these youngsters, they taught them much less than they should have. Such pupils can frequently be salvaged if their teachers only take the trouble.

BRIGHT BUT SLOW PUPILS

It has become customary to call pupils who have difficulty keeping up with the norm in learning academic material slow learners. All slow pupils are not dull pupils; neither are they necessarily poor learners or slow in all curriculum areas. Sometimes slowness is little more than a sign of the inability to read, or an indication that the pupil has never been taught how to learn by means of verbal academic material.

Quite possibly a child who has difficulty learning schoolwork based on textbooks may be quite adept at solving intricate problems involving mechanical ability, a high understanding of physical relationships, and high reasoning ability. Pupils have many different talents. The fact that a pupil lacks academic or literary talent does not preclude the possibility of his having talent, latent or active, in mechanics, arts, or social skills.

In addition, some pupils are slow because of other reasons not related to academic ability at all. Pupils from certain cultures may lack motivation to excel. Others, for a variety of reasons, are not motivated academically. Some of them hate school. Some may be slow and deliberate. Their life style may be slow. Some use up their energies in other activities so that they have none left to use on school work. Some may be late bloomers who, for one reason or another, develop slowly for a while and then pull ahead to surpass their seemingly faster age mates. To lump these types of pupils together as dull or slow is a great injustice to them.

GENERAL CHARACTERISTICS

Pupils who are truly intellectually dull are likely to be dull in other ways. The folk belief that nature usually compensates for the dull youth's lack of intellectual ability by giving him manual talents is a myth. Although both intellectually bright and dull people may be skillfull with their hands, truly dull pupils are less likely to be so than bright ones. If classes that feature manual skills are more satisfactory for dull pupils than academic classes are, it is only because the manually oriented lesson is likely to be less abstract and therefore more meaningful to them than academic classes. In this respect, as in others, dull pupils vary greatly in their potential, just as other people do.

THE READING PROBLEM

The poor learner's most common handicap is poor reading ability. Teachers should be careful when selecting reading material for these pupils. They must also give much class time to making sure that the pupils understand what they read. One step in this process is to check to see that pupils understand the words. In a social studies class, for instance, a ninth-grade girl was insistent that people in New Jersey were not hostile to Puerto Rican immigrants because the old inhabitants did not like the Puerto Ricans and did not want them around, and besides they were afraid they would take their jobs. A little questioning brought out the fact that she thought *hostile* was synonymous with *hospitable*.

With classes of pupils who read badly, the teacher can often put greater emphasis on audio-visual teaching aids and the use of nonliterary techniques. In the social studies class just mentioned, the teacher found that the pupils had difficulty following the news for current events classes in the newspaper, but that they could and did follow her assignments on the television newscasts. With television as a source of information, this "slow" group's current events discussions sometimes rivaled those of the "faster" sections.

PHYSICAL HANDICAPS AND POOR LEARNING

Sometimes poor learners are handicapped by ill health or physical disability. They seem to be particularly prone to deficiencies of sight or hearing.

If these handicaps and health problems are the cause of their poor learning, correcting the handicaps can be a step toward reducing academic deficiencies. More often, however, lack of physical fitness is another sign of their general inability, for physical and intellectual potential seem to go hand in hand. Being below par physically may be another manifestation of the fact that the poor learner is not well endowed.

Teaching the Academically Inept

The teaching techniques that are most effective for the academically inept are, for the most part, the same ones most useful for dealing with average pupils. (One must remember, however, that the best techniques for teaching average pupils are not always the ones most frequently used; sometimes the ones most frequently used are not the most effective for teaching anyone, especially not pupils of less-than-ordinary academic talent.) However, for poor learners one should ordinarily keep a slower pace and use easier materials than in other classes.

THE CURRICULUM FOR POOR LEARNERS

On the whole, the secondary school curriculum is designed for the better than average. There is little in it of real value for pupils who lack academic ability. By and large the usual subject matter offerings are too abstract for them. In addition, the divisiveness of the departmentalized school program seems to confuse them. Many of the standard secondary school courses have little relevance to their present or future lives. Even if they could profit from them academically, one wonders how much real benefit the courses could give them. Probably such pupils can be served best by block-of- time courses made up of broad units centering around preparation for citizenship and vocational adjustment.

The curriculum for poor learners should be developmental rather than remedial. Remedial work is necessary, of course, but as a rule the emphasis should be on the pupils' continuous development of skills and knowledges with only occasional reversions to short, intense doses of remedial instruction. Because these pupils' needs are more likely to be in the realm of personal development than of academic enrichment, their curriculum should contain strong guidance and homeroom programs. The content should concentrate on things important in their lives outside of school, such as consumer education and vocational and prevocational preparation, with special emphasis on things they can use in their out-of-school life now. Work-school programs have proved to be particularly good for them.

Even so, the academically inept need to learn the skills pertaining to clear thinking. These pupils need to know how to reason just as much as other people do. Because they are apt to be easy marks for propaganda, false advertising, and shady deals, they need special help in learning how to analyze propaganda and false arguments so that they can protect their own interests. To learn these skills pupils need to practice them in practical, realistic situations.

In summary, then, *the curriculum for pupils lacking in academic talent should be simple, practical, realistic, and meaningful.* There is little place in it for the purely academic. However, it is a mistake to believe that the way to help poor learners is simply to enroll them in ordinary shop and homemaking courses. Poor learners are seldom more apt in these areas than in the academic ones. Although they may profit more from such courses than from other courses because they are less abstract, the courses are not really suitable and so poor learners do not get as much from them as they would from courses designed for them specifically.

NEED FOR FREQUENT DIAGNOSIS

Diagnosis is important in all teaching, but it is doubly so in teaching poor learners. Their academic difficulties make them susceptible to misunderstanding and error. Therefore, the teacher needs to measure and evaluate their progress often. With such pupils one cannot expect success from shortcuts. To attempt to teach poor learners materials for which they are not ready is futile. Often one must repeat and reteach what has been done before. If the teacher does not constantly evaluate the progress of these pupils, they and he may become completely lost.

Constant evaluation is also necessary in teaching poor learners because of their tendency to do careless, slipshod work unless frequently reminded of the need to be careful. This tendency is, of course, present in all pupils, but in the academically inept it may be more of a problem. Because academic learning does not come easily to them, pupils who are not academically inclined may find schoolwork something of an ordeal and so are inclined to stop their work somewhat short of perfection.

NEED TO MAKE THINGS CLEAR

Because the intellectually dull have difficulty understanding, teachers of poor learners need to make special efforts to be clear. They should keep their language as simple and direct as they can. It is essentially important for teachers to refrain from speaking in generalities when they can speak in specifics. In giving instructions teachers of poor learners need to go into detail. Poor learners need plenty of instructions. Again one would be wise to avoid shortcuts, for with these pupils shortcuts will more than likely turn out to be short circuits. Because poor learners find it difficult to transfer their learnings, teachers should be careful to point out the implications of each lesson in some detail.

TECHNIQUES FOR TEACHING POOR LEARNERS

Teaching poor learners requires great patience and understanding, but patience and understanding are not enough. The teacher must also be competent in the appropriate teaching technology. These techniques are approximately the same as those that good elementary school teachers use with younger pupils. However, since poor learners in secondary schools are not children, but adolescents or young adults, they are liable to resent teaching tactics by which teachers seem to treat them as children. The secondary school teacher should guard against talking down to his poor learners or giving them childish assignments. At the same time, he must also be sure that his language and his assignments are clear and simple. The importance of making sure that what is being taught is mature enough for the pupils can not be too heavily emphasized. One young teacher of remedial mathematics in a central city high school found that he could not make any headway until he disguised the basic arithmetic he was trying to teach as algebra. When the class worked on the algebra, they began to learn their addition and subtraction and also to attend his class more regularly (although still continuing to absent themselves from other classes). To walk the tightrope between the childish and the too difficult is often quite hazardous.

Concrete, Simple Activities. In general, the usual, principally verbal teaching methods are not suitable for the academically inept. For them instruction needs to be concrete and tangible. Handwork is valuable because it makes the learning real and concrete. This type of work is important for the pupil can frequently understand the concrete when the abstract would be too much for him. For this same reason the judicious use of realia and audio-visual aids will help academically inept pupils learn. Watching demonstrations, observing phenomena, looking at motion pictures, making collections, building exhibits and models, and caring for a model home are all examples of concrete, tangible activities that can be useful.

Activities for poor learners should also be kept simple. Assignments should be kept short so as not to discourage and confuse the pupils. Lessons should be limited to a very few points. Field trips should contain only a few things for the pupils to do. If community problems or activities are used—and they can be used quite successfully—the poor learners' participation should deal only with aspects that are concrete, tangible, and not very complex. This need for simplicity is the reason for the common recommendation that when using pictures or other audio-visual aids one should use only a few at a time.

At times, of course, one must teach complex matters to poor learners. In some instances such teaching goals require large amounts of practice so as to bring about habituation. Usually, a teacher is most successful if he starts with the simple and gradually moves to the complex by an easy transition. The teacher in such a situation should make the continuity quite clear so that the pupils will be able to see the relationships as they move on. Thus it is that in teaching spelling, it is necessary to include a considerable amount of formal spelling. In doing so it would be advisable to introduce only a few words at a time and to use these words in sentences in order to make their meaning clear.

Use of Realistic Activities. Realistic activities are good for use with poor learners because they help motivate them and make transfer of learning relatively easy. Sometimes these slow pupils may find it difficult to see the relevance of many mathematics problems, but when the problem has to do with the cost of purchasing, financing, and maintaining a particular car the pertinence of the mathematics involved may become both obvious and interesting to them. So also in English classes letter writing to real people can make composition more realistic. A class newspaper may help pupils see the importance of their school work. Similarly, the presentation of an assembly or the preparation of an exhibit can be used to make the learning process real. Creative activities are also useful. Pupils are usually interested in dramatizations and can learn much from them. The value of exhibits, collections, and class newspapers made by the pupils has already been discussed. These activities have the advantage of not only being realistic, but also of activity involving the pupil.

Teaching Materials for the Academically Inept

Teaching academically inept pupils requires an assortment of materials. Particularly desirable are reading materials suitable for high school and junior high school pupils, yet written at elementary school reading levels. Fortunately, publishers and suppliers have come to realize this necessity and suitable materials are appearing on the market. At times reading material designed for younger pupils in lower grades may be used successfully with poor readers. However, pupils resent being asked to read from books they consider to be childish. Moreover, they may be ashamed to be seen with books designed for younger pupils. Since attempts to disguise the grade level of textbooks have not been very successful, teachers should not insist on pupils' using material designed for younger pupils unless they are willing.

When no stigma is attached to such books they may be excellent for slow learners. One way to use them is to pull the book apart and bind its more useful sections separately into plain cardboard binders. When this is done, the pupil does not need to carry a "kid's" book with him for any length of time. Furthermore, the practice allows the teacher to vary his assignments more easily.

In similar fashion the teacher can procure much other reading material. Fortunately, many periodicals and newspapers contain relatively easy reading materials, often of high motivational value. In a fairly short time a teacher can collect from such sources quite a selection of easy but interesting materials suitable for slow adolescents.

In some instances the teacher may find it desirable to create some of the materials himself. This is not as difficult as it may seem. If the teacher remembers to limit his vocabulary and to keep his sentences and paragraphs short and simple, he can prepare reading material of seemingly adult level which the pupils can read satisfactorily.

Since dull pupils find it difficult to learn through symbols, teachers should attempt to find materials that do not depend on words. Actually, to see things and to act things out will more likely result in learning than to hear or read about them. To this end, pictures, models, realia, and other concrete materials are explained in Part VI. However, in dealing with his less brilliant pupils, the teacher should remember to keep the material simple, clear, and realistic. To keep from confusing pupils and to keep the material within their scope, teachers should avoid presenting too much material too fast. A few pictures carefully presented are likely to be more effective than a large number of pictures presented hurriedly.

*

Is the fact that some pupils feel that there is a stigma attached to being assigned to a section of slow pupils a serious problem? What might one do to reduce this feeling in the pupils?

Is it possible to teach pupils adequately in normal classes? If so, how would you do it?

In what ways would the methods you would use in slow classes differ from those you would use in regular classes?

*

Marking and Promoting the Academically Inept

Marking the academically inept causes a serious problem that has never been solved. If a teacher marks them on their effort, he may run the danger of seeming to report achievement much greater than that they have actually attained. Similarly, to mark a poor learner on the basis of his achievement as compared to his expectations, again runs the risk of giving the recipient of the report a false impression. But, if one marks him solely on his achievements as compared to those of his peers, one dooms him to a school life of poor marks and failures.

Some schools have tried to solve this problem by reporting more than one mark, i.e., a mark based on effort, a mark based on performance as compared to his individual potential, and a mark based on performance as compared to that expected of other pupils of his age and grade. Others indicate the achievement with the usual marks plus a subscript to denote the level of the section. Unfortunately, none of these marking systems has proved to be really successful. *Perhaps the only solution is to free pupils from marks and grade levels by placing them in ungraded, continuous-progress schools or classes and to report their progress by written or graphical descriptions of their accomplishments.*

THE CHILDREN OF THE POOR[1]

Deprived youth are frequently lumped together with slow or poor learners in our thinking. Of course it is true that there is enough overlap between the two groups to make it seem that deprived children are poor learners, but appearances can be deceiving. The range of native intelligence is just as great among the culturally deprived as among the affluent. Some deprived youth are really gifted. Many deprived youth have more basic academic potential than teachers give them credit for. Because of their unusual problems and their great hidden potential, deprived youth need and deserve special consideration.

Characteristics of Poor Youth

In reality, the children of the poor are more often educationally deprived than culturally deprived,

[1] This section is based largely on the work of Riessman and others who have worked primarily with the urban disadvantaged. The experience of the present authors, however, leads them to believe that the generalizations stated here are also applicable to many other kinds of socially disadvantaged pupils.

for they all come from cultures rich in many ways and in certain aspects perhaps richer than the common middle-class American culture familiar to most of us. The difficulty seems to be that their cultures are different and therefore difficult for middle-class teachers and administrators to understand. Even the culture of the white Anglo-Saxon protestant old American poor (and there are many of them) is different, for people who live in poverty seem to develop a culture of poverty.[2] Teachers of poor youth need to develop an understanding of the culture of their pupils so that they can capitalize on its strengths and avoid competing against its mores and ideals. They should not derogate it or attempt to reform it. The nation and country may benefit more from pluralism than from conformity. Teachers need not and should not try to force all pupils into the same mold.

Nonetheless, there are numerous cultural class characteristics that make it difficult for the children of the poor in school. Poverty is, of course, one of them. In our society it is "expensive to be poor."[3] Poor people are deprived. They lack proper food, housing, and clothing. As a result they are likely to be undernourished and unhealthy. Because of their experiences, they are not oriented toward the future. They tend to be suspicious and resentful of outside influence and hostile toward those who are more affluent. They are likely to be apathetic, to trust in luck, and to depend upon others instead of relying on their own efforts, because their experience has led to feelings of futility and powerlessness. Altogether these characteristics militate against success in school.

THE LANGUAGE OF THE DISADVANTAGED

In spite of what many teachers seem to think, most poor pupils are quite verbal. In their own vernacular they can speak precisely and colorfully. Their language difficulties come from the fact that their vernacular may be quite different from the standard English of other groups. In fact, the ver-

nacular may be so different that the pupils, in effect, speak a foreign language. The ideas may be good but the words are different. In fact, their standard English vocabulary may be quite limited. Formal language, like that in books, is usually quite foreign to them. Furthermore, the pupils may have had little experience with language that deals with abstractions and abstract thought. Consequently their creative abilities and flights of fancy are likely to be lost or hidden by a language barrier in the classroom. Nevertheless it is essential for teachers to remember that because their language is different it does not necessarily mean that their language is deficient.

Increasingly, American teachers are becoming aware that large groups of pupils in our schools are literally foreign speaking. Their native tongues may be Spanish, French, Navaho, Japanese, or any one of the languages of the other ethnic groups that live in this country. They should not be penalized for being foreign language speakers. Rather they should be encouraged to capitalize on this heritage. However, it should be remembered that the language problems of the poor, e.g., lack of experience with verbal abstractions, are likely to be much the same no matter what language they speak. Furthermore, a good working knowledge of standard English is essential for success in most areas and most occupations in the United States.

PHYSICAL ORIENTATION

Although deprived pupils may be facile verbally, it is also true that they are less likely to be word-bound and word-oriented than middle-class students. Instead, they tend to react positively to what they can see and do and to approach things physically rather than verbally. Therefore poor youths are apt to learn better from physical activity and visual presentation than from listening. In short, learning by doing seems to be especially effective for them.

The tendency of the poor to be physically oriented also tends to give their culture a masculine orientation. In the urban slums and ghettos, at least, much of their life is rough and uncouth. They enjoy adventures, sports, and boisterousness. Sometimes this tendency leads to delinquency. In the classroom it may result in horsing around. It also makes it pos-

---

[2] Oscar Lewis, *Current*, December 1966, pp. 28–32.
[3] Knute Larson and Melvin R. Karpas, *Effective Secondary School Discipline* (Englewood Cliffs, N.J.: Prentice-Hall, Inc., 1963), p. 70.

sible to interest and motivate them by means of games and physical activities.

AUTHORITARIANISM AND TRADITIONALISM

The masculinity of the culture of the deprived—even when their families are matriarchal—may be responsible for, or a manifestation of, their authoritarianism and traditionalism. Pupils from such cultural backgrounds tend to like things to be definite. Often they are used to and expect rigid authoritarianism severely enforced by rough punishment. Parents, in their experience, seldom resort to reasoning, coaxing, or coddling. Rather, they enforce their desires with sharp words and blows quickly given and quickly forgotten. Because punishment is swift and hard, children seldom have doubts about why they are getting it; neither are they plagued by long drawn-out periods of nagging and threatening.

THE EXTENDED FAMILY

One reason for this punishment pattern may be the fact that in poverty areas people often live in extended families. When grandmothers, aunts, uncles, father, mother, and children all crowd together in a small house or a cramped tenement, the elders are not likely to put up with much nonsense from the young people. Such a background also explains deprived pupils' ready acceptance of authoritarianism.

It also explains their anti-intellectualism. Large poor families do not provide opportunity for amenities. Pupils raised in such situations are bound to be interested in the vocational and practical. On the whole, persons from deprived groups probably see the need for education just as clearly as other people. Parents from these groups would like to see their children educated so that they can get ahead and so that they will no longer be the dupes of sharp operators and bureaucrats. Many of them feel that only by means of education can their children ever get their rights.

The Child of Poverty in School

Children of poverty do not ordinarily like school. In the first place, their experience has taught them that school is one humiliation and failure after another. In their eyes school is just one more example of the unfairness of society. And the television has made clear to them the difference between the lives of the rich and their own niggardly existence. If they are poor and black in an integrated school, they may be reluctant to try because of fear of the whites. Seldom do they see much point in striving to learn what is taught. Most of the curriculum seems irrelevant to their lives—past, present, or future. Even though they may see value in the three Rs, science, and information that will keep them from being cheated, they are not likely to see great value in the academic studies. More often than is necessary they do badly in them and as a result drop out of school.

FAILURE, FRUSTRATION, AND HUMILIATION

The children of poverty tend to put the blame for their failures on the school. They are often right. Teachers all too often think of them as inferior and treat them as second-class citizens. After experiencing such treatment for a long time, a pupil may be convinced of his lack of ability and live *down* to the teacher's expectations.

And so the poor learn not to expect much from the school. Even if they begin with great expectations, their lack of school knowledge and middle-class know-how ends up frustrating them. Many pupils in poverty areas never get the chance to learn the qualities and skills that lead to success in school.

WHY THEY FAIL

Since for many deprived children school is just one humiliating failure after another, it is not strange that they view school and teachers with hostility. Authorities have noted many reasons why the underprivileged do not learn well in school. Most commonly mentioned are

1. The lack of an "educational tradition" in the home, few books, etc.
2. Insufficient language and reading skills.
3. Inadequate motivation to pursue a long-range educational career, and poor estimate of self.
4. Antagonism toward the school, the teacher.

5. Poor health, improper diet, frequent moving, and noisy, TV-ridden homes.[4]

Although he realizes that these reasons are partially valid, Riessman is convinced that they do not represent the problem accurately because they fail to take into account the school environment and what the school could do to attack the problem. Therefore, he has tried to reformulate a more valid list of basic deterrents to school learning in underprivileged pupils.

1. The discrimination, frequently unintentional, seen in the classroom, Parent-Teacher Association, guidance office, psychological testing program, etc., which alienates Johnny and his family.
2. Johnny's *ambivalence* toward education—not simply rejection of it—his lack of school know-how, test-taking skills, information concerning college, and his anti-intellectualism.
3. The culture of the school which overlooks and underestimates his particular skills and mode of intellectual functioning that arise out of his culture and way of life.
4. The deficits in Johnny's background which necessitate special *transitional* techniques to bring him into the academic mainstream. These do not require a "soft" approach, a lowering of standards, a capitulation to his deficiencies.[5]

Teaching the Educationally Deprived

Because many pupils from urban and rural slums enter into our secondary schools with only meager academic competencies and small expectations, to teach them successfully is liable to be difficult—so difficult that many teachers despair and give up and so compound the pupils' troubles. This faintheartedness is unfortunate, for the situation is not as hopeless as it may seem. Educationally deprived youths frequently have much more potential than surface appearances indicate. They deserve more from their schools than fainthearted teaching. The following paragraphs include several suggestions that may make the task easier.

[4] Frank Riessman, *The Culturally Deprived Child* (New York: Harper and Row, Publishers, 1962), pp. 4–15.
[5] Ibid., pp. 5–6.

DIAGNOSIS

Diagnosis is essential in all teaching. In poverty areas it is even more crucial because the pupils may have been shortchanged in their earlier schooling. Much teaching fails in secondary schools because it makes no contact with the realities of pupil knowledge, skills, interests, and aspirations. This is particularly true in poverty areas. It is not very effective, for instance, to pile reading assignment on top of reading assignment when the pupils cannot read.

The False IQ. In diagnosis, teachers in the past have depended on the IQ and past performance as principal indicators of native intelligence. As a result teachers of educationally deprived pupils are sometimes convinced that they are dealing with poor learners when they are not. It may be simply that the pupils are the victims of poor teaching in earlier grades. Their poor performance may be the result of poor study techniques or of their never having learned to read or figure properly.

It is easy to put too much faith in the intelligence quotient. The IQ can be a useful tool, but it can also be a delusion; it is not an infallible indicator of an individual's ability to learn. Good intellectual potential may be hidden by low IQ scores. Poor reading ability, lack of motivation, cultural differences, language problems, poor test conditions, and poorly designed intelligence tests are all factors which may result in false IQs. In spite of efforts to avoid injustices, there are intelligence tests that are notorious in their unfairness to persons whose culture or class is "different." In judging the potential of any youngster, it is not wise to depend on any one criterion—particularly a single test score.

Poor Reading Ability. Perhaps the most important element in the general diagnosis of poverty-stricken pupils is the determining of how well they can read. Lack of reading skills is endemic to the poor.

Teachers should be especially aware that the handicap that is holding back a deprived youth may be nothing more nor less than the inability to read well. Sometimes simply adjusting the reading level of the material to be studied may make the difference between pupil learning and pupil frustration. In any case every effort should be made to bring the pupils' reading abilities up to par as quickly as possible. Until this objective has been achieved, teachers should try to find easy reading material suitable for the age and interest levels of secondary school pupils who have difficulty reading. (Certain metropolitan newspapers are written for adult readership at quite low reading levels, for instance.) In addition, the teachers should try to utilize non-reading activities that will lead to the desired learning. Techniques that may be used to determine the reading-ability level of pupils, and the reading-difficulty level of written material as well as methods for helping pupils master reading skills, are discussed in Chapter 13.

Diagnostic Techniques. As we have already noted, teachers working in poverty areas find the need for competent diagnoses even more crucial than other teachers do. Furthermore it seems to be more difficult as the problems attending poverty —poor preparation, unfavorable attitudes, class differences, and the like—complicate diagnoses. Consequently, wherever feasible, the teacher will want to use the full range of his battery of diagnostic tools. Among the diagnositc techniques he will find useful are open-ended questions, themes, or stories concerning such topics as "What Would I Do If I Had a Million Dollars," or "What Makes Me the Maddest."[6] Such themes or stories can be written or told to a tape recorder or even acted out in an impromptu dramatization or role playing. Or they could be the subject of a group discussion. Similarly one can learn much from listening to a pupil discussion of an actual or contrived incident they have all witnessed or heard about. An interesting technique is to start a story and let the pupils finish it in open discussion. Pupil diaries can give the teacher inklings into what pupils are really like— how they feel, what they think, and what they do. Systematic observation is another important technique. Each day each teacher probably should select three or four persons to observe on a regular schedule until he has completed the class. Similarly he should make a point to set aside certain periods of time to watch the entire class for certain symbolic behaviors—does anyone seem to have vision problems, for instance.

Other techniques include sociometric tests, pupil

interviews, parent interviews, as well as standardized tests, classroom tests, and other classwork. Diagnostic devices and techniques are explained more fully in Chapter 15.

REALISTIC ASSIGNMENTS

The work the teacher of disadvantaged pupils lays out should be realistic. Disadvantaged pupils have had so much experience with failure that very challenging work may frighten them away rather than urge them forward. Still, they do not want to be insulted with childish pap below their dignity. To pick assignments that are just right requires teacher ingenuity and a thorough knowledge of one's pupils.

Consequently teachers should forget about covering the subject and concentrate on teaching well. It is far better for pupils to learn a smaller body of content well than to rush through a large body of content without real learning or understanding. The best procedure seems to be to pick a theme or topic and divide it into short segments. In teaching these segments teachers should seek out much feedback in order to be sure the steps are not too large and that the pupils learn the essentials of each segment before they move on to the next one. Because attendance of poor pupils is likely to be sporadic, teachers should try to individualize their assignments so that pupils can pick up where they left off and move through the course in an orderly fashion even when they have been absent excessively.

In giving assignments, directions should be clear and explicit. Teachers can often help pupils tremendously if they will only show them how to study. Because of the probable defects in disadvantaged pupils' home and school backgrounds teachers should be ready to teach them all sorts of skills that are usually presumed to be part of a normal secondary school pupil's equipment, for example, how to ask questions, how to study, how to take notes, or how to read.

A RELEVANT CURRICULUM

Assignments should not only be realistic in length and difficulty, they should also be realistic with respect to the experience, needs, and expectations of the pupils. Pupils from poverty areas need a cur-

6 See Hilda Taba and Deborah Elkins, *Teaching Strategies for the Culturally Disadvantaged* (Chicago: Rand, McNally & Co., 1966), for good examples of diagnostic devices and techniques.

riculum that seems valuable to them and is close enough to their own lives to have meaning. They would profit from learning from people at home and in the community. They need to learn about themselves.

Poverty-stricken people do not need or want a curriculum limited to pap. Their curriculum does not have to be kept simple and concrete. Poor people are not stupid. They can handle abstractions and think at high levels, but in developing abstract principles and generalizations one needs to begin with the simple, concrete, and familiar, and build from there. (This principle, of course, applies to everyone, poor or wealthy.) Their own experiences in their own communities can be used as the basis for instruction in the higher mental processes and standard academic subjects. Noar, for instance, reports that poor black secondary school pupils have had good experiences going out into their communities to investigate such things as the underground railroad, the history of institutions, formal groups and societies, self-help organizations, newspapers, community centers, the history of ethnic groups in occupations, and the like.[7]

COMBATING ANTI-INTELLECTUALISM

A main task of the teacher of the disadvantaged is to fight anti-intellectualism. The strategy is to crack the anti-intellectual prejudices of the pupils by any means possible at first, and then to build increasingly favorable intellectual attitudes on these small beginnings. Try to capitalize on their interests and point out the practical value of what is to be learned. Take advantage of their belief in the usefulness of the fundamentals, the vocational, and the scientific. Utilize the boys' masculinity. Let them read the sports page, science fiction, or anything else that will get them started. This is no time for intellectual snobbery.

In doing all this, the teacher must respect the pupil and his culture. Accept the pupil as a person and let him know by your behavior that you are on his side. Undoubtedly, because of unfortunate past experiences, the pupils will need a great deal of convincing. Try to overcome the hostility by deeds

[7] Gertrude Noar, *Individualized Instruction; Every Child A Winner* (New York: John Wiley and Sons, Inc., 1972).

not words. Don't talk down to the pupils. Don't be condescending. Don't demean yourself. Tend to your teaching and concentrate on getting the material across. Explain things to them carefully in good but simple English. Do not try to imitate their slang. Make it evident that you expect them to learn just like anyone else. If you convince the pupils that you respect them and are trying your best to teach them, you may find that their hostility will be replaced by loyalty and respect.

MOTIVATION AND THE CHILDREN OF THE POOR

Motivation is the key for teaching poor youth just as it is the key for teaching other youth. However, in teaching the poor, motivation is apt to be a greater problem because of their antagonisms and distrust of schools. All the techniques described in the sections on motivation in other chapters are pertinent and should be used.

Perhaps the most important step the teacher can take to motivate poor adolescents—particularly those from ethnic or racial minorities—is to prove to them by his actions that he respects and likes them, that he intends to do the best he knows how to teach them well, and that he expects them to do their best, too. The next most useful step the teacher can take is to make his course down-to-earth so that it will seem worthwhile to the pupils. It is also important to make sure that each pupil has real success. Everyone needs the feeling that he has succeeded in doing something worthwhile. Poor adolescents do not have such feelings in school often enough. Teachers need to provide these feelings. One way to do so is to use praise. If one looks hard enough, one can usually find something truly commendable in every pupil. Teachers tend to miss the good behavior of bad actors, but even the worst actor sometimes does well. When he does, the teacher should be sure to recognize him and applaud him.

On the other hand, teachers should avoid emphasis on competition. As Gardner Murphy points out, the use of competition in any school group is suspect because

> Competition . . . frustrates and benumbs most of those who fail, and, for those who succeed, it can, at best, give only the ever iterated satisfaction of winning again. This may destroy the ability to risk failure

for the sake of attempting new and more interesting goals.[8]

Since poor youth have so often faced failure in school, an emphasis on competition probably would have an effect quite the opposite of that desired.

Among the techniques that do seem to motivate poor adolescents is the fostering of "groupness" by involving them in the planning, executing, and evaluating of classroom learning experiences. If teachers let pupils tell them what they wish to know and use this information to make courses more interesting and relevant, the pupils will probably respond.

MAINTAINING CLASSROOM CONTROL

Discipline is often a problem with disadvantaged pupils. With school-caused frustration and hostilities so common, it is unreasonable to expect the situation to be otherwise. That is why it is so important to emphasize motivation when teaching disadvantaged pupils.

Probably the best way to prevent classes of disadvantaged pupils from getting out of control is by concentrating on teaching and letting the pupils know by your actions that you intend to do your best to teach them as well as you can. [In this respect it is probably best to run a rather traditional class. Disadvantaged pupils seem to distrust new approaches and particularly loose progressive techniques.]

[In addition, the teacher should set up and enforce clear, definite rules. Culturally deprived youth believe in authority. Being authoritative will probably work to the teacher's advantage.] If possible, the teacher should also determine the natural leaders in the class and solicit their support. This solicitation should be done slowly and indirectly, however.

As in any other class, consistency is a virtue. In this way you can make clear to the pupils where you and where they stand. Avoid favoritism. Treat everyone fairly and evenly. Be especially careful about accepting the advances of pupils who come to you. The pupils who first seek the friendship and attention of the teacher may well be renegades who are not accepted by the group. By gaining them you

may lose the rest of the class. If the teacher tries to treat each individual fairly, consistently, and respectfully, there is a good chance that his relations with the entire group will become easy and pleasant after a time.

Some Strategies for Teaching the Disadvantaged

Even though poor people are liable to be traditionally oriented and feel that unless classes approximate the formal authoritativeness that they associate with traditional classes they are being cheated out of a good education, teachers are not limited in the approaches that they can use to make instruction interesting and exciting. Classes can be structured without being rigid. In fact, if one uses a little caution he can successfully use his entire repertoire of teaching techniques for teaching deprived adolescents. Some teachers have had great success using the multisensory laboratory approach, for instance. The crucial consideration is that one concentrate on real learning.

EMPHASIZING CREATIVITY AND THINKING

Poor adolescents need to have opportunities to create and to learn to think. Problem-solving activities that are consistent with the ability levels and experience of the pupils seem to be excellent for these pupils. Taba and Elkins suggest the following sequence as one way of developing skill in thinking with deprived pupils.

1. Find out by written work and open discussion what the concepts, feelings, and skills of students are.
2. Read a story or two for analysis of the ideas one wishes to consider.
3. Let the students work out these points in small groups with the help of books.
4. Discuss, analyze, compare these points in class.
5. Apply the new broader view to look at their own family situation.[9]

Open-ended questions and discussions can also be used with good results. To make them most effective teachers should learn to conduct discussions as conversations. The ordinary teacher-centered dis-

---

[8] Gardner Murphy, *Human Potential*, quoted by Noar, op. cit., p. 101.

[9] Taba and Elkins, op. cit., p. 204.

cussion is liable to be more like an inquisition than a conversation. That is too bad, because it tends to stop pupils from thinking. On the other hand, a discussion that is centered on topics with which the pupils have some firsthand familiarity can be a lively, informative, thought-provoking learning experience. Thus when at Jersey City's Snyder High School one of the "difficult" classes discussed ways to improve the city, the pupils had an opportunity not only to express themselves in full discussion, but also to think seriously about problems of some importance to themselves personally. When all is said and done, poor adolescents, like other pupils, manufacture their own concepts. They will build them most effectively if they learn by means that emphasize thinking and creativity.

INTERESTING, RELEVANT, AND ACTIVE CLASSES

This illustration points up the fact that classes for deprived youth should be interesting, relevant, and active. Role playing and dramatic presentations are often very successful. In Central High School, Newark, N.J., for instance, a black studies class, noted for its high rate of absenteeism, showed an amazing amount of potential talent when they rehearsed, read, and video-taped a short play. At least one pupil who was believed to be a nonreader showed that she could not only read, but read dramatically when the occasion seemed worthwhile.

Other teachers have achieved good results from having pupils create a class book out of their own writing. A junior high school teacher in an extremely difficult slum area uses pupil-designed and -executed bulletin boards and displays very effectively. Classes that feature games are usually popular as well as classes that make use of the various media. Classes that utilize a variety of materials are always likely to be more interesting than textbook recitations. Probably books should always be thought as aids to learning. Certainly they should not be the be-all and end-all of instruction in classes in which pupils do not read well.

IMPORTANCE OF PHYSICAL ACTIVITIES

Physical activities are very useful in classes of disadvantaged pupils. Acting out scenes or role play-

ing can sometimes be very effective, particularly in teaching history or interpreting literature. The tendency of disadvantaged pupils to be physically oriented also makes it likely that they will take favorably to teaching machines and other gadgetry. Active games may also be useful to draw pupils' attention and interest. In some situations, however, such activities can lead to chaos. In any case teachers should give the pupils plenty of chances to learn by doing, for such activities will ordinarily be much more successful than lecturing and other primarily verbal techniques.

TEAM WORK

Peers can be helpful to each other in many ways. Groups in which pupils work together as teams are likely to be quite effective. This arrangement provides the pupil with allies and co-workers with whom he can share both the work and the responsibility. Because he is not alone in the learning endeavor, he can look to the other members of his team for support and therefore the fear of failure or appearing foolish is no longer so pressing. Similarly, it is sometimes very helpful for the teacher to allow or arrange for one pupil to help another when he is stuck. Frequently pupils learn better from other pupils. If the pupil tutor is a run-of-the-mill member of the group who has mastered a particular skill or concept, the experience may be even more satisfying for both pupils.

PUPIL PARTICIPATION IN PLANNING

From the preceding paragraphs one can readily see that deprived pupils, just as other pupils, benefit from taking the responsibility for charting and conducting their own learning activities. We teachers tend to do too much for pupils when we should encourage them to do things themselves. Since poor people tend to be dependent anyway, one should be especially careful to avoid this fault when teaching them. In so far as possible, one should try to involve pupils in the planning and executing of the lessons. If one starts with something familiar to them, they are usually competent enough to take a large share in the decision making if they have a little help and guidance.

Marks and Marking

In teaching the deprived it is easy to put too much emphasis on marks and marking. It would be better to emphasize how well pupils learned the important things they were supposed to learn. Thus, in correcting papers, one should beware of overusing the red pencil. These pupils are easily enough discouraged and frustrated without that. Instead, one should read the papers for ideas and perhaps a few language principles until the pupil has mastered the ideas. It is foolish to overstrain for correct language and to neglect the ideas that the language was trying to portray. To avoid drowning the paper in red, Noar suggests that instead of correcting entire themes, secondary school teachers should probably mark only a first or middle paragraph, or sentence, or problem and leave the rest for the student to check, proofread, and edit.[10]

On the other hand, teachers should tell pupils when their work is not good and why it is not good. It is unfair to them to let them think they have mastered skills when they have not. Trying is not enough; pupils have to learn to produce. However, the emphasis should not be on the deficiencies in the work but on how to improve it. In this connection self-evaluation and peer evaluation are important. Pupils can gain real insight from evaluating their own work and from the evaluations of their classmates.

*

Examine some of the textbooks for junior high school courses in your field. Are there any reasons why they would be unsatisfactory for educationally disadvantaged pupils?

What could you do to help pupils from a non-English speaking background?

Are there any things you could do to combat directly the deterrents to school learning that Riessman considers basic?

*

REMEDIAL TEACHING

Teaching designed specifically for boys and girls who have not achieved desired goals is called remedial teaching. Many teachers seem to think there

[10] Noar, op. cit., p. 95.

is something esoteric about remedial teaching. There is not. Remedial teaching is merely good teaching concentrated directly on the pupil and his needs. Usually it is more effective than ordinary teaching only because it is more thorough and more carefully designed to remedy a specific need.

Some teachers seem to feel that remedial teaching should be reserved for extraordinary pupils and for remedial classes. Nothing could be further from the truth. It is probably no exaggeration to say that every youth needs remedial teaching at one time or another. Remedial and diagnostic teaching should be a part of every unit. To provide such teaching in each unit is relatively easy to do if evaluation is continuous and the teacher centers his teaching on the youth rather than on the subject matter.

DIAGNOSING THE DIFFICULTY

If we know exactly what skills, concepts, attitudes, ideals, and appreciations we are striving for, it should be quite easy to construct devices that would tell us whether or not they have been developed. An objective or essay-type test constructed by the teacher can be excellent for showing whether or not the pupil understands, if the teacher chooses the questions carefully. However, the teacher will frequently find it necessary to rely on diagnostic techniques other than tests to get at these learnings. Examples of these devices may be found earlier in this chapter and in Part VII.

RETEACHING POORLY LEARNED MATERIAL

In the regular class remedial teaching ordinarily consists of reteaching those things that boys and girls have not learned. For instance, if the boys and girls in a class that should already have studied the fulcrum do not seem to understand what it is, the lesson should probably be repeated for all. If only a few persons did not get it, they should probably be retaught in a special group. If it becomes evident that just one youngster missed it, he should be retaught individually. To reteach in this fashion may mean spending several days with the entire class on the missed learning, or revamping the next unit to include this learning again, or it may entail no more than just a few minutes of review and explanation, or a short conference with one pupil. Similarly, when it is found that boys and girls lack basic knowledge prerequisite to any unit, the teacher must take time to reteach this understanding. In cases of this sort the ordinary techniques of teaching suffice for remedial teaching, if they are carefully aimed at the trouble. Remedial teaching is aimed firing; barrage techniques will not do.[11] Actually, this type of remedial teaching is little more than providing for individual differences; the techniques explained in Chapter 8 and elsewhere in this chapter should be very helpful; so should those described in Chapter 13.

The following illustration serves as an example of remedial teaching in the regular classroom. In going over the test papers from one of his mathematics classes, the teacher noted that one of his pupils was having considerable difficulty with the problems. An analysis of her papers showed that the pupil was neglecting to convert all the parts of the problem to the same terms. At the next class meeting the teacher pointed out to the pupil the error she was making. He then quizzed the girl to see that she understood how to convert from one unit to the other and assigned to her several special problems by which to practice the technique directly.

*

Of what value can self-correcting exercises be in remedial teaching? In what ways is remedial teaching different from regular teaching? How can practice materials be utilized in remedial teaching?

*

TEACHING THE SERIOUSLY DEFICIENT

More serious cases of inadequate learning often turn up. These require more careful handling. Frequently these disabilities warrant remedial teaching by specialists outside of the regular classroom. When such help is available the teacher should use it. However, as long as some schools limit remedial classes to pupils who are retarded at least three years, and many other schools have no such services at all, the teacher must be ready to assume the burden himself. Moreover, many of the problems

[11] Barrage firing is firing in which the artillery or missile unit covers an entire area with fire thereby hoping to deny the area to the enemy and to destroy any already there.

are not so serious that the regular classroom teacher cannot take care of them competently.

For instance, we find quite often that one reason a pupil is having trouble with higher mathematics is that he never mastered his arithmetic essentials. If this is the case, the teacher should test him to find out what the actual fault is, then teach him how to do the specific arithmetical process properly, and finally give him plenty of practice until he has mastered the difficulty.

Another example concerns a pupil who seemed to have a great deal of trouble with punctuation. Upon examination the teacher found that the pupil knew the rules for punctuation well enough, but that he did not know how to apply them. To correct this fault the instructor arranged a series of lessons in which the pupil learned to translate the rules into terms he understood, and then prescribed exercises designed to apply the rules to sentences.

As in any remedial situation, correcting severe disabilities depends upon careful diagnosis and careful reteaching. Techniques suitable for such special classes are beyond the scope of this text. Teachers would do well to take special courses in this area and read some of the excellent books on the subject.

*

Can you give examples of the need for remedial teaching of brilliant youth from your own experience? How should this type of remedial teaching best be handled?

Supposing about one third of your class missed an essential part of the last unit. You estimate that it would take about two days to reteach it properly. What would you do?

*

THE GIFTED PUPIL

By "gifted youth" we mean those who have special abilities in some subject field. A person, no matter how dull he may be in other fields, is gifted if he has a special talent. Conversely, a pupil, gifted in one field, may be below average in others. In most school situations teachers are inclined to think only of the academically bright youth as the gifted youth. Certainly intellectually bright youths are gifted, but so are the people with special talents in art, music, mechanical arts, and sports. The truly talented in these areas need to have plenty of opportunities to make the most of their special talents. At the same time, the school must see to it that in exploiting his talent, the pupil is not kept from the education best suited for his needs and abilities in other areas.

Characteristics of Talented Youth

In dealing with talented youth we should remember that their special abilities and characteristics make the teaching problem somewhat different from that of teaching normal pupils. Because of their ability, and the interest which usually accompanies ability, talented young people can accomplish more work in a shorter time than their classmates can. Not only can they do more work more quickly, they can do work of a higher order.

Academically brilliant youths like to use their brains; they are intrigued by puzzles and problems; the abstract holds no fears for them; they can maintain interests in academic problems and assignments for long hours without flagging. Therefore, work that the ordinary pupil finds difficult may bore them because of its easiness. Often they have studied and read independently to the point that they are well above the level of the normal class and even sometimes above the level of their teachers.

Yet the talented youth is in most ways a normal youth. He has most of the normal youth's traits and problems. He is not a thing apart and should not be treated as if he were. The problem is to make it possible for him to make the most of his talent while keeping the rest of his personality healthy. This is no small order, for the talented youth has probably not learned to discriminate and take care of himself any better than his less talented brother.

Teaching Talented Pupils

In many school systems special programs, and sometimes even special schools, are provided for the talented pupils. These are excellent and should be encouraged, but of more concern to most teachers is how to help the brilliant pupil in the regular classroom. To meet this problem, each one of the techniques for meeting needs of individual pupils described earlier may be used. Because of their ability, brilliant pupils should stretch their horizons by attempting high-level assignments. Where the ordinary youth may be satisfied to read about the westward movement in a text, the brilliant pupil could be reading *The Oregon Trail*. When studying World War II, the brilliant pupil might try to reconcile the accounts given by Sir Winston Churchill, General Eisenhower, and others. In metalworking the academically brilliant youth might, in addition to doing fine work, study such topics as metallurgy, the metal trades, the economics of metals, and the effect of metal on history. The importance of keeping standards high becomes extremely apparent when we realize that according to Kingsley,[12] superior pupils often work up to only 40 per cent of their capacity, although less capable pupils may work up to 80 per cent. Allowing superior youths to waste their talents creates poor work habits and slovenliness. Brilliant youths should be held to high standards that will challenge the best in them.

In addition to attempting assignments of a high order the brilliant pupil should meet high standards of workmanship. He can do choice work; the teacher must see to it that he does. The teacher must not accept careless, poorly written, or poorly executed work from talented pupils. To do so engrains in them slothfulness and mediocrity.

Furthermore, the bright pupil can accept considerable responsibility for his own direction. Brilliant youths should have experience in planning and evaluating their own work. Since they are potential leaders, they need the experience in planning, organizing, making decisions, and carrying out plans. Moreover, they should have opportunities for leadership and service in their classes.

Sometimes attempting to hold brilliant pupils to standards higher than those of their classmates may backfire. Some bright pupils may resent having to do better work than other pupils. With bright pupils this pitfall usually can be avoided by appealing to their pride, by attempting to convince them that the assignments are really worthwhile, and by making the assignments exciting and challenging rather than drudgery. Some teachers provide opportunities for recognition of the brilliant pupils in their testing by adding additional difficult extra

12 Robert W. Frederick et al., *Describing Learning* (New York: Appleton-Century-Crofts, Inc., 1938), pp. 132–134.

questions at the end of the test making it possible for a pupil to get more than 100 per cent of the questions on the test. This device has been somewhat successful. However, the threat of marks is usually of little value. Talented pupils can earn good marks without half trying. To get the most from these pupils the teacher must call upon more genuine motives. Usually this is not hard to do since the talented youth almost always enjoys challenging tasks.

*

What can be done to provide brilliant pupils with work sufficiently challenging?

A teacher complained that her bright pupils were not working up to capacity because she could not make them do more work than ordinary pupils. What would you suggest that the teacher do to help keep the bright pupils working up to capacity?

In some schools teachers use the services of brilliant pupils in teaching the less brilliant. What is your estimate of this practice?

How would you attempt to catch the interest of a brilliant pupil who was obviously bored in one of your classes?

How would you go about to tempt brilliant pupils into doing considerably more and harder work than other pupils?

*

It should not be necessary to go into detail in describing specific teaching techniques for classes of academically gifted pupils because most of the techniques ordinarily used in our secondary schools were originally developed for use with talented pupils. Similarly, as we have already pointed out, many of the techniques described in the earlier chapter concerning individual differences in regular classes are the same techniques used to teach gifted pupils. The important thing is to provide them with opportunities to use their minds to the fullest. The content they encounter should be aimed at developing generalizations, realizations, and abstractions. Moreover, it should be new to them. *Some bright high school pupils go to class month after month without ever encountering any subject matter that they have not already learned.* They really should have the chance to go into the topics more deeply or to move on to something new.

READING FOR THE GIFTED

Ordinary high school textbooks seldom meet the needs of academically gifted pupils. This lack can be filled in many ways: pupils can read their assignments from college texts, primary sources, original writings, or other works. Much use can be made of individualized reading to supplement or substitute for the ordinary assignments. In many courses the pupil himself with only a little guidance can profitably choose his own readings. Often they will profit from reading several selections on a topic. A good technique is for the pupil to make a list of proposed readings and what he hopes to learn from them, and submit it to the teacher before he begins his work. Another method is to give the gifted pupils study guides with suggested problems for investigation and a list of suitable, pertinent readings. Learning packets are good if they provide enough challenge.

Not only should gifted pupils read widely, they should also read critically. Unfortunately many gifted youths never learn the more advanced skills of critical reading. Teachers of gifted pupils must provide them with direct instruction in critical reading skills and plenty of practice if these pupils are to ever make full use of their potentials. Some suggestions for teaching these skills can be found in Chapter 13.

RESEARCH AND DEPTH STUDY

Not only should the subject matter of brilliant pupils deal with generalizations and abstractions, but the pupils themselves should have a chance to develop their own generalizations. Memorizing facts and other information is not enough for pupils with good minds. They should find things out for themselves. In science their laboratory work could include real problems. In history their work could consist of digging out real history. In literature they could write some real criticism. In music they could perform and compose. Their school projects could be actual scholarly research projects, or, at least, the study of a topic in depth. By studying in this manner, the pupil would not only be able to fix basic facts and skills securely in his mind, but he could go beyond to create new concepts for himself and his peers by making logical inferences from the information available to him. The topics to be studied can be closely allied with the course syllabus or range far from it.

THE SEMINAR APPROACH

Small seminar classes of bright pupils are excellent devices for utilizing the impact of depth study. One type of seminar consists of a member's presenting a paper on a topic he has prepared for the group to discuss. Another type consists of general discussion on topics all have studied in some detail. In either case the pupils are encouraged to bring all their knowledge and skill to bear on the problem in a penetrating, logical analysis. In such discussions the interchange must be free and open. No rules, except those of logical analysis and courtesy, should bar the way. The purpose of the seminar is to encourage hard, incisive examination of carefully researched material.

ACCELERATION

A common practice in many schools is to accelerate the gifted pupils—that is, to encourage gifted boys and girls to proceed through the curriculum more rapidly than the other pupils. By acceleration, many gifted pupils are able to complete the equivalent of four years work in three. Where classes are homogeneously grouped, it is quite common practice for the upper section to move through courses more quickly than the lower sections. Similar methods can be adopted for individuals or small groups in heterogeneous classes. Thus the brilliant student may be allowed to work through the ordinary mathematics courses more quickly than the others and then proceed to more advanced topics toward the end of the semester. If the teacher provides the pupil with study guides or similar materials, the bright youth will be able to direct himself and to check out his own work much of the time. The teacher must, of course, keep the student under his eye, but the time involved in helping the brilliant need not be excessive. Furthermore, it is usually enjoyable—so enjoyable that teachers must guard against giving too much time to the gifted when the other pupils really need their help.

When working with gifted pupils, the teacher always has the problem of determining whether to go into things deeply or to move through them quickly; that is, to accelerate or to study in depth. With heterogeneously grouped classes, depth study for the gifted is sometimes easier to conduct than

acceleration. However, it is a problem that each teacher must settle for himself in view of his own talents, the talents of his pupils, the materials available, and the subject matter concerned.

SUMMARY

Pupils who deviate from the norm create special problems in teaching. Pupils who fall into this category include the poor learners, disadvantaged pupils, and the talented.

Teaching poor learners requires much skill and patience. Careful diagnosis of each pupil is necessary so that he can receive the kind of help he needs. This diagnostic activity is particularly important because poor learning is often the result of insufficiencies in his earlier education. In general, the curriculum for poor learners should be simple, practical, realistic, and meaningful. Teaching methods should emphasize concrete, simple activities with sufficient practice and review to make the learning stick. The materials of instruction used ordinarily should be less verbal than in other classes. Reading material should be short and easy, but not childish. Consequently, teachers may find it necessary to develop their own materials.

Disadvantaged youth often have many of the problems of poor learners because of gaps and differences in their cultural backgrounds. However, there has been a tendency to underestimate the potential of disadvantaged youth. Their academic failures are more often failures of the school and the community than pupil failures. In dealing with these youth one must treat them with the respect they deserve. As a rule, they tend to accept authoritarian classes whose orientation is physical, practical, and realistic.

Much of the teaching of slow and disadvantaged youth must be remedial. So should be a considerable amount of the teaching of average and gifted youth. Remedial teaching differs from other teaching only in that as a rule it is concentrated directly on the pupil and his needs after thorough diagnosis.

The key to teaching gifted youth is to urge them forward and not hold them back. Most of the academic techniques common in secondary schools were developed for teaching the most talented youth; therefore, special techniques for teaching them need not be discussed in detail. Since they enjoy the abstract and like to learn, the gifted pupils need plenty of opportunities to exercise their minds. In doing so they can accept a great amount of the responsibility for directing and evaluating their own learnings if the teacher gives them adequate guidance.

Suggested Readings for Part IV

ABRAHAM, WILLARD, *The Slow Learner*. New York: Center for Applied Research in Education, 1964.

ABRAMOWITZ, JACK, *Diary of a Slow Learning Class*. Chicago: Follett Educational Corp., 1963.

ALEXANDER, WILLIAM, AND VYNCE HINES, *Independent Study in Secondary Schools*. New York: Holt, Rinehart and Winston, Publishers, 1970.

Association for Supervision and Curriculum Development, *Individualizing Instruction*. Washington, D.C.: The Association, 1964.

BERGESON, JOHN B., AND GEORGE S. MILLER, *Learning Activities for Disadvantaged Children*. New York: Macmillan Publishing Co., Inc., 1971.

BIENVENU, MILLARD, SR., *Helping the Slow Learner*. New York: Public Affairs Committee, 1967.

BISHOP, LLOYD, K., *Individualizing Educational Systems*. New York: Harper & Row, Publishers, Inc., 1970.

BLAIR, GLENN MYERS, *Diagnostic and Remedial Teaching*, 2nd ed. New York: Macmillan Publishing Co., Inc., 1967.

BOTTOM, R., *The Education of Disadvantaged Children*. Englewood Cliffs, N.J.: Prentice-Hall, Inc., 1970.

COPLEY, FRANK O., *The American High School and the Talented Student*. Ann Arbor, Mich.: The University of Michigan Press, 1961.

DE HAAN, ROBERT F., and ROBERT J. HAVIGHURST, *Educating Gifted Children*. Chicago: University of Chicago Press, 1961.

DELL, HELEN DAVIS, *Individualizing Instruction*. Chicago: Science Research Associates Inc., 1972.

DUANE, JAMES E., *Individualized Instruction Programs and Materials*. Englewood Cliffs, N.J.: Educational Technology Publications, 1973.

EVERETT, SAMUEL, ed. *Programs for the Gifted*. New York: Harper & Row, Publishers, 1961.

FEATHERSTONE, W. B., *Teaching the Slow Learner*, rev. ed. New York: Teachers College Press, 1951.

FLIEGLER, LOUIS, ed. *Curriculum Planning for the Gifted*. Englewood Cliffs, N.J.: Prentice-Hall, Inc., 1961.

FREEHILL, MAURICE F., *Gifted Children: Their Psychology and Education*. New York: Macmillan Publishing Co., Inc., 1961.

GALLAGHER, JAMES J., *Teaching Gifted Students: A Book of Readings*. Boston: Allyn & Bacon, Inc., 1965.

GETZELS, JACOB W., AND PHILIP W. JACKSON, *Creativity and Intelligence: Explorations with Gifted Students*. New York: John Wiley & Sons, Inc., 1962.

HOOVER, KENNETH H., *The Professional Teacher's Handbook*. Boston: Allyn & Bacon, Inc., 1973. Chs. 20–22.

Howes, Virgil M., *Individualization of Instruction: A Teaching Strategy.* New York: Macmillan Publishing Co., Inc., 1970.

Jenkins, James J., and Donald G. Paterson, *Studies in Individual Differences.* New York: Appleton-Century-Crofts, 1961.

Johnson, G. Orville, *Education for Slow Learners.* Englewood Cliffs, N.J.: Prentice-Hall, Inc., 1963.

Karlin, Muriel, and Regina Berger, *Successful Methods for Teaching the Slow Learner.* Englewood Cliffs, N.J.: Prentice-Hall, Inc., 1969.

Klaus, David J., *Instructional Innovation and Individualization.* Pittsburgh: American Institutes for Research, 1969.

Klein, Milton M., *Social Studies for the Academically Talented in the Secondary School.* Washington, D.C.: National Education Association, 1960.

Kough, Jack, *Practical Programs for the Gifted.* Chicago: Science Research Associates, Inc., 1960.

Loretan, Joseph O., and Shelley Umans, *Teaching the Disadvantaged.* New York: Teachers College Press, 1966.

Mosteller, Frederick, and Daniel P. Moynihan, *On Equality of Educational Opportunities.* New York: Random House, Inc., 1971.

National Society for the Study of Education, *Adapting the Secondary-School Program to the Needs of Youth,* Fifty-second Yearbook, Part I. Chicago: University of Chicago Press, 1953.

——, *Education for the Gifted,* Fifty-seventh Yearbook, Part II. Chicago: University of Chicago Press, 1958.

——, *Individualizing Instruction,* Sixty-first Yearbook, Part I. Chicago: University of Chicago Press, 1962.

Noar, Gertrude, *Individualized Instruction: Every Child a Winner.* New York: John Wiley & Sons, Inc., 1972.

——, *Teaching the Disadvantaged,* What Research Says to the Teacher Series, No. 33. Washington, D.C.: Association of Classroom Teachers, 1967.

Ornstein, Alan C., and Philip D. Vairo, eds., *How to Teach Disadvantaged Youth.* New York: David McKay Co., Inc., 1969

Otto, Wayne, *Remedial Teaching.* Boston: Houghton Mifflin Company, 1969.

Passow, A. Harry, ed., *Education in Depressed Areas.* New York: Teachers College Press, 1963.

——, *Nurturing Individual Potential.* Washington, D.C.: Association for Supervision and Curriculum Development, 1964.

Samalonis, Bernice L., *Methods and Materials for Today's High Schools.* New York: Van Nostrand Reinhold Company, 1970. Ch. 8.

Schreiber, Daniel, ed. *The School Drop Out.* Washington, D.C.: The National Education Association, 1964.

Shelton, B., *Teaching and Guiding the Slow Learner.* Englewood Cliffs, N.J.: Prentice-Hall, Inc., 1971.

Shiman, David A., Carmen M. Culver, and Ann Lieberman, eds. *Teachers on Individualization: The Way We Did It.* New York: McGraw-Hill Book Company, 1974.

Strom, Robert D., *Teaching in the Slum School.* Columbus, Ohio: Charles E. Merrill Publishing Company, 1965.

TABA, HILDA, AND DEBORAH ELKINS, *Teaching Strategies for the Cultural-ly Disadvantaged*. Chicago: Rand McNally & Company, 1966.

THOMAS, R. M., AND S. M. THOMAS, *Individual Differences in the Class-room*. New York: David McKay Co., Inc., 1965.

TYLER, LEONA E., *The Psychology of Human Differences*. New York: Appleton-Century-Crofts, 1965.

YOUNIE, WILLIAM J., *Instructional Approaches to Slow Learning*. New York: Teachers College Press, 1967.

V

Specific Strategies and Techniques

Discussions and Small Group Techniques

10

The skillful teacher has many methods and techniques at his command. One list of techniques contains some thirty-odd items.[1] In addition, the proficient teacher has a large repertory of teaching skills which include the ability to use both verbal and nonverbal responses, to draw out pupils, to ask the right sort of questions necessary for his purpose, to reinforce desirable behavior, to recognize the cues in student behavior that show how the class is going and what to do next, to encourage pupil motivation, to pull things together and obtain closure, to present explanations, and demonstrations using examples and so on, ad infinitum.

Although some of these methods and techniques may be better than others, not one of them can be regarded as the best, for there is no best tech-

[1] Lecture, panel discussion, debate, question, question-answer, demonstration, laboratory methods, projects, field trips, programed instruction, individualized instruction, discussion, committee work, role playing, problem solving, supervised study, textbook method, teaching machines, round-table discussion, dramatizations, written assignments, discovery method, drill, review, practice, library research, workbook method, study guide, computer-assisted instruction, and team learning.

191

nique. In fact, techniques that are good for one subject or for one group of pupils or for one objective may be quite unsatisfactory for another. The teacher should have many strings to his bow, so that he can select techniques and methods suitable to his own personality, to the pupils in his class, to the subject he is teaching, and to his educational objectives. For example, in a French class one should undoubtedly teach conversation by group techniques, but pupils can probably master irregular verbs more readily through individual study. This chapter and those following will attempt to show how some of these methods and techniques may be used to advantage.

*

What techniques and abilities should a teacher have in his repertory? Should he be skillful in all of them?

Watch your teachers or remember what techniques and skills they are adept at.

*

WORKING WITH GROUPS

Almost all school activities take place in groups. Usually the instructional group is the full class. Not so often, but still quite frequently, the class is broken down into smaller groups or committees. In spite of the current movement toward individualization very little class time is given to individual or independent study.

Under these circumstances it seems obvious that teachers need to understand the structure and behavior of groups, methods for teaching and influencing groups, group-process techniques, and methods for improving group relationships, group processes, and the group climate. This section, which is largely based on Richard A. Schmuck and Patricia A. Schmuck's excellent digest, will attempt to explain something of the nature of groups and how to teach them.[2]

Necessity for a Positive Climate

Most authorities seem to agree that a positive climate is necessary if one is to have maximum

[2] Richard A. Schmuck and Patricia A. Schmuck, *Group Processes in the Classroom* (Dubuque, Iowa: William C. Brown Company, Publishers, 1971).

learning. But determining just what constitutes a positive social climate is problematical. However, one can safely assume that a classroom with a positive social climate will be characterized by pupils who know and accept each other and are accepted by the teacher, who work well together, who understand the group goals, who know and accept what their own roles and responsibilities are in working toward the group goals, and who take satisfaction in their roles. Such pupils will have a high regard for themselves and a sense of belonging and security because they will know that they have essential roles in the decision-making process.

Characteristics of Groups

Not only is the social climate within a group important in determining the group's effectiveness, other characteristics of the group—its leadership, attraction of the members for each other, its norms, its communication patterns, the amount and kind of its cohesiveness—are equally important. Classes lacking in leadership, mutual attraction, suitable norms, pupil-centered communication pattern and cohesiveness do not function well. Fortunately it is within the power of the teacher, who is aware of these characteristics and the processes which affect them, to influence what the characteristics of any group class will be. The teacher's influence is limited, however. He should not expect to make great changes in group structure overnight; rather he should expect to make progress slowly.

LEADERSHIP IN GROUPS

Leadership is a process. People become group leaders because of what they do and how they do it, rather than because of what they are. This process involves both interpersonal relationships and leadership skills. Pupils are more likely to perform well for persons they like than for persons they dislike or for whom they have no feeling. Pupils also respond more readily to persons who have acquired skill in the functions of leadership. These functions include the task-oriented ones, such as the initiating and selling of ideas that get things done, and the social, emotional ones, such as the encouraging, harmonizing, and compromising that smooth over interpersonal relationships and maintain a congenial, productive atmosphere. To create successful leaders, teachers must cultivate in their pupils the ability to develop friendly interpersonal relations and skill in the leadership functions.

The teacher cannot depend upon his position of authority to make him the true leader of the class. Although pupils are influenced by coercion and the authority of one's position, they respond more readily to the leadership of someone they accept as an acknowledged expert (someone with expert power) or someone they consider charismatic and with whom they identify (someone with referent power). Although the teacher is a leader by virtue of his position, pupils who exert expert power or referent power are apt to be as influential —sometimes more influential.

Similarly democratic leadership is much more likely to be productive than authoritarian leadership. (Laissez-faire leadership in which the leader lets pupils do as they please is completely useless.) Although the authoritarian leader may get things done, the democratic leader usually gets better quality work in a much more positive climate. Authoritarianism tends to cause, or at least aggravate, hostility, high dependency, friction, and other negative qualities. The more pupils feel that they have some influence on the decisions that are being made, the better things are for the group. Consequently it behooves teachers to involve pupils in decision making as much as possible. Chapter 5 describes cooperative group planning techniques suitable for this purpose.

Some pupils are natural leaders. Their feelings toward the teacher and his classes have great impact on the other pupils. Other pupils have no influence at all. On the whole, the group is not much affected by teacher relationships with these low-status pupils, but his relationship with the natural leaders causes a ripple effect that carries over to the rest of the pupils. Consequently teachers would do well to seek the cooperation of high-status pupils. If they are on his side, all of the pupils will perform better. In the long run the teacher will find it very advantageous to involve these high-status pupils in decision making. Obviously the wise teacher tries to spot the

natural leaders as soon as he can. Although sociometric tools may be useful, probably the best technique for spotting the high-status pupil is careful observation. If one takes pains to set aside part each day for observation, he should soon be able to find who the leaders are. They are the pupils that other pupils turn to; they are the ones who have the ideas.

To encourage optimal performance a teacher should distribute leadership roles to as many pupils as possible. In so far as possible, he should try to arrange it so that everyone feels that he has influence and responsibility. His goal should be not to make leaders out of the low-status pupils— pupils maintain the status assigned by other pupils no matter how hard the teacher may try to change it—but to raise everyone's participation in leadership roles. He can further this objective by providing pupils with many opportunities to lead in small ways. Small group work, for instance, makes a natural setting for a large number of pupils to take part in leadership and decision making. So does entrusting some planning and decision making to a class steering committee whose personnel change from time to time. Small success in leadership and decision-making roles of this type may lead to success in larger roles in the future.

ATTRACTION AND THE GROUP PROCESS

Learning takes place more readily in a pleasant, friendly, supportive atmosphere than in a harsh one. Pupils do well in classes in which they feel they are liked by the teacher and other pupils. They do not do well in classes in which they dislike the teacher or feel that the teacher—or other pupils—dislike them. Obviously, to create an environment favorable to learning the teacher should not only demonstrate that he likes the pupils, but he must also foster an atmosphere of liking among the pupils.

Classroom groups can be divided into two main categories: diffusively structured groups and centrally structured groups. In the diffusely structured group most of the pupils like each other equally well and there are few neglected or unliked pupils and no particular subgroups of pupils who are more liked than others. On the other hand, in the centrally structured groups there are only a few pupils who are liked and a large number of pupils who are neglected. In the diffusely oriented group there is no ingroup or outgroup. In the centrally oriented group difference in status stands out. Pupils are aware of it and feel it. The pupils faced by low status do not learn as well as they otherwise might and they dislike school. In diffusely structured groups the differences are obscured. Therefore self-esteem is spread more evenly among the group. Since self-esteem tends to foster good performance, and good performance seems to reinforce self-esteem, diffusely structured groups provide the positive social climate that encourages learning. Centrally structured groups are usually threatening to pupils, and therefore to pupil learning; diffusely structured groups are not.

Evidently pupils tend to live up to what is expected of them. In centrally structured groups little is expected of all except the accepted few. Consequently, large numbers of pupils do not perform well, because they do not feel that they are expected to perform well. The teacher, therefore, needs to concentrate on building self-esteem, attractiveness, and good feeling in his group. He can do this by treating the pupils with respect and liking. When the students try hard, the teacher should encourage and compliment them. After all, we all tend to reflect other people's responses to us, and when those responses are positive our performance usually becomes more positive. Opportunities for establishing relationships of mutual respect and liking are easier in diffusely structured groups than in centrally structured groups.

To develop the wide range of friendships and mutual liking that are basic to the diffusely structured class, the teacher can use teaching techniques that force pupils to know each other and to associate with different pupils from time to time. Almost all pupil-centered teaching strategies help make the class structure more diffuse. Teacher-centered strategies will not. The more evenly the teacher can spread responsibilities and leadership roles, the more diffuse the class structure will be. Therefore, teachers should find small-group and committee work productive, especially if the committee membership is changed occasionally. A group should never be allowed to form itself into a permanent committee. Other techniques that one might use include games in which pupils mix with each other, exercises in which pupils compile biographies of other pupils, or radio or TV interviews in which pupils interact with each other. Some teachers have had considerable success with role-playing activities in which pupils act out roles different from those they normally take in the class.[3]

NORMS AND GROUP BEHAVIOR

Norms are expectations common to most of the pupils in the group. In a large measure, they determine the behavior of the group members. Thus, if the pupils expect teachers to be dictators, as they usually do, they will be suspicious of teachers who say that they want open class participation. Similarly, if pupils expect teachers to give them information, they may resist or rebel against teaching methods that require them to dig up information and think for themselves. For similar reasons, school dress codes which diametrically oppose group norms may backfire. Educational goals and curricula that do not harmonize with pupils' notions of what is valuable and relevant may result in conflict.

If the class social climate is to be positive, the group norms should allow for a wide range of behavior and individual differences. When norms are flexible, allowing for differences in individual behavior, they create an atmosphere of tolerance, encouragement, good feeling, and support. Narrow, rigid norms cause an atmosphere of restraint, threat, and anxiety.

Sometimes teachers can change group norms so as to make them more favorable. If, for instance, teachers continually encourage and support pupils who participate openly, the pupils will come to accept open participation as the norm. Teachers can also use group discussion to change group norms. Discussion allows pupils to examine the norm closely. It may turn out that the norm does not really represent the feeling of the group members. Adolescents, like adults, often have erroneous notions about what other people think and believe. Discussion also seems to bring out feelings of group solidarity so that the group members support the norm once the group has accepted it. For

3 Ibid., pp. 62–64.

that reason cooperative teacher-pupil planning is useful for fostering desirable norms. If pupils work together to make the rules or to plan the units they will study, they will be more likely to incorporate these norms into their behavior. A key to developing norms supportive of a positive social climate evidently is to involve pupils in decision-making procedures.

COMMUNICATION WITHIN THE GROUP

For a positive social climate, communication—both verbal and non-verbal—should be free, open, and supportive. There must be plenty of interaction, dialogue, and feedback among teacher and pupils, but basically the communication pattern should be pupil-centered. Optimum communication does not occur in a highly teacher-centered class (Figure 10-1).

Teachers can establish better communication in the classroom by teaching pupils such communication skills as

Paraphrasing.
Behavior descriptions.
Descriptions of one's feelings.

Perception checking.
Feedback.

Teachers need to practice these skills themselves for most teachers are less than proficient in using them. The teacher can also use a combination of direct teaching and observation of class discussion. The observation techniques described in the section on discussion and interaction analysis would also be useful as a guide for observing one's communication skills. Role-playing activities in which the spectator analyzes the communication process can also be used.

GROUP COHESIVENESS

Cohesive groups stick together and have strong goal direction; in other words, they are closely knit and purposive. In a cohesive group the pupils have high morale and are satisfied, and their feelings toward the group are positive. The pupils know where they stand, and they produce. Things are well organized because everyone knows what he is supposed to be doing and is doing it. In short, a cohesive group works together.

Classroom cohesiveness can be increased by creating a diffusely structured classroom in which pupil participation and involvement are provided and encouraged. Building self-esteem by supporting the pupils and involving them in the decision-making process also helps establish cohesiveness. Members of cohesive groups feel important. Whatever the teacher can do to engender in his students feelings of importance and influence will help to develop cohesiveness in the classroom. Similarly, the teacher can create a group feeling by fostering an atmosphere of liking in which pupils have many opportunities to become involved with each other. Pupil-centered classes are likely to be more cohesive than teacher-centered classes. Teachers can also promote cohesiveness by involving pupils in planning and evaluating their class activities. Diffused structure plus clear goals give one a cohesive group.

*

How do the characteristics of effective instructional groups differ from ineffective ones? In what ways can you as a teacher influence each of these group characteristics so as to make your teaching more effective?

*

Figure 10–1
Patterns of Group Communication.

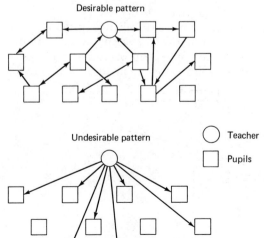

Desirable pattern

Undesirable pattern

○ Teacher

□ Pupils

DISCUSSION TECHNIQUES

Characteristics of a Good Discussion

A discussion is not just a bull session or a rap session. Rather, it is a purposeful conversation proceeding toward some goal with a minimum of rambling and bickering. For a discussion to be successful, the participants need sufficient background to know what they are talking about and to base their arguments on fact. Moreover, the topic must be discussable. The equation $a^2 + b^2 = c^2$ is a fact and so is not a subject for discussion, although perhaps one might discuss its implications.

A discussion is a conversation, not a monologue or a series of questions. In a really effective discussion, everyone should participate, although it is not always necessary for each person to talk. People can participate in different ways. Sometimes he who only sits and listens participates. In general, however, one can assume that in a discussion the more people who participate actively the better. A discussion is not a place for one person to treat his ego by dominating the conversation, nor is it a place for one person to sell his own point of view. Discussion is not another name for lecture or recitation.

A really successful discussion is not only purposeful; it also achieves its purpose. If it is at all possible, the discussion should lead to some sort of conclusion. Certainly, even if no conclusion is reached, it should always culminate in some sort of summing up. Sometimes the summary may have to include a minority report.

Although discussions should be purposeful and conclusive, true discussions are not vehicles for expressing the teacher's point of view or devices by which to win support for a particular position (although they can be very effectively used for converting people to a view). In a true discussion each member of the group thinks for himself, and every one has a chance to say his say, no matter how unpopular his position may be. At best it is informal, but it is always serious. Humor, of course, is welcome, but frivolity is not. Although the group members remain courteous at all times, there is no formal hierarchy of membership. The chairman is merely a moderator. He supervises

rather than directs the conversation. The flow of conversation should travel around the group almost at random (Figure 10-2).

Discussions which consist of questions asked by the leaders and answered by the pupils without considerable side interchange among the pupils are not really discussions at all (Figure 10-3).

Advantages of the True Discussion Method

Teachers who handle true discussions well find them to be effective. As compared to the lecture, for instance, the discussion seems to impart to the pupils better skills in thinking and clearer understandings, and it is more likely to effect changes in attitude; the lecture, however, may have the edge as far as conveying information is concerned. The discussion process—including, as it does, defending, applying, modifying, explaining, and reworking one's ideas—gives pupils the opportunity to develop concepts with deep personal meaning. Concepts developed in this way undoubtedly are more likely to stick with pupils than concepts developed by more static strategies. In addition, this process is more effective in shaping attitudes, ideals, and appreciations than the more static teaching strategies are. Discussions are also useful as a medium for training pupils in communications skills and in

Figure 10–2
Satisfactory Patterns of Discussion Flow.
Moderator's questions have elicited general responses and exchanges between pupils. (Arrows to center indicate a statement or question addressed to the entire group rather than to an individual.)

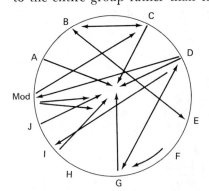

Figure 10–3
Unsatisfactory Pattern of Flow of Discussion.
All conversation emanates from the leader or
moderator.

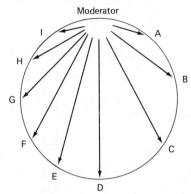

building positive social attitudes and a sense of
belongingness. Their major contribution, however,
is the opportunity they give pupils to practice
thinking—to look at their own ideas, to formulate
and apply principles, and to face up to immediate
feedback from their peers. The discussion is an
excellent tool by which to develop creative thinking.

*

What is a discussion? How does it differ from a recitation?
What value do discussions have? For what purposes
are they best suited? What sorts of things can best be
learned through discussion?
What makes a good discussion?
What can be done about discussions that seem to get
nowhere?

*

Role of the Discussion Leader

ROLE OF THE LEADER

If a discussion is to be worthwhile the leader
must ordinarily provide active, purposeful leadership. He must get the discussion started and see
to it that everyone understands the topic and purpose of the discussion. He must also keep the discussion moving by encouraging all to take part,
and by tactfully bottling up any monologuists in

the group. He attempts to draw pupils out by
skillful questioning. By clearing up errors of fact
or judgment and by recalling the group to the
problem at hand, he tries to keep the discussion
from wandering off into unproductive byways.
From time to time he summarizes to be sure that
all participants are up to date and helps the group
evaluate its progress. Sometimes he may have to
suggest next steps. Finally, when all is said and
done, he tries to tie together all the ideas, conclusions, and generalizations in the summary.

In spite of his important role, the leader should
not dominate the discussion. In the best discussions
the leader limits himself to a minor role, for a
discussion is an opportunity for participants to
share ideas. The leader tries to see that the ideas
of every participant are treated with respect and
that the discussion is kept open so that the truth—
or at least pupil ideas about truth—may come out.
At the same time, he must not turn the discussion
over to the group and let it do as it pleases. Laissez-
faire leadership seldom leads to profitable discussions. Rather the leader should seek to create a
permissive atmosphere in which participants feel
free to speak and think freely without fear of
embarrassment, but in which all the energies of
the group are kept pointed toward the goal.

An ideal discussion leader would possess such
qualities as

Evident interest in the topic at hand.
A sense of humor.
A sense of seriousness.
An interest in and respect for the opinions of
others.
The ability to suppress his own opinions.
A nonjudgmental attitude and bearing.
An accepting and encouraging manner.

Although it may seem that this list calls for
paragons who would be hard to find, many
teachers have trained pupils to be excellent discussion leaders. Figure 10-4 is an observational form
that Schmuck and Schmuck suggest that secondary
school pupils use to rank pupil discussion leaders.

ROLE OF THE RECORDER

A recorder is especially helpful in most group
discussions. He keeps a record of the important

Figure 10–4

Richard A. Schmuck and Patricia A. Schmuck, *Group Processes in the Classroom* (Dubuque, Iowa: William C. Brown Co., Publishers, 1971), p. 48.

OBSERVATION SHEET FOR GOAL-DIRECTED LEADERSHIP*

(Secondary)

Task Functions	Time				
	1	2	3	4	5
1. Initiating: proposing tasks or goals; defining a group problem; suggesting a procedure for solving a problem; suggesting other ideas for consideration.					
2. Information or opinion seeking: requesting facts on the problem; seeking relevant information; asking for suggestions and ideas.					
3. Information or opinion giving: offering facts; providing relevant information; stating a belief; giving suggestions or ideas.					
4. Clarifying or elaborating: interpreting or reflecting ideas or suggestions; clearing up confusion; indicating alternatives and issues before the group; giving examples.					
5. Summarizing: pulling related ideas together; restating suggestions after the group has discussed them.					
6. Consensus testing: sending up "trial balloons" to see if group is nearing a conclusion; checking with group to see how much agreement has been reached.					
Social Emotional Functions					
7. Encouraging: being friendly, warm and responsive to others; accepting others and their contributions; listening; showing regard for others by giving them an opportunity or recognition.					
8. Expressing group feelings: sensing feeling, mood, relationships within the group; sharing his own feelings with other members.					
9. Harmonizing: attempting to reconcile disagreements; reducing tension through "pouring oil on troubled waters"; getting people to explore their differences.					
10. Compromising: offering to compromise his own position, ideas, or status; admitting error; disciplining himself to help maintain the group.					
11. Gate-keeping: seeing that others have a chance to speak; keeping the discussion a group discussion rather than a 1-, 2-, or 3-way conversation.					
12. Setting standards: expressing standards that will help group to achieve; applying standards in evaluating group functioning and production.					

decisions and the trend of the discussion. From time to time, he sums up the status of the discussion upon the request of the leader or upon his own initiative. If necessary, he attempts to resolve conflicts between members of the group by clarifying just what the facts are and just what has been said. Like the leader, he also calls the group to task when it wanders too far afield and sees to it that they tend to the problem at hand. A good recorder can be a tremendous help to the leader of any discussion group.

The recorder's main task, of course, is to keep the record of the discussion. Because this task is a difficult one for many boys and girls, the teacher should take special pains to help the pupil recorder. Usually in classroom discussions verbatim transcripts of the discussion are not desirable. Instead, the group needs to have an account of the major positions taken and the conclusions reached. One method that will help ensure good recording by beginners is to have the recorder keep his record on the chalkboard. This technique makes it possible for all the participants to see the notes and also permits the teacher to coach the recorder if the need arises. The overhead projector can be used similarly with the added advantage that the notes recorded on the transparency can be saved for future reference or for reprojecting. In classes in which the recorder writes notes out on paper at his desk, the teacher might be wise to keep notes himself in order to supplement any lapses of the pupil recorder. As a matter of fact, this practice is a wise precaution in any case.

ROLE OF THE PARTICIPANTS

The ability to speak and listen well as participants in group discussions is a rather difficult skill that relatively few adults have truly mastered. When speaking, participants should try to be clear and precise. Although it is difficult to do so during a lively discussion, they should try to organize what they say before they say it so that they can make their points more easily. In this respect they should learn that their presentations will be more successful if they speak clearly and simply without affectation. A simply worded direct argument in which one makes one's points one by one in a simple linear order is usually much more likely to be understood than more complicated approaches. The simple technique of taping a pupil's statement and asking him to listen to himself and to try to arrange the ideas he thought he was presenting into a logical outline sometimes helps pupils understand the advantages of direct simple organization.

One danger of placing great emphasis on the way pupils present their opinions is that they may forget to listen to the discussion. Many persons, even participants in television debates and panels, are guilty of being so busy thinking about what they want to say that they never listen to the other participants or to the questions asked them. To train pupils to listen, some teachers ask each pupil to repeat the germ of the last speaker's comments before he adds his own.

ROLE OF THE TEACHER

In discussions, as in other methods, the teacher's role is to prepare, execute, and follow up. However, in the discussion his role during the execution phase should be subdued. The bulk of the discussion should be the pupils' own. Even so,

conducting the discussion is hard work for the teacher.

Before the discussion begins, the teacher must see to it that both he and the pupils are properly prepared. During the class's first experiences with real discussions he will have to act as moderator or chairman. At all times he will need to act as supervisor and observer. In these roles he must see to it that the problem to be discussed is properly defined and delimited, furnish information when it is required, set guidelines, see to it that gross errors do not remain unchallenged, pose questions, reflect the content and feeling of the comments made, relate the comments to one another and to the central topic, in general keep the discussion moving on the right track, and finally provide a follow-up. On the occasions that he acts as moderator, he will have to do all of these jobs himself directly. When a pupil is moderator, he will have to do most of them by indirection. Sometimes a hint to the moderator or recorder will suffice. Sometimes he may have to stop the discussion and restart it. However, the more unobtrusively he can do the job, the better.

Most important, during the discussion the teacher should assume the role of a consultant who is always available as a resource person or advisor for whatever contingency might arise. In discussions, perhaps more than in other strategies, the teacher acts as the servant rather than the master of the group.

Conducting the Discussion

TO PREPARE FOR A DISCUSSION

Students often think of discussions as easy periods, but really discussions are quite difficult to carry out. Both teachers and pupils must be well prepared for discussion classes if they are to be successful—perhaps they need to be better prepared for discussion classes than for any other type of class. According to Wesley and Wronski, during the period of preparation both teacher and pupils must

1. Have already in mind the topic, problem, or issue of the proposed discussion and search for pertinent information.

2. Find and utilize the best sources, such as encyclopedias, yearbooks, and specialized studies.

3. Utilize pamphlets and magazines. Remember that they are often the only source for the systematic treatment of current issues.

4. Read the newspapers. They report the latest developments in the unfoldment of a process.

5. Studying involves several processes. Scan parts of the materials and locate pertinent passages; read other parts with detailed care.

6. Read purposively. Ignore the irrelevant and concentrate upon the parts that deal with the chosen topic.

7. Read critically. Weigh statements. Note contradictions and inconsistencies. Pursue the differences to valid conclusions.

8. Read objectively. Discard preconceptions and prejudices and give the author a patient and impartial hearing.

9. Read discriminatingly. Distinguish between facts and opinions. Do not ignore opinions, for world policies are based upon them, but recognize them as interpretations rather than facts.

10. Read appreciatively. Be patient enough to secure and understand the viewpoint of the writer even though you do not accept it. A degree of intellectual humility is a prerequisite to learning.

11. Read receptively. Expand your information and be prepared to be convinced, even though it involves a change in your attitude; otherwise reading merely narrows and confirms you in your preconceived opinions.

12. Read constructively. Deduce conclusions and generalizations. As you read, reconstruct and synthesize the materials into an integrated pattern.

13. Utilize the materials to prepare an outline, a summary, a speech, or a written report. Even the most fluent participant needs a prepared outline and the less fluent may need a complete manuscript.

14. Prepare with the thought of presentation. Arrange the points in a logical sequence and imagine how they will appeal to your prospective hearers.

15. Prepare conscientiously. If the chairman has asked you to deal with one aspect of a topic, concentrate upon it. Relate it to the whole problem and be prepared to fit it into the plan rather than preempt the whole topic.[4]

During the period of preparation the teacher can make sure that pupils understand exactly what the point at issue is to be and what their roles in the discussion are. Early in the year the teacher may find it desirable to do some direct teaching concerning the how and why of carrying on discussions.

STARTING THE DISCUSSION

Not only must the teacher be well briefed on the topic to be discussed, but he needs a plan for the conducting of the discussion. In the plan, he should include provisions for getting the discussion started and questions for possible use. He should also be prepared with possible conclusions.

Starting a discussion may be something of a strain. It may take a little persuasion, or some special introductory activity. Before starting, the teacher should attempt to arrange the group in a homey, informal fashion. As a general rule, the more pleasant the atmosphere the better chance the discussion has of being successful. If possible, the pupils should be seated so that they can see each other. In actual practice a circle seems to be the best seating arrangement for a discussion, although any other arrangement that brings the participants face to face will do.

If the discussion is to be successful, the pupils must understand what it is they are to discuss and the procedure they will use in discussing it. Sometimes the introductory portion of the discussion needs to be devoted to clarifying the issues. Presenting the topic to be discussed as a problem sometimes makes the clarifying and launching of the discussion easier.

To start a discussion without some activity to develop interest among the participants is quite difficult. People need an opportunity to think and react before they can discuss anything sensibly. Consequently, it is sometimes advantageous to have

4 Edgar B. Wesley and Stanley P. Wronski, *Teaching Social Studies in High Schools*, 5th ed. (Boston: D. C. Heath & Company, 1958), p. 350.

a discussion develop out of some other activity. Buzz sessions—groups of four to six people who discuss the question for four to six minutes—sometimes help to get the discussion under way. Another common device is to start the discussion with a short introductory talk or to have someone throw some challenging questions (prepared in advance) at the group. A test, quiz, or pretest can sometimes be used to stimulate a brisk discussion.

In any case the leader will want to include an opening statement of some sort to orient the group and establish the ground rules for the discussion. Other devices to stimulate discussion include

The introduction of a specific case or problem.
Role playing.
Films.
Filmstrips.
Exhibits.
Pictures.
Visitors.
News items.
Tape recordings.
Demonstrations.
Staged incidents.
Provocative questions, especially questions emphasizing *how, why,* and *what if?*

Whatever tactic is used to get the discussion going should not take long. It should be only long enough to arouse interest and point the direction of the conversation. The discussion should follow immediately. Tomorrow may be too late, no matter how stimulating the activity. Once the mood has been lost, to reestablish it may be impossible.

No matter how dramatic or exciting an initiatory activity may seem, the teacher must be prepared for the response to be negative or for the discussants to start off in directions he never dreamed of. The wise leader always has a few spare approaches up his sleeve in case of need. Teachers must be prepared for such contingencies in order to save both their own and pupil-led discussions.

*

What can the leader do to start a discussion when the group seems reluctant to participate? Can you suggest at least five approaches which may help the discussion get started?

How would you arrange the physical setting to encourage discussion? Suppose you wished to use the board in connection with the discussion. Would that change your decision?

What can you do with pupils who monopolize the discussion?

*

GUIDING THE DISCUSSION

Once the discussion is started, the leader must keep it moving briskly in the right direction. Skillful questioning and keeping an outline of the most important points on the chalkboard will help maintain the tempo and hold the group to the topic. So will being sure that all the pupils know and accept the problem under discussion. Should a group digress, the leader can redirect them by restating the question, although the group should be allowed to pursue a digression if it seems to have promise. Occasionally groups that have become confused and cannot agree can be helped by a minute of silent consideration of the problem, an impromptu buzz session, or role playing.

Skillful Questioning. One key to successfully guiding the discussion is the skillful use of questions. The leader's role is to draw pupils out and to keep the conversation moving in the direction it should go. To draw pupils out the skillful leader asks open-ended, broad, thought-provoking questions. Divergent questions are much more likely to be successful than convergent ones. Evaluative questions are likely to be most valuable of all. Usually the leader should throw his questions out for anyone who wishes to pick them up. At other times, for some special reason—to involve a new participant, to start things moving, to reengage someone's wandering attention, or perhaps even to forestall still another comment by a monopolizer —he addresses his questions to specific individuals.

In order to involve more pupils, the leader should bounce the questions around. Asking pupils to comment on other pupil's answers may be effective. Questions such as "Do you agree with Mary, Susie?" "What would you do in such a situation?" and "If you had your druthers, which would you prefer?" tend to keep the conversation going and tend to free pupils' ideas. The leader should seldom take it upon himself to answer questions or to give his opinion except in the case of a direct question about a fact. Even then it is better to ask if anyone else can provide the information requested.

Creating a Supportive Atmosphere. The leader should strive for a supportive atmosphere, accepting all contributions graciously, even when they are not very helpful. He should refrain from expressing his approval or disapproval of the comments of the participants. He must try to ensure that all are heard with equal respect.

On the other hand, the leader cannot let error pass unchallenged. He should question inconsistencies, faulty logic, and superficialities. By using skillful questions he can get the pupils to see their own ideas and those of their colleagues clearly. He can ask them to explain why they said what they said and believe what they believe. He should try, again by questioning, to get the pupils to look beyond their statements and to see the causes and consequences of their beliefs. He should dare them to prove their statements and cite their authorities. When confusion is rife, he can try to clarify the situation by asking such questions as

Just what does that term mean?
Exactly what is the issue facing us?

One of the most difficult problems the leader has to face is that of keeping the discussion on the track. Usually he can bring the group back into focus by asking a question that deals directly with the topic at hand. Other times he may have to point out that "I think that we are forgetting the point of our discussion." At other times the leader may have to stop to reorient the group by some technique such as one of those suggested in the first paragraph of this section.

From time to time, the leader should draw the threads together by summarizing or by asking the recorder to summarize. This gives the group a chance to stop and look at its progress, to see how it stands, and perhaps to decide in which direction to proceed. To bring out these values, the leader may include any or all of the following:

1. A résumé of the major points made so far.
2. A review of the facts and evidence presented.
3. A synopsis of what has been accomplished and what remains to be finished.
4. A restatement of any conclusions that have been made.
5. An analysis of the course or conduct of the discussion up to this point.

Whatever the gist of the summary, it should be brief, well organized, and to the point. Too many or too long summaries may break up the thread of the discussion and so do more harm than good. Also harmful are summaries that do not represent the thinking of all the group. The final summary at the end of the discussion should pull together all the important ideas and conclusions. To be sure that all points of view are presented fairly, it is often advantageous to elicit the aid of other participants in developing the summary. To note these ideas and conclusions on the chalkboard for all to see will aid to emphasize their importance and to clarify their meaning.

Although a good summary is essential for the ending of a discussion, it should not end the consideration of the topic. A suitable follow-up activity that drives home the importance of the things learned or leads into the next activity can increase the value of almost any discussion.

Evaluating the Discussion

The value of discussion will ordinarily increase as the pupils learn how to carry on discussions and gain experience. Good discussion techniques must be learned and practiced. If we take stock of ourselves and our discussion from time to time, progress in those skills can be expected. Frequently self-evaluations will help to improve discussion skills. Having the group members check a form as simple as the following can be of considerable value.

1. Did the group discussion do what it set out to do?
2. In what way did we fall short?
3. Did we get off the topic?
4. Did everyone participate?
5. Did anyone monopolize the conversation?

Pupils' self-evaluation of their discussions can often be enhanced by letting them listen to taped recordings of the discussions. For evaluating a taped discussion the use of a list of criteria similar to that just mentioned or the one prepared by the A.S.C.D. (Association for Supervision and Curriculum Development) can be of great help. In spite of its obvious value, the tape recording of group discussions may present something of a problem. To

Figure 10–5
A Flow Chart

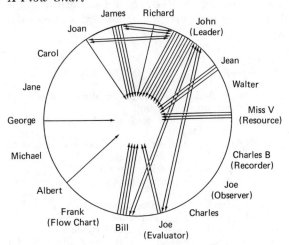

faults. Frequently the pupils will respond more positively to criticism from one of their peers acting as observer than from the teacher.

EVALUATION DEVICES

A flow chart such as the one which appears as Figure 10-5 can be of great help in evaluating the discussion.

Another way of recording the progress of the group discussion is for the evaluator to place a tally alongside a speaker's name each time he speaks as in Figure 10-6. Grambs, Carr, and Fitch recommend an alternative to this method. In this system the evaluator uses evaluative marks

— if the contribution detracts from the discussion;
+ if the contribution adds to the discussion;
0 if the contribution neither adds nor detracts;
? if the contribution is a question.[5]

Perhaps the most effective evaluative devices are discussions about the discussion in which pupils examine their own techniques and free reaction

record a large group discusion with an ordinary school tape recorder can be very difficult. For recording, the group needs to be seated in a circle with each person as close to a microphone as possible. Otherwise it may be necessary to turn up the volume so high that the recorder may pick up extraneous noises and spoil the recording. In small groups, of course, the microphone can be passed from speaker to speaker, but in most class discussions this technique is too cumbersome to be practicable. Another danger is the temptation to play the recording too long or too often. Running through a tape recording may be advantageous for training in group discussion, but overdone it can become a pernicious time-waster. Only parts of the tape should be rerun to illustrate good or poor portions of the discussion, or to reinforce the report of what happened.

Sometimes, in order to evaluate the group's discussion, one of the members is asked to act as an observer. The observer's job is to watch the group as the discussion progresses and to report his evaluation to the group. In his evaluation he may use as a guide such criteria as those mentioned in the preceding list.

The comments of the observer on the progress of the discussion and the participation of the group members are also an effective means of making the overtalkative or noncooperative person aware of his

[5] Jean D. Grambs, John C. Carr and Robert M. Fitch, *Modern Methods in Secondary Education,* 3rd ed. (New York: Holt, Rinehart and Winston, Publishers, 1970), pp. 200–201.

Figure 10–6
Discussion Analysis.

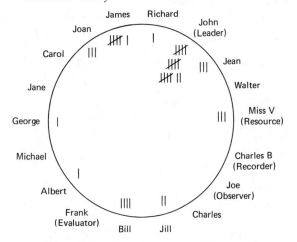

sheets in which pupils anonymously and briefly state their reactions favorable or unfavorable, and tell why they feel as they do. Simple rating forms such as the one illustrated as Figure 10-7 are also useful. The evaluations may be more honest if reaction sheets or rating forms are turned into a pupil committee charged with assessing the success of the activity rather than handed in to the teacher.

THE OVERTALKATIVE PUPIL

One pernicious problem is the person who dominates the discussion. The flow chart (Figure 10-5) is an especially good instrument for pointing out just who these people are without hurting anyone's sensibilities. A scheme sometimes used by teachers is to make the overtalkative pupil an observer, evaluator, or flow chart operator. This assignment may have two merits: it may force the pupil to silence, and it may make him aware of the danger of talking too much.

*

Make a simple rating scale with which to evaluate a group discussion.

What does the flow chart (Figure 10–5) tell you about the participating group?

Would flow charts be helpful in high school classes? How would you use them?

*

Figure 10–7
Discussion Rating Form.

```
┌─────────────────────────────────────────────────┐
│                                                   │
│   This discussion was                             │
│                                                   │
│      Excellent      Indifferent      Bad          │
│                                                   │
│   What I liked best was:                          │
│                                                   │
│                                                   │
│                                                   │
│   What I liked least was:                         │
│                                                   │
│                                                   │
│                                                   │
│   Suggestions:                                    │
│                                                   │
│                                                   │
└─────────────────────────────────────────────────┘
```

THE A.S.C.D. CHECK LIST

The following list[6] is useful for outlining the tasks of the group participants and evaluating their success.

Each Group Member and the Discussion Leader in Particular
—— Helps decide on specific problems and ways of working as a group
—— Contributes ideas and suggestions related to the problem
—— Listens to what other members say and seeks helpful ideas and insights
—— Requests clarification when needed
—— Observes the group process and makes suggestions
—— Assumes various roles as needed
—— Helps group get acquainted
—— Helps group establish ground rules
—— Reports results of preconference planning for work of group
—— Helps group proceed with planning and deciding
—— Calls on group to clarify, analyze, and summarize problems and suggested solutions
—— Draws out the "timid soul" and keeps the dominant person from monopolizing
—— Knows particular contributions which different persons can make
—— Assists the recorder
—— Summarizes the thinking of the group as needed.

The Recorder
—— Consults with the group concerning the kind of record that is developing as the discussion moves forward
—— Keeps a record of the main problems, issues, ideas, facts, and decisions as they appear in discussion
—— Summarizes the group discussion upon request
—— Requests clarification when his notes are unclear
—— Prepares resolutions and other final reports with other designated members of the group
—— Attends any scheduled clearinghouse or intergroup sharing committee sessions
—— Prepares final group report and is responsible for getting it to proper clearinghouse.

[6] Association for Supervision and Curriculum Development, *1954 Convention Program*, Washington, D.C.: the Association, a department of the National Education Association, 1954, pp. 54–55. Adapted by the 1954 Committee on Conference Orientation and Evaluation from material prepared for the 1950 Convention Program by J. Cecil Parker, University of California, Berkeley.

Each Group Member
Pays attention to the way the group:
—— States its goals clearly
—— Permits participation to be easily and widely
spread
—— Keeps its discussion clear
—— Assumes leadership responsibility
—— Uses its resources
—— Progresses toward its goals
—— Revises its goals as necessary
—— Participates in evaluation of the group process
—— Reports to the group if asked regarding observations on the group process.

Group Members as Resource Persons
Every member of a discussion group is responsible for:
—— Supplying information or other material to the
group when requested, or when the discussion seems to call for it
—— Citing his own experience freely when it is
relevant
—— Assisting the leader in moving toward the
achievement of group goals.

*

Examine the A.S.C.D. criteria for discussion groups. How can they be used in a secondary school class?

How can student leaders, recorders, and resource persons be used in secondary school classes?

*

Group Discussion and Thinking

Group discussion can be used as a thinking tool. In fact, democracy is based on the premise that problems can be thought out and solved through the group process. Evidently, properly used group discussion is a method that frees creative power in ways no other method can.[7] When a group freely discusses a problem that is real to them, their combined thinking combines many skills, insights, and backgrounds. For the discussion to be a thinking process, however, the topic must be one of importance to the discussants, and the discussion free and permissive, but at the same time disciplined and orderly. Think of what a high school group could do with topics such as the following ones which happen to be the first two topics of several included in an article on discussion in English classes.

1. Discuss objects or areas of human relations in which inventors, customs, or public policy has been highly uncreative, inflexible, or unadaptable. Have students suggest alterations for the betterment of the individual or society.

2. Have students throw a critical, yet creative eye on their own school to identify problems in school life which are not being adequately recognized or met. E.g., evaluate effectiveness of student government, co-curricular program, assemblies; discuss over-all needs in the school's program which could be improved for benefit of incoming freshmen.[8]

The procedures in a discussion that is designed to encourage problem solving are just the same as in any other discussion—after all, group discussions should be exercises in group thinking. Seldom does the thinking of the group proceed toward the solution of the problem in strictly logical fashion. However, the discussion should generally follow the steps in the usual pattern of the problem-solving process. As outlined by Burton, Kimball, and Wing, those steps, as adapted for group thinking, are

1. Discovers the existence of a problem of concern that seems to be solvable by group methods, that is, by consensus.

2. Defines the problem through group examination and discussion.

3. Analyzes the problem to find what are the facts and circumstances to be faced.

4. Attempts to find solutions to the problem. (This is likely to be a long process involving much discussion, data gathering, consulting of outside sources, and so on. In the process the group draws tentative conclusions, conducts straw votes, reviews and summarizes as it works toward consensus.)

5. Makes and tests conclusions until it finally comes to a decision.[9]

The great value of discussion in problem solving is that it opens up the process to so many ideas. Narrow, stereotypic thinking is difficult to maintain when one is bombarded by the "differing values, biases, levels of insight," standards, conclusions, and the beliefs of others. Free discussion brings these differences out in the open. It thus not only forces one to put his own values and beliefs on the line for examination, but also forces

---

[7] William H. Burton, Roland B. Kimball, and Richard L. Wing, *Education for Effective Thinking* (New York: Appleton-Century-Crofts, 1960), p. 327.

[8] Gladys Veidemanis, "A Curriculum View of Classroom Discussion," *English Journal*, 51:21–25 (January, 1962).

[9] Adapted from Burton, Kimball and Wing, op. cit., p. 328.

one to consider beliefs and values that are new and different.

Discussion and Value Clarification

Value-clarifying discussions are much like problem-solving discussions. Their purpose is not didactic but to enhance understanding. Like problem-solving discussions, they require that the pupils have freedom to think free from teacher pressure. Teachers must be nonjudgmental and accepting. They must refrain from leading questions or questions which force a pupil into a certain position. Neither can they come down hard and inform a pupil that his values are wrong. Value-clarifying discussions are always open ended. They have no correct solutions or conclusions. In the words of Raths, Harmin, and Simon

> Thus in this discussion a teacher who is concerned that students develop an intelligent and viable relationship with their worlds, that is, develop clear values, (1) helps them to examine alternatives and consequences in issues, (2) does not tell them, directly or indirectly, what is "right" for all persons and for all times, (3) is candid about his own values but insists that they not be blindly adopted by others, (4) sometimes limits behavior that he considers ill advised, but never limits the right to believe or the right to behave differently in other circumstances, and (5) points to the importance of the individual making his own choices and considering the implications for his own life.[10]

Value-clarifying discussions should be short. The minute they start to lag, they should be cut off. As springboards for value-clarifying discussions Raths, Harmin, and Simon recommend the use of provocative questions, pictures without captions, scenes from plays or movies, editorials, song lyrics, election literature, letters to the editor, advertising, cartoons, comic strips, news broadcasts, and the like. Anything that presents value judgment or possible conflict in value will usually bring on a strong discussion. Given the chance, once pupils know that their opinions and concerns will be taken seriously, they will bring in all the springboard material one needs.

[10] Louis E. Raths, Merrill Harmin, Sidney B. Simon, *Values and Teaching* (Columbus, Ohio: Charles E. Merrill Books, Inc., 1966), p. 115.

FORMAL DISCUSSION TECHNIQUES

Formal discussions have the advantage of combining audience activities with the give-and-take of the discussion. They are consequently useful as large-class activities when informal, whole-class, or small-group discussions would not be feasible. Among the type of formal discussions mentioned in the literature are

The round table—a quite informal group, usually five or fewer participants, who sit around a table and converse among themselves and with the audience.

The panel—a fairly informal setting in which four to six participants with a chairman discuss a topic among themselves, and then there is a give-and-take with the class. Each participant makes an opening statement, but there are no speeches.

The forum—a type of panel approach in which a panel gives and takes with the audience.

The symposium—a more formal setting in which the participants present speeches representing different positions and then open up for questions from the floor.

The debate—a very formal approach consisting of set speeches by participants of two opposing teams and a rebuttal by each participant.

The British debate—somewhat less formal approach in which principal presentations are given by spokesmen of each side and then the floor is opened for comment and questions from members of each side alternately.

The jury trial—approach in which the class simulates a courtroom.

In general, the procedures for preparing for these and other types of formal discussion are pretty much the same. As a matter of fact, many people use the terms very loosely so that one can never be quite sure exactly what panel, for instance, means in any given conversation and truly the techniques are so similar that distinctions may be superfluous. In any event, formal discussions are likely to be more interesting if they involve questions and discussions from members of the class other than the panelists. It is good policy to schedule either a time for general discussion or a question and answer period no matter what type of formal discussion is used.

When to Use Formal Discussion Techniques

As a preceding paragraph stated, formal discussions are useful for spicing up and personalizing large classes. These techniques need not be limited to large classes alone, however. Panels and symposia make excellent springboards for discussion in any group. They are often used to launch discussions in small classes. Teachers also find them useful

1. As culminating activities.
2. As methods of presenting committee reports.
   a. Each member of the committee becomes a panelist, or
   b. Representatives of various committees who have studied different areas or taken different portions make up the panelists.
3. As a way to get differing points of view on the floor. This technique is particularly useful when discussing controversial issues. Pupils representing differing points of view make up the panels and present their arguments.
4. As a way to present the findings of pupil research.
5. As a way to give classes a change of pace.

Suggestions for Conducting Panels, Symposia, Round Tables, and Forums

Formal discussions are best when the pupils discuss matters really important to them. For this reason, if for no other, it is wise to involve pupils in the selection of the topics to be discussed.

Most pupil panelists need help as they prepare for their panels. They should do at least part of their preparation in class during some sort of supervised study period so that the teacher can oversee the development of their presentations. It is a good policy for the teacher to require each panelist to present his plans for his presentation for approval a day or so before the panel is to occur. The procedures for preparing for panels, symposia, debates, and so on, are much the same as they would be for any other committee project, report, or research study.

Before the panel or symposium begins, the pupils should be well briefed on the procedures to be fol-

lowed. If there are to be initial presentations, the order of presentation should be arranged and time limits set. Usually these details can best be arranged by the pupils themselves in an informal planning meeting guided by the teacher. There needs to be no rehearsal although when the discussion format requires set speeches, pupils should be encouraged to rehearse their speeches.

After the formal portion of the discussion has ended, there should be an open discussion or a question-and-answer period in which everyone may participate. This should be followed by a summary of important points or portions by the chairman. In addition the teacher will usually find it advisable to follow up and tie up loose ends. If lack of time becomes a factor, the summary and follow-up can become review activities for another day.

In order to encourage pupils other than the panelists to benefit from formal discussions, teachers may take such steps as

Requiring pupils to take notes on the formal presentations and discussion.

Asking pupils to summarize the major points and different positions. (Summaries may be oral, written, or even perhaps quizzes.)

Asking pupils to evaluate the logic and accuracy of the arguments of the panelists. (Pupils should not criticize the panelists' rhetorical skill, however.)

The Chairman of the Formal Discussion

Just as in informal discussions, the chairman can make a great difference in the success of a formal discussion. At first perhaps the teacher should chair the discussion himself, but once pupils have developed some skill with the medium, pupils should be the chairmen. Among the duties the chairman must perform are these:

1. *Make the introduction.* (Announce the topic, map out the procedure to be followed, prepare the audience by setting mood, filling in necessary background, and explaining the purpose.)
2. *Control the conduct of the panel.* Introduce the participants, stop them when their time is up. Moderate give-and-take within the panel. Sum up when necessary. Redirect flow of discussion if it bogs down.

3. Moderate question, answer, and discussion period with audience. To get audience participation, sometimes it is wise to have some questions planted. Pupils can be assigned to make up questions as homework. (If you do assign questions as homework, collect them whether they were asked or not during the discussion.) In this role the chairman must solicit questions, accept and refer questions in such a way as to encourage more participation, and again sum up and redirect discussion as necessary.

4. Close the discussion. Sum up. Tie up loose ends. Thank the panelists and audience participants.

Debate

Debate is the most formal of the discussion procedures. It requires that there be (1) a formal question to be debated, e.g., *Resolved*: That all television broadcasting stations be owned and operated by the federal government; (2) two teams of debaters, one to argue for the resolution, one to argue against it; and (3) a formal procedure for debating the issue.

DEBATE PROCEDURE

1. Each of the two teams consists of two or three debators.

2. A moderator introduces the topic and the speakers. After the formal debate has ended he may conduct an open discussion in which members of the audience express their views and perhaps ask questions.

3. A timekeeper times the speeches, warns the speakers when their time is growing short, and stops them when their time has run out. Ordinarily the procedure is for the timekeeper to stand to mark the beginning of the warning period and to call the time when the time has run out.

4. Each team member makes a formal presentation for his arguments. This presentation is to be no longer than a fixed number of minutes (decided well in advance of the debate).

5. Each team member makes a rebuttal in which he tries to counter the arguments of the other team. Again the time is limited to a prearranged number of minutes.

6. The order of presentations and rebuttals runs:
First speaker pro.
First speaker con.
Second speaker pro.
Second speaker con.
First rebuttal pro.
First rebuttal con.
Second rebuttal pro.
Second rebuttal con.

7. After the formal debate has ended it is possible to open a general discussion.

8. If one wishes, one may select pupil or faculty judges who can decide on the basis of a check sheet which side argued more skillfully.

ADVANTAGES OF THE FORMAL DEBATE

The use of the formal debate is advantageous because it

1. Provides an opportunity for study in depth.
2. Can arouse interest.
3. Shows two sides of an issue.
4. Brings controversy into sharper focus.

DISADVANTAGES OF THE FORMAL DEBATE

On the other hand the formal debate has several serious drawbacks. It

1. Emphasizes dichotomous (black or white) thinking.
2. Involves too few pupils.
3. Tends to emphasize fluency in debate and winning at the expense of attempting to get at the truth of the matter.

British-Style Debate

The British-style debate is more useful for most classes than the ordinary formal debate because it opens up the discussion to more participants. The procedure for conducting the British-style debate is simple.

1. Select question or proposition to be debated.
2. Divide the class into two teams, one for the proposition, the other against it.
3. Select two principal speakers for each team.
4. Have the principal speaker of each team present his argument in a five-minute talk.

5. Have the second speaker for each team present his argument in a three-minute talk.

6. Throw the question open to comments, questions, and answers from the other team members. In order to keep things fair, alternate between members of the pro and con teams.

7. Let one member of each team summarize their case. Often the summarizer is the first speaker, but if a third principal speaker does the summarizing, it makes for better class participation.

8. Follow up with general discussion.

Jury-Trial Technique

Another debate technique that is excellent because it can involve a large number of the class in active participation is the jury trial. In this technique the class simulates courtroom procedures to discuss an issue or problem. The procedure seems to be a simple one, but it requires careful preparation if it is to go smoothly.

1. Select an issue or problem to debate. It adds interest if one of the pupils can act as a defendant.

2. Select lawyers, researchers, and witnesses for both sides. These groups can be as large as you wish, but if they are too large, they become cumbersome. The teacher can act as judge, or better yet, some responsible pupil can be named for that position. Another pupil should be selected court stenographer, or recorder, to keep a record of what transpires. All members of the class who are not lawyers, researchers, witnesses, or court officials, are the jury. (If you want to do it up brown, you can select someone to be clerk of the court, bailiff, and so on, to give the courtroom verisimilitude.)

3. All pupils should research the problems. The lawyers and witnesses should get the facts from their own research and from that of other class members.

4. Conduct the trial.
  a. The lawyers open up with their arguments.
  b. Witnesses present their evidence.
  c. Lawyers question and cross examine.
  d. Lawyers from each side sum up. Each should point out how the evidence favors his side, of course.
  e. The judge sums up, points out errors in

the arguments, fallacies, misstatements of fact, and so on.
  f. The class, acting as the jury, votes on which side won the argument.

SMALL GROUPS AND COMMITTEES

Quite often teachers divide classes into small groups. Among the various types of small groups commonly found are work groups, or committees, discussion groups, buzz groups, ability groups, and interest groups. As often as not, small groups are a combination of two or more of these types. A committee, for instance, may also be an interest or ability group. Small groups are used frequently because they are useful for many purposes.

1. Small groups allow for individual instruction and help provide for the many differences in pupils by allowing them to participate in different roles and on different committees.
2. Small-group work promotes effective learning.
  a. Small groups seem to be more successful in problem solving than individuals are.
  b. Small-group techniques tend to develop critical discrimination.
  c. Small groups provide a wide range of information.
  d. Small groups provide opportunities for depth study and wide coverage.
  e. Small groups provide opportunities to develop research and study skills.
3. Small groups provide pupils with opportunities to learn social skills and to develop good social attitudes as a result of the give-and-take.
4. Small groups can help develop leadership ability.
5. Small groups can help develop self-reliance and self-direction.
6. Small groups add variety and interest to classes.
  a. They make it possible to match method with purpose.
  b. They give a change of pace.
  c. They provide release from the tedium of the ordinary class and give pupils an opportunity to work off their energy through active participation.[11]

This section of the book will discuss small work and discussion groups. A discussion concerning the

[11] Leonard H. Clark, *Teaching Social Studies in Secondary Schools: A Handbook.* (New York: Macmillan Publishing Co., Inc., 1973), p. 95.

using of small groups as a tool for providing for individual differences in pupils can be found in Chapter 8.

Why Small Groups Fail

In spite of the many advantages of using small-group work, frequently small groups fail. Usually there is a pedagogical reason for such failures. The chances are good that it is not the group's fault. Perhaps the most common cause of failure is inadequate preparation of the group by the teacher. The goal of the groups and the role of the workers are not sufficiently defined. It is most important to establish what is to be done and who is to do it before the group begins. The teachers also must make sure that the pupils know how to do what they are supposed to do and have the material they need to do it with. Sometimes the task assigned to the group is not really the kind of job that can be done by a group. Perhaps it is too complicated, perhaps too simple, perhaps something that should be done by individual study or projects.

Sometimes the failures are caused by bad groups in which the pupils do not get along with each other or in which the members are not capable of performing the task required. Consequently teachers need to be careful when selecting group members.

Sometimes the pupils have just not learned to work together as a group. Adolescents who come to our secondary school classes may or may not have learned to work in groups in earlier grades. Many have excellent group skills; many do not. Teachers may have to work with these pupils before they will become ready to carry out small group assignments successfully.

Lack of pupil motivation can make any approach fail. The teacher should do everything he can to make the small group activity enticing. In every case group work should center as much as possible around pupil concerns and ideas. Pupils work best when the project is their own. Too much group work has little relevance to pupils' lives or concerns. It is no wonder that sometimes small groups fail; the wonder is that so many succeed in spite of their seeming uselessness.

To Launch Small Group Work

When pupils are not familiar with small group work and lack the social skills necessary to make group work successful, one should begin working with them slowly. Perhaps the best method is to start off by forming small transitory committees to perform definite tasks, e.g., the bulletin board committee, the lab-cleanup committee, the committee in charge of handing out the material for pupils to work with, and so on. The use of buzz groups is another approach often used by teachers to introduce small-group techniques to their pupils.

Buzz Groups

Buzz groups are small groups of about a half dozen pupils who discuss freely and informally for about a half dozen minutes. Because of these characteristics—six people meeting for six minutes—buzz groups are sometimes called 6 × 6 groups.[12] Buzz groups are transitory groups called together for a specific immediate purpose. As soon as its mission is accomplished, the group is dissolved.

Buzz groups are extremely useful devices because they can prevent classes from centering around the teacher or a small group of dominant (or even domineering) pupils. They are often used

To launch large group discussion.
To reformulate the objectives and background ideas of a discussion that has broken down.
To decide what to do next.
To brainstorm.
To set up rules.
To exchange ideas and experiences.
To formulate questions and problems for investigation.
To formulate questions and problems as a basis for group discussion, to put to guest speakers or panelists, and so on.
To bring out and speak frankly about controversies and differences.
To draw out pupils.

[12] 6 × 6 comes from World War II army slang for a six-wheeled vehicle with six-wheel drive. In a buzz group all the wheels are drive wheels.

To share rapidly learning gleaned from such experiences as homework, plays, films, and so on.

To provide for expression of quick reaction to issues.

TO CONDUCT BUZZ GROUPS

Buzz groups are relatively easy to organize and run. They do have to be planned, however, or they may blow up. Impromptu buzz groups organized on the spur of the moment to solve some classroom exigency (e.g., a disastrous discussion) may work well in experienced classes, but wise teachers keep impromptu buzz groups to a minimum.

Selection of the members of a buzz group is usually done by some simple informal somewhat arbitrary means. Among the methods used successfully are

1. By the seating plan (e.g., the first four persons in this row, the six pupils sitting in the first three seats in rows 1 and 2).
2. By the alphabet.
3. By sociometric test results.
4. By counting off (1, 2, 3, 4, 5, 6. 1, 2, 3, 4, 5, 6).
5. By a lottery using numbered cards. (All who draw number 1 are in group one).
6. By virtue of the teacher's knowledge of the pupils' talents, interests, background, and so on. (There may be times when one wishes to make special provisions based on these characteristics, but usually buzz groups work for such short periods of time that it seems hardly worth the effort.)

Each buzz group should have at least three but no more than six members.

To prepare pupils for the buzz group the teacher must take care that the mission for the group is clear and simple. He then should ensure that everyone understands the mission and knows what he is supposed to do. Time limits should be set explicitly. It is better that the time limits be too short than too long. Six minutes is usually about right. If the pupils need more time, the teacher can extend the time. Each group needs a leader and a recorder or secretary. The choice of leader

and secretary is not crucial because of the shortness of the buzz group's life.

FOLLOW UP THE BUZZ SESSION

At the end of the buzz session the group may report its conclusions in some fashion. When group reports are expected, the teacher should ensure that the pupils know just what the reporting procedure will be before they start working. The most common method of reporting is for each group to appoint a representative to a panel that carries on a discussion. When this is done, a recorder may keep an account of the major suggestions on the chalkboard or overhead projector. Oftentimes it is better to omit the group reports and let the class move from buzz group sessions to a whole-class discussion without any intermediate steps.

Small Discussion Groups

Discussion in small groups is carried on in the same manner as other discussion. Because pupils have a tendency to bog down and get sidetracked, the teacher must supervise such small groups with an eagle eye. In brief, the procedure is to

1. Be sure the pupils know the purpose of the discussion and what is to be discussed.
2. Be sure that someone is made discussion leader and someone is recorder.
3. Supervise carefully.
4. Follow up with some suitable activity.

The Working Committee

THE VALUE OF COMMITTEES

The working committee has a specific task to perform. Although committee groups are not supposed to be ability groups, the student should at once recognize that committees do help provide for individual differences in ability and interest. For example, let us suppose a class is studying the family. The class might form one committee to investigate the family life of animals, another to survey adolescent-parent relationships, still another to investigate family life in a polygamous society.

A pupil could choose to work on one or another of these committees on the basis of his interests. Within the committee, pupils will be allocated different tasks depending upon the committee's needs and the pupil's interests and abilities. Thus, by using committees it may be possible for pupils to assume various degrees of responsibility and to tackle tasks of varying difficulty, as well as to study things interesting to them.

In addition to providing for differences in individuals, teaching via committees has several other values. This method allows more pupils to participate actively than do the class recitation techniques. It is useful in helping pupils to develop skills of leadership, communication, socialization, cooperation, and thinking. Skillfully used it should be instrumental in teaching pupils how to search out, evaluate, and report on scholarly information. Furthermore, by its very nature committee membership should help pupils accept and carry out roles that will be theirs in adult life, for one skill, as important as it is rare in adult life, is that of organizing and carrying out effective committee work.

Committee work also has the practical advantage of eliminating unnecessary emphasis on reports and other methods. It also makes it possible to combine teaching in depth with wide coverage. Each committee can delve deeply into its area and then share its findings with the rest of the class.

SELECTING THE COMMITTEE

Ideally, a committee should consist of from four to seven members. Whenever a classroom committee grows to include eight or more members it should probably be broken into smaller committees or subcommittees. Committee members can be chosen in many ways. When teachers set up committees on the basis of interest, the nature of the pupils' individual interest largely determines the makeup of the committees. Sometimes the teacher should choose the committees himself to suit his own purposes. At other times he will want to allow the pupils to select their own committees.

In the course of time, the teacher should probably utilize all these methods of selecting committee members. As a general rule, however, it is probably wise to honor pupil preferences. For that reason, when it seems feasible, the teacher should tend toward allowing pupils to select their own members. Even when he selects the members himself, he should bear pupil preferences in mind.

In every class, pupils tend to form natural groups and follow natural leaders. By observing the class and by using sociometric devices such as those described in Chapter 15, the alert teacher can find out who the natural leaders and group members are. He should do so because, as a rule, it is advantageous to make use of these natural groups and natural leaders when forming committees. In this respect the use of sociograms can be particularly helpful.

While forming committees according to natural group lines may be advantageous, several other requirements must also be considered. Among them are the nature of the committee's task and interests of the pupils. One reason for having pupil committees is to allow pupils to work at tasks that seem important to them. The teacher should see to it, insofar as possible, that each pupil works on the committee he is most interested in. Furthermore, each committee calls for members with different abilities. In choosing committee members, provision should be made for these various abilities.

Whenever possible, committees should be made up of volunteers. This is not always feasible, of course, but the teacher may be able to approach this idea more closely if all the pupils make two or three choices in writing rather than volunteering orally. Making choices in writing allows the more timid to volunteer without embarrassment. Even so, some assignments to committees will have to be made by the teacher or by a pupil steering committee under the teacher's guidance. In either case the teacher should take care to see that the membership of each committee meets the criteria noted above.

No matter how the group members are selected, the teacher should keep a record of the committee memberships and committee assignments. Such a record will give him an insight into the relationship of the pupils in the class. Also, this record will give the teacher information he needs to be sure that all pupils have opportunities to participate to the fullest and to be sure that no one is neglected.

DETERMINING THE COMMITTEE'S PROCEDURE

Every committee should have a specific mission to perform, and the committee members should have a clear understanding of what this mission is before they start to work. This task may be assigned to the committee by a teacher or be the result of group planning. In any case, the work of each committee should further the plan worked out for the entire class.

Usually it is more satisfactory to use cooperative group planning than teacher assignments when establishing committee goals and tasks. Even when the task is teacher-assigned the committee will have to talk over the assignment and map out a plan for attacking it. In general, committee planning follows a procedure something like the following.

1. One of the first things to be done is to appoint or elect a chairman to lead the committee and a recorder to keep a record of what is done.

2. After these persons are selected, the group should decide on what it is going to do.

3. Next the pupils discuss their mission and its objectives. In their discussion they consider such questions as What might we do? What must we do? Exactly what will we do? How will we do it? and How do we report what we have done?

4. Then they work out in detail the subordinate problems and tasks and prepare an outline of how they intend to proceed. In this discussion they must find out what they will need to work with and what is available.

5. Finally they divide the tasks among the committee members and make provisions for sharing the results of their individual endeavors. For instance, the committee may ask one pupil to be responsible for securing certain material and another to be responsible for looking up a specific item of information. In the laying out of the work tasks a form similar to that in Figure 10-8 can be most useful.

Figure 10–8
Committee Assignment Form.

Committee Work

Form for assignment of committee members

Unit ______________________________

Committee ______________________________

Pupil ______________ Job ______________

1. ______________________________

2. ______________________________

3. ______________________________

4. ______________________________

Leonard H. Clark, *Teaching Social Studies in Secondary Schools: A Handbook.* (New York: Macmillan Publishing Co., Inc., 1973), p. 98.

As soon as this planning is finished, the pupils work together to complete their task. If this procedure is to succeed, the pupils must have a clear understanding of the procedures they can use as well as the mission they are supposed to accomplish. Frequently, of course, the pupils will find that their original plan was not realistic. The teacher should keep alert to detect problems as they may develop. On some occasions it will be necessary to stop and start over. Open-ended questioning may cut off deficiencies in planning before the problems develop. Even though the teacher might see faults in the proposals early in the planning, he should be careful not to interfere too quickly. Too much interference may stop the students from thinking for themselves. Usually it is better to let pupils find their own solutions without undue interference or too pointed suggestions from the teacher. After all, people learn from mistakes, it is said. However, the teacher should certainly do everything in his power to keep the committee from ending in abject failure.

HELPING PUPIL COMMITTEES

Committees usually require a great deal of teacher guidance. Inexperienced boys and girls will need much help in determining how they should go about completing their work. They need help in determining their goals, the procedures for fulfilling these goals, and ways of reporting the fruit of their labor to the total group. In advising them, the teacher should retain his role as a consultant, not as a dictator. He should point out alternatives open to the pupils and the dangers inherent in some lines of approach to the problem. Since boys and girls, like adults, are likely to take the line of least resistance and stick to the tried and true, the teacher should take special care to make pupils aware of different approaches to committee work.

TIPS FOR COMMITTEE WORK

Among the procedures that the teacher may find helpful in carrying out committee work are

1. Teach pupils how to work in committees before they start working on their own.

2. Discuss committee work and committee procedures with the entire class before they break into committees.

3. Be sure that the committees set up a reasonable time schedule.

4. Check on all groups frequently. Make sure that everyone has a job to do, knows what the job is and how to do it, and is doing it.

5. Check to be sure everyone is certain what the objective is.

6. Help groups as necessary. Use provocative questioning rather than direct suggestions. Point out alternatives. Let them make their own decisions.

7. Provide access to necessary materials. Help pupils find what they need. A little coaching in library skills may go a long way here.

8. Keep a log of what goes on. In it include committee assignments, committee members, tasks assigned, tasks completed, leadership responsibilities, and the like.

9. Keep a schedule of jobs showing when they are due for completion.

10. Ask for progress reports.

11. If a committee gets stuck, (a) recommend that the members reconsider their objective (perhaps they should change it); (b) get them to consider the strategies and tactics they have used (maybe there are others that might be better); and (c) use Socratic questioning with them to get them to see what they are doing wrong (if possible, let them find out for themselves, but sometimes you' may have to tell them what to do).

12. If a group's discipline breaks down, (a) find out what the trouble is; (b) work with the pupils who need help; (c) try role playing; and (d) talk over the problem with the group.

13. If a pupil causes trouble, (a) talk things over with him; (b) try to clarify his objectives, tasks, and strategies; (c) let him try a new role or a new group; (d) try role playing; and (e) if all else fails, take direct disciplinary action.

14. If a pupil is shy, (a) encourage him all you can; (b) do not push him; (c) help him to avoid getting into embarrassing situations; (d) make frequent evaluations and checks; and (e) see to it that his contributions are recognized.

THE COMMITTEE REPORT

Usually after the committee has accomplished its work, it should report to the class in one way or another. An oral report to the class is a common practice. Unfortunately, oral reports can become deadly, particularly if the class must listen to several of them, one following the other. The teacher who wishes to relieve the class from boredom should avoid an unending series of oral reports. Talks by skilled lecturers are difficult enough to sit through; talks by unskilled pupils can become unbearable. Therefore, the teacher should attempt to space the reports between other activities and to see to it that committees report in other different ways. Among the many possible ways to report Hock[13] includes

    Dramatic Presentations
        original plays
        role playing
        skits
        parodies of radio or television programs or movies
        monologues
    Panel Type of Discussions
        panels
        forums
        debates
        round-table sessions
        town meetings
    Written Materials
        newspapers
        notebooks
        scrapbooks

[13] Louise E. Hock, *Using Committees in the Classroom* (New York: Holt, Rinehart, and Winston, Publishers, 1958), p. 32.

duplicated material
creative writing—poems, stories, plays, songs
Visual Depictions
slides
maps
pictures
graphs
posters
models
exhibits
murals
bulletin board displays
Others
tape recordings
action projects—open house for parents, party, presentation to P.T.A. or civic groups.

*

In what other ways might a committee report to the class? Give examples of how the examples that Hock lists might be used in your classes.

*

EVALUATION OF COMMITTEE WORK

Pupils can evaluate the effectiveness of committee work as well as anyone else. Self-rating scales, such as those described in the section on the evaluating of discussion, are excellent. So are discussions in which the pupils analyze their performance and list the things that they did well and did not do well. More formal reports, such as those shown as Figure 10-9 and Figure 10-10, are also effective. Grambs, Carr, and Fitch recommend the form shown as Figure 10-10.

THE TEACHER'S ROLE

Obviously, then, the teacher's role in small group committee work is very sensitive. He must encourage the pupils to work on their own initiative, but at the same time see to it that their work is

---

Figure 10–9
An Evaluation Form.

Group Project Evaluation

1. Did you think the group project succeeded? Why? Why not?

2. Did everyone on the committee carry his load?

3. Were the members of the group interested in the project?

4. Which group member do you think contributed most?

5. Was the planning adequate?

6. If you were to do this over again, what would you do differently?

7. What exactly was your contribution?

8. How do you rank your contribution?
   Excellent———   Average———   Poor———

Figure 10–10
*Group Evaluation Form.***

	Effort	Leadership	Quality of work	Cooperation
Joe Jane etc. etc. etc. etc. etc.				

* John D. Grambs, John C. Carr, and Robert M. Fitch, *Modern Methods in Secondary Education* (New York: Holt, Rinehart and Winston, Publishers, 1970), p. 202.

productive. At all times everyone must understand that the teacher is in charge of the class no matter how much freedom he allows the pupils. He must oversee and approve pupil plans and procedures. He will have to be sure that committee work is properly scheduled and coordinated with other class activities. In this respect, one should note that it is poor practice to try to do all the instruction by means of small groups and committees. It is seldom desirable to give more than two or three consecutive days to small group or committee work. Rather, such work should be intermixed with other whole-class and individual activities of various sorts.

MAKING MATERIALS AVAILABLE

Teachers must also be sure that the pupils have suitable materials readily available for their use. At times this duty will require them to make arrangements with the library. At other times, it will mean that the teacher must collect material himself. Occasionally it will mean that he must steer the committee off in some other direction because there is no way to provide them with the material they need. A good procedure may be to require pupils to establish the availability of resources themselves before the committee is allowed to commit itself to any particular problem or course of action. Obviously, teaching by committees requires the teacher to have great knowledge of the content to be covered and the resources available in the area. For this reason, a good resource unit

or curriculum guide can be of tremendous assistance to teachers and pupils.

FOLLOWING UP COMMITTEE WORK

Teaching by small groups and committees requires the teacher to emphasize follow-up. Pupil reports may do much to tie things together, but by their very nature they tend to leave learning fragmented. The teacher's follow-up is needed to fill in gaps, smooth out rough spots, tie up loose ends, show relationships, and drive home important concepts. Without adequate follow-up the learning of the committee members may stop dead in a frustrating *cul de sac*. All too often teachers' neglect of the follow-up brings the pupils up to the door of understanding and leaves them standing there at the threshold so near to and yet so far from real learning.

Special-Interest Groups

When one divides the class into small special-interest groups, the procedures are the same as those for ability groups (which are described in Chapter 8). In general, the procedures are similar to those for conducting committee work.

1. First the teacher makes the assignment clear to the pupils and ensures that they have the things they need to do with. If feasible, the group may plan its own procedures. Specialized study guides or learning packets may be extremely useful at this point.

2. If it is a group venture, e.g., a group project, the teacher sees to it that pupils know what their roles are and that all the necessary jobs are being done. He may have to appoint pupils to do certain missions. He checks to be sure they know how to do what they are supposed to do. If it is a group within the class that is studying a topic different from that of the other pupils, this step is not necessary.

3. Then the teacher sees to it that they get to work. As the pupils go about their tasks, he supervises them, checking to be sure that they are profiting from what they are doing, guiding and helping as it seems necessary, and even teaching directly when it seems desirable.

4. After the group has finished its work, the teacher checks up on the pupils' results, evaluating, correcting, reteaching, and generally following up as necessary.

SUMMARY

The skillful teacher has many techniques and methods at his command, and so is able to vary his approach according to the instructional problem to be solved. Almost all our most common teaching methods involve working with groups, however. Little teaching is really individual, although there is a movement in the direction of individualized teaching. Consequently, teachers should understand the characteristics of groups, which include leadership, attraction, norms, communications, and cohesiveness as well as how one can influence those group characteristics. Evidently teaching is most effective when leadership is democratic and groups are diffusely structured.

Because of the characteristics of classroom groups, some of the most effective teaching is group teaching, that is, teaching by and through groups and group methods. By using committee work and discussion, teachers can quite often increase their teaching efficiency. This type of teaching is frequently effective in changing attitudes, ideals, and appreciation. It is particularly useful in raising learning above the verbalizing level. Thus, group methods often lead to thorough, permanent learning. Teaching by group methods takes considerable time and effort, but the results are usually worth it.

A discussion is not a monologue, a question-and-answer period, or a bull session. Rather, it is a controlled conversation in which participants pool their thoughts on a topic or problem in a purposeful, orderly way. The discussion leader's task is to lead the group into fruitful dialogue without dominating the participants or allowing them to meander. In this task the aid of a good recorder is extremely desirable. Observers can help the group to learn how to discuss matters more effectively. Formal discussion techniques are often not as useful as informal discussions, but techniques such as the British debate and the jury system, can be used, often with telling results, for getting pupils to examine, to think about, and to analyze critical issues and problems.

Teaching via committees has become quite popular. It is an effective means of providing for individual differences and laboratory experiences as well as involving pupils in action learning. Well done, teaching via committees helps to build a classroom climate supportive of learning. The membership of pupil committees may be determined in several ways, but when feasible, the teacher should take advantage of natural pupil leadership and groups. Although pupil committee members should do the bulk of their own planning and research, the teacher must always be ready in the background with necessary help and guidance. Sharing the results of the committee work with the rest of the class can be a particular problem. The teacher should place considerable stress on lively, original reporting and serious, careful class follow-up of committee work.

Questions, Inquiry, and Dramatic Techniques

11

USING QUESTIONS

Uses of Questions

Throughout the course of educational history, questioning has been one of the most common, if not the most common, of teaching techniques. It continues to be so in spite of modern changes in educational theory and technology for it is a fine tool both for checking memory and understanding, and getting at higher learning. It has many uses in the modern classroom. Among them are

1. To find out something one did not know.
2. To find out whether someone knows something.
3. To develop the ability to think.
4. To motivate pupil learning.
5. To provide drill or practice.
6. To help pupils organize materials.
7. To help pupils interpret materials.
8. To emphasize important points.
9. To show relationships, such as cause and effect.

10. To discover pupil interests.
11. To develop appreciation.
12. To provide review.
13. To give practice in expression.
14. To reveal mental processes.
15. To show agreement or disagreement.
16. To establish rapport with pupils.
17. To diagnose.
18. To evaluate.
19. To obtain the attention of wandering minds.

*

Can you think of a question to illustrate each one of the purposes mentioned above? After you have formed the questions, test them against the criteria in the following section. How well did you do?

Attend a class in a school or college classroom. Observe the teacher's use of questions. What techniques were used? Were they successful? Why, or why not?

*

FOUR TYPES OF QUESTIONS

Because they use a classroom for so many different purposes, teachers must use many different kinds of questions. According to Gallagher and Aschner[1] classroom questions can be arranged into four general categories.

1. Cognitive memory questions: questions that call for simple recall of information. For example, Who discovered penicillin? or What is the formula for prussic acid?

2. Convergent questions: thought questions for which there is a single correct answer. For example, Study the route of the Oregon Trail on the map. What advantages does the circuitous route via South Pass have over the much more direct route used by Lewis and Clark?

3. Divergent questions: open-ended questions that cause pupils to think but have no correct answers. These are the questions that stimulate creative thinking and imagination. For example, What would the United States be like today if King George III's government had acquiesced to the American colonists' demands?

4. Evaluative questions: questions in which pupils pass judgment on some action. For example, Do you think that President Jackson was wise to take his stand against the Bank of the United States? Which position on the role of the Federal Government was more defensible, Hamilton's or Jefferson's?

[1] James J. Gallagher and Mary Jane Aschner, "A Preliminary Report of Analyses of Classroom Interaction," *The Merrill-Palmer Quarterly of Behavior and Development*, Vol. 9 (July 1963), pp. 183–94.

BLOOM'S TAXONOMY AND QUESTIONING

As these categories illustrate, different types of questions elicit different responses. The teacher should be careful to ask questions which will further the instructional goals he wants to achieve. Sometimes the appropriate question to ask involves cognitive memory; sometimes convergent; sometimes divergent; and sometimes evaluative. In fact, skillful teachers can aim their questions so that they bring out whichever level of Bloom's Taxonomy of Cognitive Goals they wish, as the following examples show.

1. Knowledge
   1.1 Knowledge of specifics. (What is the principal ingredient in the air we breathe?)
   1.2 Knowledge of ways and means of dealing with specifics. (What steps would you have to take to become a licensed operator? What is the correct form for presenting a motion before a meeting?)
   1.3 Knowledge of universals and abstractions in a field. (What is the basic principle behind the operation of a free market?)
2. Comprehension
   2.1 Translation. (In your own words what does "laissez-faire economy" mean? What does it mean to say that to the victor belongs the spoils?)
   2.2 Interpretation. (In what ways are the Democratic and Republican positions on support for the military budget similar?)
   2.3 Extrapolation. (If the use of electrical energy continues to increase at the present rate, what will be the demand for electrical energy in A.D. 2000?)
3. Application
   (If you measure the pressure in your barometer at the foot of the mountain and then measure it again at the summit of the mountain, what difference in the reading would you expect? If of two sailing vessels leaving New York at the same time en route to London one took a route following the Gulf Stream and one kept consistently south of the Gulf Stream, which would you expect to reach London first, everything else being equal?)
4. Analysis (Questions that ask pupils to break

complex ideas down into their component elements in order to make them more understandable.)

    4.1 Analyses of elements. (Which part of the argument we have just read is fact and which is opinion? What propaganda devices can you find in this automobile advertisement?)

    4.2 Analyses of relationships. (Does the conclusion that Senator X made logically follow from the facts he presented?)

    4.3 Analysis of organizational principles. (In this poem what devices has the author used to build up the characters of the principal antagonists?)

5. Synthesis

    5.1 Production of a unique communication. (Describe the procedure you used and the results you observed in your experiment.)

    5.2 Production of a plan or a proposed set of operations. (How would you go about determining the composition of this unknown chemical?)

    5.3 Derivation of a set of abstract relations. (You have heard the description of the situation. What might be the causes of this situation?)

6. Evaluation

    6.1 Judgment in terms of internal evidence. (In what way is the argument presented illogical?)

    6.2 Judgment in terms of external criticism. (Does the theory that organically grown foods are more healthful than other foods conform to what we know of the chemical composition of these foods? Explain.)[2]

The Good Question

The criteria in this section were meant to refer to oral classroom questions. Written-test and examination questions follow a somewhat different set of rules. However, in many cases the criteria can apply just as well to written questions as to oral ones. Although these criteria are few in number, if

[2] See Frances P. Hunkins, *Questioning Strategies and Techniques* (Boston: Allyn & Bacon, Inc., 1972) for other illustrations of various types of questions.

every teacher's questions lived up to them, teaching, even by master teachers, would improve marvelously.

First of all, *a successful question asks something definite in simple, clear, straightforward English that the pupil can understand.* Therefore one must be careful to avoid ambiguity, confusing constructions, double questions, parenthetical remarks, and other verbiage that might cause the pupil to lose the point of the question.

Usually the question should be worded so as to get at a definite point consistent with the goal of the lesson. As a rule, vague generalities are usually not valuable in furthering the learning that the lesson is trying to promote. This criterion does not rule out general questions, however. Often questions calling for general answers are needed to open up the pupils' thinking, but these questions, too, should be worded so that pupils can perceive what the teacher is driving at. Vague, poorly thought-out questions tend to evoke fuzzy irrelevancies rather than to advance good thinking on the topic at hand.

A main purpose of questioning is to stimulate learning. A good question challenges the pupil to exert his intellect. To do so the question must make him think. Questions that can be answered by merely repeating some fact from a book can never be as stimulating as thought questions. In fact, as often as not, they are not stimulating at all. *A good question, then, is challenging and thought-provoking.*

A good question is consistent with the aims of the lesson, as well as being consistent with the abilities and interests of the pupils. There is no great point in embarrassing or frustrating a youngster by asking him questions he cannot answer. Neither is there much point in allowing bright youths to slide along on easy questions without stretching their intellects. Moreover, the teacher can harness the interests of various pupils by asking them questions that appeal to their special interests. For instance, the 4-H farm boy who raises stock could contribute greatly to a social studies unit on the country's resources or a general science unit on conservation. He might even be able to make a considerable contribution concerning "the lowing herd [which] winds slowly o'er the lea." In short, *the good question is adapted to the age, abilities, and interests of the pupils to whom it is addressed.*

The good question is also adapted to its purpose. Teachers must use both closed and open questions. When facts are needed, closed-ended fact questions are needed. At other times the teacher needs to ask questions that will converge pupils' thinking on a certain point. Sometimes he should ask wide-ranging questions that open up pupils' imagination. A good question is one that serves its methodological purposes. The good teacher is one who knows how and when to use all types of questions.

*

It has been said that a question should be couched in language considerably easier than the pupils' reading level. Do you agree?

Of what value is a question answerable in one word?

Suppose that one of your purposes is to stimulate the pupils' thinking. How can this be done by questioning? Just how would you word the question? Prepare some examples and try them out.

*

A Prerequisite to Good Questioning

From the foregoing account it seems evident that questioning requires skill and preparation. Good questioners usually carefully brief themselves on the subject under discussion and prepare key questions in advance. Although some teachers seem to be able to ask well-worded questions at the spur of the moment, to do so is quite difficult. The teacher who prepares in advance will usually be more successful.

In preparing key questions the teacher should consider

1. The teaching objectives.
2. What he wants the questions to do.
3. The kinds of questions that will best do the job.
4. The desirability of using questions that are in the affective domain.
5. The range of objectives covered by his questions. Unless one plans his questions in advance, it is too easy to concentrate on minutiae and irrelevancies rather than on significant learning. That is why it is wise to write key questions into one's lesson plans.

Techniques of Good Questioning

The notion of the teacher as a grand inquisitor attempting to catch the recalcitrant pupil should be foreign to the modern classroom. Questioning should be thought of as a way to get at the problems the class is trying to solve—not as an attempt to see how much the pupil knows. An inquisition is not necessary.

Many of the teacher's questions should be quite informal as he tries to help individuals and groups with their various assignments. Questions frequently may be addressed to the entire class, of course, but more often they should be addressed to an individual pupil or a small group. As a matter of fact, in a lively class the pupils will ask most of the questions.

A teacher should ask his questions in a pleasant, friendly, easy, conversational manner. If he can maintain an atmosphere of easy informality without sacrificing decorum, so much the better. He should always ask his questions in a fashion that indicates that he expects a reasonable answer. If the pupil does not know the answer, or cannot contribute at the moment, there is no point in teasing him about it. Exhortations to think will not bring back a forgotten lesson.

When using questions in a whole-class situation, the teacher usually should first ask the question, wait for the class to think about it, and then ask someone for an answer. In this way everyone has a chance to consider the question before anyone tries to answer it. There is little use in asking thought questions if you don't give the pupils time to think about them.

This technique has another merit in its favor. When the teacher asks the question first, no one knows who is going to be asked. This helps to keep the pupils alert. When the teacher calls on a pupil before asking the question, other members of the class may heave a sigh of relief and not bother to listen to the question.

As usual, there are exceptions to the rule. When one calls on an inattentive pupil, it is sometimes better to give his name first so that he will hear the question. By calling his name first, one may recapture his wandering attention and bring him back to work. Similarly, it is usually best to name a slow or shy pupil first so that he will know what is coming and be able to prepare himself.

Another technique that may help keep a class attentive is to refrain from repeating questions. If for some legitimate reason the pupil did not understand or hear, then of course to repeat the question is only fair. But if he did not hear because of inattention, the teacher should pass on to someone else. This technique also applies to repeating answers. Repeating answers merely wastes time and encourages inattention.

Distributing the questions about the class fairly equally also helps keep the pupils alert. However, one should not resort to any mechanical system for doing this. Youngsters soon catch on to these devices. The old system, for instance, of going around the class in alphabetical order, row by row, is sure death to pupil attention.

The best way to direct pupil attention to one's questions is to ask really interesting, thought-provoking questions. Leading questions, questions that give away answers, one-word-answer questions, and the like have the seeds of boredom in them. They should be avoided like poison, for they have killed many a potentially good class.

HANDLING PUPIL QUESTIONS

Teachers should encourage pupils to ask questions. If the pupils leave class with inquiring minds, the teacher will have accomplished much. But how does one encourage pupil questions? By welcoming them. If the teacher encourages a free, permissive atmosphere in which youngsters know that they will be respected, he can expect pupil questions to increase. Certainly they will if the material studied is interesting and important to them. If the teacher will only ask himself what the youngsters may want to know before he plans the lesson, he can increase the chances of his material's being interesting and important.

Not all pupil questions are as important as others. Some questions are so important that if the class is interested it would be wise to depart from the agenda and consider the question in detail, even if it is not exactly pertinent. Others are of little importance and can be answered very briefly. Some questions are so trivial that they have no place in the class at all. If the pupil asking the trivial or irrelevant question is sincere, he deserves to be answered, but briefly. The teacher should explain that class time is scarce, that class goals are important, and that there is little time for the trivial. In case the pupil is not satisfied by a brief answer in class, the teacher should arrange to go into the matter more deeply in private sometime later when the discussion would not interrupt the progress of the class. Sometimes the questions may be smart-alecky. Questions of this sort are best turned back on the questioner. If a teacher finds that many trivial or smart-alecky questions are turning up in his class, he had better check to see if this may be due to his teaching, his material, or both.

At times it is best to turn a question over to some other member of the class or to the class as a whole for discussion. In fact, there seems to be no reason why pupils should not ask each other questions directly as long as they are pertinent to the discussion and asked courteously. In "good" classes this practice is often encouraged.

Occasionally, the teacher will be asked questions he cannot answer. In that case he should promptly admit his inability. Perhaps another member of the class does know. If not, the teacher can either find out himself or ask someone to find out for him. If the latter choice is made, the teacher should look up the answer too. Thus he can check to be sure that the pupil reports back correctly.

HANDLING PUPIL ANSWERS

In order to create a permissive atmosphere, i.e., an atmosphere of friendly cooperation, in which the pupils feel free to do their best, even if their best is none too good, the teacher should accept every sincere response appreciatively. Immature thinking and lack of knowledge are not serious faults. If pupils were mature and knew all the answers, we would not need schools. Pupils should be allowed to make mistakes without fear of embarrassment, but they should not be encouraged to do careless work. When a pupil does not answer to the best of his ability, the teacher can follow up with other questions which will shake him out of his complacency. Usually he will get the point. The practice of following pupils' answers, grade book in hand—so common in the standard recitation—

has little to recommend it, although some pupils seem to be motivated by it.

In like manner, teachers should insist that the pupils make themselves understood. An answer that is not clear is not a good answer. If the pupil fails to make a point the teacher can ask him to elaborate. Each answer should be a complete thought unit—although not necessarily a sentence. If the teacher throws the incomplete thoughts back at the pupils, the pupils will probably soon learn to answer more clearly. One should not let himself get bogged down on English grammar, however. The emphasis should be on ideas. Teachers must avoid sacrificing thinking and rapport to the niceties of academic English.

Although one should listen appreciatively to all sincere answers, only the good ones should be approved. When his answer is not satisfactory, the pupil should learn why it is incorrect and how he might improve it. Any portion of an answer that is correct should be recognized, of course, but any part of an answer that is incorrect should be criticized. The teacher can do this by pointing out the error himself or by throwing the question open for discussion by other pupils.

Sometimes the teacher can use an incorrect answer as the basis for a discussion or investigation that may clear up a difficult concept. Skillful teachers also use incorrect answers as springboards for other questions, as in the Socratic technique. Such capitalization on mistakes can be achieved by asking other pupils to comment on the previously given answer or by asking additional questions that will yield a correct or more thorough understanding. These are often called probing questions.

If the question is answered well, the teacher should express approval. This does not mean that he should be effusive about it. For some questions a friendly "That's right" is quite enough. Other questions, designed to bring out major points, need to be given more emphasis. This can be done by using such questions as a basis for further discussion.

Occasionally, a question brings forth no response other than blank stares from the entire class. In such cases the chances are that the teacher has skipped some steps. Often he can get the desired response by breaking the question down into component parts or by backtracking a bit and asking

questions that will lead up to and provide background for the baffling original question. At other times the whole difficulty may be in the wording of the question. When such is the case, restating the question may clear up the problem.

*

What are the faults of the questioning techniques of teachers you have observed? How can you avoid these faults?

Prepare a list of principles to observe in questioning. Check yourself by these principles in a classroom situation. How well do you do?

*

THE USE OF THOUGHT QUESTIONS

To use thought questions well requires a little extra skill and preparation. Teachers should practice using such questions until it becomes second nature. It is particularly important to resist the temptation to favor questions whose answers are cut-and-dried repetition of what is in the book. In fact, the teacher ought to ask at least some questions whose answers are not in the book at all. Perhaps the following suggestions may be helpful for those who wish to formulate thought-provoking questions.

1. Use developmental problems emphasizing how and why rather than who, what, where, and when.

2. Follow up leads. Build on pupils' contributions. Give pupils a chance to comment on each others answers; for example, ask questions as, "Do you agree with John on that, Mary?" or "Do you think this argument would hold in such and such case, John?"

3. Be sure the pupils have the facts before you ask "thought" questions about them. One way is to ask fact questions first and then follow up with thought questions. Another way is to lead in by means of good summary questions. Other ways are to incorporate the facts in the question itself or to give the pupils fact sheets that they can consult as they try to think through suitable answers to the question. Similar results can be gained by putting the facts on the blackboard or the overhead projector, by allowing pupils to refer to their texts, or by simply telling the pupils the facts before beginning the questioning.

4. Remember that the best thought questions usually do not have correct answers. In such cases the thinking concerned is much more important than the answer derived. Be sure pupils back up their answers by valid, logical reasoning. Insist that they show evidence and demonstrate why this evidence leads to their conclusion.

5. Encourage pupils to challenge each other's thinking and even that of their teacher. Good use of thought questions leads to true discussion rather than simple question-answer teaching.[3]

The Clarifying Response

Many teachers find the clarifying response a useful tool by which to start pupils' thought processes. A clarifying response consists of a question asked of a pupil in response to one of these statements, expressions, or actions that will make him consider "what he has chosen, what he prizes, and/or what he is doing."[4] According to Raths, Harmin, and Simon the clarifying response has ten essential elements.

1. The clarifying response avoids moralizing, criticizing, giving values, or evaluating. The adult excludes all hints of "good" or "right" or "acceptable," or their opposites, in such responses.
2. It puts the responsibility on the student to look at his behavior or his ideas and to think and decide for himself what it is he wants.
3. A clarifying response also entertains the possibility that the student will *not* look or decide or think. It is permissive and stimulating, but not insistent.
4. It does not try to do big things with its small comments. It works more at stimulating thought relative to what a person does or says. It aims at setting a mood. Each clarifying response is only one of many; the effect is cumulative.
5. Clarifying responses are not used for interview purposes. The goal is not to obtain data, but for the student to clarify his ideas and life if he wants to do so.
6. It is usually not an extended discussion. The idea is for the student to think, and he usually does that best alone, without the temptation to justify his thoughts to an adult. Therefore a teacher will be advised to carry on only two or three rounds of dialogue and then offer to break off the conversation with some noncommittal but honest phrase.
7. Clarifying responses are often for individuals. A topic in which John might need clarification may be of no immediate interest to Mary. An issue that is of general concern, of course, may warrant a general

clarifying response, say to the whole class, but even here the *individual* must ultimately do the reflecting for himself. Values are personal things. The teacher often responds to one individual, although others may be listening.
8. The teacher doesn't respond to everything everyone says or does in a classroom. There are other responsibilities he has.
9. Clarifying responses operate in situations in which there are no "right" answers. They are *not* appropriate for drawing a student toward a predetermined answer. They are not questions to which the teacher has an answer already in mind.
10. Clarifying responses are not mechanical things that carefully follow a formula. They must be used creatively and with insight, but with their purpose in mind; when a response helps a student to clarify his thinking or behavior, it is considered effective.[5]

INQUIRY STRATEGIES

Inquiry teaching, one of the oldest general strategies of teaching, is the opposite of expository teaching, in which the teacher informs the pupils. In inquiry teaching pupils are expected to find out information for themselves and then draw their own conclusions and generalizations.

Inquiry teaching consists of a number of strategies and techniques all of which center on a process in which pupils seek out information and draw their own conclusions. Among these strategies and techniques are problem solving, springboards, and case studies—to name only a few. These strategies and techniques are attractive because they have high motivating value and help pupils to develop intellectual skills, including skill in thinking rationally, seeing relationships, understanding processes, and building values and attitudes. As a rule, inquiry strategies can be depended on to build firm concepts and deep understandings.

To Teach by Inquiry

In teaching by inquiry strategies the teacher must assume the role of guide rather than dictator. As a guide to pupil learning he raises problem issues and questions that will pique the pupils' interest and call for further investigation. The teacher encourages the pupils to pursue these matters and guides

[3] Leonard H. Clark, *Teaching Social Studies in Secondary Schools—A Handbook* (New York: Macmillan Publishing Co., Inc., 1973), pp. 80–81.
[4] Louis Raths, Merrill Harmin, and Sidney Simon, *Values and Teaching: Working with Values in the Classroom* (Columbus, Ohio: Charles E. Merrill Publishing Company, 1966), p. 51.

[5] Ibid., pp. 53–54.

them in their investigations, helping them to clarify the issues, the facts, and their own thinking as well as to draw reasonable conclusions. He then carries the pupils a step or two further by inducing them to test their conclusions and generalizations and apply them to other situations.

A major aim of inquiry teaching is to stimulate independent resourceful thinking. To that end the teacher uses such tactics as

Checking the pupils' data-gathering techniques.
Asking thought questions.
Asking for interpretations, explanations, and hypotheses.
Questioning the interpretations, explanations, and hypotheses that the pupils arrive at.
Asking pupils to draw conclusions from their data and information.
Asking pupils to apply their principles and conclusions to other situations.
Asking pupils to check their thinking and their logic.
Confronting pupils with problems, contradictions, fallacies, implications, value assumptions, value conflicts, and other factors that may call for reassessment of their thinking and positions.

In carrying out these tactics it is extremely important that the teacher keep the climate permissive. The pupil must be encouraged to think even though the conclusions he draws may be somewhat bizarre. To encourage thinking the teacher tries

To be supportive and acceptive.
To accentuate the positive.
To encourage pupils by showing his approval and by providing clues.
To accept for examination all legitimate hypotheses and means by which pupils attempt to arrive at truth.
To encourage the exchange and discussion of ideas.
To create an open atmosphere in which pupils feel free to contribute and to analyze the various ideas, interpretations, and logical processes.

In short, the teacher should foster an atmosphere of earnest thinking, free debate, open discussion, and, above all, freedom for the pupils to try to think things out without fear of reprisal for possible errors in their reasoning.

Inquiry teaching must be open-ended if it is to be honest. To force pupils to discover predetermined "correct" solutions is not honest. Except for problems that obviously call for one and only one answer (e.g., $1 + 1 = ?$), teachers who insist that pupils arrive at a particular conclusion that the teachers already predetermined are probably unethical and immoral.

From the preceding discussion and the one to follow, it should be evident to the reader that most inquiry teaching involves the use of some form of problem solving.

Problem-Solving Techniques

Perhaps problem solving should not be called a teaching technique. Rather it is a general strategy in which one can use many different techniques and tactics. Many theorists feel it to be the most effective of all teaching strategies. It has been used successfully both as an individual and as a group activity. The solving of problems through group activity recently has been used extensively in teaching and in the world of business and research.

THE METHOD OF PROBLEM SOLVING

Whether a problem is solved by an individual or a group, the general technique is about the same. Perhaps this explains in part the popularity of problem solving. It seems to be a natural way to learn.

In a sense, problem solving is a sophisticated form of trial-and-error learning. It provides people a chance to learn from their successes and failures. Furthermore, it leads to real understanding in a way that memorization and drill seldom can, because it provides for the pupils' becoming really involved in their learning. A brief review of the steps will show how actively the pupil participates in learning through problem solving. The steps are

1. The learner becomes aware of the problem.
2. He defines and delimits the problem.
3. He gathers evidence that may help him solve the problem.

4. He forms a hypothesis of what the solution to the problem is.
5. He tests the hypothesis.
6. He successfully solves the problem or he repeats steps 3, 4, and 5, or 4 and 5, until the problem is solved, or he gives up.[6]

Another version of the steps is

1. We become aware of a problem (it may be started by the occasion, someone else, or ourselves), isolate it, and decide to do something about it.
2. We look for clues for the solution of the problem.
   a. We think up possible solutions (hypotheses) or approaches to take in solving the problem.
   b. We test the tentative solution or approaches against criteria that will help us evaluate them adequately.
3. We reject the tentative solutions or approaches that do not meet our requirements until we find one that is suitable, or give up. In making our conclusions, we may accept the first solution or approach that appears adequate, or we may test all hypotheses to find the best one.[7]

Selecting the Problem.   Although problem solving is a natural way to learn, pupils, as a general rule, do not just naturally become expert in the techniques of problem solving. This is particularly true when the class attempts to solve problems by group techniques.

In the first place, pupils need help in finding suitable problems. Sometimes the teacher may find it necessary to suggest problems or to suggest areas in which pupils may seek problems. When suggesting a problem to a group, the teacher might propose the problem directly, or he might set the stage in such a way the problem will suggest itself to the pupils.

For instance, in a social studies class the teacher introduced a problem by telling of the number of people in the country who do not vote. She cited figures showing the lightness of the voting in the local municipal election. This led to a discussion of why citizens do not exercise their franchise. From this discussion the pupils developed two problems: the first, what causes the apathy of our citizens? and the second, what can be done to get people to

[6] Based on the analysis of the thought process by John Dewey.
[7] Clark, op. cit., p. 28.

vote at the city elections? In another class the teacher launched a group problem by asking the following question: How does a plant get its food? After a short discussion the group set out to find the answer to the problem.

No matter what the source of their problem, the pupils will probably need the teacher's guidance in the selection of a suitable one, for, left alone, even the most experienced adolescent, or group of adolescents, may flounder. Sometimes they can find no problem at all; sometimes they select problems not suitable to the course; and sometimes they select problems whose solution requires materials and equipment beyond the school's resources; sometimes they select problems too big and unyielding, and blithely setting out to solve in a weekend problems their elders have struggled with for centuries. In view of these considerations, the teacher, or the teacher and pupils cooperatively, should test the problems to be selected against such criteria as Is this problem pertinent? Is the necessary material available? Can it be completed in the time allotted?

*

Prepare a complete list of questions you feel should be considered in testing whether a problem should be selected or not.

Prepare a list of eight or ten problems that boys and girls might attempt in the study of a topic in a course in your field of major interest. Where might you advise boys and girls to search for suitable problems for such a topic?

"To be worthwhile, problems should be real and have real solutions." Explain. Do you agree? How are such problems created and carried through to a conclusion?

Why is it often claimed that all secondary school learning should be of the problem-solving variety?

*

Defining the Problem.   Once the problem has been selected, the teacher should help the pupils clarify and define the problem. This he can do by means of questions and suggestions. The important thing here is to get the problem sharply defined so that the pupil knows exactly what he wishes to find out. Beginning teachers sometimes neglect this step. When they do, pupils find it difficult to know exactly what they are expected to do. This is, of course, a handicap in solving any problem.

Let us suppose that the problem selected has

been Why does an airplane fly? The problem here is quickly and easily defined, for it is obvious to all that we are to find what it is that keeps an airplane up in the air. Yet, even in such an easily defined problem, the teacher may have to make it clear to some pupils that this problem does not refer to helicopters or to rockets.

Searching for Clues. Once the pupil has defined his problem, he should start to look for clues for its solution. This involves amassing data upon which to base a hypothesis. Here the teacher can be of great help. He can point out areas in which to look for clues. He can provide the necessary materials, or see to it that they are available. He can provide references. He can acquaint the pupils with the tools by which one can gather data.

Even in the solving of group problems, the gathering of evidence may best be done by individuals or small groups. After a period of searching for information, the group can meet to pool the data gained individually and to attempt to find a solution to the problem.

For instance, if the problem were to prepare a menu suitable for a week's camping trip for a group of teen-agers, the pupils might gather the information necessary for solving this problem individually. Once they had in their possession information concerning what the ingredients of a healthful, well-balanced diet are, what foods contain these ingredients, and any other pertinent data, they might attempt to build suitable menus individually. The final menu could be made during a class discussion using the individual suggestions. Of course, before concluding that the problem has been solved, the pupils should test the menu to be sure it meets the criteria for a healthful, well-balanced camp menu.

Solving the Problem. Preparing the menu in the foregoing example was really an example of setting up and testing a hypothesis. Each individual menu prepared was a hypothetical solution to the problem. These solutions were tested by the pupils until they found one that met the requirements of a healthful, well-balanced diet. When they found such a menu, the problem was solved.

At this stage of solving a problem, boys and girls often need assistance. Many pupils find it difficult to think of tentative solutions. Although the teacher should be careful not to solve the problem for

them, he can help put them on the track by pointing out relationships, by asking pointed questions, and by using other techniques. Similarly, the teacher can help the pupils test their proposed solutions. Unless pupils establish appropriate criteria by which to judge the worth of a solution, they may think they have a problem solved when they really have not. Consequently, the teacher may need to help the pupil set up criteria that will tell him whether he has actually solved a problem or not and help him check his solution against the criteria. Without this aid pupils often arrive at very poor solutions to their problems.

*

Select a problem that a pupil might attempt in one of your classes. Where might he look for clues? What materials should be available to the pupil? What tools of research might be needed to gather the necessary data? What skills would the pupil need? How could you prepare yourself to help a pupil gather the data for this problem?

*

THE CASE-STUDY METHOD

Case studies are detailed studies of an individual situation, institution, decision, or issue. From these detailed inquiries pupils draw conclusions concerning the type as a whole. Case studies are useful because they not only give pupils insights into knotty problems, but they also give them opportunities for study in depth. The latter result is particularly important since at present much secondary school learning is superficial.

The procedures for conducting case studies are relatively simple, but their execution is difficult. Briefly, the steps in the procedure are

1. Select a problem or topic to study.
2. Provide the pupils the wherewithal to study. They should have material that allows them to explore the problem in depth. Some of the newer texts and curriculum programs on the market provide such materials. Frequently the students and teachers will have to gather it for themselves. Usually the material will be reading matter to study, but films, pictures, tapes, laboratory experiments, and the like, may be more useful. For many social studies and science topics field work is the

best resource. For instance, in one middle school the students closely studied the flora and fauna of a small patch of the Jersey swamp which made up part of their science laboratory to see if they could establish certain ecological relationships.

3. The pupils then study the case. Before they begin their investigations, the teacher should introduce them to the problem or issue at hand, point out the goals and questions to consider, and establish the ground rules. Sometimes this orientation can be done by group planning techniques. As pupils proceed with their investigations, they will find study guides very helpful. Some of the newer books and curriculum programs have developed useful study guides. If such are available, the teacher should use them; otherwise the teacher should probably develop guides of his own.

4. Pupils should discuss what they have studied so as to share their findings and conclusions. Role playing, panels, symposia, and similar methods of presentation are often effective at this stage. Any technique that helps pupils to examine their own thinking and conclusions will do.

THE PROJECT

A Definition. A project is a natural, lifelike learning activity involving investigation and solving of problems by an individual or small group. Ideally it should consist of a task in which the pupil sets out to attain some definite goal of real value to him. As originally visualized, this goal seems to have been something tangible. Although this connotation is perhaps no longer essential, projects frequently involve the use and manipulation of physical materials and result in tangible products.

A classic example of such a project may be found in the agriculture projects in which pupils conduct farming enterprises such as raising a calf or a crop. A less ambitious project in an academic class might be making a scrapbook anthology for an English class or an illustrated history of the life of the honeybee for a science class. An unusual group project reported from a Western high school is the building and selling of a house by a group of high school apprentice pupils.

Selecting the Project. Ordinarily, the pupil

should plan, execute, and evaluate the entire project himself. Even so, the teacher's role is important. He must help and guide the pupils. One of the more important ways he can guide them is in selecting a suitable project. Sometimes the teacher will find it necessary to provide a list of possible projects from which pupils can choose. Or he might suggest readings in which the pupils might find project ideas. Occasionally, he may be able to stimulate ideas for projects by a discussion of possible projects, or by a teacher talk about what others have done, or by a demonstration of former projects. An interesting device is to have members of previous classes act as consultants and tell the class about some of the projects completed in past years. Sometimes the teacher may need only to approve the plans formed by a pupil.

In any case, the teacher should approve a project before the pupil attempts it, for selecting projects requires sound judgment. The following criteria may help in selecting useful projects. The first of these is that *the project should consist of real learning activities.* Unless one is careful, projects sometimes may turn out to be mere busywork. Scrapbooks and picture collections quite often fall into this category. An example of a supposed project which was little more than busywork was a notebook for an English class which consisted of biographies of authors, copied from the appendix of the English textbook. Teachers should guard against this danger by continually asking themselves, "What learning will result from this project?"

Not only should the learning be valuable, *it should be pertinent to the course.* Because of their very nature, projects often include materials and activities from other subjects. Consequently, there is a constant danger that the project may get out of the field completely.

Another important criterion in the selection of projects has to do with time. The teacher should consider whether or not the *learning to be gained from a project is worth the time spent on it.* Not only must the amount of time be considered, but one must also decide whether the learning might be gained more economically in another way.

Other criteria the teacher and pupil should consider include *the availability and cost of materials and equipment necessary.*

Conducting the Project. Once the project has

been selected and approved, the pupil is ready to proceed with it. As in any other activity, the teacher will find it necessary to help and guide the pupil as the latter attempts to carry out his plans. However, the pupil can carry a great deal of responsibility for executing them. He is also in a particularly good position to evaluate his own progress and its results. Consequently, the teacher should allow the pupil to accept a good share of this responsibility. Although the teacher should always be ready to help, he should be careful not to be too solicitous and thus stifle the initiative and ingenuity of the pupil.

An Example of a Good Project.   One of the best examples of the project is one which took place in a science class in a Vermont school. In this class, the pupils were attempting to study the stars, although they had no telescope. One day, during a laboratory session, a pupil asked if it might be possible to build a telescope. The teacher answered that it could be done although it would be difficult. A conference followed and the pupil, with some friends, decided to attempt to build a telescope as a project. The first thing that they had to do was to find out how to construct a telescope, i.e., they had to find out how a telescope works, what materials are necessary in making one, and how these materials can be put together. Once they had acquired this information, the boys decided on the kind of telescope they wished to build and gathered the necessary materials. Then they put it together. Hours of work and seemingly insoluable problems were part of this project, but finally the boys assembled a usable telescope. After they got through using it, they presented the telescope to the school for use in science classes. The telescope is now being used by the pupils of that high school.

This project has all the essentials of a good project. The result was well worth the effort; it was realistic and lifelike; it consisted of problem-solving situations; and it was conceived, planned, and executed by the pupils under the guidance of the teacher.

*

How might you use individual projects in your class? Group projects? Why is it sometimes said that directions for pupils may be too explicit?

*

RESEARCH PROJECTS

Independent research projects are true inquiry strategies. Pupils at all levels can profitably conduct independent research activities, but ordinarily the academically talented pupils are more likely to enjoy and profit from independent study. Less able pupils who dislike research activities should be excused from them in favor of some other activities more suitable to their endowments and temperament. They may make good contributions to group projects, however.

Research projects may be individual or group projects. Research projects that involve the whole class seem to be very successful at the secondary school level. In either case the process is the same as that of any other problem solving.

1. Decide exactly what it is that one is to try to find out.
2. Determine the problem so that it is manageable in the time available and with the materials and personnel available.
3. Decide on what tasks must be done to get the data necessary and who will do each job.
4. Gather the materials and equipment necessary.
5. Perform the data-gathering tasks.
6. Review and analyze the data gathered.
7. Draw conclusions and generalizations from the data gathered.
8. Report the findings and conclusions.

SURVEYS, QUESTIONNAIRES, AND OPINIONNAIRES

Conducting a Community Survey.   One of the more interesting types of a school project is the survey. A community survey is a study of the status of something in the community. It might consist of a study of the opinions of citizens regarding a forthcoming election or a study of sanitary conditions in a certain ward. Thus a survey can be a two-edged sword. Well planned, it can bring pupils face to face with the realities in the community. Poorly planned, it can result in erroneous learning and impaired public relations. Therefore every community survey should be prepared thoroughly and planned carefully. Before the pupils begin, they should be well versed in the topic to be investigated and the techniques they are to use. A poorly prepared survey is seldom worth the pupils' effort.

➤ Gathering and interpreting the data of the survey can be troublesome. The actual gathering of the data may be done in many ways. Among them are the interview, the questionnaire, observation, and combinations of these and other techniques. Planning for the use of these techniques should be done carefully so that the time of the respondents is not wasted and the data gathered are really useful. The interpretation of the data should be approached with even more caution. One should set up criteria to differentiate between important and unimportant data and between meaningful and meaningless data. Moreover, one should set up criteria to determine the meaning of the data. This can often be done by inspection, but in some classes one may wish to apply simple statistical procedures. High school pupils can learn to use these procedures readily. Information concerning their use may be found in any textbook on educational measurement or statistics. Many of the newer high school mathematics texts discuss these procedures as well.

Teachers and pupils are sometimes tempted to make public the results of their survey. In most cases the temptation should be resisted, and the survey should be reported to the class only. If it seems desirable to make the report public, the teacher should consult his administrative superior before releasing anything. In addition, he can sometimes consult with a group of laymen in collaboration with his superior. In any event, the report should be made public only if it is outstanding and if its public release will enhance the relationship that exists between the school and the community.

With the possible exception of requiring a little more imagination, this type of activity is not particularly different from any other. As in any other activity involving the community, the planning should be exceptionally good. If the project involves meeting the public, the pupils should be well versed in their roles.

Building Questionnaires and Opinionnaires. Pupils who plan to use questionnaires or opinionnaires need plenty of help in planning them. The following suggestions may be helpful.

1. Determine *exactly* what you want to know. Include only those things that you cannot learn from other sources with reasonable ease.

2. Write the questions as clearly as possible. Try them out on other pupils and teachers before you send them to the respondents. Beware of ambiguities. Be sure to explain any terms that may be misinterpreted.

3. Make the questions easy to answer. Where it is possible, use check lists or multiple choice items. In any case be sure to leave a place for the respondent to make a comment if he wants to. At the secondary school level questionnaire writers should avoid using forced choice items.

4. Set up a system for the respondents' answers that will make your tabulating and interpreting of the data as easy as possible.

Interview Techniques. Interview techniques are similar to questionnaire techniques. In order that the pupils actually ask the questions they should ask in the interviews, they should write out their questions beforehand. Most interviewees of status will try to put the pupils at ease, but even so, unless the questions are written out, the pupils are likely to forget them, become confused, or to word questions badly. Unless the pupil interviewer has a well-conceived interview plan and limits his questions to those things he needs to know, he is quite likely to waste his time and that of the interviewee. In surveys it is particularly important that each respondent be asked the same questions in the same way. For that reason the use of a form such as the following is recommended.

My name is _____. My class is doing a survey about student participation. I will be speaking to many students in your school and other schools. I would like to ask you a few questions.

A. Do you often discuss school issues with
   1. Friends?
   2. Class officers?
   3. School officials?
B. Have you ever attended a meeting (church, school board, union, etc.) in which school policy was discussed?
C. Have you ever taken an active part regarding school issues, such as writing a letter or presenting a petition? [8]

---

[8] Thomas S. Popkewitz, *How to Study Political Participation,* How to Do It Series No. 27 (Washington, D.C.: National Council for the Social Studies, 1974), p. 5.

This type of form is advantageous because the interviewer needs only to check off the interviewee responses. In any case, the interviewers should be trained to write down the answers to their questions immediately and not to depend on their memories for anything.

Observation Techniques. The rules for questionnaires and for interviewing also apply to observation. Again the pupils should determine exactly what they are looking for in advance and then devise some check lists, rating scales, or other devices to make recording the observed data as easy as possible.

The Discovery Approach

It should be evident by this time that the basic principle behind inquiry strategies is to help pupils discover and create their own knowledge and ideas. The premise underlying all of these techniques is that the pupil must seek out his own learning rather than just be a receiver of knowledge. This notion, which has been part of educational theory for many years, has now become substantiated firmly enough for teachers to accept it as basic, sound theory. Nevertheless, this theory does not preclude the teacher's presentation of information to pupils. For pupils to rediscover and re-create all knowledge would be most inefficient. The principal point in discovery teaching is rather to provide as many instances as possible for pupils to draw inferences from data by using logical thinking, inductive or deductive, as the case may be. Thus, if a child watches a billiard ball bouncing off the cushion at various angles, he may conclude that the "angle of incidence equals the angle of reflection" even though he does not use those words. On the other hand, if he understands the principle, he may be able to apply it to specific practical situations. In either case he utilizes the type of thinking that Dewey had in mind when he stressed problem solving.

In general, discovery teaching follows a model something like the following. (A brief study of this model should make the relationship of discovery teaching to problem solving rather obvious. In fact, all inquiry teaching is really discovery. The essential ingredient is that the pupils draw their own generalizations or build their own concepts from the experiences. The Socratic method and the directed discussion are perhaps the best known examples of the discovery approach.)

1. Select the generalization or generalizations.
2. Set up a problem situation.
3. Set up experiences that will bring out the essential elements during the problem solving, e.g., questions, demonstrations, and so on.
4. Set up experiences that will bring out contrasting elements.
5. Draw a generalization or concept.
6. Apply the generalization or concept.

THE SOCRATIC METHOD

In the fifth century B.C. Socrates, the great Athenian teacher, used the art of questioning so successfully that to this day we still speak of the Socratic method. Socrates' strategy was to ask his pupils a series of leading questions that gradually snarled them up to the point where they had to look carefully at their own ideas and to think rigorously for themselves. In several ways his technique foreshadowed the most progressive teaching of the most ardent progressivists. Socratic discussions were informal dialogues taking place in a natural, easy, pleasant enviromnent. The motivation of the students was natural and spontaneous although sometimes Socrates had to go to considerable lengths to ignite his students' intrinsic interest. In his dialogues Socrates tried to aid students develop ideas. He did not impose his own notions on the students. Rather, he encouraged the student to develop his own conclusions and to draw his own inferences. Of course, Socrates usually had preconceived notions about what the student's final learning should be and carefully aimed his questions so that the student would arrive at the conclusions desired. Still his questions were open-ended. The students were free to go wherever the facts led them.

Many modern teachers have tried to adapt the Socratic method to the secondary school. In some cases it has proved to be quite successful. However, it must be remembered that as Socrates used the method it required a one-to-one relationship between the student and the teacher. Some teachers have adapted it for ordinary class use by asking questions first of one pupil and then of another, moving about the class slowly. This technique may work well, but it is difficult because the essence of the Socratic technique is to build question on question in a logical fashion so that each question leads the student a step further toward the understanding sought. When the teacher spreads the questions around the classroom, he may find it difficult to build up the sequence desired and to keep all the pupils with the argument. Sometimes teachers in ordinary-sized classes use the Socratic method by selecting one pupil and directing all the questions at him—at least for several minutes—while the other pupils look on. This is the way Socrates did it. When the topic is interesting enough this technique can be quite successful and even exciting, but in the long run the Socratic technique works best in small-group sessions, seminars, and tutorial sessions with individual pupils.

To conduct a class by the Socratic technique

1. Pose a problem to the class.
2. Ask the pupils a series of probing questions that will cause them to examine critically the problem and their solution to the problem. The main thrust of the questioning and the key questions must be planned in advance so that the questioning will proceed logically. To think of good probing questions on the spur of the moment is too difficult.

CONTROLLED OR GUIDED DISCUSSION

The controlled or guided discussion is a variation of the Socratic discussion frequently advocated by proponents of discovery or inquiry teaching. It consists simply of (1) providing the pupils with information by means of lecture, reading, film, or some other expository device and then (2) by the use of probing questions, as in the Socratic method, guiding the pupils to derive principles and draw generalizations from the material presented. This method differs from a true discussion in that it is teacher-centered with the teacher doing most of the questioning, and from true inquiry in that the principles and generalizations to be arrived at by the pupils have been decided by the teacher in advance. The controlled discussion is not ordinarily an open-ended method of teaching, although there is no reason why it should not be.

The method of the parable used in Biblical times is really a kind of controlled discussion. Employing this type of approach, the teacher relates an incident or story and then uses it as a springboard, asking probing questions until his pupils see, from their own thinking, the principle he wishes to get across.

Springboard Techniques

Any type of presentation that can be used as a jumping-off point for a discussion, research project, or inquiry activity, is a springboard. Springboards serve both as sources of information and as motivating devices. They give the pupils something to work on and some reason for working on it. One use of the springboard can be seen in the controlled discussion technique that was explained earlier in this chapter. Moving pictures, still pictures, playlets, role playing, models, textbook selections, and anecdotes are only a few examples of what can be used for springboards. Anything that lends itself to such questions as Why? So what? How can this be true? or If this is so, then what? can be used as a springboard. Usually the teacher must follow up the springboard with questions that will bring out ideas, relationships, or conclusions to be discovered, analyzed, or evaluated. Really good springboards may be so stimulating that the pupils will eagerly investigate without further prompting.

Parables and contrived incidents are sprightly examples of springboards. When using the parable instead of answering a question or enunciating a principle, the teacher tells his audience a little anecdote and then lets them draw their conclusions from the anecdote. As used by the great teacher of yore the point of the parable often was definite and obvious, but the parable can be used to introduce open-ended debate and discussion as well.

Contrived incidents are simply exciting incidents realistically staged by the teacher to get pupils to react and think. To all appearances the incidents are real until the teacher and players let the class in on the secret. For example, a couple of pupils might come into the class and start a loud argument with each other about a controversial issue. Then on a signal they would stop the argument and the teacher launch a discussion on the merits and demerits of the proposition under discussion. Role playing techniques may be used in the same way.

VALUE SHEETS

The value sheet is a type of springboard that lends itself especially well to the teaching of attitudes or the clarifying of values and issues.[9] Basically a value sheet is a series of questions about an issue. The issue may be presented on the value sheet by a short statement, or anecdote, or by any other form of springboard technique, e.g., a role playing, tape recording, video presentation, or story. The pupils study the presentation and afterward answer the value-sheet questions in writing. Then one of the following procedures can be used as a follow-up.

1. Have a class discussion on the questions and answers in the value sheet.
2. Have small-group discussions on the value sheets.
3. Read certain selections from the value sheets without comment or identifying the writer.
4. Have the pupils turn all the value sheets over to a committee that will analyze them and present to the group the various positions taken by the pupils in the class.

Techniques for Teaching Controversial Issues

Much of the content that is most suited to teaching by inquiry and discovery techniques is controversial. Controversial issues are open-ended questions about which there are both a divergence of opinion and considerable high feeling. It is not the purpose of classroom instruction to solve such issues, but rather to give pupils an opportunity to become acquainted with the issues, the facts (where they are known), the different positions taken by the various sides, and the arguments supporting the points of view. Above all, it gives the pupils a chance to learn how to deal with controversy as objectively and wisely as possible. In teaching con-

[9] Raths, Harmin, and Simon, op. cit., pp. 98–99.

troversial issues the emphasis should be not so much on the content as on the process.

SELECTING THE CONTROVERSIAL ISSUE

Sometimes the study of controversial issues sheds more heat than light. Community feelings run high on many issues. Because controversial issues can be so touchy, teachers should be careful when they select controversial issues for class use. It is recommended that before a teacher decides whether or not to include a controversial issue in a course, he should consider such criteria as these.

1. Is the topic pertinent to your teaching goals?
2. Is it worth taking the trouble? Is it important and timely? Is it of concern to all rather than to only a few individuals?
3. Do you yourself know enough and are you skillful enough to handle the question?
4. Are the pupils mature enough for rational consideration of the issue? Do they have sufficient background?
5. Can you make enough material available so that pupils can get a fair picture of the various sides of the issue?
6. Do you have time enough to consider the issue adequately?
7. Is the issue too emotion-ridden? Some issues may be too hot to handle. It may be better to omit topics than to disrupt the class and the community.

Once it has been decided to tackle a controversial issue, the teacher has his work cut out for him. In order to see to it that all procedes smoothly and fairly, the teacher must keep on top of the topic with all the teaching skill, tact, sensitivity, and common sense he possesses. First, he must be sure to acquire all the necessary clearances from his supervisors, especially if there seems to be any possibility that the issue will cause an uproar in the community. Then he must be sure that all the necessary materials for looking up the facts and points of view are available. All sides should be fairly represented. If there is to be a classroom discussion of the controversial issue, he must be sure that both he and the pupils have the background necessary for reasonable discussion. Too often discussions of controversial issues are the airing of thoughtless prejudices. In the discussion, or study, pupils should have an opportunity to consider all points of view fairly. No pupil should be cut out simply because he represents an unpopular point of view. On the other hand, no pupil should be given more attention than he deserves. The teacher cannot allow errors in fact or logic to go unchallenged either.

In pursuing controversial issues the teacher should allow pupils to reach their own conclusions. He should not try to influence them to take one side or another. He should be particularly careful not to force his own, or an official, position on the pupils either directly or indirectly. Nevertheless, the teacher does have the right, and perhaps the responsibility, to let pupils know his own stand so that they will be aware of his biases. He can keep from overinfluencing pupils by warning them that there are no right answers and by holding back his own position until the end of the discussion.

Sometimes discussions of controversial issues get rather heated. Teachers can do much to eliminate this problem by setting up guidelines before the discussion starts. For example,

All arguments must be supported by authority.
Everyone must have a chance to be heard.
All opinions must be considered respectfully and seriously.
No name calling or personalities will be allowed.
There will be no direct dyadic argument. (To eliminate arguments the rules might specify that at least two pupils must speak before a pupil can speak again, that no one can speak unless he is recognized by the chair, or that no one can make speeches.)

SOME USEFUL STRATEGIES AND TACTICS

Among the strategies commonly used in the study of controversial issues are

Debate.
Panel discussion.
Dramatics.
Role playing.
Simulation.
Research techniques, e.g., open-ended problem solving.
Interview.

Committee work.
The case-study approach.

Other strategies and tactics that have proven successful are

When an issue is extremely hot locally, to study the problem as it has appeared at some other time or as it appears in some other place.

To use value clarifying techniques such as value clarifying responses, value sheets, value discussions, probing questions, application of logical principles to one's argument, and resquests for definition.

To present unpopular positions yourself. Play the devil's advocate when pupils can see only one side of the question. Introduce different positions that the pupils have not considered. Often pupil thinking on controversial issues becomes polarized between two opposite positions when really there are many other positions one might take. When the teacher presents a position he would do well to say, "Some people take the position that . . . ." or "Some people believe that . . . ."

To use opinion scales or fact-opinion diagrams. Let a recorder place the arguments on the scale or diagram as they are given. He can use a chalkboard, an overhead projector, or even a chart for this purpose.

Opinion	Fact

To have pupils argue against their own beliefs. This practice may clarify their thinking and reveal the position of other people.

Insist that pupils check on the sources of information and the meaning of words. After all, lots of arguments are about things that are not so or sometimes purely semantic. Try to get pupils to get at the facts underlying emotional arguments. In order for pupils to accomplish this, the teacher will probably have to train pupils in the necessary techniques.

DRAMATIZATION AND ROLE PLAYING TECHNIQUES

Role Playing

Role playing consists of an unrehearsed dramatization in which the players attempt to make a situation clear to themselves and to the audience by playing the roles of participants in the situation. Its purpose is to help people see a situation through other people's eyes. To attain this purpose the playing of the roles must be held as closely as possible to the reality of the original situation and yet at the same time allow the players to react to the situation as freely and spontaneously as the situation itself will allow.

Other types of dramatization also are useful tools for learning to understand the behavior of others, but they do not qualify as role playing unless they meet the criteria of relatively unrehearsed performance, spontaneous reproduction of real situations, and attempts to analyze, understand, and perhaps solve a problem situation. Other dramatizations will be discussed in another section. Because of the power of drama, role playing is particularly useful in making clear to pupils the motivation and feelings of others.

For instance, in order to teach how prejudice affects both the prejudiced and the prejudiced against, a group in a social studies class attempted to portray the feelings of a pair of boys who were rejected from a fraternity because of their religious beliefs. The players presented two scenes: the first, the discussion of the candidates at the fraternity just prior to the voting; the second, the scene in which the boys were notified of their rejection. In each of these scenes the players attempted to show the emotions of the characters they portrayed. They particularly emphasized how the boys felt after the rejection. Three different casts portrayed these scenes. After the presentations the entire class discussed the justice of the decision and the probable effect of the incident on the persons concerned.

Another example of role playing is an attempt to make the feelings of the American colonists more real to the pupils. In this class the players represented a group of colonists discussing the news of the stamp tax. The loyalist tried to show the reason for the tax, but the others shouted him down. From role playing of this sort it is hoped that the pupils will come to understand the tenor of the times being studied.

THE VALUE OF ROLE PLAYING

Role playing may result in other valuable learnings. If Keltner[10] is right, a more complete list of the values of role playing would show that role playing

1. Gives us insight into the effectiveness of the roles we play in real life.
2. Teaches us to examine the roles we play more objectively.
3. Teaches us to perform new roles and to experiment with new roles in order to make more adequate adjustment to the groups of which we are a part.
4. Provides us with a kind of laboratory where we can examine and experiment with roles in situations where we are not "playing for keeps" yet where a semblance of reality is present.
5. Provides us with vivid examples of behavior that are more effective than mere conversation about the situations.
6. Helps us develop clearer communication. When we cannot put an idea about human relations into words we can act it out and thus make it clearer to those who are trying to understand it.
7. Helps us to understand another point of view.

Role playing also has several advantages for the group.

1. It provides a group with a system of communication that is based on action rather than word symbols. This helps members of the group to understand one another.
2. It helps a group learn the skills necessary for effective group action.
3. It provides techniques of analyzing problems which involve human factors or items of interpersonal relations.
4. It involves the members in a consideration of the problem.

[10] John W. Keltner, *Group Discussion Processes* (New York: David McKay Co., Inc., 1957), pp. 262–263. By permission.

5. It enables a group to pretest ideas that may have significance for the future.[11]

Teachers use role playing for many purposes. Among them are

a. Clarifying attitudes and concepts.
b. Demonstrating attitudes and concepts.
c. Deepening understanding of social situations.
d. Preparing for a real situation (e.g., rehearsing the teaching of a lesson with a group of colleagues or practicing interview techniques before going out to be interviewed).
e. Planning and trying out strategies for attacking problems.
f. Testing hypothetical solutions of problems.
g. Practicing leadership and other social skills.

LIMITATIONS AND DANGERS OF ROLE PLAYING

Role playing is not a magic formula by which to solve all one's difficult teaching problems. It is a difficult technique, the improper use of which can be harmful. Among its limitations and dangers, Keltner lists the following.[12]

a. Participants must be thoroughly prepared for this kind of work. Unless the group is sensitive and open-minded enough to try new ways of working together, the process may meet serious opposition and possibly fail.
b. The cases and the problems must be realistic, practical, and complete enough for clear-cut issues to arise. Unless the role-players know the facts and the backgrounds and conditioning of the characters the whole thing may become superficial.
c. Players often tend to "ham" up their portrayal of the roles. This makes the production a farce and becomes merely a pleasant but frustrating attempt to get at real issues. The players must be cautioned to play the roles as realistically as possible.
d. Role-playing is time consuming. Properly done it takes at least an hour of highly concentrated activity. Unless there are capable leaders and directors available, this time will ge away without sufficient use of the method.

[11] Ibid.
[12] Ibid., pp. 277–278.

e. Role-playing demands some imagination on the part of the group. Unless the group has demonstrated that it has some of this ability to create ideas and use its imagination, the role-playing may be quite sterile.
f. Unless there is an atmosphere of free discussion and inquiry, the role-playing cannot be adequately developed.
g. Role-playing should involve the whole group. There is a tendency on the part of many leaders to dictate all of the conditions and the scenes that are to be portrayed. This is contradictory to the main purpose of the method —that of involving the whole group in the consideration of its problems.

Role-playing is not a device to be used for fun or entertainment. Too many groups today are using it much as they would use a skit or short dramatic production, merely to entertain the members.

h. When the members are not fully acquainted with each other, they may become known in terms of the roles they have portrayed in a session rather than as they really are. It is wise to withhold the use of the method until the members become acquainted. In the large group technique this is not possible nor so important. When stereotype perceptions of people may appear to be forming in a group, the leader should seek an opportunity for the players to be seen in several different roles so no one role will become associated with the player.

STAGING THE ROLE PLAYING

Preparing for Role Playing. Although role playing is usually done without script or rehearsal, it does require preparation. In the first place the pupils must understand the situation being presented. For this reason, the situation to be role played should be a simple one. If the situation is too complex, the role playing will probably fail. A situation involving two to four characters will probably be most effective. Once a situation that the pupils can readily comprehend has been selected, the teacher must carefully brief both the players and the rest of the class to be sure that they do understand it. The teacher should see to it that each player not only understands the situation, but also realizes the purpose of the role playing and his part in it. For this reason the players should spend some time discussing their roles with the teacher before the presentation. The teacher must also see to it that the rest of the class understands the purpose of the role playing and what they should look for as the drama is presented. Although role playing may be enjoyable, it is not entertainment. The teacher should make every effort to be sure that all the pupils realize this and treat role playing as a serious attempt to clarify a difficult social situation.

Selecting the Cast. As one can readily see, role playing requires serious effort on the part of the role player. His job is to attempt to get under the skin of another person and, as far as he possibly can, present that person's actions and emotions. This is no small task. For this reason one should select the players carefully—if possible, from volunteers. Sometimes selecting the cast is complicated by the fact that the most eager volunteers seem quite incapable of carrying out the roles. Consequently, it is not wise to commit oneself too heartily to the use of volunteers only.

At times the teacher will have to find understudies for the cast. A helpful procedure is to select several casts and have several presentations. This practice may offset poor presentations and give depth to the understanding of the class as a result of the difference in presentation and interpretation of the roles. This practice may also help to offset tendencies toward stereotypical thinking. Pupils who play roles such as that of an employer or a businessman sometimes seem to think that their representation of these types is typical of all of them. Such thinking is false. Employers and businessmen are large categories whose members run the entire gamut from conservative to radical, from outgoing to shy, from scrupulously honest to downright crooked, from stingy to generous, and so on. Different portrayals of the roles by honest persons may make these differences stand out and disabuse pupils of the notion that employers and businessmen all think alike.

Playing the Roles. Role playing is rather taxing for some pupils, and quite often the players are extremely nervous. They may need help and encouragement. Rehearsing the first few lines and preparing a general plan for the development of the dramatization may help the participants to play their roles more confidently. On the other hand, too much planning may stifle the sociodrama's spontaneity and straitjacket the role player's interpretation. Because the purpose of role playing is for the role player to place himself in his role and then, as naturally as possible, enact the role he is portraying, the teacher's part in the planning should ordinarily be limited to giving the pupils the necessary background and enough planning and direction to get started with confidence. A warm-up period is excellent, but overdone it may take the life out of the actual role playing.

The pattern in most role playing is quite loose. Consequently, there is always a danger that inexperienced role players may lose sight of their roles. The teacher can guard against this eventuality by carefully selecting the role players and thoroughly explaining their roles to them. Sometimes, however, these precautions are not sufficient. On such an occasion, if a player does get badly out of character, the teacher may have to stop the production and reorient the players. It is better to interrupt the production than to present false information to the class.

Preparing the Audience and Following Up. As with any other activity, the pupils in the audience should be well prepared for observing the sociodrama. They should understand what is going on and what to look for, or the presentation will be for naught. Similarly, if the pupils are to benefit from the acting, the dramatization must be followed up. A discussion period is excellent as a follow-up after the sociodrama. In fact, it can be the most worthwhile part of the entire presentation. Sometimes role playing a situation up to a critical point and then stopping the role playing to discuss what might or should happen next can be very effective. In any case, the pupils should discuss and analyze the action and interpret its significance. In the discussion the participants might explain just what they hoped to do and how they felt during the role playing. Finally, this discussion should end in a summary or perhaps the formulation of some generalization. The teacher should not insist that the pupils come to a definite conclusion, however. It may be much better to leave the discussion of the role playing open-ended.

Frequently it is helpful, after a period of analysis

and discussion, for a second group of pupils to role play the situation so that other interpretations can be seen.

*

What should the teacher do if a pupil seems to be badly misinterpreting his role?
What purposes may a sociodrama serve?
What sort of material is best suited to a sociodrama?

*

Dyadic Role Playing

Role playing can be a complex technique for young people to handle effectively and seriously. Zeleny and Gross[13] suggest that teachers use dyadic role playing, i.e., role playing in which only two players participate, to give pupils experience before they attempt to role play more complex situations. Dyadic role playing, like other role playing, helps pupils to understand problems and situations better and to develop empathy for people in other situations. Because only two players participate, dyadic role playing is simpler and results in learning that might be difficult to achieve in a more complex situation.

To conduct dyadic role playing, first select two opposing positions or statuses, e.g., management versus labor, and help the pupils acquire the necessary background so that they understand and identify with the different positions and statuses.

Once the pupils have been well briefed, divide the class into pairs (dyads). In each pair one pupil should represent one position and one the other. Then all the pairs role play the situation simultaneously. When their role playing is finished, they should reverse their positions and role play the situation again. Afer each person has played both roles, the pairs evaluate what they have done. In this evaluation they may discuss how well each side was presented, whether they had all the information they needed, or what the role playing showed them. If it seems that the pairs might have done better with more information, perhaps they should

find out the necessary information, and replay the roles. Finally the dyadic role playing can be followed up by a general discussion or some other suitable follow-up. Sometimes the follow-up should consist of having a dyad that did particularly well role play before the entire class. Or perhaps two pupils whose work seems promising can be formed into a new dyad for a class presentation. In either case, the role playing should be followed up by class discussion.

Focused Conversation

The focused conversation is an elementary form of role playing. In it one pupil acts as an informed spokesman and others act as informed listeners and critics. Zeleny explains the process.

As we have pointed out, the *focused conversation* is a universal means for the exchange of information and experience. It can be simulated in a high school class. Suppose a high school class desires to study the effects of rapid social change upon life in American cities . . . To interest and inform the students, the teacher could trace the major changes which have taken place in America during the last one hundred years, especially the tremendous growth of the cities. Following this, students could start their search for more detailed information, including material on the ecology of the city, the nature of stratification, and the degree of mobility among the social classes. Individual student findings may, then, be compared in focused conversations in small class groups. To repeat a point made, one student in a small group may act as *informed* spokesman while the other or others act as *informed* listeners and critics. In this way we have the talker-listener role-interaction situation. The informed listener responds knowingly, appreciatively and helpfully as well as critically. Again, as pointed out, the "warm-up" in the small groups can be excellent preparation for stimulating general class discussion. We can point out again that the procedures outlined give the teacher a good opportunity to identify and to deal with individual differences as well as to act as a resource person and consultant.[14]

A similar sort of role playing situation can be set up in which "the informed listeners and critics"

---

13 Leslie D. Zeleny and Richard E. Gross, "Dyadic Role Playing of Controversial Issues," *Social Education* 24:354–358 (December, 1960) .

14 Lesle D. Zeleny, *How to Use Simulations,* How to Do It Series No. 26 (Washington, D.C.: National Council for the Social Studies, 1973) , p. 4.

take the roles of informed questioners as in the well known television program *Meet the Press*.

Simulation

Simulation combines role playing and problem solving. In a simulation exercise pupils play roles as though they were really executing a real life situation. By acting out roles as though they were real, the pupils, it is hoped, will learn to understand the important factors in the real situation and learn either how to behave in the real situation or how persons in such situations must behave. Simulations differ from sociodramas and psychodramas in that although the role playing responses are impromptu, the roles of the actors and the scenarios are carefully drafted. Essentially simulation entails two things:

1. That pupils be assigned to perform definite roles requiring certain types of action which they must perform in a fairly well-defined situation.

2. That the pupils be confronted with simulations of real life situations in which they must take necessary action just as the character whose role they are taking would have to. As a rule, whatever action is taken leads to new incidents that require new action. In these situations the actors are not free to act in any way they please, but rather must stay in character and keep their actions within the limits prescribed by the realities of the situation being simulated. The technique is the outgrowth of the war games in which army commandants fought mock battles and has since been adopted by business, governmental, and other agencies that prepare people for important situations that they must face in the future. Consequently, the actions and scenarios should be as realistic as possible. Good simulation games are available through most of the reputable educational publishers and suppliers. An outline showing how to prepare a scenario can be found in Chapter 14. However, unless one builds his scenario carefully, it is usually better to use a professionally written one. A slipshod, hastily put together scenario may do more harm than good. Nevertheless making up their own simulation scenario can be an excellent exercise for pupils. Mapping out the scenario and delineating the role can provide much learning in depth.

Although simulations are difficult to write and to do well, the overall procedure for conducting them is quite simple.

1. Make ready any props, equipment, or material that will be needed in the simulation.
2. Introduce the simulation. Explain
   a. The reason for it.
   b. How it is played.
3. Assign pupils to roles. (Usually it is best for the teacher to assign roles in accordance with the pupils' potential as role players. Calling for volunteers is also a good method but may result in very poor casting. Sometimes the roles are described on cards that the pupils draw. If the simulation requires anything but the simplest role playing, drawing cards may be disastrous. Giving the players a card bearing a description of the role selected for them may be advantageous, however.
4. Once the pupils understand the simulation and know their roles in it, then conduct the simulation. In doing so follow the scenario to the letter. You may take on the role of umpire, referee, score keeper or consultant yourself or delegate such tasks to designated pupils, if the occasion warrants it.
5. Follow up the simulation by discussion or similar activities in which the pupils draw inferences and make generalizations from the simulated activity.

Other Dramatizations

Role playing is not the only form of dramatization used in teaching. Pupils can bring dramatics to school in all its forms from full-fledged grand opera in the music department to charades in the English classroom. Among classroom dramatic activities one may find such divergent art forms as the ballet, pantomime, pageant, choral readings, cinema, puppetry, shadow plays, mock radio and television performances, skits, and video taping.

Such dramatizations have many uses: illustration of a historical scene, portrayal of a literary character, the vitalization of a play, or the representation of a fact or an abstract idea. The impact of a well-done dramatization can drive home concepts and attitudes to both spectators and participants. Especially worth considering are the student-writ-

ten dramatizations. In addition to the benefit derived from creating the piece, the pupil may learn
many facts and figures about the topic to be dramatized as he gathers material for his presentation.

Unlike the sociodrama, dramatizations need to
be rehearsed. Before attempting to present a work
of art, the players should know pretty well what to
say, how to say it, and how to portray their roles.
Even if they are only to read a play, the pupils
should first read through the parts they are to
portray and become familiar with the vocabulary.
Impromptu classroom readings of great plays seldom lead to appreciation of the drama. A quick
rehearsal in the corridor or in a corner of the classroom will usually increase the effectiveness many
times. A more thorough preparation should be even
more beneficial.

Only on rare occasions, however, is it worthwhile
to spend long periods of time in rehearsal and line
learning. For this reason the use of pantomime, pa-
geants, and other activities in which the pupils have
few speaking parts may be advantageous. Otherwise, classroom dramatization should probably depend upon the reading of lines. This caveat should
not preclude the use of such projects as preparing
and filming a movie script or staging a play. It does
mean that one should carefully consider the relative values to be derived from the sort of activities
that require long periods of rehearsal and memorization.

*

Criticize the following practice. (Note that "criticize"
and "find fault" are not synonymous.) In a junior high
school the pupils had been reading plays for outside
reading. As a culminating activity the student teacher
asked each person to dramatize a scene from his play
using his colleagues as actors. Before the presentation the
actors consulted with one another for about five minutes
and then read their lines all from the same book.

What purposes may dramatization serve? What sort of
material is best dramatized? What types of dramatization
are possible? What are the merits of each?

When are dramatizations best used in the teaching-
learning cycle?

*

SUMMARY

Questioning is one of the oldest and most dependable tactics. Its uses are legion and range from
the checking of memory and understanding to the

bringing about of higher learning. Unfortunately,
of the four categories of questions suggested by
Gallagher and Aschner, most teachers are content
to concentrate on memory questions and neglect
convergent, divergent, and evaluative questions. Yet
it is quite possible, after a little practice, to phrase
questions that would cover each category in the
Bloom taxonomy.

Good questions are clear, simple, straightforward,
challenging, thought-provoking, adapted to the
pupils to whom they are addressed and suitable for
the purpose for which they are being used. Teachers
who use questions well prepare them in advance.
As a rule, skillful use of questions requires that one
ask questions of individuals rather than of the entire class. The best technique is to ask the question
and then call on a specific person to answer it. The
teacher should refrain from repeating questions and
should be sure to distribute questions evenly and
randomly among the class members. Thought
questions require special attention. Pupil answers
should also be handled courteously. Teachers should
support all honest attempts to answer even when
pupils do not come up with the "right" answer, but
pupil error and misunderstanding must not be allowed to go uncorrected. Pupils should also be encouraged to ask questions. The best classes are full
of pupil questions and comments. Clarifying responses are most useful for starting pupils' thought
processes.

Inquiry teaching consists of any strategy in which
the pupil attempts to seek information and to draw
from it his own generalizations and conclusions.
Most inquiry strategies involve problem solving. In
general, the problem-solving method used in schools
follows the steps outlined by Dewey as the act of a
complete thought. These steps include selecting and
defining a problem, gathering data, making hypotheses, and testing conclusions. Pupils need help in
carrying out each of these steps. It should be noted
that this technique is not the only way of solving
problems nor is it always necessary for one to follow
the steps in order. The main objective is to seek and
discover knowledge for oneself. Among the problem-solving strategies are the case study method,
value sheets, and various kinds of projects. Ideally
a project should consist of a task that the pupil
sets for himself and then carries through to com-

pletion under the teacher's guidance. It should both have intrinsic value to the pupil and be pertinent to the teacher's educational goals. Sometimes the projects are group projects, but whether group or individual, each project should be realistic, lifelike, and of innate value to the pupils, and it should be conceived, planned, and executed by the pupils under the teacher's guidance.

Discovery teaching consists of teaching in which pupils draw their own conclusions from information that they may have gleaned themselves or that teachers or others may have provided them. The famous Socratic discussion and its modern counterpart, the controlled discussion, are good examples of discovery teaching. The Socratic method, which is characterized by the logical development of concepts through open-ended, thought-provoking leading questions, is chiefly useful in teaching individuals or small classes. The controlled discussion has been developed for using Socratic techniques with full size classes. Springboard approaches are espe-

cially good for use in discovery teaching. They have been used since ancient times in the parable method and in more modern versions such as the value sheet.

Inquiry and discovery teaching usually involve controversial issues. Since controversial issues are by definition controversial, teachers should treat them as open-ended and try to see to it that all sides of any issue studied are properly represented.

One of the most powerful of the methods, when properly used, is role playing, which consists basically of trying to put oneself in the place of someone else and to act out his point of view. In order to be effective, role playing must be an unrehearsed, spontaneous attempt to analyze and understand real problem situations. Simulation is a type of role playing. The purpose of role playing and simulation is quite different from that of the many other types of dramatic presentations that may be included in the classroom. These other types should be rehearsed as carefully as the time permits in order to be effective.

Expository, Extraclass, and Management Techniques

12

Lectures and Teacher Talks

In the United States most of the teaching is done by teachers telling things to pupils. In fact, if Amidon and Flanders are right, and few observers would doubt their conclusion, the teacher talks about 45 per cent of the time in the average class.[1] For the teacher to dominate the class so much is probably not wholesome. Alcorn, Kinder, and Schunert point out that experience seems to show that pupils generally remember

10 per cent of what they READ.
20 per cent of what they HEAR.
30 per cent of what they SEE.
50 per cent of what they HEAR and SEE.
70 per cent of what they SAY.
90 per cent of what they SAY as they DO a thing.[2]

[1] Edmund J. Amidon and Ned A. Flanders, *The Role of the Teacher in the Classroom* (Minneapolis, Minn.: Paul S. Amidon and Associates, 1963), p. 57.
[2] Marvin D. Alcorn, James S. Kinder, and Jim R. Schunert, *Better Teaching in Secondary Schools*, 3rd ed. (New York:

Such experience does not argue well for the effectiveness of teacher talk as a teaching strategy. Just the same, teachers must tell pupils things. Teaching is not telling, but telling is an important ingredient in teaching. No teacher can get along without it. Almost every teacher could become effective by improving his telling techniques.

The Formal Lecture

There are three basic types of teaching telling activities: (1) the formal lecture, (2) the short informal teacher talk, and (3) teacher comment and reaction. Each one has its place. Unfortunately many teachers lean too heavily on the lecture.

In the formal lecture the teacher presents the lesson by what amounts to making a speech. There is a minimum amount of give and take in this type of teaching. This one-way formula is partly a result of the history of teaching, particularly as it was done in the medieval universities. In those days the professor was the only person who had access to the text, so he read it to the students with appropriate commentary.[3]

Lately, largely because of a reaction against its long years of misuse and overuse, it has been fashionable in some circles to downgrade the lecture, but the lecture has been used with success in the past, is being used with success at the present, and no doubt will be used with success in the future. As a matter of fact, most teachers find lectures almost indispensable for certain purposes. They use them

To introduce activities or units.
To motivate pupils.
To sum up.
To explain difficult points.
To bridge gaps between units or topics.
To establish a general point of view.
To point out a different point of view.

To provide information otherwise not readily available.
To provide additional information.
To propose a theory.

Moreover, as long as the lecture remains the predominant form of teaching in our colleges, college-bound boys and girls should have considerable experience with lectures in the last stages of their high school careers. It goes without saying that this experience with lectures should be accompanied by instruction in how to profit from lectures, most particularly in the art of taking notes.

Just the same, in spite of its values, the formal lecture is ordinarily a rather ineffective method of teaching secondary school pupils. Because learning from lectures is relatively passive learning, it may be relatively sterile learning. Lectures do not give pupils opportunity to explore, to think, or to interact. They are not conducive to study in depth, but rather tend to make pupils receivers of knowledge. They do not allow for differing responses or the exercising of one's curiosity. They are seldom useful for changing attitudes or imparting the higher cognitive skills. Except in unusual cases, very little of the lecture sticks in the pupils' minds. Pupils seem to learn better when they put themselves into the learning. Unless the pupils do something with the information presented in a lecture, their learning and retention may be rather thin. The lecture format gives very little opportunity for reinforcement to take place or for one to assess the progress in learning of either the group or individuals. Sometimes they are a waste of time. It might be better to mimeograph or ditto the information to be presented and use the class time for other purposes.

The lecture technique may also cause discipline problems. Adolescent attention spans for the typical lecture are notoriously short. This statement does not mean that secondary school boys and girls cannot pay careful attention to a good lecture for a long time. Rather, it means that it takes a good lecturer to hold any audience's interested attention for an hour. In the secondary school a stimulating lecturer, skillful enough to hold the pupils' attention and really teach them by his lecturing, is indeed a rare bird. Besides, to key himself up to the point where he can make lectures exciting four or

---

Holt, Rinehart and Winston, Publishers, 1970), p. 216. According to Alcorn, Kinder, and Schunert these figures, which were originally developed by P. J. Philips at the University of Texas, Industrial Education Department, are only approximations and should be taken as such, but experience indicates that they are reasonably accurate.

[3] The word *lecture* is derived from the Latin *legere (lectus)* to read.

five times a day, week after week, is beyond the capabilities of most mortals. New teachers who place great faith in their continuous use of the lecture day after day are foolhardy. Remember: Adolescents have a low tolerance for boredom.

PREPARING THE LECTURE

Most secondary school lectures should be short. A twenty-minute lecture is quite often more than a junior high school class can abide. Short talks of about ten minutes duration are likely to be more acceptable. Senior high school classes may be able to stand lectures that are much longer. However, it takes a really good lecturer to hold the interest of even adult groups for more than half an hour. In university graduate lectures students really have to battle to keep from day-dreaming or falling asleep.

One reason that many secondary school lectures are not more stimulating is that good lectures require more preparation than most teachers have time to give them. Very seldom can a teacher lecture effectively on the spur of the moment. If a teacher wants to have a high degree of effectiveness in his lectures, he must plan them meticulously. Not only must he plan what he wishes to say, but he should also plan how he intends to say it. If possible, it might even be wise to practice the lecture before the bedroom mirror.

*

Why is the lecture considered to be a poor technique for use in secondary schools?

You have been assigned a ninth-grade general science class. This class consists largely of slow learners. It has a reputation of being hard to handle. The youngsters are restless and not much interested. How much would you plan to lecture to such a group? What might you be able to do to hold the attention of such a group?

*

MAKING THE LECTURE CLEAR

If they are to be effective, lectures must be both clear and persuasive. With this goal in mind, the teacher planning a classroom lecture must guard against attempting too much. Because of its one-way format it is very easy for the teacher who lec-

tures to present ideas quickly and then move on to new ones before the pupils have caught the first ones. Neither secondary school pupils nor adults are likely to learn much from ideas skimmed over lightly. The capable lecturer limits his talk to a few salient points which he develops and drives home. To be sure that he achieves his purpose, he states clearly what each point is and supports it with illustrations, examples, and other details which, in themselves, may not be important, but which do tend to make the point stand out. And then, after all this has been done, he comes back to his point again, restating it clearly, in order to drive it home and clinch it as firmly as possible in a final summation. As a rule, this type of procedure will carry a lecturer's ideas across to his audience, whereas attempting to cover many points may only confuse his listeners.

MAKING THE LECTURE INTERESTING

To lecture successfully one must first secure the pupils' interest and attention and then maintain it throughout the lecture. One way to arouse attention and interest is to open the lecture with a challenging question, a problem, or a perplexing fact. If at the beginning of the lecture one can puzzle the pupils a little, they must be anxious to listen in order to solve the puzzlement.

In any case it helps if the teacher lets the pupils know what it is he intends to do and the reason for doing it. If he can establish a purpose that relates directly to the pupils' purposes and concerns, so much the better. Certainly he should point out how the information in the lecture relates to past and future content and to what they already know and like. Real and rhetorical questions, the use of humor, and above all lots of illustrations and examples will help maintain interest and make points clear. Demonstrations, pictures, exhibits, projectuals and other instructional aids all seem to spice up the lecture and to hold pupils' attention when their minds begin to wander.

In addition, illustrations, audio-visual aids, and demonstrations in lectures help to clarify and point up desired concepts. Frequently, audio-visual devices can give meaning to what would otherwise remain just a mass of words. Even when the lecture is clear and interesting without them, the use of visual aids can reinforce the learning by adding the impact of another sense. Teacher lecturers who depend solely on their voices are being unfair to themselves and their pupils.

PRESENTING THE LECTURE

Expert lecturers claim that the way to put your points across in a lecture is to

Tell them what you are going to tell them.

Tell them.

Tell them what you have told them.

This formula is a good one. It has served the best lecturers well over the years. It calls for a logical, well-ordered presentation. It is well aimed at only a few salient points, which the lecturer hits at least several times. (Using repetition is about the only way one can reinforce learning during a lecture.) To be sure to drive home his points, the lecturer summarizes frequently. There is no place for wandering in the lecture, so the formula rules out digressions and irrelevant reminiscences. Supportive examples, illustrations, forgettable details, and other trivia that help put the point across are a different matter. They may make the difference between a successful and unsuccessful lecture.

Lecturers should develop their argument logically at the listeners' comprehensive level. Some lecturers go completely over the heads of their pupils; others are insultingly childish and simple. To analyze one's audience and then to speak to it at the correct level are essential steps for every lecturer. To achieve the correct level, the lecturer must adjust his language, ideas, and sequence of ideas to the audience. In general the content should move from the concrete to the abstract, and back again to the concrete so as not to leave things hanging in midair. He should also be sure the lecture develops logically enough so that pupils have the background necessary for understanding new material. The content should be new, however. There is no excuse for lectures that parrot the textbook. The whole idea of lecturing is to give pupils new, fresh ideas or information that is not otherwise readily available.

If the teacher lectures, he must help the pupils learn from the lectures. The need for the use of repetition and other rhetorical devices has already been mentioned. Teachers should also be prepared to help pupils learn to take good notes. For this purpose an outline of the lecture on the chalkboard or overhead projector can be most helpful. The common practice of providing a skeleton outline for the pupils to fill in as the lecture goes on has much to recommend it. So does the even more common practice among good teachers of stopping to point out to the pupils that what has just been explained, or is about to be explained, should be put in their notes. Once pupils have become skilled in note taking these practices should no longer be necessary.

THE LANGUAGE OF THE LECTURE

Clarity also depends on the use of language. Beginning teachers and student teachers are inclined to talk over the heads of their pupils. Concepts and words commonplace to college seniors and recent graduates may be foreign to high school pupils. Although the teacher should avoid talking down to his pupils, he should be careful to talk to them in language they understand.

The language used should be good English, of course. Some teachers attempt to reach the pupils' level by introducing slang expressions into their talks. This is usually a poor policy. Slang and overinformality are more likely to cheapen a lecture than clarify it.[4] Furthermore, the teacher, willy-nilly, is a model of English oral composition whenever he speaks. If his influence on the pupils is to be a good one, he must see to it that his language is the type that he wishes the pupils to imitate.

The use of illustrations and figures of speech often makes lectures clearer and livelier, but their injudicious use can at times defeat their purpose. Particularly treacherous in this respect is the metaphor, which can truly be a two-edged sword. With secondary school pupils—particularly the younger and duller ones—a teacher should call things by their proper names and leave flights of poetic fancy to others. Certainly if one must use such figures of speech, one must be sure that the pupils understand to what the figures allude. Not to do so may make the entire lecture meaningless.

---

[4] Besides, the teacher's slang is frequently out of date. Teachers who try to use street argot often get it wrong.

Informal Teacher Talks

Much, if not most, of the average teacher's group instruction is done through informal talks to groups or to the entire class. These talks differ from the formal lecture in that they are usually short, extempore discourses rising out of the needs of the moment. Often they stem from class discussion or pupils' questions. Because these talks are short, teachers do not need to prepare for them as in the formal lecture. Usually they are most effective when interspersed with questions and discussions both from and to the teacher in what is sometimes called the lecture-discussion.

Because this technique will probably be one of his mainstays, each prospective teacher should become proficient in its use. He should also be aware of its dangers and shortcomings.

All of the comments about clarity of language in the lecture are applicable to the short informal talk as well, of course. So too are comments about utilizing the audio-visual aids to make the instruction clearer and more effective. The greatest danger is that the teacher will talk too much. When teachers talk, all too often pupils stop thinking. Remember the Flanders and Amidon study cited in Chapter 1 that indicated that the pupils learned better when the teaching was indirect. Oftentimes teachers must explain, but *they should try to turn many of their teacher talks into indirect teaching by asking questions, posing problems, seeking comments, and entertaining questions.* Also, the teacher should beware of the danger of thinking that pupils have learned something just because he has told it to them. Whenever it is possible to do so, pupils will misunderstand, misinterpret, or miss altogether what the teacher tells them. Teachers who make a habit of following up their explanations, and other short talks, with questions designed to check the pupils' understanding are well advised. Teachers who try to limit their talks to a minimum and substitute instead questions, discussions, Socratic techniques, and other tactics and strategies which call for the pupils to carry the load of the thinking, are even better advised.

*

For what purposes would you plan to use lectures in your secondary school teaching? What kinds of lectures are there? How can they be used?

How does one plan a lecture or informal talk? Consider objectives, outline, illustrations, motivations, length, aids, clarity, interest.

How does one tell whether a lecture or talk has been successful?

*

LARGE-CLASS INSTRUCTION

In the 1960s the practice of gathering together very large groups of seventy-five, one hundred, or more pupils for what is called large-group instruction, became something of a fad. Sometimes these large groups are part of some sort of team teaching plan, but frequently they are not. They may be simply attempts to cut instructional cost.

That some types of learning can take place equally as well in large groups as in small ones is a truism accepted by almost all teachers. Certain types of lectures, demonstrations, dramatizations, and other types of teaching in which instruction is a one-way process from the teacher to the pupil, can be just as effective with groups of a thousand as with groups of ten. As a matter of fact, the very size of a large group may cause a teacher to be more effective, or at least to try harder. Sometimes too, large groups can develop a spirit that is catching and which skillful teachers can utilize for motivational purposes.

As one might expect, large-group instruction has both merits and drawbacks. By bringing large numbers of pupils together to be instructed simultaneously, it frees time for the teachers—time that can be used for preparation, individual work, paper correction, and other professional chores. It also makes possible the elimination of much repetition. Many schools today try to take advantage of the talents of outside experts. By using large-group instruction, it is possible to bring the talents of an outside expert to all pupils without asking the guest to repeat himself to several audiences. Similarly, four or five classes can watch a moving picture all at once without tying up the equipment for four or five periods. Incidentally, showing moving pictures to large groups may make it worthwhile to schedule large blocks of time and procure feature films for use in literature or social studies courses.

The disadvantages of large-group instruction are

very serious. Large-group instruction gives little opportunity for pupil-teacher interaction. Except in the most unusual cases, it tends to be merely a period of pouring information into passive, relatively inactive minds. As a result of the size of the group and the type of instruction, the teacher can rarely make allowance for differences in individuals. Whatever is to be done for pupils who have forged ahead or fallen behind, who do not quite understand, or who wish to ask questions, must be done at some other time by some other means. All too frequently, large-group instruction tends to chain the pupils in a rigid lockstep.

Also, discipline and control often become a problem. Large groups listening to a full period of dull lecture or poorly planned demonstration sometimes become noisy and unruly. In some situations the extra time teachers were to have as a result of the large-group instruction can turn into periods of policing large classes someone else is supposed to be teaching. Another problem in large-group instruction is psychological noise—the fact that ideas seem to be harder to put across to large groups than to small ones. This difficulty perhaps results from minds that wander and woolgather during the lectures and large-group demonstrations.

From these advantages and disadvantages one can see that the large-group instruction implies the need for certain special techniques and technology. The problem of psychological noise makes it necessary for much pointing up, repeating and reemphasizing. This problem, plus the problems of control and making contact with so many individuals at once, makes it necessary for teachers to pay particular attention to the use of interest-getting and interest-holding devices. To help the pupils identify and react as *students,* teachers may use rhetorical questions, problems, and other techniques that will tend to arouse, or at least counterfeit, teacher-pupil interaction. Audio-visual devices of many sorts are especially helpful in large-group instruction. Overhead projectors, slides, demonstrations, drama, and similar devices and techniques aid the teacher by giving him other means by which to make his impact.

Under no circumstances should the large-class instruction be merely a formal lecture or speech, except in the case of assembly speakers or guest lecturers—and even then the unadorned lecture should be avoided if possible. Large-group lecture classes should be supported by other techniques in order to drive the objectives home. As a matter of fact, there can be little justification for straight lecture in large-group classes anyway. If a class is going to be only straight lecture, it would be more economical and more effective to tape or film the lecture and present it to a much wider audience, thus saving the cost of several lecturers. With our new techniques we could then individualize the large class by playing the lecture to individual pupils at the time they need it or are most ready for it.

Instructional Television

Instructional television is a form of large-group instruction. In the following paragraphs we shall discuss briefly the programming of television for classroom use. A more detailed discussion of television teaching and its use in the classroom appears in Chapter 14. Basically the techniques are the same as for any other large group instruction.

Educational television should deal primarily with the thing it can do best. Instead of being just another lecture or lecture with illustrations, the television program should aim to bring into the classroom experiences impossible otherwise, for the television program has capabilities the classroom cannot match. It can take pupils to distant places where they could not otherwise go, show them things and people they could not otherwise see, and bring to them extraordinary events (for example, the President's inauguration) that would otherwise be out of the question. It can take pupils on field trips and present demonstrations in which pupils can really see the inner workings of things. Television programming should take advantage of these capabilities. It should concentrate on opening new vistas and challenges to the pupils and enriching and deepening their concepts and attitudes. Television programming can be especially useful for culminating and tying together the various threads of a unit or course.

Obviously the programmer of educational or instructional television should utilize all the resources available to the medium. Although there is little point in using visual aids simply for the sake of using them, television programming should take full advantage of the television's ability to use film clips, charts, graphs, resource persons, demonstrations, and other materials and techniques to drive home course objectives. Educational objectives, however, should not be sacrificed for technical excellence or dramatic impact. The programs should be accurate and free from anachronisms, false emphasis, prejudice, hasty generalizations, one-sided presentations, propaganda, and other sources of error. Further, the programming should be truly educational, always aimed at furthering school objectives. The content and methodology of the program should be consistent with the educational purpose. For these reasons the program director should be an expert on educational methodology and curriculum. In planning programs he should rely heavily on the opinions and suggestions of the classroom teachers who use the programs.

In order for the programs to be most effective, the television studio should aid the classroom teachers by giving them the opportunity to preview their programs and by providing them with resource materials, suggestions for introducing and following up the programs, and study aids for pupils. From time to time, classroom teachers should have an opportunity to meet with the television programmers to evaluate the programs coming into the schools and to discuss how best to use them.

CONDUCTING PRACTICE ACTIVITIES

Sometimes one can learn something quite thoroughly as the result of a powerful, vivid experience. Unfortunately, such impressive experiences are rare in the classroom. More often the learning must be renewed through drill, practice, or review.

The differences in these words are largely differences of connotation. Drill ordinarily connotes emphasis on unthinking, meaningless repetition, whereas practice seems to connote more purposeful, varied repetition. Review, of course, implies a second look at what has been learned once before. By implication it is often thought of as less intense than drill or practice. For our purposes in this book there seems to be little merit in drawing distinctions between drill and practice. We shall use the word *practice* to denote repetition of this sort.

The Value of Repetition

Repetition is necessary in school learning for several purposes. One of them is to reinforce retention of what has been learned for some things must be learned so well that they will not be forgotten. To be sure that pupils do not forget, learning must be renewed often, much more frequently than is necessary for immediate recall. This extra renewal is called overlearning. Overlearning is essential in memorization, in making behavior automatic, and in creating desirable habits. One major purpose of practice is to provide the overlearning necessary for retention.

Another reason for practice is to develop skill. As the great pianist repeats his concert selections again and again, he continually tries to improve his rendition. He may try to play more accurately, or with more feeling; he may experiment with the tempo, or he may vary his technique. But in each instance he is trying to improve his playing by repeating his performance in a slightly different way. So it is with the learning of all skills. No one can repeat anything exactly as he did it before. Because it allows one a chance to vary his behavior, practice makes it possible for one to improve one's skill.

Practice can also increase one's understanding. As one repeats and renews the learning, the concepts may become much clearer. Just as in the high jump the jumper, through diligent practice, may learn to get his hip up and over the bar, so one may acquire new insights by restudying a topic. This clarifying can be done only if the repetition is meaningful, purposeful, and varied. New skills and new concepts seldom result from dull, dry, aimless repetition.

*

Why is repetition necessary in school learning? What sorts of things are best learned through drill techniques? Which are not?

Why was the traditional drill class ineffective? How can drill be made effective?

*

Practice and Drill

MAKING PRACTICE MEANINGFUL

In one sense one does not learn through drill or practice. Practice merely consolidates, clarifies, and emphasizes what one has already learned.[5] Therefore, before practice sessions start, the pupil should understand what he is doing and how to do it. Repeating meaningless words or actions is wasteful. When one knows what copper sulphate is, or when one understands the meaning of the verb, this is the time to overlearn $Cu\ SO_4 =$ copper sulphate, or to conjugate the verb *amare*.

Repetition is usually more meaningful in context. Pupils often find it difficult to understand just what they are doing when the material to be learned is isolated from its context. Therefore, practice should occur in as real a setting as possible. For instance, to practice foreign words in sentences and in conversation is probably more effective than to practice them in isolated lists.

Practicing by wholes rather than by parts also makes practice more meaningful. In practicing something very difficult or involved, one may need to practice the difficult parts separately, but, in general, one should practice the whole thing. Then, because no part is learned at the expense of the others, the learning becomes a unit. For example, in practicing the crawl a pupil may need to concentrate on his kick or his breathing separately; he must also practice the entire stroke if he wishes to swim well. In memorizing a passage, one can usually learn most efficiently by the whole or part-whole method. If the selection to be memorized is short, one should memorize the whole thing at once, but if the selection is long, one should divide it into meaningful divisions, each of which can be learned separately. One might learn a sonnet as a whole, but a longer poem stanza by stanza.

For similar reasons practice seems to be most successful when it consists of many different types of activities in many classes. *Making practice part of the regular classwork rather than relegating it to special practice sessions tends to make practice and the skills or knowledge to be practiced more meaningful.* This procedure also tends to give to the practice its proper proportion and emphasis. When

[5] This, too, is learning, of course.

they use special practice sessions as a means of teaching particular skills or knowledge, teachers tend to treat the practice itself as the end of the instruction. Such distortion of the teaching-learning process can lead only to confusion.

MOTIVATING PRACTICE SESSIONS

Because of its very nature practice needs to be well motivated. Moreover, practice should always occur under some pressure. The pressure should not be onerous, but it should be heavy enough to be felt so that the pupil will strive to improve. Lackadaisical practice is wasteful practice.

The hunger to learn is probably the most desirable motive, but it does not always seem to be present in pupils. Sometimes the teacher needs to use devices designed to make practice more attractive. The use of games, either individual or competitive, often serves the purpose admirably. Occasionally, someone objects to using competitive games in the classroom. However, if the teacher takes care to make them fun for all and to eliminate petty glory-seeking, such games have a place. Individual games that can be used include such things as anagrams, authors, crossword puzzles, and other puzzles of all sorts. These can be played as "solitaire"; but some of them can be competitive as well. Group games such as charades and "baseball" and "basketball" in which the questions take the place of base hits and field goals are also effective. In fact, almost every parlor game can be adapted for classroom use.

In utilizing such games, the teacher should be careful to include only the pertinent and important. He should be particularly wary of pupil-developed questions. Pupils too often search for the trivial and the obscure. Games which feature such questions help very little and should be avoided. Teachers should also avoid games which eliminate those who make errors. The old-fashioned spelling bee is not very useful because the people who need the practice most are eliminated early.

USING THE PRINCIPLE OF SPACED LEARNING

Partly because of motivation factors, learning is usually more efficient when pratice is spaced over a period of time with rather frequent breaks than when it is concentrated in long, continuous practice sessions. This phenomenon is known as the principle of spaced learning. Psychologically speaking, the principle seems to operate because of several reasons. One of them is that a person can keep motivation and effort at a high level for only a short time before he begins to tire. By keeping the practice periods relatively short and interspersing them with rest periods, one can do all one's practicing at or near his top performance level. In this way he is able to get maximum benefit from his performance. Also, the shortness of the practice sessions, plus the opportunities for rest, prevent the pupils from developing incorrect habits from practicing when overtired. Another reason for the spacing of practice is that the intervals of rest between practice give the learner a chance to forget his mistakes before he goes on to the next practice session. Because after each rest period the pupil concentrates anew on learning correctly, spaced learning tends to reinforce correct learning and to cause mistakes to drop out.

As the learning becomes more firmly entrenched, the practice periods should become shorter and the intervals longer because not so much time is needed to renew the learning. This also helps to keep the practice from becoming too deadly.

ELIMINATING UNNECESSARY DRUDGERY

Practice can be dreadfully boring, as we all have learned to our sorrow. To keep it from becoming so, the teacher should eliminate as much unnecessary work as possible. If the exercise is to punctuate a paragraph, to copy the entire paragraph is pointless. Indicating the words preceding the punctuation should be enough. It is better still to mimeograph the paragraph and punctuate directly on the mimeographed sheet.

For this very reason practice or drill should not be used unnecessarily. Teachers need to bear down on some things but not on others. If a teacher emphasizes the drill aspect too much, he runs the risk of making the class unnecessarily boring. *Hard practice should be reserved for important learning which needs to be habitualized or to be retained a long time.* In other words, one should concentrate

practice on a few skills. Also, since memorizing is at best a dreary pastime, teachers should not demand that pupils memorize things that they need not remember. There are quite enough things a person should know by heart without loading pupils up with unnecessary memorization.[6]

WHEN DRILL IS NEEDED

In spite of the warning in the previous sections, teachers should not expect to eliminate all rote learning from their teaching. Some facts and abilities simply must be developed by direct attack and repetition. Among these are such things as idiomatic expressions, conjugations, chemical formulas, and mathematical facts. Historical dates provide an excellent example of such facts. Most dates in history can be taught by always associating the event with the date during the discussion. Other techniques, such as making time lines and time charts, are also available and valuable. However, in order to have a skeleton on which to hang historical events, pupils must learn key dates. These key dates must be taught directly once the pupils have learned their significance. To ensure that pupils learn them and retain them, a few minutes at the beginning or end of the period might well be given to practice on key dates several times a week.

*

How might one adapt a spelling bee to give everyone plenty of practice?

How can one avoid the poor attitudes that often accompany drill?

Why is it recommended that practice should be under some pressure?

*

INDIVIDUALIZING PRACTICE

If practice is to be really valuable to pupils, it should be individualized. To find a practice exercise valuable and important to every teen-ager in your class is virtually impossible. Almost invariably

[6] By this we do not imply that pupils should never have an opportunity to learn a poem by heart for the pure pleasure of knowing it.

some of the pupils will have mastered the skill to the point where it would be better for them to move on to something else. On the other hand, other pupils probably do not understand well enough so that they can truly benefit from the practice at all. So, except for such things as military drill and similar mass group exercises, group practice should be used sparingly. Instead practice should be tailor-made for each pupil.

To individualize practice is easier than it sounds. Since practice ordinarily consists of experiences designed to strengthen learning that has already been acquired, the teacher can leave much of the teaching to the pupils themselves. By providing self-administering and self-correcting materials and arranging situations in which pairs and small groups can work together correcting and helping each other, the teacher can make it possible for each pupil to arrange his own work so that he can concentrate on the practice most important to him.

For this reason diagnosis, particularly self-diagnosis, is an important aid to effective practice. As the pupil realizes his weakenesses, he is more likely to see the necessity for practice. Then, if his practice is rewarded by visible progress, he may willingly redouble his efforts. Nothing is so encouraging as success.

An example of such a practice technique was one used in the teaching of ninth-grade grammar. In this class the teacher supplied the pupils with a multitude of exercises designed to give practice in each of the areas studied in grammar. Before studying each grammatical topic, the pupil took a pretest to see how well versed he was in the area. If he scored very high in the pretest, he could skip that topic and go on to another; if he did not, he practiced the exercises for that topic until he thought he had mastered the material. As he finished each exercise he corrected his own work, sometimes consulting a teacher or a neighbor about why such and such was so. When he thought he was ready, he tried another test. When he had demonstrated by the test scores that he was the master of that topic, he was allowed to move on to the next one. Of course, the teacher administered the tests and made himself available to help and guide the pupils with their practice. The result was a busy class working on those exercises which most concerned them.

Review

Review differs somewhat from practice and drill. It does not require drill techniques. What it does require is reteaching. Instead of drill activities one should use such activities as these:

1. Summarizing what has been taught.
2. Having pupils summarize or outline the essentials that were taught.
3. Reteaching the lesson in a different context.
4. Having pupils build questions to ask each other about content to be reviewed.
5. Utilizing quiz games such as jeopardy.
6. Dramatization, role playing, or simulating the content to be reviewed.
7. Building open-ended discussion around the main points of the content to be reviewed.
8. Using broad questioning techniques to get pupils to think about and apply the information in the lesson.
9. Doing problems based on the content to be reviewed.
10. Allowing pupils to build questions for a test on the subject.
11. Using the content to be reviewed in practical situations or applying it to other situations.
12. Building time lines, charts, tables, diagrams, and so on, that bring out the relationships and important points in the content to be reviewed.

Teachers should review frequently. Some teachers make it a habit to end each class with a review of the main concepts taught that day; others start each class with a short review of what has gone before. Almost all do some reviewing at the end of each unit and term, but reviewing should not be limited to the end of the unit. Rather it should be used anytime that loose ends need to be tied together or pupils' thoughts need to be regrouped or reorganized. By its use one can drive points home, make learning stick, bind ideas together, and clarify relationships among past, present, and future learning.

RECITATION

Several decades ago V. T. Thayer wrote a well-known book entitled *The Passing of the Recitation.*

In spite of the promise of that title and the progressive innovative teaching methods introduced at that time and in succeeding decades, the recitation remains a common teaching strategy.

The method in this strategy is simple. Teachers assign pupils content to study in their textbooks and then orally quiz the pupils on what they have learned in the assignment. The technique is neither very efficient nor effective, although it may have certain advantages. The question and answer technique does reinforce knowledge pupils have already acquired and does give immediate feedback concerning the accuracy of one's answers. It also gives pupils the opportunity to learn from the replies of other pupils. The fact that the pupils will be questioned on what they have studied is a motivating factor. Many a pupil has read the homework text assignment solely because he is afraid he may be called on to recite in the next class.

Still, we repeat, the recitation is neither efficient nor effective. It yields little besides the rote learning of information. It does not encourage true understanding of the information learned, to say nothing of encouraging the application of knowledge, the solving of problems, thinking of any sort, appreciation, or the development of attitudes and skills. It actually discourages the development of listening and discussion skills; not only that, it creates an unfriendly, inquisitorial class atmosphere that is really antisocial and works against the development of class cohesiveness and cooperativeness. All in all, it would be difficult to find a more anti-intellectual, antisocial pedagogical method than the recitation as it is ordinarily used. It has so little to recommend it that teachers would do well to avoid using it except on rare occasions.

To improve the ordinary recitation, teachers should try to get away from overemphasis on memory. To do this one must center the recitations around thought questions. Such questions can be first presented to the pupils when the original reading or other information-gathering activity is assigned. Studying with thought-provoking questions in mind is likely to be much more productive than simply reading or studying for information. The plan for conducting the recitation should center around key thought-provoking questions. These questions should be carefully planned in advance both as to purpose and as to sequence and wording.

The answering should emphasize thinking rather than remembering. That is why the open-text type of recitation is likely to be more advantageous than the ordinary recitation.

Open-Text Recitation

The open-text recitation differs from the ordinary recitation in that it is really a discussion in which pupils can refer to their books and other materials as the discussion progresses. It can be used effectively as part of either controlled or open discussions.

This open-text recitation has many merits. It frees pupils from the rote memorization of facts. It shows pupils that facts are not so much ends in themselves as they are means for understanding and for thinking. On the other hand by stressing the use of facts and the necessity for factual accuracy, the open-text recitation strategy emphasizes the need for factual information and getting the facts straight. The strategy also helps pupils master the intellectual skills needed to seek out and check facts and to determine which facts are important and which immaterial. All in all, the open-text method is an effective and efficient strategy—particularly when contrasted with the common recitation which is so often a waste of time.

Briefly, the procedure for conducting an open-text recitation is

1. Assign reading and study or some other information-gathering activity.

2. In the assignment include suggestions and questions that cause the pupils to read in an inquiring manner and to think and draw inferences from what they read or study (or otherwise gain information).

3. Use Socratic or open-ended thought-provoking questioning. If possible, encourage various interpretations, inferences, and conclusions from various pupils. Encourage pupils to react to and challenge each other's ideas. During the discussion pupils are free to consult their books, notes, or what have you, in order to justify their views and substantiate their opinions. In this type of recitation it is not remembering the facts but using them in the higher mental processes that matters.

4. Sum up (or have a pupil sum up). No final

conclusion or agreement is necessary. At times it may be better if no common conclusions are made.

COMMUNITY INVOLVEMENT ACTIVITIES

Conducting Field Trips

Particularly vivid learning experiences sometimes result from going out into the community. One of the most common devices used for extending the classroom into the community is the field trip. This method is a time-honored one having been used with great success for centuries. Field trips can take many forms. A nature walk is a field trip. A visit to the museum is a field trip. So is a period spent on the athletic field searching for specimens of insects.

Conducting a field trip is much the same as conducting any other instructional activity. The pupils must be introduced to it, they must be briefed on what to look for, and the activity should be followed up. However, field trips do present certain special considerations such as scheduling, permissions, transportation, expense, and control.

Early in his planning, the teacher should talk the trip over with his principal or supervisor. Bringing the principal into the planning early will help in eliciting his support. Moreover, the teacher will probably need the principal's assistance in arranging the administrative details as well as his authorization of the trip.

Before planning the trip, the teacher should make the trip himself, if possible, to see whether it would be worthwhile for the pupils and how it can be made most productive. He must arrange the details at the place to be visited. Many museums, factories, and other places of interest provide their own tour services. If they do, the teacher must be sure to let the proper persons know the purpose of the visit and what the pupils should see. He must also arrange for the necessary permissions, schedule changes, transportation, and so forth. Pupils can often help considerably in the planning and arranging of a field trip. However, the teacher should be careful to double- and triple-check himself on the details. He must also double-check to be sure that everyone has a mission to perform on the field trip.

The trip should not be a joy ride or an outing but a real learning experience.

*

What are the advantages of taking pupils on field trips? What are the disadvantages?

Why must field trips be planned? What particularly must be considered in the planning? To what extent and in what ways can the pupils participate in planning and carrying out the plans?

Many field trips are not worth the time, trouble, and expense. How can you ensure that your field trips are not merely outings?

*

Using Resource People

Undoubtedly the most important resource of a community is its people. Even in a poor rural community the number of people who have special knowledge and talent that they can share effectively with a class is amazing. Often these persons can bring to a class new authority, new interest, new information, and a new point of view. Among the people who might be good resource persons are town, county, state, or federal government employees, hobbyists, travelers, businessmen, college teachers, specialists, clergymen, and people from other lands. Alumni, and parents and relatives of the pupils are frequently available and usually interested in visiting the schools. A certain chemistry teacher aroused class interest by featuring a visit by a metallurgist from a local brass mill. A source we sometimes forget are the other teachers and school officials of our own or neighboring school systems.

Resource persons can be used for many purposes. They can provide pupils with help in specialized projects. If a pupil needs help in constructing a rocket as a science project, perhaps an officer from a nearby air defense battery would be willing to help show him how. Resource persons can also provide information not otherwise readily available. Who would know more about soil conservation in your county than the local Soil Conservation Service agent?

PREPARING FOR THE GUEST SPEAKER

Resource persons are frequently used as speakers. Before inviting a layman to speak to his class, the teacher should check to be sure that there is a reasonable chance for the success of the activity. Quite often one can find out a lot about the potential speaker from other teachers and friends. In any case, you should visit him and talk to him about his subject. In your conversation you can probably determine whether he is the type who understands and can get along with young people. You can also probably determine whether he can speak at the young people's level. If his field is engineering and he discusses reaction motors only in the language of the professional engineer, he will not contribute much to the class.

When inviting a person to speak, you should brief him carefully on what he is to talk about and the purpose of the talk. A suitable agreement should be made concerning the length of the talk, the asking of questions, visual aids, and so forth. It is wise to remind the speaker of these agreements, the time, place, and topic in a letter of confirmation. The letter should be written diplomatically. Perhaps as good a form as any is to state the agreements as you understand them and ask him if he concurs. You can also remind him of these commitments when you introduce him to the class.

The public announcement that he is to speak for ten minutes and then answer questions often has a desirable effect on a long-winded, rambling guest. Such precautions may seem far-fetched but they are sometimes necessary. It is most discouraging to have a speaker talk for forty minutes of a forty-five-minute period without letting the pupils ask one of the questions they have prepared.

The teacher should also prepare the pupils for the meeting. As with other instructional aids, they should know what to expect and what to look for. Quite often, making up questions they would like answered is good preparation for listening to the speech and for the discussion period after the speech. Pupil questions may also be given to the speaker as a guide for his speech.

As a rule, speakers cannot be counted on to hold the attention of a class for a whole period. The guest appearance is usually much more successful if the formal speaking is kept quite short and the bulk of the program devoted to discussion and pupil questions. Sometimes it is more rewarding to bring in resource persons to act as consultants for pupil discussion groups or as experts in a "Meet the Press" sort of panel.

Studying the Community

A field trip is one way to study an aspect of the community. There are other ways, of course. One of them is to read and study. A surprisingly large amount of printed information is available about almost every community. This material may include reports of the federal, state, and local governments; releases by the Chamber of Commerce and similar agencies; stories in the local press; advertising and promotional literature from local concerns; publications of local civic and fraternal organizations; and, sometimes, articles in state and national publications. Unpublished material can sometimes be used to advantage. A pupil in a New England community was allowed to use old school records to write an historical account of the founding of the local school system in the early nineteenth century.

Another common method by which to study a community is to interview its prominent citizens. This method is not always fruitful because many persons find interview techniques difficult. If pupils are to apply it in a community study, they should be properly instructed in how to carry out a successful interview. The teacher should provide demonstrations of good interview techniques, and the pupils should practice on themselves before practicing on adults. Of course adults, particularly important adults, will make allowances for the errors of pupils who interview them. Nevertheless, you will want pupils to make a good impression on the people interviewed. For this reason, if no other, the pupils should be well rehearsed in their roles before leaving for the interview.

Another excellent method to use in studying the community is observation. The familiar device of keeping a record of the foods pupils eat, so often used in health, hygiene, biology, and home economics classes, is an example of this type of study. Counting the number of cars that do not come to a full stop at a stop sign is another. Ordinarily, for observation to be successful, the observer needs to be well briefed in what he is looking for. He needs to have criteria by which to objectify his observation and some system of recording it. Usually a check list, or rating scale, or similar form is helpful to observers both for recording and for objectifying the observations. Since accurate observation is rather difficult, pupils who engage in such techniques should be instructed in their use. Quite often practice sessions will be beneficial.[7]

CONDUCTING COMMUNITY SERVICE PROJECTS

One evening in a suburban city a group of teen-agers went from house to house ringing doorbells. They were social studies pupils conducting a campaign to inform voters of the issues in the coming elections and to persuade them to vote. Such service projects are another effective way to extend the classroom into the community. Quite often such activities get at objectives which the more usual classroom activities fail to reach. The techniques for preparing pupils for community study are equally efficacious in preparing them for a service project.[8]

SECURING ADMINISTRATIVE APPROVAL

Projects like the one mentioned in the last paragraph can lead to complications if they are not carefully managed. One can well imagine that the school administrators were particularly concerned with the conduct of this activity. So it is with almost every activity involving the community. Projects of this sort have been known to upset school-community relations. For that reason the teacher should always secure the advice and consent of his administrative and supervisory superiors before attempting such activities. In communities where the climate of opinion is not right, these activities will have to be forgone. The administration may find it necessary to withhold permission for other reasons also. Perhaps the proposal would interfere with other activities or classes; perhaps the timing would not be propitious; perhaps the community has had a surfeit of school surveys or service projects; perhaps the budget would not stand the expense. The final decision about whether the activity should or should not be attempted is the administrator's responsibility.

*

What might be a community service project suitable for use in your community? If you were to attempt to

use this project, what preparations and precautions would you take?

In your own circle of friends and relatives, how many of them have special skills and knowledges which they might share with secondary school pupils? How might you use the resources of these people in a secondary school class?

*

GUIDANCE TECHNIQUES

Teacher Contribution to the Guidance Program

Ever since the first Neanderthal shaman selected a boy to apprentice for his trade, teachers have been performing guidance functions. That today's teacher should continue to do so is not surprising. Most teachers contribute to the guidance program in a large measure. Undoubtedly, the best contribution a teacher can make is to teach well. But he can also help in other ways. Even if the school did not ask them to, most teachers would perform guidance functions anyway.

One way teachers contribute is by acting as the eyes and ears of the guidance program. Because of their strategic position in the classroom and in the extracurriculum, teachers have opportunities to gather much information not available to the guidance specialist. The teacher can often spot pupils who need counseling on specific problems long before the guidance worker would ordinarily see them. By reporting this information via anecdotal or other reports, the teacher can greatly increase the efficiency of the guidance program.

Once the guidance person is working with the pupil, the teacher can help by cooperating with him. In fact, guidance specialists often do their best work through classroom teachers. Guidance workers can spend only short periods with individual pupils, whereas teachers spend considerable time with them. A teacher's sympathetic understanding of the pupil and cooperation with the guidance worker may make the difference between the success or failure of the program.

The Teacher as a Guidance Worker

Teachers sometimes play a more formal role in the guidance program. Although it is difficult to

[7] Fuller directions for conducting interviews and observation techniques can be found in Ch. 11.

[8] Techniques for conducting group projects are discussed in Ch. 11. Lately it has become stylish to include community service projects under the heading of "action learning," which is an extremely accurate description of what goes on.

conduct a satisfactory guidance program without an adequate supply of specialized guidance counselors, many classroom teachers are pressed into the counseling service either as teacher-counselors or as teachers who counsel. The reason for this practice is partly economic. Not many school systems are able to provide a sufficient number of guidance specialists to do all the counseling. In a great many schools, then, one can expect the brunt of the counseling to fall on the classroom teacher or the teacher-counselor. Since this may be the beginning teacher's lot, let us consider some of the methods and responsibilities.

COUNSELING

The guidance worker tries to help boys and girls make the most of their lives and their opportunities. He does not make decisions for the pupils, rather he tries to help them help themselves. This role is not an easy one to carry out. To live up to it the guidance worker should

1. Recognize his own abilities and limitations to counsel and guide.
2. Be familiar with the techniques appropriate for guiding individuals and groups.
3. Be able to apply appropriate principles of guidance and counseling.
4. Observe the confidential nature of the counseling and guidance process.
5. Be able to administer and interpret various types of tests.
6. Establish and maintain effective relationships with parents.
7. Recognize the ability range of the individual pupil.
8. Integrate the work of the individual pupil with the school's entire program of guidance.[9]

As the list suggests, the guidance worker needs to be master of certain professional skills. The next few paragraphs briefly discuss some techniques used by guidance workers. The first of these is the interview.

CONDUCTING GUIDANCE INTERVIEWS

The interview is perhaps the most important tool with which the guidance counselor works. It is through the interview that the counselor actually

[9] Gilbert C. Kettlekamp, *Teaching Adolescents* (Boston: D. C. Heath & Company, copyright 1954), p. 364. Quoted by permission of D. C. Heath and Company.

does the counseling. It is the heart of the guidance program. Some pupils need frequent conferences, while others require few. However, all pupils may need more help than one sometimes thinks. The secret is to make oneself available. The guidance worker should practice the open-door policy. No pupil problem should be too trivial for his attention, for questions trivial to the teacher may seem all-important to the pupil. A sympathetic, unhurried hearing of the pupil's story may well lead to ready identification and solution of the pupil's problems.

The interview is really a place for the pupil to talk. Merely talking out his problems is frequently good therapy. In order to create the atmosphere of permissiveness, some authorities advocate that the teacher must accept everything the pupil says. The key, they say, is to accept the pupil for what he is—a person, perhaps a troubled person. The counselor, they maintain, should never sit in judgment on the pupil, for to do so may disrupt the rapport or end the interview permanently. Some of them further maintain that the counselor should never advise the pupil what to do.

Although it is necessary for the counselor to accept the client and refrain from making overhasty judgments, that does not mean that the counselor should suppress himself completely. There seems little point in conducting interviews if nothing ever develops. If the interview is to amount to anything, undoubtedly the counselor sooner or later will have to give it some direction. Probably he should direct the interview toward discovery of the pupil's real problem and what can be done about it. Skillful use of questions can accomplish this. By the use of such techniques the teacher, as well as the counselor, can help the pupil draw his own value judgments and make his own decisions. Surely it is ineffective to force our own values and advice on a pupil, but, just as surely, it is ineffective and probably immoral not to try to help the pupil find the answers to his problems and to help him achieve higher values.

In the interview, if the counselor is really to be of help, he must have information about the pupil at his fingertips. If possible, he should study each case before the interview. He should also have available a wealth of information about the school, its curriculum and extracurriculum, and other matters to which the interview may lead. If he can supply the pupil with immediate information in answer to his questions, so much the better. If the pupil requires information that the counselor does not have, the counselor should find it, if at all possible. At times, of course, he needs only to direct the pupil to the information so that the pupil can look for it himself. The object is always to help the pupil to a better understanding of himself, his problems, and his potentialities so that he can make wise decisions and judgments of his own.

What career to follow and what educational program to pursue are among the problems that are of real concern to youth. To get at these problems, the pupil must know what his goals and potentialities are. Frequently he has no idea of what he can do or wants to do. Under such circumstances the counselor may have to give the pupil information by which he can appraise his own resources and the avenues open to him. The counselor can help the student form and define his goals, but the final decisions should be made by the pupil. To reiterate, no guidance counselor has the right to tell the counselee in what direction he should go; the counselor's job is to show the pupil the facts so that he can understand himself and make his decisions accordingly.

*

In what ways can you as a teacher contribute to the guidance program?

To what extent should a counselor advise a pupil?

How much direction should the counselor give during an interview?

*

Group Guidance and Homeroom Guidance

Group activities can often be used to give pupils guidance information. Some schools have formed special classes in guidance or group guidance. Others make group guidance a part of the core program. Some schools turn group guidance over to the homeroom teacher. Examples of group-guidance activities are career days, units on occupations, field trips, and orientation programs. Even student handbooks are instruments for group guidance and, of course, a great amount of group guidance may occur during regular classes.

Group guidance is, of course, a teaching function. Its purpose is to provide pupils with information that they need in order to understand themselves, their potentialities, and their opportunities. In effect, group guidance is instruction. It differs in no way from other instruction except that in group-guidance classes pupil-centered teaching is much more likely to be needed than in other classes. In group-guidance classes, therefore, one should use techniques that emphasize pupil participation in planning, problem solving, differentiated assignments, individual work, small-group work, and projects. Role playing, discussions, and the techniques of group dynamics are particularly useful.

Homeroom guidance is likely to be a combination of group guidance and counseling. The teacher is responsible not only for teaching group guidance in homeroom periods, but also for counseling his homeroom pupils. In some schools the administration gives the teacher the same homeroom group for several years so that the teacher and pupils may learn to know each other better. In such a system the homeroom teacher becomes in effect a teacher-counselor responsible for the total guidance program of his homeroom pupils.

Group Counseling

Group guidance should not be confused with group counseling. Group counseling is a form of interview in which the counselor meets with several pupils instead of just one. Many authorities maintain that counseling should never be more than a one-to-one relationship, but E. Wayne Wright and others believe that counseling in groups yields certain benefits that individual counseling cannot: (1) the lifelike setting for making decisions and choices, thus helping individuals to discover new ways of relating to others; (2) the influence of peers through group interaction and group norms; (3) the opportunity for free expression of opinion and emotions with less personal reference; and (4) the opportunity to give and receive support as a group member.[10]

[10] E. Wayne Wright, "Multiple Counseling: Why? When? How?" *Personnel and Guidance Journal,* 37:551–556 (April, 1959), in Lester D. and Alice Crow, editors, *Reading in Guidance* (New York: David McKay Company, Inc., 1962), pp. 216–224.

Referral of Difficult Cases

The counseling of difficult cases should be left to people trained in it. For that matter, teachers should be careful to limit their counseling activities to areas in which they are competent. Teacher-counselors, homeroom teachers, and other teachers are usually not guidance experts, although many approach this status after a few years of experience and training. They cannot be expected to handle all the guidance problems that may come their way. When problems of a difficult nature arise, they should be referred to the proper person. This person is usually the guidance specialist in charge, or, in smaller schools, the principal. When in doubt about what to do in any guidance matter, a teacher should go to these persons for help.

In general, teachers should not be too hasty in referring cases to the professional guidance persons. Hasty and frequent referrals may undermine the pupils' confidence in the teacher's abilities. On the other hand, the teacher should not hesitate to refer any case in which he does not feel competent. Certainly he should refer every case in which he suspects serious difficulty or difficulties beyond his scope, such as medical or serious psychological problems. Whenever the teacher feels that the pupil needs more than ordinary help, he should refer the pupil immediately. It is far better to refer too often than not refer often enough. As was pointed out earlier in the chapter, the teacher is in a strategic position to spot incipient troubles of all types. He should attempt to develop a sharp eye and report such cases early.

*

Note the difference between the advice given for referals for guidance purposes and referals in the case of discipline problems. Why the difference, do you suppose?

*

TEACHING THE EXTRACURRICULUM

The Teacher's Role in the Extracurriculum

Conducting extracurricular activities is much the same as conducting any other learning activity. The principal difference between extracurricular activities and class activities is that the coercive element is removed. Because of this lack of coercion, most pupils in an extracurricular activity are there because they want to be. Thus extracurricular activities afford unusual opportunities for utilizing natural motivation and interest.

On the other hand, because there is no coercion, activities that do not appeal to pupils are doomed to a marginal existence, if not to extinction. Such activities should be dropped in favor of activities the pupils want. An extracurricular activity that seems worthless to the pupils certainly has little valid reason for existing.

This fact imposes an increased burden for leadership on the activity sponsor. The appeal of any activity often depends upon the way the activity is conducted as much as on the activity itself. Good leadership and good planning have made more than one faltering extracurricular activity a success in every sense of the word.

The job of the sponsor or coach is to guide or direct the pupils as they conduct the activity. Delegation of responsibility is an important key in the guidance of any extracurricular activity. Guidance implies helping pupils over the hard parts by advising them on what to do and showing them how to do it. It also implies checking up on the pupils to be sure that they are carrying out their responsibilities properly. If the activity is a good one, group pressure can usually be counted on to help force do-nothings to produce. In any event, the principal duties of the sponsor, once the plan has got under way, are to see to it that the right assignments get to the proper persons, to help the pupils where they need help, and to keep checking to see that things are done and done well. If, in doing all this, the sponsor can keep in the background, so much the better.

In certain types of extracurricular activities, such as theatrical productions, athletics, and musical performances, the sponsor may have to accept a more important role in planning and direction in order to maintain high standards of performance. Even in such activities the sponsor does not need to become the dictator some teachers appear to be. The pupils can be of real help in planning them cooperatively. Still, if the pupils are ever to have the thrill of really first-class performance, much of the planning and direction must be assumed by the sponsor, director, or coach.

*

In what ways do these attributes differ from the attributes of successful classroom teachers? What attributes are more necessary for good classroom teachers? For good sponsors? How can prospective teachers develop these attributes?

In some schools extracurricular activities are held during the school day as activity periods; in others they are held in after school hours only. Can you justify giving up school time for extracurricular activities?

*

Planning Extracurricular Activities

One needs more than a good personality to lead an extracurricular activity well. As in any other teaching, planning is the key to success in conducting an extracurricular activity. In some extracurricular activities the planning can be done informally, for by their very nature many extracurricular activities lend themselves exceptionally well to teacher-pupil planning. Club activities are especially suited to such techniques. But in no activity can planning be skipped if the activity is to be successful for very long.

COOPERATIVE PLANNING

Pupils, as a rule, need help in planning extracurricular activities. Usually the pupils are eager to do things well, but they need to be shown. Consequently, the teacher must coach the responsible pupils in their duties and help them evolve good plans. For instance, club officers usually need to be taught how to conduct meetings, and school-paper editors need to be taught how to edit and proofread. Moreover, the teacher may need to suggest things for the pupils to do. Because of their lack of experience, boys and girls seldom have enough ideas concerning the things they might do to make their program successful. Part of the sponsor's task is to fill in the gaps.

Not only does the teacher need to help with ideas, but he must help the pupils set up criteria of excellence by which to judge the ideas and to maintain high standards. A case in point is the selection of a play for production. At times, youngsters are

tempted to select a hackneyed farce with no literary merit whatsoever. They can usually avoid this pitfall if they work out standards of excellence before reading the plays. Extracurricular activities should always be of high caliber.

At the same time, the teacher must keep the pupils from attempting more than they can manage. Enthusiastic youth often bite off more than they can chew readily. When the teacher thinks the pupils are considering a project that will be too much for them, he should warn them. A good method for doing this is to consider the possibilities and probabilities in a group discussion early in the planning. However, one should not be too quick to condemn plans as being too ambitious. Condemning the plans may raise the hackles of the planners; besides, what pupils can do, when they really want to, is amazing.

Because of the audience appeal of these activities, many communities have come to demand almost professional standards. These demands place great pressures on the coach or director and the pupils. Although high standards are always desirable, they should not be maintained at the expense of the total educational program or the needs of the boys and girls. When any extracurricular activity interferes with the total educational program of the school, it is time for a change.

CRITERIA FOR PLANNING EXTRACURRICULAR ACTIVITIES

In planning any extracurricular activity, the teacher should bear in mind one criterion above all others: Schools are maintained by our citizens for the education of youth. This being so, all school-sponsored activities should be learning activities. It is not the schools' business to entertain the populace, or to provide recreation for boys and girls. These worthwhile activities are the province of other agencies. This does not imply that the schools should ban all recreational activities or eliminate sports. But it does mean that each activity the school sponsors should lead toward some goal appropriate to the purposes of the school. If any activity as planned leads to no such purpose, it has no place in the school and should be dropped or changed. In other words, a dance for purely recreational purposes is probably not a proper school activity, but a dance whose purpose is to develop the social graces in boys and girls has its place, providing that it is expressly arranged for that purpose.

Another criterion is that the pupils should feel that the activities are worthwhile. Pupils quickly drop out of activities that are not worthwhile. Even such high prestige activities as football suffer from this. In order for an activity to be really successful, it must have high intrinsic value or offer important incentive. True cooperative planning is one way to ensure such value. In extracurricular activities it should be utilized to the utmost.

*

What would you do to make sure that all boys and girls had an opportunity to participate in the extra-curriculum?

As an activity sponsor how could you see to it that everyone had a chance to participate fully?

*

Business Management

The business management of any pupil organization should be carefully supervised by the teacher. Usually the school authorities will have set up explicit procedures for the collecting, expending, and accounting of money. These regulations should be followed to the letter. Carelessness in this matter can lead to embarrassment and to outright financial loss. Even though pupils may collect the money and a pupil treasurer may be charged with keeping the books, the teacher cannot escape his responsibility for safeguarding any funds in the treasury.

Money for extracurricular activities may be obtained in several ways. An allocation may be requested from the student council or some other central agency upon the basis of a budget, or money may be raised through membership dues or fund-raising projects. In general, one should keep dues and fund-raising campaigns to a minimum. Dues may embarrass some pupils; fund-raising campaigns may take too much of the pupils' time, besides being a source of annoyance to the people who must contribute the money. In any case, before venturing on such a project, the sponsor should get the principal's permission. In fact, soliciting the principal's advice on all matters concerning the financing of extracurricular activities is a wise precaution.

Ordinarily, all money is placed in the hands of the school treasurer. To leave cash in teachers' desks or pupils' lockers is very risky. In order to ensure proper accounting, most schools insist that all payments be made by check by the school treasurer on presentation of suitable vouchers by the officers and sponsors of the activity. The wise sponsor has as little to do with cash as possible and is very careful to stick to the letter of the law as far as money matters are concerned.

SUGGESTIONS CONCERNING HANDLING MONEY

Most sponsors must handle money at one time or another. Consequently, a few words of precaution may be advisable.

1. Set up a system of accounting for funds before collecting any.
2. Give receipts for all money received. Be sure to keep a duplicate or a stub.
3. Record all transactions immediately.
4. Deposit all funds with the school treasurer, safe, or bank immediately after receiving them. Get a receipt.
5. Do not keep money in your desk or on your person.
6. Do not keep school money with your personal money.
7. Do not commit the school or extracurricular activity to any indebtedness without official approval.
8. Do not authorize payments of any bills until they have been approved.
9. Do not pay any bills by cash. If possible, always pay by school check. Be sure to get receipts for any payments made.
10. Always follow to the letter school regulations concerning handling of funds.

ARRANGING THE CLASSROOM SETTING

The physical setting can make considerable difference in the effectiveness of one's teaching strategies and tactics. The more pleasant the environment, the better. Bright colors, snappy bulletin boards, good light, atttractive displays, and neatness all help to create an atmosphere conducive to efficient learning. Most helpful of all is to arrange the classroom so that it is easy for the pupil to do the activities he should do to learn what he is supposed to learn. The great majority of modern methods and techniques do not work well in traditional classroom setups.

Flexible Seating Arrangements

Most modern schools are equipped with movable chairs rather than fixed furniture. This being so, the teacher should resist the temptation to place the furniture in serried ranks, as was done with the old fixed furniture. Although arranging chairs in rows has some advantages from a control and convenience point of view, it has relatively few advantages from an instructional standpoint. As a matter of fact, no classroom seating arrangement is perfectly satisfactory for all activities and all classes. The teacher should arrange the class according to the classwork the pupils are to do. For watching a movie, working individually, or listening to a lecture, some variations of the ordinary row setup may be desirable; for committee work, small circles of chairs may be best; for a discussion, a circle or some segment of a circle may be suitable. Move the chairs to suit the activity. After all that is why the school board bought movable furniture.

Some teachers like to seat the pupils in alphabetical order or with the larger pupils in the back. In the traditional class these practices may make the routine easier, but if one uses flexible methods, such plans are pointless. To let the pupils select their own seats is probably as good a plan as any. However, for at least the first few days, the pupils should keep the same seats so that the teacher can identify them by means of a seating chart and learn their names.

Modern textbooks sometimes recommend placing the teacher's desk in the back of the classroom. This serves the purpose of removing the teacher from the front of the room and, to a degree, tends to make the class less teacher-centered. However, the position of the teacher's desk is not particularly important. The important thing is to arrange the entire room so that it will be useful and comfortable.

Some examples of possible class arrangements are shown in Figure 12–1.

*

Some teachers recommend breaking up boon companions, cliques, and troublemakers by seating them so that they can not talk to each other easily. Others say this is a useless procedure and creates more harm than good. What is your opinion on this problem?

*

The Classroom as a Laboratory

If the more modern teaching techniques are to succeed, the modern classroom should probably be arranged as a laboratory of learning. To be a laboratory in this sense, a room must have many work areas and much material and equipment with which to work. In such a laboratory the teacher is blessed with all the tables, files, cabinets, cupboards, easels, exhibit cases, tackboards, chalkboards, and other equipment necessary to carry on a full, rich, varied program.

In one corner one should find a well-stocked classroom library for research and reading. Here books, magazines, reference works, texts and vertical files may be arranged for easy classroom use.

Other areas of the classroom may be similarly arranged for other purposes. The furniture should be movable so that the class can arrange it in rows to watch a motion picture or dramatization, or in a circle for a discussion, or in a hollow square to allow for an arena stage.

Unfortunately, many classrooms are far from being classroom laboratories. Some have the seats bolted to the floor. Few have all of the equipment mentioned in the preceding paragraph. This fact, although unfortunate, should not discourage the teacher. Rich instructional programs can be carried on successfully in situations far from ideal. If the room has immovable furniture, an eager committee may be able to group together in one corner of the room, sitting sideways and backwards in the immovable chairs; they can gather round the teacher's desk, or worktable, or, if necessary, even move into the corridor. If there are no file cabinets, paper

Figure 12–1
*Diagrams of Possible
Room Arrangements.*

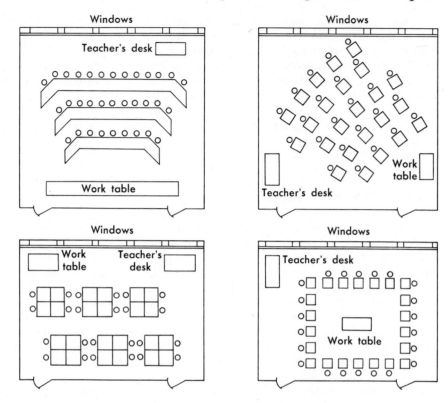

cartons can often be arranged to hold quite a sizable collection of file folders. A coat of paint or a covering of wallpaper can make such homemade filing cabinets quite attractive. With a little ingenuity one can often improvise substitutes which, although perhaps not the best, will do until something better can be obtained. Occasionally, the substitute turns out to be superior to the real thing.

In many schools, organization of classroom laboratories is a problem because one classroom must be shared by many teachers. This problem, however, is not insurmountable. The teacher who uses the classroom most should have priority, but all the teachers should share in planning the arrangement. If the teachers are reasonable and considerate, they should be able to agree on an arrangement satisfactory to all concerned.

SUMMARY

The lecture is among the most important of teaching techniques. Although its use has been severely criticized, it has a place in today's schools; it should, however, not be the teacher's mainstay. Short, informal teacher talks are much more effective for most purposes. If one wishes for quality teaching, other methods involving group process, inquiry, problem solving, and the higher mental processes are usually more effective. However, at times, the lecture is the only appropriate method. In such situations the teacher should follow the rules laid down by our best speech makers: Make it short, lively, and to the point. Tell them what you are going to tell them, tell them, tell them what you told them.

The lecture is frequently used in large-group instruction. At its best large-group instruction can yield great savings of time and effort. Badly used it can result in superficial lockstep learning. Demonstrations, dramatizations, films, and other audiovisual presentations are more likely to be successful in large classes than the ordinary lecture. In fact, the problem of psychological noise, and oftentimes real noise, makes the formal lecture very difficult to do well in a large class. Whatever method he uses, the teacher must attempt to introduce, or seem to introduce, teacher-pupil interaction and high drama.

What is true of large-group teaching is also true of television teaching. Instructional television should be treated as one more arrow for one's bow. Its purpose is to help classroom instruction—not to supplant it or hinder it. Well done, it can be a marvelous arrangement, but unless it is handled as an integral part of a total program centered around the classroom, it can easily become nothing more than a device for spreading poor instruction over great distances.

Practice makes perfect. Secondary school classes should allow plenty of opportunity for the repetition and review necessary to drive learning home. To be most effective, practice should be meaningful, varied, and as free from boredom as possible. To eliminate drudgery and to make practice efficient, one should individualize practice exercises and activities as much as possible after carefully diagnosing the needs of the individual pupils.

Recitation, as commonly practiced in our schools, is obsolete. It should have died out with the dodo. Teachers who care about learning should replace it with methods that encourage understanding and the use of the higher mental processes. The use of thought-provoking questions, Socratic questioning, open-ended discussion, and open-book recitations are examples of the types of methods that might be used instead. Inquiry, problem solving, and discovery techniques would be even more useful.

Field trips, community surveys, and community service projects are time-proven ways to utilize the community for instruction. Community activities should be planned and followed through very carefully to ensure that each activity is worthwhile and to save the school from embarrassment. In activities of this sort the teacher must always bear in mind their possible effect on school-community relations. Therefore, it is especially important that all such activities be cleared with all the authorities concerned.

The guidance program provides services by which the pupil can get help with his problems. This program can be a great boon for the classroom teacher. From it he can get information and help which should make his teaching more effective. In return, the teacher can make substantial contributions to the guidance program, since he is often the staff member closest to the pupil.

Although subordinate to actual instruction, extraclass responsibilities are a necessary part of each teacher's load. High on the list of his responsibilities are extracurricular activities. Just as much as class activities, extracurricular activities are learning experiences. Like any other learning experiences, they deserve careful planning and handling. However, the pupils should have a large share in planning and conducting them.

No matter what the method used, it will work better in pleasant, comfortable surroundings that are adapted to the method to be used. Teachers, as a rule, do not pay enough attention to the physical surroundings. Pleasant classroom laboratory setting, chairs moved into new and useful patterns, and bright and attractive colors may make the difference between a dull, drab lesson and an effective one.

Reading and Studying

13

Reading has two major functions in the school, as it has in life itself. It provides a source of information and ideas and, equally important, it is a source of enjoyment. The teacher should seek to emphasize both of these aspects in his teaching, for to be truly educated, pupils must learn to value reading as a great treasury of learning and a great source of pleasure.

Every Teacher a Reading Teacher

THE READING PROBLEM

Every secondary school teacher, no matter what his subject, must face up to the necessity for the teaching of reading in his classes.

Reading is a difficult skill that takes years to master. For most of us it is a skill we must continue to learn well into our adult lives. Even then, almost no one reads as well as he could. In the secondary schools, if Elizabeth Drews is correct, about one third of the pupils cannot read their textbooks.[1]

The reading problem becomes really acute in the junior high school years, because then the pupils are faced with more and more reading to do and less and less time to do it in. As the reading level becomes more difficult, the problem becomes greater. Faced with great amounts of reading material too hard for them to read, the pupils tend to become frustrated and bored. Some of them cope with this problem by dropping out of school as soon as they can. More than three times as many poor readers as good readers drop out of high school before graduation, most of them during the tenth grade.[2]

DEVELOPMENTAL READING

It follows, then, that programs to continue the development of reading skill in junior and senior high school are necessary. To meet this need, secondary schools all over the nation are inaugurating reading programs. Presently these programs are of three kinds.[3]

One is the program that provides training for slow boys and girls who are doing as well as can be expected considering their ability and who need continued coaching in reading to develop their limited potential to the utmost. The second type of reading program is the program for boys and girls who for some reason have not learned to read properly, although their potential ability is average or even better than average. As a result of corrective programs some of these pupils make phenomenal gains and soon learn to read at their normal ability level. The third type of reading program is for the already good readers. This program attempts to improve pupils' already adequate skills and to carry each pupil along to higher competencies so that he will be a highly efficient reader who can make the utmost of his potential abilities.

It is the third of these types that has come to be known as the developmental reading program.

[1] Cited in *Reading Instruction in Secondary Schools*, Perspectives in Reading Number 2, International Reading Associates, Newark, Delaware, 1964, p. 32.

[2] Ruth C. Penty, "Reading Ability and High School Drop Outs," in M. Jerry Weiss, *Reading in the Secondary Schools* (New York: Odyssey Press, 1961), p. 180.

[3] Leonard H. Clark, Raymond L. Klein, and John B. Burks, *The American Secondary School Curriculum*, 2nd ed. (New York: Macmillan Publishing Co., Inc., 1972), p. 218. By Permission.

Remedial reading classes are usually taught in special classes or reading laboratories; developmental reading programs are usually taught by classroom teachers. Probably the most satisfactory arrangement for developmental reading programs is a team approach in which one teacher, be it the reading teacher, the core teacher, or the English teacher, teaches the skills common to reading in all fields; the librarian teaches the library skills, and the various content teachers teach the reading skills necessary for their various subjects. In this connection, one should note that the block-of-time program lends itself well to developmental reading programs, because the block teacher has more time to learn the strengths and weaknesses of his students and teaches in a flexible organization, which lets him group his pupils, differentiate his material, and organize class time for various reading activities.[4]

M. Jerry Weiss has outlined five characteristics of a good developmental program.

1. Reading instruction must aim at individual students, taking into account their different backgrounds, abilities, and interests.
2. Flexibility of instruction depends upon the availability of a wide range of reading materials of all kinds and on all sorts of subjects. In an effective program much of the initiative passes to the student and the teacher's role changes to that of a guide, a "listener," a resource person, a critic.
3. Reading instruction means paying attention not only to the basic skills of reading, but also to the general end which education should serve; the widening of the student's intellectual, emotional, and moral horizons.
4. Reading instruction is completely successful only when the student has acquired the habit of active continuous reading and can read with ease in all of the subject areas which, by necessity or choice, he faces.
5. The reading program is not the product of one teacher, but demands the involvement of the entire faculty and administration in a wholehearted and single-minded concentration on drawing the best possible work out of each student.[5]

READING SUBJECT MATTER

Specialized subject matter teachers should expect to do their share in the teaching of reading, because each discipline presents a reading program of its own. Each discipline has its own language with its own vocabulary. Moreover, reading in dif-

[4] Ibid.

[5] M. Jerry Weiss, *Reading in the Secondary Schools* (New York: Odyssey Press, 1961), p. 10. By permission.

ferent disciplines requires different approaches. Reading a page of an algebra text differs markedly from reading a page of a novel! In addition, reading in certain disciplines requires specialized skills. Reading in history or geography requires some fluency with maps; mathematics reading assumes the ability to read equations. The only person competent and available to teach these special skills is the specialized subject matter teacher concerned. Of course, reading teachers may carry on part of the developmental reading programs by conducting classes in developmental reading designed to help the average pupil as well as special remedial classes for pupils who need special help in reading. Nevertheless, in almost any school under almost any system the brunt of a successful program of developmental reading—that is, the program designed to better the skills of normal readers—must fall on the subject-matter teachers for whose courses most secondary school reading is done. Ordinarily the subject-matter teacher should teach these skills through the regular reading material used in the course.

Selecting a Textbook

Textbooks have always had an important place in the classroom. Because this is the case, the selection of good textbooks is essential. In some schools, the teachers choose the texts for their own classes. In other schools, committees of teachers select the texts. Even when texts are selected by state or city authorities, the teacher may have a choice among various possibilities. Consequently, he should be aware of what makes a good textbook, even though he may have to use texts that have been selected by others. The following questions may serve as a guide.

1. What is the date of the copyright? Is the information and interpretation presented up to date?
2. Who is the author? Is he competent in the field? Does he write clearly and well?
3. Is the book suitable for the objectives of your course? Does it cover the proper topics with the proper emphases?
4. Are the topics arranged in a desirable se-

quence? If not, can the sequence be altered or portions omitted without disrupting the usefulness of the book?
5. Is the content accurate and accurately presented? Is the book free from bias?
6. Are the concepts presented clearly? Are they adequately developed with sufficient detail or is there a tendency to attempt to jam in too many ideas too compactly?
7. Is the vocabulary and language appropriate for the pupils of the class?
8. Does it presume background knowledge and experiences that the pupils do not yet have?
9. Does the author make good use of headings, summaries, and similar devices? Does he give opportunity for the readers to visualize, generalize, apply, and evaluate the content?
10. Are the table of contents, preface, index, appendixes, and glossary adequate?
11. Does the book provide suggestions for use of supplementary materials?
12. Does it provide a variety of suggestions for stimulating thought-provoking instructional activities?
13. Are these suggestions sufficiently varied both as to level and to kind?
14. Does the author document his sources adequately?
15. Is the book well illustrated? Are the illustrations accurate, purposeful, and properly captioned? Are they placed near the text they are designed to illustrate?
16. Does the book have suitable maps, charts, and tables? Are they clear and carefully done? Does the author refrain from trying to cram too much data onto his maps and charts?
17. Is the book well made? Does it seem to be strong and durable?
18. Does the book look good? Is the type clear and readable? Do the pages make a pleasant appearance with enough white space?

TO FIND A TEXT'S READING LEVEL

To determine the reading level of a text, the first thing to do is to check the teacher's manual or teacher's edition. If these do not give the reading levels, then you can turn to a readability formula such as the Dale and Chall or Lorge formulas.[6] To find whether or not a book is too difficult for an individual, have him first read it aloud to you and then tell you what he has read. If he can read it aloud without overmuch stumbling and can explain the gist of what he has read reasonably well, one can assume that the book is not too difficult for him.

*

How can one determine the suitability of a book's reading level for a particular pupil?

Using the criteria listed in this chapter as a basis, review several textbooks in your field. In what ways are they good? In what ways bad? If you had a choice which would you adopt?

Prepare a list of readings for pupils of different reading levels for a topic in a course you might teach.

*

ONE TEXT OR MANY READINGS?

In many schools the basic problem in selecting a textbook is whether to use a single textbook, or to use several readings.

In general, the weight of the argument seems to favor the use of several readings. A single text can lend organization and order to a course. Frequently it is the sole source for a course plan readily available to the new teacher. On the other hand, the teacher should know his own class better than any authority writing behind the ivy-clad walls of a university. Therefore, the teacher is in a better position to select and organize the material for a particular group of pupils in a particular school than the textbook writer. In addition, when a teacher adopts a single text the class is limited to a single point of view, a single reading level, and a single style.

The use of several readings has the advantage of making it possible for pupils to read material suited to their abilities and needs. If a youngster is attempting to learn the contribution of Samuel Gompers to the labor movement, it matters little whether he searches for his information in the *Encyclopaedia Americana,* a biography of Gompers, or a history of the labor movement, as long as he learns it as efficiently and effectively as he can. Since this is true, the teacher can help boys and girls pick books to study which are most suitable for their abilities and which may appeal to their interests. It is very difficult to provide adequately for individual differences if one limits the readings to one text only.

Another important possibility that presents itself in using many readings is the opportunity to read original sources. Textbooks often tell about things superficially. In many instances this treatment is justified because of the limitations of time and space, but certainly the pupil should be allowed to meet some of the originals face to face. The use of many readings makes this easily possible, especially now that much first-rate material is available in paperback.

Some teachers find it difficult to organize courses when many readings are used. If a teacher uses unit, individualized, and laboratory procedures, this difficulty should be reduced. Another solution to this problem is to adopt one textbook as a basic reader and to supplement it with other readings. In any case, the key to the technique, when one uses many texts or readings, is to be sure that each youngster knows what he is seeking in his reading. For instance, in the example above, if the youngster does not know what he wants to find out about Gompers, his search in any book is likely to be fruitless. When many readings are used, the use of study guides usually helps give the pupils direction.

Individualizing Reading

It has been said that the purpose of the textbook is to bridge the gap between the pupils' experience and knowledge and the concepts that they are going to have to master. Textbooks that can do this job are hard to find. No single textbook can do it for every member of a class. Therefore, it would seem that the only valid approach for a reading program is to match the readings and the readers in an individualized reading program. Where a truly individualized reading approach does not seem practical, then the next best thing would seem to be to divide the class into reading

[6] Edgar Dale and Jeanne L. Chall, "A Formula for Predicting Readability," *Educational Research Bulletin* (January–February 1949), 27:11–20, 37–54.

Irving Lorge, "Predicting Readability," *Teachers College Record* (March 1944), 45:404–419.

groups. Techniques for conducting such small groups are discussed in Chapter 10. The reader may wish to consult that section at this point in order to fill out his understanding of the present discussion.

An Example of Individualization. Individualized reading is based upon the assumption that pupils differ in reading ability and in background, and that pupils can acquire much the same information and concepts even though they may not read the same books or articles. Thus in the study of Ancient Man pupils with low reading ability might read such easy reading material as the Abramowitz pamphlet *World History Study Lessons,* while others read such difficult and esoteric material as the final chapter of Von Koenigswald's *The Evolution of Man.* Others might be reading in such varied works as Chapters 2 and 3 of Van Loon's *The Story of Mankind,* Ashley Montagu's *Man: His First Million Years,* a *National Geographic Magazine* article (e.g., Cynthia Irwin, Henry Irwin, and George Agogino, "Ice Age Man vs Mammoth," June 1962, 121:828–836, or Thomas R. Henry, "Ice Age Man, the First American," December, 1955), or the Dell Visual paperback *Prehistory.* Or they might be reading the first unit "Days before History" in Hartman and Saunders text *Builders of the Old World,* or Chapter I of Black's textbook *Our World History.*

Giving Individualized Reading Direction. In any unit just what it is pupils read does not really matter as much as that they read to attain certain objectives. These objectives are all grouped around the same theme—in this case prehistoric man. Each pupil is guided toward these objectives by the teacher's assignment, which should set for the pupil definite directions. In the preceeding instance, he may have asked the reader of Von Koenigswald to find out how man developed his culture and what his first tools were like. He might ask similar questions of the pupils reading the Abramowitz material or of those reading Ashley Montagu. The pupils reading the *National Geographic* articles might be searching for information about life among ice-age people—their eating habits, their hunting techniques, and their tools and weapons. And so on with the pupils reading other selections. The teacher could present the questions to the pupils orally as he gives the pupils their assign-

ments or in conferences while they are working. Another way would be to prepare a dittoed or mimeographed study guide which would list the questions that the pupils ought to look for and suggest readings in which the answers might be located. Pupils could use these guides both to direct their study and as reference lists from which to select what they would read. An example of such a study guide appears in Chapter 6.

The teacher should act as a guide for individualized readings. On the basis of his knowledge of the pupils' reading ability, interests, background, and academic needs the teacher should suggest readings appropriate to individual pupils. Insofar as possible he should match pupil reading ability with the reading level of the selection to be read. However, he should not debar a pupil from reading or attempting selections that he might enjoy and profit from merely because the selection seems to be too hard or too easy. Pupils who bite off more than they can chew should be allowed to change if they find the work frustrating. The teacher should not let good readers make a habit of working below their level; it is better to suggest challenging assignments to them rather than to forbid them access to easy reading. After all, sometimes the easiest, simplest reading is the best. Common interests and purposes may cause considerable overlap in the reading of able and less able pupils.

*

Why do authorities often condemn the use of only one text in the classroom? What is your position on this question?

What advantages does the use of multiple reading have in the subject you wish to teach? What disadvantages? How would you use such a technique in the study of mathematics?

If the pupils in your class do not all read the same readings, how can you ensure that they all have an opportunity to acquire the important learnings?

*

USING LIBRARY MATERIALS

In order to teach in the way we think one ought to teach, pupils must have plenty of material to read. To make this supply of reading material readily available, each classroom should be a library. In this classroom library, all sorts of reading matter should be readily accessible to the pupil—periodicals, pamphlets, brochures, and the like, as well as books. For record keeping a self-charging system with pupils acting as librarians from time to time may suffice. Usually one needs worry little about loss of material if such a system is used.

In addition to the classroom library one should make good use of the town and school libraries. While it is true that in some communities these libraries are rather scantily supplied, the librarians are almost invariably eager to cooperate with teachers. Teachers should make the most of this opportunity.

Few boys and girls, or men and women for that matter, use libraries well. Although instruction in the use of the library may ordinarily be the English department's responsibility, the teacher whose pupils use the library is also responsible to see that they use the library facilities efficiently. Librarians usually welcome the opportunity to explain library techniques either in the classroom or in the library. A visit to the library early in the year might well increase the efficient use of its facilities by the pupils.

*

What skills and information does a pupil need in order to learn to use the library effectively?

If your school provided no classroom library, what would you do to provide suitable reading materials?

*

BOOK REPORTS AND SUPPLEMENTARY READING

Reading reports can be useful in all courses. They can be especially helpful in multitext courses.

One interesting reporting technique is for each pupil to write a short summary and critique of each work he reads on a 5 × 8 card. The critique should allow for a frank evaluation of the reading from the point of view of the pupil and some hint of its reading difficulty. By the use of this technique the teacher can rather quickly accumulate a card catalogue of pupil criticism that may be worth more to prospective readers than any criticism other than, perhaps, word-of-mouth reports. Forms for such cards can be extremely simple. All that is needed is space for the name of the author, the title of the book, the name of the pupil critic, a short summary of what the book is about, and a critical comment.

Many teachers use more formal book reports for collateral readings. In high school honors sections quite frequently the pupils are required to write formal critical essays or book reviews. For bright, interested students this practice is commendable, but for the average pupil the accent should be placed on reading rather than reporting. A simple book-report form such as the card previously mentioned or the simple form appearing as Figure 13-1 should suffice admirably.

Learning to Use Books Properly

TEACHING THE USE OF BOOKS

The effective use of books is not a skill that comes naturally. Pupils often seem to think that books are merely to be read, but the really effective use of books is not that simple. As Bacon says, "Some books are to be tasted, others to be swallowed, and some few to be chewed and digested."

Pupils need to know how to determine which books to taste, which to swallow, and which to chew, and how to perform each of these operations well. The criteria suggested in an earlier section should be helpful in choosing one's reading material. Boys and girls can learn how to use such criteria by class discussion and by application of the criteria to various books. They may even develop their own criteria as a group project. In general, let it be said here that reference works usually are designed to be scanned, fiction and some supplementary reading may deserve only to be skimmed, and most textbooks must be chewed. In this connection, one should note that reading in science and mathematics texts almost always requires careful word by word concentration, whereas fiction quite frequently merits no more than a blithe general overview in order to catch the flavor.

LEARNING TO SKIM

Some books should be chewed and digested; others should be merely tasted. We have tried to explain how to chew and digest a book in the section in this chapter entitled "Developing Reading Comprehension." The pupil should also learn how to taste, that is, skim, for skimming allows one to

Figure 13–1
Book Report*

* Used in Lawrence High School,
Lawrence, Kansas.

HISTORY
BOOK REPORT

Hour _____

Name _____ When book was read _____

Name of book _____

Author (s) _____ Type of Book _____

Setting of story:

   Where did it take place? _____

   When did it take place? _____

Briefly tell what the book is about: _____

_____

_____

_____

_____

_____

_____

_____

_____

What do you think was the author's aim in writing this book? _____

_____

_____

What about the book was of most interest to you? _____

_____

_____

What is your opinion of this book? Where is the book weak? Strong?

_____

_____

_____

sample, to skip the old and become familiar with the new, to concentrate on the pertinent, and to brush over the irrelevant.

To learn to skim one needs to have, in the first place, a good background in the subject so that he can recognize the pertinent and the novel when he sees them. Having such a background, the pupil can glance through the preface and table of contents to see what the book is about. Perhaps he need go no further. Such a quick perusal may tell him that this book is not what he wanted. If the book seems pertinent to his problem, he may scan the book, reading the headings, introductory paragraphs, chapter summaries, and sample the opening, middle, and final paragraphs. When he finds a topic that seems provocative, he can read it carefully. Sometimes he will find that he must go back to read a previous section, but no harm is done because he is still reading only what is most essential or interesting.

To teach boys and girls to skim books effectively, teachers should first teach the techniques involved directly, and then follow up this teaching with practice. An example of practice useful for this purpose follows.

1. In a class discussion decide what the class would like to learn from the chapter.
2. Let each pupil skim the chapter to see what it has to say on these points.
3. Discuss what the class has found in the chapter.

*

How does one determine when to skim and when to read carefully?

Can you think of any exercise games that one might use to teach skimming?

Of what importance is the ability to skim in mathematics, in social studies, in science?

*

THE PARTS OF THE BOOK

Authors and publishers of textbooks go to considerable effort to provide the reader with help in using their texts. You might check through your college texts to see what aids to learning have been included. Among them you may find tables of contents, prefaces, chapter summaries, chapter intro-

ductions, chapter headings and subheadings, problems to be solved, charts, graphs, illustrations, signpost sentences, indexes, glossaries, and footnotes. Properly used, these devices can make textbook study more efficient. Every pupil should know how to use them and use them well.

Teaching the Parts of the Book. One of the best ways to teach pupils to use the parts of a book is actually to practice using them in class when the class starts a new book. The teacher might develop the lesson with questions and exercises such as the following.

"Where does one find what the book contains?"

"Examine the table of contents and see what the book is about."

"Now that we know what the book contains, what was the author's purpose in writing it? Where can we find out?"

"What else can one find out in a preface? Let us read it and see. Does this book seem good for our purposes?"

"How can the information we learned in the table of contents or the preface help us in the study of this text?"

"Does it seem that this book is better for our purposes than other texts available? How can you tell without reading the book?"

"Let us compare this book with some others we might use."

Similar exercises may be used to introduce the index and glossary, until the teacher is sure that the pupils not only know how to use them but have acquired the habit. This, of course, means recurrent practice sessions. In each unit the pupils should have plenty of opportunities to look up things in the index. More than occasionally the teacher will find that the pupils have difficulty in using the index because they do not know the alphabet. For these pupils, special instruction and practice are necessary.

A good type of practice for pupils having trouble with alphabetizing consists of scrambling the words from a page in the dictionary and asking the pupils to put them in correct order. If the words are on cards it makes it easier and saves time while being fully as effective. Pupils can also make their own lists and test other pupils. In such cases the pupil should first demonstrate his own ability to arrange his list properly before testing his peers. The teacher may have to teach directly how to find such things as "questioning, techniques of" and items that do not appear under the expected category but are listed in another.

The Parts of the Chapter. The parts of the chapter can be taught in a similar fashion. The teacher can ask the pupils to find out what the chapter is about. This they can do by checking the subheads, and by reading the introductory section or paragraph, the summary, and the marginal notes. On the basis of this information the pupils can be expected to formulate questions of their own concerning what they might learn from the chapter and similarly from the sections. Continued practice with this sort of activity should help create a habit of reading with an inquisitive open mind.

Charts, Graphs, Illustrations. When reading, pupils frequently skip charts, graphs, and illustrations. This is unfortunate because the author includes these aids for a purpose. At times, they contain the meat of what the author is trying to say. They can clarify complex ideas and obscure points. Consequently, pupils should be taught to use these materials.

Many times the reason the pupils do not use charts, graphs, illustrations and similar materials is that they do not know how. When this is true, the teacher must correct the situation. Ordinarily he can best teach the use of such materials in the usual units of his courses rather than by introducing a separate unit on this topic. In his regular classwork the teacher can ask questions that require the pupils to refer to graphs, charts, or illustrations. Sometimes the questions can be pupil-made. When a pupil does not know how to use the chart, graph, or other aid, the teacher should show him how. At first much of this instruction should probably be group instruction; later it probably will become individual and remedial. In either case exercises like the following will prove useful.

Using the graphs taken from *Americas* as a basis (Figure 13-2), answer the following questions.

1. Approximately how many Mexican movies in 1961 were produced entirely by Mexicans? How many by Mexico in collaboration with others?
2. Same for Argentina.

3. Same for Brazil.
4. In 1961 the U.S. produced 254 movies. How long would the bar representing U.S. film production be if we should add it to this graph? (The length of the bar representing Cuban movie production is one eighth of an inch. Cuba made three feature movies in 1961.)
5. According to the Inter-American Institute the information contained in Figure 13-2 is not strictly comparable. Why not?
6. How many times a year do you go to the movies? Do you go more or less frequently than the average American did in 1962?
7. In what country did the average person attend movies the fewest times? How often did he go? How could the average be less than one? Why do you suppose the people do not go to the movies more frequently in that country?

The following hints may make the teaching of charts and graphs more effective.

1. Probably you would be wise to teach charts, graphs, and tables in context during regular lessons rather than to introduce special lessons or units on such topics as "Reading and Interpreting Graphs."

2. Give definite assignments that involve the reading and interpreting of charts, graphs, and other aids from time to time. These assignments should not be special lessons on the use of charts and graphs (although sometimes they may be required). Rather, the teacher should point out important features and their significance in regular lessons as the class goes along.

3. Pupils should be asked to use charts and graphs to point out ideas and to support conclusions.

4. Teaching the use of graphs is quite difficult. Probably the teacher should do some direct teaching in the reading and interpretation of graphs. Once this is done the pupils can make comparisons and inferences from graphs.

5. The overhead projector is very useful for teaching with charts and graphs. One can project grid lines onto the chalkboard and then build the chart or graph on the board. One can also project charts and graphs as ordinary visual aids.

6. The flannel board can also be used. Graph grids or table heads can be projected on to the

Figure 13–2
*Facts and Figures of the Americas.**

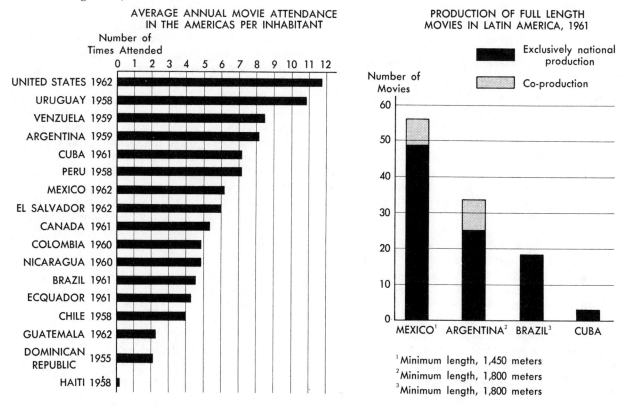

AVERAGE ANNUAL MOVIE ATTENDANCE IN THE AMERICAS PER INHABITANT

Number of Times Attended

PRODUCTION OF FULL LENGTH MOVIES IN LATIN AMERICA, 1961

Exclusively national production

Co-production

Number of Movies

MEXICO[1] ARGENTINA[2] BRAZIL[3] CUBA

[1] Minimum length, 1,450 meters
[2] Minimum length, 1,800 meters
[3] Minimum length, 1,800 meters

* Data prepared with the collaboration of the PAU Department of Statistics and the Inter-American Statistical Institute, a professional organization coordinated with the OAS.

Reprinted from *Americas,* monthly magazine published by The Pan American Union in English, Spanish, and Portuguese, Vol. 16, October 1964.

board or attached to the board. The lines and numbers of the graph can be attached to the board as the lesson moves along.

Pictures can also be useful learning aids and should be used as the basis for learning activities. When the captions are written to bring out points, one can use them for this purpose in your teaching. Another type of learning activity is for the pupils to point out relevant details in pictures and explain or interpret them.

For example, Lesson 2 of Jack Abramowitz's *World History Study Lessons,* Unit 1[7] includes sev-

eral pictures. One shows reconstructions of three kinds of "early men," another a picture of an Old Stone Age cave drawing, a third an illustrated time line, and a fourth a picture of a man making stone tools. These pictures have intrinsic interest and teaching value, but could not the teacher capitalize on these pictures by calling the pupils' attention to the features which mark the differences between the various species of *Homo,* or better yet, let the pupils spot the differences in characteristics from the pictures themselves? From there could not one go on to see where these various men seem to fit into our time line and which ones might be the artists of the stone caves and the makers of stone

[7] Chicago: Follett Publishing Company, 1962.

tools? Incidentally, this type of teaching can frequently be quite successful with pupils who ordinarily do not succeed well in book learning.

*

How much time should a biology teacher take to teach pupils how to use the parts of the biology textbook?

Build some exercise games you might use to help pupils better understand a text in your field.

*

Paperback Books

In order to provide for the differences in interests, needs, and abilities of boys and girls, and to allow the implementation of laboratory and inquiry teaching, every school and classroom should have a well-stocked library. Paperback books can fill this lack at relatively small cost.

By buying paperbacks the school library can acquire a great variety of books of all sorts to augment their more permanent collection and to build classroom libraries.

In the classroom paperbacks can supplement or even replace textbook sets. The best thing about paperbacks is that they are inexpensive enough so that pupils can buy them. In schools which have no classroom libraries pupils can pool their resources and start their own classroom libraries with paperbacks. More important, teachers should encourage pupils to build their own personal libraries, and so to become really intimate with books of their own.

When pupils own their own books, they should mark them up as they read them. Skill in marking up books is an important aid to analytical and interpretive reading. Every pupil should have a chance to learn and practice this skill in his own books in school. They should underline and label passages that seem specially significant and worthwhile and note and comment on things that strike them as good or bad, true or false, logical or illogical.

Of course, if the pupil does not own the book himself, he should not mark it up. Instead he can write notes to himself on cards or in a notebook, but it is not quite the same. Learning to mark up books properly is so important that school districts

would do well to furnish pupils with inexpensive paperbacks that the pupils can mark up to their hearts' content.

By using paperbacks, teachers make it possible for pupils to read primary sources rather than secondary or tertiary ones—whole works rather than snippets—and to explore them both extensively and intensively rather than being exposed only to a single textbook account. With inexpensive paperbacks it is much easier to provide pupils with opportunities to analyze and compare works, a practice which is almost impossible if one uses only the ordinary textbook or anthology.

Break the book into separate chapters and bind them into file folders or theme binders. Assign each chapter to a pupil to read for a report. In this way an entire book may be reported on in a day. At this rate the class could cover thirty extra books a year.

Different pupils can read different works on the same subject as a basis for discussion of a problem and a sifting of conflicting facts and interpretations.

*

What do you think of these techniques? What value do they have? Do you see any disadvantages?

*

To Improve Newspaper Reading

Most adults read newspapers more than they read anything else. Therefore it only stands to reason that schools should teach pupils how to get the most out of newspaper reading and that pupils should get plenty of experience in reading newspapers under supervision. In both English and social studies classes teachers can set up units in newspaper reading. In addition, teachers in all subjects can encourage pupils to read the newspapers profitably and make use of pertinent newspaper articles to enrich and point up their subject content.

One of the first objectives in teaching newspaper reading is to motivate pupils so that the habit of reading newspapers will carry over into their adult life. There are many techniques useful for this purpose. For example,

1. Read unusual stories aloud.
2. Display unusual headlines.

3. Hang sections of newspapers on the wall of the classroom.
4. Make up questions and problems based on the day's news.

INTERPRETING THE NEWS

The stress of course should be on interpreting and evaluating new stories. Newspapers should be read critically. In reading a news story critically one might consider questions such as
1. Does the newspaper have a reputation for accuracy?
2. What point of view (e.g., liberal or conservative) does the newspaper usually take?
3. Does the news story seem dependable?
   a. What was the source of the story: official, rumor, leak, usually reliable source, etc.?
   b. Are there evidences of bias, coloring, or sensationalizing?
   c. If the story deals with a controversial issue, does it represent the different points of view fairly?
   d. Does it check out with other known facts?
   e. Does the story distinguish facts from opinions?
   f. What is the significance of such phrases as perhaps "alleged," "the police said," "on good authority," "a source usually reliable," and so on.
4. What makes news stories newsworthy? Why are some stories worth featuring on the front page while other stories are placed inside? For example,

   p. 1 — GIRL KNIFED, FATHER HELD
          "Saucy child" is stabbed six times, left in street"
        — TRUCKS KILL TWO DEER
        — BROKEN AXLE SLOWS CITY SUBWAY CARS
   p. 12 — "DEAD" MAY LIVE AGAIN.

Pupils might look for examples of where stories are placed in different papers. Perhaps they could develop their own criteria of newsworthiness and apply them to current newsstories. Pupils might, for example, consider such questions as
Why do you think the editor buried such and such a story on an inside page?

Where would you have run the story if you were the editor?

Pupils might also discuss what should be published and what should be withheld or passed over. *The New York Times* say that it includes "All the news that is fit to print." What makes a story fit to be printed? Does an editor have the right to withhold a story because he does not think it is fit to print? Were *The New York Times* editors right to withhold news of the impending Bay of Pigs operation just because the President of the United States asked them not to print it? What are the codes and laws about what is fit to print? When is a story news?

Pupils might further discuss the role of the wire services in reporting news stories. Here one could include a study of each service and how it operates, a comparison of coverage of the various services, and their reliability.

The pupils should also have opportunities to learn the tricks of the trade in newspaper reading. The teacher might illustrate some of the methods he has found successful and conduct open discussions in which pupils share suggestions for improving their newspaper reading techniques. For example,

1. Read the conclusion of any columnist first, then read the column and reread the conclusion.
2. Read the heaviest material first, the lightest last.
3. First read all the headlines on the front page. Next read the news summary and check the index. (These condensations cover the major events). Then leaf through the whole paper, glancing at as much as you care to. Note what stories seem to be most interesting and important to you. Finally read more about the leading news stories. In doing so, pay particular attention to editors, columns, and comments on the meaning of the news.

READING OTHER DEPARTMENTS AND SECTIONS

The study of newspapers is not concerned only with the reading of news stories. Early on, pupils should become well aware of the differences in news stories and such features as editorials, columns, the op-ed page, and the like. The pupils should also learn that different skills must be used in reading various features not only because of the differences in importance and style of writing, but also because the news is supposed to be information while editorials and columnists' essays are largely statements of opinion. Some of the sections and departments of the newspaper probably should be studied in detail—e.g., general news, sports, financial, editorials, and so on. The following questions designed for the studying of the comics are typical of the kinds of questions pupils could consider when studying the sections and departments.

A. What makes for a good comic strip? A poor one?

B. Should a comic do something more than amuse? If so, what?

C. Compare the relative number of comics in several newspapers—from none in *The New York Times* to two pages or more in some of the other newspapers. How do you explain this?

D. Are comics in direct or indirect proportion to the standing of the newspaper as a purveyor of news?[8]

Also pupils can learn how the newspaper can help them in their personal lives. Reviews of books, moving pictures, television programs, stage shows, and the like, for instance, can save the reader from wasting his time and money. Advertisements can also be an aid once pupils learn to interpret them. In teaching about advertising, teachers ordinarily emphasize consumer aspects. Such things as how to recognize a bargain, how to evaluate the claims of the advertisement writers, and how to recognize the psychology used by the advertisement writers are important in teaching pupils how to get their money's worth and should be stressed. The amount of space used for advertising by various concerns, the costs of advertising, the relationship of advertising to newspaper policy, and the relationship of advertising revenues and the relatively small cost of newspapers on the retail market are also important considerations that could be studied.

[8] Carl Sailer, unpublished manuscript, slightly adapted.

USEFUL TACTICS

Among the useful means of promoting better reading of better newspapers are

1. Projects—class and individual.
   a. Scrap books: editorial cartoons, sports, "Teen Topics," "Words to Live By."
   b. Great newspaper men—present and/or past.
   c. Study of good and poor comic strips.
   d. History of newspapers or printing.
   e. Editorial cartoons drawn by students.
   f. Analysis of advertisements.
   g. The place of pictures in a newspaper.
   h. Continued study of some organization (like the U.N.) or problem, or ideas.
2. Audio-visual aids.
   Films put out by newspapers and displays borrowed from newspapers or libraries.
3. Bibliography.
   Works included should be short and to the point (which is about reading the newspaper, not about journalism). Let the class build its own bibliography.
4. Resource persons.
   a. Your own neighborhood and nearby communities.
   b. Newspapermen—sent out by the newspapers.
5. Special reports—oral and written.
6. Vocabulary—regular and special newspaper lingo.
7. Trip to newspaper offices and plants.
8. Material from newspapers, e.g., maps, teletype, and so on.
9. Bulletin board displays, both teacher- and student-made.
10. Samples of newspapers, e.g., newspapers from all over the U.S., old copies, foreign language newspapers published in the U.S., and foreign newspapers.
11. Newspaper unit combined with tape recorder.
    a. Students tell why they want to learn to read the newspaper.
    b. Pupils record what kind of help they need and in what areas of newspaper reading—list the questions they want answered.

c. Pupils include benefits derived from the unit (after its completion).

12. Other activities for pupils.
   a. Ask the editor of a local paper to brief you on his purposes and policies.
   b. Discuss the educational value of a newspaper.
   c. Discuss the importance of reading the newspapers.
   d. Discuss what lay people expect of newspapers or what newsmen think the criteria of newsworthiness should be.
   e. Discuss the influence the newspaper has in the community.[9]

TEACHING READING SKILLS

Vocabulary Building

Every teacher is responsible for helping each pupil in building his vocabulary. This is true for science, mathematics, art and music teachers as well as for teachers of English. In order to ensure that their pupils' vocabularies are adequate, teachers should introduce the study of important key words early in the course and discuss other key words as they appear. The use of vocabulary lists and word games is helpful in building an adequate vocabulary.

USING WORDS IN CONTEXT

A common practice in vocabulary building is for the pupil to keep a notebook in which he com-

[9] This section has been based heavily on Leonard H. Clark, "Social Studies and Mass Media" originally printed in *The Mass Media in Secondary Education,* 1965 Yearbook (Plainfield, N.J.; New Jersey Secondary School Teachers Association, 1965) , pp. 46–54; and Carl Sailer, *Toward Better Newspaper Reading,* unpublished manuscript, Jersey City State College.
For more complete information on the study of newspapers consult Edgar Dale, *How to Read a Newspaper* (Glenview, Ill.: Scott, Foresman and Company, 1941) and William A. Nesbit, *Interpreting the Newspaper in the Classroom,* 2nd ed. (New York: Thomas Y. Crowell, 1971) . For more ideas on how to use the newspaper as a teaching tool consult Harry Bard, Claire Eckels, Sidney Blum, and Edyth Myers, *Learning from the Sun Papers,* 2nd ed. (Baltimore, Md.: The Sun, A. S. Abell Co., n.d.) and Howard H. Cummings and Harry Bard, *How to Use Daily Newspapers,* How to Do It Series No. 5 (Washington, D.C.: National Council for the Social Studies, 1964) .

piles a glossary of terms useful in the course. If the teacher uses this technique, he should see to it that the pupils do not merely copy words and definitions in their notebooks. This practice usually amounts to little more than transferring the word from one page to another. What we want to do is transfer the words into the pupil's mind. Consequently, exercises that force the pupil to use the word in context and to learn its meaning are preferable. Defining a word in one's own words is a difficult feat which sometimes serves these purposes admirably. Similarly, acting out words is sometimes a pleasant way to bring out the meaning. So are games and exercises in which one tries to find the closest synonyms. The best practice of all, however, seems to be actually to use the words frequently in the classroom in their natural context. With strange words one should, of course, check to see that each pupil knows what the word means. This can be done by asking pupils to explain the word's meaning. The really important part in any of these exercises is that they consist of meaningful practice.

*

How can a teacher make a vocabulary notebook into a worthwhile learning experience?

*

INTRODUCING NEW WORDS

Few teachers realize how many new words face the pupils in their assignments. Teachers of the various subjects must pay particular attention to teaching new vocabulary of the lesson to come before the pupils begin to read it. In this respect the teachers must be sure not only that pupils recognize the word, but that they can attach the right meaning to the word as well. Quite frequently boys and girls can not match any reality to key words that teachers use in their lessons. Therefore, if pupils are to read these words with any understanding at all, teachers must see to it that the words are well explained before the pupils begin reading them. In this process the teacher should emphasize relationships and be sure that the pupils become familiar with the words both orally and visually, so that the words will have meaning to each pupil. There is no point in vocabulary study that is just a memory exercise.

DIRECT TEACHING

There should be direct teaching of vocabulary, however. Particularly important is the teaching of the technical meaning of words in the various disciplines. The word *root,* for instance, has greatly different meanings in language study, biology, and mathematics. Considerable attention should be placed on teaching pupils how to use suffixes, prefixes, and roots to analyze words and to build up meaning. Skill in this sort of word analysis is necessary in developing good meaningful science vocabularies since much of the nomenclature in scientific classification is a matter of considering roots with suitable prefixes and suffixes, for example, lepidoptera, hymenoptera, hemiptera, and homoptera are classes of insects whose wings (*ptera*) are scale (*lepido*), membrane (*hymen*), half (*hemi*), or all the same texture (*homo*).[10] In another instance Bamman points out that a boy who understands the *trans* of *transparent* has already won half the battle of understanding *translucent*.[11] Similar direct instruction is needed to help pupils identify words made up of two other words.

Particular care should be given to qualifying and transitional words, for these words set up the relationships in sentences and paragraphs. Soon, however, the pupil should be able to assume the burden for identifying and using such clues independently. On the other hand, idiomatic expressions and foreign words do not lend themselves to easy transfer. Teachers will always have to teach them directly, almost by rote.

Sometimes the direct teaching of the meaning of words can be made more interesting and meaningful by teaching the history of the words. Geneological charts showing the words' etymology can make interesting subjects for pupil bulletin boards. So can cartoons showing how suffixes and prefixes change the meanings of words. Other devices useful for making vocabulary study interesting are anagrams, crossword puzzles, and double crostics.

USING THE DICTIONARY

Probably the best aid to good vocabulary development, however, is the dictionary habit. Every pupil should have a dictionary of his own. Now that good, inexpensive editions like *The New American Webster Handy College Dictionary* are available in paperback editions, teachers should encourage each pupil to have a dictionary of his own, to carry it around with him, and to use it. In addition, teachers will find it necessary to teach junior high school pupils and some senior high school pupils how to use the dictionary. Among the skills one must teach, according to Jan Tausch, are the following.

> The secondary student should be able to recognize alphabetical sequence, use guide words, identify root words in both inflected and derived forms, select the definition that fits the context, and realize the differing purposes of comma and semi-colon as used in dictionary meanings. He should be capable of using the pronunciation key, the etymology key, and responding correctly to the accent mark. He should know that geographical and biographical information can be located in some dictionaries and understand also the limited nature of this information so that he uses it appropriately.[12]

Only when the pupil becomes familiar with the dictionary can one feel that he is well on his way to literacy.

TEACHING WORD-ATTACK SKILLS

Because pupils in junior and senior high schools face a much larger vocabulary than that with which their elementary school texts have made them familiar, they need to know how to decipher new and unfamiliar words. That is to say that they need skill in the use of phonetical and structural analysis and the use of context clues. Even though instruction in all of these skills is part of their elementary school instruction, most boys and girls need additional instruction and practice before

---

[10] Henry A. Bamman, "Reading in Science and Mathematics," in *Reading Instruction in Secondary Schools,* Perspectives in Reading No. 2, International Reading Association, Newark, Delaware, 1964, p. 64.

[11] Henry A. Bamman, Ursula Hogan, and Charles E. Greene, *Reading Instruction in the Secondary School* (New York: David McKay Co., Inc., 1961), p. 196.

[12] Evelyn Jan Tausch, "Teaching Developmental Reading in the Secondary School" in *Reading Instruction in Secondary Schools,* Perspectives in Reading No. 2, International Reading Association, Newark, Delaware, 1964, p. 52. By permission.

they are expert in them. Secondary school teachers must provide this additional instruction. If you have not had professional training in the use and teaching of these skills, it would be wise for you to study the manuals and handbooks which accompany the basic series used in elementary schools, or a good text in the teaching of reading. The following discussion can do little more than hint at the ways in which the secondary school teacher can help pupils learn to attack new words.

Phonetic Analysis.[13] Phonetic analysis refers to the processes of determining the sounds in words from an analysis of the letters of the words. Pupils possessing skill in phonetic analysis will be able to

1. Hear and recognize initial, final, and medial consonants.
2. Hear and recognize consonant blends.
3. Hear and recognize consonant digraphs.
4. Hear and recognize diphthongs.
5. Hear and recognize vowels.

Boys and girls who do not have these skills should practice them. For this purpose teachers should use elementary school practice materials. In these exercises the pupils should first master the simple skills and then move to the more complex ones (for example, single consonants before blends). To ensure that the benefit of these exercises is not lost, teachers should take particular care to ensure that pupils have a chance to use the skills being developed in actual reading situations. Also, teachers should make provision for enough review and practice to maintain the skills once they have been mastered.

Structural Analysis. Structural analysis has to do with the parts of words that go together to make up each word's meaning. These parts include inflectional endings, prefixes, suffixes, roots, syllables, and so on.

Inflectional endings are particularly troublesome for some pupils. The often-encountered omission of inflectional endings from words in their writing and oral reading is evidence of the prevalence of this difficulty. Pupils who make such errors need to have their direction focused on inflectional endings through exercises in locating, pronouncing, and hearing them.

All pupils should understand how prefixes and suffixes are combined with roots to make new words. They should also recognize the most important prefixes and suffixes. Bamman, Hogan, and Greene[14] list two techniques that have been used very successfully for developing skill in using prefixes and suffixes and recognizing derived forms.

1. Select a root form and build a "family" of words, substituting and adding various prefixes and suffixes. Call attention to the fact that the meaning of the root form *does not change:*

voice	convocation
vocal	vocation
vocabulary	avocation
invoke	provoke
evoke	vociferous

2. Select a derived form and examine its components, calling attention to the meaning of each part. Ask the students to name other words which contain the components:

philosophy

*phil*anthropist	theo*sophy*
mis*anthropy*	pan*the*ism
mis*ogamist*	*Pan* American
big*amist*	anti-*American*
bisect	*ant*agonist

In this connection perhaps it should be noted that the most common prefixes include, according to Stauffer, *ab, be, com, de, dis, en, ex, in* (into), *in* (not), *pre, pro, re, sub, un.*[15] The secondary school teacher should be sure that his pupils know these prefixes. Diagnostic tests for this purpose would certainly seem to be in order.

Syllabication. Similar analysis can be used to bring out the meaning of compound words to break words into syllables. Understanding of syllabication is essential for word-attack skill. Boys and girls who can recognize syllables control knowledge that shows them how to break up words into components, and so to look at their various parts.

---

[13] This section is largely based on Henry A. Bamman, Ursula Hogan, and Charles E. Greene, op. cit., pp. 94–102.

[14] Ibid., p. 99.

[15] Russell G. Stauffer, "A Study of Prefixes in the Thorndike List to Establish a List of Prefixes That Should Be Taught in the Elementary School," *Journal of Educational Research,* XXXV (February, 1942), pp. 453–58.

Syllabication also gives pupils a key to pronunciation and so directly to meaning. To teach this skill teachers should make ample use of the dictionary and instruction on determining which syllables to stress. Much of this practice must of course be done orally. Hearing the syllables may be quite as important to the pupil as seeing them.

The Context Clue. Skillful adult readers probably identify most of the strange new words they encounter by the *context clues* which give away their meaning. Among these clues Bamman, Hogan, and Greene list the following, all of which the reader will undoubtedly recognize as old friends and allies.

1. Inference: the reader's experience helps him to infer the meaning:
   The heat from our big fire came in and we were as warm as *toast.*
2. Direct explanation:
   The specialist on snakes, a *herpetologist,* showed us the poisonous and nonpoisonous snakes.
3. Use of an antonym:
   Everyone was to travel light; *excessive* weight of baggage would handicap the expedition.
4. Figures of speech:
   I watched with dismay as I observed in his face a rush of *volcanic* violence from which I had seen strong men withdraw.
5. Situation, attitude, tone, or mood of a particular writing:
   They at first thought that the snakes were wooden ones, and there was a noticeable *recoil* when they realized the reptiles were really alive.
6. Summary statement:
   Windows buckled and splintered, walls tottered and crumbled, a roof sagged weirdly, and a terrifying sheet of flame crept greedily upward and upward toward the adjacent walls of the convent; it was a *holocaust* unparalleled in my childhood experiences.[16]

Teachers should point out to pupils how these context clues can be used and give them opportunities to use them. Usually, however, it will be difficult to provide exercises that can be used successfully with a large number of pupils. In the main these skills should be learned in the context of one's ordinary reading. When pupils run up against hard words they can apply these skills to them. Exercises in which pupils individually spot words they don't

[16] Henry A. Bamman, Ursula Hogan, and Charles E. Greene, op. cit., p. 101.

know, as in the example by Elkins cited in the section in this chapter on oral reading, are useful for this purpose.

*

How can one make a vocabulary notebook a worthwhile learning experience?

Examine a few high school textbooks. What helps do you find for teaching the vocabulary? Do you find many words that seem difficult for normal pupils? For slow pupils?

*

Developing Reading Comprehension

One of the most difficult of skills seems to be to read a selection in such a way as to glean the ideas the author was trying to present. William G. Perry[17] tells us that out of 1,500 Harvard and Radcliffe freshmen assigned to read a certain chapter in a history book only one in one hundred was able to glean the sense of the chapter well enough to write a short statement on what the chapter was about. *Ninety-nine per cent of these Harvard and Radcliffe freshmen had not learned to read for comprehension well enough in their twelve years of college preparation to complete this simple task.* That secondary school teachers should exert more effort to teach pupils to read for comprehension more skillfully seems self-evident.

READING COMPREHENSION SKILLS

One uses many skills in reading. The lists of comprehension skills that appear in professional books and articles are frequently long and sometimes overwhelming. Niles, however, says that these skills can be reduced to "three skills, or abilities, which, . . . clearly differentiate between the reader who comprehends well and the reader who does not." [18] These skills are " (1) the ability to observe and to use the various and varied relationships of

[17] William G. Perry, Jr., "Students' Use and Misuse of Reading Skills: A Report to the Faculty," *Harvard Educational Review,* Summer, 1959, 29:193–200; cited in Olive S. Niles, *Improvement of Basic Comprehension Skills: An Attainable Goal in Secondary Schools,* A Scott Foresman Monograph on Education (Chicago: Scott, Foresman and Company, 1964), p. 4.
[18] Olive S. Niles, op. cit., p. 5.

ideas," for example, time, listing, comparison-contrast, cause and effect, " (2) the ability to read with adjustment to conscious purpose, and (3) the ability to make full use of the substantial backlog of real and vicarious experience which almost every reader, even the beginner, possesses." Many exercises for teaching skill in reading comprehension are available. Usually the regular textbook can and should be used for such practice exercises. The following are only a few of many possibilities. The teacher should ask the pupil to read a paragraph and then tell what it means. He should explain the meaning of key words and key sentences, paragraph leads, and topic sentences, and give the pupil practice in finding them. As soon as the pupil has learned to get the meaning out of paragraphs, the same procedure should be repeated with sections and later with chapters. Exercises of this sort can be made more interesting by using, among other things, games in which one attempts to reproduce the author's outline, by dramatizing the main ideas of a selection, by turning a book into a TV drama, and by boiling down a paragraph or section into a telegram with, of course, a penalty for any word over the limit. Sometimes these activities should be made to include the entire class. However, boys and girls who have mastered these skills and use them well should not be required to do the same exercises as pupils who have not yet learned them. The teacher can expect to find both good pupils and poor ones among those who need help in these skills.

READING IN QUESTIONS

The question is the key to learning reading comprehension skills. To learn to comprehend we must learn to read with open, inquisitive minds. It is because of the need to encourage this frame of mind that the following procedure is recommended for studying a chapter or similar reading.

1. Survey the chapter.
2. Determine what one can expect to learn in the chapter. State as questions or a question outline.
3. Read the chapter to find the answers to the questions.
4. Evaluate what has been read.
5. Apply the information to specific situations or problems.
6. Review by asking oneself the original questions.
7. Reread quickly (skim).

The heart of the method just discussed is asking oneself questions before, during, and after one's reading. Teachers should encourage such self-questioning in their pupils. At first, however, the teacher may need to do the questioning directly, either orally or by means of a study guide. If the reading were to be about the prehistoric men mentioned earlier in the chapter, for instance, one might ask the pupils to look for the answer to such questions[19] as

On page 8 the author implies that prehistoric man was probably just as smart as modern man. What evidence do you find to suport that statement?

What does the author think of prehistoric art? Do you agree with him?

In what respect do prehistoric man's achievements seem to foreshadow those of modern man?

What kinds of religious beliefs did prehistoric man seem to have? How can you explain why he had these beliefs?

Trace the development of his tools. What do the types of tools tell us about prehistoric men of various periods?

If you were to pick the one general idea as the main idea presented in this selection, what would it be?

Another technique that may be useful for developing searching attitudes in pupils is to develop the questions together in a discussion before starting on the readings. Such a discussion might be launched by the teacher's asking a question like "What do you think you want to find out from this reading?" or "What do you think that the reading might tell you?" In the case of the prehistoric men again, pupils might want to know about such things as

What did prehistoric men eat?
How did they get their food?

[19] These questions are based on Paul Hogarth and Jean-Jacques Salomon, *Prehistory—Civilization Before Writing*, Visual Series No. 6 (New York: Dell Publishing Co., Inc., 1962), pp. 7–9, 40–81.

Where did they live?
Did they believe in God?
What did they wear?
What did they do for recreation?

As such questions are developed in class discussion they could be put on the board by a pupil recorder. Then, if one wishes, these questions could be made into a formal list or study guide. In some instances at least, it would probably be better to let individual pupils adapt these questions to their own use, each one taking as many, or as few, as seems desirable for him for his own questions, adding other questions if he wishes.

Another approach would be for the pupils to write down what they expected to learn from the reading. Their lists would be used as the basis for class discussion, or could be checked over by the teacher for approval and possible additional suggestions, before beginning the reading. This approach is good when pupils' reading is individualized. Ordinarily, pupils should get the teacher's approval of their questions before they start reading. It is not wise, however, to hold up a pupil who is ready to read just because the teacher has not had time to approve his questions. When he is ready to go, let him proceed under temporary clearance. The checking can come later. In determining the questions to be asked the pupil can benefit much from knowing how to use the guides and aids put in the text by the author.

The questions asked should not be just questions of fact. Let them instead put emphasis on relationships: Why? How? So what? Of what importance is this? What's the point? These are the kinds of questions that will bring out ideas. Aim the questions at the big ideas, not the details. Perhaps the first main question in every list should be "What was the idea the author wanted to get across?" And probably the second question should be "What details did he use to try to get this idea across to his reader?" These same questions should be asked in the pupils' tests also, because it is by test questions that pupils determine what learning the teacher really values.

Questions are useful for developing comprehension skills only when they are asked *before* the pupil starts reading. One of the reasons that pupils do not learn to comprehend better is that neither they nor their teacher thinks to ask the questions beforehand. Asking questions afterward will merely tell whether or not one has understood; it will not help pupils develop skill in comprehending. The time for the reader to be active and alert is during the reading.

SIX STEPS FOR IMPROVING COMPREHENSION

Fehr[20] has suggested six steps for improving comprehension in mathematics. Bamman[21] has adapted these steps to include both mathematics and science. In the latter form the steps make a good summary of the measures necessary to teach reading comprehension in any subject. They are

1. Help the student adopt a problem consciousness.
2. Develop wide experience and broad background in mathematics and science situations.
3. Activate the problem.
4. Help students ask meaningful questions.
5. Become sensitive to the student who is using an unsuccessful attack on the problem.
6. Generalize the solution to every problem.

*

Do the six steps developed by Fehr and Bamman apply to social studies or literature? Why, or why not?

Try reading a college assignment with the use of questions and without them. Which seems more beneficial?

*

Reading Critically

EVALUATING WHAT ONE READS

"All that glitters is not gold," and all that is printed is neither true nor good. Unfortunately, many young people seem to have considerably more respect for the written word than is warranted. More than one high school pupil bases his

20 Howard F. Fehr, "Teaching High School Mathematics," *What Research Says to the Teacher*, Pamphlet No. 9, Department of Classroom Teachers and American Educational Research Association (Washington, D.C.: National Education Association, 1955), pp. 24–25.
21 Henry A. Bamman, "Reading in Science and Mathematics" in *Reading Instruction in Secondary Schools*, Perspectives in Reading No. 2, International Reading Association, Newark, Delaware, 1964, pp. 66–67.

faith on the fact that it is "in the book." Often these pupils become sadly confused when they find that what the book says is not necessarily true. Teachers should take it upon themselves to ensure that their pupils learn to read critically and to evaluate what they read.

HOW TO EVALUATE ONE'S READINGS

How does one teach pupils to evaluate what they read? One technique is to give the pupils plenty of practice. When several readings are part of each pupil's task in the various units, he soon becomes aware of the differences of opinion that exist. So perhaps the first step is to give the pupil different readings about the various topics, to consider carefully the differences of opinion, and to discuss why these differences exist.

Another step in evaluating one's reading is to try to establish the difference between fact and fancy. Early in life pupils should learn that some things are fact and some are fiction. Teachers can teach pupils how to determine the difference between fact and opinion by asking them such questions as, Is that so? How do you know? How can you check? Is this true or does the writer merely think so?

In their attempts to distinguish fact from fancy, pupils also should look for signs of bias in the writer. Assignments asking them to check their reading for such things as sensationalizing, emotionality, easy sweeping statements, disregard for facts, and loaded words will help familiarize the pupils with some of the signs of bias. Another check is to examine the writer's documentation. If the writer refers only to old works or works that are in dispute, perhaps he has not documented his work carefully. The writer who argues from anecdotes should also be distrusted. Single, isolated cases introduced into the context with the implication that they are typical are often false documentation.

Arguing from anecdote is an example of writing that violates the rules of logic. When teaching pupils to evaluate their reading, teachers should teach them to apply the test of logic to all they read. A technique useful in introducing the application of the rules of logic is to discuss violations of logic in their reading or in television materials. For instance, a television commercial implies that one gasoline is better than another because it is made in a refinery that can make its entire product 100 plus octane gas. Why does this not make good sense? Or again, one reads that a certain athlete smokes Bippos. Is this any reason why anyone else should? What does he know about it? Material of this sort can be used to teach the more obvious breaches of logic. As pupils become familiar with these errors, they can apply these tests to magazine articles and other readings.

DANGER OF POLEMICS

Pupils should also be wary of polemics, propaganda devices, and other attempts to persuade. Newspapers "Letters to the Editor" and editorials often provide excellent examples of political polemics that lend themselves to classroom instruction in critical reading. Examples of such slanted material can be found in almost any newspaper any day. Teachers can utilize them by giving pupils individual study assignments or by projecting them via the opaque projector or, after making a transparency, the overhead projector. In either case the teacher might ask the pupils to analyze the selections and to answer such questions as, Do they contain any of the faults of logic? Is the presentation just? If not, why not? Can you find instances of loaded words and other propaganda devices?

Exercises of this sort and others that the teacher may devise should help give pupils skill in evaluating. Moreover, they can be expected to encourage a questioning attitude in the pupil. It is hoped that after such teaching he will not swallow things, but will read with an active awareness of the snares of misinformation and poor logic, and also be inclined to test any idea before he gulps it down.

STYLISTIC CRITICISM

Reading critically also includes being alert to style and skill in writing. Does the style serve the thought? Is it appropriate? Does the writing bring out or obscure the meaning? Does it bring out or obscure the feelings? Does the author use symbolic language? If so, how does he use it? What does he mean to imply by means of his symbols? Are his methods effective? Any reading that brings out the answers to such questions is critical reading.

So also is any reading that results in the pupils' questioning or actively thinking about the values or implications of what they read. Especially important is the reading experience that helps to make the pupil react creatively—by drawing an illustration, by acting out the scene, by being the catalyst for making up an original poem, story, or ballet. Teachers should provide for such reactions by giving the pupils plenty of opportunity to evaluate, question, discuss, and think about what they read to encourage creative responses of all sorts.

Oral Reading

Reading aloud is considerably neglected by teachers in modern secondary schools. This neglect is unnecessary and unwise, particularly in view of the amount of excruciatingly painful oral reading that we find in some classrooms. Subject-matter teachers of all subjects who use oral reading in their classes should take time to help pupils to read better orally. Such help is necessary no matter whether the purpose of the reading is artistic (as in the reading of poetry or drama), or practical (as in reading a passage from a geography textbook).

Oral reading is not synonymous with sight reading. It is quite doubtful whether anyone really benefits from the agonizing attempts of unprepared pupils to plow through difficult material they have not read. Oral reading requires reading for effect. Therefore, pupils should always have an opportunity to read the material through silently first, so as to get some idea of the phrasing and to master the pronunciation of the strange words. Once they are ready, they should be encouraged to read in front of the class.

Before they are really prepared to read orally, however, the pupils need considerable practice. Narrative material seems to be best suited for oral reading practice. Most pupils need to have considerable help in learning to read naturally, in smooth thought units. In this respect the tape recorder can be used to a great advantage. From it a pupil can hear how he sounds naturally and how he sounds when reading. Thus he can get cues to help him improve his phrasing, emphasis, and cadence. Another common device to help pupils improve their phrasing is to have them underline the thought units in the selection they are to read. Sometimes the oral reading practice can best be done in pairs. An example in which the use of the first five minutes of each core class was routinely used for oral reading in duets is reported by Deborah Elkins.[22]

> There are times when children can share something with only one other classmate. This became evident in one routine procedure which teachers found very fruitful—the use of the first five minutes of every core session for oral reading in "duets." Each child had an outside reading book on his own level, whether it was on the Westward Movement or fantasies for young children or an adventure story. In the adventure-story sequence children were trying to come to some conclusion about what constituted adventure. Did you have to risk your life? Was there adventure in everyday life? Was the same experience adventure for everyone? A standard homework assignment was reading from that book every night. Each child had a mimeographed chart on which he made certain entries.
>
> Then he prepared the paragraph he liked best for reading to his classmate. After reading to his classmate he entered two or three words in the proper column, words he would like to be able to recognize more readily. This work was begun as soon as the children entered the classroom, even while the teacher was on hall duty. Any questions were referred to the teacher. As soon as the teacher returned he circulated around the room, listening, advising, noting progress, making comments of encouragement on the charts wherever this was warranted. In other words, at the start of each day, every child had a chance to read aloud and be heard, and the time consumed was only five minutes.

Speed Reading

For the last few years there has been much flurry about reading rapidly and efficiently. As a result some schools are conducting training in speed reading for their pupils. Possibly they should, because the average pupil does not read as rapidly as he might and the amount of print one has to get through in our modern society is staggering. On the other hand, the criterion for judging one's reading effectiveness is not so much how fast he reads, but how well he understands what he reads.

Good readers adapt their reading speed to what

[22] Deborah Elkins, *Reading Improvement in the Junior High School* (New York: Bureau of Publications, Teachers College, Columbia University, 1963), p. 41.

they are reading and their purpose in reading it. Poor readers tend to read everything at about the same rate. Classroom teachers, then, should concentrate on helping pupils learn how to adapt their reading attack to the situation. Most reading in science and mathematics, for instance, requires slow, careful study. So does studying the rule book in the physical education class, but reading in mathematics classes seldom calls for skimming or scanning, while in physical education classes one might well want to use these skills frequently to spot rules applicable to specific situations.

SPEECH

Although most classroom time is spent in talking, teachers do relatively little to help pupils learn to speak correctly and effectively. The ubiquitous television talk shows with their inarticulate celebrities who bury their thoughts in "you know," testify to the ineffectiveness of the teaching of speech in American and British schools.

Since talk is the principal ingredient in classes in all subjects, all teachers must accept the responsibility for teaching pupils to speak well. Pupils need lots of chances to talk under supervision. Oral activities, such as discussing, telling stories, reporting, chairing groups, and participating in dramatizations can, and probably should, be part of every course. When conducting these oral activities, teachers should encourage pupils to use colorful, correct, effective language. To accomplish this purpose they should work on oral vocabulary building just as they should work on written vocabulary building. The techniques used for building written vocabularies can be used equally well for building oral vocabularies. Teachers should also work to eliminate lazy speech habits such as the overuse of slang and the meaningless repetition of phrases like "you know," "I mean," and so on.

Being overcritical and picayunish in correcting the mistakes students make in speaking will not help the teacher to teach the pupils to speak effectively. The teacher will be much more likely to succeed if he sets a good example and gives pupils clear rules to follow. As far as he reasonably can, the teacher should be a model of the effective speaker of good English. However, the teacher does not have to carry the whole load himself. Tapes, recordings, and moving pictures can be used to provide examples of good speaking. Tape recordings of the pupils speaking are also effective. It shows pupils their strengths and weaknesses as well as adding a motivating factor. Sometimes just hearing and seeing himself on a videotape is enough to encourage a pupil to phenomenal efforts to learn to speak more effectively—particularly when he has an opportunity to compare his speech with that of an expert speaker he admires.

Oral reading is another helpful technique to use for teaching pupils to speak well. The oral reading techniques discussed in the section on reading may be used successfully in the teaching of speech. Choral speaking, reciting or reading poetry, speechmaking, and dramatization are also useful. Probably they should be used more frequently than they are.

When such techniques are used teachers should aim them at improving speech skills and subject-matter goals. The content of the exercises is important, but in our concern for content we should not lose sight of the importance of learning to speak well.

WRITING

Pupils need much more opportunity to learn to write than they have in most classrooms. Learning to write well takes practice, and more practice, under guidance. Therefore teachers of all subjects, not just English, should give pupils many opportunities to write.

Writing under supervision implies that whatever the pupil writes will be read and evaluated by the teacher. It does not mean, however, that the teacher should be supercritical. As in oral expression, what is important is the idea being expressed and the mode of expression. Pupils should learn to express themselves clearly and logically. Good attempts should be rewarded. The red pencil should be used sparingly. At times grammatical errors may be safely ignored, but good writing should *always* be rewarded—without fail.

Good writers revise. Secondary school pupils and some college students never seem to have heard of the word. Teachers should insist that first drafts be reworked into final drafts before papers are ultimately submitted as "contributions to the course." And final drafts should always be proof-read. Teachers who insist that pupils take back sloppy work for revision and proofreading are doing both themselves and the pupils a favor.

During the draft stages much good can come from pupils' reading and commenting on each other's papers in dyads or small groups. The criticism of a friend or colleague can be really helpful. It has the advantage of being free from the threat of a mark. Therefore consultation among writers should be welcome. Perhaps also pupils might act as editorial readers such as those used by publishing houses.[23] Perhaps also they might copy-edit each other's drafts. Another technique that may prove helpful is for the pupils to set up their own guidelines for acceptable themes and other compositions.

One of the major difficulties when writing a paper for a class is to find something to write about. In English classes pupils frequently complain that finding something worth while to write about is more difficult than writing. Teachers would do well to provide pupils with as many acceptable suggestions as they can. In English classes, particularly, teachers should consider correlating their theme writing with assignments in other classes. Pupils could then combine their work for two classes. Thus the pupil who is studying the Reconstruction period for his history class could increase and reinforce his knowledge of the period by writing an English composition on an aspect of the Reconstruction.

LISTENING

The importance of skill in listening can hardly be overemphasized. As Frank Steeves says

> Most of the time of pupils in typical classes is given to speaking and listening, especially to listening. All other pupils listen while one pupil asks a question.

All listen while the teacher discusses the question. They continue to listen while another pupil adds a comment. Even the most active discussions are largely a time of listening. If nine pupils engage in a forty-five minute discussion and each speaks an equal amount of time, each will speak for five minutes. But each will listen for forty minutes. What each *learns* from the discussion period will not be from what he said during his five minutes but from what he was able to hear during the forty minutes.[24]

Perhaps Steeves has somewhat overstated his case. Not all pupils listen when another pupil is talking, and as often as not, the pupils who do listen do not listen effectively. One of the more interesting experiments one can perform in class is to have each pupil report his version of what was said in a report or discussion. That pupils need to learn how to listen well will be self-evident.

Alert teachers find many opportunities to give pupils assignments that will help them to learn to listen. For example, listen to the radio or television and report exactly what the President said in his State of the Union address, or, more simply, what did the actors really say in the commercial advertising Product Y? Similarly the teacher can ask pupils to pick the central idea out of a short speech played on the record player. A variation of this same technique is for the pupils to pick out the principal arguments and show how a speaker's subordinate arguments supported his main thesis. Pupils can also analyze what they listen to—separating fact from opinion and information from propaganda as well as major points from minor points or even major points from folderol or window dressing. Pupils who are taught to anticipate what the speaker will probably say next learn to be alert listeners. Pupils can also build alertness by noting new technical words in what they hear or by trying to identify the feelings an oral reading expresses.

Pupils need much practice in such listening skills. Homework and classroom assignments such as those mentioned in these paragraphs will help learn to listen more attentively, to hear more correctly, and to evaluate what they hear. Direct instruction and practice in listening skills are necessities. That they have been neglected in so many classes is shameful.

---

[23] Readers are experts who go over manuscripts before they are published to suggest to the writer ways in which he might improve his book before it goes to press. They point out passages that do not make sense, errors in fact, things that were left out, places that seem illogical, and so on. The writer can accept or reject the readers' suggestions as he sees fit.

[24] Frank L. Steeves, *Fundamentals of Teaching in Secondary Schools* (New York: Odyssey Press, 1962), pp. 177–178.

GUIDING STUDY

In the past, teachers seemed to take it for granted that pupils just naturally learned to study. Seldom did teachers ever take it upon themselves to teach pupils how to go about it. "For tomorrow I want you to study Chapter 14, and you can expect a quiz on it," they would say. But not a word about how one studies or how one should get ready for the quiz.

More recently, teachers have begun to realize that boys and girls must be taught how to study. Left to themselves, few pupils develop good study techniques. If boys and girls reach the secondary grades without having learned to study well, the responsibility for seeing to it that they learn to study falls on the secondary school teacher. No pupil can do do justice to the secondary school program unless he has mastered the art of studying efficiently.

Improving Pupils' Study Habits

WHAT STUDYING IS

Some pupils seem to think that studying is the same as reading. This is not the case. Study includes all those activities that have to do with learning through planned effort. Thus, notetaking at lectures, preparation of papers, library work, reference work, problem solving, intensive reading, and skimming should all be considered study activities. They all are techniques that the pupil needs to learn before he can become an efficient student.

SUGGESTIONS FOR STUDY

When teachers first became aroused to the fact that boys and girls needed help in learning how to study, they developed rules for study as guides for the pupils. Among the admonitions often included in such rules are the following.

1. Plan your studying. Make a schedule and stick to it. Have a definite place to work. Make your studying routine and part of your routine.
2. Start off immediately. Have your material ready before you sit down to work. Be sure you understand the assignment before you begin it.
3. Space your learning. Take two- to three-minute breaks. If possible, take your rests at natural breaks in the material you are studying. Try to master one lesson or selection before moving on to the next.
4. Study actively. Develop an interest in what you are studying. Try to find out something. React to the readings. Ask yourself questions. Recite. Work out examples. Illustrate principles. Apply your learning as soon as possible.
5. Vary your study technique to suit the subject and your purpose. Learn materials in the form you expect to use them.
6. Avoid rote memorization. Memorize those things you need to memorize by the meaningful techniques of logical memory. Avoid mnemonics.
7. Evaluate your own work and study habits. Try to improve faulty habits. Try to increase your vocabulary; look up words you do not know. Make use of the aids provided in your books. Do not skip headings, marginal notes, questions, prefatory remarks, tables of contents, charts, and graphs. Use them.
8. Check your work and proofread your papers before handing them in. Take full notes but do not attempt to rewrite the text or copy down each word of the lecturer.[25]

On the whole, the advice in these suggestions is good. But the suggestions do not help a pupil's studying, unless they become a part of his behavior. How to make them part of the pupils' behavior is a problem that teachers must face.

*

Pick out several of the rules you consider important and try to devise activities that would make these rules become part of the pupils' behavior.

*

Teaching How to Study

Instruction in how to study must involve considerable practice in the classroom. In some schools

[25] The student might be wise to examine the list and apply it to his own practice. Even though each rule is not necessarily an essential, students might do well to investigate their own study habits if they diverge sharply from these rules.

a course in how to study is provided. Such courses may be helpful, but they do not relieve individual teachers of the responsibility for teaching study skills. Why not? For one thing, different subjects require different study techniques if study is to be effective. Consequently, in each of his courses, every teacher should try to teach study techniques proper to his course to any youngster who has not mastered them. Furthermore, learning how to study comes only from practicing good techniques, and where else can the pupil practice but in his ordinary courses? Thus every teacher is responsible for teaching pupils how to study for his course. Among the skills with which the pupils may need help are

1. How to read for information.
2. How to analyze a problem.
3. How to plan for study.
4. How to review.
5. How to evaluate materials.
6. How to use charts, graphs, and other audio-visual aids.
7. How to take notes.
8. How to concentrate.
9. How to analyze.
10. How to outline.
11. How to use the library.
12. How to build an adequate vocabulary both general and specialized.

THE NEED FOR DIAGNOSIS

As in any other teaching situation, one of the first prerequisites for teaching study skills is good diagnosis. By using the techniques of diagnosis described in Chapter 15, the teacher can determine what the pupil needs help with. Much of teaching pupils how to study must be done on an individual basis. As the teacher watches pupils studying, he can suggest ways and means to expedite the process. Questions like the following are often helpful.

What are you doing?
Why are you doing that?
What are you trying to do?
Will this help you?
Is what you are doing worthwhile?

Why do you think this is going to give the desired result?
What might you better be doing now?

SQ3R

Younger pupils need considerable help in learning how to study. Older ones should have acquired a great deal of this skill and should be able to work quite independently at their own level by the time they leave high school. When studying, pupils should utilize the technique of reading for comprehension discussed earlier under the heading "Reading in Questions." For the purpose of simplification and for mnemonic purposes these study procedures are often called SQ3R. These letters stand for Survey, Question, Read, Recite, and Review—basically the same techniques described earlier. Skill in these procedures must be developed by direct instruction and much supervised practice in the junior high school years.

DIRECTED-READING LESSON

For pupils who have not yet learned to direct themselves through the steps of SQ3R, one can use the directed-reading lesson. This technique is designed to teach pupils how to study and how to comprehend and retain what they read. Basically the method consists of five steps.

1. Prepare the pupils by going over new vocabulary and ideas and reviewing old material and experiences so that they can see the relationships between the new and the old.
2. Have pupils skim the selection and look at pictures, headings, and so on.
3. Help pupils formulate questions about the selection to be read, for instance:
   a. What should a pupil try to find out when studying the selection?
   b. Is this the kind of selection that must be studied carefully?
   c. How does this selection connect with other lessons studied in the past?

   Three of four questions are quite enough. Too many questions may confuse and discourage the pupils. The questions should be pupil-made rather than teacher-made, if at all possible.
4. Let the pupils read the selection to themselves.

5. Discuss the reading. By using questions, help them see the relationships among the facts presented and also relationships to what has been learned previously.[26]

TEACHING STUDY SKILLS IN THE ASSIGNMENT

In spite of their great importance, more than diagnosis and individual help is necessary in the teaching of study skills. The teacher can expect little success in this venture unless he teaches the skills directly. Although teachers often neglect it, the assignment offers a golden opportunity for teaching these skills. If the reader will turn back to the assignment discussion in Chapter 3, he will notice that the pupils developed an understanding of what they were trying to do and how they were to go about accomplishing their mission. In similar fashion they might discuss the materials and sources available, the use of the materials, and the relative merits of various study techniques in the performing of this assignment. As one can see, the assignment lends itself to such instruction.

The reverse side of the assignment coin can also be used to teach improved study skills. After an assignment has been completed, the pupils can learn about study skills and their efficiency by discussing the methods different pupils used to study the assignment and the relative success of the various methods.

In his discussions with the pupils the teacher should help them learn how to budget their time. In this connection the teacher and pupils can discuss just what they do with their time during any twenty-four hour period. An interesting exercise is for pupils to make graphs of the time they spend at different activities each day. The teacher should also encourage pupils to arrange for regular times and places for study. If his discussions are frank and fruitful he may find that some pupils truly have neither the time nor the place for home study. In such cases teachers may be able to help the pupil find time to study in school or in class. He ought to provide some time for pupils to study in class under supervision anyway. In these study sessions pupils should have oppor-

tunities to work together and to check their work with each other and the teacher. The discussions should also include the importance of learning good study habits and provide clues by which pupils may improve their learning habits. A truism many teachers forget is that it is necessary to learn how to learn if one is to learn efficiently. The more the teacher can do to help pupils to learn how to learn, the better his teaching will be.

THE PUPILS' RESPONSIBILITY FOR LEARNING

Although it is true that in his assignment, the teacher should try to ensure that the pupils know how to attack the work to be done, the teacher must also work to convince the pupils to accept the responsibilities of learning. Every pupil should learn quickly that there is no royal road to learning. Teachers should show the pupils how to attack their assignments, but they should not deprive the pupils of their initiative. The idea is to start them off, to encourage them, and to guide them—not to baby them. Rivlin[27] has suggested that the pupils discuss how they would study the material if there were no teacher, then formulate the attack, and work it out under the teacher's guidance. This method has the advantage of helping the pupils find their way under their own initiative yet with the security of the teacher's presence in case of need.

USING A GRADED SEQUENCE

No matter what methods are used to teach study skills, the material taught should be graded according to complexity and difficulty. Study skills are both difficult and complex. For this reason, they should be taught in sequence; the easier skills should precede the more difficult ones, the simple should precede the complex. The teaching of how to read for information previously cited serves as an excellent example of this point. Here the teacher first teaches the pupil how to extract the meaning from a sentence. This having been mastered, he proceeds to teach how to get the meaning from a paragraph. From there he goes on

[26] Leonard H. Clark, *Teaching Social Studies in Secondary Schools: A Handbook* (New York: Macmillan Publishing Co., Inc., 1973), p. 122.

[27] Harry N. Rivlin, *Teaching Adolescents in Secondary Schools* (New York: Appleton-Century-Crofts, 1948), p. 276.

to getting the meaning from a section, a chapter, and finally the entire book.

Building more complex skills on simple study skills is a must. To do this successfully requires the cooperative effort of the teacher in the various grade levels, and the teacher's careful diagnosis of each pupil's present level of proficiency.

*

In what ways could teachers of various grade levels cooperate in the teaching of study skills in your field?

In what ways is the studying of algebra different from studying social studies? From home economics? What skills may be used in studying these courses? Do the necessary skills vary from topic to topic within the fields? How?

*

SUPERVISED STUDY

Many teachers set aside class time for pupils to study their assignments in. This practice has several advantages. It ensures that everyone has time to do some studying. It gives the teacher a chance to guide pupils toward good study habits. It also gives teachers a chance to guide pupils in their studying—to see that they get off on the right foot, using the proper procedures and so on. In order to be sure that pupils get a proper start, when giving pupils difficult assignments in new work, it is probably always wise to start the pupils off in a supervised study session before sending them out from the class to do the assignment on their own. A short period of supervised study may eliminate pupil mistakes and make it unnecessary for the teacher to reteach and the pupils to unlearn.

To prepare for supervised study periods the teacher should establish with the pupils the purpose of the study assignment and why they should make the effort to study it. This step may not be an easy one. Pupils seldom see any *real* reason for studying assignments even when teachers think them essential. Therefore the teacher should stretch his talents to make clear the relevance and importance of the learning to the pupils. The teacher should also point out, or better help the pupils establish, what specifically should be learned. Teacher and pupil questions might include What important points should we look for? How does

the new learning relate to what has gone before? and What would you as a student or anyone else want to know about this lesson? Then, the motivation for studying the lesson having been established, the teacher can help pupils with such details as setting up their own study goals, time schedules, and methods of attacking the subject.

During the supervised study session, be it ten minutes at the beginning or end of the class period or an entire period, the teacher should keep busy supervising the pupils' studying. During his supervision he can and should observe individual study habits, keep track of each pupil's progress, and be alert for misunderstandings, poor techniques, and other difficulties that may arise. Sometimes it will be evident that the entire class does not understand how to proceed or is taking a wrong track. In such instances the teacher should stop everyone, call attention to the difficulty, and correct misapprehensions. However, occasions of this sort should be rare. The teacher who frequently interrupts the pupils when they are studying does more harm than good.

As he circulates around the classroom, the teacher should talk over progress with the pupils. He should ask pupils how things are going, but he should go further than that. Sometimes pupils don't know when things are going badly. Other times they may be unwilling to admit that they are having trouble. A little probing may give the teacher a more realistic picture of the pupils' progress.

In so far as he can, the teacher should individualize. As he observes he can find opportunities to differentiate assignments by giving different pupils work at different levels or by finding things that will appeal to pupils' peculiar interests or purposes or will help them resolve their difficulties.

There is no reason why teachers should make it routine to give over so many minutes per period, or week, to supervised study, but it is such an important technique that teachers should always include supervised study in their planning. The amount of supervised study will vary according to the lesson or unit, its aims and contents. Some days no supervised study will be needed. At other times proper planning requires that the entire period or even longer be given over to supervised study.

Outlining

Without any doubt being able to outline well is one of the most valuable skills a pupil can have and teachers in all subjects can help to be sure that pupils master it. Moreover, although having an outline of a text may not be of particular value, making an outline can be very valuable, for by the process of outlining one divides the text into its principal and subordinate points. It follows then that except for the fact that most textbook writers have reproduced the skeleton of their outline in their center heads, side heads and paragraph leads, there is no better vehicle for practicing outlining than one's own textbook.

To teach the pupils to outline correctly, the NASSP has recommended the following techniques which have been well proven over the years.[28]

1. Use easy materials and short selections in teaching pupils the mechanics of outlining. The following steps may be followed in teaching pupils to make outlines.
   a. Teacher and pupils working together select the main topics.
   b. Pupils, unaided, select the main topics.
   c. Teacher and pupils select the main topics, leaving space for subheads. Teacher and pupils then fill in these subtopics.
   d. Main topics are selected by the teachers and pupils and are written on the blackboard. Pupils then fill in the subtopics unaided.
   e. Pupils write the main topics and subheads without help.
   f. Pupils organize, in outline form, data gathered from many sources.
2. Train pupils to find the main topics and to place them in outline form. Use books with paragraph headings.
   a. Have pupils read the paragraphs and discuss the headings. Suggest other possible headings and have pupils decide why the author selected the headings he used.

   b. Match a given list of paragraph headings with numbered paragraphs.
   c. Have pupils read a paragraph with this question in mind, "What is the main idea in this paragraph?" Write a number of suggested answers on the blackboard. Choose the best one.
3. Provide practice in filling in subtopics.
   a. The teacher writes the main topics on the board or uses a text that has the main headings. Teacher and pupils then fill in the subheads.
   b. Have pupils skim other articles for more information and read carefully when additional material which is suitable for subheads is found. Add these new subheads. Do the same for new main topics.
   c. When pupils have gathered sufficient data, have them reread the complete outline and, if necessary, rearrange the order of the topics.
4. Give instructions in making a standard outline form. Many secondary school pupils do not know how to make an outline. Emphasize the fact that in a correct outline there must always be more than one item in the series under any subdivision. If there is an "a" there must also be a "b"; if there is a "1" there must also be a "2," etc. . . . A commonly accepted outline pattern is the one shown on page 292.
5. Have pupils use this outline form in preparing and giving oral reports.
6. To develop ability to draw valid conclusions, have pupils use facts and ideas which have been organized in outline form, not only as a basis for an oral report or as an exercise in outlining a chapter, but also as the basis for drawing conclusions. To check pupils' ability to make outlines, prepare lessons based on the following suggestions.
   a. List main points and subpoints consecutively. Have pupils copy these, indenting to show subordination of subtopics and writing correct numbers and letters in front of each point.
   b. List main topics and subtopics in mixed order and have pupils rearrange and number them.
   c. List main topics with Roman numerals. List subtopics (all one value) with Arabic num-

[28] "Teaching Essential Reading Skills," Reprinted by permission from the Bulletin of the National Association of Secondary-School Principals (February 1950). Copyright: Washington, D.C. Based on "How to Teach Pupils to Outline," *Teachers' Guide to Child Development in the Intermediate Grades.* Prepared under the direction of the California State Curriculum Commission. Sacramento: California State Department of Education, 1936, pp. 294–5.

erals. Have pupils organize subpoints under correct main points.

d. Present short paragraphs of well-organized material and have pupils write main topics and specified number of subtopics.

e. Present part of a skeleton outline and have students complete it.

f. Have pupils outline a problem without assistance. Class discussion is valuable in checking a lesson of this type.

Outline Pattern

```
I.
   A.
      1.
         a.
            (1)
                  (a)
                  (b)
            (2)
                  (a)
                  (b)
         b.
            (1)
            (2)
      2.
         a.
         b.
   B.
      1.
      2.
II.
   A
   B.
   etc.29
```

Taking Notes

Similar techniques should be taught to pupils who must learn to take notes from lectures. During

---

29 Another commonly used outline pattern follows the following form.

```
1.0
   1.1
   1.2
2.0
   2.1
   2.2
      2.21
      2.22
   2.3
   etc.
```

early lectures it is wise if the teacher provides a skeleton outline which pupils are to fill in with subheads and details. During the early secondary school years the lecturer should stop to point out where he is on the outline from time to time to be sure that everyone is with him. Later this help may not be necessary. As the pupils become more skillful in taking lecture notes the outline skeleton should gradually diminish until at last it finally disappears. After lectures in which pupils have taken notes following their own version of the outline, the lecturer would do well to project his outline on the screen so that the pupils can compare their version with his. Also, lecturers should give pupils plenty of clues to the structure of their lectures as they go on. Such helps as firstly's secondly's, and so on, will not only help to keep the inexperienced lecture-note taker on the track but may help keep the lecturer on it also. Skeleton outlines, dittoed or projected on the blackboard, are also excellent for this purpose. Lecturers who wander are difficult for any note takers—for beginners they are impossible!

Although many people recommend that pupils take notes on their reading, there seems to be considerable difference of opinion about the value of note taking. Certainly the mechanical production of the author's outline cannot be of much value, except as a method of learning how to outline. Obviously such outlining can help one to remember the content of the book, but there are probably other methods for gaining retention of the facts in the book that will serve better. Certainly there does not seem to be any particular advantage in making an outline of a textbook to study when one has the text itself in one's possession.

On the other hand, if the student outlines outside reading he can preserve the information so that he can study it later. Outlines consisting of questions with their answers have the additional advantage of highlighting the salient points. Notes in which the student records his reactions to chapters, sections, and passages are greatly helpful for they cause him to think about what he has read. He can also benefit from writing summaries of what he finds to be important in the various chapters he reads. Such note taking makes the pupil an active participant in his reading. All too often pupils, unless they use reaction note-taking or summary techniques, can read and outline sections of a book without turning on their minds.

Preparing for Tests

The number of pupils who do not know how to prepare for and to take tests is amazing, especially when one considers the importance of tests in school life. Experience shows that instruction in preparing for and taking tests can make substantial improvement in students' test scores. Grambs and her associates recommend that the following procedures be taught to pupils in order to prepare them for taking tests.

1. Before the test
   Review.
   Re-read.
   Relax.
   Rest.
2. Take the test with a calm realistic attitude. Be on time. Take the proper materials with you.
3. Survey the entire test before you begin. Make notes if permitted.
4. Do the easiest questions first. Skip anything that is difficult until you have completed all other items.
5. During the test, stop periodically (if it is long) and relax; close your eyes, breathe deeply, consciously work to relieve tension.[30]

HOMEWORK

Homework is a problem to all teachers. How much homework should one assign? How much should it count? What does one do to those who neglect it? What kind of homework should one give? The list could go on ad infinitum, although these problems tend to become less crucial when one uses unit planning.

HOW MUCH HOMEWORK?

How much homework should a teacher assign? The answer to this question depends upon the school, the subject, and the pupils. Quite often the school administration has established some sort of policy concerning homework. If so, the teacher must conform. Should the policy be a poor one, the teacher might work for its improvement, but under no circumstances should he flout it.

[30] Jean D. Grambs, John C. Carr, and Robert M. Fitch, *Modern Methods in Secondary Education*, 3rd ed. (New York: Holt, Rinehart and Winston, Inc., 1970) , Ch. 6.

When the school has no policy concerning homework, the teacher should probably fall in line with the school tradition, if any. In any case, one should try to ensure that pupils are neither overburdened nor underworked. Often a good unit assignment takes care of this problem automatically. At any rate, by giving long-term assignments one gives the pupil an opportunity to adjust his work so that he can avoid being overburdened by time-consuming assignments in several courses. Therefore, even if one does not use the unit approach, it may be wise to give out homework assignments for a week or more ahead. Almost invariably, it is more satisfactory to give long-term assignments in writing to prevent confusion, misunderstanding, and the need for repeating the assignment.

In making decisions about how much homework to give the teacher might want to consider the following points.

1. It has been commonly suggested that the daily homework load (study periods plus home study) of all courses combined should be

One to two hours in grades seven through eight.
Two to three hours in grades nine through ten.
Three to four hours in grades eleven through twelve.

In planning homework assignments teachers should remember that there are more important things than homework in adolescent life.

2. To avoid excessive homework assignments it is suggested that teachers in grades seven and eight stagger their assignments, e.g., science and math on Monday and Wednesday, English and social studies on Tuesday and Thursday, and no homework on Friday. The value of giving assignments to be done over the weekend is dubious. In the senior high school grades homework time can be equally divided among the various courses. At all levels due allowance should be made for major assignments and tests. As a rule college-preparatory classes seem to have more homework than other classes do.

3. The amount of time it takes a pupil to do assignment depends upon the pupil. An assignment that one pupil can do well in thirty minutes may take another pupil much more than an hour. For this reason, if no other, homework assignments should be individualized as much as possible.

4. The amount of time available for study during the school day and for a reasonable period after school hours, divided by the number of classes the pupil must prepare for daily, represents a fair estimate of the amount of time available for homework for any one class.

5. In some classes and schools pupils do not do their homework. In such cases it is futile to assign it. Instead the teacher should use supervised study and laboratory teaching while he tries to build up the attitudes and ideals that will cause the pupils to want to study in out-of-class hours. An important ingredient in this process is the introduction of assignments that seem to be worth doing.

From time to time the teacher should check on the length of time his assignments are taking. In addition to asking pupils how long an assignment took them, teachers can check by giving pupils sample homework assignments to do during class periods so as to see how long it takes pupils to complete them.

At this point a word of warning may be in order. There seems to have been a tendency for some high school teachers to illustrate how tough they are and what high standards they hold by piling great amounts of homework on their pupils. Unreasonably long assignments have no place in the secondary school for several reasons. The first is that *the emphasis should be on quality rather than quantity*. By making assignments too long teachers often force pupils to do less than their best, because there is just not enough time for them to do everything well. In addition, overdoses of homework can deprive pupils of the social and physical activities they need if they are to develop into well-balanced individuals. Sometimes unreasonable homework requirements can result in overwork or strain, and so are a threat to pupils' health. It is not necessary for a teacher to be an ogre in order to have high standards.

WHAT KIND OF HOMEWORK?

Burton[31] indicates that homework seems to make little difference in the school progress of boys and girls. Perhaps more attention to homework assignments would result in more impressive gains, although studies show little evidence of the efficacy of homework even when accompanied by such aids as questions, study guides, and the like.[32] Probably the reason that homework is ineffective now is not that home study has no merit, but that the present homework assignments, and the lessons they support, are inadequate.

Homework assignments may be of several types. One type calls for reading and studying new or old material. Another type calls for the completion of written work to be handed in. Still another type consists of solving problems, working on projects, or performing other tasks which cannot be done well in school, for example, the surveying of a portion of the community. By far the largest number of assignments at present seem to consist solely of exhortations to read certain pages in the textbook. The exception to this rule is the mathematics class where the assignment is most always to solve certain problems. In general, however, homework is most suitable for activities designed to reinforce old learning. The learning of new techniques and new materials is usually best suited to class situations in which the teacher can guide the pupil and thus guard him from learning the new techniques or new concepts incorrectly. For this same reason homework should be reviewed in class to point out errors, to correct misconceptions, and so on.

Homework assignments can, of course, be used as a basis for a lesson to follow. Moreover, they can provide opportunities for independent studying that pupils must do if they are ever to learn to think for themselves. However, assignments of new materials for study at home usually place too much emphasis on memorizing as opposed to understanding or thinking. *That is why homework assignments that carry on some activity started in class often result in better learning*, particularly when the activities are the kinds that require library or laboratory work such as digging out information from several sources, analyzing, identifying or defining problems, and doing practice exercises. Furthermore, pupils are less likely to be forgetful when the homework stems out of, or continues, an activity they are already working on and is tailored to their in-

31 William H. Burton, *The Guidance of Learning Activities,* 2nd ed. (New York: Appleton-Century-Crofts, 1952), p. 368.

32 Lloyd McCleary, "Homework," *Educational Leadership* 27:217–220, 225, (January, 1960).

terests or needs. Never should homework be just something added on or, even worse, a punishment.

Reading assignments in the text do make excellent homework assignments, but teachers tend to overwork them. The list of other types of activities that could make homework interesting as well as informative is almost endless and includes

Collateral reading.
Field trips.
Projects.
Committee assignments.
Observation.
Radio listening.
Newspaper study.
Attending meetings, hearings, and so on.
Notebook work.
Problems.
Library work.
Interviews.
Television viewing.
Magazines.
Use of community resources.
Watching films.

There seems to be no excuse for not having a variety of homework experiences.

To repeat, the emphasis in homework should be on quality rather than quantity. It should enrich the classroom study. Avoid homework assignments that are merely more of the same. The more real and significant the homework, the better. At least some of the time pupils should get out into the community to where the action is. Perhaps they can participate in the action; at least they can witness it.

Homework should consist of activities pupils can do on their own. It should be a logical extension of the classroom work that they can do without supervision or teacher assistance. To practice activities of a skill after one has learned the basic technique is excellent, but not if the practice is merely repetition for repetition's sake. Further investigating a problem that has been launched during class discussion or digging up arguments pro or con for class discussion of controversial issues are examples of the most rewarding types of homework activities. With proper encouragement and sufficient variety and recognition of pupil interests, homework can be an avenue for developing permanent interests

that carry over into adult life or even become careers.

Homework should not be used as a substitute for independent study, however. Homework can develop independence, but independent study is something else again. Independent study should be done in the classroom, in the resource center, and at home as a total strategy. It is not a tactic to be added on to ordinary teaching as homework.

Homework is most productive when it is individualized. Pupils who are having difficulty with the subject, who have schedule problems, who have missed school, who have skipped classwork because of distractions of various kinds, who have special interests or special talents, or who are involved in community and school activities will not all benefit optimally from the same homework assignment. Such pupils will profit from special homework assignments. In fact, in so far as possible, the homework of all pupils should be adjusted to fit their individual needs, abilities, aptitude and interests if homework assignments are to be maximally effective. Every pupil should participate in homework activities, but there is no reason why everyone should do the same homework. There are many reasons why at least some of them should do different homework assignments. Long-term or unit assignments that allow pupils to select homework activities from a number of options are excellent because they allow for differences in pupils.

ASSIGNING HOMEWORK

One reason homework assignments fail is that teachers do not pay enough attention to making the assignments. In making an assignment the teacher should ensure that pupils see (1) what they are supposed to do and (2) why they should do it—and the reason for having to do it should be a good one. Furthermore the teacher should make sure the pupils know how to do whatever they must do. Oftentimes pupils get nowhere with new homework because they do not have the concepts or skills basic for doing it. This is one reason why it is a good practice to start homework in supervised-study sessions during class time. If the pupils spend some time in a supervised-study period, the teacher can catch the problems that do arise and help pupils with them before they waste their time trying to do what they are not prepared to do. When assignments are planned together in group-planning sessions, many of these problems can be worked out by the pupils and the teacher together before they start.

EVALUATING HOMEWORK

Written homework presents several peculiar problems. One of them is that the written homework turned in is not always the work of the pupil, but that of his friends or relatives. Although teachers may condemn it as cheating, for parents to help their children with homework, and for friends to share their work with each other is an accepted part of our American culture which no one else, certainly not the pupils nor their parents, feels to be particularly dishonest. Because of this undoubted fact, teachers should assign written homework mainly as practice material from which the pupil may learn whether someone helps him or not. He should not count it much in making up a pupil's mark. Rather the marks should be based upon papers and tests done during class. Nevertheless, even though written homework should not carry much weight in one's marking, it should always be checked. If the homework is not self-checking, the teacher must check it himself. Unless this checking occurs, the practice value may be entirely lost. In fact, unchecked written homework may serve only to grind erroneous techniques and incorrect concepts into the pupils' minds.

Utilizing Supervised-Study Periods

A supervised-study period is an opportunity both for the pupil to study under guidance and for the teacher to supervise and guide study. This can best be done in the regular class. To a lesser extent it can also be done in study halls. Unfortunately, in some schools study halls are looked upon as merely a means for storing students who have no class at the time. This is hardly efficient. Supervised-study periods need real supervision. Merely to sit and watch the pupils is not the function of the teacher in a supervised-study period. If keeping order in the study hall were the sole function, the school would do better to hire a policeman for this duty.

Pupils who attend schools with well-run resource centers[33] have an advantage over other pupils. In the resource center the pupils can usually find the material and help they need. Teachers who work in resource centers are just as responsible for helping pupils with their work as classroom teachers are. When teachers do not do so, the resource center is not much more valuable than the ordinary sterile study hall.

*

A teacher of English says he corrects homework papers carefully about every fifth assignment. The other assignments he merely checks to see if the work has been done. Is this practice proper? Defend your answer.

In what ways might you as a study hall teacher help boys and girls improve their study hall habits?

*

SUMMARY

In spite of many changes, reading remains the heart of the secondary school curriculum. Therefore, every teacher should consider himself to be a teacher of reading. Although reading specialists may teach remedial programs and courses for slow learners, the subject-matter teacher must assume responsibility for developmental reading in his subject.

Selecting the proper reading material is essential. Probably no one text can ever be adequate. To utilize many readings in their classes and to develop techniques for individualizing instruction would usually be more satisfactory. For this reason, full use of the library and the development of classroom libraries is essential.

Boys and girls must be taught how to use books effectively and efficiently. They need to know how and when to skim, how and when to read closely, and how to use the aids provided by the author and publisher. The subject teacher must also help pupils to develop their vocabularies and to read for comprehension. Part of his job is to point out new words and ideas and to suggest methods by which the pupil can get the most from his reading. But most important of all is his obligation to teach pupils to read critically with open minds. For pu-

[33] Otherwise called learning centers or materials centers.

pils to learn to evaluate what they read is just as important as their learning to read with understanding.

Oral reading has been neglected in the secondary schools. If pupils are to be asked to read orally, they should be taught how. On the other hand, teachers must be wary of fads which cause us to emphasize the wrong objectives in our teaching. A recent example is the fad for speed reading. Going through a book quickly is not always a valid goal. Rather, the pupil should learn to adapt his reading attack to the material to be read.

Writing and listening are two of the most important skill areas in academe. Yet the secondary school does little to help its pupils to master the skills in these areas. Teachers should give their pupils plenty of opportunity to learn them and to practice them. In spite of present practice it is the rare pupil who picks up these skills incidentally and so teachers need to teach them directly through the use of prescriptive and inductive instruction, practice activities, and evaluation.

Most secondary school boys and girls need to be taught how to study. The teachers of the various subjects are responsible for seeing that each pupil learns how to study his discipline. To this end each teacher will have to show pupils how to perform a number of scholarly skills, such as analyzing problems, taking notes, and picking the meat out of lectures. Much of this teaching can be done in giving the assignment.

Homework is a problem. One seldom knows how much and what kind of homework will be best. There is no virtue in giving too much homework. Some of the problems of how much homework to give can be solved by means of term assignments in writing. Probably the best kind of homework is that which reinforces old learning or which follows up work which has been well started in class. Giving brand-new work for homework may result in incorrect learning which must be untaught in class later. Because of friends' and parents' tendency to share in the homework process, the teacher should not place too much weight on it in evaluating the pupil. Still, written homework should always be checked.

Suggested Readings for Part V

ALCORN, MARVIN D., JAMES S. KINDER, AND JIM R. SCHUNERT, *Better Teaching in Secondary Schools*, 3rd ed. New York: Holt, Rinehart and Winston, Publishers, 1970. Part III.

ARBUCKLE, DUGALD, *Counseling: Philosophy, Theory and Practice*, 2nd ed. Boston: Allyn & Bacon, Inc., 1970.

ARONSTEIN, LAURENCE W., AND EDWARD G. OLSEN, *Action Learning: Student Community Service Project*. Washington, D.C.: Association for Supervision and Curriculum Development, 1974.

BAMMAN, HENRY A., URSULA HOGAN, AND CHARLES E. GREENE, *Reading Instruction in the Secondary School*. New York: David McKay Co., Inc., 1961.

BANY, MARY A., AND LOIS V. JOHNSON, *Classroom Group Behavior*. New York: Macmillan Publishing Co., Inc., 1964.

BARBER, R. JERRY, AND W. GERALD BARBER, *The Classroom Teacher's Role in Helping Students Develop Study Skills*. El Paso, Texas: B & B Publishing Co., 1972.

BEGGS, DAVID W., III, *Team Teaching: Bold New Venture*. Indianapolis: Unified College Press, Inc., 1964.

BLAIR, GLENN MYERS, *Diagnostic and Remedial Teaching*, 2nd ed. New York: Macmillan Publishing Co., Inc., 1961.

BOOCOCK, SARANE S., AND E. O. SCHILD, *Simulation Games in Learning*. Beverly Hills, Calif.: Sage Publications, Inc., 1968.

BRADFORD, LELAND P., JACK R. GIBB, AND KENNETH D. BENNE, *T Group*

Theory and Laboratory Method. New York: John Wiley & Sons, Inc., 1964.

CALLAHAN, STERLING G., *Successful Teaching in Secondary Schools*, rev. ed. Glenview, Ill.: Scott Foresman and Company, 1971. Chs. 9–11.

CARLSON, ELLIOT, *Learning Through Games.* Washington, D.C.: Public Affairs Press, 1968.

CHESLER, MARK, AND ROBERT FOX, *Role Playing Methods in the Classroom.* Chicago: Science Research Associates Inc., 1966.

CLARK, LEONARD H., ed. *Strategies and Tactics in Secondary School Teaching, A Book of Readings.* New York: Macmillan Publishing Co., Inc., 1968.

Controversial Issues in the Classroom. Washington, D.C.: The National Education Association, 1961.

ELKINS, DEBORAH, *Reading Improvement in the Junior High School.* New York: Teachers College Press, 1963.

FARR, ROGER, AND JAMES LAFFEY, *Reading in the High School*, What Research Says to the Teacher Series, No. 11, rev. ed. Washington, D.C.: Association of Classroom Teachers, 1970.

FLANDERS, NED, *Teaching With Groups.* Minneapolis: Burgess Publishing Co., 1961.

GORDON, ALICE K., *Games for Growth: Educational Games in the Classroom.* Chicago: Science Research Associates Inc., 1970.

GORMAN, ALFRED H., *Teachers and Learners*, 2nd ed. Boston: Allyn & Bacon, Inc., 1974.

GRAMBS, JEAN D., JOHN C. CARR, AND ROBERT M. FITCH, *Modern Methods in Secondary Education*, 3rd ed. New York: Holt, Rinehart and Winston, Publishers, 1970. Chs. 5, 9–11, and 15–17.

GROISSER, PHILIP, *How to Use the Fine Art of Questioning.* Englewood Cliffs, N.J.: Prentice-Hall, Inc., 1964.

HAAS, GLEN, KIMBALL WILES, AND ARTHUR ROBERTS, *Readings in Secondary Teaching.* Boston: Allyn & Bacon, Inc., 1970.

HADDAN, EUGENE E., *Evolving Instruction.* New York: Macmillan Publishing Co., Inc., 1970.

HAFNER, LAWRENCE E., *Improving Reading in Middle and Secondary Schools*, 2nd ed. New York: Macmillan Publishing Co., Inc., 1974.

HARMIN, MERRILL, HOWARD KIRSCHENBAUM, AND SIDNEY B. SIMON, *Clarifying Values Through Subject Matter.* Minneapolis: Winston Press, Inc., 1973.

HILL, WILLIAM FAWCETT, *Learning Through Discussion: Guide for Leaders and Members of Discussion Groups.* Beverly Hills, Calif.: Sage Publications, Inc., 1969.

HIPPLE, THEODORE W., *Secondary School Teaching: Problems and Methods.* Pacific Palisades, Calif.: Goodyear Publishing Co., Inc., 1970.

HOCK, LOUISE, *Group Discussion Processes.* New York: Holt, Rinehart and Winston, Publishers, 1961.

HOOVER, KENNETH H., *The Professional Teacher's Handbook.* Boston: Allyn & Bacon, Inc., 1973. Chs. 6–17 and 24.

——, *Readings on Learning and Teaching in the Secondary School*, 2nd ed. Boston, Allyn & Bacon, Inc., 1971.

Howes, Virgil M., *Informal Teaching in the Open Classroom*. New York: Macmillan Publishing Co., Inc., 1974.

Hunkins, Francis, *Questioning: Strategies and Techniques*. Boston: Allyn & Bacon, Inc., 1972.

Hyman, Ronald T., *Teaching Vantage Points of Study*. Philadelphia: J. B. Lippincott Company, 1968.

——,*Ways of Teaching*, 2nd ed. Philadelphia: J. B. Lippincott Company, 1974.

Inlow, Gail M., *Maturity in High School Teaching*, 2nd ed. Englewood Cliffs, N.J.: Prentice-Hall, Inc., 1970.

Karlin, Robert, *Teaching Reading in High School*, 2nd ed. Indianapolis: The Bobbs-Merrill Co., Inc., 1972.

Keene, Melvin, *Beginning Secondary School Teacher's Guide, Some Problems and Suggested Solutions*. New York: Harper & Row, Publishers, 1969.

Kemp, C. Grattow, *Perspective on the Group Process*. Boston: Houghton Mifflin Company, 1964.

Kruper, Karen R., *Communication Games*. New York: The Free Press, 1973.

Leonard, Joan M., John J. Fallon, and Harold von Arx, *General Methods of Effective Teaching: A Practical Approach*. New York: Thomas Y. Crowell Company, 1972.

Livingston, Samuel, and Clarice S. Stoll, *Simulation Games*. New York: The Free Press, 1972.

McCloskey, Mildred G., *Teaching Strategies and Classroom Realities*. Englewood Cliffs, N.J.: Prentice-Hall Inc., 1971.

Massialas, Byron G., and Jack Zevin, *Creative Encounters in the Classroom*. New York: John Wiley & Sons, Inc., 1967.

Mosston, Muska, *Teaching: From Command to Discovery*. Belmont, Calif.: Wadsworth Publishing Co., Inc., 1972.

Murphy, Gardner, *Freeing Intelligence Through Teaching*. New York: Harper & Row Publishers, 1961.

National Society for the Study of Education, *Development In and Through Reading*, Sixteenth Yearbook, Part I. Chicago: University of Chicago Press, 1961.

——, *Innovation and Challenge in Reading Instruction*, Sixty-seventh Yearbook, Part II. Chicago: University of Chicago Press, 1968.

——, *The Dynamics of Instructional Groups*, Fifty-ninth Yearbook, Part II. Chicago: University of Chicago Press, 1960.

Nelson, R., *Guidance and Counseling*. New York: Holt, Rinehart and Winston, Publishers, 1972.

Nesbit, William A., *Simulation Games for the Social Studies Classroom*. New York: Thomas Y. Crowell Company, 1970.

Niles, Olive S., *Reading Skills for Young Adults*. Glenview, Ill.: Scott Foresman and Company, 1971.

Olson, Arthur V., and Wilbur S. Ames, *Teaching Reading Skills in Secondary Schools*. Scranton, Pa.: International Textbook Co., 1970.

Peters, H., and G. Farwell, *Guidance: A Developmental Approach*, 2nd ed. Chicago: Rand McNally & Company, 1967.

PLATO, *Meno.*

POPPEN, WILLIAM A., AND CHARLES L. THOMPSON, *School Counseling: Theories and Concepts.* Lincoln, Nebr.: Professional Educators Publications, Inc., 1974.

RATHS, LOUIS E., et al., *Teaching for Thinking.* Columbus, Ohio: Charles E. Merrill Publishing Company, 1967.

RATHS, LOUIS E., MERRILL HARMIN, AND SIDNEY B. SIMON, *Values and Teaching.* Columbus, Ohio: Charles E. Merrill Publishing Company, 1966.

"Responsibility and the Active Student Leader," *NASSP Bulletin,* 58:1–65; (October, 1974).

ROOT, J. H., et al., *Diagnostic Teaching, Methods and Materials.* Syracuse University Press, 1965.

SAMALONIS, BERNICE L., *Methods and Materials for Today's High Schools.* New York: Van Nostrand Reinhold Company, 1970. Chs. 9 and 13.

SAMFORD, CLARENCE D., et al., *Secondary Education.* Dubuque, Iowa: William C. Brown Company, Publishers, 1963.

SANDERS, NORRIS M., *Classroom Questions: What Kinds?* New York: Harper & Row Publishers, 1966.

SCHMUCK, RICHARD A., MARK CHESSLER, AND RONALD LIPPITT, *Problem Solving to Improve Classroom Learning.* Chicago: Science Research Associates, Inc., 1966.

SCHMUCK, RICHARD A., AND PATRICIA A. SCHMUCK, *Group Processes in the Classroom.* Dubuque, Iowa: William C. Brown Company, Publishers, 1971.

SHAFTEL, FANNIE R., AND GEORGE D. SHAFTEL, *Role-Playing for Social Values: Decision-Making in the Social Studies.* Englewood Cliffs, N.J.: Prentice-Hall, Inc., 1967.

SHAPLIN, JUDSON T., AND HENRY F. OLDS, JR., *Team Teaching.* New York: Harper & Row, Publishers, 1964.

SIMON, SIDNEY B., LELAND W. HOWE, AND HOWARD KIRSCHENBAUM, *Values Clarification.* New York: Hart Publishing Co., Inc., 1972.

STRANG, RUTH, *Guided Study and Homework,* What Research Says to the Teacher Series, No. 8, rev. ed. Washington, D.C.: Association of Classroom Teachers, 1968.

TORRANCE, E. PAUL, *Encouraging Creativity in the Classroom.* Dubuque, Iowa: William C. Brown Company, 1971.

VI

Materials of
Instruction

Use and
Selection of
Teaching
Materials

14

Mark Hopkins could conduct a school merely by sitting on one end of a log. Most teachers need more to work with than that. In fact, for most teachers the more things they have available, the better they can teach. This chapter will discuss some of the tools and materials that are available and how they may be used to aid instruction.

THE USE OF AUDIO-VISUAL MATERIALS

Among the host of things waiting to be used by the teacher are audio-visual materials of all sorts— films, filmstrips, pictures, maps, globes, charts, models, graphs, mock-ups, terrain boards, snapshots, slides, opaque projectors, microprojectors, overhead projectors, microscopes, chalkboards, phonograph records, sound tapes, radio, television, dramatizations, and realia. This list is not exhaustive. Perhaps you can add to it. With such an abundance of material, the problem becomes how to find what is best for our uses and how to best use what we select.

Purposes of Audio-Visual Materials

Although no longer fashionable, the term *audio-visual aids* is an appropriate one because it describes just what audio-visual materials are—aids to teaching and learning. Audio-visual aids cannot substitute for real teaching, however. They have an entirely different role, a powerful role, it is true, but a role in support of teaching. If one thinks of them and uses them as teaching tools, he will not go far wrong.

Audio-visual materials can help make ideas and concepts clear. As an earlier chapter points out, verbalism is one of the banes of the American secondary school. Audio-visual materials can help raise learning from verbalism to true understanding. The words "rubber bogey buffer bumper" may mean little to the reader, but if he should see a picture or model of one or watch one in operation in a moving picture, the words would probably become meaningful. Making words and phrases real is the greatest potential of audio-visual devices.

Audio-visual materials can also make learning interesting and vivid. A Chinese proverb tells us that one picture is worth a thousand words. Whether or not this is true, good audio-visual materials have eye and ear appeal. By snaring our attention they make learning more effective. Audio-visual materials can be invaluable in promoting motivation and retention.

Using Audio-Visual Materials Properly

In a suburban school a beginning teacher surprised the supervisor by asking, "Is it all right to use filmstrips for my American history class?" "Of course," he replied, "Why not?" "Well," she said, "I tried one last week and the class gave me a lot of trouble. They seemed to think the filmstrip was kid stuff and they acted up something terrible." Yet that same day the supervisor had visited a class —supposedly a class of the toughest youngsters in the school—where the teacher, who was using a filmstrip in science, had excellent interest and at-

tention. The difference seemed to be that one teacher expected the filmstrip to teach itself; the other was really teaching with the film strip as an aid.

Audio-visual aids cannot teach by themselves. They need skillful teaching to make them effective. Just like any other instructional activity, audio-visual aids should be an integral part of the total plan selected because they seem best suited for that point in the lesson. And, as with any other activity, the teacher must prepare the class for the audio-visual activity, guide the class through it, and follow-up after its completion.

*

Why is it impossible to substitute audio-visual material for good teaching?

A certain school always presents moving pictures to all its children on Friday afternoon. Criticize this practice.

*

SELECTING THE AUDIO-VISUAL MATERIAL

In selecting the audio-visual aid, a teacher should consider, in addition to its suitability, such things as visibility, clearness, level of understanding, ease of presentation, and availability of material. To be sure that the aid is effective and appropriate, if it is at all possible, the teacher should try it out before using it with the class. This is particularly important in selecting films, filmstrips, and recordings and in presenting demonstrations. Sometimes films and recordings seem to have little resemblance to their descriptions in the catalog, and a demonstration that does not come off is literally worse than useless.

PLANNING TO USE THE MATERIALS

After having previewed the audio-visual material, the teacher is ready to plan how to make the best use of it. At this point he (1) spells out the objectives that the material will best serve, (2) notes the important terms or ideas presented in the audio-visual material, and (3) identifies any words or ideas that may cause pupils difficulty without some preliminary explanation. He then makes up his plan for introducing, presenting, and following up the audio-visual material. For instance, in introducing and presenting a film clip he may plan to

(1) give a short explanation of the source and setting of the film clip, (2) play the clip through quickly without stopping or commenting, and (3) play the clip again, stopping and analyzing the action in detail. Or he might decide to play it through and discuss it. Or he might decide to stop and analyze the action from time to time in the first run through.

PREPARING FOR THE AUDIO-VISUAL ACTIVITY

Before using an audio-visual activity, the teacher must prepare the pupils for it. This he can do by introducing the audio-visual material. Sometimes a short sentence identifying the aid and its purpose will suffice. At other times, he should spend considerable time discussing the purpose of the activity and suggesting how the pupils can get the most from it. The introduction to a moving picture or a filmstrip, or a recording should point out this purpose and suggest points that pupils should watch for in their viewing or listening.

Not only must the teacher prepare the pupils for the activity, he must also prepare the activity itself. Nothing can be more embarrassing or more disruptive than movies that do not move, demonstrations that do not demonstrate, and other audio-visual fiascos. The competent teacher checks the little things. Does he have enough chalk? Are there extra fuses. Can everyone see the poster? Will the machine run? Attention to detail is especially important in preparing for an audio-visual activity. More than one class has been upset by the lack of a piece of chalk or an extension cord.

Care in preparation is particularly necessary when using projectors and other audio-visual machines. This type of equipment is effective and convenient but hardly foolproof. Before using such devices, the teacher should be sure to check everything possible. If he is going to use slides or transparencies, he should be sure that they are all there and in order. If he is going to use a tape recorder or movie projector, before the class starts he should check out the machine, be certain that it runs properly, and that it is properly adjusted. To be sure that the pupils can see and hear, he should try everything out under conditions similar to those he expects in the class.

GUIDING PUPILS THROUGH AUDIO-VISUAL ACTIVITIES

Instead of relieving the teacher of his responsibility for guiding pupils' learning, the use of the audio-visual aids gives him an opportunity to make his guidance more fruitful. In order that the pupils get the most from the audio-visual aid, the teacher should point out to the pupils what to look for and what to listen for. Often it may be necessary for the teacher to explain to the pupils what they are seeing or hearing. To do this, the teacher would do well sometimes to provide the pupils with a list of questions or a study guide to direct their attention. On other occasions, he should stop to discuss vital relationships on the spot.

*

Suppose you order a film from an audio-visual center and when it arrives it turns out not to be what you had expected. What would you do?

If you were to order a film for a class in your field, what criteria would you use in your selection?

*

FOLLOWING UP AUDIO-VISUAL ACTIVITIES

In spite of the appeal and vividness of audio-visual materials, they cannot prevent some pupils from misunderstanding or missing part of the instruction. The teacher should follow up the activity to bridge the gaps and to clear up misunderstandings. Follow-up also renews the learning and thus increases retention. Furthermore, it has motivational aspects. One danger in using films, filmstrips, television, and radio is that pupils sometimes think of these activities as recreational, and so give scant attention to them. If a teacher follows up activities featuring such audio-visual aids with discussion, review, practice, and testing, he can usually correct this misapprehension and also point up and drive home the learning desired.

USING DIFFERENT KINDS OF AUDIO-VISUAL MATERIALS

Chalkboards, Flannel Boards, Bulletin Boards, and Charts

Now that we have discussed the proper use of audio-visual material in general, let us consider how to use some of them in particular. Perhaps the most commonplace of all audio-visual aids is the old-fashioned blackboard or its brighter modern counterpart, the chalkboard. This device is so omnipresent that many of us fail to think of it as an audio-visual aid at all; yet most teachers would be hard put if they had no chalkboards available.

Closely akin to the chalkboard are bulletin boards, flannel boards, and charts. The chalkboard and flannel board are more flexible and versatile than the bulletin board and charts, although charts can be made more flexible by covering them with transparent acetate and writing on the acetate with china marking pencils. Similarly, large pieces of newsprint, cardboard, or wrapping paper can be used to draw and write on in the same manner as on a chalkboard. Chalkboards and flannel boards can best present material to be exhibited for a short time, while bulletin boards and charts may be used for more permanent exhibits.

CHALKBOARD TECHNIQUES

Perhaps because the chalkboard is so familiar, teachers seem to be careless of their chalkboard techniques. Good chalkboard techniques do exist; they apply also to bulletin boards, flannel boards, and charts. Teachers should remember to use these tools properly.

The first point in the use of the chalkboard is that people cannot learn much from a visual aid they cannot see. It is important for teachers to write legibly, to use portions of the board within the pupils' range of vision, to write large, and to stand out of the pupils' line of sight. In passing, one might add that pointers are useful tools. They do not obstruct the view nearly as much as an arm, a shoulder, or a back.

A second point is that a neat, orderly board aids learning, whereas a cluttered board can be distracting. To get the best out of a chalkboard, bulletin board, or chart, it should be neat and orderly with plenty of white space so that the material to be learned or studied will stand out.

To achieve a neat, uncluttered appearance, and to reduce distractions, one should erase anything that he no longer needs as soon as he is through with it. Too many chalkboards look like attics— full of old junk. If one must put something on the board before it is needed, it should be covered up.

One can pull down a map over it, or cover it with wrapping paper taped to the board with masking tape. Dramatically uncovering the material during a lecture is an excellent way to drive home a point.

To make important ideas stand out, one can use underlining, color, and boxes for emphasis. Stickmen, diagrams, diagramatic maps, and rough drawings can also be useful to illustrate and clarify points.

When drawing on the board, the use of stencils, patterns, or projected images will make drawing easier and more accurate. The projection of maps, pictures, and exercises on the chalkboard makes it possible for pupils to write comments, add details, fill in blanks, and so on, right on the chalkboard.

USING FLANNEL BOARDS, FELT BOARDS, HOOK-AND-LOOP BOARDS, AND MAGNETIC BOARDS

Flannel boards, felt boards, hook-and-loop boards, and magnetic boards can be used in much the same way as the chalkboard. They have certain advantages over the chalkboard, however. The material used on them can be prepared in advance and saved from year to year, and they lend themselves to techniques utilizing immediacy and drama. It has been claimed that they are 50 per cent more effective than chalkboards. With these devices the technique is to prepare materials ahead of time, and then at the propitious moments in the class presentation magically stick them onto the board. Thus as one makes each point in a lesson, he can slap the appropriate word, caption, picture, or what have you, on the flannel board to drive the point home.

BULLETIN BOARD TECHNIQUES

When teachers take advantage of their potentials, bulletin boards can be really effective teaching tools. They can motivate, interpret, supplement, and reinforce one's lessons. They should be always kept up to date and aimed at the current lessons. They should not be used simply to dress up the classroom.

To make a bulletin board effective requires planning. In order to capture the pupils' interest and direct it toward a salient point, teachers should try to arrange each bulletin board and display so that the observer's eye automatically travels toward the center of interest around which the display is focused. One can facilitate this focus by keeping the board or display free from extraneous material, by centering the most significant portion of the display, and by using lines, real or imaginary, to direct the attention from the subordinate items to the central items. In addition, titles and captions are extremely helpful in putting the central idea across. It is also a good idea to have plenty of white space. Crowding materials on a board makes it unattractive and confusing. In the use of bulletin boards, neatness and attractiveness are extremely important, and here especially the teacher should strive for an uncluttered look. Bulletin boards are more effective if they are arranged simply and tastefully. Collages and psychedelic displays can be fun, but they are more likely to obscure the idea than to point it up.

Bulletin boards should be as exciting as possible. For this purpose one can utilize ideas from magazine, newspaper, and television advertising. Eye catchers of various sorts—color, three-dimensional objects, variety, humor, lines of momentum—can be used to enliven the board. Another way to add spice is to combine the bulletin board with a table display. To do this the table is set directly in front of the bulletin board. Colored strings from the table to the bulletin board can be used to tie the two displays together.

USING CHARTS, POSTERS, MAPS, GRAPHS, AND OVERLAYS

The principles applicable to the use of chalkboards, bulletin boards, and flannel boards generally apply to the use of charts, posters, maps, and graphs. As always simplicity, clarity, and dramatic impact are the keystones. In the use of charts, as with chalkboards, it is wise to cover material prepared for display later in the lesson. When this is not done, pupils are liable to pay more attention to aids planned for later use than to the lesson in progress. This procedure can be made even more effective by covering the different sections of a chart or display in such a way that one can uncover one section at a time as it is needed. With a little imagination the teacher can make the procedure highly vivid and dramatic. One can get the same effect with an overhead projector by gradually uncovering the transparency or by adding flip-ons. Another varia-

tion is the flip chart which consists of a large pad of sheets that can be flipped over out of the way to reveal new material as the class proceeds.

Among the charts we may use in our classes are maps and graphs. Although techniques for teaching with maps and graphs are the same as for other types of charts, their use is often ineffective because the pupils do not understand how to read them. The teacher must be sure to teach the language and symbols of graphs and maps to the pupils who do not understand, or the aid will be worthless to them.

The use of overlays can also make the use of charts and maps more effective. An overlay is simply a sheet of transparent material that can be laid over the map or chart so that one can write on it without injuring it. Good ones have been made out of plastic bags such as those used by dry cleaning establishments,[1] old plastic tablecloth covers, plastic drop cloths, and the like. Individual overlays may be used with the maps and charts in books and magazines. The overlay may be preprinted or developed as the class moves along by writing on the plastic with a china marking pencil (grease pencil), or with a felt-tipped marking pen.

Similar results can be obtained by projecting maps and charts on to a chalkboard. Then additional detail can be filled in on the chalkboard itself. This technique is not quite as flexible as the overlay in the opinion of some practitioners.

*

Observe the board work of your teachers and fellow students. What makes it effective? What keeps it from being more effective?

What advantages can you see in the flannel or hook-and-loop board over an ordinary blackboard? Why is this type of board often used in television commercials rather than the chalkboard?

*

Using Projectors

Many types of projection equipment are available. Among them are opaque projectors, slide projectors, filmstrip projectors, overhead projectors,

[1] Very thin plastic sheets such as those used by dry cleaners are difficult to cut. To avoid this trouble, place the plastic on a sheet of paper—newspaper will do—and then cut both with shears. The paper adds enough bulk and stiffness so that the shears will cut the plastic easily.

microprojectors, as well as the ubiquitous motion picture projectors. These machines can bring to the entire class experiences that would otherwise be impossible, or possible only on an individual basis or at great cost. For example, if a teacher wishes to show English money to a social studies class, he can project the images of various English coins on a screen by means of an opaque projector so all can see at once. This technique allows everyone to see the coins without interrupting the presentation, something impossible if the coins should be passed around. Or, if a teacher wishes to show pupils what actually happens during the making of steel, he can show them a film or filmstrip. By using these techniques a teacher can avoid a costly field trip and at the same time actually show pupils by means of annotated drawings, exploded drawings, and magnifications much about the making of steel that the pupils could not see in a real field trip.

THE OPAQUE PROJECTOR

Even though the opaque projector requires almost complete darkness to be effective and even then may be difficult to focus and rather awkward to use, it is an extremely valuable tool. It will project on the screen the image of opaque surfaces which are too small for all pupils to see readily from their seats and it will do so in color. With it a teacher can project not only realia like the coins mentioned previously, but also pictures and pages from books, pamphlets, and magazines. It can also be used to enlarge maps and the like by projecting them on a suitable surface for copying; to project pupils' work for evaluation, correction, or exhibit; and as a basis for pupil reports.

THE OVERHEAD PROJECTOR

Overhead projectors are also extremely useful and versatile. It is not too much to say that every classroom should contain one. They can be used in lighted classrooms without darkening the room, thus allowing pupils to take notes or do other activities not possible in darkened classrooms. Some teachers, for instance, use overhead projection to present quiz questions rather than mimeographing them or writing them on the chalkboard. Moreover,

they are so constructed that one can write, draw, and point things out from the front of the room without turning his back on the class and obstructing the pupils' lines of sight.

The versatility of the overhead projector makes it particularly valuable. Not only are the transparencies easy to make, but they can be prepared in advance and used over and over, thus avoiding the tedious job of copying material on the chalkboard and tying up the board with "Do Not Erase" signs. In addition, transparencies can be placed on top of one another so as to present information in almost any combination one desires. Thus, to an outline map of Europe one could show and compare the national boundaries in 1914, the changes in boundaries after the Versailles treaties, the land grabs by Nazi Germany, and the present boundaries simply by adding and subtracting flip-ons, that is, other transparencies. On the other hand, the overhead projector can be used effectively for on-the-spot recording and illustrating. In one class during a discussion the recorder outlined the course of discussion on a transparency. Later, when a question arose concerning what had been said in the discussion, he was able to project the notes on to the screen for all to see. Such characteristics are valuable for making teaching more effective and at the same time reducing the amount of tedious busy work which sometimes interferes with more important teaching tasks.

*

What advantage does projecting a picture via the opaque projector have over showing the picture itself by passing it around or holding it up in front of the class?

What advantage does the overhead projector have over the chalkboard? The bulletin board?

*

SLIDE AND FILMSTRIP PROJECTORS

Slide projectors and filmstrip projectors can be discussed simultaneously because the two are often combined into one machine. After all, a filmstrip is little more than a series of slides joined together on a strip of film. The filmstrip has the advantage of having been put together by an expert in a ready-made sequence. Slides are more versatile, but using them requires more careful planning by the teacher. Just one slide out of order or upside down can throw a well-conceived lesson out of step.

Some filmstrips come with recorded commentary and sound effects. Although these are usually quite impressive, often teachers would rather provide their own commentary as the filmstrip progresses. Of course, if he wishes, a teacher can prerecord his own commentary and sound effects and synchronize them to a filmstrip or to a series of slides. Utilizing sound with slides is usually enhanced by the use of an automatic projector. If the teacher can influence the choice of slide projectors to be furnished him, he would do well to insist on a projector that will operate both manually and automatically.

Thirty-five millimeter filmstrip projectors and 2×2 projectors are small enough and simple enough to operate for small-group or individual use. For individual or small-group viewing the image can be thrown onto a sheet of cardboard no larger than the projector itself. It seems surprising that more teachers have not taken advantage of this capability of the thirty-five millimeter filmstrip and slide projectors.

Another machine, which seems to have been lost in the rush onward to new technology, is the $3\frac{1}{4} \times 4$ magic lantern. This machine was a mainstay of the audio-visual department of years ago and still has great potential. Its glass slides give very good fidelity and can be made easily. Those machines should not be left to gather dust in storerooms. Recently new $3\frac{1}{4} \times 4$ projectors with remote control devices have been introduced to the market.

MICROPROJECTION

The number of pupils who never see what it is they are supposed to see through the microscope is probably astronomical. The microprojector can eliminate for practical purpose much of this difficulty by enlarging and projecting the image in the microscope's field onto a screen so that all the pupils can see the image and so that the teacher can point out salient features to everyone at once. Another technique that gives much the same result is to take pictures of the slide through the microscope. This technique is not difficult. It is merely a matter of screwing a compatible thirty-five milli-

meter camera to the microscope and taking pictures by means of the optics of the microscope. The resulting 2×2 slides can be projected on a screen. In much the same way transparencies for overhead projection can be made with a Polaroid camera.

Preparing such materials takes time, but almost always they are worth the effort. In many instances much of the preparation of such aids can be done by pupils, thus giving them valuable learning experiences and saving time for the teacher.

A Word About Moving Pictures

At present, along with television, motion pictures are the most glamorous of audio-visual aids— so much so that many teachers depend upon films to do what these aids cannot do. To be effective, motion pictures must be selected with care, previewed, introduced, and followed up. Remember, a darkened classroom is an excellent place for older students to sleep and for younger pupils to commit mischief.

PRESENTING THE FILM

Checking on the equipment is essential when using motion pictures because the motion picture projector can be a particularly cranky machine. Running a little of the film immediately before the presentation to be sure all is working is a wise precaution. Once the film is in progress, projectionists should not sit back and relax; supervision of the film by checking the tension, loops, and the like can pay dividends, although improvements on newer machines have eliminated some problems of this sort.

In this day of sound movies and television we sometimes forget that the silent motion pictures can also be an effective audi-visual aid. As a matter of fact, the silent picture is sometimes more useful than the sound movie because the teacher can comment as the movie progresses, thus bringing out the salient points.

It is never wise to try to comment on a film by outshouting a sound track. Pupils cannot listen both to their teacher and to the moving picture. Nine times out of ten such comments will confuse, rather than clarify, the point a teacher wants to make unless he stops the machine before he speaks. Good planning calls for taking care of such explanations before starting the projector. In this respect the silent film has another advantage over the sound film. A teacher can emphasize and clarify by stopping the film and repeating a particular sequence as he explains and amplifies it much more easily with silent than with sound film.

TWO RECENT INNOVATIONS

In the past the use of the motion picture in the classroom has been plagued by two distinct disadvantages. One was that the projection was designed solely for large-group instruction; the other that the films had to be shown in darkened classrooms. Neither condition needs to obtain any longer. New self-threading individual eight millimeter projection devices make motion picture projection a means for providing for individual differences, and new rear projection arrangements allow moving picture projection in lighted rooms. Increased use of these devices can make motion picture projection considerably more effective.

*

What misconceptions are liable to rise from the use of aids such as the moving pictures? How can these be avoided?

What steps should you as a teacher go through before presenting a film to a class?

*

MOVING PICTURE PRODUCTION

With modern equipment production of one's own moving pictures has become relatively easy. With help pupils can carry all the tasks necessary for completing interesting, productive films. However, because film production is a highly technical subject, teachers interested in producing films should consult their school audio-visual or media-center directors, and such books as Kemp's *Planning and Producing Audio-Visual Materials*[2] and technical manuals on the subject.

[2] Jerome E. Kemp, *Planning and Producing Audio-Visual Materials* (San Francisco: Chandler Publishing Company, 1968).

Other Audio-Visual Material

USE OF PICTURES

Pictures of all sorts are available for classroom use. Pictures can be found in many places. Especially useful are the pictures in textbooks. In addition, teachers should collect as many pictures as they can. Not only are the pictures useful aids, but collecting them can also be fun. Specimens and other realia having to do with one's subject can be equally valuable and likewise fun to collect. In fact, numerous teachers have developed picture and specimen collecting into lifetime hobbies.

In selecting pictures for classroom use, teachers should consider such questions as

1. Does it fit the purpose?
2. Is it relevant and important to the lesson?
3. Is it accurate and authentic.
4. Can its point be easily understood?
5. Is it interesting?
6. Is the size, quality, color, such as to make it easily visible?

No particular technique is necessary in the use of these materials. However, if he uses a visual aid, the teacher should remember to display it in such a way that each pupil can see it clearly. The teacher should also remember to point out whatever the pupils are to learn from the aid. Here it is probably more productive to ask questions than to pontificate. Pictures can be useful for class discussion or as springboards for further study and research. Oftentimes an entire lesson can be built around a single picture. One danger to avoid is that of exhibiting pictures just because one has them. Although showing pupils a collection may be splendid fun, even for the pupils, one should be sure that the material is pertinent before using precious class time on it.

Another practice to avoid is passing pictures and other materials around the room so that pupils may look at them while the lecture, recitation, or discussion continues. Pupils cannot pay attention to two things at once. While pupils are examining the audio-visual aid they cannot concentrate on the lesson. A much better practice is to utilize the opaque projector to throw an image of the picture or object on the screen where all can see it at once.

Another alternative is to display or to pass the material around during a laboratory or work session when it is less liable to disrupt the learning process.

MODELS AND REPLICAS

Models, replicas, and sand tables also make admirable audio-visual materials, and pupils can help in constructing them. In using pupil help in building aids of any sort, teachers should be wary of two dangerous faults: one, that the pupil may spend so much time creating the aid that he neglects the things he can learn from it; and two, that inaccurate models may give pupils erroneous concepts. Teachers should be particularly on guard against incorrect proportions, historical anachronisms, and other details that can mislead pupils. Whenever it is necessary to distort in order to be effective, as is often the case in preparing three-dimensional maps, the teacher should be sure to warn the pupils of the inaccuracies.

TAPE RECORDERS AND RECORD PLAYERS

By means of recording one can bring to class the voice of an eminent mathematician discussing mathematical theory, a famous actor reading an ancient or modern play, a statesman discussing foreign policy, or a symphony orchestra playing Rimski-Korsakov. Additionally, with modern equipment, one can record a class discussion and in a playback use the recording as a basis for analyzing and evaluating the effectiveness of the discussion. Pupils can use tape recordings to analyze their own speech habits. Often after studying tape recordings of their own voices, they can identify and correct their errors. The language laboratory is based on this technique. Teachers interested in providing for individual differences and individualizing classes can prerecord assignments and lessons for certain individuals to do with the tape recorder while the teacher is busy with other groups and individuals. Truly, the possibilities of tape recording are almost limitless.

*

What audio-visual aids are available to you? What aids can you create? How could you use them? Survey the situation. You will undoubtedly find a wealth of material you had not thought of before. Consider such things as pictures, moving pictures, slides, microprojectors, chalkboards, bulletin boards, charts, graphs, diagrams, demonstrations, schematic representations, opaque projectors, records, tapes, models, maps, globes, filmstrips, radio, television, felt boards, overhead projectors, tachistoscopes, displays, exhibits, aquaria, terraria, stereoptican slides, sand tables, and realia.

How can realia be used? Is the real object, if available, always the best aid to learning? Justify your answer.

*

MULTIMEDIA

Various media can and should be used to reinforce each other. Teachers use mixed media naturally, when, for instance, they use pictures to illustrate a lecture. But teaching can be made more effective by consciously utilizing multimedia presentations to make the learning process more interesting and to drive home understanding.

Teachers can mix media by using them sequentially or simultaneously. Thus in a geography class, one might move through a carefully planned sequence involving the use of several media, e.g., a map, a pictorial representation, a model, and a film. In each step of this sequence the new medium would build upon the learning brought about by the preceding medium. Or it might be more effective to present the media simultaneously. Thus one might teach the geography lesson by presenting a picture, model, and contour map of the terrain simultaneously, moving back and forth from one to another of the media comparing and analyzing as one builds up the concept one is after. Examples of simultaneous presentations using two screens suggested by Haney and Ullmer include the following uses:

1. To hold an overview shot or complete picture on one screen, such as a laboratory experiment arrangement, while moving to a series of detailed close-up pictures on the other.
2. To show two pictures side by side for comparison, such as two works of art, each on a separate slide.
3. To hold a title of a group classification on one screen, with a series of example pictures on the other screen, providing a sort of visual paragraphing.

4. To show a line drawing or labeled schematic diagram of an object or organism next to an actual photograph.
5. To show three to six different photographs to convey a range of examples; any or all can be changed as desired.
6. To display a picture while showing a series of questions or factual notes on a second screen.[3]

Obviously in multi-media presentations the media to be used must be compatible and complimentary. Unless they work together to bring about one's teaching objectives, there is no point in using them. Misused multimedia presentations can confuse rather than clarify.

*

Think of at least a half dozen ways you could mix media in teaching your classes.

*

TELEVISION

AN UNREALIZED POTENTIAL

Schools have yet to utilize the full potentialities of television and radio. Perhaps this is not to be wondered at, because so far after fifty years the remarkable possibilities of the motion picture are far from being realized in our schools. The potential of these devices is tremendous—at first glance almost limitless. Through these techniques the pupil can be present at the critical moments of history, he can see government in the making, he can watch great experiments in science, he can visit the farthest corners of the earth, he can hear famous symphonies, and he can see great plays and operas. All these can be brought to him through television, radio, motion pictures, and recordings. These devices can bring to the pupils great experiences, but these experiences cannot take the place of teaching.

Certain school systems are conducting interesting experiments in which master teachers teach large classes by means of television. In such classes it is possible to bring to pupils teaching that they would not otherwise get. Still, television teaching does not relieve the classroom teacher of his responsibility for instruction. Even when a master teacher conducts a television lesson, the classroom teacher still has to go through his standard routine. He must plan, he must select, he must introduce, he must guide, he must follow up, in order to fill in the gaps, correct misunderstandings, and guide the pupils' learning.

ROLE OF EDUCATIONAL TELEVISION

Probably educational television's basic role should be to augment, enrich, and point up the curriculum by bringing to the school, and to the general public, experiences beyond the scope and capabilities of the ordinary classroom. According to a committee of the Northern Region of New Jersey Association for Supervision and Curriculum Development (NJASCD):

> only in unusual circumstances should educational television attempt to take on the role of classroom instruction. Rather, it should concentrate on making available to the schools and to the general public the things which it can do best. In general, these are the programs of general and special interest which are valuable to the homeviewer as well as being useful to teachers of various disciplines and grade levels to enhance their instruction. In the majority of programing, the programs should not be aimed at specific classes but should consist of experiences of more general nature from which teachers may dip as seems necessary and desirable to them.
> In certain cases instructional television is necessary and desirable. Examples of such programs are television courses for adults and other persons not regularly enrolled in school programs, and courses which are beyond the capabilities of the ordinary curriculum because of lack of facilities, competent teaching personnel, or sufficient number of pupils to justify a class.[4]

Using General Television Programs

When matters of great national or international significance are being telecast, it may be wise to stop

---

[3] John B. Haney and Eldon J. Ullmer, *Educational Media and the Teacher* (Dubuque, Iowa: William C. Brown Company, Publishers, 1970), p. 102.

[4] John Farinella, Robert Frazier, and Leonard H. Clark, *Guidelines for Educational Television,* Report of The Committee on Staff Utilization, Northern Region, New Jersey Association for Supervision and Curriculum Development, Spring 1963, unpublished. By permission.

other class activities and witness the event. When Lieutenant Commander Shepard and Lieutenant Colonel Glenn made their first space flights, in many schools all other activities ceased while the pupils viewed the telecasts of these events. Such activities are well worthwhile particularly when the telecast is skillfully introduced and followed up.

Often telecasts of significant events occur at times which do not allow direct classroom viewing. This difficulty can be circumvented by recording the program and playing significant parts during school hours. Recent advances in videotape technology are making it possible for schools to do their own video recording relatively cheaply. However, much of the material telecast by commercial and educational television stations is copyrighted and may not be available for rebroadcast to schools without permission of the copyright holder.

Another technique is to assign home viewing of telecasts. Because not all pupils have television sets available to them, it may be necessary to make such assignments selectively, with certain individuals or committees responsible for reporting them. At times, in order to get wider experiences to share in class, it may be wise to ask different pupils to view the coverage on different channels. As with other assignments, television viewing assignments should be clear so that the pupils know what to look for and what they are trying to do. The use of a bulletin board to list assignments with attendant problems, questions, and projects, has proved successful for many teachers.

Determining how best to use educational and cultural television programs can be something of a problem. Television sections of local newspapers and television magazines carry descriptions of featured programs that the teacher can use as a basis for lesson planning and assignments. Frequently, professional magazines carry study guides for exceptional programs. Sometimes teachers can secure information about both the proposed scheduling and the content of coming programs in advance by writing to local television stations or to the television networks. When such information is available, classroom activities can be planned around certain television programs, or the planned class sequence can be altered in order to take advantage of exceptional television opportunities.

Instructional Television

Too many pupils have learned well in television classes for anyone to continue to doubt whether television can be used to teach. The question now concerns what the most efficient and effective ways to teach are and where television classes should fit into the picture, if at all.

The television staff and the classroom teachers represent a team. The classroom teacher represents the heart of the team. The television teacher, if there is one, should be a consultant and resource person. The classroom teachers should determine how the television should be used and, as far as classroom-beamed telecasts are concerned, what the aims and content of the telecast should be. In other words, the classroom teacher should enter into the planning and evaluating of the television offerings. Teachers should inform television presenters and directors of program effectiveness and let them know what they want and expect from future programs.[5]

The Anaheim (California) City School District *Instructional T.V. Guide* gives a good example of the television teaching team in action.[6]

> The studio teacher indicates by the way questions and ideas are presented, the type of response that is expected of pupils observing. (He may say, "What famous man, that we have heard about before, died at the Alamo?" He may say, "Can you *think* of other types of plants that adapt to their environment in a different way?" The first question should be answered audibly by pupils in the classroom with the teacher guiding and encouraging the response. The second question requires a covert response from each pupil which the classroom teacher may wish to bring up after the telecast for further discussion.) Types of response that detract from the intimacy of the studio teacher-pupil relationship should be avoided. (The studio teacher might state, "Let's *think* about why the pioneers went west." The classroom teacher responds, "Mary, what do you think?" Mary may or may not give a correct response. The teacher in the studio cannot anticipate the timing for an oral response to this type of question and the attention and rapport exist-

[5] Farinella, Frazier, and Clark, op. cit.
[6] James D. Brier, editor, *Instructional T.V. Guide*, Anaheim City School District, Anaheim, California, 1961, p. 18. By permission.
Much of the following discussion of the duties and responsibilities of television and classroom teachers has been adapted from this excellent manual.

ing between studio teacher and pupil is divided during the discussion in the classroom.) *Participation is an important factor in learning;* it must be developed, encouraged, and controlled by both studio and classroom teacher working together during the telecast.

DUTIES OF TELEVISION TEACHERS

The television teacher should be a person of exceptional competence in his field, who possesses special talents suitable to the medium. Because of his strategic role, much of the planning of the television course falls on him. Study or lesson guides for the use of pupils and teachers, and studio scripts for the actual television lesson must be prepared well enough ahead so that the classroom teachers can make full use of them. Planning television lessons is more critical than planning ordinary lessons. They require much attention to detail. The television teacher cannot afford to leave loose ends dangling to be picked up on the way, nor can he leave his lesson plan loose so as to feel his way from the class response.[7] He must be especially careful about his timing and pacing. The lesson should not be either too fast or too slow. Somehow it should give the pupils a chance to react and give at least the appearance of teacher-pupil interaction. Until new techniques that will allow for real interaction between television teacher and individual pupils are developed, the television teacher must rely on such devices as rhetorical questions and pauses for this purpose.

The television teacher must also allow for the possibility that some pupils may not understand the first time. In a large class or a television audience the teacher must cope with the problem of psychological noise—that is, the tendency of people in large groups not to hear all that is presented. To mitigate this problem the teacher must find ways of repeating points again and again without boring the pupils who have already caught on. Clever use of visuals will often help solve the dilemma. In any case, television teachers should make optimum use of visuals. After all, the medium is television.

---

[7] Not being able to feel the class reaction is a hardship to at least some television teachers. To try to overcome this problem, some of them pretape their lessons and then during the telecast sit in the back of the classroom to watch pupils' reactions to their presentation. Because classes differ, this technique, although valuable, is not entirely satisfactory.

In addition to planning and teaching, television teachers must support the classroom teachers in other ways. They should listen carefully to the classroom teachers' suggestions, criticisms, and comments, and attempt to put teacher suggestions into the television lessons. As often as they can they should get into the classroom in order to become better acquainted with the teachers and pupils and to get something of the feeling of the classroom.

Finally, the television teacher has the important job of building public support of the television teaching program. In this role he must be a public relations agent going out to meet the parents, teachers, and the public in general so as to inform them of the program and solicit from them their support.

THE ROLE OF THE CLASSROOM TEACHER

All in all, the television teacher's role is an exacting one, but it is not as important as that of the classroom teacher, for it is he who carries the real load.

Before the television class begins, the classroom teacher prepares the setting. He must see to it that the classroom environment is arranged properly, that the necessary provisions for easily carrying out the routines of classroom management and administration have been made, and that the pupils are psychologically and intellectually ready for the lesson to be telecast. To accomplish these missions the classroom teacher must be familiar with the television teacher's plan. He should, therefore, study carefully the study guides, studio scripts, and course of study well before each lesson. The information in these documents will tell him what materials he needs to have ready and give him clues on how to best prepare the pupils for the class.

Any materials needed during the telecast must be ready and waiting before the telecast. So that the pupils will be ready also, the classroom teacher should discuss the lesson to be televised with them. In this discussion the pupils should learn something of the purpose of the television lesson—what they can expect to see and hear and what they can expect to learn. At this time the teacher can teach the pupils new vocabulary they may need and fill in any serious voids evident in their background.

This last responsibility implies the necessity for the classroom teacher to continually analyze and evaluate the present knowledge and abilities of his pupils both individually and collectively.

During the telecast the classroom teacher must continue his role as guide to learning. He must circulate among the pupils to determine whether they understand and are proceeding correctly. Sometimes he will have to supplement the television teacher's instruction, especially in work-type lessons during which the classroom teacher may need to correct and help pupils. More frequently he will prefer to take notes of pupil reactions—particularly evidences of lack of understanding or misunderstanding—for use in follow-up activities after the telecast.

Part of his follow-through during the telecast is the handling of questions put by the television teacher. Some of the questions asked will require no overt response, of course. Others should be answered aloud. The classroom teacher's plan for the television lesson should include provisions for handling these questions. A common approach is for all pupils to answer them in unison since calling on individual pupils creates a problem of timing.

AFTER THE TELEVISION CLASS

The follow-up after the television class is fully as important as the class itself. One of the most common faults in all teaching is the failure to follow through to clinch what was to be taught and then to move on to capitalize on what has been learned in a new teaching-learning situation. Class discussion following a television program might well center on What did we learn? Was this learning important? If so, why? If not, why not? and What do we do next in view of what we have already learned?

The classroom teacher should check the pupils' learning against the objectives of the lesson and reteach if necessary. He should also provide additional experiences to enrich and carry forward the learning in the television class. Since creative activity is so necessary to effective learning and since television lessons are liable to be largely passive, classroom teachers should consider the desirability of utilizing many projects, discussions, experiments, investigations, writing, and similar activities that allow pupils to engage actively in their own learning.

Physical Setup for Television Viewing

Pupils can benefit from television only if they can hear and see clearly. Both picture and sound must be kept at a reasonably high fidelity, free from interference. For that reason, teachers must pay particular attention to the tuning of the receivers and do everything in their power to see to it that the sets are properly maintained. Except in extremely unusual circumstances one should not attempt to use television in classrooms located where the reception is marginal.

To ensure good viewing one needs to observe a few rules of thumb for the physical arrangement of the classroom whether large or small. The following rules are more or less generally accepted by experts in the field.

1. Use 21- to 24-inch screen television sets with front directional speakers.
2. Place the sets so that each pupil has an unobstructed line of sight.
3. The screen should not be more than thirty feet from any pupil.
4. The set should be about five and one half feet from the floor (that is, about the same height as the teacher's face).
5. The vertical angle of sight from any pupil to the set should never be more than 30°; the horizontal angle, never more than 45°.
6. The room should be kept lighted so that pupils can see to take notes.
7. No glare should reflect from the screen. To reduce glare one can
   a. Move the set away from the windows.
   b. Tilt the set downward.
   c. Provide the set with cardboard blinders.
8. The sound should come from front directional speakers. If several sets are in use in one room, it may be better to use the sound from only one set than to have it come from several sources. In large rooms for large-class instruction it may be more satisfactory to run

the sound from one set through a public address system.

9. Pupils should have adequate surface space for writing.

10. To allow for quick, easy transition from the telecast, television classrooms should be fitted out with adequate audio-visual equipment, display space, and filing and storage space.

*

What seem to you to be the arguments for or against the use of instructional television?

Criticize the position taken by the committee of the Northern Region of the NJASCD.

What methods could you take as a classroom teacher to keep television instruction on a personal basis? What could you do as a television teacher?

*

PRINTED AND DUPLICATED MATERIALS

Pamphlets, Brochures, and Other Reading Matter

Reading materials are discussed in another chapter. Let it suffice here for us to point out the tremendous amount of materials that are available for the asking or for a small fee—one particularly rich source being the Federal and state governmental agencies. The Government Printing Office lists thousands of pamphlets and books for sale, and the various federal agencies distribute great amounts of interesting informative material for the asking. Other sources are large industrial and commercial firms; foreign governments; supragovernmental agencies, such as the United Nations, UNESCO, and NATO; civic organizations, such as the League of Women Voters; and professional organizations, such as the National Education Association.

Newspapers and magazines are a constant source of material for every one of the curriculum fields. Pertinent articles in them should be included in reading assignments. In addition, newspapers and periodicals can furnish the material for bulletin board displays and other visual aids. Gathering suitable material of this type of display can be delegated to a class committee. Sometimes this committee can combine its efforts with those of the bulletin board committee to search out pertinent material and display it effectively.

Workbooks and Exercises

Many textbook publishers provide workbooks for use by pupils in secondary school classes. Lately these books have suffered from poor reputations that are often well deserved. Workbooks need not be bad, however. Properly written and well used, they can be very helpful. Whatever is true of them can also be said of teacher-prepared exercises.

When properly used, workbooks and duplicated exercises make it possible for teachers to allow pupils to pace themselves and so provide for the differences in pupils. There is no need for all pupils to do the same exercise at the same time. As a matter of fact there is no real reason why all pupils need use the same workbook. It is quite possible to use a workbook designed for use with one text with another one. However, when so doing the teacher should take care to see that the selections used are compatible. When differences between the text and a workbook may cause confusion in the pupils, a little editing and cutting may make the content match well enough to avoid any serious difficulty.

One of the complaints against workbooks is that they encourage rote learning and discourage creative thought. These criticisms are often justified when the workbook consists of sentences from the text which the pupil completes by searching the book until he finds the missing words. Such workbooks and workbook assignments should be avoided. However, workbooks can also present problems, review material, and study guides which elicit much more than simple rote learning.

As with anything else, assignments in workbooks and locally produced materials must be followed up. Reinforcement is probably better if the follow-up is immediate. In some instances good results can be achieved by providing answer sheets so that the pupil can check his own work himself. In other cases the workbook problems lend themselves better to follow-up in classroom discussion or by the teacher's going over the problem in class. *In no case should the teacher leave the workbook work completely unchecked until he can find a propitious moment at some later time to collect and correct it.*

Mimeographed and Dittoed Material

In the better school systems, the teachers seem to provide their pupils with great amounts of duplicated materials. These materials should be used in just the same way as printed materials of the same type.

Teachers often give such material to the pupils to keep, or to use up at the time. In a good many cases this practice is desirable. On the other hand, preparing mimeographed and dittoed material costs time and money. There is no reason why duplicated exercises and supplementary reading materials should not be used again and again if the teacher takes precautions. Therefore, the teacher may wish to have the pupils write their answers to exercises and problems in a notebook, or on a separate sheet of paper, rather than on the materials directly. If one binds the duplicated, supplementary reading matter in some sort of stiff cover, it will be quite durable. Construction paper or manila file folders are excellent for this puprose. Pamphlets made this way will last longer if the copy is stapled to the cover rather than fastened with paper fasteners.

Some schools provide teachers enough secretarial service to prepare stencils and run off everything that teachers can wish for. More usually the job of preparing supplementary materials falls to the teacher himself. Consequently, as soon as he can, the prospective teacher should learn how to prepare and run off mimeograph stencils and spirit duplicator masters. Neither the mimeograph machine nor the spirit duplicator is very difficult to operate and the latter is frequently made available for teacher use in the teachers' workrooms of many schools. One merit of the spirit duplicator is that master copies can be made easily by hand. This characteristic makes it a boon for the nonexpert typist and for the teacher who needs to reproduce drawings, figures, and other devices not easily done on a typewriter.

*

It is not too soon for you to start collecting material for the classes you may sometime teach. The student who picks up and saves all the pertinent material he can find will have a start toward becoming a well-equipped teacher.

Examine several workbooks. Do they seem to encourage independent learning or rote memorizing? Examine teacher-prepared material in the same way. How can these materials be made to encourage independent thought, if they do not?

*

TEACHING MACHINES, PROGRAMED LEARNING,[8] AND COMPUTERS

The teaching machine differs from the ordinary audio-visual aid in that it actually does some of the teaching. In effect, what the machine does is to present and follow up a series of lessons, that is to say, teaching programs. In this sense the machine is a mechanical tutor that works with the pupil in a one-to-one relationship, although in reality it is the teaching program that does the actual teaching.[9] The teaching machine, whether it be a complex computer or a simple, programed text, is simply the delivery system.

Characteristics of Teaching Programs

There are two basic types of teaching programs, the linear and the intrinsic programs. Computer-assisted instruction is simply a highly sophisticated form of intrinsic programing. Well-made programs of every type have the following characteristics.

1. The objectives are clearly defined.
2. The pupil progresses toward these objectives by means of a carefully planned sequence of steps.
3. The sequence and the items in that sequence have been rigorously tested and revised to ensure that the program does in fact lead to the objective.
4. The pupil is active; it is he who does the learning.
5. The pupil assumes the responsibility for learning and sets his own pace.

[8] The state of confusion concerning programing is illustrated by the disagreement concerning the spelling of the word. Some authorities double the *m*; others do not.

[9] Students interested in the various types of machines should consult one of the numerous works on the subjects, for example, Chapter III of Lawrence Stolurow's *Teaching by Machine*, Cooperative Research Monograph No. 6, OE-34010, Office of Education, U.S. Department of Health, Education and Welfare (Washington, D.C.: U.S. Government Printing Office, 1961).

6. The program provides immediate feedback, so the pupil knows the results of his activity in one step before he goes on to the next.

Basically, the procedure in both types of programs is the same.

1. The machine or program presents the pupil with something to learn and then asks him to answer the question or solve a problem.

2. The pupil attempts to answer the question or solve the problem.

3. The machine (or program) informs the pupil whether he is correct or not and tells him what to do next.

4. In the case of the linear program, the pupil moves on to the next item. Linear programs provide no room for error. Instead they consist of easy steps from item to item so that the pupil will always answer correctly thus reinforcing the correct answer and learning by operant conditioning. In the case of the intrinsic program, including computer-assisted instruction, the answer to one question determines what the next question or activity will be. If the pupil makes an error, the program or machine reteaches him and asks him the same or similar question or problem again to determine if the pupil now understands. In a sense, by his responses the pupil builds his own program under the machine's guidance as he goes along. With its great versatility, a computer can be programed so that it will be extremely responsive to the pupil's needs.

Using Teaching Programs and Programed Instruction

Because of its flexibility and because pupils work on programs alone rather than in groups, programed instruction, especially computer programed instruction, makes it possible to provide truly individualized programs for the pupils. In addition, because it can actually teach information and skills, programed instruction can free the teacher from some of his more mundane teaching duties. While pupils are working on their programs, the teacher can work with other pupils individually or in small groups. Therefore teachers would do well to use instructional programs and machines as a basis for individualizing instruction, as a me-

dium for teaching pupils basic skills and information, as a way of providing pupils the background necessary for discussion, inquiry, and problem solving activities, and as a means for freeing themselves so that they can give pupils individual attention and concentrate on higher learnings.

Although programs will teach, one cannot expect to turn the pupils over to the machine and have it solve all one's problems. Even the most sophisticated of systems will require skilled classroom teachers always on the job. They are needed to

1. Guide and supervise the pupils.

2. Continually check the pupils' progress.

3. Select suitable programs for individual pupils and see to it that the pupils go through these programs correctly.

4. Provide follow-up activities. (Programed activities make good springboards, but teachers must provide the follow-up.)

5. Provide other types of instruction. (Programed teaching should not be overused. Some pupils find it boring. Besides too much of even a good thing quickly palls.)

6. Evaluate pupil progress. (Programed material is learning and practical material. It is not a test. It should never be graded. Teachers must provide other criteria—tests, papers, class discussion, or what have you—to use as a basis for evaluation and reporting.)

*

What reply would you make to the critics who complain that programed learning is too mechanistic and impersonal?

What types of programs seem best to you for use in your classes?

*

SOURCES OF TEACHING MATERIALS

Occasionally, teachers defend dull, humdrum teaching on the grounds that the school administration will not give them adequate materials. Usually such complaints are merely instances of teachers passing the buck, although they may be signs of incompetence; for at the expense of a little ingenuity and initiative, boundless supplies of materials are available to even the poorest schools.

The following paragraphs attempt to show how to find them.

Where to Find Materials

In the first place, materials for learning can be found almost everywhere. Among good sources of information telling where to find and how to use materials of instruction are curriculum guides and source (resource) units, and references such as those making up the following list. Note that this list is not complete but simply suggestive.[10]

The American Film Review. St. Davids, Pa.: The American Educational and Historical Film Center, Eastern Baptist College.

An Annotated Bibliography of Audiovisual Materials Related to Understanding and Teaching the Culturally Disadvantaged. Washington, D.C.: National Education Association.

Annual Paperbound Book Guide for High Schools. New York: R. R. Bowker Company.

Bibliography of Free and Inexpensive Materials for Economic Education. New York: Joint Council on Education.

Civil Aeronautics Administration, *Sources of Free and Low-Cost Materials.* Washington, D.C.: U.S. Dept. of Commerce.

CLARK, LEONARD H., *Teaching Social Studies in Secondary Schools: A Handbook.* New York: Macmillan Publishing Co., Inc., 1973. Lists sources and addresses.

Educational Film Guide. New York: The H. W. Wilson Company.

Educators' Guide to Free Films. Randolph, Wis.: Educators' Progress Service.

Educators' Guide to Free Film-Strips. Randolph, Wis.: Educators' Progress Service.

Educators' Guide to Free and Inexpensive Teaching Materials. Randolph, Wis.: Educators' Progress Service.

Educators' Guide to Free Social Studies Materials. Randolph, Wis.: Educators' Progress Service.

Film Guide for Music Educators. Washington, D.C.: Music Educators National Conference.

Free and Inexpensive Learning Materials. Nashville, Tenn.: Division of Surveys and Field Services, George Peabody College for Teachers.

FREEDOM, FLORENCE B., AND ESTHER L. BERG, *Classroom Teachers' Guide to Audio-Visual Material.* Philadelphia: Chilton Book Company, 1971.

Index to Multi-Ethnic Teaching Materials and Teaching Resources. Washington, D.C.: National Educational Association.

LEMBACHER, JAMES L., *Feature Films on 8mm and 16mm,* 3rd ed. New York: R. R. Bowker Company, 1971.

List of Free Materials Available to Secondary School Instructors. New York: The Educational Services of Dow Jones and Company, Inc.

Materials List for Use by Teachers of Modern Foreign Languages. New York: Modern Foreign Language Association.

MATHIES, LORRAINE, *Information Sources and Services in Education.* Bloomington, Ind.: The Phi Delta Kappa Educational Foundation, 1973.

MILLER, BRUCE, *Sources of Free and Inexpensive Pictures for the Classroom.* Riverside, Calif.: The Bruce Miller Publications.

——, *Sources of Free Travel Posters.* Riverside, Calif.: The Bruce Miller Publications.

——, *So You Want to Start a Picture File.* Riverside, Calif.: The Bruce Miller Publications.

National Tape Recording Catalog. Washington, D.C.: National Education Association.

New Educational Materials. Englewood Cliffs, N.J.: Citation Press.

Some Sources of 2 x 2 Inch Color Slides. Rochester, N.Y.: Eastman Kodak.

Sources of Free and Inexpensive Pictures for the Classroom. Randolph, Wis.: Educators' Progress Service.

Sources of Slides and Filmstrips, S-9. Rochester, N.Y.: Eastman Kodak.

Textbooks in Print. New York: R. R. Bowker Company.

U.S. Government Films for Educational Use. Washington, D.C.: Government Printing Office.

U.S. Government Films for Public Education Use, Superintendent of Documents. Washington, D.C.: Government Printing Office.

U.S. Government Printing Office. Thousands of publications. Catalogs available.

Using Free Materials in the Classroom. Washington,

---

[10] Because most of these lists are revised periodically, a number of publication dates have been omitted from the citations.

D.C.: Association for Supervision and Curriculum Development.

Zuckerman, David W., and Robert E. Horn, *The Guide to Simulation Games for Education and Training.* Lexington, Mass.: Information Resources, Inc., 1973.

The following periodicals are a sampling of those which carry information about instructional materials and how to procure them.

Audio-Visual Instruction
A V Communication Review
Educational Screen and Audio-Visual Guide
The English Journal
Film and A.-V. World
Journal of Business Education
Journal of Health Education, Physical Education and Recreation
Journal of Home Economics
Music Educators' Journal
The Personnel and Guidance Journal
The Mathematics Teacher
School Arts
The Science Teacher
Social Education
Social Studies

Value of Resource Units and Curriculum Guides

As we have said, resource units are excellent sources of information concerning materials of instruction. A resource unit is designed not to be taught but to serve as a source from which the teacher can build a teaching unit for classroom use. It contains suggested objectives, learning activities, lists of materials of instruction, teaching aids, and other information valuable in unit building. Some resource units are gauged for a definite grade level, but others may be used as a source for units at many levels and include tremendous amounts of material.

When such units are provided by the school system, the teacher should make use of them. If, however, none has been prepared in his school, the teacher can borrow from those available in other communities. Collections of resource units may be found in the curriculum libraries of many schools and school systems, schools of education, and state teachers' colleges. Sample copies are sometimes exhibited at conventions of educational associations. Many of them are available for purchase. Sometimes they may be obtained free. Information concerning them may be obtained from your supervisor, the state department of education, and such professional organizations as the Association for Supervision and Curriculum Development whose annual bulletin, *Curriculum Materials,* is a treasury of the best resource units and curriculum guides.

Curriculum bulletins, curriculum guides, and courses of study are also excellent sources of materials and ideas. Frequently they contain lists of materials available, addresses of places from which materials can be obtained, and other useful information. If they are provided by your school, use them. Don't let them gather dust; they are too valuable.

*

Examine a sample resource unit. Note the amount of material it presents. How could you use such a resource unit for your own teaching?
Similarly examine a number of curriculum guides.

*

Finding Free or Inexpensive Material

Much teaching material is free or inexpensive. Many teachers seem not to be aware of this fact, yet teachers can find plenty of material even if equipment and funds are scarce. Several of the works in the list of sources included in this chapter list hundreds of sources of free and inexpensive materials.

As pointed out in an earlier section, building a file of pictures is relatively easy, inexpensive, and can be considerable fun. In addition, such a file is so useful that the prospective teacher can hardly afford not to build one. He can start by collecting pictures from periodicals. Picture magazines, such as *The National Geographic Magazine* are full of potentially useful pictures. So are the special-interest magazines such as those devoted to travels, popular science, and history. He can also obtain pictures from commercial sources such as museums and publishing houses both by purchase and rental. Many libraries have pictures to lend to teachers for short or long periods.

Not only pictures but other materials, such as

slides, specimens, souvenirs, models, and the like, are readily available for the asking. Many museums will send such material to schools free of charge. In almost every hamlet in the United States some villager has a collection of interesting materials that could be used with profit in the classroom. Usually he will be pleased to let the pupils see it. Quite often the most avid collectors are other teachers, particularly college professors.

Stores, factories, commercial concerns of all sorts are usually willing, and in some instances anxious, to give samples of raw and processed materials to the schools. At times such material is accompanied by pernicious advertising, but usually the objectionable material can be eliminated. Likewise, many firms offer films, slides, filmstrips, and other similar audio-visual materials free upon request. Many of these materials are very good, although each should be carefully screened before using. The amount of excellent material available from local, state, national, foreign, and domestic government agencies, is almost boundless.

CULLING THE MATERIAL

A word of caution concerning free and inexpensive material is in order. Although much free material is available, some of it is hardly worth cluttering up one's shelves with. Consequently, one should cull the material quite thoroughly before presenting it to the pupils. In his examination of such material the teacher should be particularly alert for material that is merely advertising or propaganda.

In culling material use criteria such as the following.

1. Will the material really further educational objectives?
2. Is it free from objectionable advertising, propaganda, and so on?
3. Is it accurate, honest, free from bias (except where one wishes to illustrate dishonesty and bias, of course)?
4. Is it interesting, colorful, exciting?
5. Does it lend itself to school use?
6. Is it well made?

WRITING FOR FREE MATERIAL

To get free material all one must do is to write and ask for it. When writing for free material, the teacher should use official school stationery. The letter should state exactly what you want and why you want it. Many firms like to know just how the material will be used and how many persons will see it. Sometimes teachers ask pupils to write the letter. Although doing so is excellent practice for the pupils, some firms will honor only letters from the teacher. Of course, one can sidestep this problem by having the pupils prepare letters for the teacher's signature or by having the teacher countersign the letter.

Obtaining Classroom Films

FILMS FOR RENT

Most of the more valuable classroom films are not lent to the school gratis. Since films are usually too expensive to be purchased by any but the largest school systems, most films used in the classroom are rented from film libraries. Your school will probably have a clear policy and procedure about renting films. This policy, of course, should be followed to the letter. The critical thing is to order films early. Good films are in demand; a late order may mean that you will have to do without.

Each renting library publishes a catalog of its films. In addition, film companies and other agencies publish catalogs and announcements of films. Hints about useful films can also be found in textbooks, curriculum guides, and resource units. Through these sources teachers can usually find film suitable to their purposes. Perhaps the list of sources in this chapter may help the teacher. In using the list one should note that the list is not limited to films or even to audio-visual material alone.

USING COMMERCIAL FILM

Commercial motion pictures too are a potential teaching resource of great value both as an art form and as a source of subject matter useful in English, social studies, art, music, and other courses. Therefore, the alert teacher scans the notices of coming attractions to spot likely productions suitable for exploiting. In this connection pupils can be a great help. When exceptional productions come to town, perhaps a theater party with definite assignments would be worthwhile. Or perhaps it would be better to list it as an optional activity. In any event, the teacher should call the film to the pupils' attention and suggest how it might fit into their program. Sometimes films make excellent subjects for pupil reports either oral or written.

Many old motion pictures are classics that can add greatly to the ordinary course of study. In some instances, if asked, local theater operators will arrange to bring these films back to town. Also, quite a large number of these classic motion pictures have been reissued as sixteen millimeter films and are available for school use in both the original film length and in shorter cut versions. The shorter versions can be used in the classroom; if the film is worthwhile enough it may be possible to reschedule the periods so that one can show the full-length feature straight through at one sitting during school hours or in the evening.

Sources of Information About Television Programs

Information about television programs slated for local viewing can be obtained in much the same way as information about the theater. Much information is readily available in professional journals, for example, *Today's Education* and *NEA Reporter,* specialized magazines such as *T.V. Guide,* the television sections of newspapers and magazines, and from the television stations and networks themselves. A teacher will usually find more programs suitable for school use than he might expect.

Since it is almost impossible for any teacher to keep himself well informed concerning all the television programs that might be potentially useful, it may be wise for the teacher to enlist the aid of the pupils to scout out and report on programs of value. Many teachers regularly post billings of such programs on the chalkboard or bulletin board. These billings may be enhanced by the adding of commentary and suggested aids for viewing.

Television programs that seem to have no direct bearing on the course of study can sometimes be useful. All television dramas have plots, most of them have music, they all take place in time and space, and so almost any one of them can be used for some purpose in English, social studies, art, or music classes. The ubiquitous wild-western tele-

vision drama, for instance, can be used in a study of the customs and mores of the times, and to bring home the differences between historical fact and fiction, to illustrate plot structure, or flat versus round characterization, the use of music in the theater, and so on. Particularly useful are the many documentaries and educational programs that commercial television stations use to fill in blank periods during their off hours and that make up much of the bill of fare of educational television programs. Instructional television courses telecast for adults are often good sources of enrichment and a means for providing for individual differences. Sometimes they require high-level ability from the viewer, but usually they do not. The educational television stations telecasting such programs usually publish program schedules, reading lists, and study materials that can be purchased for a relatively small fee.

Making One's Own Materials

Frequently teachers need to make their own materials, particularly practice materials and study guides. Modern methods of duplicating written and typed materials are easy to use and very versatile. With relatively little effort and ingenuity, teachers can duplicate exercises, diagrams, reading materials, assignments, study guides, and a multitude of other things. An advantage of building one's own material is that one gets what he wants—not what some professor or merchandiser thinks one wants. Against this one must weigh the cost in time and effort. Oftentimes teachers expend great amounts of energy developing materials that are really not worth the effort. Once prepared, useful materials should be shared with other teachers. To hoard valuable teaching materials is wasteful.

An interesting technique used by a social studies teacher is to tear chapters out of old books and rebind them into pamphlets by stapling them into folders or notebook binders. By this technique the teacher amassed a considerable library of short articles on many topics pertinent to his social studies courses from discarded textbooks, *National Geographic Magazines,* and other books and periodicals at practically no expense. Not only is this a cheap method of securing reading matter, but reducing the books and periodicals to pamphlet form makes a large number of different readings accessible at the same time. The scheme had the additional advantage of cleaning out numerous school closets and family attics.

A certain English teacher uses the same procedure to provide exercises in grammar. She cuts up old textbooks to make files of exercises for use in grammar classes. Another English teacher collected exercises for punctuation study by having pupils submit sentences to be punctuated. She collected them until she had a large number of exercises which she reproduced for pupil use. A science teacher makes a habit of going around to garages and junk shops to pick up old switches and other materials which, with the help of his pupils, he turns into demonstration equipment for his laboratory. Another science teacher allows brilliant boys and girls to prepare microscope slides for class use. An art teacher prepares his own clay for ceramics classes by process-

ing, with the help of his pupils, clay dug from a bank near a river a few miles from the school.

*

These incidents illustrate a few examples of the myriad sources of materials open to the ingenious teacher. What materials could you use for a class of your own? Where might you find these materials? How might you use them?

*

DUPLICATED SPRINGBOARD MATERIALS

Springboards are materials that are used as jump-off places for inquiry, discussion, or similar activities in which pupils are encouraged to think. Springboards may be films or film clips, videotapes, dramatizations, role playing, or oral reports. Many are duplicated or printed reading matter. Much suitable material is available commercially, but homemade springboards are easy to prepare. They consist of descriptions, real or imagined, that may

Figure 14–1
Listening Questions for
The Phoenician Traders

(These questions are illustrative of the type of questions one might use in a special study guide for use with this record. They represent different levels and types of questions. In using such study guides one must guard against merely mechanical exercises.)

1. What seems to be the major business of the Phoenicians?

2. What seems to be the relationship between Tyre and Carthage?

3. What can you learn about the trade routes of the Phoenicians?

4. What was life like on a caravan?

5. What can you note about Phoenician ships and seamanship?

6. What did you learn about Phoenician trade? How did they carry it on? How did they keep accurate accounts and so on? In what way did they trade?

7. How nearly accurate is the reconstruction of Phoenician life? If you do not know how can you find out?

8. Prepare a list of questions which would emphasize or bring about the important idea expressed in this recording.

Figure 14–2

Sample Study Guide

*Twelfth–Grade Social Studies, Cheltenham, Pennsylvania.

Factors in the consideration of Means and Ends.

1. Can necessity create its own law?

2. Can "ends" be judged without previous standards of judgment?

3. Who decides, or how is it decided, that an "end" is good?

4. Are the "means" employed toward marking an "end" good?

5. When is necessity "real," when is it "imagined"?

6. Can we separate "means" from "ends"?

7. Are the "means" to be judged before or after the "ends" are achieved?

8. Is the question of the "end justifying the means" for both individuals and states?

9. Do the means determine the ends?

10. Does the pinch of necessity preclude any national consideration of means?

11. How do we consider degrees of "necessity"?

12. How can we determine whether some ends are better than others?

13. Are certain types of "means" and "ends" peculiar to specific aspects of society?

14. Are certain "means" improper, criminal, etc., even when they are not employed?

15. Can means and ends ever be considered amoral?

16. Is law a fact only when it can be enforced?

17. Can evil means ever be employed toward a good end?

18. How can we evaluate abstract ends?

19. How is the concept of what constitutes an end to be reached?

20. Can ends exist independent of the individual?*

be the source of open-ended questions. Case studies make excellent springboards. So do historical accounts, news stories, excerpts from novels, and similar provocative material. All one has to do is to duplicate the pertinent material and hand it out to the pupils with the proper instructions on how to use it.

STUDY GUIDES

Study guides give the pupils directions to follow as they guide their own learning. They are specially useful for pupils who are working alone on special assignments, independent study or research, or supplementary assignments. Directions for pupils to follow during a field trip or reaction questions for pupils to use when viewing a television program are other examples of study guides. There is no set format suitable for every study guide. Teachers design each one to suit the occasion. They may include such things as

1. Purpose and rationale of the activity.
2. Background information.
3. Directions to follow when doing the activity.
4. Problems to solve, exercises to do, questions to answer, and so on.
5. Suggested readings.
6. Suggested follow-up activities.
7. Answer sheets for self-correcting materials.

Sometimes a set of questions is quite sufficient for one's purposes as in the questions designed to accompany the recording of *The Phoenician Traders* (Figure 14–1). The study guide on means and ends used in Cheltenham, Pennsylvania (Figure 14–2), illustrates a study guide that calls for a high degree of reasoning. A more complex study guide is illustrated in Chapter 6, Planning Courses and Units.

INSTRUCTIONAL LEARNING PACKETS

Instructional learning packets or learning packets are, in a sense, special types of study guides. In addition to telling the pupils what to do, they give the pupil the material to work with. They are the heart of courses divided into modules or units as part of a continuous progress plan. The process to follow in the building of learning packets has been described in some detail in Chapter 6.

BUILDING A SIMULATION MODEL

Simulations have become increasingly popular. So many have come on the market that it seems hardly necessary for teachers to build their own. Yet, homemade simulations are often the best. Even pupil-built simulations may be very effective. To develop a simulation model

1. Select the process to be simulated.
   a. Determine the specific objectives.
   b. Decide what type of simulation would bring out these objectives.
2. Select a situation.
   a. Historical or current event.
      (1) May give a better understanding of the situation and the problems.
      (2) May be difficult to present because of biases, emotions, or lack of information.
   b. Hypothetical situation.
      (1) Good for demonstrating specific processes, skills, and pressures.
      (2) Likely to involve emotion and bias.
      (3) Teacher can control the variables easier —thus making the simulation simpler and clearer.
3. Research the situation in depth.
4. Develop the essential elements to be replicated.
   a. Try to keep all unessential elements out of the simulation model, for they tend to confuse and obscure the essential elements and complicate the simulation.
   b. Establish the relationships between the various roles (for example, power relationships).
5. Prepare the draft scenario.
   a. Read several other simulations to see how they have been developed. This may give you ideas.
   b. Set up some criteria or media for showing relationships.
   c. Try to keep the simulation from being too simple or too complicated.
   d. Write the draft scenario.
   e. Try out the draft scenario.
   f. Rewrite the draft scenario.
   g. Repeat (e) and (f) until you get a satisfactory draft.

h. Present it to the class.

i. Rewrite it (or junk it).[11]

HOMEMADE VISUAL AIDS

Many visual aids can be made easily by the teacher or the pupil. One of the simplest to make is the flannel board which can be constructed quickly by stretching a piece of flannel across a board of the desired size and tacking it down securely. Signs, pictures, letters, and so forth can be stuck on the flannel if their backs are covered with strips of sandpaper or felt. A similar device can be constructed quickly out of a sheet of iron or steel on which material can be displayed by means of magnets. Families use such magnetic boards in the kitchen or family area to remind themselves and each other of things they ought not to forget. Their use can be just as effective in the classroom.

Slides and Filmstrips. Two by two (thirty-five millimeter) film slides and filmstrips, the large glass slides, and transparencies for overhead projection are readily available from commercial sources and quite easy to make locally.

Thirty-five millimeter photography is an excellent source of slides. Thousands of slides are for sale, as one can see by thumbing through the photography magazines on display at any newsstand. Furthermore, excellent thirty-five millimeter slides can be made locally. The teacher can usually find someone to make the slides for him, if he is not equipped to make them himself. The school camera club would probably welcome such a project; if not, certainly one of the teacher's friends or pupils would be delighted to serve. Color slides are usually made by sending the exposed film to commercial concerns.

To produce filmstrips is more difficult than to make individual slides. Ordinarily the process involves copying from other slides by means of an expensive adaptation of a thirty-five millimeter camera. However, the same effect can be achieved with slides, and the slides are more versatile. Of course, camera clubs and other local personnel can develop filmstrips and even motion pictures, if they wish.

With surprisingly little extra effort it is possible to provide synchronized tape recordings for a filmstrip or series of slides. All that one needs to do is to write a script with clues, noting when the operator should change slides, and then transcribe the script on a tape recording. Not only is it fairly easy, but it is fun to do. Homemade sound-filmstrips of this sort can be used for large-group instruction in an assembly or lecture hall or for individual instruction in the classroom utilizing earphones and a miniature screen.

Making glass slides is not at all difficult. Commercial firms sell kits for making them. With these materials it is possible to make slides by typing on a special film or by writing or drawing directly on the glass. Such slides can be used with magic lantern projectors and overhead projectors.

Making Overhead Transparencies. There are many ways to make transparencies for the overhead projector. A number of photocopying or dry copying office machines will make transparencies of printed, typed, or written material or drawings. Preparing transparencies on some of these machines is something of an art. On others all one does is push a button and wait a few seconds. One can also make transparencies by using a special carbon paper or by using a china marking pencil or india ink. The popular felt-tipped pens, for example, a Magic Marker, can be used to make transparencies in color. One can also make transparencies directly with a Polaroid camera. With all these sources and acetate sheets so inexpensive (any clear acetate can be used to make transparencies by hand—the machine-made transparencies require specially treated film), there seems to be no reason why one should not have all the transparencies one needs. In order to preserve them and to keep them accessible it is recommended that one frame his transparencies and file them. Commercial frames are readily available for transparencies.

Flip-ons, which are simply additional sheets that can be placed on the original transparency to add further detail or information, are made in exactly the same way as any other transparencies. If one wishes one can fasten these to the frame of the original transparency with little metallic foil hinges.

11 Leonard H. Clark, *Teaching Social Studies in Secondary Schools: A Handbook* (New York: Macmillan Publishing Co., Inc., 1973), p. 322.

Based on Dale M. Garvey and Sancha K. Garvey, *Simulation, Role Playing and Sociodrama in the Social Studies,* The Emporia State Research Studies (Emporia: Kansas State Teachers College, 1957), Vol. 16, No. 2.

The use of frames and hinges has the advantage of keeping the transparency and its flip-ons together in proper order.

*

What sources of audio-visual material are available to you in your community?

What materials are available for use in your college classes. What could you do to make more material available if you were one of the teachers?

Pick a college course and see what audio-visual materials you could develop for it.

*

The Classroom Library

Because reading material, whether printed or duplicated, should be readily available to the pupils, the classroom should contain a library. The pupils can act as librarians. If a self-charging system is used in which the pupils select the books they want, fill out the library cards, and place them in a box set aside for that purpose, pupil librarians can carry out all the record keeping, shelving, and filing quite easily.

The Community as a Resource

Extending the classroom into the community can make a course exciting and forceful, for every community is a gold mine of resources for teaching. The experiences of the pupils as they get out into the community are not only a welcome change but also potent learning activities. Similar benefits can also come from bringing the community into a classroom. For this reason every school should have a file of community resources available. Individual teachers sometimes keep such files for use in their own classes, but probably a well-kept central file is more efficient, although the teacher will need to keep additional information applicable to his own classes. A 5x8 card file is most satisfactory for this purpose. In it should be kept such information as

1. Possible field trips.
   a. What is there.
   b. Where is it and how to get there.
   c. Whom to see about arrangements.
   d. Expense involved.
   e. Time required.
   f. Other comments.
2. Resource people.
   a. Who they are.
   b. How they can help.
   c. Addresses.
3. Resource material and instructional materials obtainable locally.
   a. What is it.
   b. How to procure it.
   c. Expense involved.
4. Community groups.
   a. Names and addresses.
   b. Function and purpose.
   c. Type of thing they can help with.
5. Local businesses, industries, and agencies.
   a. Name.
   b. Address.
   c. Key personnel.

SUMMARY

Good teachers can be better teachers when they have plenty of materials to work with. Fortunately, American teachers are blessed with materials galore, although some may have to search a little to find them. Prominent on the list are audio-visual aids—films, pictures, maps, globes, charts, models, graphs, mock-ups, terrain boards, radio, television, chalkboards, and tack boards. All of them are excellent aids to teaching if they are used well, but they are not miracle drugs. They alone cannot do the job of teaching. The same teaching techniques—introducing, explaining, problem solving, follow-up and evaluation—used in other teaching are also needed to get the most from audio-visual aids. These techniques apply particularly to the presentation of films and filmstrips. In using display devices such as chalkboards, bulletin boards, and the like, it is important to provide for impact. They should be clearly visible and uncluttered, with a clear center of interest and plenty of white space. Both the content and their presentation should be as dramatic as possible. For this reason, and because of their better visibility, the use of overhead, opaque, and other projecting is often more effective than other display methods. For the same reason flannel boards are usually more effective than chalkboards.

Recent advances in mass media have created

many opportunities for teachers to capitalize on the cinema and television. Teachers who do not utilize these commercial media may be missing opportunities to harness their undoubted appeal to youth. The use of new media, particularly television, film, and tapes, has proved valuable as a means of bringing to the classroom outstanding experiences and personalities not otherwise available. But teachers should not expect miracles of them. Television, film, and recorded presentations like anything else need to be introduced and followed up properly. On their own, they may do nothing; carefully handled they can work wonders. This is, of course, true of all tools. Perhaps the answer to the problem of effective and efficient teaching in the future lies in the building of man-machine systems that allot to each person and tool the most appropriate role.

The teaching program is a sophisticated adaptation of the workbook, utilizing scientific principles. Whether presented by machine, book, or some other means, the program acts as a mechanical tutor which presents and follows up lessons. As a rule, teachers should not attempt to build their own teaching programs. Nevertheless, all teachers should understand how the programs are constructed so they can select and use them knowledgeably. At the present there are many types of programs, the two major types being the linear and the intrinsic. Just which type is best we do not yet know. So far the only really dependable way to judge a program's worth is to try it out with pupils.

Free or inexpensive reading matter on almost any subject is available from governmental and business agencies. Still, most teachers will find it advantageous to make their own dittoed or mimeographed readings and study guides. They will probably want to duplicate their practice materials and exercises. When they do, it may be wise to consider methods by which one can preserve homemade materials for reuse.

Exercises and practice materials are also available commercially in workbooks. Workbooks have earned a bad reputation by encouraging the rote learning of inconsequential facts. Still, they can be useful for practice and review and for providing for individual differences.

Some audio-visual materials are expensive and hard to get. This is true of other materials also. But this fact should not discourage the teacher. Much material is available for the asking. Much more can be made or improvised. Hints on how to obtain and create such materials can be found in the catalogs, curriculum guides, source units, and periodicals on the subject, some of which have been listed in this chapter. Many of these materials can be procured by simply writing. Today no teacher has an excuse for not having a supply of suitable materials.

Perhaps the best resource the teacher has is the community itself. It is both a source of subject matter and a source of instructional material and resource persons. Community lay persons can be used as classroom speakers and as consultants and guides.

Suggested Readings for Part VI

ALCORN, MARVIN D., JAMES S. KINDER, AND JIM R. SCHUNERT, *Better Teaching in Secondary Schools*, 3rd ed. New York: Holt, Rinehart and Winston, Publishers, 1970. Chs. 9–11.

BROWN, JAMES W., RICHARD B. LEWIS, AND FRED R. HARCLEROAD, *AV Instruction: Technology, Media, and Methods*. New York: McGraw-Hill Book Company, 1972.

DAVIDSON, RAYMOND L., *Audiovisual Machines*. Scranton, Pa.: International Textbook Co., 1969.

DETERLINE, WILLIAM A., *An Introduction to Programed Instruction*. Englewood Cliffs, N.J.: Prentice-Hall, Inc., 1962.

EBOCH, SIDNEY C., AND GEORGE W. COCHERN, *Operating Audio-Visual Equipment*, 2nd ed. San Francisco: Chandler Publishing Company, 1970.

ELY, DONALD, AND VERNON S. GERLACH, *Teaching and Media*. Englewood Cliffs, N.J.: Prentice-Hall, Inc., 1971.

ERICKSON, CARLTON W. H., AND DAVID H. CURL, *Fundamentals of Teaching with Audiovisual Technology*, 2nd ed. New York: Macmillan Publishing Co., Inc., 1972.

GRAMBS, JEAN D., JOHN C. CARR, AND ROBERT M. FITCH, *Modern Methods in Secondary Education*, 3rd ed. New York: Holt, Rinehart and Winston, Publishers, 1970. Ch. 6.

HANEY, JOHN B., AND ELDON J. ULLMER, *Educational Media and the Teacher*. Dubuque, Iowa: William C. Brown Company, Publishers, 1970.

HEITZMANN, WM. RAY, *Educational Games and Simulations*, What Research Says to the Teacher Series. Washington, D.C.: The National Education Association, 1974.

HOOVER, KENNETH H., *The Professional Teacher's Handbook*. Boston: Allyn & Bacon, Inc., 1973. Ch. 16.

KEMP, JERROLD E., *Planning and Producing Audiovisual Materials*, rev. ed. Scranton, Pa.: International Textbook Co., 1968.

KLASEK, CHARLES B., *Instructional Media in the Modern School*. Lincoln, Nebr.: Professional Educators Publications, Inc., 1972.

National Society for the Study of Education, *Media and Symbols: The Forms of Expression, Communication, and Education*, Seventy-third Yearbook, Part I. Chicago: University of Chicago Press, 1974.

ROSSI, PETER, ed., *New Media and Education*. Chicago: Aldine Publishing Co., 1966.

SAMALONIS, BERNICE L., *Methods and Materials for Today's High Schools*. New York: Van Nostrand Reinhold Company, 1970. Chs. 10–14.

SCUORZO, HERBERT E., *The Practical Audio-Visual Handbook for Teachers*. Englewood Cliffs, N.J.: Prentice-Hall, Inc., 1967.

TAYLOR, C. W., AND FRANK E. WILLIAMS, eds. *Instructional Media and Creativity*. New York: John Wiley & Sons, Inc., 1966.

WITTICH, WALTER A., AND CHARLES F. SCHULLER, *Instructional Technology: Its Nature and Use*, 5th ed. New York: Harper & Row, Publishers, 1973.

Information on the preparation and uses of specific audio-visual devices can be found in such references as the following:

Adapting Your Tape-Recorder to the Kodak Carousel Programer, SC–1. Rochester, N.Y.: Eastman Kodak, 1969.

Applied Color Photography Indoors, E-76. Rochester, N.Y.: Eastman Kodak, 1968.

Audiovisual Projection, S-3. Rochester, N.Y.: Eastman Kodak, 1969.

Basic Copying, AM-2. Rochester, N.Y.: Eastman Kodak, 1966.

Basic Developing, Printing and Enlarging, AJ-2. Rochester, N.Y.: Eastman Kodak, 1969.

Better Bulletin Boards. Austin, Tex.: Instructional Media Center (VIB), University of Texas at Austin.

Better Movies in Minutes, AD-4. Rochester, N.Y.: Eastman Kodak, 1970.

Color Photography Outdoors, E-75. Rochester, N.Y.: Eastman Kodak, 1968.

Composition, AC-11. Rochester, N.Y.: Eastman Kodak, 1968.

COPLAN, KATE, *Poster Ideas and Bulletin Board Techniques: For Libraries and Schools*. Dobbs Ferry, N.Y.: Oceana Publications, Inc., 1962.

Copying, M-1. Rochester, N.Y.: Eastman Kodak, 1969.

Designing Instructional Visuals. Austin, Tex.: Instructional Media Center (VIB), University of Texas at Austin, 1968.

Educational Displays and Exhibits. Austin, Tex.: Instructional Media Center (VIB), University of Texas at Austin, 1966.

Effective Lecture Slides, S-22. Rochester, N.Y.: Eastman Kodak, 1970.

GASKILL, ARTHUR, AND DAVID ENGLANDER, *How to Shoot a Movie Story*. New York: Duell Sloane and Pearce, 1960.

Good Color Pictures—Quick and Easy, AE-10. Rochester, N.Y.: Eastman Kodak, 1969.

HAEMER, K., *Making the Most of Charts*. Holyoke, Mass.: Tecnifax, 1960.

Instructional Display Boards. Austin, Tex.: Instructional Media Center (VIB), University of Texas at Austin, 1968.

KOSKEY, THOMAS ARTHUR, *Bulletin Boards for Subject Areas: A Handbook for Teachers*. Palo Alto, Calif.: Fearon Publishers, 1962.

LACEY, RICHARD A., *Films in the Classroom: Seeing with Feeling*. Philadelphia, Pa.: W. B. Saunders Company, 1971.

LOUGHARY, JOHN, ed. *Man-Machine Systems in Education*. New York: Harper & Row, Publishers, Inc., 1966.

Making Black and White Transparencies for Overhead Projection, S17. Rochester, N.Y.: Eastman Kodak, 1970.

MINOR, ED., *Simplified Techniques for Preparing Visual Instructional Materials*. New York: McGraw-Hill Book Company, 1962.

Models for Teaching. Austin, Tex.: Instructional Media Center (VIB), University of Texas at Austin, 1956.

MORLAND, JOHN E., *Preparation of Inexpensive Teaching Materials*. San Francisco: Chandler Publishing Company, 1966.

The Overhead System. Austin, Tex.: Instructional Media Center (VIB), University of Texas at Austin, n.d.

Planning and Producing Visual Aids, S-13. Rochester, N.Y.: Eastman Kodak, 1969.

Producing Slides and Filmstrips, S-8, 4th ed. Rochester, N.Y.: Eastman Kodak, 1969.

Production of 2 x 2 Inch Slides. Austin, Tex.: Instructional Media Center (VIB), University of Texas at Austin, 1970.

RING, ARTHUR E., AND WILLIAM J. SKELLEY, *Creative Teaching with the Overhead Projector*. Scranton, Pa.: International Textbook Co., 1969.

SCHILLACI, ANTHONY, AND JOHN M. CULKEN, *Films Deliver*. Englewood Cliffs, N.J.: Citation Press, 1970.

SCHULTZ, MORTON J., *The Teacher and Overhead Projection: A Treasury of Ideas, Uses, and Techniques*. Englewood Cliffs, N.J.: Prentice-Hall, Inc., 1965.

The Tape Recorder. Austin, Tex.: Instructional Media Center (VIB), University of Texas at Austin, n.d.

Using Tear Sheets. Austin, Tex.: Instructional Media Center (VIB), University of Texas at Austin, n.d.

VII

Evaluation

Evaluation
and
Measurement

15

Why Evaluate?

In order to guide his ship in its proper course, a navigator must know where he is. He therefore keeps a running record of his approximate position and frequently checks to fix his exact position. He must do so in order to know in what direction to lay his course. If he does not know where he is, how can he tell in what direction to go? So it is with teaching. We must know where we are in order to know in which way to go. We must continuously appraise and reappraise our position. This appraisal of the teaching-learning situation is called evaluation.

Evaluation has many purposes. Teachers use it as basis for school marks, reporting to parents, and promotion. Administrators use it as a basis for categorizing pupils into groups. Guidance counselors use it as a basis for pupil advisement. Pupils use it as a basis for mapping out their own programs. Parents, school officials, and teachers use it as a basis for curriculum revision. But its most important role is its use in the teaching-learning process itself.

Evaluation is an essential tool for the teacher because it gives him the feedback he needs in order to know what the pupils have learned and what he should do next. Evaluation also helps him to understand his pupils, their abilities, and their needs. Further, it is useful for motivating the pupils.

EVALUATION, MOTIVATION, AND RETENTION

The evaluation process used in schools has a direct influence on what and how pupils learn. Sometimes this influence does not yield the results that teachers desire. As a rule, pupils set up their short-term goals to conform with what they think the teacher will grade them on. If the pupils expect the teacher to examine them on their knowledge of facts, then facts are what they will try to learn. But when they know that the teacher will judge them on the basis of their skill in inquiry, their learning approach will take a different direction. Similarly, evaluation effects pupil retention. Pupils tend to learn and remember what they expect to be evaluated on. But basically it is the feedback that makes evaluation so important.

EVALUATION AND DIAGNOSIS

The basic teaching pattern, as we have seen, consists of diagnosis, preparation, guidance of learning activities, evaluation, and follow-up.[1] Evaluation, then, is an essential portion of the teaching-learning process, both in its own right and as a tool for diagnosis. As Gronlund points out, the effectiveness of instruction "depends, to a large extent, on the quality of the evaluative information on which the discussions are based."[2] Furthermore, feedback makes the pupil aware of his own progress, his successes and failures, so that he can capitalize on it. Evaluation makes it possible for both pupils and teachers to find their bearings as a basis for deciding what steps to take next.

THE NEED FOR DEFINITE GOALS

To evaluate, one must know not only where he is but where he wants to go. This destination is his

[1] See Ch. 1.
[2] Norman E. Gronlund, *Measurement and Evaluation in Teaching*, 2nd ed. (New York: Macmillan Publishing Co., Inc., 1971), p. 7.

goal. One can judge one's progress by finding out how close one has come to it. In teaching, the goals are the learnings the teacher is trying to teach his pupils. These goals should be specific and definite. Unless they describe specific learning products and indicate standards of excellence, there is no way to tell how well the pupils are progressing. Effective evaluation depends upon definite goals. For this reason it is recommended that for each lesson and unit the objectives, which are the teacher's goals, be stated specifically in simple declarative sentences. If the instructional goals are stated as specific learning products or as specific behavior, it will be much easier to devise measuring instruments that will determine pupil progress accurately. In general, specific behavioral objectives are the most useful types of objectives for the evaluator.[3]

*

What is the role of diagnosis in teaching? Why is it so necessary? What is the role of evaluation in diagnosis? It is said that without good evaluation one cannot have good diagnosis. Why not?

*

Evaluation Versus Measurement

Evaluation can be defined as putting a value on or assigning worth to something. It includes both quantitative and/or qualitative description, plus a value judgment.

The basis of evaluation is judgment. This is the quality which makes evaluation differ from measurement. Measurement describes a situation; evaluation judges its worth or value. For instance, the score of a student's test may be 70. This in itself does not tell us much of anything. Is 70 good or bad? No one can say until he has more information. If 70 represents the highest score of all the students of our school, that may indicate one thing; if it represents the lowest score, it may indicate another; if it is the lowest score, but the work of a brilliant student, it may indicate something else; if it is the lowest score, but the best effort of the slowest pupil, it may indicate something else again. Evaluation is the judgment or interpretation that one draws from the information at hand about a pupil. It is

[3] See Ch. 5 for descriptions and examples of specific objectives.

the process by which a teacher puts a value on the pupil's work, talents, or other characteristics and behavior and which the teacher uses as a basis for his decision making.

Measurement gives us quantitative information on which to base judgments. It is essential for evaluation. Only by measuring can we hope to ascertain an approximation of the status of the pupil's learning at the moment. Measurement can also give us information about the approximate status of other aspects of the pupil's personality. From these measurements we can evaluate the learning or other personality traits in light of our goals. Measurement is only a tool to be used in evaluation. Used by itself it is meaningless, but without it evaluation is likely to be very erratic indeed.

SOME PRINCIPLES OF EVALUATION AND MEASUREMENT

Teachers should not allow themselves to become too enamored of measurement and evaluation. As we have seen, evaluation is a process and measurement is a tool we use in that process. Teachers and other school personnel should resist the temptation to test and measure just for the sake of measuring and evaluating. Evaluation should be a means, not an end. Unless evaluation leads to some educational action or decision, it is a waste of time.

Teachers should not expect too much of the evaluation process. All evaluation is subject to error. Measurements are only approximations at best. Educational measurements can never be precise; sometimes they are wildly inaccurate. Therefore teachers should always view the results of educational measurement and evaluation with caution. They should never accept an educational measurement or evaluation as conclusive unless it is supported by a sufficient amount of other confirmative data.

Teachers should also be certain that the evaluative data they use are pertinent to the specific decisions they must make. All too many educational decisions are based on data that are irrelevant to the problem at hand. In this connection it is important to remember that *what* is evaluated is just as important as the technique used.

If teachers are to be sure that their measuring is really relevant to the judgment they must make, they must know exactly what they need to measure.

Only then will they be ready to procure or devise instruments that will give them the needed information. That is one reason why good definitive instructional objectives are so necessary.

To be sure that the evaluation includes all the essential aspects and utilizes a proper technique, the teacher should make a plan for evaluating each unit and course before he starts to teach them. This plan should ensure (1) that the instruments used measure the progress made toward achieving each and every objective in proportion to its importance and (2) that the proper types of instruments are used to measure the progress being made.

*

What is the difference between measurement and evaluation?

What can test results be used for? What are the most valid uses of test scores?

*

EVALUATIVE DEVICES AND TECHNIQUES

THE RIGHT INSTRUMENT

Teaching objectives are of various sorts. Bloom, Kratwohl, and their associates[4] have set up taxonomies in which they list six different types of "cognitive" objectives and five different types of "affective" objectives. In order to measure these different types of learning products, one must use different types of measuring devices. The type of test item that will ascertain whether a pupil knows a fact will seldom be useful for determining his ability to analyze and will almost certainly be useless for finding out his values. Paper and pencil tests will seldom tell us how well a pupil can swim. So each measuring device and test item should be selected to do a particular job. Teachers and test builders must be very careful in building tests to select the types of items that can do what they are meant to do. Often they must turn to other techniques, such as observation and self-report techniques. Table

4 Benjamin S. Bloom, ed., *Taxonomy of Educational Objectives, Handbook I, Cognitive Domain* (New York: David McKay Co., Inc. 1956) ; David R. Kratwohl, Benjamin S. Bloom, and Bertram B. Masia, *Taxonomy of Educational Objectives, Handbook II, Affective Domain* (New York: David McKay Co., Inc., 1964) .

15–1 shows some of these techniques and the types of goals which they measure best.

*

Examine the list of objectives in Table 15–1. From what you know of these techniques, why are the items listed under understanding more suitable for checking understanding than for testing attitudes, appreciations, and ideals?

*

LIMITATIONS OF TESTS

Although paper-and-pencil tests are the commonest tool used in measuring pupil progress, they often fail to give us the most important information we want in the evaluation of a pupil. By their very nature, paper-and-pencil tests are more likely to test knowing-about than knowing, verbalizations rather than the ability to do, or platitudes rather than changes in attitude or behavior. Since understandings, abilities, and changes in attitudes or behavior are the essential goals of the unit, teachers must use other devices and techniques to supplement the formal tests and get at these important learnings. The following paragraphs will endeavor to point out how some of these devices can be used to advantage.

Four Criteria of a Good Measuring Device

When considering the worth of any measuring device, be it a standard test, teacher-made test, rat-

ing scale, or whatever, four things need to be considered.

1. How valid is it?
2. How reliable is it?
3. How objective is it?
4. How usable is it?

VALIDITY

The most important of these criteria is validity, that is, the extent to which the device measures what it is supposed to measure. A measuring device that is not valid is worthless. Validity is dependent on several things. In the first place, the instrument must be suitable to the nature of what is to be measured. A paper-and-pencil test would hardly be a valid measure of a baseball player's ability to bat, for instance. Furthermore, the instrument must measure all the significant aspects of what is to be measured in an amount proportional to their importance. If, in testing batting ability, one tested the batter's stance, but not his ability to hit, the test would give a false result because of poor sampling. Moreover, to be valid the test must also discriminate. In testing batting ability, of what use is a test that does not differentiate between the good batters and the poor batters?[5]

Test builders recognize three types of validity:

[5] In criterion-referenced testing a test would discriminate if it ascertained which pupils met the criterion and which did not.

Table 15–1
Evaluative Techniques and Goals They Best Measure*

* Leonard H. Clark, *Teaching Social Studies in Secondary Schools: A Handbook* (New York: Macmillan Publishing Co., Inc., 1973), p. 136.

Understanding	Skills	Attitudes, appreciations, ideals
Objective test items	Observation	Observation
Essay test items	Rating scales	Rating scales
Problem situations	Check lists	Check lists
Essays	Sample work	Problem situations
Discussions	Problem situations	Interest inventories
Interpreting items	Performance	Attitude tests and test items
Organizing and evaluating items	Performance tests and test items	Written work; for example, themes
Situation items		
Free-response items		

curriculum or content validity, criterion validity, and experimental or construct validity. As a rule classroom teachers are primarily concerned with curriculum validity, for curriculum validity is a particularly important criterion in establishing the worth of achievement tests. Curriculum validity indicates the extent to which a test measures what was supposed to be taught in the course. Without it, an achievement test cannot be valid. When the items of an achievement test are concerned with learning that was not part of the course, the test will give incorrect results because of its lack of curriculum validity. Commercial achievement tests sometimes give an inaccurate picture of the achievement of pupils in a particular school because the curriculum of the school may differ from that for which the commercial test was designed. In the ordinary classroom situation curriculum validity is determined by examining the instrument to be sure (1) that it does test for the specific goals of the unit or course and (2) that it gives each goal approximately the same weight that the unit or course plan calls for.[6]

RELIABILITY

A second test of the worth of an evaluative device is reliability. An instrument is reliable if it can be trusted to give the same results when it is repeated or when different forms are used. In other words, a reliable instrument is consistent and dependable. When a test is reliable one can be sure that its measurement is fairly accurate because chance errors and other inconsistencies have been largely eliminated. Just as a steel measuring tape is less likely to be stretched out of shape than a cloth tape or a fine laboratory scale is likely to be more dependable than a bathroom scale, a reliable test is less likely to be affected by irrelevant or chance factors than an unreliable one.

Statistical methods are used to determine coefficients of reliability for standardized tests, but

---

[6] Perhaps one should make a distinction between content validity and curriculum validity. A standardized test, which gives a good sample of the subject matter of the discipline but not the subject matter of the discipline as taught in a particular school, would have content validity. A test that reflects the subject matter as taught in a particular school's curriculum would have curriculum validity. Sometimes the terms are used interchangeably, as we have done.

techniques of this sort are not really suitable for use with teacher-built tests and other classroom instruments. One can make teacher-built tests fairly reliable by (1) making the tests as long as one reasonably can (so that chance errors will tend to counteract each other and cancel each other out), (2) scoring the test as objectively as possible (so that the number of inconsistencies in scoring will be reduced), (3) writing the items and directions as carefully as possible (so that pupils will not make irrelevant errors because of ambiguities, misunderstood directions, and so on), and (4) administering the test as carefully as possible (so that error will not be introduced by nonstandard conditions such as distracting noise, lack of time, and so on).

Validity and reliability are not totally independent. Reliability refers to consistency, and an instrument that is not consistent certainly cannot be counted on to give truthful information. Therefore to be valid, an instrument must be reliable. But a reliable instrument may not necessarily be valid. It can give one wrong information consistently. Consequently, to measure progress toward certain high-level objectives, an essay test item with fairly low potential reliability, but reasonably high potential validity, may be a better risk than an objective test item with much higher potential reliability, but lower potential validity.

OBJECTIVITY

Another criterion of a good instrument is objectivity. By objectivity educators mean that the personality of the scorer does not affect the scoring of the test. Thus a truly objective test will be scored in exactly the same way by every scorer. For this reason objectivity in an instrument helps make the scoring fair and the instrument reliable. As long as validity is not sacrificed, the more objective the instrument the better. However, a valid instrument may be a good instrument even though it is not objective, while an objective instrument that is not valid is always worthless.

USABILITY

A fourth criterion of a good evaluative device is its usability. Obviously a two-hour test is not suitable for a forty-minute class period. Everything else being equal, teachers should avoid instruments that are hard to administer, difficult to score, and expensive.

*

Objective-type tests are not always objective. Why not? Why might a truly objective test in composition be a bad test?

What are the most important criteria for judging the worth of a test? Rate these criteria in order of importance. Why did you choose that order? When would you use an objective test? Apply these criteria to a test in one of your college courses.

*

Evaluation by Means of Observation

Observation is one of the best means of getting to know one's pupils. It is perhaps the most common basis for judging the behavior of another person. Through its use an alert teacher, properly trained, can often find clues to the causes for a pupil's behavior. This technique is as old as mankind. Unfortunately, it has several limitations. Observers are notoriously unreliable. The behavior of the pupil is often different when he knows he is

being observed. However, to a degree, these limitations can be reduced by careful observation. A helpful technique is to determine in advance what to observe and how to observe it. Another is to set up a check list, rating scale, or some other written guide to help objectify one's observations.

RATING SCALES

Rating scales are especially helpful in judging skills, procedures, and personal social behavior. Rating scales can also be used to help objectify the evaluation of products of the pupil's work, such as a lamp shade made in an industrial arts class or a composition or theme done in an English class. Such devices have the advantage of showing the pupil an analysis of the rater's evaluation and also of preventing the rater from being unduly influenced by any one aspect of the work being evaluated.

In using such tools, the final evaluation can be made dependent upon a numerical score. However, one must always remember that often, as in the case of literary and art works and other creative activities, evaluation cannot be safely reduced to numbers. To avoid culs-de-sac, the rater should allow for the possibility that sometimes a single

Figure 15–1
Rating Scale for Posters

Design					
	Crystalline beautiful perfect	Clear well-balanced pleasing	Mediocre	Confusing poorly balanced crowded	Hodge-podge

Neatness					
	Meticulous	Excellent	Average	Fair	Sloppy

Lettering					
	Superior	Excellent	Average	Fair	Poor

Eye Appeal					
	Overwhelming	Intriguing	Catchy	Dull	Insipid

Figure 15–2
Rating Scale for Written Work

(Circle number indicating rating. Code: 5, highest; 1, lowest; NA, not applicable)

1. Originality

    5   4   3   2   1   NA

2. Vividness of expression

    5   4   3   2   1   NA

3. Clearness

    5   4   3   2   1   NA

        *   *   *

11. Spelling

    5   4   3   2   1   NA

12. Sentence structure

    5   4   3   2   1   NA

characteristic may outweigh all others and that some items may be completely inapplicable. Consequently, subjective rating after an inspection using a rating scale may be considerably superior to mechanical rating on the strength of a total score or average of the ratings.

Preparing a Rating Scale. One can make rating scales and check lists quite easily. To make a rating scale, merely decide what characteristic you wish to rate. Then arrange a scale for each of these characteristics. Since a five-point scale is about all a rater can handle, there is little point in making finer distinctions. In any case, do not use more than seven or fewer than three categories. If each point of the scale is labeled, the rating is much easier.

To illustrate this process, suppose we wish to build a scale to use as a guide for judging the excellence of some posters which pupils have prepared. First we must decide what to consider in judging the posters. Let us say that among other things we wish to include neatness, lettering, eye appeal, and design. We then provide a rating scale similar to the one in Figure 15–1. In this rating scale, the gradations are indicated by descriptive words encompassing the gamut from best to worst. These descriptions help make the teacher ratings somewhat more objective than they might be otherwise.

Another plan is to use numbers as in the following scale for evaluating themes. Five equals the highest rating and one the lowest. "NA" means "not

applicable." The scale is used by circling the number desired.

In preparing the characteristics to be rated in the scale, be sure that each is significant. Sometimes some of the characteristics included in rating scales really do not make any real difference. Be sure also that each characteristic is clearly and precisely specified so that the rater knows exactly what he is to rate. Sometimes in order to make the characteristics clear, it will be necessary to break them into components. Characteristics that are too broad are difficult to rate fairly because one time the rater may emphasize one aspect and another time, another aspect. Be sure also that the characteristics to be rated are readily observable. It is helpful to the rater if the scale allows him to make rating between categories, e.g., in Figure 15–1 the rater may feel that the lettering should be rated better than average but not quite excellent. He should also be allowed to skip any of the characteristics he feels are not applicable.

Using Rating Scales. Using rating scales is relatively easy. However, there are a few caveats that raters should be aware of. There is always the danger of a halo effect. Raters frequently rate pupils with good reputations higher than they rate pupils of lesser reputation for the same performance. Similarly, raters tend to rate certain categories higher (or lower) than they should be because associated characteristics were rated high (or low). This tendency is called the logical error. Another

Figure 15–3
Check List for Plastic Letter Opener—General Shop I

Check each item if the letter opener is up to standard in this particular:

(   ) 1. The blade is properly shaped.
(   ) 2. All saw marks are removed.
(   ) 3. The plastic is free from warping and pitting.

source of error is the common tendency to rate pupils in much the same way. Some raters rate everyone high; some raters rate everyone low; and some raters rate everyone average. Yielding to such tendencies reduces the effectiveness of the rating scale and makes it difficult to separate the good guys from the bad guys.

CHECK LISTS

Check lists differ from rating scales in that they only indicate the presence or absence of characteristics. They are most useful in the evaluating of products and procedures. They can also be used to gather evidence concerning pupils' progress toward specific objectives. They cannot be used to measure personal-social growth, however.

In building check lists one should include only characteristics where presence or absence is significant. Otherwise check lists are prepared in much the same way as rating scales, and the same procedures and precautions apply except, of course, that one provides a place for checking presence or absence of the characteristic instead of a scale.

For instance, in checking some plastic letter openers that the pupils had made in his industrial arts class, the teacher might make up a check list like that in Figure 15–3.

As the teacher inspects the letter openers, he will check the applicable items. This will give him a firm basis for evaluating the product.

In the device presented in Figure 15–4, used for rating the speech of college students preparing for teaching, spaces are left blank so that the rater can either check or make some comment for each of the various items.

*

Is it really possible to objectify observations? Explain.
Compare the various types of rating scales and check lists given above. What are the strong points and weak points of each? Why?

*

THE RANKING METHOD

Another simple procedure for rating pupils' skills and accomplishments is the rank-order method. In

Figure 15–4
Speech Qualification Rating Sheet

	Explanation	Reading	Questioning
Poised	_____	_____	_____
Direct	_____	_____	_____
Animated	_____	_____	_____
Distinct	_____	_____	_____
Audible	_____	_____	_____
Fluent	_____	_____	_____
Clear (ver)	_____	_____	_____
(vis)	_____	_____	_____
Pronunciation	_____	_____	_____

RECOMMENDATION

this procedure the rater simply ranks the characteristics of pupils or products from best to worst, or most to least. For instance, one might rank a set of themes from most original to least original or all of the posters from most eye-appealing to least eye-appealing.

In using the rank-order method it is usually best to start at the ends and rank toward the middle. Another procedure is to sort the pupils or products into five groups, e.g., best, better than average, average, less than average, least. This procedure is commonly used by teachers grading essays, essay-test questions, or projects. Usually this procedure involves considerable reshuffling among the groups before the final grouping is arrived at. If one wishes, then the pupils and projects within each group can be rearranged in rank order until one has a ranking from top to bottom of the entire group. As one can see, this last step is time consuming and cumbersome. Usually in the ordinary classroom it is unnecessary; ranking in five groups will suffice for most classroom purposes.

Rank-order methods have the advantage of ensuring that raters do not rate everyone high or low or average as they tend to do when using rating scales. However, they do not describe behavior as well as some other types of measurements and are meaningful only in the group ranked. The pupil who places lowest in a high-honors group may be doing very well indeed.

USING THE BEHAVIOR LOG

Observation of the everyday behavior of the pupils can tell the teacher much. By keeping a behavior log for each pupil the teacher can amass useful information about the attitudes, behavior, and abilities of pupils. A behavior log need not be very complicated. Usually it consists merely of a notebook with a page for each pupil. On this page the teacher notes any occurrences that seem to be significant. The entries should be brief and to the point, as in Figure 15–5.

PREPARING ANECDOTAL REPORTS

Another common method of recording observations about individual pupils is the anecdotal report. This report should record significant or unusual behavior. It should describe for a given pupil briefly and matter-of-factly what happened, when, where, and under what conditions. Sometimes if the teacher thinks it desirable, he may attempt to interpret the happening. However, he should be sure to distinguish the interpretation from the description of the incident. It is usually better to report the incident without attempting to interpret it. A form for an anecdotal report appears as Figure 15–6. Such reports may be forwarded to the guidance office or be retained by the teacher for use in his own study of the pupil. In either case they can be very helpful.

Use of Problem-Situation Tests

The teacher does not always have an opportunity to observe how his pupils act in certain situations. To fill this lack, the problem-situation test has been developed. In this type of test the examiner confronts the pupil with a problem situation. The test

---

Matthew McGuire

Date	Entry
9/27	Matthew requested permission to build a model of the solar system.
9/30	M. was involved in an argument with John at the end of the laboratory period. Cause of the argument was not determined. M. said J. was picking on him.
10/5	Conference with M. concerning his project. So far he has done nothing constructive. He says he would like to do something else.
10/6	M. was elected class treasurer at the sophomore class meeting.
10/7	M. has decided to go ahead with his project after all. He has finished his plans with working drawings. They were quite acceptable.

Figure 15–5
A Behavior Log Page

Figure 15–6
Anecdotal Report Form

Name of Pupil: Date:

Description of incident:

Interpretation:

Reported by:

Position:

---

is to see what the pupil will do. In some cases the teacher can face the pupil with an actual situation and observe what he does. For example, a common procedure in an auto-mechanics course is to give the pupil a motor that will not run and tell him to find out what the trouble is. Similarly, in a class in which one is attempting to teach pupils how to conduct a meeting according to Robert's Rules of Order, the teacher might set up a meeting and see how well various members preside.

To set up situations of this type may be quite difficult. However, teachers can create pencil-and-paper problem-situation tests to serve the same purpose. For a teacher to observe every member of his class chairing a meeting might be much too time consuming. He could, however, devise a paper-and-pencil problem-situation test as a substitute for the real thing. Such a test might consist of questions like this one.

You are senior class president. You have just called to order a special meeting of the class to discuss the class trip, the senior ball, commencement activities, and the class gift. What should the order of business be for this meeting?

In the case of a broken engine, the teacher might devise a problem-situation test with questions like this one.

A farmer's tractor will not start. What steps would you take to find out what the matter is with the motor?

The items used in a problem-situation test may be either the essay or objective type. Usually, however, some type of free recall item is better than an item that suggests possible solutions to the problem.

Use of Themes, Notebooks, Homework, and Recitation

Of course, themes, homework, papers, and oral recitations are also evidence of pupil progress. They should be checked carefully. A good rule is never to assign anything that is not going to be checked by someone. Practical material, however, need not always be checked by the teacher. Sometimes pupils can check their own and each other's work quite effectively.

In order to provide an objective basis for evaluating written work, teachers can utilize rating scales, check lists, and standards. Examples of rating scales and check lists useful in evaluating written and oral work have been included in an earlier section of this chapter. A check list for use in correcting themes might include such items as

Does the pupil develop his thought logically?
Is the central idea clearly expressed?
Does the pupil document his facts?
And so on.

Sometimes a simple set of standards to use as guidelines is all the teacher needs as he corrects the pupils' writing. In the case just mentioned, the standards might include such items as

The theme clearly expresses a central idea.
Everything in the theme presented as fact must be documented.
The writer develops his thoughts logically.
And so on.

Obviously such standards could be used to make up the items in a check list.

In any case, both writing exercises and learning devices should be used mainly as aids to instruction. The emphasis should be on diagnosis, practice, and learning rather than on rating.

*

What would be the best way to test a pupil's honesty? His ability to swim? His appreciation of a poem? His freedom from prejudices? His understanding that "all men are created equal, with certain inalienable rights"? What do your answers imply as far as a testing program is concerned?

Of what uses can a behavior log be to a classroom teacher? To a guidance worker?

*

Self-reporting Techniques

SELF-EVALUATION OF PUPILS' WORK

Too many teachers think of themselves as judges. A more important purpose of evaluation is to determine where the class is and to decide where it should go. The person most concerned in any teaching-learning situation is the pupil. *If evaluation is to be fully effective, and the pupil is to set his goals correctly, the pupil should participate in evaluating his own progress.*

Pupils can cooperate in evaluating their own progress in many ways. First, they can participate in formulating the goals for the unit. Second, they can cooperate by checking their own work. Third, they can inspect their own work to find their strengths and weaknesses. Fourth, they can often decide when they have reached the point where they should go on to something else.

For example, in a certain English class one of the major concerns was the improvement of oral language skills. Each pupil was given a small roll of recording tape to use during the semester. Every pupil learned how to run the tape recorder and could, if he so desired, use the tape during out-of-class hours. On the tape each pupil could record conversations, class discussions, oral reports, and practice material. The recordings were criticized both by the pupils and the teacher. Pupils noted their own errors and worked on them individually. They also practiced by themselves on material provided by the instructor until they thought they had improved enough to record their voices again and to listen to the playback. The other work of the class was largely individualized, so that pupils could use the tape recorder whenever they were ready. In this way the pupils were able to see their errors, and with the teacher's aid set up a program for improvement. Thus they were able to see their progress and to judge whether they had improved enough to go on to other work. The teacher felt that the class improved much more than if he had tried to teach these skills directly and had made the criticisms himself.

Another evaluation technique used in the same English class was to let the pupils criticize both their own themes and those of other pupils. The primary goal was clarity, so the teacher let the pupils read each other's themes and point out what was not clear to them. Then the teacher, or on occasion another pupil, told the writer where in the text or the supplementary readings he could find a discussion of the particular error. Sometimes the teacher gave the pupil self-correcting exercises to help remedy his fault. Ordinarily, the pupils worked on these exercises until they thought they had conquered the problem. Since the pupils knew these exercises were not to be counted into their marks, they felt no need to cheat. Again, the teacher felt that the pupils learned much more efficiently than they would have if he had corrected each paper himself and had doled out marks.

In another school the members of the class divided into groups each of which developed a plan for a utopian society. The student teacher holding this class devised a rating scale (Figure 15–7) by which the class members rated each group's plan for its utopia and its class presentation.

As Gronlund points out, pupil self-evaluation helps a pupil to

1. Understand objectives better.
2. Recognize his own progress.
3. Diagnose his strengths and weaknesses.
4. Develop skill in self-evaluation.[7]

Aids to Self-evaluation. Pupils can keep anecdotal reports and behavior logs to measure their own work. For instance, a pupil working on a project can keep a daily log or diary of his progress and a record of his successes and difficulties. In a unit a pupil might submit short reports on himself at the culmination of different aspects of the work and estimate the worth of his product and the benefits he has gained from the activity. In many classes pupils keep records and report "The Things I Have Done During This Unit." This report can be

[7] Gronlund, op. cit., p. 432.

a free-response type of paper in which the pupil simply lists what he has accomplished, or a more sophisticated paper in which the pupil evaluates his accomplishments. Some teachers prepare a list of things the pupils might do and let the pupils check the things they have done. In some cases pupils check off things as they do them; in others they complete the check list at the end of the unit. Pupils can also keep profiles of what they have done. Such records as activity check lists and profiles (see Figure 15–8) are especially useful in individualized classes.

The use of cameras and tape recorders may make it easier for pupils to judge their own progress. They also make it possible for teachers to analyze pupils' actions, to diagnose errors, and to measure progress. Teachers can also use these devices to show pupils how well they are getting on and what their faults and strengths are. Motion pictures are commonly used by coaches and physical education directors for these purposes. Similarly, tape recorders are often used in speech classes and in the evaluation of discussions, panels, and other group activities.

The pupil may also participate in the evaluation of his own work through conferences with the teacher. In the conference the pupil has an opportunity to ask the teacher for help on difficult points,

Figure 15–7
Creation of a Utopian Society.

Category	Excellent	Good	Average	Fair	Poor	Comments
Believability: Might you want to see this place? Does it exist? Can it?						
Appeal: Are you ready to jump up and join this society?						
Justice: Are the laws plausible? Fair?						
Group Participation: Did each member of the panel seem important?						
Preparation: Did they know what they wanted to say?						
Presentation: Could you follow the logic?						

Figure 15–8
Profile.

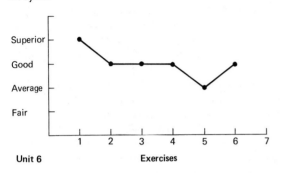

Unit 6   Exercises

Personal history.
Education.
Nonschool activities.
Health.
Personal characteristics—shy, friendly, lazy, and
so on.
Future plans.

Questionnaires As a Source of Information. The
information sought might also be gathered by the
use of a pupil questionnaire. The interest finder,
the social distance scale, and the guess-who test[8]
are all specialized examples of the questionnaire.
To prepare a questionnaire is quite simple even
though it requires care. The author of a questionnaire merely determines what he wishes to know
and then designs questions that will get that information. Whenever possible, the questionnaire
should call for short answers only. In fact, when
feasible a check list will probably be most satisfactory. However, the teacher should always allow
the pupil a chance to comment freely on any item.

Another way to get pupils to give information
about themselves is to ask the pupils to examine
themselves and to report *Things About Myself to
Improve.* This device can be made more effective by
using a questionnaire as a framework on which to
base the report. Open-ended questions, which allow
pupils to elaborate their answers as they please, may
give a teacher considerable insight into his pupils'
attitudes and values.

Individual Conferences. To know one's pupils
and to provide for their needs the teacher should
have individual conferences with them. These conferences may vary from brief comments on some
work or a question about one's health to long conversations about the youth's life objectives, adjustment problems, or difficulties with his school work.
Conferences will take place for many reasons: to
settle matters of discipline, to help pupils plan their
learning activities, to help with difficult assignments,
to diagnose pupil difficulties, to discuss pupils' academic or vocational goals, and many others. At
times the conference can be the most important tool
in the teacher's worktchest.

while the teacher has an opportunity to evaluate
the pupil's work, to point out errors, to encourage
him, and to diagnose his performance. The conference need not be formal. A few words at the
teacher's desk or at the pupil's work station may
serve just as well as a full-dress interview. In fact,
the more informal the conference, the more valuable it is likely to be.

OTHER SELF-REPORTING DEVICES

Pupil Autobiographies. Pupil autobiographies
are another excellent source of information about
pupils. From a pupil autobiography one may learn
the pupil's likes and dislikes, his background, family
history, and other pertinent facts. The beginning of
the school year is perhaps the best time for the
pupil to write his autobiography. A subject teacher
may make the assignment as part of one of the
pupil's regular classes, or it may be assigned by a
homeroom or guidance teacher. In any case, the
teachers should be careful to coordinate their assignments so that the pupil will not need to write more
than one autobiography during a given period. The
teachers should also cooperate in sharing and using
the information from the autobiographies. Too
often such information is allowed to stagnate in
some teacher's file and never gets to the persons
who should use it.

Autobiographies might include such items as
Birth—place and date.
Family information.
Home—past and present.
Home life.

Teacher-pupil conferences take time. Teachers
may have difficulty in finding time for conferences
with all their pupils. Considering that a teacher who

[8] See the following section for descriptions of these devices.

has five classes of 30 pupils each teaches 150 pupils a day, finding time for individual conferences can be a real problem. Fortunately, the situation is not as formidable as it may seem. Many of the conferences need not be long. In fact, many of them will be very short and almost recreational in nature. Moreover, the teacher has many opportunities to confer with pupils if he will only take advantage of them—before class, after school, during study periods, and so on. Class time devoted to working with pupils individually can be well worth the effort. Therefore, the competent teacher tries to arrange his class periods so as to allow for such individual work.

Opportunities for becoming acquainted with the pupil are always present. The teacher is constantly learning about the pupil from observation, other teachers, other pupils, parents, and from the many devices open to him.

*

What devices and techniques does the teacher have available for estimating the progress of pupils? How can each be best used?

How much reliance would you place on pupils' self-evaluation in your own teaching?

*

SOCIOMETRIC DEVICES

Reports from other teachers are helpful, but they can seldom give one all the information he needs. Fortunately, many devices by which one may find information are available. Particularly useful are the devices that show the social aspects of the class and the natural grouping and friendships of the pupils. Both the social distance scale and sociogram are useful for this purpose.

The Sociogram

In every class, pupils tend to form natural groups and follow natural leaders. By observing the class and by using devices such as those described in this chapter, the alert teacher can find out who the natural leaders and group members are. He should do so because, as a rule, it is advantageous to make use of these natural groups and natural leaders, par-

ticularly when forming committees.

A device particularly useful for this purpose is the sociogram. This is nothing more than a diagrammatic representation of what seems to be the structure of the group in a class. Any teacher can make a sociogram easily by using the following procedure:

1. Ask the pupils to answer in secret such questions as: Which two pupils would you like to work with on a topic for an oral report? If we should change the seating plan, whom would you like to sit beside? Or, with whom would you most like to work on a class committee in planning? Sometimes one might also ask questions such as With whom would you rather not work?

2. Tabulate the choices of each pupil. Keep the boys and girls in separate columns.

3. Construct the sociogram.

   a. Select a symbol for boy and another for girl.

   b. Place the symbols representing the most popular pupils near the center of the page, those of the less popular farther out, and those of the least popular on the fringes. It may be helpful to place the boys on one side of the page and the girls on the other.

   c. Draw lines to represent the choices. Show the direction of the choice by an arrow. Show mutual choices by a double arrow. Dislike may be shown by using dotted or colored lines.[9]

Figure 15–9 is a sociogram depicting the composition of an eighth-grade mathematics class.

*

In the sample sociogram what natural groups do you find? Do you see any indications of group leaders? If you were to form four committees, would this particular sociogram be of any help?

What other information might a sociogram give? What evidence does the sociogram give of mutual choices, rejections, mutual rejections, cliques, friendships, isolates, chains?

How might one use the data to create new patterns in the class?

How might one use natural relationships to encourage learning?

*

[9] Norman E. Gronlund and other authors recommend more ornate forms of sociograms. These sociograms are excellent for many purposes, but for ordinary classroom use they seem to be gilding the lily.

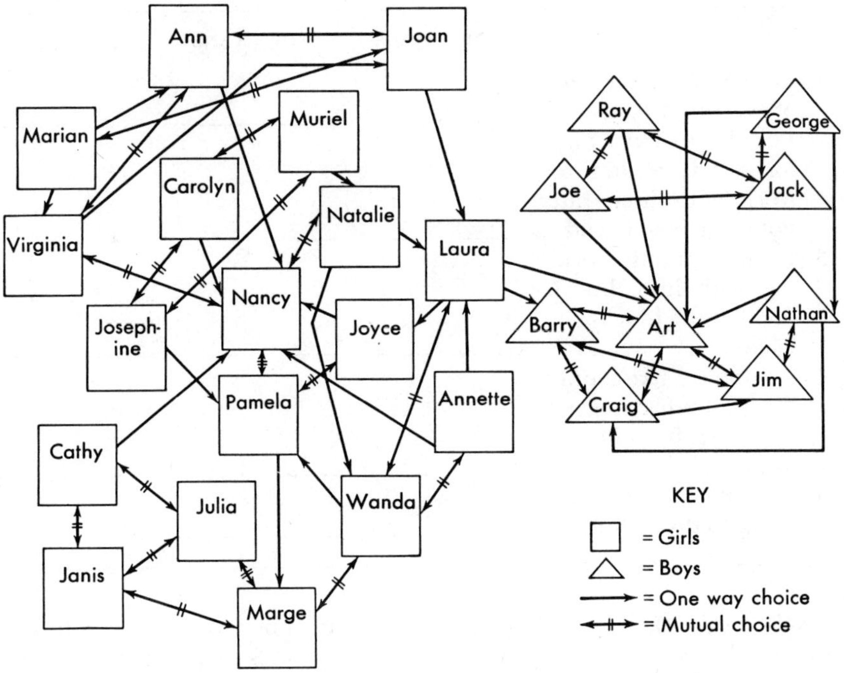

Figure 15–9
A Sociogram.

KEY

☐ = Girls
△ = Boys
→ = One way choice
←+→ = Mutual choice

The Social Distance Scale

Another useful device for obtaining information about pupils is the social distance scale. This, too, is a very simple device. One merely asks each pupil to indicate his opinion of each of the other pupils on a scale such as that shown in Figure 15–10.

The social distance scale can give the teacher valuable information concerning the natural grouping of the pupils in his class. It can point out fairly clearly which pupils are likely to work together congenially.

The Guess Who Test

Another device helpful in determining some of the social characteristics of the class is the guess-who test. Actually, this test may be used to find out many things about your pupils—interests, friendships, hobbies, habits, problems, even emotional problems at times. To buy such a test is not necessary. A teacher or a group of teachers can construct one quite easily by making up a series of statements like the follow-

ing and asking the pupils to identify which of their classmates the statements best describe.

This person is always daydreaming.
This person likes to read.
This person seems to be always worrying about something.
This person is always putting things off.

*

How might you use a Guess Who Test. What limitations does it have? Do you see any dangers in using it with high school pupils? With junior high school pupils? Make a Guess Who Test of your own.

*

STANDARDIZED TESTS

Although the teacher-built test will always remain the mainstay in the teacher's tool kit, standardized tests are important supplementary measuring devices. In general, there are three basic types: achievement tests, personality and character tests, and aptitude and intelligence tests. They differ from teacher-built tests in that they are carefully built to provide

Figure 15–10

A Social Distance Scale *

* This social distance scale and the guess-who test following are adapted from ones presented in Ruth Cunningham and Associates, *Understanding Group Behavior of Boys and Girls* (New York: Teachers College Bureau of Publications, Columbia University, 1951). *See also* Helen Jennings, *Sociometry in Group Relations* (Washington, D.C.: American Council on Education, 1948).

	JIM	JACK	NANCY	WANDA	RITA	SAM
1. I'd like him for one of my best friends.	___	___	___	___	___	___
2. I'd like to have him for a friend and to work with him, but not as a best friend.	___	___	___	___	___	___
3. I don't mind working with him, but I don't want him for a friend.	___	___	___	___	___	___
4. I don't like him much. Prefer not to work with him, if possible.	___	___	___	___	___	___
5. I don't want anything to do with him.	___	___	___	___	___	___

a common unit of measurement just as the yardstick provides a common measure for length. To this end, the procedures for administering, scoring, and interpreting the tests have been standardized so that the results may be compared all over the country.

Kinds of Standardized Tests

ACHIEVEMENT TESTS

The standardized achievement test is a most useful tool. It comes in two basic types: (1) that which shows strengths and weaknesses of pupils as a basis for diagnosis and (2) that which shows the status of individual pupils as compared with boys and girls throughout the nation. Standardized tests are useful for these purposes, but they are not valuable for determining achievement in any particular course or for evaluating the effectiveness of any particular teacher's teaching. In the first place, they rarely measure exactly what was taught in the course. Second, since standardized tests are liable to emphasize facts rather than understandings, abilities, attitudes, and skills, they frequently fail to indicate achievement in the most important aspects of the pupils' learning. Moreover, if a course or course sequence differs markedly in content from the courses in the schools which were used for standardizing the test, the latter will not measure the true

achievement of the pupils or report accurately how their achievement compares with that of other pupils.

PERSONALITY AND CHARACTER TESTS

Personality and character tests are also important tools for the teacher. That they can be a useful source of information about pupils has been pointed out in an earlier chapter. Tests of this sort are not only useful for such purposes, but they can also help ascertain to what extent such teaching goals as attitudes, ideals, and other personality and character traits have been achieved. They are essential, of course, as a source of information in the guidance program.

APTITUDE AND INTELLIGENCE TESTS

Aptitude tests are another source of information for the teacher. They attempt to show what a person's aptitudes or innate abilities are. Among the aptitude tests available are intelligence tests that seek to show one's aptitude for intellectual work, and tests designed to show one's aptitude for music, art, and various types of tasks. Probably the best-known type of these is the intelligence test. Tests of true intelligence are extremely difficult to construct. It is doubtful that any intelligence test really measures intelligence. However, the scores from such tests are extremely helpful in understanding the individual and should be used—but with caution. Similarly, tests for other aptitudes, such as musical, artistic, and vocational aptitudes, give important contributions to the teacher's knowledge of the pupil and are a great aid in guidance.

Selecting a Standardized Test

Standardized tests should be selected with care. There are many of them. Some are excellent, others are far from satisfactory. In searching for a suitable test, the teacher can receive considerable help from such sources as curriculum laboratories and test files maintained by local and state departments of education and by colleges and universities. Textbooks on tests and measurements often list and criticize tests both in the text and appendixes. Catalogs of the various test publishing houses tell what they have to offer. Critical analyses may be found in the *Mental Measurement Yearbooks*[10] compiled under the editorship of O. K. Buros, probably the most dependable sources of information concerning standardized tests. In these books the various tests are discussed without fear or favor by competent analysts. New tests are frequently listed in such journals as the *Education Index, Psychological Abstracts, Review of Educational Research,* and *Educational and Psychological Measurement.* Textbooks in specific methods courses often discuss standardized achievement tests in the field with which they are concerned. Another source is the various bibliographies of tests.

These references will usually provide considerable information about the tests' content, validity, reliability, and usability. By using these references it should be relatively easy to eliminate the instruments that are patently not appropriate for one's purpose and thus narrow down the number which one should examine most carefully in making the final selection.

In the final selection the test buyer should carefully consult sample copies of the test and its manual. (Any test that lacks a manual should be viewed

with particular caution.) The first thing one should check for is the validity of the test. Is it designed to do what you wish it to do? If it is an achievement test, does it fit in with the philosophy and objectives of the school and courses concerned? How was the validity established? From what type of population were the norms derived? If the population was greatly different from the type of class you have, the test will not be valid for your group. How were the items selected? Does a careful, logical, and psycological analysis of the test and its manual indicate that the items measure what they purport to measure?

If the test is valid, then one may go on to check the test's reliability and usability. In so doing, the teacher should bear in mind that a test bearing a reliability coefficient of less than .70 is proably a bad risk, and that ease in administering, scoring, and interpreting can lighten what is at best a difficult job.

Administering a Standardized Test

Any standardized test worth its salt will give clear, detailed directions for the administering of the test. Teachers should follow these directions exactly. Failure to do so may give false scores. As much as possible, standardized tests should be treated as routine classroom activities. A great to-do about the giving of a standardized test may cause tensions and upset the purpose of the test. Particularly reprehensible is coaching pupils for the test. A standardized test is a sampling. If boys and girls are coached on the sample the test will be much in error and it will be impossible to find out what the test might have told you. The only sure way to give a test a chance to do what you wish it do is to administer it exactly as the manual prescribes.

*

If you were to select a standardized test to measure the achievement of pupils in one of your classes, how would you go about it?

What three qualities would you have to check?

Where does cost appear in your answer?

How would you find out if a standardized achievement test was valid in your situation?

In what ways might poor administering of a standardized test upset the test results?

*

[10] O. K. Buros, *Mental Measurement Yearbook* (Highland Park, N.J.: The Gryphon Press. Various noncumulative editions).

Interpreting Standardized Test Scores

The value of a standardized test comes in the interpretation of the scores. Consequently, a standardized test should provide norms that permit the comparison of one group with other groups. Norms should not be confused with standards. A standard is a level of achievement or ability required for some purpose. A norm is quite a different thing. It is an average. Usually we deal with grade norms or age norms. A ninth-grade norm, for instance, is simply the average or mean score of the ninth graders. It is a theoretical point at which the average of the scores of all the ninth graders falls. Similarly, an age norm is the average of the scores of all the pupils of that age. This means that in an average group at any particular level, half of the pupils should be higher, and half of the pupils lower, than the norm. Thus any pupil who is reading at the tenth-grade level is reading as well as the average tenth-grader. Without further information one cannot tell whether this is good or bad.

USING DERIVED SCORES

Norms of standardized tests are really derived scores provided by the test makers to aid the user in the interpretation of the test. Grade norms and age norms, however, are not the only types of derived scores that may be used. One of the most familiar types is the ratio intelligence quotient. This score represents the ratio between the mental age of a child and his chronological age, i.e., $IQ = \dfrac{MA}{CA} \times 100$. It is, in effect, a refinement of the age norm.

This ratio IQ and other scores such as the Education Quotient and Achievement Quotient derived from ratio IQs are now obsolete. They are being replaced by the deviation IQ which is simply a standardized score having, for the most intelligence tests, a mean of 100 and a standard deviation of 16 (or sometimes 15). But even these IQ scores should be viewed with caution.

Estimating an individual's intelligence is too complicated a matter to be based on a single test score. Different tests of intelligence do not yield the same scores. Also, scores from the same tests vary considerably. IQs may be accepted as general indexes of brightness, but they cannot be accepted at their face value. A good rule might be to assume that the chances are good that the actual index of brightness would fall within a range of five points above or below the IQ derived from the test. To judge how bright a particular youngster is requires the use of other criteria in addition to the IQ.

PERCENTILE SCORES

Another type of derived score is the centile or percentile norm. The percentile score indicates the per cent of the sample population who reached that score. For example, if a youngster receives a percentile score of 10, 10 per cent of the group did less well than or as well as he, and 90 per cent did better. The 50th percentile, of course, is average.

T AND Z SCORES

Other derived scores are the z score[11] and T score, which are based upon the normal curve of probability and the standard deviation from the mean. Usually the z score tells the number of standard deviations a person's score is above or below the mean. For instance, a z score of $+0.5$ means that the person's score was one half a standard deviation above the mean of the scores of all persons taking the test. In order to eliminate fractions and plus and minus signs, McCall invented the T scale in which the mean is represented by 50 and each standard deviation is given the value of 10. In this scale $+0.5$ would become 55. Some writers call these Z scores when the original distribution of raw scores is not normal. They use the term T score only for normal or normalized distribution. The z score itself has been varied to eliminate the signs by taking 5 or 10 as the mean and expressing the deviation from the mean as a multiple of the standard deviations. Thus our score of $+0.5$ may become 5.5 or 55 or 110, depending upon the values used.

STANINE SCORES

Another useful score is the stanine score. This is a nine point score in which each unit represents a band equal to one half a standard deviation and the

11 Or sigma score.

mean is equal to 5 and the standard deviation, 2. Table 15–2 is an attempt to compare these scales.

From this table we see that a T score of 70 can be interpreted to mean that the pupil is rated at two standard deviations above the mean or within the top 3 per cent (97th percentile) of those taking the test. Presumably this is a good score, but one cannot really tell until he knows more about the pupil and the test situation. To make decisions on the basis of test scores alone can be very dangerous.

USING TEST NORMS

Norms are useful in that they provide a basis for comparing pupils from different school systems. They are valuable in evaluating school programs, and they can also tell the approximate standing of pupils with respect to their peers. Thus they can be extremely useful in developing individual programs for pupils and in providing for individual differences. For instance, if a teacher finds that an eighth grader seems to have ability at the tenth-grade level, he should investigate the feasibility of giving him work that would be challenging at that level.

*

In a certain seventh grade a test indicated that 25 percent of the pupils were reading below the seventh-grade level. The teacher claimed that there was no cause to worry. Would you agree? Why, or why not? Do you need more information on which to decide?

The parents of a brilliant boy have just been informed that their youngster has achieved his grade norm in all areas and is slightly above norm in one area. They are well pleased. Should they be?

Some schools segregate boys and girls into homogeneous groups on the basis of an IQ score alone. After reading this short discussion do you think this practice is proper? Why, or why not?

*

Criterion-Referenced Tests

Recently educators have been turning to the use of criterion-referenced tests instead of norm-based tests. As we have seen, rather than showing the differences in individual achievement these tests show whether pupils have achieved a standard. These tests are basically what the space workers call go–no go tests. If the standard requires the pupil to answer ten of twelve questions correctly, then the pupil who answers ten, eleven, or twelve questions correctly succeeds; the pupil who answers nine questions correctly does not. Such tests are particularly important in classrooms and schools that employ continuous promotion schemes. Mastery tests are, or should be, of this type.

Test builders have had relatively little experience with these tests at the formal level. At the present state of the art, procedures for developing standardized criterion-referenced tests and criteria of excellence for tests of this type have not been fully determined, but there is no doubht that if the competency-based education, assessment, and accountability movements continue, we educators must have criterion-referenced standardized tests.

Table 15–2
*Comparison of Various Derived Scores**

Note: Deviation IQs are computed with a standard deviation of 16; stanine scores represent ranges or bands rather than points.

Standard deviations	−3	−2	−1	0	1	2	3		
z scores	−3.0	−2.0	−1.0	0	−1.0	2.0	3.0		
Converted z scores	70	80	90	100	110	120	130		
T scores	20	30	40	50	60	70	80		
Z scores	20	30	40	50	60	70	80		
Deviation IQ's	52	68	84	100	110	132	148		
Percentiles	0.1	2.3	15.9	5.0	84.1	97.7	99.9		
Stanines		1	2	3	4	5	6	7	8	9

DIAGNOSIS

The Need for Diagnosis

The major point of the introductory section of this chapter was that the principal value of evaluation and measurement is their potential as tools to use in diagnosing the teaching-learning situation. This use of evaluation and measurement is most important, for good diagnosis is essential for good teaching.

In treating an ill patient, a physician must first find out what the patient's illness is and, if possible, what is causing it. Then, and then only, can he treat the disease successfully, for, if he cannot determine what the disease is, he can treat only the symptoms. Even if the patient is free from disease, the physician finds diagnosis a necessary part of his campaign to keep his patient in good health.

So it is with a teacher. Much of our work has to do with boys and girls who are in poor academic health. In order to improve their health the teacher must

1. Find that a difficulty exists.
2. Find exactly what the difficulty is.
3. Find the cause of the difficulty.

This is diagnosis. Without it, teaching flounders. To be sure, these steps must be followed up by teaching directed toward correcting whatever seems to be wrong or lacking. But without diagnosis, teaching can have little direction. It is as necessary when pupils are in good academic health as when they are ailing, for if a teacher is to teach his pupils well, he must know their academic strengths and weaknesses. Diagnosis is also essential as a basis for motivation, the selection of educational objectives, and the determination of the most suitable methods and content.

*

Suppose that after studying the lever in a physics class, you gave a test and found that all of the pupils did not measure up to your expectations in their understanding of the fulcrum. What would your diagnosis of the situation be? Would it be different if most of the pupils did understand and only a few did not? Would it be different if only one or two did not understand? What could have caused these pupils to fail to learn as well as you expected?

*

The Tools of Diagnosis

DIAGNOSTIC TESTS

The tools used in the diagnostic process are the tools of evaluation and measurement. Perhaps the most common are the criterion-referenced diagnostic or mastery tests. Such tests may be either teacher-made or procured from commercial test houses. Listings of diagnostic tests available commercially may be found in such references as Buros' Mental Measurement Yearbooks.[12] Before selecting a commercial diagnostic test for any particular mission, the teacher should examine several and compare them carefully. Not all of the tests are equally good. In fact, some tests are downright bad. Moreover, not all of the good tests do each job equally well. The teacher in search of a diagnostic test should consult the references and apply the criteria for commercial-test selection noted elsewhere in this chapter.

The most important criterion to check is whether or not the test items actually test the presence or absence of the specific skills, understandings, and attitudes that you wish to find out about. You can obtain this information by examining the test manual furnished by the publisher and by inspecting the instrument itself and comparing it with your teaching objectives. Teachers can make their own diagnostic instruments by

1. Setting up specific (preferably criterion-referenced) behavioral objectives.
2. Building test items that test the various behavioral objectives. There usually should be several items for each objective. It helps in analyzing the test result if each item tests only one objective.
3. Arranging the items into an instrument.

OTHER DIAGNOSTIC DEVICES

In addition to diagnostic tests, many other devices may be used for diagnosis. One example of a device that might be employed is the following scheme, previously cited, sometimes used to determine whether or not a book is beyond a certain pupil's reading ability. The technique is amazingly simple. One just gives to the pupil a portion of the

12 Buros, op. cit.

book to read and then tests him on it. If he can answer the questions, the work is probably not too difficult for him; if he stumbles, the teacher can try him on increasingly less difficult material until a book he can read and understand is found. If the teacher takes the selections from a graded series, he can also ascertain the pupil's approximate reading level by this technique. However, before using the technique as an index of reading level, the teacher should note that all books reported to be at a given level are not equally difficult and also that some pupils find it more difficult to read in some subject matter areas than in others. Another example also concerns reading. One of the most common of pupils' reading problems is an inability to grasp the point of a paragraph. A simple method for testing this ability is to have the pupil read a paragraph and then ask him what it said. This technique may also be used in mathematics to see whether or not the pupil can read and understand a problem.

The preceding techniques described are forms of controlled observation. Other useful techniques include analysis of written work, analysis of oral work, analysis of records, check lists, rating scales, and conferences. Thus questioning a pupil about his mathematics paper might disclose that he does not know how to marshal his facts in order to attack a problem. In mathematics again, and in other subjects as well, analysis of the pupils' papers might show errors in their thinking, poor problem-solving techniques, or a lack of understanding of the fundamental processes. Questionnaires and conferences with the pupil or his parents can often be very useful in uncovering faulty study habits and procedures. Descriptions of specific techniques can be found in works on diagnostic and remedial teaching such as those by O. K. Buros[13] and Blair and Powell's *Diagnostic and Remedial Teaching.*[14]

*

A student teacher suggests that one method of diagnosing pupil difficulty is to ask the pupil about his troubles. What do you think of this technique?

A pupil in one of your classes, although seemingly bright enough in class discussion, invariably does poorly on the tests. What could you do to find out why this is so?

*

[13] Ibid.
[14] (New York: Macmillan Publishing Co., Inc., 1967).

A Procedure for Diagnosis

INITIAL DIAGNOSIS IN THE CLASSROOM

Diagnosis should be going on every day in every classroom. For the most efficient teaching the teacher should make a general diagnosis of the status of each pupil's learning at the beginning of the year and continue with similar diagnoses as each unit of work is carried to completion. For an initial diagnosis one can give a standardized survey test to ascertain each pupil's initial position in relation to the goals of the course. Frequently teacher-made tests are as satisfactory for this purpose as standardized tests. In many courses an objective paper-and-pencil test would be a good device to show how each pupil stands, while in others another type of test would be more desirable. Paper-and-pencil tests are usually not the best device for measuring skills, attitudes, appreciations, and ideals. To get at these learnings, the teacher might do better with check lists, observation, analysis of papers, rating of skills, rating of products, questionnaires, and reports of previous teachers. While the initial diagnosis cannot always be completed immediately, it should be developed during the first unit. The more information the teacher has at the beginning of the course, the better and sooner will he be able to make this diagnosis.

CONTINUING THE DIAGNOSIS

After the initial diagnosis the teacher should continue to diagnose, revising, if necessary, as he goes along. Certainly the teacher should attempt to take stock at the end of every unit. This can be done simply by testing the pupils to see where they stand in relation to the goals of the unit. For this purpose one should use a diagnostic or mastery test. For example, two specific objectives might be

1. Strong ties of friendship have developed between the United States and Great Britain during the twentieth century.
2. The American State Department, beginning with the days of John Hay and continuing to the present, has cooperated with the British Foreign Office in matters of international importance to both nations.

In an objective test the teacher might use items like the following to see how well the pupils had achieved these objectives.

1. During the first half of the twentieth century, relations between the United States and Great Britain have been
   a. friendly
   b. neutral
   c. unfriendly
   d. inimical.
   (Designed to check the first objective: Strong ties of friendship have developed between the United States and Great Britain during the twentieth century.)
2. Give five examples of how the British Foreign Office has cooperated with the United States in matters of international importance to both nations.
   (Designed to check the second objective: The American State Department, beginning with the days of John Hay and continuing to the present, has cooperated with the British Foreign Office in matters of international importance to both nations.)

Essay test items can be used in the same way. In this unit one specific objective was "The ties [of friendship] which draw the United States closer to the Commonwealth are based upon our common language, customs, and traditions."

To test this objective one might use the following essay item: Describe the ties that tend to draw the United States and Great Britain together.

ASSESSING ATTITUDES, IDEALS, AND APPRECIATIONS

To test attitudes, ideals, and appreciations by means of paper-and-pencil tests is more difficult. Pupils are likely to give the answer the teacher wants rather than what they really believe. For instance, one of the attitudes that might be a goal in this same unit is: In international affairs, as well as private affairs, one should deal justly with all. If, to test this attitude, one should ask, "Should the United States respect the rights of other nations?" the clever pupils would answer "Yes," because they know that is the answer the teacher expects. However, if the teacher poses for discussion a problem in which the United States can gain an advantage by violating the rights of a small nation, one may learn individuals' true attitudes by observing their reaction to the problem. Other methods of getting at attitudes are observation, rating scales, check lists, questionnaires, and analysis of papers.

*

Following are four other attitudes, ideals, and appreciations which might be goals for the unit "From Empire to Commonwealth." How might one get at these objectives?

1. No nation can depend entirely on itself.
2. The achievements of the British deserve our respect.
3. Cooperation is more desirable than warfare in international relations.
4. One should respect the rights and feelings of others.

*

USING THE ITEM ANALYSIS

After the test has been given and scored, what does it tell us? If the test items have been aimed at specific objectives, an item analysis can give us the information fairly easily. All the teacher needs to do is to see how well each pupil responded to the items designed to test the various objectives. Table 15–3 is an example of an item analysis.

Table 15–3
An Item Analysis

	Item	A	B	C	D	E	F	G	H	I	J	K
Obj. I	1	√	√	√		√	√	√	√	√	√	√
	2	√	√	√	√			√				
	3	√		√			√					
	4	√	√	√		√	√	√			√	
Obj. II	5											
	6	√			√							√
	7											
	8					√						
Obj. III	9	√	√	√	√		√	√		√	√	√
	10	√		√	√	√	√		√		√	√
	11		√	√	√			√				
	12	√	√	√	√	√	√	√		√		√

A quick look at this table shows us that none of the pupils seems to have attained the second objective very well. Also it seems that although pupils D and K have mastered the third objective quite well, neither of them has done very well with the first or second objective. Pupil H, on the other hand, does not seem to have done well on any three of the objectives. Obviously the teacher would do well to give additional instruction to the entire class on objective 2 and individual or small group instruction to certain people in the other areas.

A BASIS FOR REMEDIAL PROCEDURES

At times it will become evident that some pupils are falling behind. Their difficulties may be more serious than their inability to reach the goal of a unit—in some cases much more serious. For these persons other techniques are necessary. Some pupils may need the specialized help of remedial classes and teachers, if available. Others can perhaps be helped by the classroom teacher.

The first thing to do, after ascertaining that a difficulty exists, is to determine exactly what the nature of the difficulty is. For example, John is doing very badly in algebra. A check of his papers shows that one cause of his trouble seems to be his arithmetic. Consequently, the next step would be to try to find what about his arithmetic is faulty and why it is so. Perhaps a diagnostic arithmetic test can find the answers to these questions. If no such test is available, perhaps one can find out the trouble in a conference, or by a more minute study of the pupil's papers, or by giving him specific work in arithmetic and checking to see just what type of errors he makes. In any case, a painstaking search for the exact trouble is imperative if the remedial teaching is to be of any value at all. An item analysis of the pupil's test responses may be particularly helpful at this point.

SUMMARY

If we are to keep from drifting aimlessly like so much flotsam and jetsam in the surf, we need to determine where we are and where we should go. This process is evaluation. It differs from measurement in that it involves judgment of worth, while measurement merely describes the pupil's status. Many devices can be used to measure the status of the learning of boys and girls. We should use more of these devices than we ordinarily do, but evaluations can be made only by the evaluator himself. Consequently, goals and standards must be established to give the evaluator touchstones against which to compare the value of what he is judging.

But the purpose of evaluation is not merely to determine a pupil's worth. Evaluation should be the basis for determining what comes next, or where to go on to. Evaluation can also be useful as a basis for remedial action or as a basis for deciding whether retention or promotion will be better for a pupil. Evaluation is a concomitant of good teaching.

Evaluation instruments stand or fall on the basis of their validity. If an instrument is reliable, objective, and usable, so much the better. But one that is not valid is worthless. The key to test building is to choose items that will ascertain whether or not the pupils have attained the teaching objectives. Consequently, the test builder should aim his items at specific goals. The same criteria that hold for teacher-built tests also hold for standardized tests. Although statistical procedures and other esoteric techniques are useful for the professional tester, the basic ingredients necessary for the classroom user and builder of tests are good judgment and careful thought.

Although teachers tend to use test scores as the basis for a large share of their evaluations, they have many other tools and devices for evaluation available to them. Among them are rating scales, check lists, behavior logs, anecdotal reports, problem-situation tests, themes, notebooks, other written work, homework, class recitation and participation, and various sociometric devices. Pupils can profitably take on some of the responsibility for their own work. Self-report forms and rating scales make pupil self-evaluation easier and more profitable. Among the sociometric devices that can be very useful are the sociogram, social distance scale, and guess-who test.

Standardized tests come in all shapes and sizes. Some are very good and some very bad. Before using them one should check out their worth carefully. For this purpose references like Buros' *Mental Measurement Yearbook* can be most helpful. The administration of a standardized test can make the difference between obtaining good data and misinformation, therefore the tests should be given exactly as the test's manual prescribes. Any variation from the prescribed procedure may invalidate the test. In interpreting standardized scores it should be remembered that most of them are norm-based. So far test experts have not settled on procedures for standardizing criterion-referenced tests. Most modern standardized tests are scored on the basis of percentile or standard scores of a norm group. Versions of the standard score commonly used are z score, T score, Z score, deviation IQs, and stanines. Grade and age norms are obtained by

averaging the scores of all the pupils in the norm group who are of a particular age. Test users should remember that these norms are not standards but averages.

The principal function of measurement and evaluation in teaching should be diagnosis. For that purpose one can use diagnostic tests, observation, and other procedures and devices. Item analyses of mastery and diagnostic tests can be particularly helpful. However, we repeat that the most important tool in this, as in other aspects of evaluation, is good judgment.

Classroom
Testing

16

A test is "a systematic procedure for measuring an individual's behavior."[1] According to Brown, tests can be used

1. To determine present levels of skills, abilities, and characteristics.
2. To judge students' skills and characteristics as a basis for placing them in the educational sequence.
3. To monitor the progress of students' learning.
4. To determine degree of students' mastery of the skill or material being taught.
5. To measure the amount of retention, transfer and/or integration resulting from the learning experience.[2]

Classroom tests, Brown continues, have the following functions:

1. To find out how well the pupils have mastered what was taught.
2. As a basis for grading.
3. To motivate pupils.
4. As a basis for planning.
5. Review.[3]

[1] Frederick G. Brown, *Measurement and Evaluation* (Itasca, Ill.: F. E. Peacock Publishers, Inc., 1971), p. 8.
[2] Ibid., Ch. 1.
[3] Ibid., pp. 48–49.

357

Types of Tests

There are many types of tests. According to Gronlund these include

Oral and written tests.
Informal and standardized tests.
Essay and objective tests.
Mastery, survey, and diagnostic tests.
Individual and group tests.
Performance, verbal and nonverbal tests.
Speed and power tests.[4]

No matter what types of tests are used, they are subject to numerous limitations. There is always some error in sampling. There is always some error inherent in the test itself (e.g., true-false tests encourage guessing). There is always some error in the process by which we administer and score tests (e.g., scoring of essay tests is often wildly inconsistent). There is always some error in our interpretation of test results. (Consequently teachers should be careful to get several test scores and to gather as many other data as possible before making irrevocable decisions.)

INFORMAL AND STANDARDIZED TESTS

Most classroom tests are informal tests of achievement in the cognitive and psychomotor domains. Although there is increased effort by teachers to gather information about the progress of pupils in the affective domain, most attempts to gain such information must be done by the use of observational and self-report techniques.[5] As a rule, formal standardized tests are used only on special occasions for special purposes. Their use is discussed in another section of this chapter.

MASTERY, SURVEY, OR DIAGNOSTIC TESTS

Classroom tests may be either mastery, survey, or diagnostic in nature. The mastery test is designed to determine whether or not pupils have achieved a minimum standard. It does not attempt to compare the worth of various pupils' performance. The survey test is designed to find the differences in

pupils' achievement as an indicator of their general ability in the area being tested. It is used to compare pupils' scores so as to give them grades. The diagnostic test is used to find where pupils' abilities and disabilities lie. Diagnostic tests are usually designed so that there are a number of items pointed at each objective. This procedure makes it possible for the teacher to analyze the test results so as to find the strengths and weaknesses of individual pupils and of the class as a whole. Although the differences among the different types of tests tend to blur in ordinary classroom testing, if teachers bear the differences in mind when they are making out their test plans, their testing should be more effective.

CRITERION-REFERENCED VERSUS NORM-REFERENCED TESTS

Well-built mastery and diagnostic tests are criterion-referenced tests. Survey tests are more often norm-referenced. These terms have been explained earlier. The difference between them is that in criterion-referenced tests the pupil's performance on the test is rated against a set standard while in norm-referenced tests the pupil's performance is rated against the performance of other pupils, i.e., the norm of the group. Criterion-referenced tests are therefore more likely to be based on the achievement of definite objectives. Criterion-referenced tests and test items are not very efficient for determining classmarks, however. Even so, they are probably of more real value for use in the classroom than achievement tests of the survey type are.

SPEED VERSUS POWER TESTS

No matter what the test type, except in unusual cases, classroom tests should be power tests, not speed tests. Therefore when building and administering a classroom test, the teacher should try to ensure that all pupils have plenty of time to do their best on every part of the test. Hurried test situations are grossly unfair to the thorough and methodical pupil. They also tend to defeat the purpose of testing. One never can be sure whether pupils could not answer the later portions of the test because of lack of knowledge or lack of time.

---

[4] Norman E. Gronlund, *Measurement and Evaluation in Teaching*, 2nd ed. (New York: Macmillan Publishing Co., Inc., 1971), p. 25.
[5] Rating scales, check lists, rankings, anecdotal reports, behavioral logs, guess-who, sociometric techniques, and so on.

OBJECTIVE VERSUS ESSAY TESTS

In uninformed circles there is quite a bit of debate about the relative merit of objective and essay tests. Such debate is fruitless. Each type of test has merits and each has limitations. The good test builder does not depend entirely on one or the other, but rather uses each for the purposes for which it is best fitted.

In several ways and for certain purposes the objective-test item is better than the essay-test item. With it teachers can provide a relatively adequate sampling quite easily. Furthermore, since objective test items limit the pupil's choice, the answers do not wander from the point in the way essay answers sometimes do. Also, they are not likely to include irrelevant material or to be affected by environmental conditions. For these reasons objective tests are often more reliable than essay tests. In addition, they are easier to score. In fact, the scoring is often so easy that it may be farmed out to clerks or other nonprofessionals. Moreover, the use of keys and automatic scoring devices can make the objective test really objective. It is only when the scorer departs from the key that the test becomes subjective. Objective tests have the additional advantage of being less time-consuming than essay tests. As a matter of fact, objective tests can often do in a single period more than an essay test can do in a double period.

In spite of their virtues objective-type tests have many serious faults. In the first place, good objective-test items are difficult to write. Even in carefully built tests some items are liable to be ambiguous or to contain clues that may give away the answers. Second, to test high-level learning with this type of test is difficult. Although objective-test items can test the ability to organize, the ability to use what has been learned, the ability to show relationships, and the ability to evaluate, such items are extremely difficult to build and frequently even more difficult to key. The objective-type test often tests only isolated facts with a resultant emphasis on verbalism rather than true understanding.

The essay item has several distinct advantages over the objective-test item for testing certain types of learning. Being a pure recall type of item, it tests a higher level of knowledge than do many objective-test items. It can also test the ability to organize, to use materials, to show relationships, to apply knowledge, and to write—abilities that are not easily tested by objective-test items. Furthermore, pupils seem to put more effort into studying for essay tests.

In spite of its virtues, the essay test has many innate faults. First, the validity of an essay test is liable to be low. This lack of validity stems from the fact that in essay testing it is very difficult to get an adequate sample of the pupils' knowledge of what was to be learned. Irrelevancies are likely to enter into the essay item. The validity and reliability of the test are lowered by the tendency of some pupils to wander off the subject, to shoot the bull, and to speak in vague generalities. The reliability of the essay test is also lowered by the tendency of the scorers to mistake skill in expression, style, glibness, handwriting, neatness, and other irrelevant qualities for knowledge of what was to be learned. Scoring essay items, when done properly, is a slow, difficult process. This greatly reduces the test's usability.

Because the essay-test item is prone to these faults—low objectivity, low reliability, and low usability—the teacher should use them with discrimination. As a rule, the essay test should be reserved for occasions in which the teacher wishes to test a high level of recall and in which he wishes to test the ability to organize material, to apply what has been learned, to evaluate, to show relationships, and to write well. In determining whether or not to use such items, the teacher should also consider whether or not essays instead of essay tests might not be a better measure. The pupil who has time to sit and develop his thoughts in a theme or essay may demonstrate his skills in these areas more accurately than in the rush of an examination. Table 16–1 shows a comparison of the advantages and limitations of these two types of test items.

*

What criteria would you use in deciding whether or not to use an essay or objective test for a specific unit?

What advantages does the use of performance testing have over the ordinary essay or objective test?

*

Table 16–1

Comparative Advantages of Objective and Essay Tests*

	Objective Test	Essay Test
Learning outcomes measured	Efficient for measuring knowledge of facts. Some types (e.g., multiple choice) can also measure understandings, thinking skills, and other complex outcomes. Inefficient or inappropriate for measuring ability to select and organize ideas, writing abilities, and some types of problem-solving skills.	Inefficient for measuring knowledge of facts. Can measure understanding, thinking skills, and other complex learning outcomes (especially useful where originality of response is desired). Appropriate for measuring ability to select and organize ideas, writing abilities, and problem-solving skills requiring originality.
Preparation of questions	A relatively large number of questions needed for a test. Preparation is difficult and time consuming.	Only a few questions are needed for a test. Preparation is relatively easy (but more difficult than generally assumed).
Sampling of course content	Provides an extensive sampling of course content, owing to the large number of questions that can be included in a test.	Sampling of course content is usually limited, owing to the small number of questions that can be included in the test.
Control of pupil's response	Complete structuring of task limits pupil to type of response called for. Prevents bluffing and avoids influence of writing skill. However, selection-type items are subject to guessing.	Freedom to respond in own words enables bluffing and writing skill to influence the score. However, guessing is minimized.
Scoring	Objective scoring, which is quick, easy, and consistent.	Subjective scoring, which is slow, difficult, and inconsistent.
Influence on learning	Usually encourages pupils to develop a comprehensive knowledge of specific facts and the ability to make fine discriminations among them. Can encourage the development of understandings, thinking skills, and other complex outcomes, if properly constructed .	Encourages pupils to concentrate on larger units of subject matter, with special emphasis on the ability to organize, integrate, and express ideas effectively.

* Norman E. Gronlund, *Measurement and Evaluation in Teaching,* 2nd ed. (New York: Macmillan Publishing Co., Inc., 1971), p. 25.

BUILDING THE CLASSROOM TEST

General Rules for Test Construction

As in all other teaching, the first step in test construction is to plan. Every teacher should set up objectives for each lesson or unit he teaches. He should use these objectives for the basis of his test plan. To a large measure they should determine what kind of test to give and what items to include. Some learning products may be tested best by performance tests, some by essay tests, some by objective tests, and some by observation. The test builder attempts to pick the type of item that will best suit the objectives of a particular lesson. After consideration he may find it advisable to use several types of test items and devices. Whatever choice he makes usually depends upon the time and materials available as well as the objectives to be tested. In short, then, the steps to follow in building a test are

1. Determine what the specific instructional objectives of the unit are going to be. Define these objectives as specific pupil behavior.
2. Outline the subject matter content to be included.
3. Draw up a table of specifications which will show the objectives, the content, and the number or weight of test items (or other measuring devices) to be given to each area. An example of a table of specifications appears as Table 16–2.
4. Build the test items in accordance with the table of specifications.

Note that steps 1, 2, and 3 of this procedure should be completed before the teaching of the unit begins. Building the table of specifications should influence instruction as well as evaluation in the unit.

DESIGNING THE TEST

Designing the test should be done with care, for the task is to build a test that will allow the pupils to show just how well they have progressed. The test builder should avoid any extraneous influences that might affect the test score. In designing the test, he should bear the following rules of thumb in mind.

1. All teaching objectives should be tested in proportion to their importance.
2. The test should include items easy enough for the slowest pupils and items difficult enough to challenge the brightest ones—except in mastery tests when the items should be designed to find out whether or not the pupils know and can perform up to a certain standard. In mastery tests it is not necessary to include difficult items—just items that show whether or not the pupil has reached the objective. In any case there should be some easy items so that pupils will not be discouraged and so not try.
3. To avoid confusion, only a few types of items should be used in the test.
4. All items of the same type should be placed together.
5. Items should be arranged from the easiest to the most difficult so as not to discourage the less bright at the beginning of the test.

6. Directions, format, and wording should be crystal clear. There is no room for trick questions or obscurity. A test is neither a joke nor a puzzle.
7. The test items should fit the objectives to be tested. They should call for the same type of behavior that the objectives call for. It is easy to write items that check memory so almost everyone tends to overuse memory questions unless he is wary.
8. The test should provide the pupils with all the information necessary for the completion of the items. Any additional materials necessary should be provided before the test begins.
9. The reading level of the test should not be too difficult.
10. There should be several items aimed at each objective.
11. The test should not be affected by irrelevancies such as the pupils' ability to write well or their reading skill. The only criterion should be how well they have learned those things they were supposed to have learned.
12. The test should be so constructed that it "contributes to improved teaching-learning practice." [6]

*

Of what value are the objectives of a lesson or unit when one is devising a test?

Why is it sometimes stated that there is no such thing as an objective test?

In constructing a teacher-built test, what procedure would you follow? Outline what you would do step by step.

*

SELECTION OF THE ITEMS

Once the teacher has developed his test plan, he is ready to select the test items. In order to ensure curriculum validity, without which an achievement test is of little value, the teacher should see to it that each item selected is directed toward a specific teaching objective. Moreover, he must be careful to select items that point up the objectives in proportion to their importance. A test that emphasizes some goals at the expense of others is not valid. Following a well-drawn table of specifications will ensure that the proper weight to each objective is given.

If the teacher has taught the unit or lesson before, he should have a file of test items. Good test items are too difficult to build to be thrown away. Consequently, whenever a teacher gives a test he should save the good items and file them away for future

[6] Gronlund, op. cit., p. 144.

Table 16–2
*Table of Specifications for a Weather Unit in Junior High School Science**

| | Knows | | Understands | Skill in | | | |
Content	Symbols and Terms	Specific Facts	Influence of Each Factor on Weather Formation	Use of Measuring Devices	Constructing Weather Maps	Interpreting Weather Maps	Total Number of Items
Air pressure	2	3	3			3	11
Wind	4	2	8	Observe pupils using measuring devices (rating scale)	Evaluate maps constructed by pupils (check list)	2	16
Temperature	2	2	2			2	8
Humidity and Precipitation	2	1	2			5	10
Clouds	2	2	1				5
Total number of Items	12	10	16			12	50
Per cent of Items	24	20	32			24	Items

* Gronlund, op. cit., p. 65.

use. Keeping such a file is easy, since all the teacher needs to do is to clip the good items from his test as he uses them, paste them to 5 × 8 cards, and file them. A little painless filing may save much laborious item building. It goes without saying that the teacher will find it desirable to construct additional new items for every test. Fortunately, the item builder has many types of items from which to choose.

ARRANGING THE TEST ITEMS

Once the test items have been selected, they should be arranged by types—e.g., true-false, (alternative response), matching, completion, short answer, multiple choice, interpretation, and essay,[7] in that order—and by learning products—e.g., knowledge of facts, knowledge of principles, application of principles, and so on. If the test is to be a diagnostic test, the items can be arranged according to subject matter in order to make the diagnosis easier. In any case, it is important that they be arranged in order of increasing difficulty in so far as possible.[8]

DIRECTIONS FOR THE TEST

After the test has been arranged, it is time to write the directions. Be sure the directions are clear and complete. Many otherwise good tests are spoiled by faulty directions. The directions should include

The purpose of the test.
Time allowance for the entire test.
Suggested time allowances for specific items or sections.
Bases for answering.
Procedure for recording answers.
What to do about guessing.
Amount of credit for the various items or sections.

Some of these directions can be given orally. For instance, the purpose of the test may be explained to the pupils well ahead of the test period. No matter how or what the directions are given, the teach-

er should be sure that everyone understands before the pupils start to work on their answers.[9]

LENGTH OF THE TEST

It is always difficult to estimate how long pupils will take to answer test questions. This is especially true of essay tests. According to test experts, however, it is probably safe to allow a minute for each multiple choice, short-answer, and completion item, and a half-minute for each true-false item at the senior high school level. Junior high school and middle school pupils will probably need more time. Since the ordinary classroom test is a power test, not a speed test, it is better to err on the side of allowing too much time. Tests which not all the pupils finish are almost always extremely unreliable and therefore unfair.[10]

REPRODUCING THE TEST

It is too bad to spoil a good test by a sloppy job of reproduction. If the test is illegible or hard to read, it will be unreliable. The following are suggested as guidelines for the physical format of the test.

Avoid cramming things too close together. Provide for reasonable borders, white space between items, and ample room for the answers.
List multiple choice alternatives in columns.
Do not allow any items to go over the page. All items should start and end on the same page. This is especially true of matching items.
Either use an answer sheet or list the answers in a column on the left side of the page.
When possible, have pupils draw a circle around the correct answers.
Above all, be sure to proofread for grammatical, spelling, and typographical errors.[11]

Building an Objective Test

The procedures outlined for constructing tests in general, apply specifically to the building of objective tests. Although further discussion of such matters as arranging of items, directions for the test, length of the test, and reproduction of the test

[7] Of course not all these types of items should be included in a single test.
[8] Gronlund, op. cit., p. 238.

[9] Ibid., p. 239; Frederick G. Brown, op. cit., pp. 70–71.
[10] Gronlund, op. cit., p. 240.
[11] Ibid., pp. 243–244.

would be redundant, there are so many different types of objective test items that it is important to consider the uses, merits and demerits, and writing of each of the various types. Many teachers do not use the most productive types of objective-test items. With a little study and practice you should be able to become familiar with, and relatively expert in, writing the more sophisticated objective-test items.

ALTERNATIVE-RESPONSE ITEMS

Probably the most familiar type of objective-test item is the alternative-response item, in which the pupil has a choice between two possible responses, for example, true-false or yes-no. Some examples are

Circle the correct answer (or underline the correct answer).

True-False   1. Milton was a sense realist.

Right-Wrong   2. Reliability is the degree to which the test agrees with itself.

Yes-No   3. Most early scientific discoveries were made by university professors.

Were-Were not   4. Girls _____ allowed to attend school beyond elementary level in Colonial New England.

Forward-Rearward   5. The clutch lever of the Bell and Howell projector must be in the _____ position before it will run.

This type of item can be found in many forms. An interesting variation is the following in which the pupil must identify synonymous words.

In the following, write S in the space provided if the words are essentially the same; write D if they are different.

( ) 1. reliability-consistency
( ) 2. scoring-grading
( ) 3. measure-evaluating
( ) 4. norm-average.

The most common type of alternative-response item is the true-false item. True-false items have had great popularity, but they are looked on with disfavor by some authorities because they encourage guessing. Probably one should avoid using them except when no other type of item will serve. They can be useful to find if pupils can discriminate fact from opinion, cause from effect, valid generalizations from invalid ones, or cases in which there is a clear dichotomy. As a rule multiple-choice items are preferable.

True-false items seem to be easy to write. Actually this ease is quite illusory. To make true-false items free from ambiguity or irrelevant clues is not easy. Most statements are neither true, nor false, but iffy. Taking precautions such as the following may help one produce successful true-false items.

Avoid broad, general statements. (They are too difficult to key true or false.)

Avoid trivia. (Trivia obscure the major ideas.)

Avoid negative statements. (They confuse pupils.)

Avoid introducing more than one central idea in a single true-false item. (You cannot tell which idea he knew and which he did not.)

Make the test reasonably long. (Short true-false tests are unreliable.)

Avoid such words as usual and always. (They give away the answer.)

Try to have about an equal number of true and false statements. (A test should never be made up entirely of true [or false] statements. A 60–40 per cent ratio is about right.)

Avoid any pattern of true-false responses. Scatter the true and false items haphazardly throughout the test.

CHECK-LIST ITEMS

Check-list items are much like alternative response items. Usually these items consist of fairly long lists from which the pupil checks the items which apply. In the following example the list might well consist of ten items.

Check the duties of the local board of education that appear in the following list.
_____ 1. Hire teachers.
_____ 2. Adopt school budget.

_____ 3. Select superintendent.
_____ 4. Etc.

MATCHING-TEST ITEMS

Another common type of objective test is the matching test. Again we find several variations of the basic form which consists of two unequal columns of items to be matched as in the following.

On the line to the left of each score tested in column I write the letter from column II of the phrase or statement that accurately describes in whole or in part that type of score. Each statement in column II may be used once, more than once, or not at all.

I	II
_____ 1. z score	a. Has a mean of 50 and a standard deviation of 10.
_____ 2. T score	
_____ 3. Stanine score	b. Its units are equal to one half a standard deviation.
_____ 4. Percentile score	
_____ 5. Deviation IQ. score	c. Is computed by a ratio formula.
	d. Gives scores in plus or minus qualities.
	e. Gives scores in fractions.
	f. Has a mean of 100.
	g. Has a median of 50.

Teachers sometimes overuse matching items because they seem to be easy to write. Once again appearances are deceiving. To make good matching items the test builder must be sure that the content of the stimuli (left-hand column) is homogeneous and that there are several plausible responses for each stimulus. Otherwise pupils can guess the correct answers by elimination. The column should not be too long, however. Five to eight stimuli and a few more responses are quite sufficient. To cut down on guessing by elimination there should always be more responses than stimuli, and pupils should be directed that they may use each response once, more than once, or not at all. The directions should also clearly state what the basis for matching is to be. It is particularly important that the entire item appear on the same page. Pupils are likely to make accidental errors if they have to turn the page back and forth in the search for correct answers.

Matching items have only limited usefulness. They can be used for little other than the measurement of rote memorization, facts, and simple associations. For most purposes multiple-choice items are preferable.

MULTIPLE-CHOICE ITEMS

Multiple-choice items have the advantage of being relatively free from guessing if four or more alternative responses are used and if reasonable care is used in picking the incorrect responses. However, if these distracters (i.e., incorrect answers) do not seem reasonable, they can easily give the answer away. Following are two examples of multiple-choice questions.

Select the best answer and write its letter in the space in the margin.
_____ 1. The U.S. Commissioner of Education is
   a. elected by the people.
   b. elected by the Senate.
   c. appointed by the President with the approval of the Senate.
   d. elected by the House of Representatives.
   e. appointed by the Secretary of Health, Education, and Welfare.

Underline the right answer (or circle or cross out the right answer).
1. Which was the first college established?
   a. Brown
   b. Columbia
   c. Harvard
   d. Princeton
   e. Yale

The multiple-choice test question is probably the most versatile type of test item in the teacher's repertory. It can be used both to measure simple memory and many of the complex higher mental processes, although it is difficult to write multiple-choice items that measure problem-solving ability. As a general rule, multiple-choice items that call for "best answers" are more useful for measuring higher learnings than ones that call for correct answers. These latter are most useful for measuring knowledge of fact.

Multiple-choice items are relatively easy to write if one keeps the following guidelines in mind.

1. Write the stem of the multiple-choice question as a direct question. Then, if there seems to be some reason for doing so, it may be changed to an incomplete statement; but often a direct question plus a list of alternative answers makes the best multiple-choice item. Probably the best way to make up a list of alternatives is to ask the stem as a short-answer item and then pick distracters from the incorrect answers.

2. Be sure the items are clearly written. Beware of purple prose and heavy vocabulary loads.

3. Be sure that the alternatives all seem plausible, but that there is one, and only one, correct response. All responses should be independent and mutually exclusive.

4. Be sure that the stem presents a clear, meaningful central problem. Beware of irrelevancies and window dressing.

5. Include in the stem as much of the item as possible. In so far as possible it should include all words that would be repeated in the alternatives.

6. Avoid use of the negative except when it is absolutely essential. It is seldom important for pupils to know what was the "least important," the "poorest reason," or the "principle that does not apply." Besides negatives tend to confuse pupils. Particularly beware of double negatives.

7. Be sure that the item is grammatically correct and free from rote verbal associations, grammatical inconsistencies, correct responses that are longer (or shorter) than the other alternatives, and other extraneous clues. As far as possible list alternatives in random, numerical, or alphabetical order.

8. Avoid using "none of the above" or "all of the above."

CATEGORY OR IDENTIFICATION ITEMS

A variation of the multiple-choice item which differs in substance as well as form is the category or identification item. Usually these are used with long lists. For example,

Mark the items which result from action of the sympathetic nervous system, S; those which result from action of the parasympathetic nervous system, P; if neither of these systems controls an item, mark it X.

( ) 1. Increases heart beat.
( ) 2. Dilates pupils of eyes.
( ) 3. Increases sweating.
( ) 4. Checks flow of saliva.
( ) 5. Etc.

ORGANIZATION AND EVALUATION ITEMS

Skillfully made organization and evaluation items can test a high level of learning and the ability to use knowledge. Items that require the pupils to organize are especially useful in testing learning above the verbalization level. The following item in which the pupils are asked to place a list of events in chronological sequence requires more than mere verbalization on the part of the pupil.

Place the following in chronological order by numbering the first event 1, the second event 2, and so on.
_____ The Declaration of Independence.
_____ The Articles of Confederation.
_____ The battle of Lexington.
_____ Washington's assumption of command of the Continental Army.

Items that ask pupils to evaluate and rate practices can not only test knowledge, but can also test the ability to draw fine distinctions. Questions of this sort are excellent for getting at the higher mental processes.

Rate the following techniques according to the following scheme: G, good; D, doubtful; X, poor. Place your responses in the parentheses.
( ) a. Encouraging pupils by accepting, at least tentatively, all answers to oral questions that can be used at all.
( ) b. Scolding pupils whenever they are unable to answer oral questions.
And so on.

SITUATION-TEST ITEMS

Situation items also demand that the pupils be able to use their knowledge. In this example the pupils must know how to do an item analysis in order to answer correctly.

What does the following item analysis tell you about the items in the text? Put your answer in the space below.

STUDENTS	ITEMS						TOTAL SCORE
	1	2	3	4	5	6	
John	+	0	0	+	0	+	111
Mary	+	+	0	+	0	+	109
Susan	+	+	0	+	0	0	100
Mike	+	+	0	+	0	+	96
Don	+	0	+	+	0	+	94
Harry	+	0	0	+	0	0	60
George	+	0	+	0	0	+	58
Anne	+	0	+	+	0	0	57
Tom	+	0	+	0	0	0	42
Sally	+	0	+	0	0	0	40

1. Item 1 _____
2. Item 2 _____
3. Item 3 _____
4. Item 4 _____
5. Item 5 _____
6. Item 6 _____

INTERPRETIVE ITEMS

Interpretive items consist of an introductory statement and a series of questions which ask the pupil to interpret the data in the introductory presentation. The introductory material may be presented by a picture, graph, chart, formula, statistical table, film or recording as well as an expository statement. The individual test items are ordinarily multiple-choice or alternative--response items. Short-answer items are sometimes used, but they are harder to key and score. In any case the items should require analysis or interpretation of the introductory material. This type of item, like all others that test higher learnings, is difficult to construct. The introductory material should be brief and clear and lend itself to interpretation or analysis. Usually the test writer will have to revise the introduction several times before it is satisfactory. Therefore one should include enough items to make the effort of writing it and reading it worthwhile. Of course, these items must be written

just as carefully as any other short-answer, alternative-response, or multiple-choice questions.

The following is an example of a free-response interpretive item.

The two pie graphs presented here show the per cent of the world's gold possessed by various countries in December 1913 and June 1931. Study the graphs and then answer the questions in the place provided.

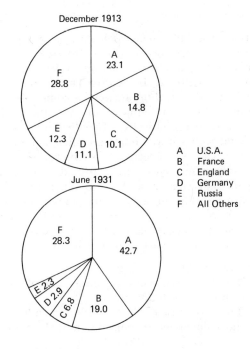

1. Which of the countries possessed the most gold in 1913? _____
2. Which European country had the biggest increase in gold supply between 1913 and 1931? _____
3. Which of the countries listed had the smallest supply in 1931? _____
4. What two countries held 60 per cent of the world's gold supply in 1931? _____
5. In which year was the gold more equally distributed? _____

The item could be turned into several multiple-choice interpretation items quite easily as in the following examples.

Which of the countries listed possessed the most gold in 1913?   ( )
    a. England; b. France; c. Germany;
    d. Russia.

Which European country had the largest increase in gold supply between 1913 and 1931?
                                  ( )
    a. England; b. France; c. Germany;
    d. Russia.

FREE-RESPONSE ITEMS

Strictly speaking free-response items are not objective-type items. Because they are free response, their answers are open to considerable interpretation. Frequently their scoring must be quite subjective. In fact, short-answer items may be considerably closer to being short-essay items than they are to being objective. Usually both completion- and short-answer items are included in tests that are basically objective type, however.

Free-response items which provide the pupils with no suggested responses also test a high level of learning. The most common representative of this type of item in objective tests is the completion item. In the completion item the pupil merely places the correct answer in the blank.

Fill in the blanks.
1. The first permanent secondary school in this country was founded at _____ .
2. The Committee of Ten recommended that the elementary schools be limited to grades _____ through _____ .

To make scoring easier, teachers often require that the answers to the completion questions be placed in an answer column.

*

Place the answers in the blanks in the space provided in the margin.
( ) 1. The student body of the average American high school numbers approximately ——— pupils per school.
( ) 2. A stanine is equal to ——— of a standard deviation.

*

When using completion items, teachers should be wary of ambiguous questions and unexpected correct responses. Good completion items that call for more than isolated, pinpointed facts are difficult to build. In order to avoid these faults, the teacher should try to word the item so that only one answer can be correct and so that the pupils know just what type of answer is expected. To be sure that the pupils can decipher the item, the teacher probably should never allow more than one or two blanks in any one completion item. He should make sure that blanks represent only key words and that they are placed near the end of the sentence so that the pupil will not have to waste his time figuring out what is being asked.

The best procedure for writing completion items seems to be to write the item as a short-answer question and then turn it into a completion item if it seems desirable. Sometimes teachers are tempted to use phrases and sentences copied from the book as completion items. This practice is undesirable. It encourages rote learning and usually results in items that are hard to key because they have a number of unexpected correct answers.

SHORT-ANSWER ITEMS

Short-answer questions are exactly what the name implies, questions than can be answered in a word or phrase. They are extremely useful, but, as with completion questions, it is difficult to write the items so that they will rule out undesirable responses. In writing short-answer items the teacher needs to be especially careful to be sure each pupil knows what is expected of him. He should indicate in the directions, or in the wording of the item, how long and how detailed the answer should be. As in the completion item it would be helpful if the wording made only one correct answer possible.

Each of the following can be answered by a single word or phrase. Place the answer to each of the following questions in the space provided.
_____ 1. In an algebra test a boy scored exactly one standard deviation below the mean. What is his T score?
_____ 2. What do Crow and Crow consider to be the best size for a local school board?

*

For what may the various types of test items be best used? Criticize the items used as illustrations. In what ways might they be improved?

What are the characteristics of a good objective-test item?

Make a chart showing for each type of objective and short free-response item (1) what type of objective it tests best; (2) its advantages; (3) its limitations.

*

Designing the Essay Test

Designing an essay test is much like designing an objective test. The object is to find out the pupil's progress. The teacher selects items that will ascertain what that progress is. Because of the time factor, the problem of adequate sampling becomes extremely important. As a rule of thumb, one should use many short essay items rather than a few long ones.

Here are some other rules of thumb to keep in mind in constructing essay tests.

1. Limit the questions to something the pupil can answer adequately in the allotted time and be sure each question is worded so that the pupil realizes these delimitations.
2. Be sure the sample is adequate and that the test will actually show how well the pupils have acquired the learning products that were the goals.
3. Be sure each question tests specific products and that the information necessary for the correct answer was included in the course.
4. Be specific. Be sure each question indicates just what the pupil is to write about. To do this, it may be necessary to write several sentences explaining the question. Avoid "discuss" questions. They are too vague and general.
5. Decide what the standards are for scoring the answers before you commit yourself to any question.
6. Be clear.

Building Criterion-Referenced Tests

One builds a criterion-referenced test in about the same way that one builds any other test. The basic difference is that in criterion-referenced tests, e.g., diagnostic and mastery tests, it is most important that the test items clearly measure the degree to which the objectives have been achieved. This requirement means that the objective must be clearly stated, preferably in terms of terminal behavior. If the standard for deciding whether the goal has been attained has been written into each objective, it is easy to write criterion-referenced items. This is the beauty of using specific behavioral objectives.

Briefly, the basic procedures for building criterion-referenced tests are

1. Define the specific objectives in detail, as criterion-referenced behavioral objectives. Be sure to include in the objectives the standard that will be considered acceptable.
2. Build test items that will show whether or not these standards have been attained.
   a. Be sure each objective is tested in proportion to its importance.
   b. Have several items for each objective.
   c. Use items that show whether the pupils can actually perform the required behavior.

*

When would you use criterion-referenced tests rather than norm-referenced survey tests? Why?

*

ADMINISTERING, SCORING AND EVALUATING TEACHER-BUILT TESTS

Giving the Test

At first glance it would seem as though there was nothing at all to giving a test. This is not the case, however. Both essay and objective tests must be administered carefully. Once the test and key have been prepared, the first thing to do is to check the test to be sure it contains no errors. Little slips in typing may cause items to turn out quite differently from what was intended. The teacher should also note any directions that may be unclear and any items that need to be explained. A good way to spot unclear items and directions is to ask another teacher to read the test critically.

If possible, any errors or obscurities should be corrected before one takes the test to class. Announcing and correcting errors in class take valuable time away from the test itself, and there is usually someone who misses the correction and is thus penalized. Since correcting the test before class is not always possible, the teacher may have to explain items and procedures to the class orally. If so, he should do so before the class begins. If in addition he writes the explanation or correction on the chalkboard, the pupils can refer to it as the test progresses and thus will not be penalized if they forget or miss the announcement. Interrupting the test to make announcements is a poor practice because it may break a pupil's train of thought and upset him.

To avoid distracting the pupils once the test has started, the teacher should be sure that each pupil has everything he needs before the test begins. It is important that the pupils check to see that each one of them has a good copy of the complete test. Even the most carefully prepared test may have poorly mimeographed, blank, or missing pages, so the teacher should have extra copies of the test to substitute for defective ones, if necessary. If this checking is completed before the test starts, it will eliminate confusion and interruptions during the test itself. Confusion and delay may also be minimized by setting up a routine for distributing and collecting the tests.

Preparing the Classroom for the Test

The physical condition of the classroom may make a tremendous difference in the test situation. The comfortable pupil can do his best work, the uncomfortable pupil often cannot. For this reason the teacher should consider the light, heat, and ventilation in the room. If possible, he should prevent any noises, interruptions, or other distractions. Common practice when giving standardized tests is to post a notice. "TESTING: PLEASE DO NOT DISTURB." There is no reason why such a practice should not be used for ordinary teacher-built achievement tests also. Many teachers are

guilty of carrying on conversations with pupils or other teachers during a test. Some leave the classroom doors open while other classes are moving in the corridors. Such disturbances are liable to distract the pupils and reduce the reliability of the test.

Scoring the Essay Test

After the test has been given, it must be scored. Ordinarily, the test should be scored immediately. Otherwise the teacher loses the opportunity to capitalize on the test's motivational and diagnostic aspects.

Essay tests are notoriously hard to score. To score them objectively is almost impossible. However, the teacher must try to score them as objectively as he can. This is no easy task, but the following procedure can somewhat reduce the difficulty.

1. Before giving the test, answer each question yourself. (*Sometimes you will not want to use the item after you try to answer it.*) Note all the acceptable points and the relative importance of each. If you wish, give each point a numerical value or weight. This is the key.

2. After the test has been given, read the first essay question in each of the papers and assign scores on the basis of the key. If a pupil has mentioned an acceptable point not in the key, add the point to the key and reread the papers already scored to be sure that everyone gets credit for the point.

3. After completing the first question in all of the papers, repeat the process with the second question. It is much easier to read one question in all of the papers at once because the scorer can concentrate on that one question.

Scoring the Objective Test

The objective test is considerably easier to score than the essay test. The questions lend themselves to easy automatic scoring. In fact, scoring such questions is often so automatic that they can be scored more profitably by a clerk, pupil, or machine than by the teacher.

As in the essay test, the key should be made out before the test is given. A good method is to indicate the acceptable answers as the test is being made out. Then the teacher should let the test sit for a day or so, after which he should retest himself to see whether he still believes that the answers are acceptable. If they are, the teacher is ready to make his key. One of the easiest methods of making a key, if the test is arranged so that the responses are in a column, is simply to take an extra copy of the test and fill in all the responses correctly. The key can be placed against the test and the answers compared. Often, the teacher will find it easier to cut off the text of the test so that his key will be a strip which can be laid along either side of the answers on the test being corrected. This makes it easier to correct answers listed on the left side of the page if the scorer is right-handed. Some teachers find it easier to score by simply checking all correct items, that is, items which agree with the key. Others prefer to mark the wrong answers. Of course, if one intends to correct for guessing, one must indicate both right and wrong items.

Example:

key	test
a	(a) John Smith was: (a) an explorer, (b) a merchant, (c) an admiral, (d) a general.
c	(a) Pocahontas married: (a) John Smith, (b) Myles Standish, (c) John Rolfe, (d) John Winthrop.

USING A MASK

Another common type of key is the mask. Masks are stiff pieces of paper or cardboard which, when placed over the test, cover up all the incorrect responses and allow only the correct responses to appear. They can be made easily. All one needs to do is to cover the test with the paper and then make holes in the mask where the correct answer should appear. With this type of key all the scorer needs to do is to mark correct all answers that show through the mask.

Example:

TEST

1. a b c d	John Smith was (a) an explorer, (b) a merchant, (c) an admiral, (d) a general.
2. a b c d	Pocahontas married (a) John Smith, (b) Myles Standish, (c) John Rolfe, (d) John Winthrop.

MASK

1. O
2.   O

CORRECTING FOR GUESSING

Since in testing one is attempting to determine progress toward the desired learning products, one should not conduct a guessing contest. When items have fewer than four responses, pupils can guess the answers relatively easily. Consequently, some teachers correct for guessing when scoring items with fewer than four responses. This is easily done. The formula is

$$S = R - \frac{(C - 1)}{W}$$

S is the corrected score, R is the number of correct responses, W the number of incorrect responses, and C the number of choices provided for each item. Substituting in the formula we find that for alternate-answer items the formula becomes Rights minus Wrongs.

$$S = R - \frac{W}{(2 - 1)} \quad \text{or} \quad S = R - W$$

For items having three choices we find that the formula becomes Rights minus $\frac{1}{2}$ Wrongs.

$$S = R - \frac{W}{(3 - 1)} \quad \text{or} \quad S = R - \frac{W}{2}$$

These are the only two instances in which the formula is used.

Many teachers and writers in the field of measurement prefer not to use the correction formula at all. They feel that the correction is not worth the trouble because it seldoms changes the relative rating of the pupils. Besides, pupils do not understand it very well and do not like it. In addition it may introduce additional errors in measurement caused by pupils' attitudes.

Perhaps the best answer to the problem is to use items with at least four choices as much as possible. If it is necessary or advisable to use alternate-answer questions, the teacher should probably make the test long enough to accommodate several items directed at each learning product. This will tend to compensate for guessing without using the formula.

Evaluating Teacher-Built Tests

Much of the evaluation of a test can be done before it is given. The most important criterion of a test's worth is its validity. Does it test what it was supposed to test? Perhaps the easiest and best way to check the validity of a teacher-built achievement test is by inspection. Do the items test the goals of the course? Does the test cover the various goals in proper proportion? Is it free from catch questions and ambiguous items? Is the physical format correct? Are questions of the same type grouped together? Are the test items arranged from easy to difficult? Is the test free from format blunders such as matching items that go over the page? In other words, is it valid, reliable, objective, and usable?

After the test has been given, it can be evaluated more fully. Things that can be checked are

1. Length.
2. Directions.
3. Item discrimination.
4. Difficulty of items.
5. Clearness.
6. Balance.

ITEM ANALYSIS

An item analysis can be very helpful in evaluating a test. The procedure for such an analysis is quite simple. On a sheet of graph paper list the pupils' names on the stub at the left, and items of the test in the heading. We are interested only in the upper and lower quarters, but it is best to list all the pupils in rank order because the chart can also be used for diagnosis. By using plus

(+) and minus (−) signs, indicate whether each of the pupils answered each of the items correctly or incorrectly, as in the following chart.

Upper Quarter

	1	2	3	4	5	6	7	and so on
Jerry	+	+	+	−	−	+	−	
John	+	+	+	+	−	+	−	
Sally	−	−	+	+	−	+	−	

Lower Quarter

	1	2	3	4	5	6	7
Mike	+	−	−	−	−	+	−
Susy	+	−	+	−	−	−	+
Tom	−	−	−	+	−	−	+
George	+	−	−	+	−	−	+

By studying this chart one can learn how well the items discriminated and how difficult they were. The chart also gives clues to items that are not well written, are ambiguous, or were not learned.

An achievement test of the survey type should have some items that very few people can answer and some that almost everyone can answer. The first are needed to find out who the high achievers are; the second, to encourage the low achievers. Ordinarily, most items should be answered correctly by about half of the pupils. An item that is answered correctly by fewer than 20 per cent of the pupils may well be a bad item. One should examine it to see if it is not too difficult, if it tests any of the objectives, if it is pertinent to the course, or if it is poorly written. On the other hand, if the item is answered correctly by more than 80 per cent of the pupils, one should check to see if it is too easy or if the wording gives the answer away. These criteria hold for all tests in which the scores of pupils are compared with each other but not for mastery tests and diagnostic tests, as we shall see.

By comparing the answers of the upper-quarter pupils with those of the lower-quarter pupils, one can find other things that help to evaluate the items. If the upper quarter of the pupils answered an item correctly and the lower quarter of the pupils answered it incorrectly, the item discriminates between them. If both upper-quarter and lower-quarter pupils answered the question equally well, it does not discriminate. If an item is answered correctly more frequently by the lower-quarter pupils than the upper-quarter pupils, something is very wrong indeed. Perhaps the key is wrong, or perhaps the item needs to be rewritten.

*

Often you hear it said that an achievement test on which pupils make perfect scores is a poor test. Discuss the merits and faults of such tests.

Compare the type of item analysis recommended for use in diagnosis with the type of item analysis recommended in this section. In what ways do they differ? Could both be used for the evaluation of test items? Could both be used for diagnosis?

*

ANALYSIS OF CRITERION-REFERENCED TESTS

The factors of discrimination and difficulty are not really important in mastery and diagnostic tests. Such tests should be criterion referenced. If they are, the items will tell whether or not the pupil knows or can do what he was supposed to have learned. The touchstone in these cases is the objective. If the items show whether or not the objective has been attained, they are good items. For instance, in one college one of the physical education requirements is for the pupils to demonstrate the ability to swim two lengths of the pool. The test for this requirement is for the student to swim the length of the pool and back. Either the student can do it or he cannot. How well he swims, how fast he swims, and how much farther he can swim are all irrelevant.

SUMMARY

A test is a systematic procedure for measuring behavior. Classroom tests determine how much and how well pupils have learned. They are used as a basis for grading and motivating pupils and for planning and review. There are many types of tests. Most classroom tests are informal tests of cognitive or psychomotor achievement. They may be survey, diagnostic, or mastery in nature. Norm-referenced classroom tests are better as a basis for marking, but criterion-referenced tests are more useful for most classroom purposes. Both essay-test items and objective-test items have good and bad points. For most purposes the objective-test item when well written is the better of the two. How-

ever, it is the purpose of the test that should determine the type of item used rather than some notion about the innate worth of objective- or essay-test items.

To build a classroom test, one should follow these procedures: (1) define the objectives; (2) outline the content to be tested; (3) draw up a table of specifications; and (4) construct test items to meet the specifications. In designing the test itself one should make sure that all objectives are tested in proportion to their importance, that there are at least some relatively easy items included so that pupils will not become quickly discouraged, that only a few types of items are used in the test, that all items of the same type are placed together, that the items are arranged from easiest to most difficult, that the items are appropriate for their purpose and for the sophistication of the pupils, and that the test provides the pupils with clear directions and the information and materials they need for completing it. Classroom tests are designed not as jokes or puzzles, but to find out how well the pupils have learned what it was hoped they would learn.

There are many types of objective-test items. Each type has its merits, and each has its faults. Probably the most useful of them all is the multiple-choice item. However, teachers should be careful to use each type of item to do only the type of thing it is designed to do. Organization and evaluation items, situation items, and interpretation items are excellent for testing higher intellectual learnings and are not used as much as they should be.

Free-response items include completion items, short-answer items, and essay items. They can test a high level of recall but are much more difficult to write than one might expect. Essay tests are also difficult to design, although, again, few people realize it. In designing an essay test one should be sure to (1) limit the number and scope of questions to the time allotted for the test; (2) sample the teaching objectives adequately; (3) test specific learning products that were in the course; (4) write items that specify what answers are called for; (5) write "correct" answers to the items before you decide whether or not to use them; and last and most important, (6) be clear.

In designing criterion-referenced tests there are

only two major steps: (1) determine the objectives; and (2) build items that test those objectives adequately. These steps are basically those outlined earlier as the general procedure for test construction.

Tests should be carefully administered, scored, and interpreted. In so far as possible, scoring should be objective. It is extremely good policy, once a test has been given, to analyze it and save those items that have proven to be good for use another time. Item analyses may be very useful for this purpose.

Marking and Reporting to Parents

17

Marks hold an extremely high position in our school system. They are used as a basis for reporting pupil progress to parents and to other interested persons and as a basis for promotion, graduation, and honors. Teachers frequently use marks as a means of motivating pupils to greater effort. Guidance personnel use marks in guiding boys and girls for college entrance or employment. College admission officers and prospective employers use pupil marks as one basis of their decision making.

To determine marks, most school systems use a system based on a five-point scale. The most common version is the A B C D F scale. Variations of this scale use the numbers 1 2 3 4 5 or the terms "Superior," "Above Average," "Average," "Below Average," and "Unsatisfactory." Some schools use a scale based on 100 per cent, while others merely indicate the work to be passing or failing, or in some cases outstanding, passing, or failing.

Criticism of Marking Systems

Unfortunately none of the variations mentioned has been quite satisfactory primarily because marks and marking systems are based on certain fallacious assumptions. According to Wrinkle[1] these fallacies are six in number.

1. The belief that anyone can tell from the mark assigned what the student's level of achievement is or what progress he has made.
2. The belief that any student can achieve any mark he wishes—if he is willing to make the effort.
3. The belief that the student's success in his after-school life compares favorably with his success in school.
4. The belief that the student's mark is comparable to the worker's pay check.
5. The belief that the competitive marking system provides a worthwhile and justifiable introduction to competitive adult life.
6. The belief that school marks can be used as a means to an end without their becoming thought of by students as ends in themselves.

The truth of the matter is that these beliefs have little or no basis in fact. The errors contained in some of them are quite plain. Obviously the ordinary school marking system does not allow adequately for individual differences in pupils. School marks and worldly success do not always correlate well. Although learning rather than marks should be the object of education, because of the system marks are much more important than learning to the average student. Marks seldom tell what a student's level of achievement is or what progress he has made.

In this respect at least, marks may give more misinformation than information. A prestigious committee of the Association for Supervision and Curriculum Development concluded that because of these various inadequacies, grades, marks, and credits as presently used should be discarded. Unfortunately we have no hard proof that any of the various substitutes for marks and marking systems that have been proposed are really more satisfactory than the system now being used.

MARKS AS AN INDICATION OF PUPIL PROGRESS

Because the average student may find it difficult to believe that marks do not tell what a student's

[1] William L. Wrinkle, *Improving Marking and Reporting Practices* (New York: Rinehart and Company, Inc.), copyright 1947, permission of Rinehart and Company, Inc.

level of achievement is or what progress he has made, let us briefly examine marks as indicators of pupil progress.

Marks do not tell one as much about a pupil's progress as one might suppose. For example, if someone says that Johnny received an A in ninth-grade social studies, what does that tell you? Does it mean he worked hard or that he is a bright loafer? Does it mean that he has mastered some particular bit of subject matter, or does it mean he has a charming personality?

Letter and percentage marks do not give the answers to such questions. They do not show what skills, concepts, attitudes, appreciations, or ideals the pupil has learned. They give no indication of the pupil's strengths or weaknesses in a subject, nor do they tell how much he has progressed. In fact, as often as not, they hide information. For instance, because of his excellence in literature, reading, grammar, or written composition, Jack receives an A in English. However, he may be quite poor in conversational skill. The mark of A, therefore, hides the fact that he is deficient in one area of English. Such a marking system is of little value to anyone who really wants to know much about the pupil's progress in school. Still, it does predict fairly well a pupil's continued success in a subject and does give a rough index of his teacher's estimate of his worth.

Even as an indication of the teacher's estimate of a pupil's worth, marks are not always very valuable. Teachers' marks are often influenced by extraneous matters such as sex, effort, extracurricular activities, neatness, school behavior, attitudes, and attendance. Obviously, such inconsistencies may result in many inequities.

Particularly futile are marking systems that attempt to give precise marks. No human being can make the fine distinctions in the schoolwork of pupils that the percentage system requires. Neither have we been able to develop testing instruments capable of such fine distinctions. Since the data on which pupil marks are based are so rough, the computing of percentage marks hardly seems worth the trouble.

MARKS AS A MENTAL-HEALTH HAZARD

A frequent criticism of marks is that they are a mental-health hazard. Some critics feel that marks place an undue emphasis on competition and success. This emphasis, they believe, endangers pupils' mental health. Others feel that these pressures represent nothing more than the ordinary give-and-take in life, so that these objectives should not be taken seriously. However, it is certainly true that marks often cause anxieties and worries out of proportion to their importance in pupils' lives. It seems, therefore, that the advisability of using marks is at least questionable from a mental-health standpoint.

MARKS AS A MOTIVATIONAL DEVICE

Probably the only valid argument for using letter or percentage marks is that they have a certain motivational effect, particularly with the better pupils. Even this effect, however, may be illusory. If marks really motivated effectively, would not fewer pupils fail?

As a matter of fact, sometimes marks have a very poor motivational effect. This is true when the mark rather than the learning becomes the major goal. In such circumstances the pupils concentrate on getting marks rather than on learning something worthwhile. The result often is cheating, cramming, electing easy courses, and expending only enough energy to pass.

*

Of what value are marks? Do they serve the purposes to which they pretend? If they do, how do they do it?

What do you think of competitive marking? What value does it have? What weaknesses?

For what purposes should marks be used?

*

MARKING TESTS AND PAPERS

At best, assigning marks is a thankless task. In the following paragraphs several ways to do this job will be suggested. However, the teacher must remember that no procedure can relieve him of the responsibility for making decisions, some of which will be difficult.

Teachers may assign marks on the basis of either some absolute (or more properly, arbitrary) standard or a relative scale. The old-fashioned tests in which pupils had to have 90 per cent or better of the items right in order to achieve an A, 80 to 90 per cent right for a B, 70 to 80 per cent for a C, and 60 to 70 per cent for a D furnish one example of the use of an arbitrary standard for marking. Another example is the more modern criterion referenced, or mastery, test which requires a pupil to answer 18 problems out of 20 correctly in order to pass. In relative scales a pupil's mark depends upon the relationship of his score or his performance to the scores or performance of the other pupils in the group.

Marking on the Curve

In the past many teachers have used the normal curve as a relative scale to use in marking. Unfortunately, in ordinary practice the theory of the normal curve does not hold for secondary school marks. As a rule, secondary school teachers should not base class marks on the normal curve. Schemes based on modifications of the curve may be acceptable, however.

According to the theory of the normal curve, which is based on the laws of chance, any continuous variable will be distributed according to a perfectly smooth bell-shaped curve (Figure 17–1), if no factors are present to throw things off balance. Thus, according to the laws of chance, in a large group marks should tend to fall according to the normal curve. In other words, letter marks would, according to this theory, be distributed about as follows: A, 7 per cent; B, 23 per cent; C, 40 per cent; D, 23 per cent; E (or F), 7 per cent. Just what the exact percentages should be is debatable.

Note that the theory of the normal curve assumes that the variable varies according to pure chance. This condition rarely exists in a secondary school class. For one thing, a secondary school class is not a normal, or average, group but a select group of people. For instance, many of the slow-learning pupils drop out when they are sixteen or so. Therefore, the distribution of marks should vary from the normal curve because of the selection that has taken place. Thus, one should expect that the marks of twelfth graders in a high school are more likely to fall according to the following proportions: A, 15 per cent; B, 25 per cent; C, 40 per cent; D, 15 per cent; E (or F), 5 per cent.

Figure 17–1
The Normal Curve of Probability.

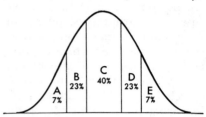

When one considers the other factors that may be operating (for instance, ability grouping, selective curriculum tracks, and so on), it seems obvious that the curve in any single class will probably be far from normal. In an honors section the proper distribution of marks might be 40 per cent, A; 60 per cent, B; in an advanced section, 25 per cent, A; 50 per cent, B; 25 per cent, C; in a slow section, 50 per cent, C, 30 per cent, D, 20 per cent, F; and so on.

Secondly, few classes are large enough to warrant using the normal curve. In order for the theory of the normal curve to operate, one needs at least several hundred pupils to be marked against the same criteria. To use the normal curve as a basis for marks in a smaller group may lead to errors in marking. Therefore, when marking, the teacher must depend largely upon his own judgment. Statistical procedures such as using the normal curve are seldom worthwhile.

Thirdly, the ordinary classroom teacher-built test is not designed so as to give a normal distribution according to Terwilliger. In his investigations he found that classroom tests are usually skewed negatively.[2]

Using Relative-Growth Groups

In spite of its faults, the normal curve can be used to indicate the relative growth of pupils with respect to each other. Billett recommends that teachers do this by setting up a five-point, relative-growth scale.[3] In such a scale the percentage of

[2] James S. Terwilliger, *Assigning Grades to Students* (Glenview, Ill.: Scott, Foresman and Company, 1971), pp. 77–78.
[3] Roy O. Billett, *Fundamentals of Secondary School Teaching* (Boston: Houghton Mifflin Company, 1940), p. 633–41.

members in each of the relative-growth groups will be distributed in the same proportion as when marking by the normal curve, i.e., I = 7 per cent; II = 23 per cent; III = 40 per cent; IV = 23 per cent; V = 7 per cent. These groups do not represent marks, however, but comparisons within the class. They merely show each pupil's progress in relation to that of his classmates.

The following method of determining relative growth within class groups has been used with some success.[4]

1. Subtract the lowest score from the highest and add 1 to find the range.
2. Determine the approximate standard deviation by dividing the range by 5.[5]
3. Find the mid-score.
4. Add $\frac{1}{2}$ the approximate standard deviation to the mid-score and subtract $\frac{1}{2}$ approximate standard deviation from the mid-score to find the boundaries of the middle group.
5. Find the other group boundaries by adding (or subtracting) the standard deviation from the group limit already established.

For example: We have a test whose scores range from 63 through 117. The mid-score of the test is 89. Seventy-three pupils took the test. The range of the test is 117 minus 63 plus 1, or 55. The approximate standard deviation is 55 divided by 5, or 11. The middle relative-growth group falls between 94 − 84; the next higher relative-growth group ranges from 95 − 105; the highest ranges from 106 up. The other two groups become 83 − 73 and 72 − 62. However, if the scores fall so that there are natural breaks at places near the end of the groups, one might use these natural breaks for group limits instead of the limits computed.

Although the relative-growth groups can be quite useful, pupils and parents have become so mark-oriented that they do not always willingly accept this practice.

Blount and Klausmeier recommend a somewhat

[4] Ibid.
[5] Dividing the range by 4 would probably give a more accurate approximation of the standard deviation. However, if 4 is used as the divisor there will be four groups, two above the midpoint and two below it. The use of 5 gives one an average group straddling the midpoint. This is of some advantage in interpreting scores.

simpler method of dividing the class into relative growth groups.[6] They suggest that instead of reporting marks the teacher might use the highest lowest or middle third or quarter of the class. For an example they say a teacher might report a pupil's standing in various areas to be

    Speaking: In the highest third of the class.
    Listening: In the middle third of the class.
    Reading: In the lowest third of the class.
    Spelling: In the lowest third of the class.
    Composition: In the lowest third of the class.[7]

Comparative groups of this sort will be used for reporting test results or pupil standings at the end of the marking period.

Use of Standard Scores and Percentiles

Some authorities feel that perhaps the marks of the future will consist of standard scores or stanine scores. These scores are of course relative scales based upon standard deviations. Such scores are difficult to compute, however.

The standard score most useful for use in marking classroom tests and exercises is the T score, or Z score.[8] This score is computed by the formula

$$\text{T score} = 10 \, \frac{(X - M)}{SD} + 50$$

where

    X = any raw score
    M = arithmetic mean of raw scores
    SD = *standard deviation of raw scores.*

[6] Although they do not use the terms *relative growth groups.*
[7] Nathan S. Blount and Herbert S. Klausmeier, *Teaching in Secondary School*, 3rd ed. (New York: Harper & Row, Publishers, 1968), pp. 430–431.
[8] The terms T score and Z score both refer to scores derived by the formula T score = $50 + 10 \frac{(X - M)}{SD}$. Some authorities call any set of scores derived from these scores T scores. Others use the term T score to refer only to normalized scores, and the term Z score to any score derived from the formula Z score = $50 + 10 \frac{(X - M)}{SD}$. See the preceding chapter for an explanation.

When one has a small distribution and a fairly normal curve, one can find an approximation of the standard deviation (SD) by dividing the range of the raw scores by 4. If the extremes of the distribution deviate from the normal multiply the range between the 10th and 90th percentiles by 4.

Stanine scores can be approximated easily by the following procedure.

1. Find the standard deviation.
2. Find the mean of the raw scores.
3. Measure $\frac{1}{4}$ standard deviation down from the mean and $\frac{1}{4}$ standard deviation up from the mean. This will establish the limits of stanine 5.
4. Find the limits of the other stanines by measuring down or up $\frac{1}{2}$ standard deviation for each stanine.

Thus if the standard deviation is 6 and the mean score 40, the stanines would be[9]

1	$0 - 29$		6	$42 - 44$
2	$30 - 32$		7	$45 - 47$
3	$33 - 35$		8	$48 - 50$
4	$36 - 38$		9	$50 +$
5	$39 - 41$	$(38.5 - 41.5)$		

Test results may also be reported as percentiles. However there is a danger that pupils and parents may confuse percentiles with per cents and so misunderstand.

Using Raw Scores Instead of Marks

Another effective procedure is to give the results of objective tests in raw scores, telling the pupils the range of the scores and the range of the relative-growth groups. By comparing their scores, high school pupils soon realize how they stand in comparison with their classmates. If the scores are accompanied by comments such as, "I think you have missed the point of . . ., and should reread it," or "You did not provide enough illustrations," or "You have not differentiated between major and

[9] Although the statistical procedures suggested here give only approximations, they are quite accurate enough for most class marks. See works on statistics and tests and measurements for computing by accurate procedures.

minor points," and so on, the pupil can learn how he stands in relation to his own potential and the standards of the course. Conferences also help make these points clear. This procedure is probably the fairest of all marking systems. It also has the advantage of being the procedure least likely to be misused by beginners.

Assigning Marks to Tests

Both the raw-score plan and the relative-growth plan avoid giving actual marks to tests. Experts in the field of measurement feel that

> Teachers should consider these instruments [e.g., quizzes, tests, homework assignments, term papers, laboratory exercises, etc.] as data-collection devices that yield numerical results which will subsequently provide a basis for value judgments concerning individual students. Scoring procedures, however crude, should be devised so that the results of all classroom measurement can be recorded in quantitative terms. Grades (e.g., A, B, C, D, F) should *not* be assigned every time measurement occurs but, instead, should be withheld until official reports are required.[10]

However, if one must give marks, the only satisfactory solution seems to be to establish certain criteria for each mark and then mark on the basis of those criteria.

One might also base one's test mark on a distribution scheme such as

A = 10 per cent.
B = 25 per cent.
C = 45 per cent.
D = 15 per cent.
F = 5 per cent.

In this method one simply finds the raw score of the tests, lists them from highest to lowest, and then apportions the letter grades according to the proportions decreed—taking advantage of the natural breaks wherever possible. Thus in the example in Figure 17–2 in a class of 25, the teacher assigned 1 A, 9 Bs, 12 Cs, 2 Ds, and 1 F. These marks do not quite correspond to the distribution scheme, but they are close enough given the nature of the distribution of the raw scores. The decreed distribution should not be held sacred. When the

[10] Terwilliger, op. cit., p. 23.

Figure 17–2
Distribution of Test Scores and Assigned Letter Grades

1	83	A
	78	
	77	
	76	
	74	
9	73	B
	70	
	68	
	68	
	68	
	65	
	64	
	63	
	62	
	59	
12	58	C
	58	
	57	
	56	
	54	
	53	
	53	
2	50	D
	48	
1	40	F

raw scores cluster together in an obviously skewed distribution, one should not hold rigidly to the distribution. In marking tests, teachers should remember that the purposes of tests are primarily to evaluate pupil progress and to diagnose pupil learning rather than to give marks.

*

How would you grade an objective test if your school used the five-letter system of marking? Would you use a different procedure for marking an essay test? If so, what?

Why do authorities generally condemn the percentage system of grading tests?

What are z scores, T scores, and Z scores? What are their good and bad points? How might they be used in marking tests?

In a certain school the school policy holds that pupils' marks should approximate the normal curve. A teacher of an honors section found that all of his fifteen pupils did exceptionally well on one of his tests. He decided to give each a mark of A. Can his action be justified?

*

Assigning Marks to Compositions and Other Creative Work

Compositions and other creative work are difficult to mark. Perhaps the following technique used by a veteran teacher of English is as good as any in marking original written work:

First, he selects a comfortable chair with plenty of floor space around him. Then he reads each paper carefully, making notes as he reads them. On the basis of this reading he judges whether the paper is "Superior," "Excellent," "Average," "Fair," or "Poor." Then, without placing any mark on the paper, he places it on a portion of the floor designated for papers of that category. After reading all the papers, he places them into piles according to their categories and lets them lie fallow for a while. Later, refreshed, he rereads each paper in each group to test his previous judgment, and moves from pile to pile those papers which he feels he has rated too high or too low. He then assigns marks to the papers in the piles. He could have just as easily assigned them to relative-growth groups or even assigned them point scores. Although this technique is not foolproof, with a little ingenuity it can be adapted for marking various types of original work.

Another method is to rate each paper according to each of various qualities such as originality, expression, mechanics, and so on. Rating scales and check lists are particularly useful for this purpose. The ratings produced by these procedures can be converted into point scores in accordance with Terwilliger's suggestion that measurements be recorded in quantitative terms if one desires.[11]

TERM AND COURSE MARKS

Purpose of Term Marks

As we have already seen, the more one reads about marks and marking, the more one is tempted

to believe that there can be no such thing as a truly satisfactory mark or marking system. The experts seem to view none of the marking schemes yet devised as statistically sound (or feasible) or fair to all of the pupils. Yet marks seem to be necessary. As long as there are schools, there will have to be some sort of marking and reporting system.

Marks serve many purposes—administration, guidance, information, motivation and discipline.[12]

More specifically marks are used

1. To inform pupils, parents, and other interested persons such as teachers, prospective employers, and college admissions officers of the pupil's achievement in his secondary school work.
2. To motivate pupils by giving them feedback on their progress.
3. To identify the strengths and weaknesses of pupils.
4. To inform those concerned of the progress or achievement of pupils in comparison with other pupils.
5. As a basis for guiding the pupil in his choice of courses, activities, curriculum, and career.
6. As a basis for promotion, grouping, graduation, honors, college entrance, and eligibility for certain awards, activities, or programs.
7. To show parents and others the objectives of the school.
8. To indicate pupils' personal social development.

Criteria for Marks and Marking Systems

To carry out their purposes marks and marking systems should be based on sound principles.

1. Marks should indicate the attainment of definite worthwhile goals. These goals should be well defined, or the marks themselves will become the goals.
2. Marks should be easily understood by pupils and parents.
3. Marks should be as objective as possible.

11 See Ch. 15 for information on the use of rating devices.

12 Wrinkle, op. cit., pp. 31–32.

4. Marks should be free from bias and the influence of other irrelevant considerations.
5. Marks should be based on an abundance of evidence.
6. Pupils should be informed in advance what will be counted in computing the mark.
7. The method used to compute the marks should be objective and statistically valid.
8. Marks for achievement and personal social development should be separated.
9. Marks should be based on positive evidence.
10. Marks should be used as means to an end. They should not be ends in themselves. Overemphasis on marks distorts the teaching-learning process.

The Basis of Term Marks

Subject marks should be based on the teacher's best estimate of the pupil's achievement in the course. No basis other than achievement is valid for granting subject marks. Because of the nature of education and educational measurement, no teacher can be completely objective or accurate in determining pupil achievement. The best he can do is to gather all the evidence he can find and then make a judgment. But the amount of energy the pupil expended, his attendance, and his classroom behavior should not be included in his mark. That such things should be noted and reported to school officials, guidance persons, new teachers, and parents is axiomatic, but they should be reported as separate entities not as part of a subject mark. A subject mark should be *an index of achievement* in a course, nothing less. That is why Oliva and Scrafford recommend that one should give three types of marks:

> (1) A subject matter achievement grade determined competitively in relation to the performance of pupils at a particular grade level; (2) information concerning the relationship of the pupils' attainment and ability; and (3) information concerning personal traits, social skills, and study habits.[13]

Some teachers and theoreticians have proposed the theory that a person should be marked on the

[13] Peter F. Oliva and Ralph A. Scrafford, *Teaching in a Modern Secondary School* (Columbus, Ohio: Charles E. Merrill Books, Inc., 1965), p. 186.

amount of progress he has made during a year. On the face of it, progress is an admirable criterion for marking. However, if the mark is also to be an index of the pupil's level of achievement, then a mark based solely on the amount of progress made during the period is misleading, as the following case demonstrates.

When they arrived at the first class of their drawing course, John already had great—almost professional—skill in drawing, while Jim had no skill whatsoever. After a year in class, John has progressed comparatively little, although he can still draw much better than anyone else in the class. Jim, however, has become interested in drawing and has made swift progress. He is now slightly better than the average pupil in the class, although still not nearly as good as John. How should one mark the two boys? If one bases the marks on progress, then Jim should get the higher mark, but this would lead to the ridiculous situation of giving the higher mark to the less skilled student. To be fair and to give a reasonably accurate picture in a mark the criterion must be achievement rather than progress.

Other teachers and experts seem to feel that pupils' marks should be related to native ability. Thus a pupil who did the very best he could would be marked A, while the pupil who did not come up to his promise would be marked less. Again the system can lead us into ridiculous situations in which the ignoramus whose best turns out to be very little would receive a higher mark than the brilliant pupil who does infinitely better work without half trying.

*

Suppose you are an eleventh-grade English teacher. What should you wish to know about a pupil coming to you from the tenth grade? Would the fact that he got a B help you? If not, what information would be more helpful?

*

Determining Term Marks

COMBINING UNIT MARKS

A way to determine term marks for a course is to give the pupils marks for each unit. The final mark can be computed by taking an average of the units, making due allowance for those units that may be more important than others. Unit marks can be arrived at quite easily. Since marks should be based on as much evidence as possible, an excellent method is for the teacher to rate all the test results, oral reports, written work, observation, and other pupil activities on a five-point scale as described in preceding sections. Then the teacher can determine the unit mark by inspecting all the evidence recorded for each pupil and weighing each according to its importance. No attempt to derive an average arithmetically need be made. Obviously, the resultant mark will be based on largely subjective considerations, but then, marks are always subjective, no matter how one marks. A mark arrived at by this procedure is probably as fair as a mark arrived at by any other. Perhaps a better way to determine the unit mark is to use the total-performance-score technique described in the following section.

Some schools require that marks be recorded and reported as percentages. This presents a problem to the conscientious teacher because percentage scores often require judgments finer than the human mind can make. However, such scores may be approximated by assigning values to the unit marks. For instance, if the passing grade is 70 per cent, then the teacher can assign the following values: A, 95 per cent; B, 87 per cent; C, 80 per cent; D, 73 per cent; F, 65 per cent, or less if you wish. To attempt to give finer evaluations for the various units may be merely deceiving oneself and one's clientele.

Other methods for determining term marks will be discussed in succeeding paragraphs. These methods can also be used to establish unit marks.

TOTAL-PERFORMANCE SCORES

Another highly recommended system of calculating term marks is to rank every pupil according to his total-performance score. In this system the teacher records a point score for each and every activity he wishes reflected in the course mark. He then totals all of the activity scores (tests, quizzes, themes, papers, class recitations, and so on). Once he has the total scores he assigns marks using as a basis some such scheme as

A	10 per cent	C	45 per cent
B	25 per cent	D	15 per cent
	F	5 per cent	

The percent of pupils in each category would be an arbitrary decision based on the teacher's estimate of the ability of the class as a whole. It would be patently unfair to use the same per cent breakdown for an honors' group or for a class of low achievers. If natural breaks occur, it is usually better to use these breaks as cutoff points rather than to hew strictly to the per cent scheme. The total performance score technique is perhaps the fairest of all the methods we shall discuss.

A METHOD FOR COMPUTING FINAL MARKS

Where the teacher has given marks to pupils as the class moved on through the course, the following procedure for combining the marks into a final mark works quite well.

Decide what weight is to be given to each mark. For instance, if we should plan to base our marks on daily work, 25 per cent; papers and themes, 50 per cent; tests, 25 per cent, we could follow the following procedure:

1. Change the letter marks to numerical values: A = 4; B = 3; C = 2; D = 1; F = 0.

2. Combine the daily marks by averaging. For instance, supposing the pupil had earned the following daily marks, A, B, B, A, C, A, D, we would use the following computation to find his average score;

$$
\begin{aligned}
A &= 4 \\
B &= 3 \\
B &= 3 \\
A &= 4 \\
C &= 2 \\
A &= 4 \\
D &= 1 \\
\hline
21 &: 7 = 3.00
\end{aligned}
$$

3. Average the marks on the themes and papers. (For purposes of illustration let us assume that there are three themes and one major paper, and that the paper is equivalent to three themes, and that the pupil received a mark of A on one theme

and marks of B on the other themes and the major paper).

First Theme	A	4	4
Second Theme	B	3	3
Third Theme	B	3	3
Major Paper	B	3×3	9

$$19 : 6 = 3.17$$

(Note that the major paper is counted as three themes and so the divisor is 6).

4. Combine the test scores. In this case just one test.

$$A = 4$$

5. Combine the averages:

Daily Work	3.00	3.00
Themes & Papers	3.17×2	6.34
Test	4	4.00

$$13.34 : 4 = 3.34$$

(Note that since our original plan was to weigh the mark on the basis of daily work 25 per cent, themes and papers are given twice the weight of the other items and so the divisor is 4).

Final score is 3.34 or B.

TO BUILD MULTI-CLASS NORMS

When the content and different sections of a course are much the same, it is quite possible to combine the score distribution of the sections or of classes taught in successive years into performance norms. To make this plan feasible, the measurement for the course must be planned so that the possible number of points that can be earned is the same in all sections. Usually this means that the teacher or teachers must use the same or comparable tests and assignments in all sections and score and weigh the tests and assignments in the same way. To make the norms the teachers simply combine the score distribution of the sections into one distribution. Marks can be assigned from the combined raw scores, e.g., top 10 per cent, A; next 25 per cent, B; next 45 per cent, C; next 15 per cent, D; and last 5 per cent, F. Standard scores or stanine scores could be combined in the same manner.

However, unless the teacher has a desk calculator available, computing of standard scores is probably too time consuming for ordinary class use,[14] although they can be approximated by procedures explained in a preceding section of this chapter.

TO COMBINE STANDARD SCORES

To combine scores recorded as standard scores is quite easy. If, for instance, the daily marks were to count 50 per cent; quizzes, 25 per cent; and tests, 25 per cent; and the marks were recorded as T scores, the computation of a pupil's mark would follow the pattern:

Daily work	Quizzes	Test
55	50	52
71	65	52
63	65	
59	$180 : 3 = 60$	
68		
64		
60		
65		
60		

$$565 : 9 = 62.78$$

Daily work	62.78×2	=	125.56
Quizzes		=	60
Test		=	52

$$237.56$$

The pupil's letter mark could then be determined by the position of his total score in the total distribution. If, for instance, it fell in the middle 45 per cent of the total scores, the letter grade would probably be C.

Teacher's Responsibility for the Grade

The reader will notice that in each of the examples no matter how much computation the teacher did, in the end he had to decide what mark to give the pupil on the basis of his best judgment. Measuring techniques may make the basis for the judgment more objective, but it cannot make marking an automatic process.

[14] See Terwilliger, op. cit., Ch. 6, for instructions by which to build norms based on standard scores.

*

Is it possible to devise a means whereby all teachers' marks will mean the same thing? If not, why not? If so, what do you advise?

*

Marks in Attitude, Citizenship, Behavior, Effort

Most report cards call for the reporting of social-personal qualities as well as subject marks. Sometimes these marks are broken into categories as in the West Hartford Schools (Figure 17–3 and Figure 17–4) or sometimes all the categories are lumped under the heading Attitudes or Citizenship as in Woodbridge Township (Figure 17–8 and Figure 17–8b). The teacher's basis for making such marks is usually observation sometimes bolstered with inferences from the pupil's school work, behavior, or sometimes sociometric devices. These marks should be made out more carefully than they usually are. Probably the best method to use is to rate all pupils as average at the beginning of the marking period; raise the marks of those pupils whose attitude, effort, or behavior is excellent; or lower the marks for those pupils whose behavior, attitude, or effort is bad.

Criterion-Referenced Marking and Reporting Systems

The methods for deriving term marks already described have all been based upon normative or relative marking. In some schools we now find a movement toward criterion-referenced marking systems. Such systems base marks on an absolute or arbitrary standard or set of standards. If the pupil achieves the standard, he succeeds; if he does not, he fails. Or if he achieves the standard for C, he gets a C; if he does not, he does not. How well other pupils do is irrelevant to his mark. For example, let us suppose the teacher gives a 65 item mastery test for which he has determined each pupil must get 55 items correctly to pass. The standard, or criterion, set is 55 items. Of the thirty pupils in his class, twenty-eight get from 55 to 63 items correct; they pass. The other two pupils get 54 items

correct; they fail. If it were the other way around and of the thirty pupils twenty-eight scored in the 50–54 range, and two scored in the 55 plus range, then the twenty-eight would fail and the two would pass.[15] Similarly, the teacher could set up standards for letter marks, e.g., A = 63 and above; B = 60–62; C = 55–59; D = 52–54; F = 50 and below. The per cent correct marking system, so common in the past, is theoretically based on absolute standards (e.g., 90 per cent and above, A; 80–89 per cent, B; 70–79 per cent, C; 60–69 per cent, D; 59 per cent and below, F). In reality teachers seldom kept to the absolute standards, but rather based the per cent on the pupils' standing instead of basing the pupils' standing on the per cent. In fact, criterion-referenced tests or marks based on absolute standards do not work well in most courses as presently organized because there are no real criteria or standards by which to gauge the marking.

Criterion-referenced testing is most useful for mastery situations in which the pupil proceeds through a sequence of modules or units on a continuous-progress plan. In such a system the criterion-referenced marking could be based on a go–no go or pass–fail system. To carry out the system

1. The teacher, or higher authority, sets up a series of behavioral objectives which the pupil must achieve.
2. The teacher, or other authority, devises instruments that will measure whether or not the pupils can perform the behavior required.
3. If the pupil performs the behavior as required, he passes. If he does not, he does not pass. In a modulated continuous progress course he could go back, restudy, and then try again.

For example, the objective may be that the pupil will be able to type 40 words per minute without making more than one error per minute. If the pupil meets this standard, he has met the requirement and may go on. Although we have spoken of criterion-referenced system marking in terms of pass-fail, there is no reason that the same sort of criteria cannot be set up for other letter marks, i.e., for a C the pupil must be able to type Y words

---

[15] Few teachers would have enough gumption to let these disastrous results stand, however.

Figure 17–3

Interim Report, Mathematics, West Hartford, Conn.

TO PARENTS OF: _____

MATH TEACHER: _____

DECIMAL UNIT

Please call the Math Teacher if you have any questions or would like a personal conference.	BASIC DEVELOPMENT OF DECIMALS	ADDITION AND SUBTRACTION	MULTIPLICATION	DIVISION	ADVANCED TOPICS IN DECIMALS	PROBLEM SOLVING
PROGRESS						
Test results indicate:						
1. Significant Growth						
2. Reasonable Growth						
3. Little or No Growth						
Progress was hindered by frequent absence from class.						
I believe more growth has taken place than the test data indicate.						
SKILL DEVELOPMENT						
Is at an introductory stage.						
Demonstrates an understanding of the process and is working toward mastery.						
Has demonstrated mastery of the skills involved.						
No work was assigned because:						
1. The pre-test indicated previous mastery.						
2. Work in other topics was deemed more important.						

COMMENTS REGARDING THE STUDENT AS A LEARNER

____ Demonstrates conscientious effort.

____ Demonstrates reasonable effort.

____ Does not seem to be making a reasonable effort.

____ Makes a real attempt to learn from assigned work.

____ Views work as a task to be completed rather than a means of learning.

____ Persists even if understanding does not come immediately.

____ Is willing to settle for incomplete understanding.

____ Tends to seek help prematurely.

____ Seeks help effectively.

____ Seems unwilling to seek help.

____ Uses resources to gather information.

____ Draws conclusions based on well-organized data.

____ Demonstrates a willingness to test conclusions.

____ Effectively seeks alternate or additional assignments.

____ Demonstrates a willingness to evaluate his or her work and set objectives to correct weaknesses.

COMMENTS REGARDING STUDENT AS A CLASS MEMBER

____ Generally cooperates with class.

____ Distracts other members of the class.

____ Contributes positively to class welfare.

____ Is easily distracted.

STUDENT'S NAME: _____ HOME ROOM: _____

SUBJECT: ENGLISH   SOCIAL STUDIES   AMERICAN STUDIES   TRIMESTER: 1 2 3

	Outstanding	Above Average	Average	Below Average	Unsatisfactory	Insufficient Observation	Not Applicable
I. SKILLS							
Use of resources.							
Use of maps, graphs, and charts.							
Ability to organize.							
Ability to follow directions.							
Ability to sense problems.							
Ability to develop hypotheses.							
Ability to interpret data.							
Reads with understanding.							
Mechanics:							
Spelling.							
Punctuation.							
Capitalization.							
II. SKILLS—Written Work							
Quality of content.							
Appearance.							
Creativity.							
Ability to express ideas clearly.							
III. The Student As a Learner							
Individual Contribution:							
Quality.							
Frequency of individual presentations.							
Works well with others.							
Initiates.							
Accepts responsibility.							
Meets deadlines.							
IV. Knowledge of Subject							
V. Effort							
VI. Citizenship							

Comments:

Signature: _____

If you have any questions concerning this report, please call
to arrange for an appointment with your child's teacher.

Figure 17–4
*Interim Report, Sedgwick
Junior High School, West
Hartford, Conn.*

per minute and for a B, Z words per minute. Such standards are easiest to establish in skill subjects, but they can be built for other subjects too as the discussion of behavioral objectives in Chapter 5 shows. Creating worthwhile behavioral objectives in some subjects (e.g., literature and most of the social studies areas) may be extremely difficult, however.

In some schools the mark in a criterion-referenced system simply acknowledges that the pupil has achieved the objective. The pupil or teacher might simply record that a unit has been completed satisfactorily on such and such a day. In some systems the pupil fills in a square on a bar graph whenever he finishes a unit satisfactorily (Figure 17-9), or the teacher may record and initial the date the pupil completed the unit to his satisfaction. These marks may be turned into letter marks representing pupil progress or combined with other factors to give letter marks. In reporting to the parents the marking system usually provides other information concerning the pupil progress as in the West Hartford report shown as Figure 17-3 and Figure 17-4.

In some schools a judgment concerning how well the pupil did the work or to what degree he had reached the objective is recorded as his mark. This type of mark can be given in otherwise criterion-referenced programs. Thus in the Plant Junior High School in West Hartford, Connecticut, the pupil understanding of each social studies unit and tool skill studied is marked on an achievement scale of "Considerable," "Adequate," or "Inadequate."

Combination Marking Systems

Perhaps the most satisfactory marking system would be a combination of the normative and criterion-referenced systems.[16] Terwilliger recommends that passing or failing should be determined by the use of absolute criteria. He suggests that every pupil be required to take a test referenced to minimal instructional objectives. On this test (which, of course, could be a performance exercise) the pupil must achieve the minimum score determined before the administering of the test—usually

[16] Terwilliger, op. cit., pp. 97–99.

the minimum score should be at least 80 per cent of the possible score. Higher marks such as A, B, or C would be figured on the same basis as in any normative marking system.

*

Which of the various marking systems described seems the fairest? Why?

Which marking system would you rather use? Why?

Which is preferable, a criterion-referenced marking system or a normative marking system?

*

REPORTING TO PARENTS

The Right to Know

Every parent has the right to know how his children are progressing in school. In fact, he probably is obligated to know whether he wants to or not. Following is a list of what a parent should know about the progress of his child in school.

1. How well is the pupil progressing in each of his subjects?
2. How does his progress compare with that of other boys and girls in his age group and in his class?
3. What are his potentialities? Is he developing any particular talents or interests?
4. How does his progress compare with his potentialities?
5. What specific difficulties does he have, if any?
6. In what has he done well?
7. How does he behave in school?
8. How does he get along with his peers? With his teachers?
9. Is there any way the parent can help him?
10. Is there any way the parent can help his teachers?

Such information should be passed on to the parent at regular intervals in some fashion or other. This process is called reporting to parents. It is an important part of the school's program for many reasons. In the first place, it is through this reporting that the school can fulfill its responsibilities of telling parents of their children's status in school. Second, it gives the school an opportunity to enlist the parent's help in educating his child. Third, it gives the school an opportunity to explain its program to the parent and to solicit his understanding and assistance. All of these things are done by various means. The most common are report cards, parent conferences, and letters to parents.

Report Cards

By far the most common medium for reporting to parents is the report card. Different types of cards are used, but most schools report pupil progess by means of the ubiquitous A B C D F marking system in one guise or another. Because of the inadequacies of A B C D F marks, there is a definite trend toward supplementing these marks by adding to report cards marks in such things as effort, behavior, study habits, and attitudes. Also, many schools provide considerable opportunity for the teacher's comments and, increasingly, an opportunity for parents to comment in reply.

The report card is a vital link in the teacher's relationship with pupils and parents. Improper marking can upset pupils' morale and destroy home relationships. However, if a mark is consistent with what has been going on in class, the pupils will usually accept it without question. So will most parents if they are forwarned.

At any rate, the teacher must be careful in making out report cards. Quite often the school provides definite instructions for preparing them. When this is done, the teacher should follow the instructions exactly. If instructions are not available, the teacher should be sure to find out from a supervisor or experienced teacher just what the procedures are. It is always better to find out before one makes a faux pas than afterward.

*

Several report cards have been included in this chapter (Figure 17–3 through 17–9). Note the difference in procedure. Note what is included on each card. Criticize the cards. Which do you think is most satisfactory? Attempt to fill out the report for some youth. Doing so may point out several things you had not thought of. Which do you prefer? Why?

Look at the report card files in your curriculum library. Consider the merits of the various pupil progress cards and marking systems.

*

Supplementary Reports

Many schools find the report card alone insufficient as a basis for reporting pupil progress, even when some information over and above marks is supplied to parents. To meet this need, several schools issue supplementary progress reports from time to time. Preparing these reports may be the responsibility of the classroom teacher, the homeroom teacher, or the guidance personnel. More often than not, supplementary reports take the form of warnings of possible failure or reports of unsatisfactory progress. In a few school systems such reports are sent on other occasions, for example, to notify the parent that the pupil is doing well. These reports may be made as notes to parents, warning slips, check lists, conferences, and letters of commendation.

Letters to Parents

Letters to parents are of two types: (1) routine letters used as reports to parents in addition to, or in place of, report cards; and (2) letters for special occasions—requests to see the parent, invitations to class functions, letters notifying the parent about the pupil's work, and letters calling the parent's attention to some abnormality in the child's behavior.

Letters to parents—no matter what their purpose —should be carefully written. They should always be correct as to form and style. Errors in spelling, composition, grammar, and sentence structure should be avoided at all costs. Errors that might never be noticed in the letter of a lawyer, doctor, or dentist may be very embarrassing if made by a teacher. This is particularly true in the so-called better neighborhoods. Teachers should not take offense at parents' expecting such high standards in English usage. It is the price of being a teacher. "Teachers *should* know, you know."

Letters used as progress reports should be short and to the point. Unless one is careful, such letters soon become stereotyped. If possible, each letter

Figure 17–5
Social Studies Report, Plant Junior High School, West Hartford, Conn.

TO PARENTS OF _____

SOCIAL STUDIES TEACHER: _____

SOCIAL STUDIES PROGRAM	PUPIL ACHIEVEMENT		
	Considerable	Adequate	Inadequate
I. Units Taught Pupil understanding of the unit was judged according to test scores, projects, participation in class activities and teacher observation.			
1.			
2.			
3.			
II. Social Studies Tool Skills Pupils practiced the following skills during the marking period:			
III. Pupil As A Learner This section refers to pupil progress toward becoming an independent and effective learner.* 1. Skills a. Asks appropriate questions			
b. Finds necessary information			
c. Organizes information logically			
d. Develops answers to questions			
e. Evaluates own work			
2. Attitudes Toward Learning a. Seems eager to ask questions			
b. Promptly and freely collects information			
c. Readily organizes data			
d. Enthusiastically develops answers to questions			
e. Willingly evaluates own work.			

Topic   IV. Independent Study (where applicable)
Teacher Comments:

V. Teacher Comments (optional)

*A more detailed explanation of section III will accompany this form the first time it
is distributed during the school year.

should be a personal message to the parents, but even a stereotyped letter is better than one that is not clear. In writing to parents, teachers should remember that parents may not be familiar with the professional jargon of teachers. Consequently, the teacher should attempt to write in clear, idio-matic English. Sentences like, "Mary seems to have difficulty adjusting to the group," may be crystal clear to you but mean little to some parents. In a report concerning a seventh grader, the statement that "Lucy seems to be a little immature" may seem appropriate enough to you and your col-

Figure 17–6a
Report Card Used in Hartford, Conn. High Schools.

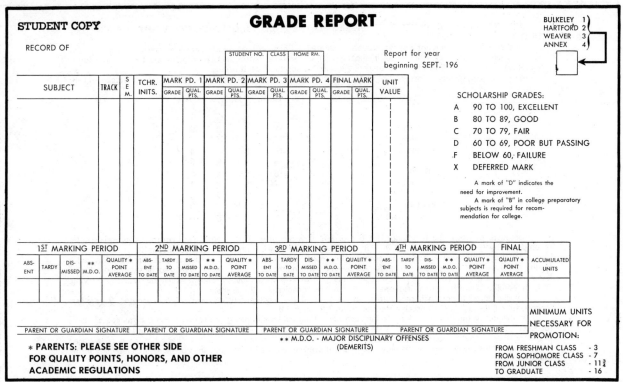

leagues, but it can make you the laughing stock of the country club set.

In writing such letters it is usually best to start and end on a pleasant note. A frequent recommendation is always to commence by reporting something favorable about the pupil and ending in an optimistic vein. This is sound advice. However, the effort to be pleasant must not outweigh truthfulness. The parent is entitled to an accurate report which reflects the teacher's best judgment concerning the child. Sometimes teachers are so careful not to hurt the parent's feelings and so eager to establish amicable relations with the parent that they fail to point out clearly the pupil's failings. This is not fair to the parent. While the teacher should not be tactless, he should let the parent know the facts about his child. The best rule is to decide what you wish the parent to know and then say it simply and pleasantly.

The body of the report should estimate the progress of the pupil as accurately as possible. This estimate should indicate the pupil's progress in relation to his ability and also in relation to the normal achievement for pupils at his grade level. It should point out the pupil's strong and weak points, and show where he needs help. The report should not be limited to achievement in subject matter alone, but should also provide information concerning the pupil's social behavior and other aspects of his activities in school. At times, the teacher will wish to ask the parent for his cooperation in some specific way. Certainly he should always ask the parent for his comments.

AN EXAMPLE OF A LETTER TO A PARENT

When writing a letter to a parent, be brief, clear, pleasant, honest, and factual. An example of a

Figure 17–6b
Reverse Side of Report Card Used in Hartford, Conn., High Schools.

THE ATTENTION OF PARENTS IS CALLED TO THE FOLLOWING ACADEMIC REGULATIONS OF THE SCHOOL:

On the basis of the amount and type of work required, all high-school subjects have been classified in one of five groups: Advanced-Placement, Honors, Academic, General, or Personal. After the title of each subject which your son or daughter is taking you will find a letter to indicate the classification to which it belongs.

In each subject, quality points will be granted according to the classification of the subject and the mark earned in it:

Mark		Quality Points			
	AP	H	A	G	P
95–100	14	12	10	8	6
90–94	13	11	9	7	5
85–89	12	10	8	6	4
80–84	11	9	7	5	3
75–79	10	8	6	4	2
70–74	9	7	5	3	1
65–69	8	6	4	2	0
60–64	7	5	3	1	0
Less than 60	0	0	0	0	0

Any mark in which the last figure is a five or higher is recorded on the report card with the appropriate letter accompanied by +. For example, 75, 76, 77, 78, and 79 are indicated as C+; 85, 86, 87, 88, and 89, as B+.

Each marking period a student receives on his report card a letter mark for each subject that he takes and a quality-point average. The parent can verify this average by using the table listed above. To do so, he should convert the letter marks into quality points, total them, and divide that total by the number of subjects which the student is carrying. Only those subjects which count at least one-half unit will be considered in this average.

Marking-period honors will be awarded on the basis of the quality-point average; Highest Honors, 9 or more; Honors, from 8 through 8.9; Honorable Mention, from 7 through 7.9.

At the end of the fourth marking period each subject-matter teacher, using the conventional 0 through 100 marks for each marking period, will average the year's work in his subject and will convert that average into a letter-mark and the proper number of quality points. These points and those which the student receives in his other subjects will be averaged for the year. This average will be the only quality-point average recorded on the student's permanent record card during the school year.

homeroom teacher's letter to a ninth grader's parents follows.

Dear Mr. and Mrs. Smith:

Joan's teachers have reported to me the results of her first quarter's work. They are quite satisfactory except for algebra, in which she is experiencing some difficulty. Her difficulty seems to be caused by a lack of understanding of mathematical principles. Mr. Courtney, her algebra teacher, feels that she should have extra help in his course. In all other respects, Joan seems to be making an excellent start this year.

If you have any suggestions or comments to make about Joan's school work, we should welcome them. Also, we should very much like to have you visit our school whenever it is convenient for you.

Cordially yours,
Jennie Jones

*

Compare the merits and faults of the following as a means of reporting to parents:

letter marks
percentage marks
pass-fail marks
letters to parents
conferences with parents
descriptive marks

Which would be the most informative? Which would you rather receive if you were a parent?

*

Conferences with Parents

Parent-teacher conferences are an increasingly popular method of reporting pupil progress to parents. This procedure has many advantages. It allows the teacher and the parent to discuss the pupil face-to-face. The conference should serve to create better understanding between parents and teachers and to obviate parental misunderstand-

Figure 17–7
Report Card Used in Chatham Township High School, Chatham, N.J.

CHATHAM TOWNSHIP HIGH SCHOOL
REPORT CARD

A Excellent	D Basic (Poor)	MD Medical Excuse
B Good	E Failure	NG No Grade
C⁺ College Credit	WD Withdrawn	I Incomplete
C Average		

To Parents or Guardian: This is a report of the progress of the student in the subjects being studied this year. The report card value depends largely upon the interest you show in it. We suggest that you talk over this report with the student each time it is received. If the report is satisfactory a word of encouragement will mean much to him. If unsatisfactory, the cause of poor work should be sought and remedied. The school is always ready to cooperate with parents in seeking remedies. Please do not hesitate to call. Appointment may be made by telephone. Call 635-9075.

STUDENT'S NAME						GRADE
HOMEROOM			YEAR GRAD.			
SUBJECT	1st M.P.	2nd M.P.	3rd M.P.	4th M.P.	EXAM.	FINAL GRADE
1. Physical Education						
2.						
3.						
4.						
5.						
6.						
7.						
8.						
ATTENDANCE Absent					Totals	
Tardy						

ings that sometimes result from teachers' letters and report forms. The conference gives the parent an opportunity to ask questions and to make suggestions. It also gives the teacher an opportunity to solicit additional information from the parent and to suggest ways in which the parent can cooperate to improve the child's work.

Conferences can be very helpful as supplements to the written reports of pupil progress to parents. It is doubtful whether they should be the sole medium for reporting, although some elementary schools rely almost wholly upon them. In secondary schools, conferences are more likely to be arranged to meet certain definite problems.

In spite of their many advantages parent-teacher conferences have certain inherent drawbacks. They are often time-consuming and difficult to schedule. Sometimes they must be scheduled at hours that are inconvenient for the teacher. Occasionally, instead of clearing up misunderstandings between parents and teachers, conferences add to them. At times the parent may be difficult to deal with. Some parents are emotional, domineering, or excessively talkative. Some are opinionated and overly critical

of the school. The competent teacher attempts to plan and conduct parent-teacher conferences so as to avoid these difficulties as much as he can.

Some suggestions for conducting parent-teacher conferences follow.

1. Plan what you wish to say and how you wish to conduct the conference. Do not make a fetish of your plan, but do try to keep to the purpose of the conference at least. If possible, keep the conference moving. On the other hand do not rush the parent. In your planning allow enough time to talk things over thoroughly and leisurely.

2. Be pleasant, courteous, tactful, and patient. Remember that the visit to the school may often be upsetting to the parent. Listen to him and try to understand his point of view. Remember that he has much information valuable to you. Let him tell it to you. If he is running hot, keep cool and let him talk it out. This is often an effective way to calm an irate parent. However, do not be obsequious. One does not need to agree with a parent to be

Figure 17–8a
Report Card Used in Woodbridge Township Junior High Schools, Woodbridge, N.J.

Fords Junior High School
Woodbridge Township,
GRADE 7–8   **WOODBRIDGE, NEW JERSEY**   19____ 19____
JUNIOR HIGH SCHOOL

NAME _____   GRADE ____   HOMEROOM ____

		1	2	3	4	YEAR M	A	CR.			1	2	3	4	YEAR M	A	CR.
ENGLISH	M								COMMERCE	M							
	A									A							
PHYS. ED.	M									M							
	A									A							
HYGIENE	M								ART	M							
	A									A							
LANGUAGE	M								VOCAL MUSIC	M							
	A									A							
	M								INSTR. MUSIC	M							
	A									A							
SOCIAL SC.	M								COOKING	M							
	A									A							
	M								SEWING	M							
	A									A							
SCIENCE	M								WOODSHOP	M							
	A									A							
	M								METAL SHOP	M							
	A									A							
MATH.	M									M							
	A									A							
ABSENT									TARDY								

polite. If the parent is severely critical of the school, arrange for him to talk to the principal or someone else in authority. Remember at all times that a conference is serious business and should be conducted with care and dignity.

3. Be clear and specific. Try to be sure the parent understands you. Talk to him in simple English and avoid technical terms. Make specific points and back them up with specific examples. Avoid vague, unsubstantiated generalizations which may lead to misunderstanding. Summarizing at critical points during the conference and at its end may help eliminate confusion and ensure a common understanding of what has transpired.

4. Avoid criticizing other teachers and school officials. First, it is unethical. Second, it will surely hurt your standing with your colleagues. Third, it will probably cause the parent to form a poor impression of you.

5. Solicit the parent's cooperation. The school is as much his as it is yours, and he has as much at stake in its success as you do. His interest in his own children is presumably greater than yours. Many parents would be eager to help if they only knew how. On the other hand, the teacher should be cautious

WOODBRIDGE TOWNSHIP JUNIOR HIGH SCHOOLS
Woodbridge, New Jersey

Grade 7-8

REPORT CARD

SIGNIFICANCE OF MARKS

<u>Academic</u>
(Designated by M)

<u>Attitude</u>
(Designated by A)

A = Superior

B = Good

C = Average

D = Poor

I = Incomplete

O = Outstanding
(Above Average)

S = Satisfactory

U = Unsatisfactory

X = Probation
(Parental Conference
Required)

F = Failure

Academic marks are based
on subject matter
achievement only.

Attitude marks are based
on behavior, effort, and
citizenship.

Two period marks of F in achievement constitute
failure in that subject for the year.

Parents should recognize that good attendance has
a positive effect on student achievement.

                                                  Principal

Parents are requested to study this report carefully,
sign, and return it immediately.

1. _____

2. _____

3. _____

4. _____

Figure 17–8b
*Reverse Side, Woodbridge
Township Junior High School
Report Card, Woodbridge, N.J.*

about making suggestions which the parent might resent as intrusions on his own privacy, home life, or social life. If any suggestions of this sort need to be made, the teacher should be sure that his suggestions are constructive and that the parent is ready to act upon them. Frequently the better part of discretion is to leave such suggestions to guidance personnel, an administrator, or a supervisor.

6. After the conference the teacher should note

Figure 17–9

*Bar Graph Recording Pupil Progress.** *

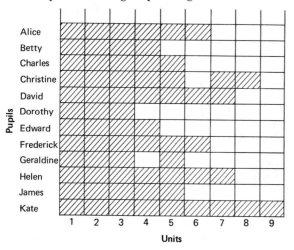

* *Note:* Some pupils have skipped units. Some teachers record progress on such a chart by dating and initialing the proper square when the pupil has satisfactorily completed a unit.

down what has been said, what suggestions have been made, and what conclusions have been reached. This should be done as soon as possible lest some of the information be forgotten.

7. Ordinarily there should be some follow-up on every teacher-parent conference.

*

Marks quite often become a bone of contention between parents and the school. Why? How can this be avoided?

In a conference the parent strongly criticizes the school administration or another teacher. You wholeheartedly agree with the parent. What should you do?

Describe what you consider the best system of marking and reporting to parents.

*

PROMOTION

Desirability of Continuous Progress

Promotion is an exceedingly difficult problem. Most logically promotion should be based on readi-

ness. Pupils should progress through their course work in orderly fashion, staying with a particular course or unit only long enough to learn the material well and then moving on. In other words, the pupil should be promoted when he is ready. Promotion based on readiness is called continuous progress.

Unfortunately, the secondary school is seldom organized in a manner suitable for continuous progress. The difficulty preventing continuous promotions is that our schools are graded. At the end of a year the youngster must go on to the next grade or return to the beginning of his present grade. This system makes little sense. Our present pass-or-fail promotion policies may either make the pupil repeat material he has already learned, or force him ahead to more difficult material before he is ready. The establishment of nongraded high schools may foreshadow the end of this perplexing problem. Continuous progress is the heart of the nongraded high school idea.

CONDUCTING A CONTINUOUS-PROGRESS SYSTEM

To organize a school for a continuous-progress system one can divide the course work into units or modules. For each of these units one sets up minimum requirements in terms of minimal instructional objectives which the pupil must achieve in order to complete the unit successfully. Instruction in these units is individualized so that pupils may achieve these minimal objectives at their own speed and by different pathways. When the pupil feels that he is ready, he is given a criterion-referenced test or other device which determines whether he has met the goal or not. If he is successful, he is free to go on to the next unit. If at the end of the year he has not completed all of the units for the year, he picks up where he left off next year. If he finishes the year's work early, he can immediately proceed to the new year's units. In this way pupils are kept from having to mark time or having to move on to new material when they have not mastered the old material. The construction of units (modules) and individualized instructional materials for use in such units (modules) is discussed in other chapters.

Setting Standards for Promotion

Although most secondary schools are not organized for continuous promotion, the principles behind it do apply to promotion in general. The basic criterion for deciding if a pupil should be promoted is whether or not he is ready to profit from the next higher course in the subject. Even though the pupil does not intend to go on to the next course, the principle still holds in general, although perhaps it need not be applied quite so stringently in this instance. In other words, teachers should have standards of minimum achievement for their courses, and these standards should represent what is required of the pupil before he is ready for the next higher course.

THE ROLE OF SOCIAL PROMOTION

Although a teacher should ordinarily promote only those pupils who are ready, on occasion pupils are promoted whether they are ready or not. Usually when this is done, it is an attempt to keep the pupil in a social group with which he is compatible. This practice is called social promotion. On occasion, it is justified. The old practice of keeping sixteen-year-old youths in third-grade classes was cruel. An example of a well-justified social promotion follows.

A junior high school boy was reading well below his grade level. Although evidently of at least normal intelligence, he was quite incapable of doing junior high school work. The boy also suffered from an acute speech defect and certain other emotional problems. The school psychiatrist examined the boy and recommended a social promotion as a means of helping him find himself. In this case the promotion was justified. But automatic promotions are never justified. Too often the young people are promoted to free the classrooms and because of a mistaken attempt to be democratic. Except in cases such as the one just noted, pupils should be required to meet minimum standards before they move on.

*

To what extent can one apply the principle of continuous progress in the ordinary secondary school? To what extent should it be applied?

Do you agree that social promotion was justified in the preceding example?

*

TWO FINAL CONSIDERATIONS

Although the teacher should maintain standards, these standards should be flexible. The fact that a pupil has not mastered the material of a course may not be sufficient reason for keeping him back. On the other hand, merely spending a year in a classroom is not sufficient reason for promoting him either. Some pupils should repeat courses. Each problem of promotion should be decided on its own merits. In applying promotion standards to a particular case, one should bear in mind two main questions: (1) How will the decision affect the pupil concerned? and (2) How will the decision affect the other pupils? Probably the final criterion should be: Which would benefit the pupil more? If it seems that the youngster would benefit from repeating the course another year, let him repeat it; if, on the other hand, there seems to be no reason to think that another year would be beneficial, let him move on. However, one should also consider the other pupils. How will promoting this pupil affect them? How will it affect pupil motivation and morale? Will promoting him be fair to the others? If promoting a pupil will injure pupil motivation and morale in any way, one should weigh the case carefully before deciding to promote the pupil.

To Pass or Not to Pass

Deciding if a pupil should pass or fail often calls for difficult decisions. To illustrate the complexity of the problem let us consider the following situation. In your Algebra I class you have a youngster who has done poor work. It is your considered opinion that he is just not a mathematician. He is unable to do the work, no matter how hard he tries—and he seems to have tried very hard. He and his family are determined that he go on to college and insist that he continue with mathematics. Presumably, if he passes Algebra I, he will try Algebra II for which he is definitely not ready. What should you do? What would be best for the boy? To pass and attempt Algebra II? To fail and to repeat Algebra I? Is there some other way out? What about the effect on the other pupils? What information do you need and what must you consider to answer this problem intelligently?

As you can see, if you try to think this problem through, it probably has no truly satisfactory answer. Even though we have stated categorically that when a pupil has not been able to achieve the minimum standard he shall not pass, is this perhaps not the case where justice should be tempered with mercy? Fortunately, many schools help the teacher in making this decision by establishing quite definite school policies concerning promotion. When they do, the teacher should try to follow the policy. Other schools have no formal policy, although there may be an informal one. Even if there is no policy at all, the principal can advise one on what he ought to do. Even so, the decision of whether or not to promote must be made by the teacher on the basis of what is best for the pupil himself and for other pupils in the school within the limits set by school policy. In spite of statistics and theory, in the end all decisions concerning marks and marking come down to teacher judgment.

*

A boy is completing his second year in Latin I. He is definitely not yet capable of doing the work of Latin II. What do you recommend the teachers do as far as promotion is concerned?

*

SUMMARY

Parents have the right to know how well their children are doing in school, and teachers have a duty to keep the parents informed. For many years teachers have used marks to meet this obligation. Although many parents, pupils, and teachers do not realize it, marks, unfortunately, do not inform anyone of much of anything. Moreover, present-day marking systems tend to emphasize the mark rather than the learning. About the only value they have is a certain amount of incentive value, and even that seems to be overrated.

As teachers have come to recognize these facts, they have made numerous attempts to create better methods of evaluating and reporting pupils' progress. So far none of these attempts has been completely successful. Probably what is needed is a system that explains in writing how well a pupil is doing in relation to the standard for the group and to his own potentialities. In reporting to parents and pupils, such devices should undoubtedly be supplemented by conferences. Modern systems of reporting to parents seem to be moving in that direction. However, in many cases they still have a long distance to go. In the meantime, we shall have to do the best we can with what we have.

Promotion has always been a problem for the conscientious teacher. Promotion should be based on readiness, but this principle of continuous progress is not readily feasible in the secondary school as now organized. The need for continuous progress is one of the major arguments for the establishment of nongraded secondary schools.

There is no truly satisfactory answer to the problem of promotion. The final decision, however, should rest with the teacher, and his decision should be based on what is best for the student himself and for the other students in the class and school.

Suggested Reading for Part VII

ADAMS, SAM, AND FRED M. SMITH, *Educational Measurement for the Classroom Teacher.* New York: Harper & Row, Publishers, 1966.

AHMANN, J. STANLEY, AND MARVIN D. GLOCK, *Evaluating Pupil Growth.* Boston: Allyn & Bacon, Inc., 1963.

ALCORN, MARVIN D., JAMES S. KINDER, AND JIM R. SCHUNERT, *Better Teaching in Secondary Schools,* 3rd ed. New York: Holt, Rinehart and Winston, Publishers, 1970. Chs. 16–18.

BERG, HARRY D., ed. *Evaluation in Social Studies,* Thirty-fifth Yearbook. Washington, D.C.: National Council for the Social Studies, 1965.

BLOOD, DON F., AND WILLIAM C. BUDD, *Educational Measurement and Evaluation.* New York: Harper & Row, Publishers, 1972.

BLOOM, BENJAMIN S., J. THOMAS HASTINGS, AND GEORGE F. MADAOS, *Handbook on Formative and Summative Evaluation of Student Learning.* New York: McGraw-Hill Book Company, 1971.

BROWN, FREDERICK G., *Measurement and Evaluation.* Itasca, Ill.: F. E. Peacock Publishers, Inc., 1971.

BUROS, OSCAR, *Mental Measurements Yearbook.* Highland Park, N.J.: The Gryphon Press. Various noncumulative editions.

CRONBACH, L. J., *Essentials of Psychological Testing*, 3rd ed. New York: Harper & Row, Publishers, Inc., 1970.

DIZNEY, HENRY, *Classroom Evaluation for Teachers.* Dubuque, Iowa: William C. Brown Company, Publishers, 1971.

———, *Evaluation in the Classroom.* Dubuque, Iowa: William C. Brown Company, Publishers, 1971.

DUROST, WALTER N., AND GEORGE A. PRESCOTT, *Essentials of Measurement for Teachers.* New York: Harcourt Brace and World, Inc., 1964.

ENGLEHART, MAX D., *Improving Classroom Testing*, What Research Says to the Teacher Series, No. 31. Washington, D.C.: The National Education Association, 1964.

FOX, ROBERT, MARGARET B. LUSZKI, AND RICHARD SCHMUCK, *Diagnosing Classroom Learning.* Chicago: Science Research Associates Inc., 1966.

GOROW, FRANK F., *Better Classroom Testing.* San Francisco: Chandler Publishing Company, 1966.

GRAMBS, JEAN D., JOHN C. CARR, AND ROBERT M. FITCH, *Modern Methods in Secondary Education,* 3rd ed. New York: Holt, Rinehart and Winston, Publishers, 1970. Chs. 13 and 14.

GRONLUND, NORMAN E., *Improving Marketing and Reporting in Classroom Instruction.* New York: Macmillan Publishing Co., Inc., 1974.

———, *Measurement and Evaluation in Teaching,* 3rd ed. New York: Macmillan Publishing Co., Inc., 1970.

———, *Preparing Criterion-Referenced Tests for Classroom Instruction.* New York: Macmillan Publishing Co., Inc., 1973.

GROSSE, LOIS M., DOROTHY MILLER, AND ERWIN R. STEINBERG, eds. *Suggestions for Evaluating Junior High School Writing.* Pittsburg, Pa.: Association of English Teachers of Western Pennsylvania, n.d. Distributed by National Council of Teachers of English.

HOOVER, KENNETH H., *The Professional Teacher's Handbook.* Boston: Allyn & Bacon, Inc., 1973. Chs. 7 and 18.

JANSEN, V. H., *Marking and Reporting Procedures in the Secondary Schools of Texas.* Austin, Tex.: Texas Study of Secondary Education, 1966.

JENNINGS, HELEN HALL, *Sociometry in Group Relations.* Washington, D.C.: American Council on Education, 1948.

KRATWOHL, DAVID R., BENJAMIN S. BLOOM, AND BERTRAM M. MASIA, *Taxonomy of Educational Objectives, Handbook II, Affective Domain.* New York: David McKay Company, Inc., 1964.

KRYSPIN, WILLIAM J., AND JOHN F. FELDHUSEN, *Developing Classroom Tests: A Guide for Writing and Evaluating Test Items.* Minneapolis: Burgess Publishing Company, 1974.

KURFMAN, DANA, ed. "Teacher Made Test Items in American History: Emphasis Junior High School," Bulletin No. 40. Washington, D.C.: National Council for the Social Studies, 1968.

MAGER, ROBERT F., *Measuring Instructional Intent.* San Francisco: Fearon Publishers, 1973.

Making the Classroom Test, 2nd ed. Princeton, N.J.: Educational Testing Service, 1961.

Marking and Reporting Pupil Progress, Research Summary 1971–Sl. Washington, D.C.: The National Education Association, 1970.

MARSHALL, JON CLARK, AND LOYDE WESLEY HALES, *Classroom Test Construction.* Reading, Mass.: Addison-Wesley Publishing Co., Inc. 1971.

McLAUGHLIN, KENNETH F., *Interpretation of Test Results,* Bulletin 1964, No. 7, OE 25–038, U.S. Office of Education, U.S. Dept. of Health, Education and Welfare. Washington, D.C.: U.S. Government Printing Office, 1964.

MEHRENS, WILLIAM A., AND IRVIN J. LEHMANN, *Measurment and Evaluation in Education and Psychology.* New York: Holt, Rinehart and Winston, Publishers, 1973.

MORSE, HORACE T., AND GEORGE H. McCUNE, "Selected Items for the Testing of Study Skills and Critical Thinking," Bulletin No. 15. Washington, D.C.: National Council for the Social Studies, 1964.

Multiple Choice Questions: A Close Look. Princeton, N.J.: Educational Testing Service, 1963.

National Society for the Study of Education, *Educational Evaluation: New Role, New Means,* Sixty-eighth Yearbook, Part II. Chicago: University of Chicago Press, 1969.

NELSON, CLARENCE H., *Measurement and Evaluation in the Classroom.* New York: Macmillan Publishing Co., Inc., 1970.

PAYNE, D. A., AND R. F. McMORRIS, eds. *Educational and Psychological Measurement.* Waltham, Mass.: Ginn/Blaisdell, 1967.

POPHAM, W. JAMES, ed. *Criterion-Referenced Measurement.* Englewood Cliffs, N.J.: Educational Technology Publications, 1971.

SAMALONIS, BERNICE L., *Methods and Materials for Today's High Schools.* New York: Van Nostrand Reinhold Company, 1970. Ch. 7.

SCHOER, LOWELL A., *Test Construction: A Programed Guide.* Boston: Allyn & Bacon, Inc., 1970.

Selecting an Achievement Test: Principles and Procedures, 2nd ed. Princeton, N.J.: Educational Testing Service, 1961.

SMITH, FRED M., AND SAM ADAMS, *Educational Measurement for the Classroom Teachers,* 2nd ed. New York: Harper & Row, Publishers, 1972.

Standards for Educational and Psychological Tests and Manuals. Washington, D.C.: American Psychological Association, 1966.

STODOLA, Q., *Making the Classroom Test.* Princeton, N.J.: Educational Testing Service, 1961.

TATE, MERLE W., AND RICHARD C. CLELLAND, *Nonparametric and Short-*

cut Statistics. Danville, Ill.: The Interstate Printers and Publishers, Inc., 1957.

TEN BRINK, TERRY D., *Evaluation.* New York: McGraw-Hill Book Company, 1974.

TERWILLIGER, JAMES S., *Assigning Grades to Students.* Glenview, Ill.: Scott Foresman and Company, 1971.

——, "Self-Reported Marking Practices and Policies in Secondary Schools," The Bulletin of the National Association of Secondary-School Principals, 50:5–37 (March, 1966).

THORNDIKE, ROBERT L., ed. *Educational Measurement*, 2nd ed. Washington, D.C.: American Council on Education, 1971.

THORNDIKE, ROBERT L., AND ELIZABETH HAGER, *Measurement and Evaluation in Psychology and Education*, 3rd ed. New York: John Wiley & Sons, Inc., 1969.

TOWNSEND, EDWARD ARTHUR, AND PAUL J. BURKE, *Statistics for the Classroom Teacher: A Self-teaching Unit.* New York: Macmillan Publishing Co., Inc., 1963.

TYLER, RALPH W., AND RICHARD M. WOLF, *Crucial Issues in Testing.* Berkeley, Calif.: McCutchan Publishing Corporation, 1974.

WORTHER, BLAINE R., AND JAMES R. SANDERS, *Educational Evaluation.* Worthington, Ohio: Charles A. Jones Publishing Company, 1973.

VIII

The Beginning Teacher

Becoming a Professional

18

To the beginning teacher the prospect of the first job can be both exciting and frightening. Many students find the advent of student teaching or internship equally challenging and alarming. In these situations things take on a degree of seriousness that does not always apply to ordinary college classes. Here one is playing for keeps. The prize may well be success—or failure—in one's career. This chapter is an attempt to help make the beginners' first teaching experiences more enjoyable and profitable.

THE PROFESSIONAL TEACHER

The word *professional* has at least two connotations. One connotation refers to the type of work that is done by professional workers; the other connotation is that which is expressed in the common expression "being a real pro," that is to say, a really competent performer.

Although it may be some time before you can

become a real pro, you should try to be a thoroughly professional teacher from the day you start teaching. The truly professional teacher gives a full measure of professional service. He does a fine job at the highest possible level; he undertakes all professional responsibilities willingly, and he carries out to the best of his abilities whatever he undertakes. In return, he expects to be paid adequately for these services. In other words, in dealing with his colleagues and employers, he does unto them as he would have them do unto him.

Above all, the professional teacher is proud of his profession, although it is arduous and exacting and in the past has not always been rewarded as well as it should have been. The professional teacher works to secure satisfactory tangible rewards, but he will always give a little more than he is paid for.

It takes a little longer to become a real pro. When one first starts to teach, one is only beginning to learn his trade. A retired superintendent of schools says that, judging from his more than thirty years of experience in the superintendency, it takes a beginning teacher at least two years to become worth his salt. As one teaches, the experience should help him to become more expert. Unfortunately, some teachers do not improve with experience.

A real pro is truly competent in what he does. He is well prepared in the three things essential for teaching—he knows his pupils, his subject, and how to teach. He has mastered a vast repertoire of techniques and strategies and can adapt them skillfully to whatever type of teaching situation he is faced with. He has learned how to get the most out of his pupils and to adapt the curriculum to their needs and abilities. In short, he is a master teacher.

STUDENT TEACHING AND INTERNSHIPS

The first major step in moving from amateur status toward gaining the competencies that mark the real pro, is the student-teaching or internship program. It is in this experience that the neophyte has his first real opportunity to put educational theory and methods into practice. Simulations, mini-lessons, and microteaching are all excellent learning opportunities, but they do not match the

reality one finds in the internship or student teaching. Even these experiences are not completely real teaching experiences. They are designed to be learning experiences and so are likely to be somewhat artificial.

That student teaching[1] is first and foremost a learning situation cannot be emphasized too much. This is the time for the teacher-to-be to master the rudiments of his craft before he has to put his skills on the line in his own classroom. Here is a chance for the neophyte in teaching to make mistakes and learn from his mistakes without causing harm to the pupils. Here is the time the beginner can try his wings and find out the strategies, tactics, and teaching styles that best suit him. It is a time of trial and error and for growing confidence and beginning expertness. It is not a time of perfectness but of striving for competence.

Some Facts of Life

The comments in this section are based upon many years of watching student teachers. They were written in the hope that they can make your life as a student teacher easier and more rewarding. They are not intended to preach; rather, they are intended to point out some pitfalls and ways to avoid them and to suggest ways to make the most of the student-teaching experience.

BECOMING PREPARED

First one should know that student teaching is a difficult experience requiring a lot of hard work. Do not underestimate its demands. Most students find it to be much more time consuming than any other college work they have had. Students who try to combine full-time student teaching assignments with additional courses or part-time jobs usually find themselves overwhelmed. It is much wiser to concentrate all one's time on the student teaching from the very beginning than to have to drop out later on.

Because student teaching is hard work, the student teacher needs to find out as much as he can

---

[1] We shall use the term *student teaching* to cover both student teaching and internship in this section from this point on.

about his assignment as soon as he can—long before the student-teaching period begins If possible, he should find out what topics he is to teach and prepare himself for these topics. Most student teachers do not have perfect command of the content that secondary school pupils study. For instance, mathematics student teachers seldom are at their best in high school geometry; English student teachers cannot possibly be familiar with all the works secondary school pupils may read; and social studies student teachers are not likely to have recently studied all the history, geography, economics, political science, and sociology they may be called on to teach. *The wise student teacher uses the period before student teaching begins to master his content!*

Probably the first thing the student teacher should do is to procure the curriculum guide, textbook, and other readings used in each of the courses he is to teach and then master them. In addition it might be wise to study a review book. Such works may give you a basis for organizing units and lessons and ideas for building lessons and tactics. One can also find many ideas in the curriculum guide, question banks, and other materials developed by various school systems and on file in the local or university curriculum library. If it is feasible, the student teacher should build himself a resource unit covering each of the areas he will have to teach. Unless this early preparation is done carefully, the student teacher may find himself having to become an instant expert on something about which he knows little or nothing.

Even students whose college background should fit them perfectly for their student-teaching assignment may find the content difficult. It takes only a little teaching to show one how much he does not know about a subject. If one does a great share of his studying and preparation before the student teaching period begins, it will be a great advantage. Many student teachers must spend so much of their time trying to master the content, that they never learn to teach it well.

A LEARNING EXPERIENCE

Student teaching is a learning experience. It is not expected that the student teacher will be a master teacher from the first day. As a matter of fact, few teachers become real masters of the art of teaching in the first few years. Student teachers who find that their lessons do not always go as well as they had hoped should not be surprised. Every beginner makes mistakes. Many student teachers find that it takes many weeks before they begin really to master the techniques of teaching and start to become easy and effective in the classroom. Often teachers who find the first few weeks hard going develop into the best of teachers if they are sensitive and learn as they go along. On the other hand, student teachers who find that things at first go very well should not become overconfident. Many of our poorest teachers are young people who, having had a fair amount of success at first, became overconfident and self-satisfied, and so did not strive to become real pros. As a result, they have remained amateurish ever since.

NO LONGER JUST A STUDENT

Although the student-teaching or internship experience is designed to be a learning experience, the student teacher should remember that student teaching is also a job, and the cooperating teacher, and other supervisors, are his bosses. Student teachers are expected to toe the mark just as other employees are. If they do not, they may be fired. Looseness or slackness that may be allowed in ordinary college classes has no place in student teaching.

Because the local cooperating teacher and his college supervisor are the student teacher's immediate supervisors, they must be pleased and satisfied with his performance. Therefore, the student teacher must carry out their instructions, directions, and suggestions without "ifs," "ands" or "buts." Unfortunately the student teacher's job may be complicated by the fact that the instructions, directions, and suggestions of his various supervisors sometimes differ. They may be incompatible. In such cases the student teacher should go to the college supervisor for help and advice.

Some student teachers worry about the restraints on their behavior during the student-teaching period. In certain ways student teachers are in a peculiarly anomalous situation. They are neophytes learning, and at the same time they are teachers. Therefore student teaching can be quite trying. Some student teachers rebel against the demands of student teaching, which admittedly are great. Some believe that these demands infringe on their rights. However, it is not wise to press one's rights overmuch during one's student teaching because it is doubtful how many rights one really has—at least as far as the cooperating school is concerned. Student teachers are guests of the school and their cooperating teacher. They are in the school mostly on sufferance. The teacher-education institution can only try to persuade the local personnel. It cannot dictate or demand. Consequently, both student teachers and college supervisors must do their best to meet the expectations of the school.

RELATIONS WITH SUPERVISORS

It is extremely important for the student teacher to establish and maintain good relationships with his supervisors. In most student-teaching situations the student teacher's immediate supervisor is a cooperating teacher. This teacher is the professional person with whom the student teacher comes in close contact during his teacher education program. One of the advantages of student teaching ordinarily is that the cooperating teacher provides the student teacher with close supervision and a knowledgeable adviser who is close to the situation and immediately available in time of need. Nevertheless such intimate relationships can be trying. They require tact, patience, understanding, and forbearance on the part of both the individuals concerned.

The student-teaching period can be very bothersome to the cooperating teacher. To be a good cooperating teacher is a difficult job. He may find it more difficult to supervise another's teaching than to do it himself. Furthermore the student teacher may seem to be a threat to the success of his own teaching. He may fear that if the student teacher does not do well, the progress of the class may suffer, the discipline of the class may disintegrate, or the class atmosphere may deteriorate. Many a cooperating teacher has had to work extra hard for several weeks in order to whip back into shape a class that has gone sour under a student teacher. For the insecure teacher merely for another adult to be in the room may seem threatening.

Sometimes student teachers commit tactical errors that cause the relationship with their supervisors to fall apart. Let us consider some of these mistakes

that supervisors complain about so much. Some of them seem so obvious that it would seem ridiculous to mention them, but for the fact that they cause so many student teaching failures.

Preparedness.   Some student teachers do not prepare well enough. Soon the pupils become aware that the student teacher does not know his stuff or what he is trying to do. Once this happens, the student teacher is through. To reestablish the confidence of pupils and supervisors in such cases is a monumental task. Student teachers who must continually improvise are anathema to most supervisors.

Attention to Detail.   Some student teachers neglect their duties. If unit plans or lesson plans are due on Friday, supervisors expect them on Friday —not Monday. If attendance is to be taken at the beginning of the period, then supervisors expect it to be taken at the beginning of the period. If the student teacher plans to use audio-visual aids, the supervisor expects the student teacher to make all the arrangements in plenty of time and, insofar as he possibly can, to be sure that all the equipment and materials are ready. If the student teacher does not attend to details of this sort, he goes down in the supervisor's book as irresponsible.

Responsibility and Dependability.   Being responsible and dependable rate very high with most supervisors. They expect student teachers to do what they are supposed to do or at least try their utmost to do it. They appreciate honest attempts even when they are unsuccessful, but they are very suspicious of alibis and excuses. The quickest way to earn the supervisor's disfavor is to try to alibi one's self out of one's failure to deliver.

Punctuality and Attendance.   Supervisors consider tardiness and unnecessary absence as particularly heinous offences. As a rule they consider them to be inexcusable.

Complaining and Criticizing.   In no case should the student teacher criticize the school or the teaching of his cooperating teachers. He should be particularly careful about what he says in conversations with other teachers or other student teachers. He should also avoid going to the principal or department head with complaints. When he finds that he needs to complain or criticize, he should go to his college supervisor. If any action needs to be taken, the college supervisor should be the one to negotiate with the school personnel concerned. If any onus is to fall on anyone because of disagreements over policy and method, it is better that it fall on the broad shoulders of the college supervisor than on the student teacher.

Conforming to the School's Expectations. To keep relationships pleasant, the student teacher should try his best to conform to the standards and customs of the school. Drastic departures from the norm in language, dress, appearance, and so on, can be upsetting to principals and cooperating teachers. If the student teacher can find out what is expected of him in these matters early and then live up to these expectations, he will find that things will go more smoothly than if he does not.

In this connection a word about appearance may be in order. How one carries himself, his expression, his posture, and how he dresses make a difference in how his pupils and his colleagues perceive him. Obviously a person who is sprightly, attractive, and pleasant-appearing is more prepossessing than one who is sullen or withdrawn. One's dress can make a difference in how pupils perceive the teacher also. Strangely enough, many pupils hold quite different dress standards for their teachers than they do for themselves. Consequently it is usually helpful for the student teacher to conform to the standard and style of dress common to the older teachers. Being a little on the conservative side does not hurt. Some young looking student teachers find it helpful to dress so as to look older. After all, the age difference between college seniors and high school seniors is not great. Anything that accentuates the maturity of the student teacher may help him establish himself.[2]

Listen! One complaint constantly heard is that the student teacher does not listen. College teachers and college supervisors say they have to repeat instructions or advice over and over again before the student teacher heeds it. Sometimes this is because the student teacher does not really listen— perhaps because he is too busy thinking of reasons why he did not do better. If the student teacher listens carefully, asks questions to be sure he understands, and then makes a sincere effort to follow the advice or instructions given him, relations with his supervisors will usually be easy and cordial.

[2] If nothing more, it may help one from being embarrassingly mistaken for a pupil.

Avoid Competing with the Teacher. The student teacher must avoid any appearance of competing with his cooperating teacher. He is there to learn from the cooperating teacher, and there are very few cooperating teachers he cannot learn from. Consequently he should consult the cooperating teacher before he undertakes anything, and then he should follow the advice given him to the best of his ability. In this connection, sometimes the pupils tell student teachers how well the student teachers teach and that they prefer the student teachers to their regular teachers. No matter how flattering this may be, student teachers should pass off such remarks without comment. Do not allow yourself to get in the position of discussing any other teacher's teaching with a pupil. To do so can lead only to misunderstanding and unhappiness.

Show Initiative. The student teacher can raise his stock with his supervisors and cooperating teachers by showing initiative and volunteering to do things before he has to be asked to do them. If the student teacher takes on arduous tasks willingly and readily, he will endear himself to his cooperating teacher. Sometimes student teachers feel that they are being used if the cooperating teacher asks them to read papers or to correct tests that he has assigned. Actually a student teacher should be glad to do tasks of this sort. Such tasks are an important part of a teacher's job and the student teacher should show his mettle here as in other tasks. Also many cooperating teachers feel that they can learn much about a student teacher's capabilities by the way he handles jobs of this sort. In this connection, most cooperating teachers and supervisors expect the student teacher to do his share in cafeteria supervision, extracurricular activities, attendance at PTA, student activities, and all the other additional tasks that make up the teacher's professional life. Principals and department heads find participation in these extras by student teachers quite impressive.

The Student Teaching Experience

When the student teacher arrives at his student teaching assignment, it is expected that he will bring with him certain knowledge and competencies. These include, according to Wiggins,

An understanding of the school and community.

Subject matter competence.

An understanding of pupils.

A supply of instructional materials.

An understanding of and ability to use sound educational principles and techniques.

An understanding of and ability to use the principles and techniques of evaluation and measurement.

An understanding of what the job is, its ethical, moral, and legal requirements, and the willingness to live up to its requirements.[3]

Any student who measures up reasonably well to the standards implied by this list should expect his student-teaching experience to be satisfying. Any student who finds himself very deficient in these competencies and understandings would probably be wise not to attempt student teaching until he has brought himself up to the standard.

OBSERVATION

Before the student teacher begins his teaching, he usually spends a few days observing the classes he is going to teach. During this observation he should try to learn as much as he can about the school and how it works—its customs, procedures, requirements, and the like. In particular he should become acquainted with the personality and customs of each of the classes he will teach. The more he can learn about the pupils and the basic situation and routines, e.g., the materials available and the procedures for requisitioning and distributing materials, the better off he will be. It will be especially helpful for him to observe what the pupils expect from the class and the teacher, what the teacher expects from each pupil, and how the teacher deals with them both as a group and as individuals.

A wise step to take during this period is to learn the names of the pupils. Sitting down with the seating chart and attempting to match names and faces may pay dividends when one begins to teach the class. If one also learns something about the personalities of the pupils, it is much easier to create a smooth, personalized atmosphere in the class when you begin to teach.

[3] Sam P. Wiggins, *The Student Teacher in Action* (Boston: Allyn & Bacon, Inc., 1957), Ch. 2.

BEGINNING TO TEACH

Most student teachers find their first teaching experience somewhat traumatic. Of course they are nervous. Probably anyone who is not nervous is not sensitive enough to be a good teacher. To compensate for this nervousness and to build up one's confidence, skill, and understanding, student teachers would probaly do well to begin their student teaching in small ways—e.g., by taking the roll, acting as assistant teacher, working with a small group, introducing a movie, or attempting similar tasks.

DIFFERENT STYLES AND METHODS

Student teaching gives the student teacher a chance to try out a variety of teaching styles and methods. By trying out a variety of methods the student teacher not only broadens his repertory of teaching skills, but he also learns which types of approaches are most comfortable to him. The teaching style one teacher find easy and comfortable, another teacher may find to be disagreeable.

Since teaching styles differ, the student teacher who finds himself working with two cooperating teachers whose modes of teaching differ may be fortunate. He can see the different styles in action and try them under supervision. Sometimes these differences in style cause conflicts, however. When they do, the student teacher should consult with his college supervisor.

Although one should try various techniques, it is not wise to be too innovative at first. Pupils, like adults, feel most secure in their established routines. They may not accept new ways of teaching or learning willingly. Further, some cooperating teachers are suspicious of new methods which, they fear, may upset the even tenor of the class. Cooperating teachers, too, sometimes feel threatened by too much change. Therefore the best policy is to introduce innovations slowly. Besides, as a neophyte it is best if you master the tried and true methods the class is used to before you branch out. Sometimes it is necessary to learn to walk before one learns to run.

On the other hand, one should not be too quick to drop an innovative method that does not seem to work. The reason the method does not work may have nothing to do with the method itself. Perhaps your technique was not quite right, or you may have rushed the pupils into it before they were ready, or the technique was ill-adapted to the class or situation in which you used it. When a technique falls flat, rather than concluding that the method is no good, the student teacher should determine why it went wrong. Usually he will find it was because of some ineptness on his part rather than because of a fault in the method itself.

Before attempting new approaches the student teacher should talk over the approach with his cooperating teacher. Sometimes the cooperating teacher will resist the innovation. Perhaps he sees a flaw in the plan that the student teacher does not realize. Perhaps his orientation is such that he dislikes the new method. In any case, when the cooperating teacher turns down a student teacher's suggestion, the student teacher should immediately defer to the cooperating teacher's judgment. Should he desire, he can talk the matter over with his college supervisor.

Many times student teachers who are progressively oriented find themselves in very conservative situations in which they cannot use the innovative ideas that they are eager to try. Such situations are hard but are not without their merits. Anyone who is to become a really professional teacher should know how to use both conservative and progressive strategies and tactics. In our present state of knowledge concerning teaching and learning we really do not know what the best way to teach is anyway. Probably there is no best way. Consequently the student teacher should use his teaching experience to become expert in whatever methods are compatible with the school and teaching situation in which he finds himself. Later, in his own classes, he should try to expand his repertoire until he has a complete battery of methods in which he is expert.

PLANNING IN STUDENT TEACHING

Planning is crucial in student teaching. When student teachers fail in their teaching it is almost always because they have not planned adequately. Every student teacher needs specific detailed plans.

He should know, and have written down, exactly what he wants the pupils to learn during the lesson, exactly what content will be covered, exactly what methods he plans to use, and how he plans to use them, and what materials he needs. He should try to anticipate every contingency as best he can. Very little should be left to chance. For that reason key questions, major points to be covered in the summary, and other details should be worked out ahead of time and included in the plan. Once he becomes experienced, such detailed planning may not be necessary, but he will never outgrow the need to plan thoroughly.

MAKING ASSIGNMENTS

Frequently student teachers find determining the length and difficulty of assignments bothersome. Here is an area in which the cooperating teacher can help. The wise student teacher follows his cooperating teacher's lead because any quick change from the accustomed length and difficulty may upset the class.

In making assignments the student teacher should strive to be crystal clear so that the pupils know exactly what to do and how to do it. He should also try to make the assignment challenging but not so difficult as to be discouraging. Assignments that lack challenge, or are fairly long or difficult, or are not clear to the pupils, may lead to confusion, undone work, and perhaps disruptions.

SEEKING HELP

Old hands are usually very glad to give beginners the benefit of their experience. Usually their advice is good and their opinions valid, although sometimes their suggestions should be listened to politely and then forgotten as quickly as possible. (The old truism that some teachers have twenty years of experience while others have only one year of experience twenty times still holds.) In any event the student teacher would be wise to ask for advice and suggestions. It never hurts a beginner to ask an old hand for help. If nothing else, it makes the old hand feel important.

Many student teachers find themselves overwhelmed by the demands on their time during the student-teaching period. This problem can be alleviated somewhat by developing a time budget. By allocating reasonable amounts of time to the different tasks he must perform during the day before, during, and after school, one may be able to ensure that all the tasks get done reasonably well. In making such a time budget the student teacher should be as realistic as he can. If one's time budget is too demanding it may be worse than no budget at all.

Evaluating One's Student Teaching

The student teacher's supervisors will evaluate his student teaching from time to time and confer with him on his strengths and weaknesses. In addition, each student teacher should evaluate himself in order to learn from his successes and his mistakes. In this process he should be critical, but not too critical. Sometimes student teachers demand of themselves more than they have a right to expect. Nevertheless each day the student teacher should set aside some time to think about his lessons and try to determine what went well and what poorly and why. Techniques for somewhat more sophisticated techniques for self-evaluation may be found later in this chapter. They can be extremely helpful to the teacher who wants to learn how to teach more effectively.

THE FIRST JOB

Preparing for the New Job

In teaching, as in any other profession, the time literally on the job represents only a fraction of one's work time. Just as a lawyer does most of his work before entering the courtroom, the teacher should do much of his work before entering the classroom. This is especially true of young teachers who do not have a reservoir of experience and previous study to rely on. The beginning teacher should allow himself plenty of time to prepare for his new job. A summer's work is none too long.

As soon as you learn what your teaching assignment is to be, you should start reviewing for your courses. Much of the reviewing can be done in the textbooks the pupils are to use. This practice has several advantages. Although you will probably find the material quite elementary, it will orient you to what is expected of the pupils. Moreover, as you review for the course, you can prepare general plans for conducting it. Finally, studying a secondary school text is a relatively easy way to review. If you are tempted to map out a more ambitious project, remember that an easy program that you finish is much better than an arduous program that you never complete.

The type of review program you plan is not so important, but do review and study during the summer. The time for study is all too scarce once the actual hurly-burly of teaching starts. The life of a high school or junior high school teacher is a full and sometimes hectic one. Long, quiet hours for study are rare indeed, particularly in the first years of teaching.

During the summer months you should not only become familiar with the subject matter, but you should also learn as much as you can about the community and pupils with whom you will be working. In some schools class rosters are not drawn up in final form until the term is well started; other schools are much more stable. In either case, even if you cannot identify the individual pupils, gathering information about them that will give you a general picture of the makeup of the class and will assist you in your planning. Having on hand information gathered from cumulative record folders and other sources makes it possible to become acquainted with individual pupils more quickly and should help you spot pupils with problems, special interests, or handicaps. An additional advantage of getting this information before school opens is that then you will probably have more time to go through the records carefully than you would in the fall. Thus you can eliminate one activity from the busy first weeks of school.

The First Day

In every endeavor a good start is a distinct advantage; teaching is no exception. Therefore, you should get your classes off to a good beginning on the first day of school. On this day the pupils are often in a mood to learn. They have hopes that the new course and new teacher may have something worthwhile for them. So your first lesson should be one of your best. If you can possibly do so, use an interesting experiment, a demonstration, an exciting story, an intriguing problem, or something equally appealing. The initial activity may set the tone for the entire course.

Some teachers devote most of the first class period to administrative work; some spend the period outlining what the class is going to do for the year; others review or test during this period in order to relate the course to previous courses. All of these activities are good and necessary, but do not allow them to prevent your course from getting off to a good start. If you cannot make these activities part of an exciting initial class, you had better leave them for another day.

Usually, however, these activities can be fitted into an exciting start. Some teachers devote the first day to a discussion of what one might study in the course. Others introduce an interesting problem. Then, while their pupils search for the solution, the teacher records the book numbers and performs other necessary administrative duties. Another possibility is to conduct a review in the form of a game or a television quiz program. Whatever approach you use, the beginning class should include something lively, new, and worthwhile.

*

If you were going to teach next September, what would you need to review and study? What could you do in the summer to make your work easier in the fall?

Plan a first day for a course you may teach. What introductory activities would you try? How might you work in administrative tasks? What would you do to motivate the pupils?

*

Relationships with Pupils

ESTABLISHING TEACHER CONTROL

The first days of school will bring you together with new pupils in a new situation. In this situa-

tion your position is much the same as that of a stage star at an opening performance. Under the circumstances, it is not at all unusual for a beginning teacher to feel nervous. You will certainly be tense; you may even suffer from stage fright. But no matter how nervous you are, you should display as much confidence as you can muster and go ahead with your work. If you act as though this were a commonplace occurrence which you are enjoying, the pupils will probably be convinced by your performance.

However, you are new and you can expect some boys and girls to try you out. In the interest of good discipline, it may be wise to be fairly strict for a few days. During this period, minimize the amount of movement around the classroom. A wise precaution is to have a written assignment ready so that you can give the class written work if the pupils become restless. In any event you should have an alternate plan of some sort to fall back on if your first plan does not work.

In order to establish good teacher-pupil relationships and teacher control, learn the names of the pupils immediately. During the first period you should probably prepare a seating plan. One way to do so is to assign some written work to the pupils and then circulate about the room to copy their names from their papers. Another method is to have the names of the pupils written on a slip of paper before the period starts, and, as you call the roll, to put these slips in the proper places in a pocket-type seating plan. No matter how you prepare the seating plan, associate the names of the pupils with their faces as quickly as possible. You will more readily establish good rapport with pupils when they realize you know them by name.

HANDLING CLASSROOM ROUTINE

As a general rule, classes will make better progress if the more usual tasks are routinized. Routines make it possible for boys and girls to know what to do without being told over and over again. For instance, there should be no question about whether to write on both sides of a paper, or whether a pupil should give his oral report from his desk or from the front of the room, for we *always* write on only one side of a sheet and we *always* give oral reports from the front of the classroom.

Time is critical in any class. Routinization of housekeeping activities is an effective way to save time. The more time we can save for active instruction the better. However, too much routinizing can lead to boredom and loss of interest. A good rule is to routinize as many of the administrative and managerial aspects of the classroom as possible but to leave the instructional activities free from unnecessary routine.

Routinization can be applied to such administrative matters as attendance, tardy slips, and excuses. In handling these, the teacher must, of course, carry out the school regulations. However, in order to save time and interruptions, all of this work should be completed before the class starts. Attendance should be taken by some quick method such as noting the unfilled chairs. Calling the roll is a time-wasting procedure. In order to take attendance quickly it is usually a good practice to have pupils start off at the beginning of the class in their assigned stations, even though they move to other work stations later.

In order for the class to get started with a minimum of confusion, the teacher should routinize the issuing of equipment and materials. The issuing of papers and books can often be delegated to pupils. Before the class starts, materials to be used during the period should be ready for instant distribution. A good way to keep confusion to a minimum is to list on the board those things which will be needed during the various periods. Thus the pupils can equip themselves with the necessary materials without asking a single question. A similar routine can be set up for putting things away at the end of the period. In some classes the teacher will want to routinize the collection and distribution of pupil papers. This is usually done by passing the papers to, or from, the ends of rows, or to the head of the table. However, in a classroom laboratory perhaps a better way is to circulate unobtrusively about the class and to collect or distribute the papers without interrupting the pupils' work.

One should never become a slave to routine, but if certain tasks must be done again and again, a properly used routine can make the class more efficient and pleasant.

CLASSROOM ROUTINE IN "INNOVATIVE" CLASSROOMS

The recent birth of new technologies and the resurrection of old ones have had little real impact on classroom management except to make attention to detail more important. Because of the one-way nature of most large-group and television instruction, and the size of the group, distractions can become much more bothersome than in ordinary classes. Also in large-group classes discomfort and distraction can increase the psychological noise attendant upon any large-group presentation, and worse yet, may lead to the real noise of collapsing discipline. For this reason, too, the teacher should carefully check sight lines and acoustics before large-group instruction. Routines for passing and collecting things, moving in and out of the room, and so on, need to be worked out carefully and carried out quite formally in order to avoid confusion and the wasting of time.

The small group and individual study require far less formality than the large group. However, they do require adequate surroundings suitable to the task before them. Work groups and individual researchers need to have materials readily available so that they may go to them with the least amount of difficulty. In some cases they can be best served by classroom libraries and laboratories, and at others, by central sources such as libraries and materials' centers. In any event, the processes for getting materials and equipment for use should be simple and quick. When pupils have to wait around to draw a tape or program with which they should be working, the system may break down.

Considerable attention needs to be given to work space for small groups and individual workers. Small discussion groups should be housed where they can discuss freely without disturbing others— a situation that does not always obtain when groups are separated by movable partitions. Work groups and individuals need adequate provision for storage and sometimes space in which to leave work in progress so that they can come back to it. Not many schools have really adequate facilities for the encouragement of independent study. To improvise good work space may be difficult, but teachers and administrators should be alert to the need so as to take steps when the opportunity offers.

Flexible schedules and no-bell systems present no great problem to the teacher except that he may have to learn to be a clock watcher. To keep from disturbing others it will, however, be necessary to keep good order and quiet in groups that move about the corridors at odd times. Although control of pupil movement is really an administrative problem, the teacher must be ready to help keep these movements under control.

SHOWING RESPECT FOR EACH PUPIL'S INDIVIDUALITY

Teachers should learn the pupils' names not only because it helps control them, but because it is one of their rights. Pupils are people and should be recognized as such. They should be treated courteously and tactfully. The fact that they are youthful does not give the teacher the right to be rude to them or to override their rights as persons. "Minding one's manners" is as important for teachers as it is for pupils.

Show your pupils that you have confidence in them. Secondary school pupils are not children, although their actions will sometimes be childlike. They are approaching adulthood. Although their lack of experience necessitates giving them plenty of guidance, pupils can behave themselves if you give them the opportunity. They can also plan, execute, and evaluate their own work. If your pupils feel that you really have faith in their good sense and judgment, they will seldom let you down.

You should also develop a real interest in your pupils. Everyone reacts well to people who are truly interested in them. To demonstrate your interest, you should learn all you can about your pupils and their problems. You should also establish an "open-door" policy so that your pupils will know that you are ready to listen to their problems and help them when you can. What the pupil wishes to discuss may be trivial, but you should listen if the pupil considers it important. Problems that seem unimportant to adults frequently appear serious to adolescents.

But it is not only the pupils' problems that you should be concerned about. You should also take an interest in their activities. Their ideas, their hobbies, and their occupations are often fascinating. The teacher who participates wholeheartedly in the extracurriculum, who attends the athletic games and school dances, who knows the school traditions and cooperates in furthering them, and who shows a real interest in all of his pupils' activities is likely to be readily accepted by the pupils.

EARNING THE PUPILS' RESPECT

In building good teacher-pupil relationships, mutual respect is the best foundation. This does not come naturally. Although respect for the teacher's position is something each child should have acquired by the time he reaches the secondary school, respect for the teacher as a person is something else. Each teacher must earn that respect himself.

Respect can be earned in many ways. The best way, of course, is to do an outstanding job of teaching. Another is to treat all pupils fairly and impartially. Sociological studies indicate that teachers often do not give boys and girls from "underprivileged homes" the same treatment they give to pupils from "better homes."[4] If this is true, these pupils are really underprivileged. You must treat every pupil fairly and impartially regardless of his color, ethnic background, or social position. Pupils will respect you if you do, and the ethics of the profession require it.

Sometimes young teachers attempt to seek popularity by becoming overfriendly with the pupils. This procedure seldom works. In dealing with your pupils, you should be friendly, not chummy. Seek respect rather than popularity. If you are the type of person who can inculcate respect, a good teacher with a well-developed sense of humor, a wholesome personality, and a good character, popularity will take care of itself.

*

An experienced teacher once told a new colleague that he did not care whether the pupils liked him or not, but he did want them to respect him. What do you think of this philosophy?

Think of the teacher in your high school whom you most respected. What qualities did he have which earned

4 See for instance, August B. Hollingshead, *Elmtown's Youth* (New York: John Wiley & Sons, Inc., 1949).

him this respect? Think of a teacher whom pupils did not respect. What caused him to lose their respect?

*

Relationships with Parents

IMPROVING PARENT-TEACHER RELATIONSHIPS

Friendly relationships between teachers and their pupils' parents can contribute considerably to effective teaching, since parents and teachers should be seeking the same objective, the welfare of the pupils. One way to avoid friction with parents is to learn to know them as well as possible. If the teacher becomes acquainted with parents at school functions, at parent-teacher association meetings, in community activities, and in their homes, and in other social situations, teacher-parent relationships can become much more pleasant. Establishing and maintaining good relations with parents and parent groups is so advantageous to teachers that they would do well to take the initiative in formal and informal communication and in socialization with parents.

In meeting parents you may find your role a little difficult. Parents are often nervous about meeting their children's teachers just as teachers are often nervous about meeting parents, and for much the same reasons. After all, the teacher is in a strategic position for judging the parent's success as a parent. The teacher sits in judgment over the activities and efforts and, to some extent, the future of the parent's child. Knowledge of this is enough to make the parent a little apprehensive when he meets the teacher. Therefore, when talking to parents, you should try to be as relaxed and friendly as possible. Above all, try to guard against the didactic tone that comes so naturally to many teachers. If parents find you a pleasant, intelligent, well-informed adult, you will probably get along with them quite well and also dissipate any fears you may have concerning their judgments of your abilities as a teacher of their children.

In this connection it would be helpful if teachers would on occasion take time to notify parents of some of the good things their children are doing. Too often we in the schools only communicate with the parents when something is wrong.

SEEKING PARENTAL COOPERATION

Because parents are more interested than anyone else in the welfare of their children, they almost always wish to do everything possible to help them. The teacher who so desires can often enlist the parents' aid. Many parents are glad to serve on committees and to engage in other tasks to help the school. Parents frequently have talents the teacher can put to good use in class activities. However, before soliciting the services of parents, it is wise to consult your principal. He may be able to help you avoid mistakes.

Parents can be particularly helpful by providing information about their children. Usually parents respond readily to such an approach as, "I seem to be having trouble teaching Jack to spell. I wonder if you can help me." Quite often the parent will not only cooperate in furnishing information about his child, but will also cooperate with any reasonable program for helping the youngster.

Relationships with the Community

Parent-teacher relationships lead us directly to teachers' relationships with the community in general. These relationships should be the normal ones that might be found among any adult members of the community. However, because of the teacher's peculiar position as a leader of children, the community usually expects him to adhere to a fairly high standard of behavior similar to that expected of clergymen, physicians, and lawyers. These expectations should be regarded not as a burden but as a recognition of the high status that teachers hold. The community is asking you to provide leadership which it feels that others cannot give.

Under no circumstances should the reader interpret *professionalism* to mean that teachers must avoid their obligations as citizens to espouse causes, to take stands, and to participate as their consciences direct in civil, moral, and political affairs. Professional leadership is not compatible with conformity or timidity; neither does being a teacher deprive, or relieve, anyone of his rights and responsibilities as an American and a citizen.

The members of the various professions are considered to be community leaders and therefore should act as leaders. As a professional person, you should take part in community activities. These include civic affairs, parent-teachers' organizations, churches, service clubs, and so on. Participating in such activities will not only help to make your life fuller and more enjoyable but will give you splendid contacts with the community.

*

What advantages are there in becoming acquainted with your pupils' parents socially? Are there any disadvantages? In what ways would you attempt to become acquainted with them?

In one high school the teachers were required to visit the home of each of their classroom pupils some time during the school year. What do you think of this practice?

To what extent should you as a teacher become involved in community affairs? What organizations would you join?

*

Relationships with Other Staff Members

ESTABLISHING CORDIAL RELATIONSHIPS WITH OTHER TEACHERS

Second only in importance to your relationships with your pupils are those with your fellow teachers. You must get along with them. Some of them will undoubtedly become your good friends; others you may find not so agreeable. But you will be in close contact with them every working day. Your relationships with them can make the difference between happiness and success in your work, and unhappiness and even failure. Therefore, you should do everything you can to make these relationships cordial. Until you have been accepted by the group, you would do well to look, listen, and learn.

Not only should the new teacher look, listen, and learn, he should also pitch in to cooperate willingly. In some schools there is a tendency to give the less desirable tasks to the new teacher. This practice is also common in most business and professional establishments. It represents one of the perquisites of seniority in an organization. Most supervisors and administrators, however, try to see to it that the beginning teacher's assignment,

even if not the easiest and most desirable, is a reasonable one. But whatever his assignment, the beginning teacher would do well to take it on with good grace and give it his very best effort with the sure knowledge that he will not be the junior faculty member for long. In addition, most new teachers find that they have numerous opportunities to contribute to the school program not included in their assigned tasks. Although it is not wise to volunteer for more than you can manage well, it is better to err on the side of attempting to contribute too much than too little.

As a new teacher, you will find that you have much to learn, but you will also discover that your colleagues will be pleased to teach you. They will give you much friendly advice—some good, some bad. Accept it in the spirit it is given in, but act only on that which you are convinced is good. Some of your colleagues will be outstanding teachers, while others may be lazy, incompetent, or embittered. Although you should listen courteously to the advice of all, you should heed particularly that of the more successful teachers.

Undoubtedly you will find things in your school of which you do not approve. In this case, *keep your criticisms to yourself until you are better established.* Otherwise, the older teachers may resent your criticisms and you. Members of a faculty are much like families. They find fault themselves, but bitterly resent fault-finding by outsiders. Until you have been accepted, which may take some time, you are an outsider and should refrain from criticisms. Besides, once you understand the situation better, you may change your opinion.

You should be courteous, friendly, and sociable. Join other teachers for coffee, attend the faculty parties, and accept invitations with pleasure. Try to show your colleagues that you would like to be a member of the group, but do not let yourself become identified with any clique until you become well acquainted with the entire faculty.

Faculty relationships are pleasant when teachers remember the common courtesies. "Please" and "Thank you" are important. So are other little things. For instance, if you share a classroom with another teacher, do not move the chairs and tables without moving them back again before you leave. Be sure to leave the blackboards clean, and do not usurp all the bulletin board space. In short, give consideration at all times to the use of the class-room by other teachers.

Administrators and supervisors can help the teacher in all sorts of ways. Although one's relationships with them may not become as intimate as those with other teachers, they are fully as important. The administrator aids the teacher by furnishing supplies, equipment, and other services and facilities, while the supervisor aids the teacher with instructional activities. Sometimes the supervisor and the administrator are the same person. In any case, make use of their services. That is why they are there.

Principals, department heads, and supervisors can be of tremendous help to beginning teachers in planning their classroom activities, in organizing classroom routine, in working with difficult pupils, and in promoting good parent-teacher relationships. They know firsthand some of the difficulties you may encounter during your first year, and will be glad to suggest ways of meeting them. Seek their advice, cooperation, and help.

Carrying Out Administrative Duties. Supposedly administrative procedures are designed to aid instruction and to make life more pleasant in the school. By following these procedures, the teacher can usually make things easier for everyone. Occasionally, administrative details become somewhat oppressive and at times downright ridiculous. Nevertheless, part of the teacher's job is to carry out the administrative procedures as well as he can. If he takes care of these administrative details, usually the school runs more smoothly and his relationships with his superiors are more pleasant.

Among the teacher's administrative responsibilities are record keeping, the making of reports, and procedures having to do with the requisitioning and accounting for supplies and equipment. There are many more. Early in one's career one should make a special effort to learn the administrative procedures of one's school. The regulations and directions for the various administrative tasks may often be found in the teachers' manual or handbook. Study the manual carefully before you attend your first class. If the school does not furnish

a manual, make one of your own. When in doubt of what your procedure should be, consult your department head or principal. Doing so may save you much embarrassment, confusion, and delay.

*

What legal complications could result from an improperly filled-out register?

What materials and supplies would you need to keep records of in your classes?

What pupil personnel records would you expect to work with as a teacher?

*

Keeping Administrators and Supervisors Informed. You would be wise to consult your supervisor before you try anything that is decidedly new or unusual. He may be able to help you do it more successfully and avoid mistakes you might otherwise make. It is especially important that before you depart markedly from the practice that is usual in the school, you should talk things over with your supervisor. New methods and techniques may cause parental concern. If the supervisor knows what you are attempting, he will be prepared to answer parents' questions and to support you in what you want to do. Seeking his advice may also prevent you from inadvertently violating school board policy.

It is particularly wise to let the administrators know of serious incidents involving the school or the pupils especially if they may lead to adverse criticism and undesirable publicity. Administrators do not like unpleasant surprises. When a principal first learns of a fiasco in his school from a harrassed superintendent, or an irate parent, or worse yet, from headlines in the local press, he is greatly handicapped. If the principal has prior information of the incident, he may be able to take constructive action. Otherwise he can do little more than be embarrassed.

Relationships with Nonprofessional Personnel

Secretaries, clerks, and custodians can also be helpful to the teacher. Teachers should always try to keep on good terms with these people and other nonprofessional personnel. Try to be reasonable in your demands on the secretaries and custodians.

For instance, if mimeographing is to be done for you, submit the copy in ample time. One can cooperate in other ways. In some schools the heating system is designed to work with the windows closed. By noting this detail, you can make it much easier for the custodian to heat the entire building. You can also help the custodian by maintaining a neat and orderly classroom. The teacher who keeps in the good graces of the custodial and secretarial staffs may find that he can get good cooperation when it is particularly needed.

*

Suppose that early in your teaching, one of the older teachers complains to you about what he considers the deterioration of the school's instructional program under the present principal and superintendent. What should you do?

What practical advantages may be obtained from maintaining good relationships with the custodial personnel? What would you do to keep up favorable relationships?

*

BECOMING A MASTER TEACHER

Learning One's Business

To become a real pro one must combine experience with diligent efforts to learn one's business. It requires that one be wide awake to new ideas, to be aware of innovations in teaching technology (including teaching methods) and of other developments in the field of pedagogy, and to utilize these in his own teaching. Similarly the real pro develops competency in his subject field and the use of the nature of the pupil.

Teachers use many different methods to increase their competencies. For example

Teacher A spends each Saturday morning taking graduate courses in her major at the state university.

Teacher B is planning to attend a workshop in methods of teaching his subject conducted by a national study group.

Teacher C, a science teacher, has arranged to work in a major research laboratory during the summer months in order to brush up some of her skills.

Teacher D, a French teacher, spent his vacation traveling through the French Riviera.

Teacher E, a social science teacher, spent her summer as part of a team building a course guide for a new integrated humanities course.

Teacher F is conducting an action-research project in which she is experimenting with a new method of teaching history to slow learners.[5]

Teacher G, an English teacher, makes it a point to read extensively in the professional journals to find ideas that will help him with his teaching. He also belongs to the local and national English teachers organizations and attends their meetings. Here he learns of new developments and shares the experiences of others who face the same problems. He finds the journals of the organizations especially valuable.

Teacher H is constantly on the alert for new ideas. He visits other teachers, talks to them, and tries to get ideas from them. He tries out the material and techniques other teachers have found successful. He attends teacher conventions and other professional meetings in search of new ideas. A fine source of ideas for teaching is the book exhibit at conventions. But he does more than make use of the work of others, he shares his own successful experiences. One way he does this is to write about his experiences for publication in a professional journal. He finds that editors are anxious to obtain articles that tell what teachers are doing. Moreover, setting down his thoughts seems to help him clarify his own professional thinking.

Evaluating One's Own Teaching

All teachers, but especially student teachers and beginning teachers, should stop, step back and look

---

[5] Action research is aimed at finding solutions for specific practical problems. One does not expect to draw conclusions suitable for all situations from it. Consequently, it is not subject to some of the rigors of more formal research. Yet it is rigorous enough for the teacher to take specific action on the basis of its findings. School systems have found it exceptionally helpful for drawing conclusions in curriculum revisions. Basically the process is merely to identify a problem, to hypothesize a solution, and to try the solution out under reasonable controls to see whether or not it works. Step-by-step procedures for carrying out action research may be found in Hilda Taba and Elizabeth Noel, *Action Research: A Case Study* (Washington, D.C.: Association for Supervision and Curriculum Development, 1957).

critically at their teaching from time to time. It is much too easy to spend one's entire professional life in the same deadly rut. Self-criticism will keep one from stagnating.

To evaluate one's own teaching objectively may be asking too much of any teacher. Yet any teacher can do a number of things that will give him a fair idea of his effectiveness and perhaps a few clues for self-improvement.

The use of a self-analysis form such as that appearing as Figure 18–1 can be very helpful. For student teachers it is recommended that they use such a form to analyze one lesson each day for the first three weeks of their student teaching and then once a week thereafter. Teachers in service should analyze their teaching on some regular time schedule, e.g., once a week or even once a month. Ordinarily it is suggested that one use the self-analysis form to analyze his best classes. However, the form may be useful for analyzing troublesome classes also.

TEST ANALYSIS

Analysis of the results of one's own teacher-built tests can give one much information about the effectiveness of the instruction. In some ways classroom tests can be more revealing than standardized tests or other external tests are. If well-constructed, classroom tests have the advantage of indicating how well pupils learned what the teacher wanted to teach. (Standardized tests may have very little relationship to the goals the teacher believed to be important.)

If classroom tests are to be useful in assessing one's teaching success, the teacher must

1. Set up clear, definite, specific teaching objectives.
2. Design measurement instruments that measure how well pupils have achieved each of these objectives.

If these procedures have been carried out successfully, the test analyses described in Chapter 16 will give one a good description of the teacher's successes and failures. Vague, general objectives and vague general questions in one's measuring device render such analyses worthless, however.

PUPIL JUDGMENTS

The pupils' reaction to one's teaching is a fairly reliable indicator of its success. Probably the easiest way to find out what pupils think of one's teaching

Figure 18–1
Self-analysis of a Lesson

Use this form to analyze the class you thought went best this day.

1. Do you feel good about this class? Why, or why not?
2. In what way was the lesson most successful?
3. If you were to teach this lesson again, what would you do differently? Why?
4. Was your plan adequate? In what ways would you change it?
5. Did you achieve your major objectives?
6. Was the class atmosphere pleasant, productive, and supportive?
7. Were there signs of strain or misbehavior? If so, what do you think was the cause?
8. How much class participation was there?
9. Which pupils did extremely well?
10. Were there pupils who did not learn? How might you help them?
11. Were the provisions for motivation adequate?
12. Was the lesson individualized so that pupils had opportunities to learn something according to their abilities, interests, and needs?
13. Did the pupils have any opportunities to think?

is to observe their reaction to one's classes. Apathetic, bored, surly, inattentive, restless classes indicate that the instruction is not going very well. Interested, attentive classes, on the other hand, indicate that the teacher must be doing at least something right.

Another simple way to determine what pupils think of one's teaching is to ask them. Simple questionnaires or rating sheets may be used for this purpose. Usually teachers collect such data at the end of the school year. However, if the information is to be useful, it may be that one should collect the data earlier. In any case, the ratings should be anonymous. If pupils feel that the teacher can identify them, they are likely to be less than truthful when filling out the sheet or questionnaire. For that reason forms that call for checking rather than handwritten comments are recommended. Even so, free-response questions that ask pupils to suggest ways instruction can be made more effective or more interesting are very useful. Pupils feel flattered to be asked for their opinions and will not feel too threatened to respond honestly in such a format.

INTERACTION ANALYSIS

Interaction analysis attempts to give a picture of the talking that goes on in a class. Obviously analyses of classroom interaction can be useful for certain types of classes and for certain purposes. Interaction analysis, however, simply describes what occurred during the class. Whether what has been described by the analysis should be judged to be good or bad depends upon the objectives of the instruction and other elements of the teaching situation.

Some interaction analysis techniques are rather simple and can be carried out easily by any neophyte. The basic data gathering can be done live by an observer during the actual class session or by the teacher himself from a tape recording of one of his own class sessions. Either an audiotape or videotape recording is satisfactory.

Simple Interaction Analysis Techniques. The simplest method of gathering interaction analyses data is for the observer to record *T* every time the teacher talks and *P* every time a pupil talks. This technique gives some idea of the number of times

pupils talk as compared to the teacher.

A more useful refinement of this same technique is for the observer to mark down who is talking at regular intervals, e.g., three seconds. Again the observer uses the symbol *T* to indicate that the teacher is talking and *P* to indicate that a pupil is talking. Thus for one minute period the observer's record might take the following form: T P T T T P TTT P P T T TTT P P TTT. Such an analysis would show the amount of time that is given to teacher talk as compared to pupil talk.

A more complex refinement of the technique is for the observer to sit at the back of the class with a seating chart and to tally the number of times each person speaks. (Figure 18–2.)

In another version, as in the earlier example, the observer could record who was talking at stated intervals, e.g., every five seconds. This type of analysis has the advantage of showing just which persons were interacting, how much, and how often. The chart shown in Figure 18–2 would be suitable for recording such analysis. In discussions, flow charts of the type discussed in Chapter 10 can be used for the same purpose.

The VICS System. Several writers and researchers have devised much more sophisticated interaction analyses techniques. Because these procedures

Figure 18–2
Form of Interaction Analysis.

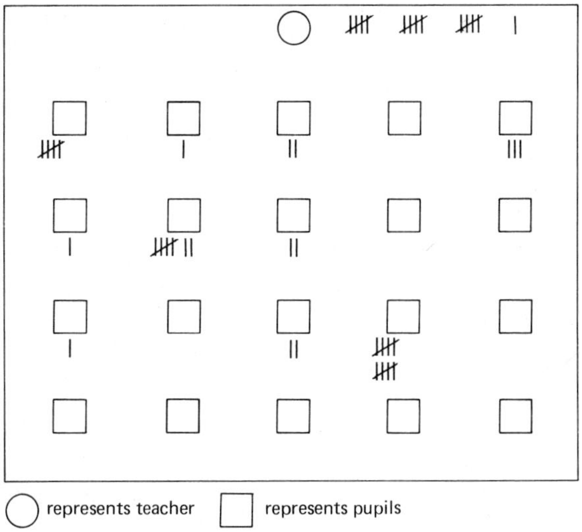

⬭ represents teacher ☐ represents pupils

provide means for indicating the kind of inter-action going on at any moment, they give a much more complete picture of what has happened in a class. One of the best of these techniques is the Verbal Interaction Category System. In this technique classroom interaction is divided into the following categories.

Teacher-Initiated Talk
1. Gives Information or Opinion: presents content or own ideas, explains, orients, asks rhetorical questions. May be short statements or extended lecture.
2. Gives Direction: tells pupil to take some specific action; gives orders; commands.
3. Asks Narrow Question: asks drill questions, questions requiring one or two word replies or yes-or-no answers; questions to which the specific nature of the response can be predicted.
4. Asks Broad Question: asks relatively open-ended questions which call for unpredictable responses; questions which are thought-provoking. Apt to elicit a longer response than 3.

Teacher Response
5. Accepts   (5a) Ideas: reflects, clarifies, encourages or praises ideas of pupils. Summarizes, or comments without rejection.
            (5b) Behavior: responds in ways which commend or encourage pupil behavior.
            (5c) Feeling: responds in ways which reflect or encourage expression of pupil feeling.
6. Rejects   (6a) Ideas: criticizes, ignores or discourages pupil ideas.
            (6b) Behavior: discourages or criticizes pupil behavior. Designed to stop undesirable behavior. May be stated in question form, but differentiated from category 3 or 4, and from category 2. Gives Direction, by tone of voice and resultant effect on pupils.
            (6c) Feeling: ignores, discourages or rejects pupil expression of feeling.

Pupil Response
7. Responds (7a) Predictably: relatively short replies, usually, which follow category 3. May also follow category 2, i.e., "David, you may read next."
to
Teacher:
            (7b) Unpredictably: replies which usually follow category 4.
8. Responds to Another Pupil: replies occurring in conversation between pupils.

Pupil-Initiated Talk
9. Initiates Talk to Teacher: statements which pupils direct to teacher without solicitation from teacher.

10. Initiates Talk to Another Pupil: statements which pupils direct to another pupil which are not solicited.

Other
11. Silence: pauses or short periods of silence during a time of classroom conversation.
Z. Confusion, considerable noise which disrupts planned activities. This category may accompany other categories or may totally preclude the use of other categories.[6]

The observer records which type of action is in progress at three-second intervals. He then arranges his observations into a matrix from which one can read not only what happened during the class, but also the class atmosphere.

Criteria for Satisfactory Interaction. Although in any particular lesson the objectives and design of the lesson plan plus other factors in the specific situation determine what types and amounts of interaction are desirable, there are certain criteria that apply to most lessons in general:

Pupils should be actively participating at least half of the time. (If the teacher finds himself to be talking more than half of the time, he should check his procedures.)

As far as possible, every pupil should participate in some way. (Classes that are dominated by only a few pupils are hardly satisfactory.)

A good share of the classtime should be given to thoughtful, creative activity rather than to mere recitation of information by either teacher or pupils.

AUDIO AND VIDEO PLAYBACK

One never quite realizes how one sounds or how he appears until he hears or sees himself on tape. Taping allows one to see both the little things he does that distress him and also the ways that he comes through larger than life. We have already seen how recording can be used in self-analysis and interaction analyses. It is also a wonderful tool for studying one's skill in lecturing, questioning, leading a discussion, and so on. One can greatly improve one's teaching skill by reviewing tapes of his lessons and asking himself questions such as

[6] Edmund Amidon and Elizabeth Hunter, *Improving Teaching* (Holt, Rinehart and Winston, Publishers, 1966), p. 11.

Are my explanations clear?

Do I speak well and clearly?

Do I speak in a monotone? Do I slur my words? Do my sentences drop off so that ends are difficult to hear?

Do I involve everyone in the class or do I direct my teaching only to a few?

Are my questions clear and unambiguous? Do I use broad or narrow questions?

Do I dominate class discussion?

Do I allow certain pupils to dominate the class? And so on.

*

Make a list of check questions that you might use to evaluate your own teaching.

*

Whatever questions you decide to use, it is wise to concentrate on only a few areas when reviewing a tape of your teaching. If you limit yourself to studying your questioning technique in one session and to studying your discussion technique in another, you may find it easier to pinpoint your merits and deficiencies than if you do not concentrate your observation on a particular technique. Nevertheless generally reviewing the entire lesson can be helpful, particularly if one uses a self-analysis form similar to the one described earlier in this chapter.

GETTING A JOB

Selecting the Proper Program

The first step, of course, is to get the job. Actually one should start planning for a job early in his college course. Early planning may make considerable difference in one's career. A major consideration is, for instance, what is the market for my service? After finding out what the market is, you may want to change your preparation somewhat. If you are headed for a field which is crowded, perhaps you should reconsider your choice. For example, English or social science teachers may be a drug on the market, but there may be demand for teachers ready and willing to handle the junior high school English–social studies block.

In planning one's college program you should carefully consider the certification requirements of the state in which you wish to teach. Do this early. To find, at graduation time, that you are deficient in one of the state requirements can be disconcerting. Sometimes a small change in your program can make quite a difference in your certification. For instance, you may have an excellent program mapped out in biology. A glance at the certification requirements may show you that by substituting a course in chemistry for one biology course you can certify for general science as well as biology. Thus a three-hour course may make a tremendous difference in your worth to a potential employer.

You should also bear in mind what courses are offered in typical secondary schools and select college courses that prepare you for them. Although Nordic literature may be an excellent course, it may be that some other course, e.g., a course in writing, would be more helpful to you as a beginning English teacher.

You should probably also bear in mind that often teaching positions call for subject combinations. Most secondary school social studies departments, for instance, offer courses in sociology, geography, government, economics, and perhaps other social sciences as well as American and European history. Principals and department heads hope to find teachers who can teach several of these areas. A candidate who can teach only sociology may not be of much use to a department, but a sociology major who also has background in U.S. history and economics may be just what the department needs. Similarly a school may not need another full-time French teacher but have great need for someone who can teach both French and English.

Finding Leads on Vacancies

How does one find where job openings are? There are several sources of information available to you. The most readily accessible and often the most effective is the local placement office at your college or university. As well as usually being effective and dependable, these bureaus have the added attraction of rendering their services without charge. Similar placement services are operated by state teachers' associations in some states. These agencies, however, usually restrict their services to association members and charge a fee if one is employed through them. Leads for jobs can also be obtained from your professors and from the state departments of education. In some states the state departments conduct formal placement services.

Many teachers obtain positions through commercial agencies. These agencies are usually quite helpful and efficient, but it is wise to check on an agency's reputation before registering with it. Some agencies may not be good risks. Your college teachers or college placement service can usually tell you about the reputation of the various agencies. Although efficient and honest, the commercial agencies are relatively expensive; however, since their bread and butter comes from finding teachers jobs the agencies usually try to give good service.

Agencies and placement services can serve you only as well as you let them. When you register you will be asked to fill out forms, to send out references, and so on. Be sure to do everything promptly just as requested. Be particularly careful to give the agency all the information for which it asks. Double check to be sure that everything is correct. The number of prospective teachers who omit vital information is amazing. Be particularly careful to give the agency addresses and telephone numbers where you may be located at all times.

Applications

Once you have learned of a vacancy, you must apply. Usually the actual application is by letter, although sometimes a telephone call may be in order. The writing of a letter of application is a serious undertaking. Usually it is your first contact with the prospective employer. Consequently, in writing the letter, you should try to put your best foot forward. A surprisingly large number of letters of application are sloppily written, replete with errors, in poor careless handwriting. Do not let this be said of you. Write your letters with care.

The text should be brief and businesslike. In a few short paragraphs state your purpose, explain why you are a good prospect, and suggest

an interview. Keep your presentation dignified, conservative, and formal, both in style and format. Conservative styles are never incorrect and run no risk of offending the reader. Many schoolmen resent brash, modern innovations in letter writing. Remember, your purpose is to sell yourself to your prospective employer, so make your letter the acme of clarity, simplicity, brevity, and good taste.

To be sure that the letter of application is free from errors in form, composition, and clarity, have someone you trust read the letter carefully and critically before you send it off. Usually your advisor or some other professor will be glad to do you this favor.

With your letter you should also send a data sheet. In the data sheet you can state simply in outline form important information concerning yourself and your qualifications. Some of the items you might wish to include are

1. Personal data.
   Date of birth.
   Age.
   Sex.
   Marital status (plans, if any).
2. Education.
   High School.
   College.
     Major.
     Minor.
     Honors.
   University.
     Major.
     Minor.
3. Current teaching certificate.
4. Professional experience (Include nonteaching experiences with teaching, such as camp counselor, Scout work, and playground work).
5. Other work experience.
6. Hobbies.
7. Extracurricular activities.
8. Travel.
9. Publications, if any (Include theses).
10. Professional organizations.
11. Other organizations.
12. Honors.
13. Name of some persons who will act as references.

Probably the district will ask you to fill out an

application form anyway, but a good letter of application never hurt one's chances.

Recommendations

Prospective teachers are careless in selecting persons to recommend them. When you pick people to recommend you, be sure to select persons who know you well and who, you think, have a good opinion of you. A note from a reference that the applicant is unknown to him does not favorably impress a prospective employer. To avoid embarrassment and unpleasantness one should always ask permission before submitting anyone's name as a reference.

In passing it might be wise to mention that most employers consider open letters of recommendation to be worthless. Superintendents pay attention only to confidential letters of recommendation.

The Interview

Perhaps the most crucial step in securing a position is the interview with the prospective employer. Here it is that the principals in the little drama come face-to-face and here it is that the prospective employer makes his decision. Although we have been speaking of the interview, quite often the interview is really a series of interviews. Not only may you talk with the superintendent or his assistant, but you may also have the opportunity to speak to the principal with whom you may work, the prospective department head, the director of secondary education, and, in some schools, some classroom teachers.

Since the interview is so important, you would be wise to think through what you wish to say in your interview beforehand. Usually your interviewer will not ask you about your academic background—he has already found out about that —but he will ask questions on a variety of subjetcs perhaps ranging from philosophy of education to why you think you would be an asset to his school system. He will undoubtedly be anxious to determine whether you can control your classes, whether you will plan to stay in the system a while or whether you are a floater, what extracurricular activities you can handle, and so on. You will probably be able to answer these questions most successfully if you have thought about them before the interview.

Your interviewer will also expect you to ask some questions. Before going to the interview you should also decide what you wish to know about the school. Do not be afraid to ask questions. Intelligent questions will be welcome. They give the interviewer a chance to get to know you a little better, and they also take the burden for the interview off the interviewer's shoulder for a minute and allow him to relax.

Of course you yourself should be as natural and relaxed as possible during the interview. A calm, collected, easy manner will help make the interview pleasant for both of you. However, sometimes such a manner is more than you can assume. If so, do not be concerned; administrators realize that interviewees are under something of a strain. Besides, there are many other things one can do to make the interview successful.

An important help in any interview is one's dress. Dress your best in conservative good taste. Not only will your appearance help create a good impression, but the knowledge that you are well and correctly dressed will give you added confidence. Simple clothes are the safest for this type of interview. Remember that you are trying to show the world that you are a cultured young leader of youth. Consequently you should avoid anything which might make you look cheap and bizarre. For this same reason the candidate never chews gum. It is also wise not to smoke (unless the interviewer invites you to and *lights up himself*). Some interviewers react unfavorably to smoking.

Your conduct during the interview should also be determined by good taste. Answer all the questions you can forthrightly. Do not attempt to bluff. If you do not know the answer, say so. It makes a considerably better impression than attempting to cover up. When the interviewer has finished his questions you may ask the questions you have. Try not to appear inquisitive, but do find out as much as you can about the position, the school, and the system. Then, when you have finished, thank the interviewer, say your goodbyes, and leave. Usually the administrator will help you know when he thinks it is time to close the interview. Take the hint and depart gracefully. (More than one person has spoiled a good interview by overstaying his welcome.)

Really the rules for the interview are very simple. If you just remember your manners, all will go well. As in all other human relations courtesy and good taste are unbeatable.

Selecting a Job

If the interview goes well and you are offered the job, the problem of whether you really should accept it comes up. Of course in all honesty you should not apply for a job which you do not want. However, accepting a position is an important step and should not be rushed into. Once you have accepted a position, you are committed, so that you should be careful to select the right one.

In making your decision some of the questions you should consider are these:

Is the philosophy of the school congenial?
Would you like to spend the rest of your life in this community?
Does the load seem reasonable?
Would you be happy working with this faculty and this principal?
Does the system have adequate provisions for sick leave, retirement, fringe benefits, and so on?

These are only a few of the many things you might wish to investigate before making a decision. Compile a list of all the things that you would really want to know about the job.

Perhaps you have noted that so far the matter of salary has not been mentioned. Salary is, of course, an important consideration in selecting a job. However, it is not the most important. Probably it is not as important as you think it is. Usually the salaries which you will be offered will not differ much from school to school. Starting off in a congenial atmosphere at a job suited to you is much more important than a couple of hundred dollars in salary. If you can, pick a position in which you think you will get a good start. Everything else is secondary.

LAST WORDS

This chapter begins by stating that one should try to be a professional teacher from the day he starts teaching. That is a rather high standard.

Teaching is hard, difficult work. It is always demanding. To become a real master of the trade one must be a pretty special person, for the master teacher is a person of quality—a person with a sense of high commitment and a great faith in the value of what he is doing; a person with a great respect for himself, his pupils, and learning; and perhaps most importantly a person who cares about the pupils, about himself, about society, about the content he teaches, and about education. He does his best to help youth develop into self-sufficient, knowledgeable adults who will face the future with a repertoire of skills, attitudes, and knowledge that will make them able to cope with the experiences of an unpredictable and perhaps perilous future.

The task may be difficult and arduous, but it is not without its rewards. No professional life can be more exciting, interesting, or important than that of the master teacher. When a master teacher works with young minds, there is never a dull moment. His influence is great. Through his pupils he can contribute to the shaping of the community. Teaching is a profession to be proud of. The really professional teacher glories in being able to say, "I am a teacher." There is no greater praise of anyone in any walk of life than for people to say of one, "There goes a master teacher."

Suggested Readings for Part VIII

ALCORN, MARVIN D., JAMES L. KINDER, AND JIM R. SCHUNERT, *Better Teaching in Secondary Schools,* 3rd ed. New York: Holt, Rinehart and Winston, Publishers, 1970. Chs. 3 and 20.

ALLEN, PAUL, et al., *Teacher Self-Appraisal.* Worthington, Ohio: Charles A. Jones Publishing Company, 1970.

AMIDON, EDMUND J., AND ELIZABETH HUNTER, *Improving Teaching.* New York: Holt, Rinehart and Winston, Publishers, 1966.

AMIDON, EDMUND J., AND NED A. FLANDERS, *The Role of the Teacher in the Classroom.* Minneapolis: Paul S. Amidon and Associates, 1963.

ANDREW, MICHAEL D., *Teachers Should be Human Too.* Washington, D.C.: Association of Teacher Educators, 1972.

BIDDLE, BRUCE J., AND WILLIAM J. ELLENA, eds. *Contemporary Research in Teacher Effectiveness.* New York: Holt, Rinehart and Winston, Publishers, 1964.

FAUNCE, ROLAND C., AND CARROLL L. MUNSHAW, *Teaching and Learning in Secondary Schools.* Belmont, Calif.: Wadsworth Publishing Co. Inc., 1964.

GORMAN, ALFRED H., *Teachers and Learners,* 2nd ed. Boston: Allyn & Bacon, Inc., 1974.

GRAMBS, JEAN D., JOHN C. CARR, AND ROBERT M. FITCH, *Modern Methods in Secondary Education,* 3rd ed. New York: Holt, Rinehart and Winston, Publishers, 1970. Ch. 2.

HENSON, KENNETH T., *Secondary Teaching: A Personal Approach.* Itasca, Ill.: F. E. Peacock Publishers, Inc., 1974.

HIGHET, GILBERT, *The Art of Teaching.* New York: Vintage Books, 1955.

HYMAN, RONALD T., *Ways of Teaching,* 2nd ed. Philadelphia, Pa.: J. B. Lippincott Company, 1974.

JAMES, DEBORAH, *The Taming.* New York: McGraw-Hill Book Company, 1969.

JOHNSON, JAMES A., AND ROGER A. ANDERSON, *Secondary Student Teaching Readings.* Glenview, Ill.: Scott Foresman and Company, 1971.

SHARP, D. LOUISE, *Why Teach?* New York: Holt, Rinehart and Winston, Publishers, 1957.

STINNETT, T. M., AND ALBERT J. HUGGETT, *Professional Problems of Teachers,* 2nd ed. New York: Macmillan Publishing Co., Inc., 1963.

STUART, JESSE, *To Teach, To Love.* New York: Penguin Books Inc., 1973.

WILSON, CHARLES H., *A Teacher Is a Person.* New York: Holt, Rinehart and Winston Publishers, 1956

WILSON, ELIZABETH C., *Needed: A New Kind of Teacher.* Bloomington, Ind.: The Phi Delta Kappa Educational Foundation, 1973.

*Appendix: Colonial America and the French and Indian War**

INSTRUCTIONS FOR USE
OF THIS PACKET

This packet is divided into several sections. Each section is designed to aid you in acquiring specific information and skills. The following suggestions will aid you in using this packet.

1. Take time to explore the *whole* packet.
2. Read the rationale and the primary and secondary ideas for this packet. If you've read these you'll know the WHY and the WHAT you'll be studying.
3. There are goals or objectives in each packet you'll use. For each goal there are activities to aid you in achieving the goal. Familiarize yourself with goals and activities.
4. Your assignments while using these packets

* By Dennis Salk, Washington Irving Junior High School, Colorado Springs, Colorado. Reprinted by permission of the author.

are given DIRECTLY THROUGH THE ACTIVITIES, SO READ CAREFULLY.

5. All assignments resulting from activities completed in reaching the goals or objectives will be recorded by YOU in your personal folder.

6. Remember that you *do not* have to complete all activities. If and when you feel you've fulfilled the goal or objective go on to another.

7. Most of the materials you'll use in working on these packets will be found in the library, the resource center, the audio-visual bank, teacher-led discussions, and your textbook. Be sure you keep your notes from these sources as they will help you later.

8. There are corresponding *Annexes* in the back of the packets to aid you in your study. These annexes include the following: lists of films, tapes, records, and so on; outlines of information and other material. When working with audio-visual materials you select what you need and use them. If what you are looking for is not listed, ask your teacher to help you.

9. At times in the packet you will finish activities and be expected to report to a certain teacher for a small group lecture over certain important topics. If the teacher leading the discussion has only two or three people in a group he will have you sign up and then call on you to come into the discussion later. In the meantime you may go on with another activity.

10. There are self-assessments at the end of each objective. If you can answer the questions and fulfill the goals you are ready to take the unit test. If you can't answer the self-assessment questions, review the activities until you can do so.

11. When you have finished the self-assessment and have satisfied yourself that you can answer all questions, report to your teacher for the UNIT TEST. This unit test will evaluate the objectives of the unit as well as the content knowledge you should have acquired while doing the activities.

12. If you have a grade of 76 per cent or better you may go on to the next packet. If, however, you have a grade of 75 per cent or below you *must* complete the recycling activities in the packet before going on.

13. You may move as rapidly as you like through this packet. Remember you only cheat yourself if you don't fulfill the goals as they are set up.

14. If you are having any problems with this packet report to one of the teachers for help. This way, they will aid you early, and straighten out the problem.

15. DO NOT WRITE IN THIS PACKET!

PACKET # 1
COLONIAL AMERICA AND THE FRENCH AND INDIAN WAR

Rationale

The chance to earn a living brought many people to the English colonies. In the northern area, New England, people worked at lumbering and fishing. They were also sailors, shippers, and merchants.

Most people in the middle colonies were farmers. They raised wheat and other grains. Because their agriculture produced chiefly grain for flour-making, these middle colonies were called the "bread colonies."

The people in the southern colonies also engaged in agriculture. Southern farmers grew rice, tobacco, indigo, and hemp. Southern farmers often used slaves from Africa to raise their crops.

The chance to earn a living was not the only reason settlers came to the English colonies. Many people came to America because they wanted religious freedom. They wanted to worship God in their own way. In most parts of Europe, they could not. They had to belong to a national church.

Quakers, Catholics, Puritans, and Jews were among the people who came to America for religious reasons. Catholics found refuge in Maryland. Puritans founded Massachusetts. The Quakers first settled Pennsylvania. The idea of free worship came early to America.

Political rights of Englishmen also brought settlers. England allowed the colonists a considerable amount of self-rule, and this also made people want to live in the English colonies.

English colonists had helped fight for their liberties. They fought alongside British soldiers in the wars against France. In 1763, the French lost their lands in North America to England. After that, the colonists did not have to fear attack by the French, or Indian raids from Canada.

Defeating the French had cost England a great deal of money. England needed money for her empty treasury and decided to collect taxes from her colonies. England had placed taxes on the colonists before but, until 1763, she had not tried very hard to collect them. When England did try to seriously collect these taxes, it led to trouble with the colonists.

Primary Idea

The people who came to America to set up colonies did so mainly to have a better way of life.

SECONDARY IDEAS

1. Early colonization in the New World was carried out by the English, French, and Dutch.
2. Three distinct sections developed in the thirteen colonies. They were the northern or New England colonies, the Middle colonies, and the Southern colonies.
3. Because of geographical conditions each section (New England, Middle, and Southern) had different patterns of living.
4. French settlement in the New World was not based primarily on religion as had been true of English settlement.
5. Rivalry between France and England in Europe led to wars which extended to North America.
6. France was defeated in the French and Indian War and her territorial claims were lost.
7. French influence is still present in North America.

Objective A

You will be able to write a paragraph for at least three (3) of the four reasons explaining why the English came to settle colonies in the New World between 1607 and 1733.

ACTIVITY 1

Read section 1 of Chapter 4, page 81, in *This Is America's Story*, or Chapter 4, page 37, in *Adventures in American History*. Also see the filmstrip *England Prepares to Colonize*. Take notes on your reading and viewing.

ACTIVITY 2

Make a list of four (4) causes for English colonization in America. Could you write a paragraph summary of each cause?

ACTIVITY 3

Make a chart showing the thirteen English Colonies. Use these headings for your chart: *Name of Colony; Date Founded; Who* (leader or group) *Founded It;* and *Reasons for Founding.* Now research and fill in the chart.

ACTIVITY 4

With the information you've gathered from activities 2 and 3, write four (4) paragraphs. Each paragraph will describe a reason for English colonization.

ACTIVITY 5

Imagine you have been hired by the Pilgrims, Lord Baltimore, or William Penn to make posters to attract settlers to one of the three colonies. Before you make your poster, decide what point or points you want to emphasize, then illustrate these in your poster.

SELF-ASSESSMENT

At this point, can you write four (4) paragraphs explaining the four main reasons for English colonization, 1607–1733? If not, see your teacher.

Objective B

You will be able to construct an outline or a chart which will give the order of settlement of the New England, the Middle, and the Southern colonies between 1607 and 1733.

ACTIVITY 1

Read and take notes on sections 2, 3, 4, and 5 in Chapter 4 of *This Is America's Story*, or review Chapter 4 in *Adventures in American History*. You may group with three (3) other students to go over these notes.

ACTIVITY 2

Make a chart or an outline pointing out how the New England, Middle, and Southern colonies were founded. Make sure you get the names under the right heading or sections of colonies. Hint! Activity #3 for objective A may help you in doing this activity.

ACTIVITY 3

Write entries in an imaginary diary kept by a boy or girl who went to the New World with (a) the Jamestown settlers in 1607, (b) the Pilgrims in 1620, (c) the Puritans in 1630.

ACTIVITY 4

Find pictures showing costumes worn by French, English, Spanish, and Dutch colonists. Show these to the class or prepare a bulletin board display.

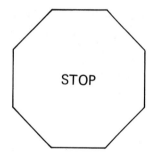

Take your chart or outline to a teacher and, using it, explain how the three colonial areas were founded.

Objective C

You will be able to fill in the names of the thirteen colonies on a blank map.

ACTIVITY 1

Review the activities you've completed for the previous two objectives.

ACTIVITY 2

Study the map on page 87 in *This Is America's Story,* or page 50 in *Adventures in American History.* Be sure you can spell correctly the name of each colony.

ACTIVITY 3

With a blank outline map of the eastern coast of America fill in the names of the colonies. Your teacher will give you the map.

ACTIVITY 4 (OPTIONAL)

Include on your map for Activity #3 the major topographical features (major rivers, mountain ranges, and so on) of the eastern America colonial area.

Now—Put your name on your map and post it on the bulletin board.

Self-assessment

If you were given a blank map of the thirteen colonies could you fill in the names of the colonies in their right locations?

Index